Civil Procedure

Civil Procedure

by Linda S. Mullenix

Morris and Rita Atlas Chair in Advocacy
University of Texas School of Law

SECOND EDITION

WEST
ACADEMIC
PUBLISHING

Mat #41181733

© 2004 West, a Thomson business
© 2014 LEG, Inc. d/b/a West Academic
    444 Cedar Street, Suite 700
    St. Paul, MN 55101
    1–877–888–1330

West, West Academic Publishing, and West Academic are trademarks of West Publishing Corporation, used under license.

Printed in the United States of America

ISBN: 978–0–314–27771–8

Summary of Contents

Table of Contents

Flow Chart of a Civil Litigation

This chart illustrates the basic stages in the trial of a civil case. It is intended as a study aid for first-year law students. It is not a complete description of the civil process, nor is it a description of the process in any specific state jurisdiction.

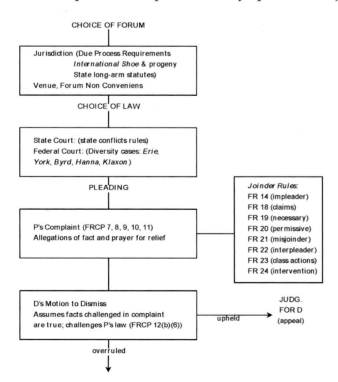

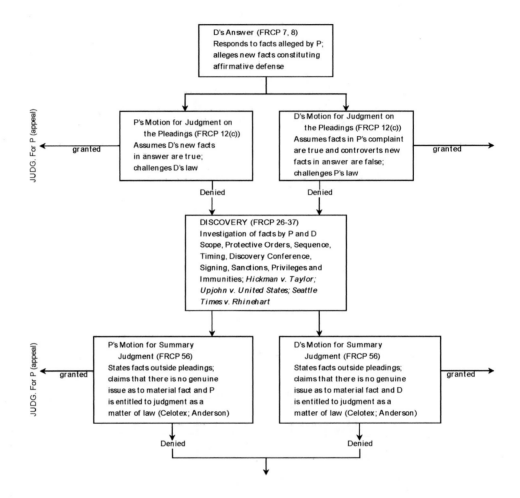

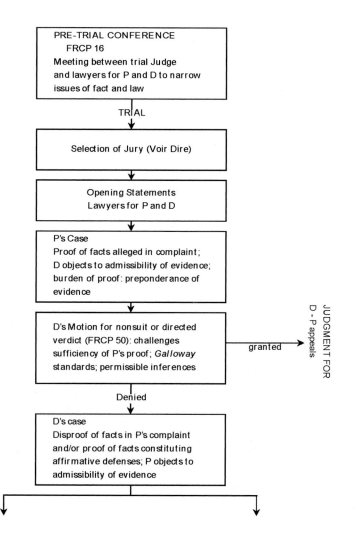

PRE-TRIAL CONFERENCE
  FRCP 16
Meeting between trial Judge
and lawyers for P and D to narrow
issues of fact and law

TRIAL

Selection of Jury (Voir Dire)

Opening Statements
Lawyers for P and D

P's Case
Proof of facts alleged in complaint;
D objects to admissibility of evidence;
burden of proof: preponderance of
evidence

D's Motion for nonsuit or directed
verdict (FRCP 50): challenges
sufficiency of P's proof; *Galloway*
standards; permissible inferences

granted

JUDGMENT FOR
D - P appeals

Denied

D's case
Disproof of facts in P's complaint
and/or proof of facts constituting
affirmative defenses; P objects to
admissibility of evidence

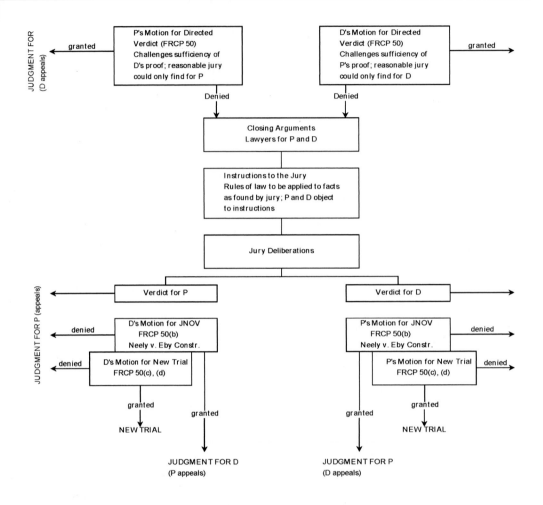

Capsule Summary of Civil Procedure

■ I. CHOOSING THE FORUM: PERSONAL JURISDICTION

A. JURISDICTION IN ANGLO–AMERICAN LAW

1. Definition of Terms

"Jurisdiction" refers to the power or authority of a court to hear and determine a case. The term "jurisdiction" is used to describe a court's territorial reach over its own citizens, citizens of other states, or foreign nationals. A court must have two kinds of jurisdiction in order to enter a legally enforceable judgment over a defendant: personal jurisdiction over the parties to the dispute, and subject matter jurisdiction over the claims presented to the court.

a. Due Process Concerns

In addition to having the territorial and subject matter power to decide a dispute, litigants must be afforded adequate notice of a proceeding against them as well as an opportunity to be heard. A court cannot render a valid, binding judgment in absence of territorial power and notice.

b. Jurisdictional Facts

Jurisdictional facts are the information a court must have in order to determine whether it has the competency and may properly exercise its adjudicatory powers to render a binding judgment. Jurisdictional facts typically include—but are not limited to—the citizenship or residency of the parties to the dispute; the location and nature of any defendant's property; the defendant's affiliating circumstances with the forum; whether and how the defendant was served with process or notice of the action; and the amount in controversy involved in the litigation.

c. Challenges to Jurisdiction

Challenges to jurisdiction may be raised in motions to quash service of process, motions to dismiss (under **Federal Rules of Civil Procedure 12(b)(1)** and **(2)**) (Federal Rules of Civil Procedure will hereinafter be referred to simply by the word "Rules."), or on direct appeal to a superior court. A non-resident defendant may make a "special appearance" to challenge a court's jurisdiction without thereby submitting to the court's jurisdiction. If the defendant fails to appear and contest jurisdiction, and suffers a default judgment, the defendant may subsequently collaterally attack the first court's personal jurisdiction determination in another court.

2. Personal Jurisdiction

With regard to the power of courts, there are basically three territorial bases for asserting jurisdiction: *in personam* jurisdiction, *in rem* jurisdiction, and *quasi in rem* jurisdiction.

a. *In Personam* Jurisdiction

In personam jurisdiction refers to the authority of the court to render a personally binding judgment against a defendant within its territory. Actions brought *in personam* typically are to obtain a judgment against a defendant for monetary or compensatory relief, to be satisfied by the defendant's general assets (legal relief). In addition, an action *in personam* may be brought to require a defendant to perform some act or to refrain from performing some act (equitable relief). A plaintiff also may bring an action *in personam* that requests a court to declare the rights of the parties to a contract or other similar relationship (declaratory judgment).

b. *In Rem* Jurisdiction

In rem jurisdiction, or actions *in rem*, refers to adjudication by claimants concerning their respective interests in a specific thing (a res), usually a piece of property. The historical basis for a court's *in rem* jurisdiction is the state's absolute authority over all property within its borders, without regard to the location of the defendant. In contrast to *in personam* actions, actions *in rem* typically do not seek to determine a defendant's liability for the defendant's actions. Rather, actions *in rem* seek to determine and affect the interests of persons in the property. Modern examples of actions *in rem* are actions to quiet title to real estate, to foreclose a lien upon property, or to partition a piece of land. *In rem* jurisdiction also extends to certain actions to determine legal status, as in divorce proceedings. *In rem* jurisdiction also is the means for establishing jurisdiction in actions in admiralty.

c. *Quasi In Rem* Jurisdiction

There are two types of *quasi in rem* actions. In the first instance, a plaintiff may assert *quasi in rem* jurisdiction over a piece of property owned by a defendant, in order to adjudicate personal rights related to the property under the court's control. The property serves as the basis for jurisdiction, and in such *quasi in rem* actions the property itself usually is not involved in the underlying substantive action for relief. An example of this form of *quasi in rem* jurisdiction is an action for specific performance on a contract to convey land.

3. Subject Matter Jurisdiction

In addition to having personal jurisdiction over the parties to the dispute, a court must have valid subject matter jurisdiction. "Subject matter" jurisdiction refers to whether the court has the competency to adjudicate the particular types of claims or controversies presented to it for resolution.

a. State Court Subject Matter Jurisdiction

States determine the jurisdiction of their courts by legislative enactment in their state codes, setting forth the substantive bases for relief and actionable claims. Typically, state statutes set forth the substantive law relating to contracts, property, torts, domestic relations, estates, commercial transactions, and so on. In addition to setting forth the substantive bases for relief, state statutes also will determine court subject matter jurisdiction by the amount in controversy involved in a dispute. Hence, disputes involving relatively small amounts of monetary damages will be assigned to small claims courts; litigation involving increasingly higher compensatory damages will be assigned to other state courts of general jurisdiction. Some state courts handle only particular subject matters, such as surrogates courts, which deal exclusively with matters relating to probate, estates, wills, and trusts.

b. Federal Court Subject Matter Jurisdiction

Federal court subject matter jurisdiction is constitutionally authorized in **Article III § 2** of the United States Constitution. There are two primary statutory bases for federal court jurisdiction: federal question jurisdiction (as provided in **28 U.S.C. § 1331**) and federal diversity jurisdiction (as provided in **28 U.S.C. § 1332**). In addition, **Title 28 of the United States Code** provides special subject matter jurisdiction for numerous actions of peculiarly federal interest, such as actions involving patents, copyright, antitrust, securities, civil rights, and so on.

4. Other Types of Jurisdiction

In addition to personal (or territorial) jurisdiction and subject matter jurisdiction, there are many other types of jurisdiction defining the ability of courts to exercise authority over cases and controversies.

a. Ancillary Jurisdiction

Ancillary jurisdiction refers to the ability of a court to adjudicate additional claims that are logically related to the plaintiff's claims. The concept of ancillary jurisdiction is codified in federal court as part of the federal supplemental jurisdiction statute, **28 U.S.C. § 1367**.

b. Appellate Jurisdiction

Appellate jurisdiction refers to the ability of state or federal court superior tribunals to hear appeals from lower court orders, decisions, or judgments, based on claims of legal error or abuse of discretion, among other legal standards for appellate review. Appellate jurisdiction is defined by statutes and rules of appellate procedure.

c. Concurrent Jurisdiction

Concurrent jurisdiction refers to the ability of two different courts to adjudicate a dispute at the same time, usually within the same territory. It is possible for state and federal courts simultaneously to adjudicate the same dispute in their concurrent jurisdictions. It is also possible for two or more state or federal courts independently to have jurisdiction over separate actions involving the same parties and claims. When two or more lawsuits are filed in state and federal courts, this is often referred to as parallel, repetitive or duplicative litigation. When a defendant files an independent lawsuit in another forum involving the same parties and claims, this concurrent litigation is often referred to as a parallel, reactive lawsuit.

d. Exclusive Jurisdiction

Some federal statutes provide that federal courts have exclusive jurisdiction over certain types of federal claims or actions, such as the federal antitrust laws. In such instances, if state litigation is filed containing exclusive federal claims, the state court is without power to adjudicate claims that are within the exclusive jurisdiction of the federal courts.

e. Original Jurisdiction

Original jurisdiction refers to subject matter jurisdiction conferred as a matter of first instance on federal or state trial level courts, to adjudicate claims and render a judgment. Many federal statutes specify that federal district courts have original jurisdiction over federal statutory claims. Original jurisdiction is distinguished from appellate jurisdiction.

f. Pendent Claim and Pendent Party Jurisdiction

In federal court, pendent claim jurisdiction refers to the competency of courts to adjudicate additional claims that lack an independent federal subject matter jurisdictional basis—such as a state-based claim. Pendent party jurisdiction similarly refers to the ability of the court to render a judgment against an additional party for whom there is no independent federal jurisdictional base. Pendent claim and pendent party jurisdiction are now provided for in federal court subject to the provisions of the supplemental jurisdiction statute, **28 U.S.C. § 1367.**

g. Removal Jurisdiction

Removal jurisdiction refers to the ability of a federal court to assume federal court jurisdiction over a lawsuit originally filed in state court. Federal statutes provide for removal of state cases from state court to the federal system at **28 U.S.C. § 1441** *et seq.* The defendant in the state court litigation petitions for the removal to federal court. The federal court then has jurisdiction to determine its valid federal subject matter jurisdiction. If the case has been improvidently removed because there is no proper federal subject matter jurisdiction, the federal court will hold that there is no removal jurisdiction and remand the case back to state court.

h. Supplemental Jurisdiction

In federal court, supplemental jurisdiction refers to the ability of the federal court to adjudicate additional claims and render judgments over additional parties, where the court lacks federal subject matter jurisdiction over those claims and parties independently. Supplemental jurisdiction basically refers to the older doctrines of pendent claim, pendent party, and ancillary jurisdiction. These doctrines have now been codified in the federal supplemental jurisdiction statute, at **28 U.S.C. § 1367**.

B. CHOOSING A FORUM IN A DUAL–COURT SYSTEM

1. The Consequences of Federalism

The United States government is based on a federalist system, consisting of fifty separate state governments, the District of Columbia, United States territories, and the federal government. One consequence of this system is the existence of a dual-court system consisting of separate federal and state courts, virtually independent of each other.

The Tenth Amendment constrains the federal government from interfering with state court systems. In addition, each state as an independent sovereign has virtually no ability to interfere with a sister state's court system or legal process. However, the Full Faith and Credit Clause to the United States Constitution (**Article IV § 1** and its enabling statute, **28 U.S.C. § 1738**) requires states to give full faith and credit to the statutes, proceedings, and judgments of other courts.

2. The State Court System

Each of the fifty states, as well as the District of Columbia, the Commonwealth of Puerto Rico, and United States territories have their own court systems and distinct procedural rules.

a. Structure of State Court Systems

Some state court systems have three-tier court systems consisting of trial-level courts, intermediate appellate courts, and highest appellate courts (courts-of-last-resort). Other states such as Nebraska have a two-tier court system consisting of trial level and appellate courts. Each state denominates its various courts by different names, so a state's superior court may actually be a trial level court, and a state's supreme court may actually be an intermediate appellate court. Forty-eight states have "unified" high courts which hear both criminal and civil appeals. Two states have bifurcated supreme courts, one for civil appeals and the other exclusively for criminal appeals.

b. State Court Judges

Each state has its own method for selecting judges. In some states judges may be appointed by the governor or a judicial selection commission; in other states judges run for office in contested or uncontested elections. State judges may sit for varying terms.

c. Relationship of State Courts to Federal Courts

Litigation commenced in a state court generally will remain in the state court system, unless a defendant in the state litigation exercises the right to remove the case to a federal district court. Appeals from adverse state court rulings or judgments must be pursued within the state appellate system. In certain limited circumstances, if a constitutional question is involved, litigants may appeal an adverse decision from the highest state court to the United States Supreme Court.

3. The Federal Court System

The federal court system is a three-tier system of trial level and appellate courts.

a. United States Federal District Courts

Federal trial-level courts are called district courts, and the United States is divided into 94 federal judicial districts. Some less populous states, such as Utah and Montana, consist of one federal judicial district. More populous states such as Texas, New York, and California, have four or five judicial districts (typically denominated as the Northern, Eastern, Western, Southern and Central districts). Many federal district courts also are divided into divisions, usually the place where a federal judge sits. Federal district courts have a "unified" docket and hear both federal civil and criminal cases.

b. United States Federal Courts of Appeal

The United States is divided into eleven judicial circuits and there are eleven intermediate courts of appeal. In addition, there is a separate Court of Appeals for the District of Columbia, and one for the Federal Circuit, which hears appeals from certain specialized federal tribunals, such as the Court of Claims. The Circuits have a minimum of four or more federal appellate judges, who sit in three-judge panels to decide appeals from the district courts within their judicial circuit. Circuit courts hear appeals in both criminal and civil cases.

c.   United States Supreme Court

The United States Supreme Court is the highest court of appeals in the federal system, and for certain state court decisions involving constitutional issues. The Supreme Court consists of nine justices and the Court hears and decides approximately ninety cases per term (October through June), chiefly on appeal from Circuit Court decisions. The Supreme Court used to have both mandatory and discretionary dockets, but the Court's mandatory docket is very small. Thus, almost the entire current Supreme Court docket is discretionary. This is known as the Court's "certoriari" docket. The Court hears appeals in both criminal and civil cases.

d.   Appointment and Tenure of Federal Judges

All federal judges are nominated by the President of the United States and appointed with the advice and consent of the United States Senate. If there is a judicial opening for a federal district or circuit judgeship, the President usually confers with the two Senators from the particular judicial district as a matter of "senatorial courtesy." Judicial nominations are reviewed by the Senate Judiciary Committee, which reports its vote and recommendation to the full Senate. This process is the same for all federal judgeships, including appointments to the Supreme Court. Federal judges have life tenure and may only be removed by impeachment, resignation, or death.

4.   Strategic Considerations in Choosing Between State and Federal Court: The Parity Debate

As an initial litigation matter, parties must decide the forum in which they wish to seek relief. Subject to jurisdictional and venue rules, litigants may sue either in state or federal court. As indicated above, litigants also may pursue relief in both court systems simultaneously, provided there is concurrent jurisdiction in the state and federal courts. In consultation with the client, the attorney will evaluate various strategic and legal considerations before choosing the forum for litigation. Academic commentators describe the controversy over the comparative strengths and weaknesses of state and federal courts as the "parity debate." Among the strategic factors relating to the choice of forum are:

a. Docket Congestion

State and federal courts within a particular jurisdiction may be more or less current on their civil docket, and parties seeking an expeditious resolution of their litigation may choose a court system with the least crowded docket. State defendants may seek to take advantage of federal court docket congestion by exercising a right of removal.

b. Jury Pools

State and federal courts draw their jury pools by different methods and from different geographical locations. Parties seeking more local and sympathetic jury pools typically will prefer state courts. Parties seeking jurors drawn from a broader geographical area will prefer federal courts.

c. Judges

Some attorneys may be more familiar with local state court judges; other attorneys may be more familiar with federal district judges. Because federal judges have life tenure, in theory they are conceived of as more impartial and less subject to political influence. Conversely, elected state court judges sometimes are viewed as less impartial than federal judges and more subject to political influence. Depending on local legal culture and knowledge of judicial performance on the bench, lawyers either will prefer a state court venue or choose to avoid particular local judges.

d. Procedural Rules

Each state has its own procedural rules. Some states have adopted procedural rules closely based on the Federal Rules of Civil Procedure. Other states have not. The Federal Rules of Civil Procedure tend to be more liberal than comparative state procedural rules. Attorneys will assess whether they wish to litigate in a federal court under liberal federal procedural rules, or in state court under more restrictive procedural rules.

e. Location and Convenience of the Courthouse

The physical location of state and federal courts may be in different geographical locations throughout the state, and more or less convenient for litigants and witnesses. In general, plaintiffs' lawyers will choose a courthouse venue most convenient to the plaintiff and plaintiff's witnesses. Defense attorneys may attempt to change the plaintiff's choice of venue by seeking a transfer or change of venue.

5. Legal Considerations in Choosing a Court

In addition to weighing various strategic considerations relating to the possible choice of forum, a litigant's choice of forum also must satisfy the jurisdictional requirements relating to personal jurisdiction, subject matter jurisdiction, and venue. Litigants also may assess the possible substantive law that will apply to the litigation, including statutes of limitation and available remedies.

a. Jurisdictional Requirements

As indicated above, the plaintiff must choose a forum that has valid personal and subject matter jurisdiction and also is an appropriate venue. A defendant may consent to the plaintiff's choice of forum and waive defects in personal jurisdiction and venue. However, the forum must have valid subject matter jurisdiction in order to render a binding, enforceable judgment and litigants cannot waive defects in a court's subject matter jurisdiction.

b. Applicable Law

In choosing a forum for litigation, plaintiffs frequently will take into account the substantive and procedural law that will apply to the case. Litigants may attempt to "forum shop" for preferable law. With regard to procedural law, state courts follow their own procedural rules and federal cases are subject to the Federal Rules of Civil Procedure. With regard to substantive law, state courts will apply their own substantive law to disputes involving parties and transactions or events within the state's territorial boundaries. In multi-party lawsuits involving events occurring in multiple states, the forum will apply its choice-of-law rules to determine which state's substantive law applies. Under various standards, a state may determine either to apply its own substantive law or another state's law. This includes applicable statute of limitations and available remedies. In federal cases within the court's diversity jurisdiction, the federal court will first apply the state's choice-of-law rules to determine which state's substantive law applies to the federal diversity case. In federal cases within the court's federal question jurisdiction, the court will apply federal law and doctrine.

C. PERSONAL JURISDICTION

1. Introductory Notes

a. Personal Jurisdiction over Plaintiffs

Personal jurisdiction concerns the power and authority of a court to render a binding enforceable judgment over the parties to the dispute.

There generally are few issues relating to a court's personal jurisdiction over a plaintiff, because the plaintiff chooses the forum, institutes the action, and voluntarily consents to the court's jurisdiction.

b. Personal Jurisdiction over Resident Defendants

There are also relatively few personal jurisdictional problems relating to resident defendants, or defendants owning property within a state. Historically, states have claimed exclusive jurisdiction over persons and property within the state's borders. Almost all problems relating to personal jurisdiction involve the ability of state courts to exercise jurisdiction over non-resident defendants. In order to assert jurisdiction over non-resident defendants, various traditional common law doctrines have supported such assertions of jurisdiction. Contemporary notions of personal jurisdiction are determined by statutory provisions and constitutional requirements. Most problems relating to the proper assertion of jurisdiction over defendants relate to business associations and corporate entities, whose "presence" in the state for jurisdictional purposes frequently present more complicated questions than that of individual defendants.

2. Traditional Bases: Territorial Theories

The two most prevalent theories supporting assertions of personal jurisdiction at common law are presence within the state (*in personam* jurisdiction) or ownership of property within the state (*in rem* and *quasi in rem* jurisdiction). The basis for this authority is the sovereign power of each state over persons and property within its borders.

a. Transient Presence within the State

This power extends to persons who are temporarily or transiently within a state. As long as a person is served with process while visiting a state, this presence supports an assertion of personal jurisdiction over the defendant (**Burnham v. Superior Court,** 495 U.S. 604 (1990)). A state has the power to issue an *in personam* judgment against defendants within the state's borders, which judgment must be given full faith and credit by other states under **Article IV § 1** of the Constitution. Conversely, a state may not legitimately exercise jurisdiction over citizens outside its borders, as this would violate other states' sovereignty and compromise comity among states.

b. Property

The presence of property within the state provides a basis for assertion of valid *in rem* jurisdiction. The presence of property within the state, regardless of the location of the defendant, provides a basis for valid assertion of *quasi in rem* jurisdiction, provided that the property is seized or attached prior to the institution of legal proceedings. **Pennoyer v. Neff**, 95 U.S. 714 (1877).

3. Expanding Bases: Consent

The Supreme Court in **Pennoyer v. Neff** indicated that consent to a state's authority could provide a basis for rendering a binding *in personam* judgment against non-resident defendants. Consent doctrines assumed increased importance in the twentieth century, as a consequence of the advent of modern means of transportation such as the automobile and increased interstate commerce. Consent to jurisdiction either may be expressly given or implied by certain actions or waivers.

a. Express Consent

Parties may give express consent to a court's assertion of personal jurisdiction in different ways, including (1) appointment of an in-state agent and (2) contractual forum selection clauses. Parties contractually may consent to have their disputes litigated in a particular forum, through use of "forum selection clauses." (**M/S Bremen v. Zapata Off–Shore Co.,** 407 U.S. 1 (1972); **Carnival Cruise Lines, Inc. v. Shute,** 499 U.S. 585 (1991).) Most state and federal courts will uphold these contractual agreements specifying a particular forum, subject to rules relating to contract unconscionability and duress. Although litigants may consent to a court's assertion of personal jurisdiction, litigants may not contractually agree to a court's subject matter jurisdiction.

b. Implied Consent

In addition to giving express consent to a court's assertion of personal jurisdiction over non-resident litigants, modern jurisprudence has developed expanded concepts of implied consent. Thus, there are many circumstances in which parties may impliedly consent to a court's jurisdiction. Consent may be implied from (1) non-resident motorist statutes involving inherently dangerous activity; (2) the sale of securities involving inherently dangerous business activity; and (3) certain activities after commencement of an action.

c. Waiver or Consent by Failure to Object

A defendant can impliedly consent to a court's jurisdiction by failing to raise any available objections to the court's personal jurisdiction in a timely manner. **Federal Rule of Civil Procedure 12(h)(1)** provides that a defendant may waive objections to personal jurisdiction by failing to raise those objections either in a **Rule 12** motion or in an answer to a complaint.

d. Waiver or Consent by Failure to Comply with Discovery Requests Regarding Jurisdictional Facts

A defendant who contests personal jurisdiction but then fails to comply with court orders to divulge information needed by the plaintiff to support the burden of establishing personal jurisdiction may presumptively be held to have waived objections to personal jurisdiction. The Supreme Court upheld such a waiver as a sanction under federal discovery **Rule 37(b)(2)(A)** in **Insurance Corp. of Ireland v. Compagnie Des Bauxites de Guinee,** 456 U.S. 694 (1982).

e. Defendant's "General Appearance"

A defendant who wishes to challenge a court's personal jurisdiction may elect to make a special appearance before the court to contest jurisdiction without thereby subjecting itself to the court's jurisdiction. However, if the defendant appears and presents any other defenses or objections, the defendant will be deemed to have made a general appearance and to thereby have impliedly consented to the court's jurisdiction.

f. Non-Resident Plaintiffs and Counterclaims

A non-resident plaintiff who enters a forum and institutes a legal proceeding impliedly consents to personal jurisdiction over any cross-actions or counterclaims asserted by a defendant to the action. Consent is implied by the plaintiff's availing itself of the forum in the first instance. (**Adam v. Saenger,** 303 U.S. 59 (1938).)

4. Modern Constitutional Due Process Approaches

The Supreme Court's decision in **Pennoyer v. Neff** embodied a nineteenth-century approach to jurisdictional questions, which was embedded in notions of state sovereignty and strict territoriality. These territoriality concerns continued well into the twentieth and twenty-first centuries with regard to litigation based on or relating to property: actions *in rem* and *quasi in rem*. However, with the expansion of commercial activities nationally and globally, traditional notions of *in personam* jurisdiction strictly based on presence within the state have been modified to conform to changing notions of due process requirements. Thus, since the Supreme Court's decision in

International Shoe Co. v. Washington, 326 U.S. 310 (1945), almost all state assertions of *in personam* jurisdiction are now measured against an array of standards assessing the fairness and reasonableness of subjecting a non-resident defendant to a forum state's personal jurisdiction.

a. Defining Constitutional Power: Minimum Contacts and Fairness

The Supreme Court's original formulation of a due process standard for a state's assertion of jurisdiction required a two-part inquiry, asking whether the defendant had sufficient minimum contacts with the forum so as not to violate due process, and also whether such an assertion of jurisdiction would be fair.

b. Supreme Court's Decision in *International Shoe Co.*

Recognizing the *Pennoyer* Court's requirement of presence within the state in order to assert jurisdiction over a defendant, the Supreme Court articulated the modern due process standard for such assertions of state power: "due process requires only that in order to subject a defendant to a judgment *in personam*, if he be not present within the territory of the forum, he have certain minimum contacts with it such that the maintenance of the suit does not offend 'traditional notions of fair play and substantial justice.' "

c. Minimum Contacts Defined; No Quantitative Test; Quality and Nature of Contacts

International Shoe itself articulates no criteria for assessing a corporation's contacts or activities within the forum state. Instead, the Court indicated that the operative standard whether due process is satisfied "must depend rather upon the quality and nature of the activity in relation to the fair and orderly administration of the laws which it is the purpose of the Due Process Clause to ensure."

d. No Contacts

A state may not render a binding *in personam* judgment against an individual or corporate defendant that has no contacts, ties, or relations with the forum state. Such a judgment would violate the Due Process Clause of the Fourteenth Amendment.

e. Single Acts or Contacts

The Supreme Court in *International Shoe* stated the generally recognized principle that "the causal presence of the corporate agent or even his conduct of single or isolated items of activities in a state in the corporation's behalf are not enough to subject it to suit on causes of action unconnected with the activities there." Notwithstanding the Supreme Court's suggestion, however, some states have asserted jurisdiction over non-resident defendants with very few contacts with the forum.

f. Systematic and Continuous Business Activities within the State

A state legitimately may assert personal jurisdiction over a non-resident corporation if that business's activities within the state are "systematic and continuous," as opposed to "irregular or casual." The Court in *International Shoe* found that corporation's activities in Washington State sufficient to meet this standard; its operations made it reasonable and just according to "traditional notions of fair play and substantial justice" to permit the state to enforce obligations against the defendant corporation.

g. Purposeful Availment of Benefits and Protections of the State

Due process is not violated to the extent that a corporation, in conducting its business activities within a state, benefits from those activities as well as the protection of the state. Conducting business within a state is considered a privilege which may give rise to obligations, including the obligation to answer to legal proceedings. Among the "benefits" that courts will assess are the profits or revenues a corporation derives from its business within the state. "Protections" afforded to the defendant may include access to the state's legal system, as well as other health, welfare, and police protection benefits. In addition, the defendant must have "purposefully" availed itself of these benefits and protections. These standards sometimes are difficult to satisfy.

h. "Unilateral Activity" Qualification to the Purposeful Availment Standard

The "minimum contacts" standard cannot be satisfied by the unilateral activities of someone—usually a third party or an outsider to the litigation—who has a relationship to the defendant. The Supreme Court has held that "It is essential in each case that there be some act by which the defendant purposefully avails itself of the privilege of conducting activities within the forum State, invoking the benefits and protections of its law. . . . " **Hanson v. Denckla,** 357 U.S. 235 (1958). In addition, the "unilateral activity" of the plaintiff also cannot supply the contacts sufficient to support a defendant's purposeful availment of a forum. **World–Wide Volkswagen Corp. v. Woodson,** 444 U.S. 286 (1980).

i. "Center of Gravity" Qualification to the Purposeful Availment Standard

The fact that a number of events relating to an action cluster within a certain forum will not support an assertion of personal jurisdiction over a non-resident defendant in that forum. Hence, plaintiffs may not successfully urge that a court assert jurisdiction over a non-resident defendant because the forum is the "center of gravity" of the dispute. **Hanson v. Denckla,** 357 U.S. 235 (1958).

j. "Reasonable Foreseeability" Qualification to the Purposeful Availment Requirement

In order to subject a non-resident defendant to a forum's personal jurisdiction, a defendant that purposefully avails itself of the benefits and protections of a forum also must reasonably foresee that as a consequence of its activities it may be subject to suit in the state. **World–Wide Volkswagen Corp. v. Woodson,** 444 U.S. 286 (1980). Courts will assess the defendant's conduct or activities outside the state to determine whether that conduct was of such a nature that the non-resident defendant could reasonably have anticipated being "haled into court."

k. Applicable Law

The fact that a particular state's law—especially forum law—may apply to a controversy usually is not a factor or "contact" that enters into a due process minimum contact analysis. **Hanson v. Denckla,** 357 U.S. 235 (1958) ("The issue is personal jurisdiction, not choice of law. . . . "). However, when parties have contractually stipulated that the forum's law will apply to any future disputes related to the contract, this contract provision will support a finding of reasonable foreseeability of being sued in that forum. **Burger King Corp. v. Rudzewicz,** 471 U.S. 462 (1985).

l. Fairness Considerations—Burdens and Inconvenience

In addition to assessing whether the defendant has constitutionally sufficient minimum contacts, the second prong of the *International Shoe* due process standard requires courts to evaluate the fairness of asserting jurisdiction over the defendant (assuming the defendant has sufficient minimum contacts with the forum). In assessing the reasonableness or fairness of the assertion of jurisdiction against a non-resident defendant, the Court indicated that the relevant consideration is "an 'estimate of the inconveniences' that would result to the corporation from a trial away from its home or principal place of business." It is considered an unreasonable burden to require a corporation to defend a suit away from the jurisdiction where it carries on more substantial activities than the forum state.

m. First Amendment Limitations

A non-resident defendant may not invoke the First Amendment to invalidate an otherwise proper assertion of personal jurisdiction under the Due Process Clause. Writers and publishers have attempted to argue that constitutional First Amendment free speech and press concerns should override assertions of personal jurisdiction in distant forums. The Supreme Court has rejected this argument.

n. Commerce Clause Limitations

The potential burden on interstate commerce of a state court's assertion of personal jurisdiction over a non-resident defendant corporation may be taken into account in a court's assessment of *International Shoe* minimum contacts. Such constitutional Commerce Clause objections to state assertions of personal jurisdiction are rare.

o. General and Specific Jurisdiction

The *International Shoe* decision very broadly suggests the concepts of both general and specific jurisdiction. In **Helicopteros Nacionales de Colombia, S.A. v. Hall,** 466 U.S. 408 (1984), the Supreme Court endorsed the concept of general jurisdiction but refused to approve any particular formulation of specific jurisdiction. In **Goodyear Dunlop Tires Operations v. Brown,** ___ U.S. ___, 131 S.Ct. 2846 (2011), the Supreme Court held that "specific jurisdiction is confined to adjudication of issues deriving from, or connected with, the very controversy that establishes jurisdiction."

5. State Long-Arm Statutes

The Supreme Court's expansive decision in *International Shoe* left the states to elaborate on the requirements of minimum contacts jurisprudence. Since 1945 almost all states have enacted so-called "long-arm" statutes which permit states to expand their jurisdictional reach beyond state borders and assert jurisdiction over non-resident defendants. Typically these statutes specify the acts or conduct of a defendant both within and outside the state that can subject a defendant to the court's authority.

a. Characteristics of State Long-Arm Statutes

Most state long-arm statutes differ in the degree of detail enumerating the specific acts that can subject a defendant to jurisdiction, while other long-arm statutes may subject a defendant to jurisdiction based on the defendant's general activities within the state.

b. Judicial Construction of State Long-Arm Statutes

Since the enactment of state long-arm statutes, plaintiffs must now satisfy state statutory requirements for the assertion of personal jurisdiction over non-resident defendants. Thus, at the outset of every jurisdictional inquiry, the state court must construe and apply its own long-arm statute (except if the parties have contractually agreed to the forum, or the basis for jurisdiction is transient presence in the state, discussed below).

c. Jurisdictional Analysis Now Typically Requires a Two-Step Process

A court must first examine its own long-arm statute to determine whether a defendant's conduct or activities brings that defendant within the enumerated bases for jurisdiction as determined by the state legislature. If the defendant is subject to the state long-arm statute, then the court will examine whether the state's assertion of jurisdiction comports with the requirements of constitutional due process. **World–Wide Volkswagen Corp. v. Woodson,** 444 U.S. 286 (1980).

d. Specific Jurisdiction Tests

Some states have long-arm provisions authorizing the assertion of jurisdiction over a defendant if a cause of action arises from the transaction of any business within the state. In construing these broad provisions, many states and some federal courts have permitted the assertion of jurisdiction over non-resident defendants based on so-called "specific jurisdiction" tests. Some courts have adopted the "but for" causation standard to satisfy "arising from" statutory language. Other states and federal courts have construed the same statutory language to require that a plaintiff show that the plaintiff's cause of action is "related to" or "substantially related to" the defendant's business transacted within the state. In **Goodyear Dunlop Tires Operations v. Brown,** ___ U.S. ___, 131 S.Ct. 2846 (2011), the Supreme Court held that adjudicatory authority is specific when the suit arises out of or relates to the defendant's contacts with the forum.

e. Judicial Construction of California-Style Long-Arm Statutes

California-style long-arm statutes authorize states to assert jurisdiction to the full extent of the Constitution. This means that the court must assess the forum's assertion of jurisdiction in relation to due process minimum contacts jurisprudence as elaborated in *International Shoe* and subsequent cases. In states with California-style long-arm statutes, the usual two-stage jurisdictional inquiry effectively is conflated into a constitutional due process inquiry. Furthermore, several states interpret their own detailed long-arm statutes as authorizing assertion of jurisdiction to the full extent of the Constitution. In these states with long-arm statutes that resemble Illinois-style statutes, the jurisdictional inquiry typically evaluates constitutional due process requirements only.

f. Specific and General Jurisdiction Distinguished

Theories of specific jurisdiction support assertions of jurisdiction over non-resident defendants if a defendant's acts or conduct within the forum relate to the plaintiff's claims (in absence of more systematic and continuous contacts that would support an assertion of general jurisdiction unrelated to those contacts). General jurisdiction, on the other hand, permits an assertion of jurisdiction over a non-resident defendant by virtue of the defendant's systematic and continuous activities in the state, which may be totally unrelated to the plaintiff's claim.

6. Stream-of-Commerce Theory

With the transformation of the national economy in the twentieth century and the increased shipment of goods and services across state lines, state courts adapted *International Shoe* due process standards to a "stream-of-commerce" theory for assertions of personal jurisdiction over businesses that place their products in interstate commerce. Stream-of-commerce theories place less weight on "inconvenience" factors in due process analysis. Current issues concern whether state courts, using stream-of-commerce rationales, can extend their reach globally to foreign corporations.

a. Classical Statement of Stream-of-Commerce Theory Rationales

The trend towards expanding state jurisdiction over non-residents is "[i]n part . . . attributable to the fundamental transformation of our national economy over the years. Today many commercial transactions touch two or more States and may involve parties separated by the full continent. With this increasing nationalization of commerce has come a great increase in the amount of business conducted by mail across state lines. At the same time modern transportation and communication have made it much less burdensome for a party sued to defend himself in a State where he engages in economic activity." **McGee v. International Life Insurance Co.,** 355 U.S. 220 (1957); *see also* **Gray v. American Radiator & Standard Sanitary Corp.,** 22 Ill.2d 432 (1961).

b. Stream of Commerce and Foreseeability

Early formulations of the stream-of-commerce theory expansively permitted assertions of jurisdiction over corporations that placed their products into the stream of commerce, even without precise knowledge of where those products eventually might wind up. Jurisdiction also would extend even if a middleman purchased the product or someone other than the defendant shipped the product interstate. **Gray v. American Radiator & Standard Sanitary Corp.,** 22 Ill.2d 432 (1961).

c. *World–Wide Volkswagen* and Reasonable Expectations

The Supreme Court in 1980 endorsed the "stream-of-commerce" theory for assertions of personal jurisdiction over non-resident product manufacturers and distributors, but added a requirement that the defendant have some reasonable expectation that its products would wind up in the forum. Thus, the Court stated that a state could constitutionally exercise jurisdiction over "a corporation that delivers its products into the stream of commerce with the expectation that they will be purchased by consumers in the forum State." **World–Wide Volkswagen Corp. v. Woodson,** 444 U.S. 286 (1980). Otherwise, "every seller of chattels would in effect appoint the chattel his agent for service of process." *Id.*

d. Foreseeability Test Stated

". . . the foreseeability that is critical to due process analysis is not the mere likelihood that a product will find its way into the forum State. Rather, it is that the defendant's conduct and connection with the forum State are such that he should reasonably anticipate being haled into court there. . . . " **World–Wide Volkswagen Corp. v. Woodson,** 444 U.S. 286 (1980).

e. "Unilateral Activity" Corollary

The defendant corporation must place its product in the stream of commerce in order to be held to answer for a lawsuit in a distant forum. It is unfair to make a defendant answerable where the product is brought to the forum by the plaintiff or some other person. **World–Wide Volkswagen v. Woodson,** 444 U.S. 286 (1980), relying on **Hanson v. Denckla,** 357 U.S. 235 (1958).

f.   Stream of Commerce and "Purposeful Availment"

A state legitimately may assert personal jurisdiction over a non-resident manufacturer or distributor if the non-resident defendant makes efforts to directly or indirectly serve a market and purposefully avails itself of the privilege of conducting activities within a state. Absent such purposeful availment, an out-of-state business cannot be held accountable for the random, fortuitous, or isolated possibility that its products might wind up in a particular market.

g.   Stream of Commerce and "Purposeful Direction" of Products Into the Forum

Some courts require that a defendant product manufacturer or distributor not only place its product into the stream of commerce, but that the defendant "purposefully direct [the product] to the forum state." Absent such "purposeful direction" a distant forum may not assert jurisdiction over the non-resident defendant consistent with due process. **Asahi Metal Industry Co. v. Superior Court,** 480 U.S. 102 (1987).

h.   Stream-of-Commerce Theory in a Global Economy: International Dimensions

In contemporary minimum contacts analysis, under expanded *World–Wide Volkswagen* standards, courts are to take into consideration the interests of the "several states" in the efficient judicial resolution of disputes. The reasonableness of asserting jurisdiction over a foreign corporate defendant must be assessed in the context of federal interests in its foreign-relations policies. The Supreme Court has cautioned that "Great care and reserve should be exercised when extending our notions of personal jurisdiction into the international field." **Asahi Metal Industry Co. v. Superior Court,** 480 U.S. 102 (1987).

i.   Post-*Asahi* Stream-of-Commerce Applications

Some state and federal courts have adopted Justice O'Connor's "purposeful direction" standard in stream-of-commerce cases after *Asahi;* other courts have followed Justice Brennan in repudiating a stream-of-commerce standard that requires "additional conduct." The Supreme Court recently has indicated that Justice O'Connor's purposeful availment test in *Asahi* does not itself resolve many difficult questions of jurisdiction that arise in particular cases. **J. McIntyre Machinery Ltd. v. Nicastro,** ___ U.S. ___, 131 S.Ct. 2780 (2011).

j.   Stream of Commerce and Sovereign Authority

In 2011, the Supreme Court announced that jurisdiction is, in the first instance, a question of sovereign authority rather than fairness. Whether a judgment is lawful depends on whether the sovereign has authority to render it. A defendant's purposeful contacts with a state, not with the entire United States, are what is relevant. **J. McIntyre Machinery Ltd. v. Nicastro,** ___ U.S. ___, 131 S.Ct. 2780 (2011).

7.   Redefined Minimum Contacts Jurisprudence

In 1980, the Supreme Court synthesized existing minimum contacts jurisprudence as it had developed in the state and lower federal courts in the thirty-five years after *International Shoe*. In **World–Wide Volkswagen Corp. v. Woodson,** the Supreme Court reaffirmed some old standards and set forth some new factors to be evaluated in considering the due process dimension of state assertions of personal jurisdiction.

a.   Redefined Concept of Minimum Contacts (Purposes)

Minimum contacts jurisprudence "performs two related, but distinguishable functions:" the protection of states as co-equal sovereigns (the so-called "sovereignty branch" of jurisdictional analysis), and the protection of defendants against the burdens of litigating in a distant or inconvenient forum (the so-called "convenience branch" of jurisdictional analysis, also described in terms of "reasonableness" or "fairness").

b.   Additional Factors in Determining the Reasonableness of a Forum's Assertion of Personal Jurisdiction over a Non-Resident Defendant ("Affiliating Circumstances" Test)

Courts consider the burden on the defendant; the forum state's interest in adjudicating the dispute; the plaintiff's interest in obtaining convenient and effective relief; the interstate judicial system's interest in obtaining the most efficient resolution of controversies; and the shared interests of the several states in furthering fundamental substantive social policies.

c.   Significance of *World–Wide Volkswagen*'s Reformulated Minimum Contacts Jurisprudence

The Court's decision in *World–Wide Volkswagen* broadened minimum contacts jurisprudence by shifting analysis to other considerations beyond the defendant's contacts with the forum. On the other hand, the Court's definition of a foreseeability standard narrowed application of jurisdiction possibilities.

8. Property as a Basis for Jurisdiction, Revisited

State assertions of jurisdiction based on the presence of property in the state, except for purely *in rem* actions, must be assessed against *International Shoe* minimum contacts due process jurisprudence. Assertions of jurisdiction either *in personam* and *quasi in rem* must be measured by the same due process requirements. **Shaffer v. Heitner,** 433 U.S. 186 (1977).

a. Supreme Court's Holding in *Shaffer v. Heitner*

The Court held that "all state assertions of state-court jurisdiction must be evaluated according to the standards set forth in *International Shoe* and its progeny."

b. Impact of Shaffer v. Heitner on *In Rem* and *Quasi In Rem* Jurisdiction

Shaffer v. Heitner does not affect actions purely in a court's *in rem* jurisdiction, but it has affected *quasi in rem* actions. The rules relating to assertions of jurisdiction based on the presence of property within the state are as follows:

i. Pure *In Rem* Actions

Jurisdiction is permissible where the presence of property within the state is itself the subject matter of the dispute—whether tangible or intangible—and is directly related to the plaintiff's cause of action. The presence of property within the state supplies the contacts necessary and sufficient to permit the exercise of jurisdiction. Recovery is limited to the value of the property underlying the dispute.

ii. *Quasi In Rem* Actions

Jurisdiction is permissible where the plaintiff's claims relate to rights and obligations arising out of the defendant's ownership of property within the state, provided the defendant meets *International Shoe* minimum contacts requirements. The *Shaffer* rule has its greatest impact on assertions of *quasi in rem* jurisdiction where the plaintiff's cause of action is completely unrelated to the defendant's property.

9. Personal Service Within the Jurisdiction: Transient or "Tag" Jurisdiction

A state legitimately may assert jurisdiction over a non-resident defendant who is temporarily within the state and who is served with process while within the state. This is called "transient" or "tag" jurisdiction and is one of the oldest forms of assertion of personal jurisdiction. The Supreme Court in **Pennoyer v. Neff** recognized transient jurisdiction as one of the legitimate bases for a state's assertion of personal jurisdiction. The Supreme Court's decision in **Shaffer v. Heitner** has not modified the doctrine of transient jurisdiction. Assertions of transient jurisdiction, then, do not have to satisfy *International Shoe* minimum contacts jurisprudence. **Burnham v. Superior Court,** 495 U.S. 604 (1990).

10. Modern Consent: Choice-of-Forum and Choice-of-Law Clauses

Assertions of jurisdiction based on contractual agreements to litigate in a particular forum fall outside minimum contacts jurisprudence.

a. Choice-of-Forum Clauses

The presence of a choice-of-forum clause ("forum selection clause") is binding on the parties. Such agreements are presumably valid and courts will enforce such agreements unless it would be unreasonable. (**M/S Bremen v. Zapata Off–Shore Co.,** 407 U.S. 1 (1972), **Carnival Cruise Lines, Inc. v. Shute,** 499 U.S. 585 (1991).)

b. *The Bremen* and *Carnival Cruise Lines* "Reasonableness Factors" for Evaluating the Reasonableness of a Forum Selection Clause

Courts consider whether the forum selection clause was freely negotiated and unaffected by fraud, undue influence, or overweening bargaining power; the business sophistication of the bargaining parties; the serious difficulty or inconvenience of the contractual forum to one or both of the parties; whether in light of commercial realities and expanding international trade the forum selection clause should control; and whether enforcement of the forum selection clause would contravene a strong public policy of the state in which the suit was brought.

c. Choice-of-Law Provisions

A contractual provision specifying that a forum's law is to apply to disputes arising from a contract may support an assertion of that forum's jurisdiction, even in the absence of a forum selection clause. **Burger King Corp. v. Rudzewicz,** 471 U.S. 462 (1985).

11. Jurisdictional Reach of Federal Courts

The jurisdictional reach of federal courts over defendants located both inside and outside a federal judicial district is governed by a complicated, interrelated set of Federal Rules provisions as well as independent federal statutory authority. The primary authority for federal assertions of personal jurisdiction are located in **Rule 4 (Summons).** In general, the jurisdictional reach of the federal courts is no broader than the states in which those district courts sit. However, some federal statutes explicitly provide for nationwide jurisdiction over defendants in particular actions and in such instances the defendants need only have "minimum contacts" with the United States. Moreover, **Rule 4** was amended to permit federal court to assert jurisdiction over defendants in claims arising under federal law when the defendant would not otherwise be subject to a state's personal jurisdiction.

a. Actions *In Personam*: Defendants Located within the Federal Judicial District

Defendants who are located within the federal judicial district are subject to the federal court's personal jurisdiction by reference to the state's jurisdiction statutes and interpretations of those statutes. **Rule 4(k)(1)(A)** provides that the federal court may establish jurisdiction over a defendant who could be subjected to the jurisdiction of a court of general jurisdiction in the state in which the district court is located.

b. Defendants Located within 100 Miles of the Federal District Courthouse: The 100–Mile Bulge Rule

Federal courts may exert personal jurisdiction over certain defendants who may be located within 100 miles of the federal courthouse, but are in another state. **Rule 4(k)(1)(B).** This "100–mile bulge" rule applies only to third parties who are impleaded in an action under **Rule 14,** or parties who are needed for a just adjudication under **Rule 19.**

c. Federal Interpleader Actions

Federal courts may assert personal jurisdiction over any parties who are joined in a federal interpleader action under **28 U.S.C. § 1335, Rule 4(k)(1)(C).**

d. Federal Question Cases Involving Defendants Not Subject to Any State's Law

Federal courts may assert personal jurisdiction over defendants if the action involves a federal question and the defendant is not otherwise subject to the jurisdiction of the courts of general jurisdiction of any state. **Rule 4(k)(2).**

e. Actions *In Rem*

Federal courts may assert jurisdiction in actions *in rem* in two different manners: (1) by seizure of property as provided by federal statute, **Rule 4(n)(1);** or (2) by seizure of a defendant's assets found within the district in the circumstances and manner as provided by the law of the state in which the district court is located. **Rule 4(n)(2).**

12. Challenging Assertions of Personal Jurisdiction

Parties may challenge a court's assertion of personal jurisdiction either directly in a first action, or, in limited circumstances, collaterally in a subsequent action to enforce a prior judgment.

a. Direct Attacks on Personal Jurisdiction in State Court: Special Appearance

Challenges to a state court's assertion of personal jurisdiction typically are brought on a motion to dismiss or a motion to quash service of process. A non-resident defendant may appear specially to contest the sole issue of the court's personal jurisdiction without thereby submitting to the court's jurisdiction. However, if the defendant appears and presents other claims or defenses, the defendant will be deemed to have made a general appearance and to have consented to the court's jurisdiction. A defendant who makes a special appearance and loses the jurisdictional issue may not subsequently collaterally attack the court's adverse ruling on jurisdiction.

b. Federal Court Litigation: How Asserted—Rules 12(b)(2), 12(g), and 12(h)(1)

A federal defendant may challenge the court's personal jurisdiction in a motion prior to the filing of a responsive pleading such as the defendant's answer, **Rule 12(b)(2),** although if the objection is not raised by motion it may still be made in the defendant's answer (or an amendment permitted by **Rule 15(a)**). **Rule 12(h).**

c. Waivable Defect

The failure to object to a federal court's assertion of personal jurisdiction is a waivable defect, and it will be lost if it is not asserted in a timely fashion. **Rule 12(h)(1).**

d. Burdens of Proof on Motions to Dismiss for Lack of Personal Jurisdiction

The mode of determination of a motion to dismiss for lack of personal jurisdiction is left to the trial court, which may either consider the motion on written affidavits, or request an evidentiary hearing. The trial court also may defer consideration of the jurisdictional issue until trial, in which instance the jurisdictional inquiry may become intertwined with the merits of the litigation. In general, however, pretrial determinations of personal jurisdiction are not supposed to involve a consideration of the litigation's merits.

e. Default

A defendant who believes that a court lacks jurisdiction may elect not to appear at all either to contest jurisdiction or to defend on the merits of the lawsuit. A defendant who fails to appear will suffer a default judgment. In federal courts, defaults are governed by **Rule 55**. A defaulting defendant may subsequently "collaterally" attack the court's jurisdiction if the plaintiff seeks to enforce that judgment in another forum. The defendant may argue that the second court does not have to give full faith and credit to a judgment rendered by a court that lacked personal jurisdiction over the defendant.

f. Direct Appeal

If a defendant makes a special appearance and litigates the jurisdictional issue, the defendant may renew the issue on direct appeal to a higher court.

g. Collateral Attacks on Personal Jurisdiction

Defendants may or may not be able to collaterally attack a first court's judgment on personal jurisdiction grounds in a subsequent enforcement action in another forum, based on the Constitution's Full Faith and Credit Clause.

■ II. CHOOSING THE FORUM: SUBJECT MATTER JURISDICTION

A. THE CONCEPT OF SUBJECT MATTER JURISDICTION: COMPETENCY OF THE COURT

1. Subject Matter Jurisdiction Defined

Subject matter jurisdiction concerns the power or authority of a court to adjudicate the case or controversy presented to the court for resolution. The subject matter of both state and federal courts is based in the Constitution and statutes setting forth the subject matter jurisdiction of the courts.

a. Requisite for Binding Judgment

Subject matter jurisdiction must exist in order for a court to render a binding, enforceable judgment. Sister states are under no obligation to give full faith and credit to state court judgments rendered by courts lacking subject matter jurisdiction.

b. Not Waivable. Subject Matter Either Exists or Does Not Exist

Subject matter jurisdiction is not a waivable defect and parties may not consent to a court's subject matter jurisdiction. Challenges to subject matter jurisdiction may be raised at any point during legal proceedings. A trial court or appellate court may question its own subject matter jurisdiction even if the issue is not raised by the parties.

c. Jurisdiction to Determine Jurisdiction

Courts have jurisdiction to determine the validity of their own subject matter jurisdiction.

2. Distinguished from Personal or Territorial Jurisdiction

Personal or territorial jurisdiction refers to the territorial reach of the courts over parties to the litigation. It is particularly concerned with the authority of courts to render binding judgments against defendants not found within the borders of the state. Unlike subject matter jurisdiction, personal jurisdiction is a waivable defect. Personal jurisdiction chiefly is governed by statutory provisions, subject to constitutional due process constraints.

3. Distinguished from Justiciability or Prudential Doctrines

Courts must have subject matter jurisdiction to render an enforceable judgment binding the parties. In addition, the parties must present the court with a "justiciable" case or controversy under Article III of the Constitution. Justiciability refers to the competence of a court hearing a particular matter—some disputes present "non-justiciable" controversies that a court may decline to adjudicate even though the court has subject matter jurisdiction to render a decision. The doctrines relating to justiciability usually are studied in either constitutional law or federal courts. Justiciability doctrines include standing, ripeness, mootness, political questions, and advisory opinions.

B. SUBJECT MATTER JURISDICTION IN STATE COURT

1. General Jurisdiction

State courts are courts of general jurisdiction. This mean that state courts have the ability to adjudicate any and all types of cases as provided for in state statutory provisions. State codes provide for the substantive rights of action in state courts. In many states, the jurisdiction of various courts is circumscribed by amount-in-controversy requirements, so disputes involving small claims will be assigned to municipal or small claims courts.

2. Specialized Jurisdiction

Many states have created courts with specialized subject matter jurisdiction, such as courts handling criminal matters, probate matters, domestic relations issues, etc. Some specialized courts also may have their subject matter jurisdiction circumscribed by amount-in-controversy requirements, such as small claims courts.

3. Federalism Concerns

The existence of a federal system raises issues about the power of state courts to adjudicate claims based on the laws of other states. In addition, the dual-court system raises issues about the ability of state courts to adjudicate claims within the federal courts' jurisdiction, and federal courts' ability to adjudicate state-based claims in their diversity jurisdiction.

a. Interstate Subject Matter Jurisdiction

A state may open its courts—and may be constitutionally required to do so—to claims based on the laws of another state.

b. Limitation on Intersystem Claim Assertion: Valid State Policies

Even if a state must open its courts to claims based on other state's laws, a state may apply its own law to vindicate policies related to the conduct of litigation in its own courts, such as statutes of limitation or tolling provisions.

c. Concurrent Federal-State Subject Matter Jurisdiction

State courts are competent to adjudicate claims within federal subject matter jurisdiction, except claims with the federal court's exclusive jurisdiction. However, even where some claims are within the federal court's exclusive jurisdiction, in some instances both federal and state courts can exercise concurrent jurisdiction over the same conduct.

d. Exclusive Federal Subject Matter Jurisdiction with Concurrent State Jurisdiction over Common Law Claims

Although Congress may have conferred exclusive jurisdiction on federal courts over some subject matters by statute, this does not prohibit a state court from having concurrent jurisdiction over state law claims related to the federal claim within the federal court's exclusive jurisdiction.

e. Requirement that State Courts Hear Federal Claims: Supremacy Clause Concerns

The refusal of a state court to hear a claim arising under federal law may violate the Supremacy Clause of the U.S. Constitution.

C. SUBJECT MATTER JURISDICTION IN FEDERAL COURTS

1. Constitutional and Statutory Bases for Federal Court Jurisdiction

Subject matter jurisdiction of federal courts is based both in constitutional and statutory provisions. Unresolved questions remain whether the statutory reach of federal court jurisdiction is as broad as the federal courts' constitutional reach.

a. Congressional Power to Create Federal Courts

Article III § 1 of the Constitution vests judicial power "in one supreme Court, and in such inferior Courts as the Congress may from time to time ordain and establish." Thus, the Constitution provides only for the United States Supreme Court. All other federal courts have been created by Congress, which has the power to create new federal courts and to determine the size of the federal judiciary. In theory, Congress could reduce the size of the federal judiciary and eliminate federal courts if it chose to do so.

b. Constitutional Scope of Federal Court Jurisdiction

Article III § 2 sets forth the scope of federal court subject matter jurisdiction, providing for both federal question jurisdiction and federal diversity jurisdiction.

c. Congressional Statutory Bases for Federal Court Jurisdiction

Congress must by statute provide federal subject matter jurisdiction to the inferior federal courts that it creates. Until 1875, Congress only provided the federal courts with diversity jurisdiction. In 1875 Congress statutorily enacted federal question jurisdiction (current **28 U.S.C. § 1331**). Congress also has statutorily provided for federal court removal jurisdiction (**28 U.S.C. § 1441** et seq.) and, in **1990**, for federal court supplemental jurisdiction (**28 U.S.C. § 1367**).

d. Limited Jurisdiction

Unlike state courts, federal courts are viewed as courts of limited jurisdiction, able to hear only cases within their constitutional or statutory authority. Federal courts thus may not hear all cases presented to them.

2. Federal Diversity Jurisdiction

Federal court diversity jurisdiction is based both in the Constitution and federal statutory provisions. Congress could, if it wished, abolish the federal statutory basis for federal court jurisdiction and has, from time to time, modified the diversity statute. In addition, federal courts have variously construed the scope of its diversity jurisdiction under the diversity statute. There is a long-standing and continuing debate over whether federal courts ought to continue to have diversity jurisdiction to hear diversity cases.

a. Constitutional Basis for Diversity Jurisdiction

Article III § 2 of the Constitution provides that the "judicial power of the United States shall extend to controversies between Citizens of different States . . . and between a State, or Citizens thereof, and Foreign States, Citizens or Subjects."

b. Congressional Statutory Basis for Diversity Jurisdiction: 28 U.S.C. § 1332

The statutory authorization for federal diversity jurisdiction is **28 U.S.C. § 1332,** which provides that district courts shall have original jurisdiction of all civil actions where the matter in controversy exceeds the sum or value of $75,000 (exclusive of interests and costs) and the controversy is among the four following possibilities of diverse parties: (1) citizens of different states; (2) citizens of a state and citizens or subjects of a foreign state; (3) citizens of different states and in which citizens or subjects of a foreign state are additional parties; and (4) a foreign state (as plaintiff) and citizens of a state or different states.

c.   Rationale for Diversity Jurisdiction

The rationales underlying diversity subject matter jurisdiction in federal court have been the subject of much controversy and continue to play a part in the ongoing debate over whether to eliminate or modify federal diversity jurisdiction. The major rationale is to protect litigants against possible local bias. **Bank of the United States v. Deveaux,** 9 U.S. (5 Cranch) 61, 3 L.Ed. 38 (1809).

d.   Policy Debate over Continued Existence of Federal Diversity Jurisdiction

Critics of diversity jurisdiction have advanced a number of arguments for eliminating or curtailing the federal court's diversity jurisdiction. Efforts to eliminate diversity jurisdiction have not been successful.

e.   Judicial Exceptions to Federal Diversity Jurisdiction

In some areas of law, federal courts have carved out long-standing exceptions to their own diversity jurisdiction. The two most prominent exceptions to federal diversity jurisdiction concern probate matters and cases involving domestic relations. **Ankenbrandt v. Richards,** 504 U.S. 689 (1992).

f.   Complete Diversity Rule: *Strawbridge v. Curtiss*, 7 U.S. (3 Cranch) 267, 2 L. Ed. 435 (1806)

Federal diversity jurisdiction requires "complete" diversity between all plaintiffs and all defendants: That is, no plaintiff may be from the same state as any defendant (but plaintiffs and defendants need not be diverse among themselves). The complete diversity rule has a long lineage. Although Chief Justice John Marshall announced the complete diversity rule in 1806, historical research has suggested that the Chief Justice may not have intended it as a constitutional limitation on federal court jurisdiction.

i.   Exceptions to the Complete Diversity Rule

Congress may provide for exceptions to the complete diversity rule by statute (*see, e.g.,* the **Federal Interpleader Statute, 28 U.S.C.**

§ 1335), or the federal courts may create such exceptions by judicial construction (*see, e.g.,* **Supreme Tribe of Ben Hur v. Cauble,** 255 U.S. 356 (1921) (class actions exception to complete diversity rule)).

g. Establishing Citizenship for the Purposes of the Diversity Rule

The basic diversity statute requires diversity of citizenship, but **28 U.S.C. § 1332** does not itself define "citizenship" for the purposes of diversity jurisdiction. In contrast, federal venue provisions are based on party residence. **28 U.S.C. § 1391** *et seq.,* discussed below. In general, citizenship for diversity purposes is the same as a party's domicile—as distinguished from a party's residence. Moreover, diversity of citizenship requirements depends on party status.

i. Citizenship Defined. Citizenship for Federal Diversity Purposes Means a Party's Domicile

A domicile is a person's fixed place of abode, coupled with an intention to remain. A person has only one domicile; a person may have more than one residence.

ii. Citizenship Requirements Based on Status

The federal diversity statute has different requirements based on the status of the parties to the dispute; that is, whether the parties involved are individuals, legal representatives, insurance companies, aliens, corporations, unincorporated associations, partnerships, or foreign states.

iii. Corporate Citizenship

For the purpose of establishing diversity of citizenship, a corporation is deemed to be a citizen of the corporation's headquarters. **The Hertz Corp. v. Friend,** 559 U.S. 77 (2010).

h. Collusive Creation or Destruction of Diversity Jurisdiction

Some plaintiffs may prefer to have their case heard in federal court and may attempt, through various devices, to "create" federal court jurisdiction in order to gain access to the federal courts. Conversely, some plaintiffs may wish to have their cases heard exclusively in state courts, and may attempt to frustrate a defendant's right to remove the case to federal court by ensuring that the litigation involves no basis for federal jurisdiction. There is a federal statutory prohibition against manipulative efforts to create federal diversity jurisdiction. *See* **28 U.S.C. § 1359.**

However, that statute does not per se prohibit efforts to destroy federal diversity jurisdiction. Federal courts will nonetheless repudiate blatant manipulative efforts to evade or destroy federal diversity jurisdiction, and federal law prohibits collusive or improper joinder of parties or assignment of a right (usually a contract right) for the purpose of creating federal jurisdiction.

i. The Amount-in-Controversy Requirement: 28 U.S.C. § 1332(a)

In order to satisfy federal diversity jurisdiction requirements, the controversy also must "exceed the sum or value of $75,000, exclusive of interests or costs."

i. The Good Faith Pleading and "Legal Certainty" Standard

The amount claimed by a plaintiff in the plaintiff's complaint controls "if the claim is apparently made in good faith. It must appear to a *legal certainty* that the claim is really for less than the jurisdictional amount to justify a dismissal." **St. Paul Mercury Indemnity Co. v. Red Cab Co.,** 303 U.S. 283 (1938).

ii. Multiple Parties and Claims: Special Aggregation Problems

Under the Federal Rules of Civil Procedure, plaintiffs may liberally join multiple claims and parties in a single, unified complaint. The presence of multiple claims and parties raises issues as to whether parties' claims may be aggregated to meet the amount-in-controversy requirement, and the federal courts have developed a complex series of rules delineating when claims may or may not be aggregated.

iii. Failure to Meet Amount-In-Controversy Requirements at Trial

The plaintiff's failure to recover the minimum amount in controversy required by the diversity statute during trial or at judgment does not cause a dismissal for lack of subject matter jurisdiction. Instead, the court may impose costs on the plaintiff (and deny costs to the plaintiff). This will be calculated without regard to any set-offs or counterclaim amounts due to the defendant. **28 U.S.C. § 1332(b).**

j. Timing Requirements for Determining Diversity Jurisdiction

The requirements for diversity jurisdiction must exist at the time of the commencement or filing of the action in federal court. Before filing a lawsuit, individuals may change their domicile or corporations may reincorporate in another state in order to create diversity jurisdiction. Any events occurring after commencement of the suit, such as a change in the parties' domicile, will not affect the court's subject matter jurisdiction. A post-filing change in a party's citizenship cannot serve to cure defects in diversity jurisdiction. **Grupo Dataflux v. Atlas Global Group,** 541 U.S. 567 (2004) (affirming longstanding "time-of-filing" rule).

k. Realignment of Parties: Involuntary Plaintiffs and Defendants

In some rare instances, courts may "realign" the parties to a lawsuit in order to determine whether diversity requirements are satisfied. If a defendant is realigned on the plaintiff's side of the suit, the defendant is called an "involuntary plaintiff"; conversely, a realigned plaintiff is called an "involuntary defendant." The court will realign the parties to correspond to their real interests in the litigation, which may be tied to substantive law.

l. Diversity Class Actions

In 2005, Congress enacted the Class Action Fairness Act which created new diversity jurisdiction for class actions in **28 U.S.C. § 1332(d)**. In order to establish a diversity class action the proponents must demonstrate (1) diversity of citizenship between a class member and the defendant, (2) the matter in controversy exceeds $5 million, and (3) there are at least 100 members of the class. The provision contains several exceptions and exemptions from federal court jurisdiction based on local state controversies.

3. Federal Question Jurisdiction

Federal question jurisdiction is based on both the Constitution and statutory provisions. In general, the scope of federal courts' constitutional jurisdiction is viewed as more expansive than the courts' statutory reach, but difficult interpretation problems exist for both constitutional and statutory federal question jurisdiction.

a. Constitutional Federal Question Jurisdiction

Article III § 2 of the Constitution provides for federal question jurisdiction over the following kinds of cases: cases arising under the Constitution; cases arising under the laws and treaties of the United States; cases affecting ambassadors, other public ministers, and consuls; cases involving admiralty and maritime jurisdiction; and cases in which the United States is a party.

b. Other Constitutional Provisions: Bankruptcy Matters

Article I § 2 of the United States Constitution is the primary constitutional basis for the federal courts' constitutional reach. In addition, **Article I § 8** of the Constitution authorizes Congress to "establish uniform Laws on the subject of Bankruptcies." Congress has created federal bankruptcy courts as adjuncts to federal district courts to handle bankruptcy matters. Bankruptcy courts, however, are not Article III courts and the Supreme Court has held unconstitutional the broad delegation of jurisdiction in bankruptcy matters under **28 U.S.C. § 1471(c). (Northern Pipeline Construction Co. v. Marathon Pipeline Co.,** 458 U.S. 50 (1982).)

c. Constitutional "Arising Under" Jurisdiction: Interpretation Problems

The "arising under" language in **Article III § 2** is repeated in the statutory enabling legislation, **28 U.S.C. § 1331,** first enacted by Congress in 1875. The Supreme Court and federal courts generally have construed the **Article III** provision as conferring more expansive jurisdiction than § 1331. Both the constitutional and statutory bases for federal question jurisdiction have presented difficult interpretation problems for the courts.

i. "Original Ingredient Theory"

This theory posits that federal courts have jurisdiction over a plaintiff's cause of action ("the original cause") if it is based in part on federal law. **Osborn v. Bank of the United States,** 22 U.S. (9 Wheat) 738, 6 L. Ed. 204 (1824).

ii. Other Expansive Constitutional Theories of "Arising Under" Jurisdiction (Extensions of the *Osborn* Theory)

The most extreme view of *Osborn* is that there is federal question jurisdiction whenever there is a potential federal question in the case. Justice Frankfurter expressed this view in his dissent in **Textile Workers Union v. Lincoln Mills,** 353 U.S. 448 (1957), suggesting that such an interpretation of *Osborn* would authorize federal court jurisdiction "whenever there exists in the background some federal proposition that might be challenged, despite the remoteness of the likelihood of actual presentation of such a federal question."

d. Statutory Bases for Federal Question Jurisdiction

The general federal question jurisdiction of the federal courts is provided for in **28 U.S.C. § 1331.** In addition, numerous federal statutes also provide for "special federal question" jurisdiction.

i. Special Federal Question Jurisdiction; Concurrent and Exclusive Jurisdiction

Special federal question jurisdiction simply means original jurisdiction conferred on the federal district courts by some provision other than the general statute **28 U.S.C. § 1331.** For example, federal statutes provide for original jurisdiction of the federal courts over actions involving commerce and antitrust regulations (**28 U.S.C. § 1337**); patents, copyright, and trademarks (**28 U.S.C. § 1338**); and civil rights and elective franchise (**28 U.S.C. § 1343**). There are many other such statutory provisions. State courts may exercise concurrent jurisdiction over the same subject matters unless the federal jurisdictional statute explicitly indicates that the federal courts are to exercise exclusive jurisdiction. If the federal statute provides for exclusive federal court jurisdiction, the matter may only be heard in federal court.

ii. Statutory "Arising Under" Jurisdiction: 28 U.S.C. § 1331

The general federal question jurisdictional statute provides that federal courts shall have original jurisdiction of all civil actions "arising under the Constitution, laws, or treaties of the United States." Although the statute repeats the language of Article III, federal courts have interpreted the scope of statutory federal question jurisdiction as less broad than the federal court's constitutional reach. **T.B. Harms Co. v. Eliscu,** 339 F.2d 823 (2d Cir. 1964) (rejecting Justice Marshall's broad "original ingredient" standard for the statutory jurisdictional grant in **28 U.S.C. § 1331**).

e. The "Well-Pleaded" Complaint Rule

The federal cause of action must appear in the plaintiff's complaint and may not be found or supplied by the defendant's answer, or by an anticipated defense. **Louisville & Nashville R. Co. v. Mottley,** 211 U.S. 149 (1908).

i.   The Well-Pleaded Complaint Rule and Federal Declaratory Judgment Actions: The *Skelly Oil* Rule

Actions brought seeking a declaratory judgment in federal court present special problems under the well-pleaded complaint rule. It is important to understand the usual procedural posture of a declaratory judgment action. Typically, declaratory judgment actions are "anticipatory" actions. The party seeking a declaratory judgment does so in anticipation of being a defendant in a litigated action and hopes that the favorable determination of rights or duties will foreclose such litigation. Federal courts, however, will not permit declaratory judgment actions that essentially violate the well-pleaded complaint rule and will look beyond the pleadings to ascertain the true adverse interests of the parties if those interests were presented in a real litigation. **Skelly Oil Co. v. Phillips Petroleum Co.,** 339 U.S. 667 (1950).

f.   Artful Pleading to Avoid Federal Jurisdiction

Usually, a plaintiff is considered to be "the master of his [or her] own complaint" and courts will not interfere with a plaintiff's statement or characterization of the grounds for relief. However, federal courts will exert jurisdiction if the defendant convinces the court that the plaintiff has "artfully pleaded" the complaint to mask claims truly based in federal law for the purpose of avoiding federal jurisdiction.

4.   Supplemental Jurisdiction

In addition to diversity and federal question jurisdiction, federal courts have expanded their jurisdictional reach through the doctrine of "supplemental" jurisdiction. The doctrine of supplemental jurisdiction allows a federal court, in its discretion, to add parties to a dispute who otherwise would not have a valid jurisdictional basis to be in federal court, or to add claims that independently lack a federal jurisdictional basis (such as state-based claims). Until 1990, the principles permitting federal court supplemental jurisdiction were judicially-created doctrines. In 1990 Congress enacted **28 U.S.C. § 1367,** which is the current supplemental jurisdiction statute. Now, all assertions of supplemental jurisdiction in federal court are governed by the statute.

a.   Types of Supplemental Jurisdiction

The supplemental jurisdiction statute basically codifies three possible types of supplemental jurisdiction. Prior to 1990, these forms of supplemental jurisdiction were defined and limited by judicially-created principles:

i. Pendent Claim Jurisdiction

Pendent claim jurisdiction usually is the easiest form of supplemental jurisdiction to recognize. This typically involves a situation where a plaintiff in federal court asserts a federal claim for relief, but also includes a claim or claims for state-based relief that otherwise, standing alone, would not be permitted to be pursued in federal court. Federal courts lack subject matter jurisdiction over state-based claims. Under the theory of pendent claim jurisdiction, the general rule was that if the federal claim had a valid federal jurisdictional basis, then the federal court also could exercise jurisdiction over the state-based claim as long as the federal and state claims "arose from a common nucleus of operative facts." In this sense, then, the state-based claim was "appended" to the federal claim. **United Mine Workers v. Gibbs,** 383 U.S. 715 (1966).

ii. Pendent Claim Jurisdiction Codified at 28 U.S.C. § 1367(a) and (c)

The supplemental jurisdiction statute in subsection (a) states that "district courts shall have supplemental jurisdiction over all other claims that are so related to claims in the action within such original jurisdiction that they form part of the same case or controversy under Article III of the United States Constitution."

iii. Relationship of § 1367(a) to the *Gibbs* Decision

The legislative history to the supplemental jurisdiction statute and its drafters have indicated that subsection (a) of the decision was intended to codify the *Gibbs* decision permitting pendent claim jurisdiction. The statute, however, does not set forth the "common nucleus of operative facts" test. Instead, the provision uses the *Gibbs* formulation of "one constitutional case." Some lower federal courts, in applying statutory pendent claim jurisdiction have looked to the *Gibbs* "common nucleus of operative facts" test to determine whether to exercise pendent claim jurisdiction.

iv. Discretionary Jurisdiction

Subsection (c) of the supplemental jurisdiction statute provides federal courts the discretion to decline to exercise supplemental claim jurisdiction under subsection (a) under certain delineated circumstances. Subsection (c) of the supplemental jurisdiction statute basically codifies the discretionary ability of federal courts to decline to exercise supplemental claim jurisdiction on the same grounds delineated in *Gibbs.*

v.   Pendent Party Jurisdiction

Pendent party jurisdiction refers to the ability of a federal court to exercise jurisdiction over an additional party brought into a lawsuit under various joinder rules, for whom there is no independent federal jurisdictional basis, but whose joinder is logically related to the plaintiff and defendant's case-in-chief. Prior to 1989, lower federal courts were split in their decisions concerning whether pendent party jurisdiction was permitted, even though the Supreme Court had repudiated the doctrine of pendent party jurisdiction. The Supreme Court had rejected an extension of the *Gibbs* doctrine to pendent parties in **Aldinger v. Howard,** 427 U.S. 1 (1976), and in **Finley v. United States,** 490 U.S. 545 (1989).

vi.   Pendent Party Jurisdiction Codified at § 1367(a) and (b)

In 1990, in direct response to the *Finley* decision and Justice Scalia's invitation to Congress to codify the doctrine of pendent party jurisdiction by statute, the second sentence of **28 U.S.C. § 1367(a)** specifically provides for supplemental jurisdiction over claims adding pendent parties. The intention of this subsection was to overrule *Finley* and cases like *Finley* where lower federal courts had repudiated pendent party jurisdiction.

vii.   Common Law Limitations on Party Joinder in Diversity Supplemental Jurisdiction

The judicially-created doctrine of ancillary jurisdiction (*see* **Owen Equipment & Erection Co. v. Kroger,** 437 U.S. 365 (1978)) permitted federal courts to exercise jurisdiction over additional claims or parties brought into a lawsuit as a result of impleader (**Rule 14**), permissive joinder of parties **(Rule 20),** intervention (**Rule 24**), or parties joined because their presence in the lawsuit was necessary for a just adjudication (**Rule 24**). Ancillary jurisdiction traditionally was available to support a court's assertion of jurisdiction over counterclaims and cross-claims that lacked an independent federal jurisdictional basis, but which were "logically related" to the case-in-chief between the plaintiff and the defendant. Similar to the rationales supporting pendent claim jurisdiction, the doctrine of ancillary jurisdiction rests on considerations of judicial economy and convenience to the parties.

viii. Statutory Codification of the *Owen Equipment* Rule in § 1367(b)

The 1990 supplemental jurisdiction statute attempted to codify the *Owen Equipment* rule in **§ 1367(b).** This subsection of the statute basically provides that in federal actions brought in diversity jurisdiction, the federal court may not exercise supplemental jurisdiction over claims by plaintiffs against parties joined under **Rules 14, 19, 20,** or **24** if to do so would violate the requirements of diversity jurisdiction.

ix. Supplemental Jurisdiction in Class Actions and Joinder Cases

Where at least one named plaintiff satisfies the amount-in-controversy requirement, **§ 1367** authorizes supplemental jurisdiction over the claims of other plaintiffs in the same **Article III** case or controversy, even if those claims are for less than the jurisdictional amount specified in the statute setting forth the requirements for diversity jurisdiction. **Exxon Mobil Corp. v. Allapattah Services, Inc.,** 545 U.S. 546 (2005). This decision overturned the contrary holding in **Zahn v. International Paper Co.,** 414 U.S. 291 (1973).

5. Removal Jurisdiction

Removal jurisdiction refers to the ability of a defendant to move or shift a case that the plaintiff originally filed in state court to a federal district court.

a. Scope and Basis of Defendant's Removal Right

The right to remove a case from state court to federal court is a defendant's right, not a plaintiff's right. **Shamrock Oil & Gas Corp. v. Sheets,** 313 U.S. 100 (1941). This makes sense because the plaintiff is viewed as being "the master of his [or her] complaint" and if the plaintiff wanted to sue in federal court, the plaintiff could have made that decision initially. Removal is a very old right and was provided for by **Section 12** of the Judiciary Act of 1789. Removal is not a constitutionally-based right.

b. Modern Statutory Basis

The removal statute, **28 U.S.C. § 1441** and subsequent provisions, has been amended several times. The basic removal statute at **§ 1441(a)** provides that any civil action brought in a state court "may be removed by the defendant or defendants."

c. No Reverse-Removal Right

Removal is a procedure that is only available to state court defendants to move a case from state court into the federal court system. Currently, there is no parallel right of federal court litigants to move a case out of the federal court system into the state court system. However, a federal litigant, in appropriate circumstances, may ask the federal court to invoke an abstention doctrine and decline to exercise its validly conferred jurisdiction in deference to a state court's jurisdiction.

d. Removable Actions; Parties Who May Remove: Statutory Provisions

The general removal statute is **28 U.S.C. § 1441.** Sections **1442–1444** delineate the removal power of specific defendants in specific kinds of cases.

e. Removal Procedure: 28 U.S.C. § 1446

In general, a defendant seeking to remove a case from state court files a **notice** or **petition for removal** in the appropriate federal district court. The state court no longer has any jurisdiction over the action; the federal district court has physical possession of any pleadings, papers, or motions relating to the case. Removal procedure is subject to certain technical requirements.

f. Procedure After Removal: 28 U.S.C. § 1447—Federal Court Authority

After removal the federal district court may issue all necessary orders and process to bring the parties to the dispute before the court. **§ 1447(a).** The federal court also may order that all state court papers be filed with the federal court. **§ 1447(b).** Once a case has been removed to federal court it is governed by federal procedure.

i. Grounds for Remand

The federal district court (not the state court) will determine whether appropriate grounds for removal exist to permit federal court assertion of jurisdiction over the litigation. The standard for assessing proper removal is: "If at any time before final judgment it appears that the district court lacks subject matter jurisdiction, the case shall be remanded." **§ 1447(c).** The federal district court will decide this either on the written papers or after a hearing on the motion. If the federal court determines that it is without removal jurisdiction, it will order a *remand* of the case back to state court.

ii. Impermissible Remand Grounds: Federal Docket Congestion

A federal district judge may not remand a removed case that is validly within the federal court's jurisdiction because the judge's docket is overcrowded. **Thermtron Prods., Inc. v. Hermansdorfer,** 423 U.S. 336 (1976).

iii. Appellate Review

Federal court orders remanding cases to state court are not reviewable (except for civil rights cases). **§ 1447(d).**

iv. Subsequent Actions Affecting Federal Jurisdiction: 28 U.S.C. § 1447(e) (Added by Congress in 1988)

If a plaintiff, after removal, attempts to add defendants whose presence in the lawsuit would destroy diversity jurisdiction, the federal court may either (a) deny joinder of the additional defendants, or (b) permit the joinder of the additional defendants and then remand the case back to state court.

g. Separate and Independent Claims (28 U.S.C. § 1441(c)); Relationship to Supplemental Jurisdiction Statute (28 U.S.C. § 1367)

The general removal statute provides that whenever a state court plaintiff's complaint sets forth state-based claims but also contains a "separate and independent claim or cause of action" that is within federal question jurisdiction, then the defendant may remove the entire case to the federal district court. After such a removal, the federal district court either may hear the entire case, including the state-based claims, or the court may retain the federal question and remand the state claims back to the state court. **§ 1441(c).**

h. Removal of Class Actions

In 2005, Congress created a new special removal provision for class actions filed in state courts. Any defendant may remove a state class action without the consent of other defendants. **28 U.S.C. § 1453**.

D. RESTRAINTS ON JURISDICTIONAL POWER

1. Venue Provisions

Venue refers to the place or geographical location of a litigation and it usually is determined with reference to the possible burdens or inconvenience to the parties of litigating in a particular place. Both federal and state courts have venue rules, which are typically defined in intricate detail in statutory provisions. A plaintiff's choice of forum must satisfy venue rules in addition to establishing valid personal and subject matter jurisdiction. However, venue is a waivable defect and if a plaintiff selects a court that is in a improper venue, the court can either dismiss the case or, in the federal system, transfer the case to the proper venue. **Hoffman v. Blaski,** 363 U.S. 335 (1960).

a. Local and Transitory Actions Distinguished

Historically, state courts have distinguished venue based on the concepts of "local" and "transitory" actions. The federal venue statutes are not couched in the terminology of "local" and "transitory" actions. However, many state common law decisions still rely on these distinctions, and some federal authorities make reference to these concepts.

b. Venue in Federal Court

Venue in federal court is determined by reference to a highly detailed statutory scheme that delineates appropriate venue for federal cases depending on the subject matter jurisdiction of the case, the status of the parties, or the nature of the claim. The "general venue statute" is **28 U.S.C. § 1391.** Similar to the removal provisions, the venue statutes contain a number of separate, additional venue provisions for specialized cases or controversies.

i. General Venue Provision § 1391(b)

Federal venue refers to the appropriate federal judicial district court in which a plaintiff may bring a civil action. There are ninety-four federal district courts, so venue must be established with reference to one or more of these federal judicial districts. In actions based either in federal question or diversity jurisdiction, appropriate venue for a civil action may be based on party status, residence, or the location in which the party is doing business, or a variety of other factors set forth in the venue provisions.

ii. **Special Venue Based on Case Types: Additional and Exclusive Venues**

Various provisions of the federal venue statutes provide special venue rules for certain types of cases, such as tax cases or interpleader actions. In some instances, these provisions permit venue in courts other than the venue indicated by the general venue statute. In other instances, the special venue statutes require that certain kinds of cases be brought in only one particular venue.

c. **Venue in State Court**

Venue in state court is similarly defined by state statutory provisions. Venue in state court is typically defined by the appropriate county in which to pursue relief. Each state varies in the grounds for determining venue, and all states permit change-of-venue or transfer to another location within the state to mitigate problems of local bias and inconvenience. In general, state venue rules are more stringently applied to in-state defendants and more liberally applied to non-resident defendants.

d. **Challenging Venue: Method and Timing of a Challenge**

In federal cases, defects in venue typically are raised in federal court by a **Rule 12(b)(3)** motion or in a responsive pleading (or to an amended pleading) such as the defendant's answer. If the defendant fails to raise defects relating to venue in either circumstance, then the defendant is deemed to have consented to the venue and waives any objections to that venue. **Rule 12(h)(1).** *See also* **28 U.S.C. § 1406(b):** "Nothing in this chapter shall impair the jurisdiction of a district court of any matter involving a party who does not interpose timely and sufficient objection to venue."

e. **Transfer of Venue**

Actions filed in federal court may be transferred to another judicial district either upon the request of the parties, or *sua sponte* by the court itself. Venue transfers are subject to a set of statutory provisions and judicially-created rules.

i. Convenience Transfers

In addition, a federal judge may, "for the convenience of parties and witnesses, in the interests of justice," either dismiss the action or (as is more usual) transfer the case to "any district or division in which it could have been brought." **28 U.S.C. § 1404(a).**

ii. Improper Venue

If a plaintiff "lays venue" in the wrong district court (or division of a district court), then the judge may either dismiss the case or transfer it to any other district where the case could have been brought. **28 U.S.C. § 1406(a).** This provision is distinguished from transfers under **§ 1404(a),** which presume that the first forum had proper venue.

iii. Multidistrict Litigation: 28 U.S.C. § 1407

Federal courts have the power to transfer cases already filed in the federal judicial system to one particular federal district court for consolidated pretrial proceedings. This is commonly called an "MDL transfer" and the case becomes an "MDL" proceeding. In order to create an MDL proceeding, the separate federal cases must be pending in different judicial districts and must involve "one or more common questions of fact." **28 U.S.C. § 1407(a).**

f. Contractual Venue

Parties may stipulate contractually to a particular court's venue.

2. Discretionary Decline of Jurisdiction: Forum Non Conveniens

Federal courts may decline to exercise their jurisdiction under the judicially-created doctrine of forum non conveniens. In general, a greater showing of "inconvenience" is required for a forum non conveniens dismissal than for a "convenience" transfer under **28 U.S.C. § 1404(a).** The two leading Supreme Court cases setting forth the factors to be evaluated in determining whether to dismiss a case on a forum non conveniens motion are **Gulf Oil Corp. v. Gilbert,** 330 U.S. 501 (1947), and **Piper Aircraft Co. v. Reyno,** 454 U.S. 235 (1981).

a. Factors Relevant to a Forum Non Conveniens Determination Include Both Private and Public Interests

i. Private Interest Factors

Courts consider the private interests of the litigants in: the ease of access to available sources of proof; availability of compulsory process for attendance of unwilling witnesses; costs of obtaining attendance of willing witnesses; possibility of view of the premises, if appropriate for the action; all other practical problems relating to ease, speed, and expense; enforceability of a judgment if obtained; relative advantages and obstacles to a fair trial; the existence of an alternative forum that will provide adequate relief.

ii. Public Interest Factors

Courts also consider the public interest in: administrative difficulties for courts; burdens of jury duty on a community which may have little or no relationship to the litigation; interest of the local community in having a trial touching on the community's interest tried locally, rather than in a distant forum where citizens can learn of it only by report; interest in diversity cases in having the litigation tried in the home forum with the state law that must govern the case, rather than having some distant forum interpret the state's laws; interest in avoiding having courts interpret other state's laws or foreign law.

b. Standard for Granting an Appellate Review

A forum non conveniens determination is within a federal judge's discretion and may be reversed only for a clear abuse of discretion. **Piper Aircraft v. Reyno,** 454 U.S. 235 (1981).

c. Alternative Forum

A requirement for a forum non conveniens dismissal is that there be another more convenient forum where the plaintiff may obtain adequate relief. Some courts condition forum non conveniens dismissals on stipulations from the defendant waiving defendant's objections to personal jurisdiction and statutes of limitations in the alternative forum. **In re Union Carbide Corp. Gas Plant Disaster at Bhopal, India in Dec. 1984,** 809 F.2d 195 (2d Cir. 1987). However, in forum non conveniens dismissals to an alternative foreign state's court, the federal courts lack the ability to impose such conditions as adherence to federal discovery rules. **In re Union Carbide Corp. Gas Plant Disaster at Bhopal,** *id.*

d. Applicable Law

The possibility that a forum non conveniens dismissal will preclude the plaintiff from being able to take advantage of a forum's more favorable law is not a dispositive factor in a forum non conveniens determination.

Piper Aircraft Co. v. Reyno, 454 U.S. 235 (1981). However, some lower federal courts take possible applicable law into consideration in assessing whether to grant or deny a forum non conveniens dismissal.

e. Pre-Emption of State Law

Federal forum non conveniens doctrine does not pre-empt state law in a state court suit between domestic parties. **American Dredging Co. v. Miller,** 510 U.S. 443 (1994).

■ III. ASCERTAINING APPLICABLE LAW

A. DEFINING THE PROBLEM OF APPLICABLE LAW

Both state and federal courts must determine what substantive and procedural law applies to the case. The question of what law applies arises as a consequence of the American federal system of government, and the two-tier or dual-court system. Students should be aware that there is not "one law," but the possibility of multiple states' laws, or federal law. The problem of determining what applicable law applies to resolve a dispute is called "choice of law" or "conflicts of law."

1. The Applicable Law Problem in State Courts: "Horizontal" Choice of Law

State courts may either apply the forum state's law, the law of some other state, or federal law. What law applies will depend on the parties to the lawsuit, the claims, and the events or transactions giving rise to the claims.

a. Apply Forum Law

States will apply their own, or *forum,* law to completely localized disputes where the parties, claims, and events giving rise to the litigation all are contained within the state's jurisdiction. The court will apply both the state's substantive legal principles (i.e., tort, contract, property, etc.) as well as the state's procedural rules for the conduct of the action.

b. Apply Some Other State's Law

If a litigation involves out-of-state parties, or if the claims arise from events with contacts in other states (such as a dispersed tort), then a state may determine to apply some other state's law, rather than forum law. This choice-of-law determination is called "horizontal" choice of law, because it requires states to look "horizontally" across sister states for the appropriate choice-of-law. This is distinguished from a "vertical" choice of law, or choice of law between the federal and state court systems.

c. Apply Federal Law

State courts are competent to interpret and apply federal law in a state case that contains federal claims. A state's application of federal law is called a "reverse *Erie*" problem.

d. Procedural Law

In all instances, whether a state court applies forum law, some other state's law, or federal law, the state court will apply its own procedural rules to the conduct of the litigation.

i. Special Limitations Problems

Whether a state's statute of limitations (and related concepts such as tolling) are part of procedural law has caused great difficulties in both horizontal and vertical choice-of-law problems. Some states and federal courts "borrow" another state's limitations periods; other states do not and apply their own forum limitations to foreign substantive law.

2. The Applicable Law Problem in Federal Courts

Determining applicable law in federal court chiefly (but not always) is tied to the jurisdictional basis for the lawsuit—either federal question jurisdiction or diversity jurisdiction.

a. Applicable Law in Federal Question Cases

In federal cases based on federal question jurisdiction—raising a claim under the United States Constitution, or a treaty—federal courts apply federal law. Constitutional questions are determined by federal constitutional law principles. For federal substantive claims, Congress either may statutorily supply federal substantive law or may authorize the federal courts to create federal common law to give content to newly created substantive rights.

b. Applicable Law in Federal Diversity Cases: Vertical Choice of Law

By definition, cases within the federal court's diversity jurisdiction involve at least two adverse parties from different states, and the claims in the lawsuit are state-based claims. In federal cases based on the federal court's diversity jurisdiction, federal courts will apply state substantive law and federal procedural law. These two principles constitute the so-called *Erie* **doctrine,** discussed at length below.

c. Applicable Procedural Law

In all federal cases, federal courts apply the Federal Rules of Civil Procedure. Federal courts will apply state statutes of limitation, however, if the federal court determines that the state statute of limitations is substantive in effect. *See* **Guaranty Trust Co. v. York,** 326 U.S. 99 (1945).

B. STATE LAW IN FEDERAL COURTS: THE *ERIE* PROBLEM

Until 1938, federal courts freely applied notions of "federal common law" to all federal cases, including cases within the court's diversity jurisdiction. The reign of federal common law was repudiated by the Supreme Court's 1938 decision in **Erie R.R. Co. v. Tompkins,** 304 U.S. 64 (1938).

1. The Rule of Swift v. Tyson

The long-standing reign of federal common law derived from the Supreme Court's interpretation of the **Rules of Decision Act, 28 U.S.C. § 1652** in **Swift v. Tyson,** 41 U.S. 1, 16 Pet. 1, 10 L.Ed. 865 (1842). This Act requires that federal courts apply "the laws of the several states" as their rules of decision, except when the Constitution, federal law, or a treaty provides otherwise.

a. Construction of "Laws" In Section 34 of the Judiciary Act of 1789 and the Rules of Decision Act

In *Swift,* the Supreme Court, in a decision written by Justice Story, interpreted "laws" to mean only state statutes or state common law on issues that were peculiarly local in character. "Laws" did not apply to the decisions of state judicial tribunals, or to issues of broader national character, such as issues involving commercial paper.

b. General Federal Common Law

In litigation involving non-localized issues, federal judges were free to make recourse to "general principles" of "federal common law" to resolve a dispute.

2. *Erie* Doctrine

In 1938 the Supreme Court in **Erie Railroad Co. v. Tompkins** repudiated the earlier Court's interpretation of **Section 34** and the **Rules of Decision Act** and overruled **Swift v. Tyson.** The practical import of the *Erie* decision was its rejection of the concept that federal judges were empowered to ascertain and apply principles of "general federal common law" in federal diversity cases. Perhaps the most famous statement in the *Erie* decision is the Court's declaration that there is "no general federal common law."

a. "Laws" and Section 34 and the Rules of Decision Act

The Supreme Court, based on "newly discovered evidence" in a law review article written by Charles Warren concerning the intent of the drafters of **Section 34** of the **Judiciary Act of 1789,** determined that "laws" in the Act included judge-made law.

b. Effect of *Erie* Interpretation of What Constitutes "Law"

The *Erie* decision basically requires federal judges to look to both statutory law and judge-made law (that is, judicial development of common law precedent) and to apply that law under the **Rules of Decision Act.**

c. Rationales Underlying *Erie* Decisions: The "Twin Aims of *Erie*"

The *Erie* decision was intended to remedy the "mischievous" practices that had developed under the reign of *Swift*-based federal common law.

i. Forum-Shopping, Inequitable Discrimination, and Lack of Equal Protection of the Law

The *Swift* rule encouraged litigants to forum-shop for a better choice of law, usually by seeking federal diversity jurisdiction in order to benefit from a federal court willing to apply federal common law. *See, e.g.,* **Black & White Taxicab & Transfer Co. v. Brown & Yellow Taxicab & Transfer Co.,** 276 U.S. 518 (1928). In extreme instances, such as the *Black & White Taxi* case, a corporation would reincorporate in another state.

ii. Rejection of Fallacy of Transcendental Body of Federal Common Law

The *Erie* Court also suggested that the *Swift* decision rested on the erroneous assumption that there is a "transcendental body of law outside of any particular State but obligatory within it unless and until changed by statute." In another famous sentence, Justice Brandeis explained that law is not a "brooding omnipresence in the sky"—rejecting the existence of a transcendental body of general federal common law "discoverable" by federal judges.

d. Constitutional Basis for the *Erie* Decision

The Court in *Erie* did not hold Section 34 of the **Judiciary Act of 1789** unconstitutional. However, the Court suggested that in applying the *Swift* doctrine, the federal courts "h[ad] invaded rights which in our opinion are reserved by the Constitution to the several states." A major academic debate has long centered on the issue whether the *Erie* decision is constitutionally based. Many consider the *Erie* decision's discussion of its constitutional basis as *dicta*.

3. Modes of *Erie* Analysis

Although the *Erie* decision overruled *Swift* and effectively ended the reign of general federal common law, the *Erie* decision itself provided very little guidance to federal courts concerning what state law to apply, and how to ascertain that state law. This methodology for ascertaining applicable state law in federal cases has developed over a series of Supreme Court decisions since 1938, and this group of cases provides the modes of analysis collectively known as **"*Erie* doctrine."**

a. Two Branches of *Erie* Analysis

Erie analysis has developed two major branches, known as the **Rules of Decision Act** branch and the **Rules Enabling Act** branch. Almost all *Erie* problems may be classified as a problem of applicable law falling within one mode of analysis or the other.

b. *Erie* Analysis under the Rules of Decision Act

After *Erie*, federal courts have no power to create federal substantive common law, but rather must follow the substantive statutory or common law of the states. Although the *Erie* decision instructed federal courts to apply state substantive law, that decision did not indicate how to classify the law or issues involved as substantive or procedural. Subsequent Supreme Court cases have attempted to offer some analytical guidance to the lower federal courts.

i. No Conflict between State and Federal Law

In federal diversity cases, if there is no conflict between possible applicable state and federal law, then there is no *Erie* problem and the federal court is not confronted with the need to choose between conflicting law. However, if a conflict does exist between possible applicable state and federal law, then the court is confronted with an *Erie* problem.

ii. **The "Outcome Determination" Test:** *Guaranty Trust Co. v. York*, **326 U.S. 99 (1945)**

Shortly after the *Erie* decision, the Supreme Court issued a clarifying decision to assist federal courts in distinguishing between substantive and procedural issues. In *Guaranty Trust,* the Supreme Court suggested principles to follow in assessing whether an issue is substantive or procedural under *Erie:*

- Is the issue one which is tightly or loosely bound up with the creation of the rights being sued on?

- Would application of a different rule in federal court *determine the outcome* of the litigation differently (and more favorably) than application of the state rule?

- Would the application of the federal rule be *outcome determinative* because it would induce forum-shopping in favor of the federal courts and result in unequal administration of the laws?

iii. **The** *Byrd* **"Balancing Test":** *Byrd v. Blue Ridge Rural Electric Cooperative, Inc.*, **356 U.S. 525 (1958)**

In *Byrd,* the Supreme Court articulated a test requiring federal courts to balance the relative federal and state interests in application of their respective rules, asking: What is the federal interest in avoiding state law or the federal policy to be fostered by applying state law? Would the use of a federal standard have an adverse impact on federalism? Would application of the federal rule intrude on a state's ability to regulate a legitimate *area of state interest?*

c. *Erie* **Analysis under the Rules Enabling Act: Federal Procedural Rulemaking Power**

The **Rules of Decision Act** does not apply to the resolution of conflicts between federal and state procedural rules. Such conflicts implicate the procedural rulemaking power, and federal courts analyze these problems using analysis derived from the **Rules Enabling Act. 28 U.S.C. § 2072.**

i. Constitutional Authorization for the Federal Courts

Article III § 2 of the **United States Constitution** creates one Supreme Court and such inferior courts as the Congress chooses to establish. Pursuant to this authority, Congress created the lower federal courts. Inherent in the power to create federal courts is the power to prescribe rules of procedure governing procedures in those courts.

ii. Constitutional Basis for Federal Rulemaking Authority

Congress, under the authority to make all laws "necessary and proper" to carry out the functions of a federal government, enacted the Rules Enabling Act to authorize Congress and the federal judiciary to create federal rules of civil procedure. *See* **U.S. Const. Art. I § 8; 28 U.S.C. § 2072.** Congress and the federal judiciary share rulemaking power to create and revise federal rules of procedure.

iii. The Rules Enabling Act and the Federal Rules of Civil Procedure

In 1934 Congress enacted the Rules Enabling Act, which provided the statutory authority for the Federal Judicial Conference, working through an advisory committee, to promulgate the original Federal Rules of Civil Procedure in 1938. The Rules Enabling Act provides that the Supreme Court may promulgate rules of procedure for the federal courts so long as those rules do not enlarge, abridge, or modify substantive rights.

iv. Presumptively Valid Federal Rules of Civil Procedure

If the Supreme Court and Congress approve a Federal Rule of Civil Procedure (or a subsequent amendment to a rule), the **Federal Rule** is virtually presumptively valid. *See* **Sibbach v. Wilson & Co.,** 312 U.S. 1 (1941) (concluding that promulgation of **Rule 35** on mental and physical exams was within congressional power); **Schlagenhauf v. Holder,** 379 U.S. 104 (1964) (same).

v. *Erie* Conflicts between a State Rule of Procedure and a Federal Rule of Procedure

If a question presents a conflict between a state rule of procedure and a Federal Rule of Civil Procedure that is exactly on point, then *Erie* doctrine requires that the federal court apply the Federal Rule of Procedure over any conflicting state rule of procedure. **Hanna v.**

Plumer, 380 U.S. 460 (1965) (applying more liberal provisions of **Rule 4,** relating to service of process, over conflicting and more narrow Massachusetts state law service requirements).

vi. Rationale for Application of Federal Procedural Rules

The federal judiciary has a legitimate interest in establishing and maintaining a uniform system of procedural rules within the federal court system. As long as Congress and the judiciary validly promulgated the rule, and it does not contravene the Rules Enabling Act by enlarging, abridging, or modifying substantive rights, then federal courts are entitled to apply the federal rule pursuant to the Supremacy Clause. **U.S. Const. Art. VI.**

vii. No Direct Conflict between Federal Rule and State Rule: Tolling Statutes

If a federal rule and state statute appear to conflict but actually are designed for different purposes, then *Hanna* analysis does not apply and the federal court may comfortably apply both rules. See, *e.g.,* **Walker v. Armco Steel Corp.,** 446 U.S. 740 (1980) **(Rule 3** governs timing consideration in federal actions, but not tolling of state limitations periods; Oklahoma tolling statute applied. There was no direct conflict between the **Federal Rule** and the state law; *Hanna* analysis did not apply).

viii. Conflicts between Federal Statutes and State Law

If a conflict exists between a federal statute (as opposed to a Federal Rule of Civil Procedure) and a state law, *Hanna* analysis applies and the federal statute governs under the Supremacy Clause, **U.S. Const. Art. VI.** *See* **Stewart Organization, Inc. v. Ricoh Corp.,** 487 U.S. 22 (1988) (federal venue transfer statute, **28 U.S.C. § 1404(a)** applies rather than state law denying enforceability of contractual forum selection clauses).

C. DETERMINING STATE LAW FOR *ERIE* PURPOSES

Erie analysis presumes that federal courts can determine existing state law on a contested issue. Sometimes state law is not evident, especially if state law is in flux. Additionally, complex problems of ascertaining applicable law arise when state courts have not considered an issue (or there is no governing statute).

1. Determining Which State's Law Governs: *Erie* and Conflicts Principles

If a federal court determines that it must apply state substantive law, then the threshold question arises: "which state's law?" The Supreme Court answered this basic problem in **Klaxon Co. v. Stentor Electric Mfg. Co.,** 313 U.S. 487 (1941).

a.   The *"Klaxon"* Rule

Federal courts in diversity cases must apply the conflicts-of-law rules of the state in which the district court sits. For example, in federal diversity cases, the District Court for the Southern District of Texas must apply Texas state choice-of-law rules.

i.   Rationale for the *Klaxon* Rule

The *Klaxon* rule is intended to promote the uniform application of substantive law within a state.

ii.   Practical Implications of the *Klaxon* Rule

In practice, a federal judge in a diversity case sits as though he or she were a state court judge. The judge's first inquiry is to determine the state's choice-of-law regime, and then to determine whether, under the state's choice-of-law principles, the court should apply forum state law or some other state's law.

b.   Transferred Cases within the Federal System: The *Van Dusen* and *Ferens* Rules

If litigants file a federal diversity lawsuit and then transfer the case to another judicial district, the law of the transferor court applies in the transferee court. This rule applies whether the transfer is initiated by either the defendant or the plaintiff under **28 U.S.C. § 1404(a).** *See* **Van Dusen v. Barrack,** 376 U.S. 612 (1964) (defendant-initiated transfers) and **Ferens v. John Deere Co., Inc.,** 494 U.S. 516 (1990) (plaintiff-initiated transfers).

i.   Rationale for the *Van Dusen* and *Ferens* Rules

The basic rationale underlying these rules is to prevent forum-shopping. Thus, if the law of the transferor court did not follow the case, litigants would have a great incentive to file a lawsuit in one federal forum and then transfer it to another in order to take advantage of federal law. In order to defeat such forum-shopping opportunities, the rules require that the applicable state law (including the state conflicts rules) travel with the case. All the transfer changes is the courtroom, not the applicable law.

2. Ascertaining State Law

Once a federal judge determines which state's law applies, the judge must ascertain the sources of authority for, and content of, that law.

a. Hierarchy of Authority

Federal courts look to state statutes and state common law decisions as the authoritative basis for ascertaining state law. The federal judge will first look to decisions of the state's highest court, and if there is no decision on point, then to decisions of intermediate state court. Although decisions of lower state courts are entitled to some weight in *Erie* determinations, lower state court decisions do not necessarily control a federal court's reading of state law in diversity cases. *See* **Commissioner v. Bosch's Estate,** 387 U.S. 456 (1967).

b. State Law in Flux

In some federal diversity cases, federal judges may be presented with a legal question where the state law is in flux because lower state courts have repudiated older doctrine, but the highest state court has not yet definitively overturned existing precedent. Alternatively, a case may simply present an issue on which the highest state court has not yet ruled.

i. Federal Court Predictions of State Law

Federal courts may, in situations where state law is in flux (or where a state high court has not yet considered the issue), forecast what the state's highest courts might do if confronted with the legal issue.

ii. State Certification Procedures

Many states have adopted "certification" procedures that permit a federal court to petition a state's highest court for a decision on how that state court might rule on an issue of law on which the court has not yet spoken. *See, e.g.,* **Ill. Sup. Ct. Rule 20.**

D. FEDERAL LAW IN STATE COURTS: THE "REVERSE *ERIE*" PROBLEM

Many federal statutes create concurrent jurisdiction with state courts and permit litigants to pursue relief for federal law violations in state court. In such instances, the Supremacy Clause, **U.S. Const. Art. VI,** requires that state courts apply federal law. This situation is called a *"reverse Erie"* problem.

1. Federally–Created Claims

When a state case involves a federally-created claim, state courts must apply governing federal law. *See* **Dice v. Akron, Canton & Youngstown R.R. Co.,** 342 U.S. 359 (1952) (Federal Employers' Liability Act concerning validity of releases raises federal question to be determined by federal, and not state, law); **Testa v. Katt,** 330 U.S. 386 (1947).

2. Federally Conferred Right to Jury Trial

If a federal statute creating rights also supplies a right to a jury trial on an issue, states are duty-bound to supply a jury trial even though state law would not permit this. *See* **Dice v. Akron, Canton & Youngstown, supra.**

3. Federal Defenses

When a plaintiff asserts a state-based claim, a defendant may interpose a federal defense. For example, in a state contract action for recovery of royalties under a patent, the defendant may assert as a defense the invalidity of the patent, or that it has been used in violation of federal antitrust laws. The application of these defenses requires the state court to apply federal law.

4. Federal Rules of Procedure in State Courts

Congress may require that state courts use the federal procedural rules when litigants seek to enforce certain statutory rights in state court (effectively displacing state procedures). *See* **Federal Energy Regulatory Commn. v. Mississippi,** 456 U.S. 742 (1982) (upholding provisions of the **Public Utilities Regulatory Policies Act of 1978** requiring state public utility commissions to observe federal procedures in regulating energy use).

E. FEDERAL COMMON LAW

Even though the Supreme Court declared in *Erie* that there is no "general federal common law," that limitation applies only to federal courts sitting in their diversity jurisdiction. Thus, federal courts have continued to apply notions of federal common law in certain limited circumstances.

1. Traditional Bases for Federal Common Law

Federal courts have most typically applied federal common law in cases implicating important federal interests.

a. Interstate Disputes

A classic arena in which federal courts have articulated and applied federal common law is in the resolution of interstate disputes, such as over water rights, where it would be unfair to apply the law of a particular state. *See, e.g.,* **Hinderlider v. La Plata River & Cherry Creek Ditch Co.,** 304 U.S. 92 (1938).

b. Admiralty and Maritime Cases

The Constitution vests jurisdiction over admiralty cases in the federal courts, and federal courts have long created federal common law to develop a uniform body of admiralty law in these cases. *See, e.g.,* **Kossick v. United Fruit Co.,** 365 U.S. 731 (1961).

c. International Relations

In order to "speak with one voice," federal courts frequently resolve cases involving international disputes, including commercial disputes between United States citizens and foreign nationals, according to principles of federal common law. *See, e.g.,* **Banco Nacional de Cuba v. Sabbatino,** 376 U.S. 398 (1964).

d. Legal Activities of the United States: Commercial Paper

The rights and duties of the United States government on commercial paper are issues governed by federal common law, rather than by local law. **Clearfield Trust Co. v. United States,** 318 U.S. 363 (1943). The application of state law in this area would subject the rights and duties of the United States to "exceptional uncertainty."

i. Test for Determining Federal Common Law under *Clearfield Trust*

See **United States v. Kimbell Foods, Inc.,** 440 U.S. 715 (1979).

(a) Does the question involve a right of the United States arising under the operation of a nationwide program?

(b) Is there a need for a national body of uniform law? Would the application of state law frustrate the specific objectives of the federal program?

2. Interstitial Federal Common Law

Federal courts are empowered to create federal common law when there is a "statutory gap" that does not supply applicable substantive law to enforce a congressionally-created right. This type of federal common law is called "interstitial federal common law."

a. Implied Congressional Directive: Labor Law

The federal courts have been able to fashion federal common law in the labor area, based on an implied congressional directive authorizing the federal courts to develop a uniform, national body of collective bargaining law. *See* **Textile Workers Union v. Lincoln Mills,** 353 U.S. 448 (1957) (federal common law governs the decision whether federal court had jurisdiction to enforce collective bargaining agreement under the **Labor Management Relations Act of 1947).**

b. Statutes of Limitations

In instances where a federal statute is silent and does not supply an applicable statute of limitations, federal courts may draw timeliness rules from federal law (either express limitation periods from related federal statutes, or alternatives such as laches). *See* **Del Costello v. International Bhd. of Teamsters,** 462 U.S. 151 (1983). This is especially true where state statutes of limitation are unsatisfactory vehicles for the enforcement of federal law.

c. Exceptions

When a federal statute is silent, federal courts will not always create federal common law to fill the gap. *See, e.g.,* **Texas Indus., Inc. v. Radcliff Materials, Inc.,** 451 U.S. 630 (1981) (federal court not permitted to fashion federal common law of contribution among antitrust violators; presumption is strong that Congress deliberately omitted remedy when it enacts a comprehensive, integrated scheme of enforcement procedures).

■ IV. COMMENCING THE ACTION: NOTICE AND SERVICE OF PROCESS

A. THE REQUIREMENT OF REASONABLE NOTICE

1. Constitutional Notice and Due Process

The Fifth and Fourteenth Amendments to the Constitution provide that no person may be deprived of life, liberty, or property without due process of law. The Supreme Court has held: "An elementary and fundamental requirement of due process in any proceeding which is to be accorded finality is notice reasonably calculated, under all the circumstances, to apprise interested parties of the pendency of the action and to afford them an opportunity to present their objections." **Mullane v. Central Hanover Bank & Trust Co.,** 339 U.S. 306 (1950).

2. ***Mullane* Notice Requirements: *Mullane v. Central Hanover Bank & Trust Co.*, 339 U.S. 306 (1950)**

Notice must be reasonably calculated, under all the circumstances, to apprise interested parties of the pendency of the action and afford them an opportunity to present their objections. The notice must be of such nature as reasonably to convey the required information concerning the nature of the action. The notice must afford a reasonable time for those interested to make their appearance. The court should have "due regard" for the "practicalities and peculiarities" of the case.

a. **Notice and Actions Involving Real Property**

Attachment of a chattel or real estate, together with publication, may provide adequate notice. Where the names and addresses of property owners are known, then publication alone may be insufficient to provide property owners of notice in condemnation proceedings, *see, e.g.,* **Walker v. City of Hutchinson,** 352 U.S. 112 (1956).

b. **Notice Requirements for Known Parties**

Mullane requires that known parties be given notice in a manner reasonably calculated to reach them directly, such as by personal or mail service. Personal service, however, is not absolutely required. Where the names and post office addresses of parties are known, newspaper publication is constitutionally inadequate to provide notice to known parties. Courts will not require the impracticable.

c. **Notice Requirements for Unknown Parties: Publication or Constructive Notice**

Mullane indicates that notice by publication is constitutionally sufficient for unknown parties or missing parties. Notice by publication alone is a disfavored method of providing notice. However, resort to publication as a substitute for other means of actual or constructive notice is permissible in certain cases where it is not reasonably practicable or possible to provide more adequate warning of a lawsuit. Such cases typically involve unknown or missing persons.

B. THE MECHANICS OF GIVING NOTICE: SERVICE OF PROCESS

1. Commencement of an Action under State Law

State law provides different methods for determining the official commencement of an action. The date of the commencement of an action is important because this date typically triggers the filing requirements for responsive pleadings—such as the defendant's answer—or other pretrial motions, such as motions to dismiss or demurrers. Fixing the official date of the commencement of an action also is important because actions must be commenced prior to the running of any applicable statutes of limitations. In some states, a civil action is officially commenced when a complaint is filed in court. In other states, an action is commenced only when the complaint has been filed in court and the defendant has been properly served. In the latter instance, a plaintiff who files a complaint very close to a statute of limitations deadline may run into problems if the defendant cannot be properly served prior to the running of the statute of limitations.

2. Commencement of an Action in Federal Court

In federal court, "a civil action is commenced by filing a complaint with the court." **Rule 3.**

a. Timing Requirements from Service

In federal court, the timing requirements for many responsive pleadings and motions typically run from the service of process of the complaint and summons, rather than filing of the complaint. For example, a defendant's answer or motions to dismiss must be served within 21 days of the defendant's being served with the summons and complaint, unless the defendant waived service of the summons (in which case the defendant has 60 days to respond). A defendant has 90 days to answer if served outside the U.S. **Rule 12(a)(1)(A).**

3. Service of Process Provisions: Rule 4

a. Historical Note on Revisions of the Federal Service of Process Rule

The federal service of process rule, **Rule 4,** has been one of the most frequently amended rules, which Rule has grown lengthier and more detailed with each successive amendment. Prior to 1983, the primary means for accomplishing service in federal court was through the United States Marshal's Service. In 1983, **Rule 4** was extensively amended to provide for service of process by first-class mail with the return of an acknowledgment form. After a decade of problems with this mail procedure, the **Advisory Committee on Civil Rules** largely abandoned the mail-service-and-acknowledgment form in a 1993 revision of **Rule 4**. **Rule 4** was amended again in 2000, in provisions in subsection 4(i) relating to actions involving United States employees.

b. The 1993 Amendments to Rule 4 Service of Process

Rule 4 was completely rewritten as of 1993, and significant provisions of the old Rule were revised, eliminated, or renumbered. Thus, case law prior to 1993 may refer to **Rule 4** provisions that have been eliminated or moved to another place within the Rule. **Amended Rule 4** addresses both the manner and form of service of process and the assertion of personal (*in personam*) jurisdiction over defendants.

c. Major Change: Waiver of Service

The most significant 1993 change to **Rule 4** concerns the provisions for a defendant's waiver of service, contained in **Rule 4(d)** and described below.

d. Complaint; Form and Issuance of the Summons

As indicated above, a federal civil action is commenced by the filing of a complaint. **Rule 3.** The defendant must be served with a copy of the complaint and a summons. After filing the complaint, a plaintiff presents a summons to the court clerk for signing. The summons must indicate the name of the parties, the court, and the plaintiff's attorney (or the name of the plaintiff, if the plaintiff does not have a lawyer). The summons also must indicate the time in which the defendant must appear or suffer a default judgment for failure to respond within that time. A court clerk must sign the summons, which should bear the court's seal. If there are multiple defendants in the action, a summons must be issued to each. **Rules 4(a), (b).**

e. Proof of Service

Under the 1993 amendments to **Rule 4,** a defendant may waive service of process altogether. *See* **Rule 4(d)** (discussed below). However, if a defendant does not waive service, then the plaintiff must effect service of process and provide proof of that service to the court. **Rule 4(l).** This proof may be furnished by an affidavit sworn by the person who has served the process on the defendant. If the defendant is outside the United States, proof of service may be furnished according to any means agreed to by treaty, or by a receipt signed by the addressee (or other evidence of delivery to the addressee). A plaintiff's failure to make proof of service of process does not effect the validity of the process, and proof of service may be amended. **Rule 4(l).**

f. Time Limits for Service: Federal Rule 4(m)

i. In General

A defendant must be served within 120 days after the filing of the complaint.

ii. Failure to Effect Service within 120 Days

If a plaintiff fails to make service within 120 days, the court may do one of two things: either (1) dismiss the action against the defendant, without prejudice to the plaintiff's ability to refile the action (provided that any relevant statutes of limitation have not run); or, (2) if the plaintiff can show *good cause* for the failure to accomplish service, the court may extend the time for making service and direct that such service be accomplished within a specified time.

iii. Time Limits: United States as a Party

A plaintiff has a "reasonable time" to accomplish service where service is made on a U.S. attorney or the Attorney General of the United States. This special provision is "for the purpose of curing the failure to serve multiple officers, agencies, or corporations of the United States." **Rule 4(i)(4).** An amendment to this subdivision in 2000 added a new subsection **(3)** relating to the proper manner of service on a United States employee.

iv. Time Limits: Waiver (Rule 4(d)(1)(F))

If a plaintiff notifies a defendant of commencement of an action and requests a waiver of service, the defendant is entitled to a "reasonable time" to return the waiver.

g. Manner of Service on Individuals and Entities

The **Federal Rules** provide for different methods of service on individuals and entities such as corporations or associations. Service rules also relate to whether the named party is located in the United States or abroad. An individual or entity may waive service of process under **Rule 4(d).**

h. Property Seizure as the Basis for Jurisdiction and Notice: Federal Rule 4(n)

i. Authorized by United States Statute

A court may assert jurisdiction over property if it is authorized by federal statute. Once the federal government has seized such property, notice must be given to claimants of that property either as the federal seizure statute provides, or by the regular service provisions in **Rule 4. Rule 4(n)(1).**

ii. Seizure of Assets under State Law

If a court cannot obtain personal jurisdiction over a defendant by reasonable efforts to serve process, then a court may assert jurisdiction over any of the defendant's assets found within the jurisdiction as provided for by state seizure laws (the state laws in which the federal district court is located). **Rule 4(n)(2).**

i. Territorial Limits: Rule 4(k)

i. Jurisdictional Effects of Service of Process: In General

In a federal action, service of process or the filing of a waiver of service is effective to establish personal jurisdiction over party defendants, impleaded parties and interpleaded parties. Service of process also may establish valid personal jurisdiction where authorized by a federal statute. **Rule 4(k)(1).**

ii. Jurisdictional Effects of Service of Process: Federal Claims

In actions based on federal claims, service of process (or waiver of service of process) is effective to establish personal jurisdiction over a defendant who is not subject to the jurisdiction of any state— provided that exercise of jurisdiction comports with constitutional due process requirements. **Rule 4(k)(2).**

j. Waiver of Service: Rule 4(d)

The centerpiece of the 1993 amendment of **Rule 4** was the addition of provisions for waiver of service of process by the defendant in an action. If the defendant waives service and the plaintiff files the waiver with the court, the plaintiff is not required to furnish proof of service. **Rule 4(d)(4), (5).**

i.   Shift in Notice Philosophy: Duty to Avoid Unnecessary Costs: Burden on Plaintiff to Request Waiver

The 1993 amendment reflects a shift in the relative obligations of the parties with regard to notice; the new waiver provisions place an *affirmative duty* "to avoid the unnecessary costs of serving the summons." To avoid costs, a plaintiff must notify the defendant(s) of the filing of a complaint, and provide the defendant with an opportunity to waive service. **Rule 4(d)(1).**

ii.   Duty to Avoid Unnecessary Costs: Burden on Defendant to Grant Waiver

A defendant who fails to comply with a request for waiver is required to pay the plaintiff's costs in effecting service on the defendant, unless the defendant can show *good cause* for failing to comply with the plaintiff's request for a waiver. **Rule 4(d)(2).**

iii.   Implementation Provisions

A plaintiff is obligated to send a notice of the action, a copy of the complaint, and a request for waiver to the defendant (or the defendant's agent) by first-class mail or other reliable means. The defendant has to be informed of the consequences of failure to comply with the request for waiver, and the time period in which to comply. **Rule 4(d)(2)(A)–(C).**

iv.   Time Limits: Return of Waiver (Rule 4(d)(2)(F))

If a plaintiff notifies a defendant of commencement of an action and requests a waiver of service, the defendant is entitled to a *reasonable time* to return the waiver.

v.   Waiver and Time Limits for Responsive Pleadings

A defendant who returns a waiver is not required to serve an answer until 60 days after the date on which the plaintiff sent the request for the waiver, or 90 days if the defendant is outside the country.

4. Service of Process and Statutes of Limitations

a. Timing Considerations: Limitations, Accrual, and Tolling Distinguished

i. Statutes of Limitations

States have statutes of limitations that describe or limit the period in which an action may be brought. Different substantive claims, such as contract, tort, or property actions typically have different limitations periods. The failure to bring an action within the statutory limitation period bars the action and the defendant may raise the statute of limitations as an affirmative defense. *See* **Rule 8(c)** (affirmative defenses). In many federal actions based on federal statutes that lack a specific limitation period, federal courts will "borrow" a limitations period from the closest analogous state or common law form of action.

ii. Accrual

Accrual refers to the time when an action begins to run for the statute of limitations period. State and federal law determine when a particular claim or action begins to accrue. This may depend on the substantive nature of the claim. For example, in some states certain personal-injury tort claims accrue from the date of the *discovery* of the injury, rather than the date of the injury.

iii. Tolling

Tolling refers to the suspension of the running of the statute-of-limitations period. State and federal law determine under what circumstances tolling may occur. Tolling usually is contemplated when a plaintiff, for some reason, is unable to assert his or her claim in a timely fashion.

b. Service of Process and Timing Provisions

i. State Law: Commencement of an Action and Statutes of Limitation

In some states, an action is not deemed commenced until the plaintiff has effected service of process. Hence, a defect in either the process or service of process can be fatal to the plaintiff's lawsuit if service is not validly effected prior to the running of the statute of limitations. In other states, an action is commenced with the filing of the complaint, which event relates to any applicable statute of limitations periods. *See, e.g.,* **Cal. Code Civ. Proc. §§ 411.10, 583.210.** In California, a plaintiff has up to three years after filing the complaint to serve process.

ii. Federal Court: Commencement of an Action and Statutes of Limitations

Commencement of an action in federal court, for statute of limitations purposes, depends on whether the action is based on a federal claim or a state-based diversity claim.

C. IMMUNITY FROM PROCESS AND FRAUDULENT INDUCEMENT

1. General Immunity Rule

Non-resident attorneys, parties, and witnesses are immune from service of process in an unrelated action during the period they are traveling to appear at, or are appearing at, a criminal or civil action within a state.

a. Settlement Discussions Included

Immunity from service extends to litigation participants who appear in a jurisdiction for the purpose of negotiating a settlement.

b. Special Statutory Immunity

Representatives of foreign governments and their families are entitled to immunity from service of process by federal statute. Other federal statutes similarly afford immunity from process to specially designated persons.

c. Exceptions to General Immunity Rule

i. Counterclaims Against Non-Resident Plaintiff

If a non-resident plaintiff brings a lawsuit in a state, then that non-resident plaintiff is not immune from service of a counterclaim asserted by the defendant. The rationale is that the non-resident plaintiff has consented to the jurisdiction of the court by availing itself of the opportunity to sue within the state.

ii. Defendants Entering Jurisdiction Prior to Commencement of an Action

Immunity from process will not extend to a defendant who enters a jurisdiction prior to the commencement of a legal action against that defendant, and who is involuntarily detained and then served with process.

iii. Non-Resident Defendants Subject to Long-Arm Jurisdiction

Immunity from process also does not apply to non-resident defendants who otherwise are subject to a state valid long-arm jurisdiction. In other words, a non-resident defendant cannot avoid service of process simply by staying outside a state's borders.

2. Rationale for Immunity Rule

Immunity from service under such circumstances is granted to non-residents in order to encourage active participation in legal proceedings.

a. Original Purpose

The original purpose of the process immunity rule was as a privilege of the court to secure the administration of justice free from outside interference or influence. **State ex rel. Sivnksty v. Duffield,** 137 W.Va. 112 (W. Va. 1952).

b. Modern Rationale

In absence of immunity, lawyers, parties, and witnesses might refuse to attend legal proceedings if they feared being subject to service in an unrelated matter.

3. Fraudulent Inducement

A plaintiff may not effect service of process on a defendant by fraudulently inducing the defendant into the jurisdiction for the purpose of serving process and conferring jurisdiction.

a. Rationale

A judgment procured fraudulently lacks jurisdiction and is null and void. A fraud affecting jurisdiction is the equivalent of a lack of jurisdiction. **Wyman v. Newhouse,** 93 F.2d 313 (2d Cir. 1937).

D. CHALLENGING DEFECTIVE OR IMPROPER SERVICE OF PROCESS

1. Two Types of Challenges

Under **Rule 12,** there are two available grounds for challenging improper service of process: insufficiency of process, **Rule 12(b)(4),** and insufficiency of service of process, **Rule 12(b)(5).** These two challenges are distinct, and have distinct consequences.

a. Insufficiency of Process: Rule 12(b)(4)

Insufficiency of process refers to a defect in the form or content of the summons.

i. Consequences of Insufficiency of Process

If the form or content of the summons is defective, the court will invalidate the process and dismiss the action without prejudice to the plaintiff's ability to re-file the action and re-serve the defendant.

b. Insufficiency of Service of Process: Rule 12(b)(5)

Insufficiency of service of process refers to the improper manner of service on the defendant(s). The failure to accomplish sufficient service of process is a jurisdictional defect; the court lacks jurisdiction over the improperly served defendant.

2. Methods for Asserting Challenges to Service of Process

a. Insufficient Process or Insufficient Service of Process

May be challenged by a motion to quash service, a plea in abatement, or a motion to dismiss (**Rule 12(b)(4), (5)).**

E. PROVISIONAL REMEDIES AND DUE PROCESS REQUIREMENTS

1. Due Process Notice Requirements Revisited

Constitutional due process requires that a defendant have adequate notice of an action as well as a meaningful opportunity to be heard in response to that action. *See* **Mullane v. Central Hanover Bank & Trust Company,** 339 U.S. 306 (1950).

2. Provisional Remedies Defined

"Provisional remedies" are forms of relief that a court affords a plaintiff prior to an actual adjudicated trial of the merits asserted by a plaintiff against a defendant. The most common form of relief prior to trial involves seizure or attachment of the defendant's property, or other restraints enjoining the defendant from using, wasting, or alienating the property. Provisional remedies include temporary restraining orders, preliminary injunctions, and prejudgment attachments, seizures, or sequestrations.

3. Provisional Remedies and Due Process: The Constitutional Issue

Many provisional remedies are equitable, and are obtained on an expedited or emergency basis. Since most provisional remedies involve prejudgment attachment or seizure of the defendant's property, the constitutional issue concerns what due process is required to protect the defendant's property interests, particularly where the state law defines the manner of effecting the prejudgment seizure.

a. Constitutional Basis

In actions where state law defines the availability and manner of prejudgment seizure (or other provisional relief), such statutes are subject to the Fourteenth Amendment to the United States Constitution: "No state shall make any law . . . depriving any person of life, liberty, or property without due process of law. . . . "

b. Property Interests Protected under the Fourteenth Amendment in Provisional Remedies Situations

i. What Constitutes a "Taking"

A person's property interests are protected by the Fourteenth Amendment without regard to the length of a possible deprivation. Hence, even a temporary seizure of property through a provisional remedy must meet constitutional standards. The Fourteenth Amendment does not distinguish between temporary or permanent deprivations of property. **Fuentes v. Shevin,** 407 U.S. 67 (1972).

ii. What Constitutes "Property"

The Fourteenth Amendment extends protection to any significant property interest and has never been interpreted to protect only the rights of undisputed ownership of property. Hence, the Fourteenth Amendment protection extends to conditional sales contracts where a person may not yet possess full legal title to goods. **Fuentes v. Shevin,** 407 U.S. 67 (1972).

4. Governmental Deprivations of Property: Due Process Requirements

a. General Constitutional Principles: *Fuentes v. Shevin*, 407 U.S. 67 (1972)

Constitutional due process in prejudgment provisional remedies cases requires: (1) the right to notice and an opportunity to be heard at a meaningful time and in a meaningful manner; (2) notice and an opportunity to be heard *before* the seizure (i.e., a time when the deprivation can still be prevented); (3) informed evaluation of the claims to the property by a neutral official.

b.   *Mathews v. Eldridge* Analytical Framework

When a government seeks to deprive a defendant of property on its own initiative, a court is required to evaluate: (1) the private interest that will be affected by the official action; (2) the risk of an erroneous deprivation of such interest through the procedures used; (3) the probable value, if any, of additional or substitute safeguards; and (4) the "government's interest, including the function involved and the fiscal and administrative burdens that the additional or substitute procedural requirement would entail." *See* **Mathews v. Eldridge,** 424 U.S. 319 (1976).

c.   Garnishment Statutes: *Sniadach v. Family Finance Corp.*, 395 U.S. 337 (1969)

The Supreme Court struck down a Wisconsin prejudgment wage garnishment procedure as violative of due process; the statute did not provide for notice or an opportunity to be heard prior to the garnishment.

d.   "Extraordinary Situations" Exception

Certain situations may justify an exception to the due process requirements for prejudgment notice and a hearing. These situations, however, "must be truly unusual." **Boddie v. Connecticut,** 401 U.S. 371 (1971). Such seizures must: (1) be directly necessary to secure an important governmental or general public interest; (2) be a special need for very prompt action; (3) be kept under strict control by the government possessing a monopoly of legitimate force; (4) be initiated by a government official responsible for determining under the standards of a narrowly drawn statute that such an emergency seizure was necessary or justified in the particular instance.

5.   Private–Party Disputes and Prejudgment Seizures

Mathews v. Eldridge supplies the analytical framework for assessing due process requirements of prejudgment seizures in disputes between individuals and the government (*see* above).

a.   Different Focus in Private Disputes

The Supreme Court has suggested that the prejudgment seizure due process inquiry has a *different focus* in disputes between private parties.

Connecticut v. Doehr, 501 U.S. 1 (1991). In disputes involving private parties, the appropriate analytical framework for evaluating the due process sufficiency of prejudgment seizure statutes involves consideration of: (1) the private interest that will be affected by the prejudgment measure; (2) the risk of erroneous deprivation through the procedures under attack; (3) the probable value of additional or alternative safeguards; (4) principal attention to the interest of the party seeking the prejudgment remedy; and (5) due regard to the ancillary interest the government may have in providing the procedure or foregoing the added burden of providing greater protections.

6. *Mathews* and *Doehr* Standards Compared

The *Mathews* analytical framework is properly used in prejudgment seizure cases where the government itself initiates the seizure or attachment of property, such as garnishment of an employee's wages. The *Doehr* standards apply in disputes between private parties, where the government is not the party seizing the property. The focus of the *Doehr* standards is on the interests of the private party seeking the prejudgment remedy; under the *Doehr* standards, the government's interests are *ancillary* to those of the parties.

■ V. PLEADINGS

A. THE DEVELOPMENT OF MODERN PLEADING—HISTORICAL CONTEXT

1. Importance of Historical Pleading Rules to Understanding Modern Federal Pleading Rules

The philosophy underlying the 1938 Federal Rules of Civil Procedure represents a marked departure from the English common law system of pleading and state "code" pleading regimes. Modern federal pleading reforms were enacted in response to perceived problems with existing common law or code pleading systems. Hence, it is important to understand English common law and code pleading as the basis for appreciating modern civil procedural rules.

2. Common Law Pleading and Divided Power

a. The Writ System

In the English common law system, the writ was the document or paper by which an action was commenced. The modern analog of the English writ is the summons. Technically, a person with a grievance sought justice from the king; the king issued the writ that ordered a sheriff to bring the defendant before the king's judges to answer the complaint.

b. Relationship of Writs to Forms of Action

Over time, English common law developed a particular writ for each distinctive "form of action." The failure of the plaintiff's lawyer to swear out the appropriate writ for the particular cause of action was fatally defective to the case and would result in a dismissal.

c. Purpose of Common Law Pleading Requirements

The basic purpose of common law pleading was to reduce the dispute to a single issue of law or fact. Common law pleading did not permit multiple parties or multiple claims to be present in an action.

d. Detailed Structure of Successive Rounds of Common Law Pleading

Pleading at English common law was characterized by multiple, successive rounds of responsive pleading. Many of these pleading forms have analogs under modern pleading systems.

i. The Declaration

A civil action at common law was instituted with a declaration, which set forth the plaintiff's claim. The complaint is the modern analog of the common law declaration.

ii. Defendant's Responses: Demurrer or Plea

In response to the plaintiff's declaration, the defendant either had to demur to the declaration, or respond in a plea.

iii. Plaintiff's Responses to the Defendant's Plea

If the defendant entered a plea, then the plaintiff had to respond in another pleading. The plaintiff had two possible methods for responding to the defendant's confession-and-avoidance.

iv. Defendant's Response to Plaintiff's Replication Pleading a Confession-and-Avoidance

If the plaintiff pleaded a confession-and-avoidance in response, the defendant could respond with another pleading.

v. Successive Rounds of Pleading

Since at each round of pleading either party could assert a confession-and-avoidance by way of defense, in theory common law pleading could go on indefinitely. Such successive pleadings were denominated as surrejoinders, rebutters, and surrebutters.

e. Problems with English Common Law Pleading

i. "Traps for the Unwary Pleader"

A plaintiff was required to choose the appropriate writ for each substantive claim, and failure to swear out the appropriate writ for a particular form of action was a fatal defect and subject to dismissal on demurrer.

ii. Delay

The multiple, successive rounds of permissible pleading led to lengthy periods for pleading the claim.

iii. Inability to Hear Claims on the Merits

Under common law pleading, the process of pleading became an end in itself, and the technical requirements plus the length of time for responsive pleading frustrated the ability of the courts to hear claims on the merits.

iv. Limitations on Joinder of Parties and Claims

One of the major purposes of common law pleading was to produce a single issue; therefore, it was necessary to prohibit duplication in pleading. A person was prohibited from raising more than one issue of fact or law in a pleading, or joining multiple parties.

f. Chancery and the Rise of Equity Procedure

Equity courts and procedure began to develop at the end of the thirteenth century, in the king's Chancery. Equity developed as a parallel, alternative system to afford relief to petitioners unable to obtain justice or a remedy at law. Such petitions were referred by the king to the Chancellor, and by the end of the fourteenth century, directly to the Chancellor. Equity developed its own distinctive characteristics.

i. Common Law Jurisdiction Distinguished

The Chancellor was not empowered to hear claims that were cognizable at common law in the ordinary law courts, which could provide legal relief for a claimant. Thus, equity would not lie for actions involving claims relating to property, torts, or contracts.

Actions at law were entitled to a trial by jury. A judgment at law declared a legal relationship between the parties; if the plaintiff prevailed, the plaintiff was entitled to relief from the defendant, but the judgment did not order the defendant to do anything. If the defendant failed to pay, the plaintiff needed to enforce the judgment.

ii. Equity Jurisdiction

Other disputes were considered highly appropriate for handling in the equity courts, such as matters involving wills and trusts, fraud or breach of trust, or injunctive relief. Actions in equity were tried to a judge and not a jury. A decree in equity (unlike a judgment at law) was directed at the defendant, and an equity court could order imprisonment or fines to enforce compliance. The maxim describing this relationship states that "equity acts *in personam* and not in rem." The primary means of equitable relief was the injunction, an order directing a defendant to perform (or to cease performing) certain conduct.

iii. Equitable Procedure

Over time, equity developed its own separate court system and procedural rules.

iv. Equity in Colonial America

Generally, in the United States northern courts did not retain the English distinction between law and equity courts. Many southern states, however, did retain the distinctive two-court system, recognizing separate actions at law and in equity, as well as the distinctive procedural prerequisites and remedies for each system.

v. Modern Equity Practice

The Federal Rules of Civil Procedure have merged law and equity into one unified civil action. Both legal and equitable relief may be sought in a federal civil action in the same court. **Rules 1** and **2.** Requests for equitable relief, however, still retain their distinctive procedural and substantive prerequisites. A few states still retain separate equity courts and procedure.

3. Reform: New Pleading, Abolition of Forms of Action, and Merger of Law and Equity

a. Reforms in Nineteenth-Century England

The Common Law Procedure Acts of 1852, 1854, and 1860 were the major statutory bills that reformed English pleading. These statutes liberalized pleading rules, weakened the forms of action, and expanded joinder possibilities. English legal reform culminated in the Judicature Acts of 1873 and 1875, which merged the common law courts and Chancery into the Supreme Court of Judicature. These acts merged law and equity and abolished the forms of action.

b. American Reforms in the Nineteenth Century: The Field Code and the Merger of Law and Equity

New York State led the nineteenth-century American reform of procedure. In 1846 a new state constitution abolished the Chancery court, and the legislature authorized a commission to reform civil procedure. As a result of the commission's report, the legislature enacted a Code of Civil Procedure, commonly called the Field Code (after David Dudley Field, the most prominent of the commission's members). The most prominent features of the Field Code included: abolition of the distinction of actions at law and suits in equity; creation of one form of action—the civil action; and abolition of all prior forms of pleading.

c. Code Pleading and Persistent Problems

Many states followed New York's model and enacted "code pleading" regimes similar to the Field Code. Although the intent of code pleading was to effect a clean break with the problems of common law pleading, many state courts persisted in interpreting code pleadings in light of common law rules and restrictions.

B. MODERN PLEADING UNDER THE FEDERAL RULES OF CIVIL PROCEDURE

1. Introductory Notes on the Federal Rules and Rulemaking Authority

In 1934 Congress enacted the **Rules Enabling Act, 28 U.S.C. §§ 2071–72,** which authorized the Supreme Court to promulgate rules of procedure for the federal district courts. After a four-year rulemaking process, Congress enacted the Federal Rules of Civil Procedure in 1938. Since 1938 the Federal Rules have been amended and revised several times, although the underlying philosophy of the Federal Rules has remained constant since 1938.

a. Theory of Transsubstantive Rules

The Federal Rules of Civil Procedure are intended to be "transsubstantive"— that is, to apply uniformly to all substantive claims and actions. With very few exceptions (such as shareholder derivative lawsuits, *see* **Rule 23.1)**, the Federal Rules are not case-specific. Federal pleading rules are the antithesis of common law forms of action and writs, a substance-specific pleading regime.

b. Goals of the Federal Rules

Rule 1 sets forth the declared purpose of the Federal Rules, to secure the "just, speedy, and inexpensive determination of every action and proceeding." Federal judges are to construe and administer the rules to ensure these purposes. **Rule 1** was amended in 1993 to add the phrase "and administered," indicating an intent that federal judges actively manage federal cases to ensure these goals.

c. General Reforms

The Federal Rules were patterned after the Field Code and nineteenth-century procedural reforms, merging law and equity, simplifying pleading, and abolishing forms of action as well as multiple rounds of pleading.

d. Limitations on Pleadings

The Federal Rules permit only three types of pleadings: a complaint, an answer, and a plaintiff's reply to defendant's counterclaim. **Rule 7(a).** If the defendant does not assert a counterclaim, then the plaintiff is not permitted to file a reply.

e. Policy Favoring Merits Resolution

The Federal Rules were intended to permit a resolution of claims on the merits, and prevent pleadings from serving as a barrier to reaching the merits. Dismissals based on technical pleadings defects were discouraged, and pleaders were not expected to know all the facts at the time of pleading.

f. Creation of Liberal Discovery Regime

The Federal Rules created a system of liberal discovery provisions to assist in fact development after filing the complaint.

g. Fostering Liberal Joinder

The Federal Rules permitted and encouraged liberal joinder of parties and claims.

h. Intent of Liberal Construction

The Federal Rules were intended to be liberally construed, including amendments to pleadings and joinder of parties and claims.

i. Postponed Claim Screening

Rules 11, 12, and **56** were intended to filter out baseless claims through pretrial motions to dismiss factually or legally deficient claims.

2. The Complaint

a. Statement of Claims: General Principles and the Problem of Specificity

The major function of pleading under the Federal Rules is to provide parties with notice of the nature of claims or defenses.

i. Notice Pleading

The Federal Rules require a complaint to contain simply "a short and plain statement of the claim showing that the pleader is entitled to relief." **Rule 8(a)(2).** The pleader also must state the grounds for the court's jurisdiction, **Rule 8(a)(1),** and a demand for relief, **Rule 8(a)(3).**

ii. Fact Pleading versus Notice Pleading

For nearly fifty years, the Supreme Court affirmed that federal pleading rules did not require a plaintiff to set out in great detail the facts upon which the claim is based. **Conley v. Gibson,** 355 U.S. 41 (1957). In 2007 and 2009, the Supreme Court reversed course and repudiated its prior liberal holding in **Conley v. Gibson.** The Court held that a plaintiff has an obligation to provide the grounds for his entitlement to relief; requires more than labels and conclusions; and rejects formulaic recitations of the elements of a cause of action. **Bell Atlantic Corp. v. Twombly,** 550 U.S. 544 (2007); **Ashcroft v. Iqbal,** 556 U.S. 662 (2009).

iii. The *Twombly/Iqbal* "Plausibility" Standard

Under **Rule 8(a)(2),** to survive a motion to dismiss, a plaintiff must allege sufficient factual matter, accepted as true, to state a claim that is plausible on its face. A claim has facial plausibility when the plaintiff pleads factual content that allows the court to draw the reasonable inference that the defendant is liable for the misconduct alleged. **Bell Atlantic v. Twombly; Ashcroft v. Iqbal.**

iv. The Plausibility Standard Applied

The plausibility standard is not akin to a "probability requirement," but it asks for more than a sheer possibility that a defendant acted unlawfully. **Bell Atlantic v. Twombly; Ashcroft v. Iqbal.**

v.   Pleading Requirements under the Private Securities Litigation Reform Act of 1995 (PSLRA)

In alleging a securities' fraud violation pleading facts that give rise to a strong inference of scienter, an inference of scienter must be more than merely plausible or reasonable—it must be cogent and at least as compelling as any opposing inference of non-fraudulent intent. **Tellabs, Inc. v. Makor Issues & Rights, Ltd.,** 551 U.S. 308 (2007).

vi.   Insufficient Facts: Motion for More Definite Statement (Rule 12(e))

A plaintiff must state a claim with a level of specificity sufficient for the defendant to frame a response. If a plaintiff's complaint is factually too vague, a defendant, in a "motion for a more definite statement," may request the plaintiff to state more facts specifically detailing the claim. **Rule 12(e).**

vii.   Illustrative Pleading Forms

The pleading forms contained in the **Appendix** to the rules are presumptively sufficient to state a claim in federal court. **Rule 84.** The forms "are intended to indicate the simplicity and brevity of statement which the rules contemplate." **Rule 84.**

b.   Consistency and Honesty in Pleading

i.   Alternative and Inconsistent Allegations: Rule 8(d)(2)

Under the Federal Rules, a pleader (either the plaintiff or the defendant) may state alternative or hypothetical allegations, if made in good faith, either in the complaint or a responsive pleading, such as a defense. **Rule 8(d)(2).** Such alternative or inconsistent allegations are subject to the requirements of **Rule 11.** Many states also permit the assertion of inconsistent allegations.

ii.   Signature and Certification Requirements: Federal Rule of Civil Procedure 11

Every pleading, motion, and paper filed in federal court must be signed by an attorney of record or, if a party is not represented by a lawyer, then by the party. In general, pleadings do not need to be verified (that is, by sworn oath before a notary—under penalty of perjury) or accompanied by an affidavit. **Rule 11(a).** A few exceptions require verified pleadings, such as shareholder derivative complaints. *See* **Rule 23.1.**

iii. Purpose of the Signature Requirement

The purpose of the signature requirement is to make the attorney or party pleader responsible for truthfulness of the allegations contained in the complaint.

iv. Reasonable Inquiry Standard

A pleader certifies that the allegations made in the complaint were formed after "an inquiry reasonable under the circumstances." In addition, the pleader certifies that, to the person's best knowledge, information, and belief that the complaint is not being presented for any improper purpose, such as to harass or cause unnecessary delay or needless increase in the cost of litigation; the claims, defenses, and other legal contentions are warranted by existing law or by a nonfrivolous argument for the extension, modification, or reversal of existing law, or the establishment of new law; the allegations or other factual contentions have evidentiary support or are likely to have evidentiary support after a reasonable opportunity for further investigation or discovery; and denials of factual contentions are warranted on the evidence, or are reasonably based on a lack of information or belief.

v. Sanctions Available

Prior to the amendment of **Rule 11** in 1993, a court was required to impose a monetary sanction against a **Rule 11** violator. The 1993 amendments of **Rule 11** substantially modified the available array of sanctions under the rule and additionally provided that sanctions may be imposed in the court's discretion.

vi. Notice; Safe Harbor Provision; Opportunity to Be Heard

A person seeking sanctions for a **Rule 11** violation is required to serve notice on the person who has filed the challenged paper. That person then has 21 days (a "safe harbor") either to withdraw or correct the challenged claim, defense, contention, or allegation. If the challenged paper is not corrected or withdrawn within 21 days, then the person seeking sanctions may file the request for sanctions with the court. The pleader has to be given an opportunity to respond to the alleged **Rule 11** violation. **Rule 11(c)(1).**

vii. Certification Requirements: Other Provisions—Shareholder's Derivative Suits under Rule 23.1

Although the Federal Rules do not require a pleader to verify the pleadings by notarization or affidavit, certain actions require verification. An example is the shareholder's derivative suit, which requires the plaintiff to sign a verified complaint. **Rule 23.1.** A verified signature subjects the signer to penalty of perjury for false statements. A falsely verified complaint may also result in dismissal of the action as a "sham pleading."

viii. State Verification Requirements

Some states require certain types of pleadings to be verified, such as petitions for divorce, state petitions to enjoin a nuisance, or complaints to obtain support of an illegitimate child.

c. Pleading Special Matters: Rule 9

Rule 9 requires that certain matters have to be pleaded with greater specificity or particularity.

i. Fraud or Mistake

The circumstances constituting fraud or mistake needed to be pleaded with particularity. **Rule 9(b).**

ii. Special Damages

Special damages also must be specifically stated and claimed, or they will be forfeited. **Rule (9)(g).**

iii. Denial of Performance or Occurrence of Conditions Precedent

A pleader is required to plead specifically and particularly the denial of performance or occurrence of conditions precedent. **Rule 9(c).** However, a pleader *may generally state* the performance or occurrence of conditions precedent.

d. Pleading Damages; Prayer for Relief

i. The Demand for Relief

The concluding paragraphs of the complaint typically contain the "prayer for relief" setting forth the legal or equitable remedies the pleader seeks for the claims set forth in the complaint. The paragraph requesting monetary damages is called an ad damnum clause.

ii. Federal Practice

In federal court a pleader must set forth "a demand for judgment for the relief the pleader seeks." A pleader may seek alternative relief, or several different types of relief (such as a combination of legal and equitable remedies). **Rule 8(a)(3).** There is some sentiment that the ad damnum clause also is anachronistic in federal practice, but it is still a requirement of the rules.

iii. Judgment Exceeding the Demand: Permissible Recovery of Damages

A federal pleader is entitled to recover an amount exceeding what was demanded in the complaint. **Rule 54(c); Bail v. Cunningham,** 452 F.2d 182 (7th Cir. 1971). Most states follow the Federal Rule with regard to the recovery of excessive damages.

iv. Amending the Prayer for Relief

Some states that do not follow **Rule 54(c)** (damages in excess of the ad damnum clause) instead allow the plaintiff to amend the complaint to increase the amount of damages, in order to permit full recovery. *See, e.g.,* **Haney v. Burgin,** 106 N.H. 213, 208 A.2d 448 (1965) (permitting plaintiff to successively amend complaint four times, increasing amount of damages with each amendment).

v. Damages in Excess of Jurisdictional Amount

State court jurisdiction often is circumscribed by amount-in-controversy limitations, but plaintiffs may plead damages in excess of the court's jurisdiction.

vi. Pleading Special Damages: Rule 9(g)

Special damages must be specifically stated in a federal complaint. **Rule 9(g).** Many states also require that special damages be specially pleaded.

3. Responding to the Complaint: Responsive Motions and Pleadings

a. General Considerations

Defendants have two possible ways of responding to a complaint. The defendant may either challenge the complaint by a motion prior to answering, or if not by a motion, then by filing an answer to the complaint.

i. Defenses and Objections Made Pursuant to Rule 12

Rule 12 motions must be asserted within the time period in which a defendant has to answer a complaint (or in which a plaintiff must respond to a defendant's counterclaim). Thus, a defendant who wishes to raise any defenses or objections permitted in **Rule 12** must do so before filing an answer. Similarly, a plaintiff who wishes to raise **Rule 12** objections or defenses to a counterclaim must do so prior to filing a reply to the counterclaim. **Rule 12(b).**

ii. Answer

A defendant has a different amount of time to file an answer, depending on whether the defendant waived service of process, or declined to waive process and was actually served.

iii. Effect of Rule 12 Motions on Timing of Responsive Pleadings

In general, a **Rule 12** motion extends the time for filing a responsive pleading such as an answer for 14 days after notice of the court's action. **Rule 12(a)(4)(A), (B).**

iv. Extensions of Time

Attorneys frequently request extensions of time in which to file responsive pleadings, which is permitted under the rules. *See* **Rule 6(b).** Generally, the parties mutually agree to extensions of time. Judges also may order extensions of time by written stipulation (i.e., agreement) of the parties.

b. Pre-Answer Motions: Motions to Dismiss—Rule 12

i. Motion to Dismiss for Failure to State a Claim

The modern motion to dismiss for failure to state a claim upon which relief can be granted has its historical antecedents in the common law demurrer. The concept of the demurrer was incorporated into state code pleading systems, which permitted a complaint to be dismissed for a failure to state facts sufficient to constitute a cause of action, for deficiencies in the form of pleading, or for lack of subject matter jurisdiction.

ii. Other Jurisdictional Defects: Common Law Analogs

Federal motions to dismiss based on technical defects in jurisdiction, venue, process, and failure to join necessary parties. **(Rules 12(b)(1)** through **12(b)(5)** and **12(b)(7)** contain modern counterparts to common law pleas in abatement.)

iii. Rule 12 Motions to Dismiss: Available Challenges and Defenses

Rule 12 provides for seven separate grounds for dismissing a complaint: lack of subject matter jurisdiction (**Rule 12(b)(1)**); lack of personal jurisdiction (**Rule 12(b)(2)**); improper venue **(Rule 12(b)(3))**; insufficient process (**Rule 12(b)(4)**); insufficient service of process (**Rule 12(b)(5)**); failure to state a claim upon which relief can be granted (**Rule 12(b)(6)**); and failure to join a party needed for a just adjudication under **Rule 19 (Rule 12(b)(7))**.

iv. Consolidation Requirement

A defendant who wishes to raise more than one **Rule 12** objection or defense—or any other motion available under the rule—must join all those objections into one consolidated motion. **Rule 12(g)**.

v. Waiver of Defenses

Four defenses must be timely asserted either in a **Rule 12** motion, the answer, or an amended pleading (permitted under **Rule 15)**. These are: lack of personal jurisdiction, improper venue, insufficient process, or insufficient service of process. The failure to raise these defenses constitutes a waiver of these objections. **Rule 12(h)(1)**.

vi. Subject Matter Jurisdiction Non-Waivable Defense

Objections to the court's subject matter jurisdiction are not waivable and are never lost. Objections to the court's subject matter jurisdiction may be raised prior to, during, and after trial. If the court finds that it lacks subject matter jurisdiction, it must dismiss the case. **Rule 12(h)(3)**.

vii. Motion to Dismiss for Failure to State a Claim: Rule 12(b)(6)

The Federal Rules permit a defendant to challenge the factual sufficiency of a complaint in a motion to dismiss for failure to state a claim upon which relief can be granted. **Rule 12(b)(6)**. The standard applied to **Rule 12(b)(6)** motions is the plausibility standard set forth in **Bell Atlantic Corp. v. Twombly** and **Ashcroft v. Iqbal**.

viii. Motion for a Judgment on the Pleadings: Rule 12(c)

This motion is the means for challenging the substantive sufficiency of the opposing party's pleadings once all the pleadings have been completed.

ix. Motion to Strike: Rule 12(f)

The motion to strike is the means by which a party challenges the substantive sufficiency of defenses raised in an answer (or in a plaintiff's reply), or any redundant, impertinent, or scandalous matter.

x. Motion for a More Definite Statement: Rule 12(e)

A party may request a more definite statement from a pleader if the party is unable to frame a responsive pleading.

xi. Affirmative Defenses

Preliminary motion practice in federal courts is not restricted to the objections and defenses enumerated in **Rule 12.** Many federal courts also permit affirmative defenses (available in **Rule 8(c)**) to be raised in a pretrial motion, although these defenses probably were intended to be raised solely in the answer.

xii. Summary Judgment

Defendants may move for a summary judgment dismissal prior to filing a responsive pleading. **Rule 56(a).** In addition, **Rule 12** motions may be converted into summary judgment motions if material outside the pleadings is introduced in support of those **Rule 12** motions. **Rule 12(d).**

4. The Answer

a. Timing

An answer must be filed by the defendant either 21, 60, or 90 days after waiver of process or actual service of process, depending on whether the defendant is located in the United States or outside the United States. This time period is extended if the defendant instead chooses to file a **Rule 12** motion, or other motions (such as a summary judgment motion).

b. Signing and Verification

An answer under the Federal Rules must be signed by the pleader and is subject to **Rule 11** requirements. Answers do not need to be verified or accompanied by an affidavit. Some states require that answers be verified.

c. Defendant's Possible Responses in the Answer under Rule 8(b)

Rule 8(b) requires that a defendant make one of three possible responses to the averments or allegations in the plaintiff's complaint. These three possible responses are to: admit each allegation; deny each allegation; or plead that the defendant lacks knowledge or sufficient information to form a belief as to the truth of an averment.

d. The General Denial

A federal pleader may "generally deny" all the allegations contained in a complaint, including the jurisdictional allegations. **Rule 8(b)(3).** Some states permit general denials; other states do not permit a defendant to generally deny the entire complaint. In California, for example, an answer cannot contain a general denial and must also be verified. The effect of a general denial is to place each and every averment stated in the complaint in issue, as a contested fact. This means that the plaintiff at trial must offer proof as to every averment or allegation in the complaint.

e. Evasive Denials

A defendant may respond to allegations in a complaint by stating that the pleader "neither admits nor denies" the plaintiff's allegations. **Rule 8(b)** does not particularly prohibit evasive denials, but such a response may fail to comport with the requirement that denials fairly meet the substance of the averments denied. Some states specifically prohibit such evasive denials.

f. Specific Denials; Form of Denials

If a defendant does not make a general denial, then the answer typically will contain numbered paragraphs corresponding to the complaint that specifically admit some allegations and deny others. A defendant may partially admit and deny statements contained within a plaintiff's paragraphs. *See* **Zielinski v. Philadelphia Piers, Inc.,** 139 F.Supp. 408 (E.D. Pa. 1956). A specific denial places the particular statement or averment in issue and the plaintiff must offer proof in support of the contested allegation at trial. In contrast, allegations that the defendant admits are not in issue and the plaintiff need not prove these facts at trial.

g. Consequence of Failure to Deny

All averments to which a defendant does not specifically respond are deemed admitted. This means that the plaintiff will not be required to present evidence in support of the averment, and the defendant will not be able to contest the claims at trial.

h. Affirmative Defenses: Rule 8(c)

Affirmative defenses are available under both state procedural rules and **Rule 8(c).** In federal diversity cases, the federal court usually will look to state law to determine the availability of an affirmative defense, but not always. *See, e.g.,* **Taylor v. United States,** 821 F.2d 1428 (9th Cir. 1987), *cert denied,* 485 U.S. 992 (1988) (declining to give effect to California affirmative defense of limitation of liability on noneconomic damages).

i. Types of Affirmative Defenses Available

Rule 8(c) lists affirmative defenses that a party may set forth in a responsive pleading: accord and satisfaction; arbitration and award; assumption of risk; contributory negligence; duress; estoppel; failure of consideration; fraud; illegality; injury by fellow servant; laches; license; payment; release; res judicata; statute of frauds; statute of limitations; and waiver.

ii. Other Affirmative Defenses

The list of available affirmative defenses in **Rule 8(c)** is not exhaustive.

iii. Mistaken Denomination of an Affirmative Defense

If a pleader mistakenly labels a defense as a counterclaim or a counterclaim as a defense, a court may treat the allegations as if they were properly designated ("if justice so requires"). The purpose of this rule is to alleviate the harshness of common law technical pleading defects as a result of mis-naming claims or defenses. **Rule 8(c)(2).**

i. Counterclaims

A defendant in the answer or a plaintiff in a reply may assert any counterclaims that are available to the pleader. In some instances the pleader is *required* to assert certain compulsory counterclaims. *See* **Rule 13(a), (b).**

j. Cross-Claims

A defendant in the answer may assert any cross-claims it has against co-defendants in the lawsuit. *See* **Rule 13(g).** Similarly, a plaintiff in its reply to a counterclaim also may assert any claims the plaintiff has against co-plaintiffs, although this is more unusual.

5. The Reply: Rule 7(a)

Reply is one of the three forms of pleading permitted under federal pleading rules.

a. Relationship to Common Law Pleading

The reply in federal practice (and most states) is the third permissible responsive pleading. This reflects a reaction to common law pleading, which permitted multiple successive rounds of pleading until disputed issues were identified.

b. Federal Practice

A plaintiff may file a reply if the defendant asserts a counterclaim. A court may order a reply to an answer. A third-party plaintiff also may file a reply to a third-party answer. *See* third-party practice and **Rule 14** generally.

c. Court-Ordered Replies

A federal court may order a reply to allegations other than a counterclaim, but are reluctant to do so unless there is "a clear and convincing factual showing of necessity or other extraordinary circumstances of a compelling nature."

d. State Practice

In some states, the failure to deny the allegations of a defendant's affirmative defenses in a responsive reply results in those affirmative defenses being deemed admitted.

e. Replies and Jury Demands

Rule 38(b) provides, in relevant part, that a pleader may demand a jury trial "no later than 14 days after service of the last pleading directed to the issue is served."

f. Consequences of Failure to Reply

If a reply is not filed, any allegations requiring a responsive pleading are deemed admitted. Any matter not denied in a reply also is deemed admitted.

6. Amendments to the Pleadings: Rule 15

a. Liberal Amendment Philosophy

In general, amendments of pleadings under the Federal Rules are liberally permitted in the early stages of a litigation, especially before responsive pleadings are served. This liberal amendment philosophy supports many of the goals of federal notice pleading, in that pleaders are not expected to have all the facts at the time of the filing of the complaint. In addition, liberal amendment helps to avoid unnecessary costs and delay, and is consistent with desiring a trial on the merits.

b. Scope

The amendment provisions apply to all pleadings: the plaintiff's complaint, the defendant's answer, and the plaintiff's reply (if filed), as well as all pleadings filed relating to cross-claims and third-party claims.

c. Timing Considerations: When Amendments May Be Sought

Technically, a federal pleader may amend its pleadings at any time after filing a pleading, as well as during or after trial (although this is most unusual). The earlier a pleader seeks to amend the pleadings, the more likely a court will grant a request to amend (if court permission is required).

i. Amendment as a Matter of Course: Rule 15(a)

A party may amend its pleadings as a *matter of course,* (that is, without the other party's or the court's permission) 21 days after serving the pleading or, if a responsive pleading is required (such as an answer), 21 days after service of that responsive pleading. A pleader may amend as a matter of course within 21 days after service of a motion under **Rule 12(b), (e),** or **(f).**

ii. Amendment at All Other Times

If a party does not amend its pleadings within these early windows for amendment, then at all other times a party may amend either by leave of court or with the written permission of the other parties. The court should "freely give leave when justice so requires." **Rule 15(a)(2).**

iii. Responding to Amended Pleadings

If a party serves an amended pleading on the opposing party, the opposing party may respond to the amended pleading within any time that remains for answering the original pleading. Alternatively, the opposing party may respond within 14 days after service of the amended pleading—whichever period is later.

d. Amendments to Conform the Pleadings: Rule 15(b)

i. When Used

A party may at any time during or after trial ask the court for permission to amend the party's pleadings to "conform" those pleadings to the proof offered at trial. This situation arises when a party has not pleaded certain issues in its complaint or answer, raises these issues at trial, and offers proof in support.

ii. Who May Raise; Timing

Any party, at any time (even after trial) may assert a motion to conform the pleadings to the proof, even after a judgment. **Rule 15(b)(2).**

iii. Failure to Plead Issues: Express and Implied Consent

If a party fails to plead certain issues in the case, those issues may be tried either by express or implied consent. **Rule 15(b).**

e. Permissive Amendments and Statute of Limitations Problems: The Relation-Back Doctrine: Rule 15(c)

i. Statute of Limitations Problems

In general, a party may amend its pleadings at any time, subject to the limitations indicated above. However, if a statute of limitations has expired on a claim, then a party may not be able to amend a pleading.

ii. Relation-Back Doctrine

In certain special circumstances, a party may be permitted to amend a pleading after a statute of limitations has run, and the amended pleading "relates back" to the date of the original pleading. The relation-back doctrine permits otherwise expired claims to be asserted, or mis-named or omitted parties to be changed or added to the litigation.

iii. Circumstances Permitting Relation-Back of Amendments

A party may amend a pleading to relate-back if the statute supplying the limitations permits the relation-back of an amendment. **Rule**

15(c)(1)(A). A federal pleader may amend if the allegations in the amended pleading arose out of the same conduct, transaction, or occurrence set forth in the original pleading (or attempted to be set forth in the original pleading). **Rule 15(c)(1)(B).**

iv. Amendment of Parties: General Standards

A federal pleader may amend to change the name of a party if (a) the amended pleading arose out of the same conduct, transaction, or occurrence set forth (or attempted to be set forth) in the original pleading; (b) the amendment is made within the period specified in **Rule 4(m)** for service of the summons and complaint to the party to be brought in by the amendment; (c) the party brought in has received notice of the institution of the action such that the party will not be prejudiced in maintaining a defense on the merits; and (d) the party brought in knew or should have known that, but for a mistake concerning the identity of the proper party, the action would not have been brought against the party. **Rule 15(c)(1)(C).** The question under **Rule 15(c)(1)(C)(ii)** is what a prospective defendant reasonably should have understood about a plaintiff's intent in filing the original complaint against the first defendant. **Krupski v. Costa Crociere S.p.A.**, 560 U.S. 538 (2010).

v. 1991 Rule 15(c) Amendment Relating to Notice Requirement

Current **Rule 15(c)** requires that a party to be changed in an amendment must have had notice of the institution of the lawsuit within 120 days of filing the complaint. Congress enacted this rule change in 1991 to effectively overturn the Supreme Court's decision in **Schiavone v. Fortune,** 477 U.S. 21 (1986).

vi. Amendment of Parties: Calculating the Time in Which to Amend

Rule 15(c) ties timing of its notice provision to the **Rule 4(m)** time period for effecting service of process, which is 120 days after filing the complaint. In order for a plaintiff to be permitted to amend to change a party, that party would have had to have known of the institution of the action within that 120 day period.

vii. Amendment of Parties: Purpose of Notice Provisions

Rule 15(c) has additional requirements for amendments that seek to change parties in order to avoid unfair surprise or prejudice to the party who is added through the amended pleading. Unfair surprise is eliminated because the rule requires that the changed party have had notice of the action within 120 days of its institution.

viii. Amendment of Parties: Misnomers and New Parties

Most federal courts will liberally permit an amendment to correct a party's name that is a misnomer or spelling defect. Federal courts are split, however, concerning whether amendment is available to add a new party altogether who was not originally named in the complaint.

ix. New or Substituted Plaintiffs

Rule 15(c) does not deal with new or substituted plaintiffs after a statute of limitations has run. There is no need for a rule relating to change of plaintiffs since the defendant will already be on notice of the suit and it is not inconsistent with statutes of limitations to permit a new plaintiff to be substituted for an original one after the complaint has been filed.

7. Supplemental Pleadings: Rules 7(a) and 15(d)

a. State Practice

Some states prohibit pleaders from asserting a new cause of action in a supplemental pleading. Other states, however, very liberally permit a pleader to add new claims or issues filed as supplemental pleadings even if the pleader had no cause of action at the time of filing the original complaint.

b. Federal Practice: Rule 15(d)

i. When Available and How Made

A party must seek permission of the court to serve supplemental pleadings. The supplemental pleadings must satisfy three requirements: (a) reasonable notice to the opposing party of the supplemental pleadings; (b) under terms that are just; and (c) setting forth transactions, occurrences, or events that have happened since the date of the pleading that is being supplemented.

ii. New Claims

There is substantial authority in lower federal courts that a plaintiff (or other pleader) is permitted to bring new claims in a supplemental pleading. This is based on the rationale that allowing such supplemental pleadings promotes the economical and speedy disposition of the controversy. A minority of federal courts take the position that newly arising claims can only be asserted in a new action.

iii. Curative Supplemental Pleadings

A plaintiff may correct a factually deficient pleading through supplemental pleadings (a supplemental pleading is allowed "even though the original pleading is defective in stating a claim or defense.").

■ VI. JOINDER

A. JOINDER OF CLAIMS

1. Historical Background and Modern Federal Rules Approach

a. Common Law Joinder Rules

At common law the ability to join distinct causes of action was limited by the forms of action and writ system.

b. Joinder Rules under Code Pleading Systems

Code pleading systems abolished the common law forms of action and consequently liberalized joinder rules. Code pleading also merged law and equity and made it possible to state claims seeking both types of relief.

2. Methods of Claim Joinder and Severability

a. Liberal Joinder of Claims: Rule 18(a)

Rule 18(a) sets forth the basic liberal joinder-of-claims provision in the Federal Rules. Under this rule a pleader may join as many claims as the party has against an opposing party, and all legal and equitable claims.

i. Permissive Joinder

A federal plaintiff may join any and all claims in one action against a defendant, but is not compelled to do so. The rule is not mandatory.

ii. Jurisdictional Limitations

The only restriction on the joinder of claims is imposed by subject matter jurisdictional requirements. Every claim and party in a litigation must have an independent jurisdictional basis.

iii. Rationale for Federal Liberal Joinder Rule

Similar to the code pleading reforms of common law joinder rules, the major purpose of **Rule 18(a)** is to avoid a multiplicity of lawsuits.

iv. Severance under Rule 42

The problems of jury confusion and prejudice may be remedied in federal practice by severing the claims under **Rule 42(b).**

b. Counterclaims and Cross-Claims: Rule 13

i. Counterclaims at Common Law

The modern counterclaim did not exist at common law.

ii. Counterclaims in Code Pleading Systems

The 1848 original Field Code made no mention of counterclaims. Amendment of the Field Code in 1852 permitted counterclaims for a cause of action arising out of the contract or transaction set forth in the complaint, as the foundation of the plaintiff's claim, or connected with the subject of the action, and in an action arising on contract, any other cause of action arising on contract, and existing at the commencement of the action.

iii. Counterclaims under Rules 13(a)–(e)

The modern Federal Rules of Civil Procedure are even more expansive concerning counterclaims than English or code pleading practice. Under the Federal Rules, not only are counterclaims *permissive,* but some other counterclaims are *compulsory* and *must be raised.*

iv. Compulsory Counterclaims: Rule 13(a)

A pleader must assert a compulsory counterclaim against the opposing party that exists at the time of service. The counterclaim is compulsory if it arises out of the same transaction or occurrence that is the subject matter of the opposing party's claim, and does not require the joinder of third parties over whom the court cannot acquire jurisdiction.

v. Consequences of Failing to Plead a Compulsory Counterclaim

Rule 13(a) does not indicate the consequences of failing to assert a compulsory counterclaim. However, a pleader who fails to assert a compulsory counterclaim in a federal action may be barred from asserting the claim in a subsequent federal suit.

vi. Compulsory Counterclaims in State Practice

States have widely different rules and approaches to compulsory counterclaims. For example, Minnesota's compulsory counterclaim rule omits the word "occurrence" and that provision has been construed more narrowly than **Rule 13(a).**

vii. Permissive Counterclaims

A pleader may state as a counterclaim against the opposing party any claim that is not compulsory. **Rule 13(b).**

viii. Later-Maturing Counterclaims

A federal pleader may use supplemental pleadings, with the court's permission, to assert any counterclaim which matures or is acquired after service of process. **Rule 13(e).**

ix. Omitted Counterclaims

A pleader, with the court's permission, may amend its pleading to assert any counterclaim that matured or was acquired by the party after serving an earlier pleading. **Rule 13(e).**

x. Cross-Claims Against Co-Parties: Rule 13(g)

Cross-claims are permitted under the Federal Rules and may be asserted by a party against a co-party.

xi. Joinder of Additional Parties to Answer for Cross-Claims and Counterclaims

Additional persons may be added or joined in a federal lawsuit (under **Rules 19** and **20)** to be made parties to asserted cross-claims or counterclaims. **Rule 13(h).**

xii. State Practice Relating to Cross-Claims

Some states have very narrow definitions of "transaction" for cross-claim purposes. Wisconsin limits cross-claims to situations where only the rights of the plaintiff are necessarily involved, so that the plaintiff will not be "compelled to become a mere observer in a contest between two defendants which in no way concerns her."

c. Consolidation: Rule 42(a)

i. Consolidation Defined and Distinguished from Other Joinder Devices

Consolidation refers to combining separate actions in one federal court. Typically, the individual actions retain their separate nature and individual counsel, but the common issues may be tried together in a joint trial. A court may order a consolidated action if there are separate actions pending before the court that involve common questions of law or fact.

ii. Consequences of Consolidation: Joint Hearing, Separate Judgments

The court may order a joint hearing of any or all matters in issue in the separate cases. The court also may make any other orders "to avoid unnecessary costs or delay." However, in the typical consolidation each action retains its distinct character and requires a separate judgment.

d. Separate Trials: Rule 42(b)

i. Standards for Ordering Separate Trials

A court may order separate trials of any claims or issues in an action in the interests of convenience, to avoid prejudice, or to expedite and economize. Under **Rule 42(b),** a court also may sever claims for separate resolution from an action involving multiple parties and claims. A court will balance convenience, prejudice, and expense in deciding whether to order separate trials of issues, or the severance of claims.

ii. Separation and Severance Distinguished

Technically, there is a distinction between the separate trial of issues and the "severance" of claims, but many courts interchangeably refer to separation and severance.

iii. Purpose of Separate Trials and Severance

The separate trial of issues or severance of claims allows more efficient processing of a complicated case. Separate trial of issues may expedite resolution of an entire case. Severance of claims may facilitate other procedural techniques, or may reduce jury confusion.

iv. Seventh Amendment Trial by Jury Concerns

A judge may order severance or separate trial of issues or claims, but must preserve any federal right to jury trial.

B. JOINDER OF PARTIES

1. Identifying Parties Who May Sue and Be Sued

Whether a party may sue and be sued involves three different concerns: (1) "standing" to sue, (2) capacity, and (3) "real party in interest." A litigant must be the real party in interest, have the requisite capacity to sue or be sued, and have standing. It is possible for a litigant to be the real party in interest, but to lack capacity or standing.

a. Standing to Sue

Standing refers to a doctrine federal courts have derived from Article III of the Constitution to ensure that only adverse litigants with actual injury sue in federal court. This doctrine primarily protects the judicial system's interest in hearing only real cases and controversies. Standing is related to other justiciability doctrines prohibiting collusive lawsuits, advisory opinions, and political questions. State courts employ various standing concepts similar to federal doctrine.

b. Capacity

Capacity refers to the ability of a person or an entity to enforce rights (or to be sued by someone else). Capacity is specially defined for "artificial persons" such as corporations, partnerships, and unincorporated associations. Special capacity rules apply for children and incompetents. Generally, capacity is determined by state law, and federal courts follow state capacity rules. **Rules 17(b)** and **(c).**

c. The Real Party in Interest

In addition to having standing and capacity, the person who sues (or is sued) must be the "real party in interest." This rule applies to every party asserting a claim in an action. **Federal Rule 17(a).**

i. Determining the Real Party in Interest

The real party in interest generally is the person who, under substantive law, possesses the right to be enforced.

ii. Modern Practice

In modern practice, courts look to the nature of the substantive right to determine if the person asserting the right is the real party in interest. A person who might benefit from a litigation may not always be the real party in interest.

iii. Failure to Name Real Party in Interest

A federal court will not dismiss a lawsuit for the failure to designate the real party in interest as the plaintiff. Rather, the parties have a reasonable time to substitute the real party. **Rule 17(a).** A court will dismiss an action if the real party is not substituted, but this is not a dismissal on the merits. The real party in interest may later bring an action on the same claim, provided that any relevant statute of limitations has not expired.

iv. Abolition of the Real-Party-in-Interest Concept

Some commentators have urged that the real-party-in-interest rule is antiquated, superfluous, and unnecessary because state substantive law defines the real party, and the law would be the same without any express rule. New York State, the originator of the real party rule, has abolished it.

2. Claims Involving Multiple Parties

a. Permissive Joinder of Parties: Rules 20 and 21

i. Historical Practice and Common Law Rules

At common law the ability to join parties in a legal action depended on whether the parties' rights were jointly or severally held. If rights were jointly held, then parties could be joined in one action. If rights were severally held, parties could not be joined. Problems in determining the nature and scope of joint and several rights led to the development of modern liberal party joinder rules.

ii. Modern Permissive Party Joinder Practice

Modern party joinder rules are considerably more flexible than common law practice, requiring some loose overlap of interest. Parties may be joined if their interests are joint, several, or in the alternative. In federal court, parties to be joined must satisfy both a transaction and occurrence standard and a common question test.

iii. Elimination of Joint and Several Criteria

Rule 20(a) (and many states) permit permissive joinder of parties who assert any right to relief either jointly or severally. In addition, federal courts permit a plaintiff to sue defendants in the alternative. Parties may be joined if they assert some right to relief arising out of the same transaction or occurrence that comprises the subject of the action. **Rule 20(a).** Courts generally ask whether there is a logical relationship between the case and the claim of the party to be joined (*see* **Moore v. New York Cotton Exchange,** 270 U.S. 593 (1926)), and whether it is efficient to have the parties litigate together. Courts often flexibly interpret and apply this standard.

iv. Separate Trials: Rule 20(b)

Federal courts flexibly balance the interests of efficiency against possible prejudice in allowing party joinder. If party joinder will result in embarrassment, delay, or additional expense, a court may order a separate trial to prevent or mitigate delay or prejudice.

v. Misjoinder or Nonjoinder of Parties: Rule 21

A court may not dismiss an action for misjoined parties. At any stage of a litigation and "on just terms," a court may order that parties be added or dropped on a motion by any party or on the court's own initiative.

vi. Relationship to Joinder of Claims

Courts evaluate the joinder of parties independently of joinder of claims. Even if claim joinder rules are satisfied, party joinder rules must also be satisfied before parties can be added with regard to new claims.

b. Compulsory Joinder of Parties: Rule 19

Permissive joinder of parties deals with who may be present in a lawsuit and the expansive outer limits of the size of a litigation. Compulsory joinder, on the other hand, specifies not who may be present in the litigation, but who must be present in the lawsuit. Hence, compulsory joinder of parties is governed by more restrictive rules than permissive joinder.

i. Historical Background: Necessary and Indispensable Parties

Compulsory joinder principles traditionally distinguished between two types of parties: those who are "necessary" to the litigation, and those who were "indispensable."

ii. Historical Note on Terminology

Until 1966, the federal compulsory joinder rule (**Rule 19**) was entitled: "Necessary Joinder of Parties." In 1966 **Rule 19** was amended to read "Joinder of Persons Needed for a Just Adjudication." This change reflected the **Advisory Committee on Civil Rules'** decision to eliminate references to "necessary" and "indispensable" parties, which terms had caused interpretation difficulties in the lower federal courts. As part of the judiciary's style project, **Rule 19** is now denominated: "Required Joinder of Parties."

iii. Necessary Parties

Necessary parties are those who are so interested in a controversy that they must be joined if it is feasible to do so, but if these parties cannot be joined, the lawsuit can still proceed and the court does not have to dismiss it. *See* **Bank of California Natl. Assn. v. Superior Court,** 16 Cal.2d 516, 106 P.2d 879 (1940).

iv. Indispensable Parties

Indispensable parties are those parties who must be joined in the lawsuit and, if they cannot be joined for any reason, the lawsuit cannot proceed without them and the court must dismiss the action. *See Bank of California, id.*

v. Modern Federal Practice: Amended Rule 19

Rule 19 was amended in 1966 to provide a pragmatic basis for resolving the policy dilemmas raised by the older necessary and indispensable party classifications. The amended rule requires courts to analyze factors balancing various considerations relating to absent parties. A defendant typically challenges a person's absence in the lawsuit through a motion based on **Rule 12(b)(7):** a "failure to join a party under **Rule 19.**" This objection also may be raised in the answer, and in some states, through a demurrer.

vi. Persons to Be Joined If Feasible: Rule 19(a)

If an absent person is subject to service of process and that person will not deprive the court of its jurisdiction (for example, by destroying diversity jurisdiction), then the court must determine whether to join the absent party. This portion of amended **Rule 19** parallels the older concept of "necessary" parties. In making this evaluation, the court will consider the absent party's interest in the litigation, asking if (a) in the person's absence complete relief cannot be accorded among those already parties; (b) the person claims an interest relating to the subject of the action and is so situated that the disposition of the action may as a practical matter impair or impede the person's ability to protect that interest, or leave any of the persons already parties subject to a substantial risk of incurring double, multiple, or inconsistent obligations by reason of the claimed interest. **Provident Tradesmens Bank & Trust Co. v. Patterson,** 390 U.S. 102 (1968).

vii. Joinder Not Feasible: Rule 19(b)

In certain circumstances an absent party may satisfy **Rule 19(a)** criteria, but it may not be feasible to join them. Among the possible reasons are (a) joinder will defeat diversity jurisdiction; (b) the court cannot obtain personal jurisdiction over the absent party; or (c) the absent party has a valid venue objection.

viii. Equitable Assessment

When joinder is not feasible, the court must determine whether it can proceed "in equity and good conscience," or whether it must dismiss the action altogether, evaluating the possible prejudice to those already parties as well as the absent person. **Provident Tradesmens Bank & Trust Co. v. Patterson,** 390 U.S. 102 (1968).

3. Impleader: Third–Party Practice under Rule 14

a. Terminology

Impleader is the procedural means by which a defendant may bring into the lawsuit another party who the defendant believes is or may be liable to the defendant as a consequence of the plaintiff's claim. When the defendant asserts such a claim and brings a new party into the lawsuit, this is called "third-party practice." Impleader practice in federal court is governed by **Rule 14;** state courts have identical or similar impleader rules.

i. The Third-Party Plaintiff

The original defendant who asserts a claim against a person who is not already a party to the lawsuit is called the "third-party plaintiff." The original defendant (the third-party plaintiff) is said to "implead" the third-party defendant. **Rule 14(a).**

ii. The Third-Party Defendant

The person whom the original defendant brings into the lawsuit is called the "third-party defendant." This defendant is "impleaded" into the lawsuit. **Rule 14(a)(2).**

b. Who May Implead Third Parties

i. Defendant Impleader

Typically, defendants implead or bring other persons into the lawsuit based on various theories of liability and/or contribution. **Rule 14(a).**

ii. Plaintiff Impleader

Plaintiffs also may implead persons who are not already in the lawsuit, when a claim is asserted against the plaintiff. Under these circumstances, a plaintiff may implead a third party in the same fashion as a defendant may under the rules. **Rule 14(b).**

c. Principles Supporting Impleader of Third Parties

i. Derivative Liability

Rule 14(a) provides that a third-party defendant may be impleaded when a person not a party to the action "is or may be liable to the third-party plaintiff for all or part of the claim against it." Principles supporting impleader include indemnity, subrogation, contribution, breach of warranty, and other theories of derivative liability.

ii. Recognized by Relevant Substantive Law

The relevant substantive law must recognize the concept of derivative liability. **Rule 14** cannot be used to create any form of derivative liability, because this would violate the **Rules Enabling Act, 28 U.S.C. § 2072,** which prohibits federal procedural rules from abridging, enlarging, or modifying substantive rights.

d. Timing Considerations, Complaint, and Service

i. Impleader without Leave of Court

Anytime after the commencement of an action, a defendant may bring a person into the lawsuit, without the court's permission, if the defendant serves a third-party complaint *not later than 14 days* after the defendant serves its original answer on the original plaintiff. **Rule 14(a)(1).**

ii. Impleader with Leave of Court

If *more than 14 days* have elapsed since the defendant served its answer in the original action, then the defendant must obtain "leave" or permission from the court to implead a third party. **Rule 14(a)(1).**

iii. Complaint and Service

A defendant who seeks to implead a third-party defendant accomplishes this by serving a "third-party complaint" and summons, which are subject to the federal pleading and service rules. **Rule 14(a)(1).**

iv. Acceleration Effect

Rule 14(a) permits impleader of a person who "is or may be liable to" the defendant. Consequently, federal impleader allows a defendant to bring in a third party against whom the original defendant's claim has not yet accrued unless and until the plaintiff wins the lawsuit. The effect of permitting impleader in these circumstances is to accelerate determination of the defendant's contingent claim against the impleaded party.

e. Rationale for Impleader; Discretionary Procedure

i. Efficiency Rationale

Similar to many of the joinder rules, one of the underlying purposes of impleader is to serve the interests of judicial efficiency and economy. This is accomplished by joining all transactionally-related parties and claims in one litigation, and avoiding splitting parties and claims into several successive lawsuits.

ii. Discretionary Joinder

Impleader is not a matter of litigant rights. Even though the requisites for impleader may be satisfied, the court has the discretion to permit or deny the joinder. The court weighs the efficiency of permitting the impleader balanced against the possibility of prejudice to the existing parties by complicating the lawsuit with additional parties.

f. Status of Impleaded Parties; Consequences of Impleader

i. Persons Not Party to the Action

Only persons who are not parties to the original action may be impleaded or brought into the action. It is technically impossible to implead an existing defendant. A person who is impleaded into a litigation then has the status of a party to the action.

ii. Rule 12 Defenses

Once a person is impleaded into a litigation as a third-party defendant, that third-party defendant must assert any **Rule 12** defenses against the original defendant (that is, the third-party plaintiff who filed the third-party complaint against the third-party defendant). **Rule 14(a)(2).**

iii. Counterclaims

A third-party defendant also must assert any counterclaims it may have against the third-party plaintiff. If there are other defendants in the lawsuit, the third-party defendant may assert any cross-claims against those defendants. **Rule 14(a)(2).**

g. Severance or Separate Trial

Any party may move to strike a third-party claim, or to move for its severance or separate trial. **Rule 14(a)(4).**

h. Jurisdiction over Impleaded Parties

Courts must have appropriate subject matter and personal jurisdiction over impleaded parties.

i. Subject Matter Jurisdiction

Jurisdiction over impleaded parties is governed by the supplemental jurisdiction statute, **28 U.S.C. § 1367,** which provides such supplemental jurisdiction over additional claims so long as they are part of the same case or controversy as the action over which the court has original jurisdiction.

ii. Personal Jurisdiction

Although the supplemental jurisdiction statute expansively provides a subject matter jurisdiction basis for impleaded parties, federal courts have not relaxed personal jurisdiction requirements for impleaded parties. These requirements still must be independently satisfied for the court to have good jurisdiction over impleaded parties.

4. Interpleader: Rule 22 and 28 U.S.C. § 1335

a. Definition; Equitable Basis

Interpleader is an equitable device that permits multiple claimants to money or property to resolve their competing claims in one lawsuit. The person who has the obligation to pay, or who holds the property, is known as the stakeholder.

b. Concept of the Stakeholder

In interpleader actions, the stakeholder is the person who has some obligation to others, but is uncertain which claims are legitimate and how to satisfy the competing claims. The stakeholder deposits the "stake" (money or property) with the court. The court serves notice on the competing claimants and resolves those claims.

c. Modern Practice

In modern practice the person seeking an interpleader action need only show a stake with competing claimants that gives rise to the possibility of multiple vexatious litigation. Interpleader actions typically occur in two stages. The court determines whether an interpleader action is proper (a controversy between a stakeholder and competing claimants). If granted, the stakeholder deposits the property with the court and withdraws from the litigation. The court then determines the competing claims to the stake or the fund.

d. Limitations on Interpleader Actions

i. Equitable Limitations

Equitable principles apply and may limit or prevent an interpleader. For example, the doctrine of laches applies if the stakeholder has delayed in seeking a resolution of the claims.

ii. Jurisdictional Limitations: State Court

Interpleader actions are *in personam* and state courts must have valid personal jurisdiction over the claimants to render a valid binding judgment. **New York Life Ins. Co. v. Dunlevy,** 241 U.S. 518 (1916).

e. Federal Rule and Statutory Interpleader

There are two possible bases for interpleader in federal court, either under **Rule 22** or through a series of statutory provisions. The former is called "rule interpleader" and the latter is called "statutory interpleader." In general, **Rule 22** serves as a mere joinder device and is more limited than statutory interpleader.

i. Characteristics of Rule 22 Interpleader

Claimants must meet normal jurisdiction requirements (i.e., there must be complete diversity among the parties and more than $75,000 must be at issue). Personal jurisdiction is governed by the state law in which the district court sits. Most state long-arm statutes do not permit assertion of personal jurisdiction over non-resident claimants to a stake. **Rule 22** interpleader, therefore, typically is limited to claimants who reside within the state.

ii. Statutory Interpleader

Statutory interpleader is governed by a series of related statutes at **28 U.S.C. §§ 1335, 1397,** and **2361.** In general, statutory interpleader requirements are more liberal than **Rule 22** interpleader. Only minimal diversity is required among parties and only $500 need be in controversy. The stockholder's citizenship is irrelevant. **28 U.S.C. § 1335; State Farm Fire & Cas. Co. v. Tashire,** 386 U.S. 523 (1967). Nationwide service of process is available and therefore personal jurisdiction is co-extensive with contacts with the United States. **28 U.S.C. § 2361.**

5. Intervention: Rule 24

a. Definition and Statutory Basis

Intervention is the means by which a person (or groups) who are not named in a lawsuit may join the litigation if they have an interest they seek to protect. Intervention is largely a modern statutory invention.

b. Purposes of Intervention

Intervention serves three basic purposes: (1) protection of non-parties to the litigation; (2) efficient judicial administration and trial convenience; and (3) protection of the original parties to the litigation.

c. General Grounds for Intervention

State standards for intervention vary, but focus on the similar principle that an intervenor's right or interest must be of a direct or immediate character such that the intervenor will either gain or lose by the direct legal operation of the judgment.

d. Competing Policy Concerns

Intervention embodies conflicting policy concerns. On the one hand, intervention supports the judicial system's interest in efficient adjudication through the joinder of all interested parties in one litigation. On the other hand, intervention may undermine judicial efficiency by increasing complexity and possible jury confusion.

e. Federal Intervention

There are two types of intervention in federal court: intervention of right and permissive intervention.

i. Timing Considerations

A person seeking to intervene, either permissively or by right, may do so at any time "on timely motion." **Rule 24(a)** and **(b).** The earlier a person seeks to intervene mitigates the possible prejudicial effects of the intervention. However, courts have permitted intervention even as late as on appeal. *See, e.g.,* **Smuck v. Hobson,** 408 F.2d 175 (D.C. Cir. 1969), although such intervention will be permitted only in very few unique situations where the intervention will not prejudice the rights of existing parties or interfere with the "orderly processes of the court."

ii. Procedure for Initiating Intervention

A person who seeks to intervene files a pleading—a complaint in intervention—which must be served on the parties already in the lawsuit. **Rule 24(c)** and **Rule 5.** The complaint in intervention must set forth the grounds that are the basis for the intervention.

iii. Standards for Intervention of Right—Rule 24(a)

There are two grounds that provide a person a right to intervene. A person has a right to intervene when a federal statute confers an unconditional right to intervene. **Rule 24(a)(1).** A person also has a right to intervene when the applicant claims an interest relating to the property or transaction that is the subject of the action, and the disposition of the action may as a practical matter impair or impede the applicant's ability to protect that interest, unless the applicant's interest is adequately represented by the existing parties.

iv. **Standards for Permissive Intervention—Rule 24(b)**

An applicant permissively may intervene when a federal statute confers a conditional right to intervene, or, the applicant's claim or defense and the main action have a common question of law or fact.

f. **Consequences of Intervention—Status of the Intervenor**

Applicants granted intervention become parties to the lawsuit and, in general, have all the rights of other parties to the suit, including service of pleadings, motions, and papers in the litigation. However, courts may limit the nature or scope of the intervenor's involvement in the litigation, in the interests of sound judicial case management. If the court denies intervention, it may suggest that the applicant file a "friend of the court" brief (amicus curiae) in lieu of intervention, to apprise the court of the person's interests.

g. **Jurisdictional Considerations: Supplemental Jurisdiction**

i. **Intervention of Right: 1990 Legislative Change**

Prior to 1990, intervenors of right automatically came within the court's ancillary jurisdiction. The 1990 supplemental jurisdiction statute, **28 U.S.C. § 1367(b)** specifically excludes intervenors from supplemental jurisdiction. Hence, nondiverse persons may not intervene in an action.

ii. **Permissive Intervention**

Permissive intervenors must satisfy subject matter jurisdictional requirements. This is true for both pre-1990 intervention and post-1990 intervention.

h. **Relationship to Indispensable Party Requirements and Rule 19(a)**

The "impairment" requirement for intervention of right under **Rule 24(a)(2)** repeats the same language of **Rule 19(a)(2)(i).** There is some suggestion that a person who satisfies the requirements to intervene as of right should have been joined as an indispensable party under **Rule 19.**

i. **Relationship to Amicus Curiae Participation**

Some courts that deny intervention will instead recommend that persons file a friend of the court brief to apprise the court of the applicant's special interests in the litigation. Amicus curiae status is perceived as a less-desirable alternative to intervention, because it is questionable whether amicus curiae briefs have the same influence on a litigation as intervention in the proceedings.

j. Appellate Review of Intervention Decisions

i. Grant of Intervention

In general, an order granting intervention is not final and not appealable. Parties opposing intervention must await the conclusion of trial to bring a direct appeal.

ii. Denial of Intervention: Split of Authority

Lower federal courts are split concerning whether the denial of a motion to intervene is immediately appealable. The Supreme Court has held that an order denying intervention of right, but permitting permissive intervention, is nonappealable under the final judgment rule. **Stringfellow v. Concerned Neighbors in Action,** 480 U.S. 370 (1987). Many courts have held that denial of intervention of right is appealable under the so-called "collateral order" doctrine, but that denial of permissive intervention is only appealable for abuse of discretion. At least one federal court has held that all orders denying intervention are final for purposes of immediate review.

C. CLASS ACTIONS: RULE 23

1. History of Class Actions

a. Equitable Origins

The concept of group or aggregative litigation originated in medieval English equity procedure in the "bill of peace." Chancery courts permitted a representative action when (1) many people were involved who were too numerous to permit joinder, (2) the group members possessed a joint interest, and (3) the named parties would adequately represent the group. A judgment bound all members of the represented group.

b. State Codes

In the nineteenth and early twentieth centuries, many states adopting code procedure included precursors of the modern class action rule.

c. Federal Equity Rules

Prior to the enactment of the Federal Rules of Civil Procedure in 1938, the Federal Equity Rules provided for class action procedure.

d. Rule 23

The **Federal Rules** enacted in 1938 contained the original modern class action rule. With the merger of law and equity, class actions could be pursued in actions at law and equity.

i. The Modern Class Action Rule: 1966 Amendments

The **Advisory Committee on Civil Rules** extensively revised **Rule 23** in 1966 to eliminate the existing rigid class action categories. The major purpose of the 1966 revision of the class action rule was to create functional tests for types of class actions. The 1996 amendments to **Rule 23** created the three **Rule 23(b)** categories. In addition, the 1966 amendments invented the so-called **(b)(3)** "opt-out" class, a device that had not existed under the original class action rule.

ii. Further Revisions to the Class Action Rule: 1998 and 2003

In 1998, a new subsection **(f)** was added to **Rule 23,** to provide an avenue for appellate review of court orders either granting or denying class certification. In December 2003, a more extensive set of **Rule 23** revisions became effective. These revisions changed existing provisions of **Rule 23(c)** and **(e)**, and added new subsections **(g)** and **(h)**, dealing with appointment of class counsel and attorney fees.

iii. Settlement Classes

In the late 1990s, the Supreme Court decided two major appeals concerning class action settlements in **Amchem Prods. Inc. v. Windsor,** 521 U.S. 591 (1997) and **Ortiz v. Fibreboard Corp.,** 527 U.S. 815 (1999). The Court upheld the validity of settlement classes, and provided guidelines concerning requirements for adequacy of representation and due process in settlement classes.

2. Modern Class Action Procedure: Due Process Considerations

a. Class Actions as Representational Litigation

The distinguishing feature of the class action is that it is a representational litigation. Most class members are not actually present and do not individually litigate their claims. Instead, a designated plaintiff (the "class representative") and class counsel virtually represent the interests of class members. Many class actions include more than one named class plaintiff. Class members other than the class representatives are called "absent" or "unnamed" class members.

b. Consequences of Representational Litigation

Class members (especially absent class members) do not have a traditional relationship with the class lawyer or the prosecution of their individual claims. Class action litigation has the potential for conflicts-of-interest between the class representatives, class members, and class counsel.

c. Binding Effects of Judgments

In general, a person cannot be bound to an *in personam* judgment unless that person has been designated as a party, is properly served, and is subject the court's jurisdiction. Class actions are an exception to this rule. The judgment in a class action suit binds the named parties and all the class members identified in the class description.

i. Adequacy of Representation

Procedural due process requires that the class representative must fairly and adequately represent the interests of absent class members. Due process is lacking if the class representative and class members have actual or potentially conflicting interests. **Hansberry v. Lee,** 311 U.S. 32 (1940); *see also* **Amchem Prods. Inc. v. Windsor,** 521 U.S. 591 (1997) and **Ortiz v. Fibreboard Corp.,** 527 U.S. 815 (1999).

ii. Notice

Due process requires that members of a **Rule 23(b)(3)** opt-out class receive notice of the class action. **Eisen v. Carlisle & Jacquelin,** 417 U.S. 156 (1974). In their discretion courts may order that notice be given to class members in **Rule 23(b)(1)** or **(b)(2)** classes.

iii. Personal Jurisdiction over Absent Class Members

A state court may render a binding judgment over absent class members who do not choose to opt-out of a (b)(3) class action, even though they lack minimum contacts with the forum state. **Phillips Petroleum Co. v. Shutts,** 472 U.S. 797 (1985). By not opting-out, such absent class members are deemed to have consented to the court's jurisdiction.

d. Class Settlements

A class action may not be settled, compromised, or dismissed unless a federal judge reviews and approves the settlement. **Rule 23(e).** A judge must hold a fairness hearing prior to approving a proposed class action settlement, to determine whether the proposed class settlement is fair, adequate, and reasonable. In non-class litigation, by contrast, the court does not review a settlement agreed to by the parties and their lawyers. In class action litigation, the requirement of court approval is a further due process protection to ensure that absent class members' interests are not compromised by fellow class members or class counsel. Proposed settlement classes are subject to the same certification requirements as litigation classes, except for **Rule 23(b)(3)** classes, which do not need to satisfy the "manageability" requirement for certification. **Amchem Prods. Inc. v. Windsor,** 521 U.S. 591 (1997) and **Ortiz v. Fibreboard Corp.,** 527 U.S. 815 (1999). **Rule 23(e)** specifies that notice must be given of the proposed settlement, and makes provision for objectors to the settlement.

3. Operation of the Class Action Device

a. Initiation of Class Action

A court may initiate a class action on its own **(sua sponte).** A single plaintiff may initiate a class action. Plaintiffs' lawyers typically initiate class actions, especially in certain actions such as shareholder's derivative litigation or mass tort cases. In such instances, the plaintiff's lawyer initiates the class action by filing a class complaint on behalf of a named plaintiff and other similarly-situated claimants.

i. Class Complaint

The class complaint is designated as a class action. The complaint names the class representatives as plaintiffs. Frequently counsel will name more than one class representative. The class complaint also will contain a definition of the class membership.

ii. Consent of Class Members: Notification

A plaintiff or class counsel may file a class complaint without first seeking the consent or permission of unnamed class members. Some potential class members may not desire the class action and may oppose class certification at a certification hearing.

b. Certification Requirements

Unlike simple litigation, a court must certify an action that is to be resolved as a class action. **Rule 23(c)(1).** The certification requirement is another due process protection for absent class members, providing court scrutiny of the proposed class action.

i. Timing of Class Certification

A court must determine whether a proposed action may be maintained as a class action "at any early practicable time" after parties sue or are sued in a class complaint. **Rule 23(c)(1)(A).** The rule does not specify when this certification must occur.

ii. Certification Hearing

To determine whether a class action may be maintained, a court may review class certification requirements based on the complaint and other papers the lawyers submit on the certification motion. Opponents to the class action may retain counsel and oppose the class certification. In other instances, judges hold a certification hearing at which the parties supporting and opposing the class certification present their arguments.

iii. Threshold Requirements

A proposed class action must satisfy two general threshold requirements not codified in the class action rule. There must be a class, and the class representative must be a member of the class.

iv. Class Action Prerequisites: Rule 23(a)

A proposed class must satisfy four prerequisites: numerosity, commonality, typicality, and adequacy. Only if the proposed class satisfies these prerequisites will a court then determine whether the action may be maintained as a particular type of class.

v. Types of Class Actions

The current class action rule provides for three different types of class actions, the so-called **"Rule 23(b)"** actions. In general, **(b)(1)** and **(b)(2)** class actions are mandatory classes; the **(b)(3)** class is a non-mandatory opt-out class. The contemporary mandatory classes existed under the original 1938 version of the class action rule; the **(b)(3)** class was newly created as part of the 1966 rule revisions and had no analog in the older class action rule.

vi. Appointment of Class Counsel

Rule 23 was amended in 2003 to add a new subsection **(g)** relating to the appointment of class counsel. **Rule 23(g)** provides a set of standards for courts to consider in the appointment of class counsel as part of the class certification process.

vii. Attorney Fees

Rule 23 was amended in 2003 to add a new subsection **(h)** that provides standards and guidance for judicial determination of attorney fees in class action litigation. **Rule 23(g)** provides for a motion for the award of attorney fees, objections to the motion, a hearing and findings on fees, and the possibility for referral of fees issues to a special master or magistrate.

c. Appellate Review of Class Certification Decisions

i. Pre-1998: Lack of Interlocutory Review and the Final Judgment Rule

Prior to 1998, it was somewhat difficult for litigants to obtain review of a judge's order either granting or denying class certification. This was because a judge's order granting or denying class certification was not immediately appealable to a higher court. Such orders were not a final judgment under **28 U.S.C. § 1291,** because class certification orders can be decertified, amended, or altered by the court prior to the litigation's conclusion. *See* **Coopers & Lybrand v. Livesay,** 437 U.S. 463 (1978). However, a judge's class certification order was immediately appealable if the judge certified that order for immediate review under **28 U.S.C. § 1292(b),** certifying that the order involved "a controlling question of law as to which there is a substantial ground for difference of opinion and an immediate appeal from the order may materially advance the ultimate termination of the litigation." Alternatively, litigants could seek a writ of mandamus pursuant to **28 U.S.C. § 1651** on the grounds of judicial abuse of discretion in granting or denying the class certification. Mandamus was a disfavored means for supplying appellate jurisdiction of class certification decisions. *See* **In the Matter of Rhone–Poulenc Rorer, Inc.,** 51 F.3d 1293 (7th Cir. 1995).

ii. Rule 23(f) Appeals

In 1998 **Rule 23** was amended to add a new provision **(f)** to provide for interlocutory appeals of class certification orders. This provision was added to ameliorate the problems relating to difficulties in seeking review of class certification orders. **Rule 23(f)** now authorizes immediate appellate review (within ten days after entry of the order) of class certifications decisions. Jurisdiction of such appeals is within the discretion of the appellate court, which may consider the opinions and recommendations of the lower court judge who certified (or denied certification) of a proposed class. An appeal does not stay class proceedings in the district court unless the judge or court of appeals orders such a stay.

d. Class Notice Requirements

i. When Required and Permitted

Members of damage classes certified under **Rule 23(b)(3)** must receive "the best notice practicable under the circumstances" **Rule 23(c)(2)(B)**. This notice language tracks the due process standard the Supreme Court articulated in **Mullane v. Central Hanover Bank & Trust,** 339 U.S. 306 (1950). **Rule 23(c)(2)(A)** was added to provide that a court may direct notice to classes certified under subsections **Rule 23(b)(1)** and **(b)(2).** Prior to 2003, classes certified under the **(b)(1)** and **(b)(2)** subsections did not require nor direct notice.

ii. Who Must Provide Notice

The wording of the class action rule is ambiguous concerning who is responsible for supplying notice—the court or the litigants. *See* **Rule 23(c)(2)(A)** and **(B).**

iii. Content of Notice: Damage Classes

In Rule 23(b)(3) class actions, the notice to class members must advise the class members of (1) the nature of the action, (2) the class claims, issues, or defenses, (3) the definition of the certified class, (4) that a class member can enter an appearance through counsel, (5) that any member may request to be excluded from the class, (6) the time and manner for requesting exclusion, and (7) the binding effect of a class action judgment. The judge either may order notice to individual class members, or more general notice by publication.

e. Orders Regulating Pretrial and Trial Proceedings

In addition to certification and notice orders, judges are authorized to issue any other case management orders that will assist in the conduct of the proceedings. **Rule 23(d).** Frequently, class action procedure will be governed by procedures and recommendations set forth in the *Manual for Complex Litigation* (Federal Judicial Center 4th ed. 2004).

f. Proving Class Claims and Administering Class Relief

Judges have many options for structuring class actions trials and relief. Again, courts will make recourse to the *Manual for Complex Litigation* for recommendations relating to these complex procedures.

i. Fluid Recovery Relief

A court may order a "fluid recovery" in different circumstances. One instance is where it is impossible to identify individually all the claimants in the class and the recovery exceeds the number of claimants. Another instance is where the class distribution does not exhaust the recovery, leaving a fund remaining. In such instances courts may order some remedy that provides a general benefit to all class members (rather than individual compensation).

g. Class Settlement

Class actions differ from simple litigation in that the class action may not be "compromised" or dismissed unless the court approves. In practice, this means that the court reviews the terms of the proposed class settlement. Court scrutiny of proposed settlements is another due process protection for absent class members, to ensure that the terms of the settlement do not compromise or prejudice their rights. *See* **Amchem Prods. Inc. v. Windsor,** 521 U.S. 591 (1997) and **Ortiz v. Fibreboard Corp.,** 527 U.S. 815 (1999).

i. Manner of Review

Rule 23(e) was amended effective December 1, 2003 to require that a judge hold an evidentiary hearing before approving a proposed class settlement. This is known as a "fairness hearing." The court will hear testimony and receive evidence from the proponents and opponents of the settlement. **Rule 23(e)** was extensively amended to provide additional guidance to courts, litigants, and objectors concerning applicable procedures for submitting and approving class action settlements.

ii. Standard of Review

The judge must determine whether the proposed settlement is fair, adequate, and reasonable. It is not necessary that all members of the class agree to the settlement, and the court may approve a settlement even when some class members do not want the settlement. Settlements also may be approved over the objections of the class representatives. **Rule 23(e)** was amended in 2003 to provide an opportunity for objectors to appear and object to proposed class settlements.

iii. Burdens

The proponents of the settlement carry the burden of demonstrating that the settlement is fair, adequate, and reasonable.

iv. Ability to Modify

The court has no power to change or modify the terms of a class action settlement. The court must approve or reject the settlement in its entirety.

v. Timing Considerations: "Settlement Classes"

Class settlements may occur at any time during proceedings. In the usual instance, a class is certified at the outset of the litigation and the court reviews a settlement of pre-existing certified classes. In recent years, however, some federal courts have reviewed class certification simultaneous with the court's review of the terms of a negotiated settlement. Hence, class certification is part of the agreement, with no pre-existing certification prior to the settlement. This mechanism or procedure is called a "settlement class." In the late 1990s, in two landmark cases, the Supreme Court held that when class certification is sought along with approval of a proposed settlement, the proposed class must satisfy all the same requirements for certification as litigation classes, except for the "manageability" factor. *See* **Amchem Prods. Inc. v. Windsor,** 521 U.S. 591 (1997) and **Ortiz v. Fibreboard Corp.,** 527 U.S. 815 (1999).

vi. Objectors to Class Settlements

The Supreme Court has ruled that nonnamed class members who have objected in a timely manner to a proposed class settlement, at a fairness hearing, have a subsequent right to appeal the court's judgment approving the settlement, without formally intervening in the action. **Devlin v. Scardelletti,** 536 U.S. 1 (2002).

h. Special Problems: Role of Attorneys, Ethical Issues, Attorneys' Fees

Class action litigation, as representational litigation, departs from the traditional model of the attorney-client relationship in simple litigation.

i. **Role of the Attorneys**

Class action litigation often involves more than one class lawyer and in extremely complex cases, the court may organize plaintiffs' and defense lawyers into committees.

ii. **Ethical Issues**

Class action litigation raises significant ethical issues that are heightened by the representational nature of the litigation. The most pressing ethical dilemmas include improper solicitation, conflicts-of-interest, and maintaining client confidences and secrets.

iii. **Attorney's Fees; Cost and Expenses**

Attorneys may subsidize the ongoing costs and expenses of class litigation, which costs and expenses are chargeable to and recoverable from the class. **Rule 23** was amended in 2003 to add a new subsection **(h)** that provides standards and guidance for judicial determination of attorney fees in class action litigation. **Rule 23(g)** provides for a motion for the award of attorney fees, objections to the motion, a hearing and findings on fees, and the possibility for referral of fees issues to a special master or magistrate. Attorney's fees in class actions may be determined in a number of different manners, such as by statutory provisions, contingency fee arrangements, hourly rate fee agreements, or the lodestar formula.

i. **Defendant Classes**

Most class actions are structured as plaintiffs' class actions. However, **Rule 23(a)** permits certification of a defendant class: "one or more members of a class *may sue or be sued* as representative parties. . . . " Defendant classes are very rare. A defendant class must meet the same **Rule 23** requirements as a plaintiffs' class.

j. **Intervention into Class Actions**

It is possible for a person who is not included by the class description to intervene in the class to protect that nonparty's interests in the litigation.

i. **Criteria for Intervention in a Class Action**

Intervention in a class action litigation is governed by the criteria of **Rule 24.** The consensus is that intervention in class actions is governed by the same principles as in any other proceeding.

ii. **Orders Relating to Intervenors**

A judge may issue any orders "imposing conditions . . . on intervenors." **Rule 23(d)(1)(C).**

iii. Relationship of Intervention to Objectors

The Supreme Court has ruled that nonnamed class members who have objected in a timely manner to a proposed class settlement, at a fairness hearing, have a subsequent right to appeal the court's judgment approving the settlement without formally intervening in the action. **Devlin v. Scardelletti,** 536 U.S. 1 (2002).

k. "Limited Issues" Classes and Subclasses

i. "Limited Issues" Classes

A judge has the ability to authorize or create class actions that are limited to the trial of specific issues, rather than the entire claim. **Rule 23(c)(4)** ("an action may be brought or maintained as a class action with respect to particular issues"). For example, a judge may authorize a class action limited to a trial of the causation issue, or state of the art defense.

ii. Subclasses

Judges and the litigants also may structure a class action to include subclasses. **Rule 23(c)(5).** Each subclass is treated the same as any other class action, and must satisfy all class requirements. Subclasses are one means of resolving lack of commonality and typicality problems in heterogeneous damage class actions under **Rule 23(b)(3).** Similar claimants may then be grouped together in subclasses.

l. Class Actions and Mass Tort Litigation

i. Unsuitability for Aggregate Tort Litigation: 1966 Advisory Committee Note

In the late 1970s and early 1980s, federal courts were resistant to certifying mass tort cases as class actions. This refusal was based largely on the 1966 Advisory Committee Note stating that "mass accident" cases resulting in injuries to numerous persons was not appropriate for class action treatment. Additionally, federal courts held that such class actions failed to satisfy threshold commonality, typicality, and adequacy requirements, and that attempted (b)(3) classes also failed the predominance and superiority tests. *See, e.g.,* **In re Northern Dist. Cal. Dalkon Shield IUD Prods. Liab. Litig.,** 693 F.2d 847 (9th Cir. 1982); **Yandle v. PPG Industries, Inc.,** 65 F.R.D. 566 (E.D. Tex. 1974) (refusal to certify asbestos class action).

ii. Mass Tort Litigation Class Actions Authorized

Although the general trend was to refuse to certify mass tort class actions, in the early 1980s courts in the Second, Third, and Fifth Circuits upheld class actions in significant mass tort litigations.

iii. Mass Tort Litigation Class Actions Repudiated

Receptivity to use of the class action rule to adjudicate mass torts has been mixed. In the 1990s, federal courts renewed their rejection of proposed mass tort class actions in a series of decisions. *See, e.g.,* **In re Fibreboard Corp.,** 893 F.2d 706 (5th Cir. 1990) (reversing proposed four-phase **Rule 23(b)(3)** class action trial plan of asbestos personal injury claims); **In re Keene Corp.,** 14 F.3d 726 (2d Cir. 1993) (repudiating attempted **Rule 23(b)(1)(B)** limited fund class action involving present and future asbestos claimants); **In the Matter of Rhone–Poulenc Rorer, Inc.,** 51 F.3d 1293 (7th Cir. 1995) (reversing nationwide class certification in contaminated blood products litigation); **In re Medical Systems, Inc.,** 75 F.3d 1069 (6th Cir. 1996) (reversing certification of **Rule 23(b)(3)** nationwide class of defective penile implants claimants); **Castano v. American Tobacco Co.,** 84 F.3d 734 (5th Cir. 1996) (reversing certification of a **Rule 23(b)(3)** nationwide class of all smokers addicted to tobacco products).

iv. Mass Tort Settlement Classes

Proposed settlement classes are subject to the same certification requirements as litigation classes, except for **Rule 23(b)(3)** classes, which do not need to satisfy the "manageability" requirement for certification. **Amchem Prods. Inc. v. Windsor,** 521 U.S. 591 (1997) and **Ortiz v. Fibreboard Corp.,** 527 U.S. 815 (1999). Federal courts have upheld some mass tort settlement classes, *see, e.g.,* **In re A.H. Robins Co.,** 880 F.2d 709 (4th Cir. 1989) (Dalkon Shield settlement class), but repudiated others. *See, e.g.,* **In re General Motors Corp. Pick–Up Truck Fuel Tank Products Liab. Litig.,** 55 F.3d 768 (3d Cir. 1995) (proposed settlement not fair, adequate, and reasonable).

■ VII. OBTAINING INFORMATION PRIOR TO TRIAL: DISCOVERY

A. MODERN DISCOVERY: HISTORICAL CONTEXT

1. At Common Law and Equity

The ability to obtain information about the opponent's or one's own case was not an integral part of the litigation process at common law. The American concept of "discovery" was largely unknown in the English courts, a tradition that continues into modern times. Many other legal systems also do not recognize the modern American concept of discovery.

a. At Common Law

At common law a defendant could obtain information about the plaintiff's case through a bill of particulars. The defendant could only require the plaintiff to set forth in detail the items of account that the plaintiff was suing on.

b. In Equity

A litigant could file an equitable action asking for a bill of discovery. This procedure, however, only allowed a litigant to uncover facts to support the litigant's own case. The bill of discovery could not be used to learn about the evidence and information the opposing parties had for trial.

2. Discovery under the Federal Rules of Civil Procedure

In American practice, discovery techniques existed prior to the promulgation of the Federal Rules of Civil Procedure in 1938. The 1938 rules, however, set forth a detailed system for broad discovery of information relating to the litigation.

a. Relationship of Modern Federal Discovery Rules to Modern Pleading

The modern federal discovery rules are a hand-maiden to the liberal pleading philosophy embodied in the 1938 rules. Because the new federal rules permitted notice pleading, there was no expectation that a pleader would know all the facts underlying the claims at the time the person filed the lawsuit. The new federal discovery rules, then, were conceived as the means by which litigants could obtain more information about their own and their opponent's case even after commencement of the action.

b. Impact of the Modern Federal Discovery Rules

i. Local Federal District Court Rules

Although many federal district courts follow the general federal discovery rules, local federal district courts have modified discovery procedures by local rule (**Federal Rule 83**). In addition, almost all federal district courts have modified discovery procedures as a consequence of the reforms mandated by the **1990 Civil Justice Reform Act.**

ii. State Court Discovery

The modern federal discovery rules provide a model for many state courts. However, some states, such as Arizona, New Jersey, and Texas have been in the vanguard in the 1990s in modifying discovery rules to cope with increasing problems of discovery abuse. In general, these state reforms have required increased mandatory disclosure and have restricted non-disclosure based on various privileges and immunities.

3. Purposes of Discovery

The modern discovery rules greatly expanded the nature and scope of the information that litigants may obtain during an ongoing litigation. The expansive nature of discovery has, in some instances, led to abuse of the discovery system, raising questions relating to harassment and privacy. In general modem discovery is intended to serve three purposes.

a. Preservation of Evidence

One of the primary functions of discovery is to preserve relevant evidence that might not be available at trial. *See* **Rule 27** and **Rule 32(a)(4)**.

b. Ascertainment of Issues in Controversy

Another purpose of discovery is to ascertain and isolate those issues that are in controversy and disputed. Often pleadings in federal court contain many facts that are not in dispute. If the pleadings have put a claim in issue, it is legitimate to ask whether the pleader contests the facts underlying that issue. If certain facts are not contested, then trial time does not have to be wasted proving these facts. This goes far beyond the function intended by the complaint and answer.

c. Evidence on Issues in Dispute: Prelude to Trial

Discovery also is used to ascertain relevant evidence to disputed factual issues that will be contested at trial.

i. Necessity for Pretrial Formal Discovery Devices

The discovery devices provide a coercive means to obtain information from people who might not otherwise cooperate in supplying needed information. For example, certain witnesses might not want to become involved in a litigation, or to provide documents. The discovery rules enable parties to require that witnesses submit to depositions and provide whatever knowledge or information they have relating to the litigation. Similarly, the discovery devices enable one party to obtain documents from another.

4. Tension in Modern Discovery Practice: Competing Concerns

Modern discovery practice, particularly in federal court, has sometimes been characterized as either a game of "show and tell," or "hide and seek." Both models capture an inherent tension that has inspired an on-going debate about the scope and limits of modern discovery.

a. Broad-Discovery Proponents

Some litigants favor broad discovery based on a model of "show and tell." The underlying rationale is that voluntary disclosure of as much information as possible, without formal request or coercion, supports and accomplishes the goal of **Rule 1** to ensure the just, speedy, and inexpensive resolution of disputes. These supporters of the liberal discovery provisions believe that eliciting fact information should not be reduced to a game of "hide and seek." A related reason for permitting widespread liberal fact discovery is to reduce or eliminate surprise at trial. Attorneys can evaluate the relative strengths or weaknesses of their respective cases and often settle the dispute.

b. Limited-Discovery Proponents

The prime concern of opponents of liberal discovery relates to the sweeping scope of permissible discovery. Hence, the concern is that the

Federal Rules permit (and encourage) "fishing expeditions" into an opposing party's personal life or corporate affairs. Second, opponents contend that liberal discovery invades privacy rights. Third, opponents argue that liberal discovery costs very little to the party seeking discovery and therefore encourages abusive behavior such as expansive, burdensome, or potentially embarrassing discovery requests. Fourth, opponents contend that liberal discovery encourages some litigants to sit back and do very little, instead living off the "borrowed wits" of their opponents. Fifth, open discovery is antithetical to the adversary process.

B. SCOPE AND DISCRETIONARY LIMITS ON DISCOVERY

1. The Scope of Discovery

The scope of discovery under the Federal Rules and analogous state practice is very broad.

a. General Problem

The purpose of discovery is to permit the litigants to discover as much factual information as possible about both their own claims as well as the opposing party's defenses. In this sense, discovery enhances the "truth-seeking" function of the judicial process. However, the concept of liberal discovery is in tension with the idea that each litigant should prepare his or her own case, and not sit back and allow the opponent to do all the work.

b. Standard

Litigants may discover any matter relevant to the subject matter in the action whether admissible or not at trial that is reasonably calculated to lead to the discovery of admissible evidence and that is not privileged. **Rule 26(b)(1).**

2. Timing and Sequence of Discovery

a. Discovery Prior to the Commencement of an Action

The Federal Rules and state practice provide for very limited discovery prior to the formal commencement of an action.

i. Depositions before Action: Rule 27(a)

Before filing a complaint, a person who intends to file a lawsuit may "perpetuate the testimony" of an adverse party, by taking that party's deposition. The person seeking to take this deposition must file a verified petition in a district court where the deponent resides, stating that the person intends to file an action but is presently unable to do so (without violating **Rule 11).** The petition also has to state the subject matter of the forthcoming litigation, the testimony to be elicited, and the reasons for wishing to perpetuate that testimony.

ii. Fact Elicitation before Filing

Courts disagree whether litigants may use discovery before filing a lawsuit merely in order to discover facts. Courts generally agree that discovery may not be used to learn if one has a case at all.

b. Initial Discovery Scheduling and Conferences: Rules 26(d), (f) and 16(b)

i. General Prohibition

Parties generally may not seek discovery from any source before they have met and conferred as required by **Rule 26(f).**

ii. Local Rules Exemption (Rule 83)

Rules 26(d), (f) and **16(b)** prescribe when parties must meet, discuss, and plan discovery. Federal district courts, however, may exempt themselves from this Federal Rule and specify any other discovery timing rule for the district.

iii. Discovery Meeting and Agreement

Attorneys of record and all unrepresented parties must meet at least 21 days prior to a scheduling conference with a federal district judge magistrate. **Rule 26(f).** At this meeting, the parties must, in good faith, discuss their claims and defenses and possible settlement, arrange for informal exchange of the information required under **Rule 26(a)(1),** and develop a proposed formal discovery plan.

iv. Court-Mandated Scheduling Order: Rule 16(b)(1)

When the federal court receives the parties' **Rule 26(f)** written report, the court will confer with the attorneys by phone, mail, or in person and issue a scheduling order.

c. Mandatory Informal Exchange of Information: Rule 26(a)(1)

The centerpiece of the 1993 amendment of the Federal Rules was the addition of the new **Rule 26(a)(1),** mandating early informal exchange of information. **Rule 26(a)(1)** was further amended in 2000, to establish a nationally uniform practice relating to initial disclosures.

i. Background to the 1993 Rule Revision

The addition of **Rule 26(a)(1)** to the federal discovery provisions was part of a civil justice reform initiative in state and federal courts. The federal rule was patterned after a similar rule in Arizona and a few federal district courts (Southern District of Florida and the Central District of California). Congress also recommended that local district courts adopt informal discovery exchanges as part of the **Civil Justice Reform Act of 1990.**

ii. Required Disclosures

Without awaiting a discovery request parties must now disclose the names, addresses, and telephone numbers of individuals likely to have discoverable information that the disclosing party may use to support its claims and defenses, unless solely for impeachment, identifying the subjects of the information; descriptions and locations of documents, data compilations, and tangible things in the possession, custody or control of a party that are relevant to the disputed facts alleged with particularity in the pleadings; a computation of damages the disclosing party claims, as well as documents or other evidence supporting the calculation of those damages (and including materials bearing on the nature and extent of injuries); and any insurance agreement which may satisfy or indemnify all or part of a judgment. This provision also exempts various categories of information from initial disclosure.

iii. Timing of Informal Information Exchange

Parties are required to exchange **Rule 26(a)(1)** information at or within 14 days after they meet to discuss the litigation required in **Rule 26(f)** (*see* above). **Rule 26(f)** requires the attorneys meet at least 21 days before the **Rule 16** scheduling conference, and to submit a written report no later than 14 days after their meeting. The **Rule 16** scheduling conference, at the latest, will occur either 90 or 120 days after the defendant makes an appearance or the plaintiff serves the complaint.

iv. No Excuses

Parties must make the required disclosure of the information listed in **Rule 26(a)(1)(E)** "based on the information then reasonably available to it." A party is not excused from making the required disclosures because the party has not completed its investigation, or the party challenges the sufficiency of the opposing party's disclosures, or another party has not made its disclosures.

d. Expert Witnesses: Rule 26(a)(2)

The amended discovery rules require parties to disclose the identity of any expert witness to be used at trial to present evidence under **Rules 702, 703,** or **705.**

i. Expert Witness Report and Opinions

Parties must supply expert witness reports of retained, testifying expert witnesses. The report must state the expert's opinions, the basis for those opinions, exhibits, the expert's qualifications, publications, and other cases in which the expert has testified within four years.

e. Pretrial Disclosures: Rule 26(a)(3)

Prior to trial, in addition to early disclosure and expert witness information, parties also must disclose certain evidentiary material that will be used for other than impeachment purposes.

f. Discovery in Other Special Circumstances

i. Class Certification

In general, most courts do not permit plaintiffs to conduct discovery prior to class certification. However, some federal courts may order discovery limited to ascertainment of facts in support of class certification.

ii. Summary Judgment

Courts may order additional discovery in support of a summary judgment motion, particularly after a responding party has satisfied its burden of production and the burden of proof shifts to the moving party. **Rule 56(e).**

3. Discretionary Limits on Scope of Discovery in Adversary System

There are three primary ways of protecting information from disclosure during discovery: through invocation of a valid privilege, immunity, or protective order.

a. Privileges in General

Rule 26(b)(1) permits discovery of any "non-privileged matter that is relevant to any party's claim or defense." In general, the same rules of privilege that apply at trial also apply during discovery, and the "reasonably calculated to lead to discovery of admissible evidence" standard does not circumvent privilege. When a person invokes a validly-held privilege, that person does not have to disclose the requested information; the privilege usually attaches to a communication.

i. Privileges at Common Law

The common law has long recognized various testimonial privileges, including communications between attorney and client, doctor and patient, clergy and congregant, and husband and wife. State law determines the existence and scope of these privileges. Some states have limited spousal immunity. In addition, almost no jurisdiction recognizes a privilege for reporter and source.

ii. Testimonial Privileges

Testimonial privileges include the privilege against self-incrimination, testifying against a spouse, and revealing the identity of confidential police informants. These privileges protect the individuals involved from harm, as against the possible benefit from disclosure. Protection of informants assists police in obtaining information. In recent years, spousal immunity and protection of informants has eroded in certain circumstances.

b. Attorney-Client Privilege

All American state and federal courts recognize attorney-client privilege. The attorney-client privilege is the oldest common law principle protecting confidential communications.

i. Attorney-Client Privilege in Federal Court: Source of Authority

In purely federal claims, attorney-client privilege is a matter of federal law. In federal diversity cases, attorney-client privilege is governed by state common law principles. *See* **Federal Rule of Evidence 501** ("the privilege of a witness . . . shall be governed by the principles of the common law as they may be interpreted by the courts of the United States").

ii. Rationale or Purpose of the Attorney-Client Privilege

The purpose of the attorney-client privilege is to encourage full and frank communication between the attorney and client. "The privilege recognizes that sound legal advice or advocacy serves public ends and that such advice or advocacy depends upon the lawyer's being fully informed by the client." **Upjohn v. United States,** 449 U.S. 383 (1981).

iii. Scope of the Attorney-Client Privilege and Standards for Invoking the Privilege

If the attorney-client privilege is validly invoked, it attaches to all communications between the client and the client's attorney, with limited exceptions noted below.

iv. How Invoked; Burdens of Proof

The person claiming the attorney-client privilege must invoke it in response to a discovery request, and carries the burden of establishing the existence of the privilege. The 1993 amendments to the federal discovery provisions added a specific provision requiring parties to expressly claim the privilege in response to a discovery request. **Rule 26(b)(5).**

v. Possessor of the Privilege

The client possesses the privilege and must invoke it. As a practical matter, the attorney invokes the privilege on the client's behalf.

vi. Corporations and Attorney-Client Privilege

Attorney-client privilege extends to all corporate employees who seek or secure legal advice from counsel. **Upjohn Co. v. United States,** 449 U.S. 383 (1981). The protection is not limited to a "control group" of upper-echelon management, but applies as well to middle-level and lower-level employees. *Id.*

vii. Nature of the Privilege

Attorney-client privilege is *absolute.* If the privilege exists, it bars disclosure of the protected information. It is not a qualified privilege, and cannot be overcome on a showing of need for the information by the party requesting disclosure (compare work product doctrine, which is a *qualified immunity*).

viii. Qualifications, Waivers, and Exceptions

Attorney-client privilege is subject to certain qualifications, exceptions, and waivers. The following information is not protected by attorney-client privilege: facts; disclosures by consent or waiver; involuntary or inadvertent disclosures; ongoing or future crimes, frauds, or torts.

c. Attorney Work Product Doctrine

Unlike attorney-client privilege, which has a long heritage at common law, attorney work product immunity is a relatively recent twentieth-century American invention in federal practice. Work product immunity is primarily a protection of the lawyer, rather than the client.

i. Attorney Work Product Doctrine in Federal Court: Sources of Authority

The two major authoritative sources for work product doctrine in federal court are the Supreme Court's 1947 decision in **Hickman v. Taylor,** 329 U.S. 495 (1947) and the Advisory Committee's 1970 codification of the doctrine in **Rule 26(b)(3)** ("Trial Preparation: Materials").

ii. Ordinary and Opinion Work Product: Rule 26(b)(3)

In 1970, the **Advisory Committee on Civil Rules** partially codified the principles of **Hickman v. Taylor** in **Rule 26(b)(3).** The federal work product rule distinguishes between discovery of "ordinary" work product and "opinion" work product. **Rule 26(b)(3)** permits discovery of documents and tangible things prepared in anticipation of litigation or for trial by or for another party, or, by or for that other party's representative (including the other party's attorney, surety, consultant, indemnitor, insurer, or agent). Opinion work product consists of an attorney's "mental impressions, conclusions, opinions, or legal theories." The protection extends to the opinion work product of other party representatives. **Rule 26(b)(3)** requires courts to protect opinion work product from disclosure. Required disclosure of opinion work product would be too much of an intrusion on the adversary process.

iii. *Hickman* and Rule 23(b)(3) Compared

The federal work product rule is considered to be a partial codification of the Supreme Court's holding in *Hickman.* For example, the federal rule covers only "documents and tangible things," but *Hickman* extends work product protection to intangible work product, such as oral statements. Federal courts typically refer to both the Supreme Court's holding in *Hickman* and **Rule 23(b)(3)** as authoritative sources for the work product doctrine.

iv. Rationale or Purpose of the Attorney Work Product Immunity

The attorney work product immunity is based on a number of supporting rationales protecting a zone of privacy for the lawyer; reducing the potential for sharp practices; reducing the potential for professional demoraliziation; and avoiding attorneys' practicing off the "borrowed wits" of their adversaries.

v. How Invoked; Burdens of Proof

The person claiming attorney work product immunity must invoke it in response to a discovery request, and carries the burden of establishing the existence of the immunity. **Rule 26(b)(5)** also applies to work product immunity. The 1993 amendments to the federal discovery provisions added a specific provision requiring parties to expressly claim the immunity in response to a discovery request. **Rule 26(b)(5).**

vi. Overcoming the Immunity

Once the party invoking the immunity states the grounds for the immunity's existence, the party seeking disclosure carries the burden of overcoming the immunity by showing substantial need for the requested materials and an inability to obtain a substantial equivalent by other means. **Rule 26(b)(3)(A)(ii).**

vii. Possessor of the Immunity

Attorney work product immunity primarily exists to protect the lawyer's trial preparation materials and thought processes, and thus chiefly is the lawyer's immunity. **Rule 26(b)(3)** extends the protection to any materials prepared by or for the party's representatives, including all agents working for the lawyer or the client, such as paralegals, investigators, and the like. Although attorneys usually invoke the protection, the client also may invoke the work product immunity if the lawyer does not wish to seek this protection.

viii. Qualifications, Waivers, and Exceptions

Attorney work product immunity is subject to the same qualifications, waivers, and exceptions as attorney-client privilege. In addition to this list of exceptions, work product immunity also excludes "party statements" from work product protection.

d. Protective Orders: Rule 26(c)

Although the Federal Rules enable liberal discovery, the manner and scope of discovery may be tailored to protect against embarrassment, harassment, or release of certain proprietary information (such as trade secrets). Parties may shield such information through a "protective order."

i. Stipulated Agreements

Parties may negotiate protective orders or confidentiality agreements, and may *stipulate* to the terms of such agreements. If the parties cannot agree, then a person seeking to shield information may file a motion for a protective order.

ii. Umbrella Protective Orders

Lawyers in complex litigation sometimes agree to an "umbrella" protective order at the outset of the litigation, that covers entire categories of materials that the producing party designates as confidential. This arrangement avoids the necessity of having a court determine whether to issue a protective order on a document-by-document basis. *See, e.g.,* **Zenith Radio Corp. v. Matsushita Elec. Indus. Co.,** 529 F.Supp. 866 (E.D. Pa. 1981).

iii. Court-Mandated Protective Orders: Who May Seek

A party or person may seek a protective order to shield information an opposing party seeks through a discovery request. Prior to seeking a protective order, the attorneys must confer (or attempt to confer) to resolve the dispute relating to disclosure of the requested material. If the lawyers are unable to agree, then the party seeking a protective order must furnish the court with a certificate that the lawyers have conferred in good faith and attempted to resolve the discovery dispute. **Rule 26(c)(1).**

iv. Motion for Protective Order: Where Made

A party who seeks a protective order may do so either in the court in which the action is pending, or if the protective order seeks to shield possible deposition testimony, in the district where a deposition is to be taken. **Rule 26(c)(1).**

v. Standards

In its discretion, a court may issue an order "which justice requires to protect a party or person from undue annoyance, embarrassment, oppression, or undue burden or expense." **Rule 26(c)(1).**

vi. In Camera Inspection

When a party seeks a protective order relating to information contained in documents, courts frequently examine the documents in an in camera *ex parte* proceeding. This means a judge reviews the materials in chambers, without the presence of the party seeking discovery. *See, e.g.,* **Marrese v. American Academy of Orthopaedic Surgeons.**

vii. Scope of the Protective Order

A judge has wide latitude in fashioning a protective order. In most instances, the judge will not totally deny discovery. Instead, the judge will structure a protective order to permit access to as much information as the requesting party needs, without invading the privacy of the objecting party. *See* **Marrese v. American Academy of Orthopaedic Surgeons.**

viii. Denial of Protective Orders: Expenses

If a court denies a motion for a protective order, the court may order discovery. The court also may award expenses incurred in relation to the motion. **Rule 26(c)(2); Rule 26(c)(3); Rule 37(a)(5).**

ix. Modification of Protective Orders

Whether to lift or modify a protective order is committed to the sound discretion of the court. Most courts generally will not modify a protective order once granted. A party seeking to modify a protective order must show that the protective order was improvidently granted or must demonstrate some extraordinary compelling need for disclosure of the information.

x. Duration of Protective Orders; Public Purpose Exception

Lawyers may stipulate that material covered by a protective order remains shielded even after a litigation is concluded. Courts disagree, however, whether a judge may rescind a protective order and unseal protected documents if the judge concludes that the underlying litigation was imbued with a public purpose, and disclosure of documents or information would prevent future harm. *See, e.g.,* **In re Agent Orange Prod. Liab. Litig.,** 821 F.2d 139 (2d Cir. 1987) (upholding order by Judge Weinstein unsealing materials produced during Agent Orange litigation and protected by settlement agreement); *cf.* **Mirak v. McGhan Medical Corp.,** 142 F.R.D. 34 (D. Mass. 1992) (denying intervenor's motion to vacate protective order concerning confidential documents in the Silicone Breast Implant litigation).

xi. First Amendment Concerns

There is no First Amendment right to obtain or disseminate information obtained through discovery. *See* **Seattle Times Co. v. Rhinehart,** 467 U.S. 20 (1984) (upholding as constitutional a protective order prohibiting a newspaper from publishing donor's list of a religious foundation).

4. Formal Discovery Devices: 1993 Amendments

The 1993 amendments to the discovery provisions added a number of provisions permitting federal judges greater latitude in managing formal discovery and controlling potential and actual discovery abuse. Many of the 1993 amendments provide that district courts may alter the general federal rule by local rules, and many local district courts have done so.

a. Timing and Sequencing: Rules 26(d) and (f)

Parties may not seek to conduct formal discovery until they have met as soon as practicable to discuss and plan discovery. After the initial discovery conference, parties may use formal discovery methods in any sequence. The fact that one person is conducting discovery shall not operate to delay another party's discovery These requirements may be modified either by local rule or by court order.

b. Limits on Formal Discovery: Rule 26(b) (to Curb Discovery Abuse)

Federal judges, either on their own initiative or on a motion by a party, may limit the frequency or extent of discovery methods if the court determines that (1) the discovery sought is unreasonably cumulative or duplicative, or it is obtainable from some other source that is more convenient, less burdensome, or less expensive; (2) the party seeking discovery has had ample opportunity by discovery in the action to obtain the information sought; (3) the burden or expense of the proposed discovery outweighs its likely benefit, taking into account the needs of the case, the amount in controversy, the parties' resources, the importance of the issues at stake in the litigation, and the importance of the proposed discovery in resolving the issues. **Rule 26(b)(2)(B)** imposes requirements and limitations on discovery of electronically stored information.

c. Interrogatories: Rule 33

Interrogatories are a series of questions directed at the opposing party. Interrogatories typically are one of the first methods of formal discovery, often used to obtain leads to other information helpful in depositions or requests for documents.

d. Depositions: Rules 28, 30, and 31

Depositions are a discovery method where a party may summons a party or a non-party and ask that person questions regarding the subject matter of the case while under oath. The person who is questioned is called the "deponent."

e. Depositions on Written Interrogatories: Rule 31

A deposition on written questions operates the same way as an oral deposition, except the attorneys are not present. Questions are sent to an officer who reads the question aloud to the deponent, whose answers are recorded.

f. Document Production and Inspection of Things: Scope of Rule 34

A party may compel an opposing party to produce documents or other tangible things for inspection. **Rule 34(a)(1)(A)** contains specific directives concerning the storage, retrieval, and production of electronically created documents and data. A party may also compel the opposing party to allow them to come onto property to inspect, measure, survey, photograph, test or sample the property, or to observe an operation taking place on the property. **Rule 34(a).**

g. Physical and Mental Examinations: Rule 35

A person whose physical or mental condition is in controversy in a litigation may be compelled to submit to a medical examination.

h. Requests for Admission: Rule 36

A party may serve on another party a written request to admit the truth of certain matters of fact, or the application of law to fact, or the genuineness of a document or other evidence.

5. The Duty to Supplement Responses: Rule 26(e)

In federal court and many state courts, parties have a duty to update or supplement material they disclose during discovery. The federal rule relating to the duty to supplement discovery responses was substantially rewritten as part of the 1993 amendments to the discovery rules, chiefly to eliminate confusing language in the earlier rule.

a. Duty to Supplement Information Disclosed as Part of Initial Mandatory Disclosure

The 1993 amendments added a new provision requiring early mandatory informal exchange of information at the outset of the litigation. A party is under a duty to supplement these initial disclosures, or to correct the disclosure, if the party acquires information after the disclosure. The amended rule does not specify any particular form of supplementation.

i. Standard for Duty to Supplement

A party must supplement or correct a response if the party "learns that in some material respect the information disclosed is incomplete or incorrect and if the additional or corrective information has not been made known to the other parties during the discovery process or in writing." **Rule 26(e)(1)(A).** This eliminates the need for parties to keep resubmitting the same discovery requests to make sure nothing has changed since the last response.

b. Formal Discovery Methods: Duty to Supplement

A party is under the same duty to supplement or correct information disclosed through formal discovery procedures.

c. Sanctions for Failure to Supplement

Prior to the 1993 amendments to the discovery provision, there was no specific sanction for the failure to supplement. The 1993 **Rule 37** amendments include a sanction for a failure to supplement responses as required in **Rule 26(e).** *See* **Rule 37(c)(1),** barring the use of any witness or information the responding party did not supplement or correct.

6. The Use of Discovery at Trial: Rules 32, 33(c), 36(b)

The discovery rules contain specific provisions indicating when parties may use discovery materials at trial. **Rule 32** indicates the appropriate uses of deposition testimony at trial, and **Rule 33(c)** indicates the permissible use of interrogatory answers at trial. **Rule 36(b)** provides that a party need not adduce evidence at trial in support of admissions. Use of discovery materials at trial also is governed by state and federal evidence rules.

a. Relevant Party Statements

Evidence rules permit a party to introduce any relevant statement of an opposing party, even if the opposing party does testify. **Federal Rule of Evidence 801(d)(2).**

b. Statements of Party Agents or Employees

Parties also may use at trial the statements of managing agents or persons authorized to speak for the party, as well as an employee statement about his or her duties.

c. Impeachment Purposes

The classic use of discovery materials at trial is to impeach a witness with former inconsistent statements made under oath in an earlier deposition or discovery response, or to refresh recollection. *See* **Rule 32(a)(2); Federal Rule of Evidence 613.**

d. Unavailable Witnesses

The discovery rules permit reading deposition testimony at trial if the deponent is dead, ill, incompetent, or beyond the subpoena power of the court. **Rule 32(a)(4).** In this respect, the discovery rules provide an exception to the evidentiary rule barring hearsay or out-of-court statements from being introduced at trial.

7. Judicial Supervision of Discovery and Sanctions: Rules 26 and 37

The general sanctioning provisions for failure to cooperate or respond to discovery requests is contained in **Rule 37,** which provides an array of possible sanctions a court may impose for discovery abuse. Prior to the 1993 amendment of the discovery rules, litigants did not often seek discovery sanctions and courts did not frequently impose them.

a. Availability of Discovery Sanctions, In General

Discovery typically is conducted by the parties, without court orders implementing the discovery requests. Sanctions are available, then, only when the discovery process breaks down and an aggrieved party seeks a court order requiring a person to attend a deposition, answer interrogatories, or produce requested documents. **Rule 37(a)(3). Rule 11** sanctions are inapplicable to discovery disputes.

i. Contempt

Contempt sanctions usually cannot be issued for failure to comply with discovery requests, because the initial discovery request typically is not made under compulsion of a court order.

ii. Jurisdictional Issues

Only a court with personal jurisdiction over a witness may issue an order compelling the witness to make responses to discovery requests. The court in which an action is pending, therefore, may not be able to compel or sanction a witness outside the court's territorial reach. **Rule 37(a)(2).**

b. Signature Requirements: 1993 Amendments to Rule 26(g)

The 1993 amendments to the discovery provisions added extensive provisions to subsection **(g)** relating to the attorney's duties to sign all discovery requests, as well as responses to discovery requests.

i. Signature Requirements for Early Mandatory Exchange of Information: Rule 26(g)(1)

Lawyers who disclose information as part of the new mandatory informal discovery provisions (*see* **Rules 26(a)(1)** and **(3)**) must sign those disclosures. Unrepresented parties also must sign such disclosures. The signature serves as a certification that to the best of the signer's knowledge, information, and belief formed after a reasonable inquiry, the disclosure is complete and correct as of the time it is made.

ii. Signature Requirements for Discovery Requests and Responses: Rule 26(g)(1)

The signature requirement for discovery requests was modified to parallel the language of **Rule 11** relating to truth-in-pleading, although **Rule 11** does not itself apply to discovery requests. The attorney's signature constitutes the lawyer's certification that to the best of the signer's knowledge, information, and belief, formed after a reasonable inquiry, that a request, response or objection is consistent with the discovery rules and warranted by existing law or a good faith argument for the extension, modification, or reversal of existing law; not interposed for any improper purpose, such as to harass or cause unnecessary delay or needless increase in the cost of litigation; and not unreasonable or unduly burdensome or expensive, given the needs of the case, the discovery already had in the case, the amount in controversy, and the importance of the issues at stake in the litigation.

c. Court-Ordered Discovery: Possible Sanctions

Even where discovery is court ordered, federal courts have been reluctant to sanction non-complying parties, and generally will do so only if there is willful non-compliance. However, when a party fails to comply, courts have an array of possible sanctions. **Rules 37(b), (c), (d), (e), and (f).**

i. Severity of Sanctions

Sanctions must be tailored to the conduct of the non-responding party and must not be overly harsh or violate the party's due process rights. "Considerations of fair play may dictate that courts eschew the harshest sanctions provided by **Rule 37** where failure to comply is due to a mere oversight of counsel amounting to no more than simple negligence." **Cine Forty–Second Street Theatre Corp. v. Allied Artists Pictures Corp.,** 602 F.2d 1062 (2d Cir. 1979).

ii. Contempt

Once a court has issued a discovery order, a non-responding party may be held in contempt for failure to comply with the court order. A party held in contempt may be fined or jailed until such time as he or she complies with the discovery request. **Rule 37(b)(2).**

iii. Attorney's Fees

A party that has been unreasonable in refusing to comply with a discovery request may be assessed the opposing counsel's attorney's fees incurred in seeking the motion. **Rules 37(a)(5); (b)(2)(C); (b)(2)(F).**

iv. Striking Portions of Claims or Defenses

A court may sanction a party who fails to obey a discovery request by striking all or a portion of a claim or defense. **Rule 37(b)(2)(A)(iii).**

v. Other Possible Sanctions: Default, Dismissal, Limiting Trial Testimony

In addition to contempt and striking portions of claims and defenses, courts may issue an array of sanctions for discovery abuse, including granting a default judgment, dismissing the action, or limiting the testimony available at trial **Rule 37(b)(2).**

d. Other 1993 Amendments to Rule 37

Rule 37 was substantially amended in 1993. The Advisory Committee added several provisions requiring attorneys seeking relief to have in good faith conferred or attempted to confer with the party against whom relief is sought.

i. In General

Rule 37 was amended at several points to include sanctions for failure to provide early mandatory disclosure information required under new **Rule 26(a)(1),** or to supplement responses as required in **Rule 26(e).**

ii. Sanctions for Failure to Provide Mandatory Exchange of Information under Rule 26(a)(1)

A lawyer who fails to comply and disclose information listed in **Rule 26(a)(1)** may not offer as evidence at trial information that, without substantial justification, was not included in the attorney's initial disclosures or by supplemental disclosure. **Rule 37(c)(1).**

iii. Additional or Supplemental Sanctions

For failure to comply with **Rules 26(a)(1)** or **26(e),** the court may impose any substitute or additional sanctions. **Rule 37(c)(1).**

iv. Informing Jury

The court also may inform the jury of a party's failure to make required disclosures. **Rule 37(c)(1).**

8. Discovery Problems in International Litigation

a. Discovery Located Abroad

General Problem. Frequently litigation involves parties or documentary evidence located abroad. The fundamental problems relating to such discovery concern the territorial reach of the Federal Rules of Civil Procedure, as well as international comity concerns.

b. Hague Convention on the Taking of Evidence Abroad

This convention provides procedures on requesting evidence that is located in foreign countries. **Hague Convention on the Taking of Evidence Abroad in Civil or Commercial Matters,** 23 U.S.T. 2555 (text of Convention located at **28 U.S.C. § 1781).**

c. Relationship of Federal Discovery Rules to the Hague Convention

The Hague Convention provisions do not replace the federal rules of discovery, but are rather a supplemental consideration that a court may take into account when a litigation entails discovery abroad. **Société Nationale Industrielle Aerospatiale v. United States Dist. Court,** 482 U.S. 522 (1987).

■ VIII. RESOLUTION WITHOUT TRIAL

A. VOLUNTARY DISMISSAL, DEFAULT, AND INVOLUNTARY DISMISSAL

1. Voluntary Dismissal: Common Law

At common law a plaintiff was viewed as the master of the case until a judgment was rendered, and therefore permitted to withdraw the lawsuit voluntarily and without prejudice at any time prior to a judgment. Modern state and federal rules limit the period in which a plaintiff voluntarily may withdraw a lawsuit without consequences, and have rejected the common law approach.

2. Voluntary Dismissal: Rule 41(a)

In general, a plaintiff is permitted to withdraw a lawsuit so long as the defendant is not unduly burdened by the plaintiff's actions. In most jurisdictions, this is usually codified as some time before "trial" or the "commencement" of trial (which is a matter of judicial construction). In federal court, a plaintiff may voluntarily dismiss the action without a court order in one of two ways.

a. Before Service of Process

By filing a notice of dismissal at any time before service by the opposing party of an answer or a motion for summary judgment, whichever occurs first.

b. After Appearance of Parties

By filing a stipulation of dismissal signed by all the parties who appeared in the action.

c. Effect of Voluntary Dismissal

A voluntary dismissal either by notice or stipulation is "without prejudice," meaning that the plaintiff may institute another action at a later time, provided the action is not barred by an applicable statute of limitations. **Rule 41(a)(1)(B).**

i. The Two Dismissal Rule: Repetitive Dismissals

A plaintiff may dismiss an action as a matter of right only once. If, however, the plaintiff already has previously filed and dismissed the same claim in a state or federal court, then the subsequent voluntary dismissal will operate as an adjudication on the merits. **Rule 41(a)(1)(B).**

ii. Costs of Previously Dismissed Action

If a plaintiff previously has dismissed an action and then commences an action based on the same claim against the same defendant, the court may make any order for payment of costs of the previously dismissed action "as it may deem proper." The court also may stay the pending proceeding until the plaintiff complies with the order to pay costs for the previously dismissed action. **Rule 41(d).**

iii. Counterclaims

If the defendant pleads a counterclaim prior to the plaintiff's motion to dismiss the complaint, the action cannot be dismissed against the defendant's objection unless the counterclaim remains pending for independent adjudication by the court. A dismissal under these circumstances is also without prejudice to the plaintiff's ability to re-institute a subsequent lawsuit on the same claim or issues. **Rule 41(a)(2); Rule 41(c).**

3. Involuntary Dismissal: Rule 41(b)

A court, in its discretion, may dismiss a lawsuit under three circumstances.

a. Failure to Prosecute the Case

A plaintiff is expected to go forward with its case with "due diligence." If the plaintiff fails to prosecute its own litigation, the court has the authority to dismiss the case with prejudice. This power is derived from the judiciary's inherent powers to manage its affairs and ensure the orderly disposition of cases.

i. Timing

Some states set time limits before which an involuntary dismissal cannot occur; other jurisdictions set time limits beyond which such a dismissal is mandatory. In most jurisdictions, including federal courts, the timing of an involuntary dismissal is entirely within the court's discretion.

ii. Standards

There is a general disinclination to involuntarily dismiss a lawsuit because the law favors deciding cases on the merits. However, courts will look to the entire factual circumstances involved in the failure to prosecute the case. The defendant does not have to show prejudice because it is presumed from the delay. **Link v. Wabash R.R. Co.,** 370 U.S. 626 (1962).

b. Failure to Comply with the Federal Rules

Under the inherent powers of the court, a judge may dismiss a case for failure to comply with the Federal Rules of Civil Procedure. Such a sanction is an extreme penalty and is used only for the most egregious and willful disregard of the rules. *See, e.g.,* **Link v. Wabash R.R. Co.,** 370 U.S. 626 (1962) (dismissal for failure to conduct discovery and failure to appear at pretrial conference as mandated under the federal rules). Frequently such dismissals are with prejudice.

c. Failure to Comply with a Court Order

Under the inherent powers of the court, a judge also may dismiss a case for a party's failure to comply with a court order. This is an extremely harsh sanction for noncompliance, however, and is used only rarely in extreme cases of noncompliance. Frequently such dismissals are with prejudice.

d. Effect of Involuntary Dismissal

A court-ordered dismissal operates as an *adjudication on the merits.* This does not apply to dismissals based on a lack of jurisdiction, improper venue, or failure to join a party needed for a just adjudication under **Rule 19. Rule 42(b).**

4. Default: Rule 55

There are two types of defaults: an "entry of default" which is a court notation of the defendant's failure to appear and defend, and a court-ordered default judgment. An "entry of default" is not itself a judgment. **Rule 55(b)(1), (2).**

a. Occasions for Default

A defendant may suffer a default in three circumstances: failure to appear or answer the plaintiff's complaint; appear in the action, but then fail to file an answer or appear at trial; or failure to comply with a procedural requirement or court order during pre-trial proceedings (default serves as a sanction).

b. Entry of Default

If a party does not appear in the litigation and plead or present defenses, then the court may enter a default against the nonappearing party. **Rule 55(a).** Default is considered a drastic remedy because it runs counter to the judicial system's preference for an adjudication of a dispute on the merits.

c. Calculation of Damages

The party that has brought the suit may request the court to enter a default judgment in the amount of damages, plus costs, if it is clear from the complaint that a certain sum and only that sum is due the complainant. **Rule 55(b)(1).** The court may hold a hearing to assess those damages. **Rule 55(b)(2).**

d. Exceptions for Infants, Incompetents

Default judgments may not be entered against infants or incompetents unless they have been represented by a guardian, conservator, or other representative. **Rule 55(b)(2).**

e. Setting Aside Defaults

A court may set aside an "entry of default . . . for good cause". **Rule 55(c).** A default judgment may be set aside under the conditions specified for relief from a final judgment, including mistake, inadvertence, excusable neglect, newly discovered evidence, or fraud. *See* **Rule 60(b).**

B. SUMMARY JUDGMENT: RULE 56

1. Purpose of Summary Judgment

The purpose of summary judgment is to end a litigation where there are no disputed factual issues and therefore one of the parties is entitled to a judgment. In these circumstances, a summary judgment eliminates the need for a trial.

a. Practical Effect of Granting a Summary Judgment

The practical effect of a court's granting a summary judgment is that the case does not go to trial and is not decided by a jury. If a summary judgment motion is denied, then the case will go to trial. If the court grants a partial summary judgment as to certain issues or claims, then the case proceeds to trial, but the issues for which summary judgment has been granted are not tried to the jury. *See* **Rule 56(g).**

b. Disfavored Motion until 1986

From 1938 through 1986, the summary judgment was a disfavored motion and rarely granted in many federal courts, especially in some circuits, such as the Second Circuit. Judges generally favored allowing cases to be tried to juries, rather than disposing of the litigation on paper motions. In 1986, in a trilogy of decisions interpreting the nature and scope of summary judgment procedure, the Supreme Court signaled its desire that the lower federal courts more aggressively employ summary judgment as a tool to eliminate cases where it is clear that a trial is unnecessary. *See* **Celotex Corp. v. Catrett,** 477 U.S. 317 (1986); **Anderson v. Liberty Lobby, Inc.,** 477 U.S. 242 (1986), and **Matsushita Elec. Indus. Corp. v. Zenith Radio Corp.,** 475 U.S. 574 (1986).

2. Terminology

Either a plaintiff or defendant, or any party added who asserts claims, counterclaims, or cross-claims, may ask the court for a summary judgment. The summary judgment rule is not organized with reference to plaintiffs or defendants. Rather, the rule refers to "claimants" and "defending parties."

3. Timing: When a Party May Seek a Summary Judgment

Parties may seek a summary judgment relatively early in the proceedings, but typically parties do not seek summary judgment until discovery is conducted and further fact information is elicited to support or refute disputed issues. A party may file a motion for summary judgment at any time until 30 days after the close of all discovery.

a. Relationship to Rule 12(d): Motion for a Judgment on the Pleadings

If, after the close of pleadings, a party moves for a judgment on the pleadings and supports that motion with materials outside the pleadings, such as affidavits or other documentary evidence, then the **Rule**

12(d) motion is "converted" in a summary judgment motion and will be evaluated according to the standards required for a summary judgment motion made under **Rule 56.**

4. Procedure for Seeking Summary Judgment

a. How Presented

A motion for summary judgment is presented to the court, along with a supporting memoranda of law and materials attached in support of the summary judgment. Such materials may be pleadings, depositions, portions of depositions, answers to interrogatories, answers to admissions, documents, electronically stored information, affidavits, declarations, stipulations or other materials.

b. Initial Burden on Movant

The party seeking a summary judgment—either a claimant or defending party—may move for a summary judgment. There is, however, no affirmative requirement that the moving party support its motion with any materials in support of the motion. **Celotex Corp. v. Catrett,** 477 U.S. 317 (1986). Usually, however, moving parties do supply the court with more information than what is alleged in the party's pleadings.

c. Standard

A court is required to grant a summary judgment if the pleadings and other supporting materials "show that there is no genuine issue as to any material fact and that the moving party is entitled to a judgment as a matter of law." **Rule 56(a).**

d. Relationship to Directed Verdicts

The standard for summary judgment generally mirrors the standard for a directed verdict under **Rule 50(a).** A trial judge must direct a verdict if, under governing law, there can be but "one reasonable conclusion as to the verdict . . . if reasonable minds could differ as to the import of the evidence, a verdict should not be directed. . . . " **Anderson v. Liberty Lobby,** *supra.* The difference between the two motions is a timing consideration; summary judgment occurs prior to trial, and directed verdict occurs at trial.

e. Inferences and Credibility Issues

When a party is unable to establish the existence of a central act or event directly through affidavits, documents, or other evidence, courts generally may not allow inferences to be taken into account on summary judgment. *See, e.g.,* **Cross v. United States,** 336 F.2d 431 (2d Cir. 1964). Similarly, as discussed below, where issues of witness credibility or demeanor are involved, courts are reluctant to grant summary judgment. *Cross, id.; see also* **Lundeen v. Cordner,** 354 F.2d 401 (8th Cir. 1966).

f. Shifting Burdens of Production, Persuasion, and Proof

Until 1986, there was a great deal of confusion in the lower federal courts concerning the appropriate allocation of burdens of production, persuasion, and proof on a summary judgment motion. In a 1986 trilogy of cases addressed to this issue, the Supreme Court attempted to clarify the burdens on the movant and adverse party in a summary judgment proceeding. *See* **Celotex Corp. v. Catrett,** 477 U.S. 317 (1986); **Anderson v. Liberty Lobby, Inc.,** 477 U.S. 242 (1986), and **Matsushita Electric Industrial Corp. v. Zenith Radio Corp.,** 475 U.S. 574 (1986). The major insight of the *Celotex* decision is to relate burdens of production and proof on the summary judgment motion to the party that carries those burdens at trial.

g. Shifted Burden of Production and Persuasion: Burden on the Party Opposing the Motion

Once the movant has satisfied its initial burden of production on the motion, then the burden of production shifts to the party opposing the motion—the adverse party. Again, the nature of the shifted burden depends on who bears the burden of persuasion at trial.

h. Evidentiary Standards on the Motion

A court must evaluate the summary judgment materials in light of the applicable substantive standards of proof required at trial. **Anderson v. Liberty Lobby, Inc.,** 477 U.S. 242 (1986).

5. Special Problems Relating to Summary Judgment

a. Credibility and Demeanor Issues

Summary judgment traditionally is considered inappropriate in cases that require assessment or evaluation of a witness's credibility or demeanor. This is especially true because summary judgment, if granted, effectively forecloses the non-movant's ability to cross-examine a witness at trial. *See, e.g.,* **Cross v. United States,** 336 F.2d 431 (2d Cir. 1964) (summary judgment improvidently granted where Internal Revenue

Service should have opportunity to call at trial a taxpayer claiming travel deductions; government should have benefit of jury determination of taxpayer's credibility for claimed deductions). *Cf.* **Lundeen v. Cordner,** 354 F.2d 401 (8th Cir. 1966) (no need for cross-examination where there is no indication that affiant is biased, dishonest, or unaware or unsure of facts).

b. State of Mind

Some jurisdictions prohibit summary judgment when a moving party's state of mind is in issue. The only way to counter a moving party's affidavit as to the person's state of mind or intent is to call that person at trial and subject the person to formal examination and cross-examination.

c. Complex Litigation

In general, courts have been reluctant to grant summary judgment in certain types of complex litigation, especially antitrust litigation. This resistance, however, has been substantially eroded by the Supreme Court's 1986 decision in **Matsushita Elec. Indus. Co. v. Zenith Radio Corp.,** *supra,* a complex antitrust suit, where the Court upheld a summary judgment motion granted on the basis of no showing of an antitrust conspiracy.

6. Partial Summary Judgment: Rules 56(g) and 54(b)

a. Partial Summary Judgment

Courts may grant partial summary judgment if they cannot grant summary judgment on the entire action. By this method, the court can reduce the number of claims or issues that need be tried to the jury. **Rule 56(g).**

b. Final Judgment

In a multi-claim case, the court may enter a final judgment on the claim that has been resolved by summary judgment. This permits a losing litigant to bring a direct appeal from the claim decided by the summary judgment motion. *See* **Rule 54(b)** and **28 U.S.C. § 1291.**

■ IX. PRETRIAL JUDICIAL CASE MANAGEMENT

A. JUDICIAL CASE MANAGEMENT, GENERALLY

1. Traditional Model of Litigation, Judicial Function, and the Adversary System

The traditional model of litigation, described by Professor Abram Chayes, is characterized by five features: (1) the lawsuit is bipolar—between a single plaintiff and single defendant; (2) the litigation is retrospective, concerning past events; (3) the right and the remedy are interdependent; (4) the lawsuit is a self-contained episode; and (5) the process is party-initiated and party-controlled. *See* Abram Chayes, *The Role of the Judge in Public Law Litigation*, 89 Harv. L. Rev. 1281 (1976).

2. Development of Modern Public Law Litigation

Although many state cases and some federal litigation still resemble the traditional model, most litigation does not. Professor Chayes posited the modern litigation paradigm of "public law" litigation. *Id.* Characteristics of the public litigation model include a sprawling and amorphous litigation, including multiple parties and multiple claims; a litigation that changes over the course of the dispute resolution process; a litigation suffused and intermixed with negotiating and mediating processes at every point; and a judge who is the dominant figure in organizing and conducting the case, as well as continuing involvement in administration and implementation of relief.

3. Modern Case Management Movement: Managerial Judges

The "judicial case management" movement originated in the development of the modern sprawling, amorphous case involving multiple parties and multiple claims. Additionally, liberal discovery rules inspire numerous disputes among attorneys concerning pretrial access to information. These pretrial disputes often require the active intervention or supervision by a judicial officer. Once involved, judges often assume the roles of mediators, negotiators, or trial planners—functions well removed from the traditional concept of the neutral, disengaged judge ("mere referee").

a. Mandated Case Management

Active case management is a method of implementing the values embodied in **Rule 1,** which requires *administration* of the Federal Rules to achieve the *speedy, efficient and inexpensive* resolution of civil disputes.

i. Rule 1 and 16 Amendments

The **Advisory Committee on Civil Rules** amended **Rule 1** in 1993 to add the requirement that federal courts "administer" the Federal Rules to accomplish the three goals. Prior to 1993, federal judges only were required to construe the rules to achieve these ends. The amendment, along with revisions to **Rule 16,** were intended to prod federal judges into active case management.

b. Criticisms of Judicial Case Management

The "judicial case management movement" is not universally approved or lauded, for a number of reasons. *See* Judith Resnik, *Managerial Judges,* 96 Harv. L. Rev. 374 (1982).

i. Traditional Role of Judge

Active judicial case management transgresses the traditional notion of the role and function of the judge as a neutral arbiter of disputes, who only decides questions framed by adversarial litigants.

ii. Rejection of Adversarial System

Judicial case management undermines or subverts the adversarial system by permitting the litigation to be judicially directed, rather than controlled by the litigants. Under the judicial case management model, the judicial system has an independent interest in the litigation and the judge shares power with the parties in processing the lawsuit.

iii. Disservice to Litigants

Some managerial judges may place the court's interests in expeditious dispute resolution above the litigants' interests. Thus, judges concerned about congested dockets may impair litigants' interests through docket-clearing techniques, under the guise of calendar control or other supervisory powers. Judges also may improperly pressure parties to settle.

c. Positive Support for Judicial Case Management

Supporters of judicial case management argue that judges are not mere referees, but that they actively ensure that justice is done through close case supervision.

4. Civil Justice Reform Act of 1990

Congress enacted the **Civil Justice Reform Act** in 1990, which required every federal judicial district to create a CJRA Advisory Committee. These committees were required to conduct an assessment of the district's docket and write a report and plan for reform. By the end of 1993, all 94 federal district courts complied with the CJRA and implemented plans incorporating a wide array of judicial case management techniques. Many of the CJRA recommendations also have been implemented by local rules of court (*see* **Rule 83**).

5. The Manual for Complex Litigation

In addition to a judge's powers to manage and control a litigation under **Rule 16** and other inherent powers (discussed below), the Federal Judicial Center publishes a *Manual for Complex Litigation* (4th ed. 2004) which contains numerous recommendations to federal judges for organizing and supervising complex litigation. The *Manual's* recommendations do not have the status of Federal Rules of Civil Procedure and are not binding on the parties, unless the judge formally incorporates a recommended procedure into a court order.

B. PRETRIAL CONFERENCE: RULE 16

The pretrial conference rule is the chief means through which a federal judge manages and controls the course of a litigation. In theory, a federal judge may schedule as many pretrial conferences as the judge deems appropriate to the litigation. Prior to 1993, there was no requirement for any pretrial conference or scheduling order, and many federal judges did not wish to use their time in this fashion. The 1993 amendments to **Rule 16** now affirmatively require that the judge prepare a scheduling order, even in the absence of an early pretrial conference. Local district courts may exempt certain cases from this requirement, and many courts have exempted routine simple cases, such as Social Security appeals, from this rule. In addition, the Advisory Committee Note indicates that the 1993 changes were to alter the focus of pretrial conferences to encompass all aspects of case management, and not merely the conduct of trial.

1. Objectives of the Pretrial Conference: Rule 16(a)

Judges have discretionary power to order attorneys or unrepresented parties to appear at a pretrial conference. The purposes of the pretrial conference include expediting the disposition of the action; establishing early and continuing control so that the case will not be protracted because of a lack of management; discouraging wasteful pretrial activities; improving the quality of the trial through more thorough preparation; and facilitating settlement of the case.

2. Initial Pretrial Scheduling Conference and Order: Rule 16(b)

After the lawyers have met and conferred at the outset of the litigation to discuss mandatory informal exchange of discovery, as well as subsequent formal discovery, the lawyers must submit a report to the court. **Rule 26(f)** (*see* discussion above). After receiving the lawyer's report, the court either may arrange a conference in person with the lawyers, or by other means such as telephone or mail.

a. Timing of the Scheduling Order

The court must issue a scheduling order within 90 days after the appearance of the defendant in the lawsuit or within 120 days after the plaintiff serves the complaint on the defendant.

b. Content of the Scheduling Order

The scheduling order must limit the time (1) to join other parties and amend the pleadings; (2) to file motions, and (3) to complete discovery. The scheduling order also may include modifications of the times for disclosures of mandatory information required to be exchanged under **Rule 26(a)** and **26(e)(1)** and of the extent of permissible discovery; the date or dates for other pretrial conferences, a final pretrial conference, and trial; and any other matters appropriate in the circumstances of the case.

c. Modifications of the Scheduling Order

A scheduling order may not be modified except upon a *showing of good cause* and by leave of a district judge or if authorized by local rule, by a magistrate judge.

3. Subjects for Consideration at Pretrial Conferences: Rule 16(c)

Rule 16(c) was substantially amended in 1993 to greatly expand the nature and scope of subjects a court may take action regarding, at pretrial conference. These revisions reflect an endorsement and encouragement of increased judicial case management.

4. Pretrial Orders

The court may issue any pretrial orders as a result of pretrial conferences. The order controls the course of the proceedings, unless the court modifies the order by a subsequent order. **Rule 16(d).**

5. Final Pretrial Conference and Pretrial Order: Rule 16(e)

a. Timing

The final pretrial conference takes place as close to the time of trial as reasonable under the circumstances. A final pretrial conference is not absolutely required, and the judge will determine if a final pretrial conference is appropriate.

b. Attendance

The final pretrial conference must be attended by at least one lawyer who will try the case for each side, and by any unrepresented parties.

c. Duties

Lawyers attending the final pretrial conference must be prepared, in good faith, to discuss the case and any subjects listed in subsection (c). Lawyers participating in any pretrial conference must have authority to enter into stipulations and make admissions regarding all matters that the participants may reasonably anticipate being discussed. **Rule 16(c).**

i. Settlement

The court may require that a party or its representative be present or reasonably available by telephone in order to consider possible settlement of the dispute. **Rule 16(c).**

d. Final Pretrial Order

The court will issue a final pretrial order memorializing the actions concluded at the pretrial conference, which are absolutely binding on the subsequent trial. *See* **Payne v. S.S. Nabob,** 302 F.2d 803 (3d Cir. 1962). The final pretrial order may be modified *only to prevent manifest injustice.* **Rule 16(e).**

6. Duties and Sanctions: Rule 16(f)

a. Duties

Parties and their attorneys are required to appear on behalf of a party at a scheduling or pretrial conference; be prepared to participate in the conference; and participate in good faith. An attorney may be sanctioned for failing to obey a scheduling or other pretrial order.

b. Sanctions for Failure to Comply with Pretrial Conference Duties

A court may sanction a party or lawyer who fails to comply with duties relating to pretrial conferences. Another party may seek a sanction by motion, or the judge may sanction the offending lawyer on the judge's own initiative.

i. "Just Orders"

The judge may make any orders that are just, or available under the discovery sanctioning provisions contained in **Rule 37(b)(2)(A).**

ii. Attorney's Fees

The court also may order an attorney to pay any reasonable expenses and attorney's fees incurred in connection with non-compliance, unless the judge finds that the attorney's noncompliance was substantially justified or other circumstances make award of expenses unjust. **Rule 16(f)(2).**

C. EXTRAJUDICIAL PERSONNEL: MASTERS AND MAGISTRATES

1. Special Masters: Rule 53

"Special masters" are court-appointed personnel to assist the court in performing a wide array of functions. Special masters have a long history in English law, although their use in civil litigation was disfavored. Under the old **Federal Equity Rule 59,** the appointment of a special master was to be used in exceptional circumstances only. **Rule 53** was effectively re-written and extensively amended in 2003, to reflect the modern practice of appointment of special masters and the various tasks special masters may perform.

a. Modern Special Masters under the Federal Rules 53

A court may appoint a special master in any pending action. Masters can be appointed to perform duties consented to by the parties, hold trial proceedings, and address pre-trial and post-trial matters. Masters traditionally have served as referees, auditors, examiners, assessors, trial planners, or any other role for which the court seeks assistance. **Rule 53(a).**

b. Order Appointing Special Master; Appointment of Magistrate Judges

The court must give the parties notice and an opportunity to be heard prior to appointing a special master. The court must issue and order appointing a special master delineating the scope and authority of the special master, as well as method and terms for determining the master's compensation. **Rule 53(b).** A matter may be referred to a magistrate judge under the special master rule only when the order referring the matter to the magistrate judge expressly provides that the reference is made under **Rule 53. Rule 53(h).**

c.   Special Master's Authority

Special masters have authority to regulate all proceedings and take appropriate actions to perform assigned duties. Masters may impose any non-contempt sanctions provided by **Rules 37** or **45. Rule 53(c).**

d.   Evidentiary Hearings, Orders, Reports

A special master may conduct evidentiary hearings and compel, take, and record evidence. **Rule 53(c).** The special master may issue orders, **Rule 53(d),** and must issue a report to the court as required by the special master's order of appointment. **Rule 53(e).** A court subsequently may act on the special master's report, affording parties an opportunity to be heard on the report, to object, and to modify the report. **Rule 53(f).**

e.   Special Master Compensation

The appointing court has the power to determine and fix the special master's compensation based on terms stated in the order of appointment. **Rule 53(g).**

2.   Magistrate Judges: 28 U.S.C. §§ 631–639 and Rule 72

The **Federal Magistrates Act of 1968** created a system of federal magistrates. Federal magistrates may serve in a wide array of functions and capacities as defined both by statute and by the Federal Rules. A 1990 amendment to the Act provides that magistrates "be designated as United States magistrate judges."

a.   Constitutional Status of Magistrate Judges

Magistrate judges are not Article III judges and do not enjoy life tenure or the salary protections of Article III judges. Magistrate judges, however, perform many of the same functions as Article III judges, including conducting trials by consent of the parties. There is some controversy whether magistrates are unconstitutional, but the consensus of expert witnesses at the time of enactment of the Magistrates Act was that the legislation creating magistrates was constitutional.

b.   Powers and Functions of Magistrate Judges

The scope of magistrates' authority is very broad. Magistrates may supervise discovery, pretrial motions, and conduct trials by party consent.

■ X. TRIAL

A. CHOOSING THE TRIER: JUDGE OR JURY?

1. The Province of the Judge and Jury

Traditionally, the jury is the "finder of fact" and the judge applies the law. This development of the judge-jury relationship evolved over a lengthy period into this modern dichotomy. For example, in colonial America, juries could decide questions of law, especially in criminal cases. Prior to 1850, juries in many jurisdictions could decide questions of both fact and law.

a. Historical Basis for Choice of Trier: The Institution of Trial by Jury

Modern American jury practice derives from the development of the jury in England. William the Conqueror introduced the jury system in England in the eleventh century. By the end of the fifteenth century the jury was the central method of fact-finding (replacing the medieval practice of trial by ordeal). By the seventeenth century, juries served as checks against the absolutist Stuart kings.

b. Historical Function of the Jury

Originally jurors were chosen on the basis for their fitness as a witness with knowledge and background about the local community. Jurors were entitled to decided a case based on personal knowledge even when this contradicted testimony at trial. Jurors could consult and communicate directly with the parties in an inquisitorial fashion. Over time this inquisitorial role shifted to that of impartial finder-of-fact, and jurors became dependent on evidence the parties presented at trial.

c. Criticisms of Jury Structure and Practice

Notwithstanding its long privileged historical lineage, the jury in contemporary practice frequently is under attack.

i. Juries as an Oppressive, Unregulated Force

Populist juries are viewed as an oppressive force—unknowledgeable, unpredictable, and operating in a largely unregulated manner.

ii. Jury Nullification

Jury critics point to the phenomenon of "jury nullification," when juries essentially disregard the factual evidence presented at trial, disregard the law, and use their power to "send a message" through their verdict. Jury nullification is more a phenomenon in criminal prosecutions, because judges in civil cases have greater control over the litigation outcome through **Rule 50.**

iii. Waste of Resources

Jury trials also are perceived as a waste of time and resources, consuming a disproportionate part of societal resources. The costs of jury trials outweigh the benefits derived from them; bench trials are equally efficacious and less costly.

iv. Lack of Expertise

Critics have argued that juries are composed of non-experts who are not capable of understanding complex litigation and often base verdicts on improper criteria or sympathies.

d. Modern Jury Functions

Modern jury functions include determining facts; determining the legal consequences of the facts through application of the law as the judge instructs the jury; and presenting the results of the jury's deliberation in a verdict.

e. Modern Judicial Functions

Modern judicial functions include ruling on pretrial motions and pre-liminary issues; determining threshold issues such as questions relating to jurisdiction, joinder, pleading, and defenses; the structure of the trial; questions of admissibility of evidence and exclusion of evidence; questions of privilege and immunity; taking "judicial notice" of undisputed and uncontroverted facts; the sufficiency of evidence relative to the allocation of burdens of production, persuasion, and proof; the rules of substantive law to be applied; how to instruct the jury concerning the substantive law and what type of verdict to be rendered; and whether a jury's determination is unreasonable or needs to be reduced or in-creased.

2. Sources of the Right to a Jury Trial

There are three sources for the right to a jury trial: (1) the Seventh Amendment or state constitutional provisions; (2) statutorily-created rights providing for a jury trial; and (3) discretionary jury panels in equity proceedings.

a. Federal Constitutional Right to Jury Trial: The Seventh Amendment Right to Trial by Jury

The Seventh Amendment to the Constitution, effective in 1791, provides: "In suits at common law, where the value in controversy shall exceed twenty dollars, the right to trial by jury shall be preserved, and no fact tried by a jury, shall be otherwise re-examined in any court of the United States, than according to the rules of the common law."

i. "Preservation of Right"

The Seventh Amendment does not create a right to trial by jury. Rather, it "preserves" the right as it existed at the time the amendment was ratified in 1791. This does not mean that jury trials are frozen only as to those actions that existed at common law in 1791. Rather, this language provides the interpretative basis for modern federal courts to determine what contemporary statutory causes of action are entitled to a jury trial.

ii. Rules

Rule 38 also preserves "the right of trial by jury as declared by the Seventh Amendment . . . to the parties inviolate."

iii. Jury Demand and Waiver

The federal right to a jury is waivable. **Rule 38(d).** A party desiring a jury trial must make a jury demand in a timely fashion. **Rule 38(b).**

iv. Implementation of the Right to a Jury Trial: Problem Created by the Merger of Law and Equity

With promulgation of the Federal Rules in 1938, the rules merged actions at law and equity into one "civil action." A party could now assert any legal or equitable claims in a unified federal complaint.

v. Consequences of the Merger of Law and Equity for Jury Trial Right

The merger of law and equity permitted the presentation of a single form of action in a unitary federal lawsuit. However, the merger did not abrogate the differences between the substantive and remedial rules of the two systems. Actions at law are entitled to be tried to a jury; equitable claims to a judge.

vi. The Equitable "Clean-Up" Doctrine

Before the merger of law and equity, equity practice developed the "clean-up" doctrine which allowed a court with equity jurisdiction to decide ("clean-up") any incidental legal issues involved in the litigation.

vii. Applying the Seventh Amendment Guarantee in Modern Non-Statutory Cases

In determining whether litigants are entitled to a jury, federal courts focus on the *nature of the issue* involved in the litigation. If the underlying issue involved in the case is legal (i.e., the parties seek money damages), then the litigant is entitled to a jury trial on the legal issue. **Ross v. Bernhard,** 396 U.S. 531 (1970). In actions that contain both legal and equitable claims, if there is a common factual issue then the legal issue must be tried first to a jury. The judge may then rule on the equitable claim. **Beacon Theatres, Inc. v. Westover,** 359 U.S. 500 (1959).

viii. Complexity Exception

The Supreme Court also has suggested that there may be a "complexity exception" to the Seventh Amendment right to a trial by jury. **Ross v. Bernhard.** In addition to evaluating whether an issue is legal or equitable, courts also may assess the "practical abilities and limitations of juries." *Id.* That is, some cases are so complex that a jury cannot reasonably decide the issues. To date the Supreme Court has not elaborated further on this standard and lower federal courts are split concerning applicability of this "complexity" standard.

ix. Right to Trial by Jury in Statutory Actions

When Congress creates a new right of action it may expressly or impliedly create a right to a jury trial. *See* **Beacon Theatres, Inc. v. Westover.** Congress has the power to confer a jury trial right broader than the Seventh Amendment guarantee. Congress also expressly or impliedly may deny a jury trial. Further, a statute may be silent concerning a jury trial right.

x. Right to Jury Panel in Equitable Actions: Rule 39(c)

The right to a jury panel in equitable actions historically is based in the equity advisory jury. The Chancellor had discretion to empanel a jury to render an advisory verdict. These verdicts were not binding and the Chancellor could enforce or disregard the advisory jury's conclusions. Equity juries determined questions for which they were thought especially suited, such as assessing witness credibility. Modern federal and state practice has retained the equity advisory jury to assist the judge in any issue the judge requests. Advisory juries may decide equitable issues for which there is no jury right. *See* **Rule 39(c).**

b. Right to Jury Trial in State Court

The federal constitutional right to a jury trial is not binding on the states because the Seventh Amendment has not been "incorporated" through the Fourteenth Amendment, as have many other provisions of the Bill of Rights. *See* **Chicago, Rock Island & Pacific Ry. Co. v. Cole,** 251 U.S. 54 (1919); **Walker v. Sauvinet,** 92 U.S. (2 Otto) 90, 23 L.Ed. 678 (1875).

i. State Constitutional Provisions

Most state constitutions contain a right to trial by jury. In state practice, the right to a jury trial typically is determined with reference to the date of the ratification of the state constitutional provisions. Since most states have merged law and equity and have constitutional or statutory provisions identical or similar to the Seventh Amendment, the same law-and-equity problems that exist in federal court are replicated in state court.

c. Conflicts between Federal and State Jury Trial Right

i. Actions Asserting Federally-Created Rights in State Court

If a federal statute confers a jury trial right as an integral part of the relief, then federal rather than state law applies regarding the jury function. This is especially true when Congress has indicated a strong federal policy in favor of a jury trial in a particular case. **Dice v. Akron, Canton & Youngstown Railroad Company,** 342 U.S. 359 (1952).

ii. Actions Involving State-Created Rights in Federal Court

In federal diversity cases, federal jury standards apply. Although state law characterizes the state claim as legal or equitable, federal law determines whether the case is entitled to a jury trial. *See* **Byrd v. Blue Ridge Rural Elec. Cooperative Inc.,** 356 U.S. 525 (1958); **Herron v. Southern Pacific Co.,** 283 U.S. 91 (1931) (state law cannot alter the character or function of federal courts).

3. Demand or Waiver of Jury Trial: Rule 38(b)

In a few states, a jury trial is used unless the parties request a bench trial. In most states, however, and federal court, the right to trial by jury is waived unless a litigant demands a jury within the time period provided by rule. Both plaintiffs and defendants have the right to make a jury demand. The loss of the right to a jury trial because of a failure to make a jury demand does not violate the Seventh Amendment (and therefore is not unconstitutional). **Moore v. United States,** 196 F.2d 906 (5th Cir. 1952).

a. Jury Demand in Federal Court

A party requesting a jury trial must make an affirmative demand and failure to do so results in a waiver. **Rule 38(b), (d).**

i. How Made; Timing

A jury demand must be made in writing and served on the opposing party. The jury demand may be made no later than 14 days after the service of the last pleading directed to such issue. **Rule 38(b).**

ii. Specified Issues

A litigant may effectively extend the time for making a jury demand by requesting a jury for only specified issues. This provides the responding party with time within which to make a jury demand on the issue. **Rule 38(c).**

iii. Withdrawal of Jury Demand

A jury demand may only be withdrawn on the consent of all the parties. This is to protect those parties who have relied on the jury demand and prepared their case for presentation to a jury (rather than a judge).

iv. Removed Cases: Rule 81(c)

A timely express demand for a jury trial in state court secures the right to a trial by jury in federal court. A demand need not be made, however, if the state court does not require an express jury trial demand. *But see* **Segal v. American Cas. Co.,** 250 F.Supp. 936 (D. Md. 1966) (plaintiffs not entitled to jury on removal where no demand was necessary under state law, and federal demand was untimely).

v. Discretionary Jury Trial: Rule 39(b)

If parties fail to make a timely jury demand and have waived their right to a jury trial, they may request that the court exercise its discretion and order a jury trial anyway. **Rule 39(b).** Some federal courts have indicated that there should be good grounds for exercise of this discretion.

B. IMPLEMENTATION OF THE JURY TRIAL RIGHT

1. Selection and Composition of the Jury

The selection and composition of juries varies in state and federal practice. In federal practice, district courts implement the jury right through local rules, pursuant to authority in **Rule 83.**

a. Jury Pools; Size

State and federal courts determine the methods for summoning jurors and the geographic area from which jurors are drawn to constitute the jury pool or array. Generally, federal courts draw a jury pool from a wider geographic area than do local state courts.

b. Empanelling the Jury; Voir Dire; Challenges

i. Empanelling the Jury

State courts draw jury pools from property and tax lists, local residency, and such. Federal jury pools are summoned from voter registration lists, with supplemental sources (such as driver's licenses, public utilities lists, state tax rolls, telephone lists) when necessary to ensure adequate representation. *See* **28 U.S.C. §§ 1861– 66.**

ii. Composition of the Jury Pool

The jury pool is supposed to be drawn from a cross-section of the community, without systematic or intentional exclusion of any groups. This does not mean that every jury pool or jury must contain representatives of every social, economic, religious, racial, political, and geographical segments of the community. **Thiel v. Southern Pac. Co.,** 328 U.S. 217 (1946) (improper jury panel selection where court clerk intentionally excluded all daily wage earners from jury service, regardless of whether actual hardship existed).

iii. Blue Ribbon Juries

So-called "blue ribbon" juries consist of jurors selected for their above-average intelligence, presumably to decide complex litigation. The Supreme Court has upheld a New York state statute empowering a judge to empanel such blue ribbon juries.

iv. Voir Dire: Rule 47(a)

Voir dire is the process of questioning jurors for suitability to sit on a jury. In state courts, judges or the attorneys conduct the voir dire, or the judge may conduct the voir dire with suggestions from the attorney. In federal court, judges have discretion to determine the method of voir dire, although most federal judges conduct the voir dire. *See* **Rule 47(a).**

v. Challenges to Jurors

Jurors may be disqualified from a jury for two reasons: either "for cause" or through a "pre-emptory challenge." A challenge for cause removes a prospective juror who evidences bias or other prejudice that might impair the juror's ability to fairly and impartially weigh the evidence and render a verdict. In order to disqualify, the state of mind of the juror must lead to the inference that the juror will not or could not act with impartiality. Pre-emptory challenges allow an attorney to disqualify or strike a juror without having to give a reason. Attorneys typically use pre-emptory challenges to remove jurors the attorney believes will not be sympathetic to the client.

C. THE SCOPE AND ORDER OF TRIAL

1. Order of Trial in Jury Cases

After a jury is selected and the judge instructs the jurors of their duties, a jury trial typically is presented in successive rounds of opening statements, direct and cross examination, motions for directed verdicts, closing arguments, and post-verdict motions.

a. Non-Jury Trials

In bench trials the court dispenses with many of the formal proceedings in jury trials, such as opening and closing arguments. In addition, bench trials do not require jury instructions or deliberation.

2. Allocating Burdens of Production, Persuasion, and Proof

The term "burden of proof" actually encompasses three different types of burdens, which "shift" during the course of trial. These are the burdens of production, persuasion, and proof.

a. Burden of Production

The burden of production refers to the requirement that a party come forward or produce some threshold level of evidence in support of a claim needed to satisfy the standard of proof. Typically the initial burden of production is on the plaintiff. If a plaintiff fails to satisfy its burden of production on a claim, the plaintiff loses. However, a plaintiff may satisfy its burden of production, but nonetheless lose the case for failing to ultimately persuade the fact finder. The burden of production must be met for the case to go to the fact finder (usually the jury). If the plaintiff fails in this burden before trial, the plaintiff may suffer a summary judgment. At trial, if the plaintiff fails to carry its burden, the plaintiff will suffer a "directed verdict," or under new terminology, a "judgment as a matter of law."

b. Burden of Persuasion

If the plaintiff satisfies the burden of production, it also must satisfy the burden of persuasion and convince the fact-finder that the plaintiff should prevail based on the weight of the evidence. The defendant will produce its own evidence, or attempt to cast doubt on the plaintiff's evidence by attacking witness credibility or reliability. If the fact finder is convinced that the plaintiff's evidence is not sufficiently reliable or credible, the defendant will win. Plaintiffs and the prosecution must satisfy one of three standards in civil and criminal cases. These standards assessing the quantity and quality of the evidence proffered are the "preponderance of the evidence"; "clear and convincing evidence"; and "beyond a reasonable doubt" (criminal standard).

c. Shifting Burdens

Typically the burden of production and persuasion rests on the party asserting a claim, so the plaintiff carries both burdens. In some actions, however, once the burden of production has been satisfied, the burden of persuasion shifts to the opposing party.

3. Opening Statements

The plaintiff's lawyer typically makes the opening statement because the plaintiff carries the burden of proof. If the defendant carries the burden of proof as to all issues (a trial solely on affirmative defenses), then the defendant has the right to make the opening statement. In most jurisdictions the defendant has an option to make an opening statement after the plaintiff, a choice guided by tactical considerations. The attorneys may not make legal arguments during opening statements, but may only present a road map of what the evidence is to show.

4. Presentation of Evidence: Direct and Cross Examination

Each side presents its case in-chief and rebuttal (if necessary) through witness testimony or by offering other evidence into the record, such as documents or exhibits. A party questions its own witnesses through direct examination. The opposing party has the opportunity to cross-examine the same witness. The major purpose of cross examination is to impeach or impair the credibility or reliability of a witness's testimony. The party then can "rehabilitate" its witnesses by re-direct examination. The scope of cross examination is limited by the scope of the direct examination.

5. Closing Argument

In final arguments, the attorneys summarize the evidence and draw out the logical implications of the evidence for the jury. Final argument is in three parts. The plaintiff, who typically carries the burden of production and persuasion, speaks first and last. If the defendant carries the burden of proof, the order of closing is reversed. In many jurisdictions, the court limits the length of closing argument.

D. JUDICIAL CONTROL OF JURY ACTION

1. Enforcing Burdens: Taking Cases from the Jury

a. Motion for Judgment as a Matter of Law (Formerly Directed Verdicts and Judgments Notwithstanding the Verdict): Rule 50(a)

Either party, at the conclusion of the party's presentation of its case, may ask the court to "direct a verdict"; that is, to decide the case in the moving party's favor. If the judge directs the verdict, the case effectively is taken away from the jury, because the case ends and never goes to the jury for decision. Typically the defendant moves for a directed verdict at the conclusion of the plaintiff's presentation of evidence, but it is possible for the court to direct a verdict in the plaintiff's favor if the defendant fails to prove a defense. *See* **Daniel J. Hartwig Assocs., Inc. v. Kanner,** 913 F.2d 1213 (7th Cir. 1990) (directed verdict for plaintiff where defendant failed to prove a defense to a contract).

i. Terminology

State court systems provide for directed verdicts. In 1991, **Rule 50** was amended to change the terms "directed verdict" and "judgment notwithstanding the verdict" to be called "judgment as a matter of law." This change supports the concept that directed verdicts, judgments notwithstanding the verdict, and summary judgment all are governed by identical standards. The singular difference is the time at which these motions typically are raised.

ii. Standard: Directed Verdicts

A judge is to grant a directed verdict if "there is no legally sufficient evidentiary basis for a reasonable jury to find for the party on that issue." Directed verdicts are granted where the party carrying the burden of production initially fails to come forward with sufficient evidence in support of its claim, or an issue that is part of the claim.

iii. Evaluation of the Evidence

In evaluating the evidence on a directed verdict motion, the court views the evidence in the light most favorable to the non-moving party. Typically the court will view all the evidence, but decide credibility problems in favor of the non-movant.

iv. Quantum and Weight of the Evidence

Historically courts have used two different tests (the "scintilla" test and the "substantial evidence" test) to assess whether the evidence supports a directed verdict. The court is not supposed to weigh the evidence, but rather determine whether the party carrying the burden of proof has produced sufficient evidence to support a favorable verdict.

v. Reasonable Inferences

On motions for directed verdict and judgment notwithstanding the verdict, courts are permitted to draw reasonable inferences from the evidence. Impermissible inferences require the court (or jury) to span large gaps in the testimony in order to reach a conclusion. *See* **Galloway v. United States,** 319 U.S. 372 (1943).

vi. Constitutionality of Judgments as a Matter of Law

The directed verdict does not violate the Seventh Amendment right to a jury trial because the procedure has analogs at common law, such as the demurrer. *See* **Galloway v. United States,** *supra.* Judgments as a matter of law also withstand constitutional challenge, provided the moving litigant makes a prior directed verdict motion, because JNOVs are viewed as derivative of the directed verdict motion.

vii. Judgments Notwithstanding the Verdict: Rule 50(b)

Judgments notwithstanding the verdict (so-called "JNOVs" from the Latin judgment non obstante veredicto) are virtually the same as directed verdicts, except the JNOV motion is made after the jury has rendered its verdict. JNOVs are now also denominated as "judgments as a matter of law." The losing attorney basically asks the court to render a judgment in its favor, despite what the jury has done. Similar to the directed verdict, the effect of the JNOV is to take the case away from the jury. Also similar to directed verdicts, JNOVs are not an unconstitutional violation of the Seventh Amendment, but they do require the moving party to have made a prior directed verdict motion.

viii. Standard for the JNOV

The standard for granting a JNOV is that the party carrying the burden of proof at trial failed to support its claim with sufficient evidence, and therefore no reasonable jury could have found the verdict it did. Similar to the directed verdict motion, the court is not supposed to weigh the evidence. The court is to evaluate whether, under the requirements of the substantive law and applicable evidentiary burdens, there is any evidence supporting the jury's verdict. In assessing the jury's conclusion, the jury may make reasonable inferences from the evidence, but may not base a decision on mere possibilities.

ix. Conditional Rulings on Motions for a Judgment as a Matter of Law and New Trial Motions

Rules 50(c) and **(d)** provide for the judge to simultaneously rule on a losing party's motion for a judgment as a matter of law, and the losing party's new trial motion. The purpose of the "conditional" rulings is to allow the trial judge to preserve the ability to grant a new trial in the eventuality that an appellate court overturns the judge's ruling on the JNOV. The appellate court independently may order a new trial from a reversal of the trial judge's JNOV. If the judge makes a conditional new trial ruling, the judge must specify the grounds for granting or denying the motion. **Rules 50(c), (d).** *See also* **Neely v. Martin K. Eby Constr. Co.,** 386 U.S. 317 (1967).

x. **Consequences and Benefits of the JNOV**

Because the JNOV is available to reverse a jury's verdict after all the evidence at trial, this reduces pressure on the judge to make an earlier directed verdict ruling. With the JNOV, the judge has the ability to reverse the jury's verdict after all the evidence is in. Also, if a judge orders a directed verdict and an appellate court reverses this ruling, then a new trial must be ordered. If an appellate court reverses a JNOV, however, the appellate court can reinstitute the jury's verdict and there will be no need for a new trial.

2. Instructions and Verdicts

Before the jury retires to deliberate, the judge will "instruct" the jury in the law and the jury's fact-finding function.

a. Instructions to the Jury

Practice varies in state and federal court concerning whether the judge instructs the jury before or after the attorneys' closing arguments. **Rule 51** gives the judge discretion to instruct the jury at any time before the jury is discharged.

i. Form of the Instructions; Objections

In many jurisdictions, the judge permits the attorneys to submit proposed jury instructions. The judge then determines what jury instructions to provide the jury. In most jurisdictions, a party cannot appeal a judge's failure to give a jury instruction the attorney did not request. In federal court, party must state objections to jury instructions on the record. **Rule 51(c).**

b. Commenting on the Evidence

The ability of judges to comment on the evidence is derived from the common law. A minority of states have retained this power, which includes the ability to express opinions on evidence and witness credibility.

i. Federal Practice

In federal court judges are permitted to comment on the evidence when submitting the case to the jury. **Quercia v. United States,** 289 U.S. 466 (1933). *But see* **Nunley v. Pettway Oil Co.,** 346 F.2d 95 (6th Cir. 1965) (judge improperly gave opinion on ultimate fact question—

amounting to a directed verdict—that was peculiarly for the jury to decide).

ii.   State Practice

The majority of states restrict the ability of judges to comment on the evidence.

c.   Submission to the Jury

After the judge instructs the jury, the jury retires to deliberate and render a judgment.

i.   Unanimity Requirement

Federal courts require a unanimous verdict by the jury. The unanimity requirement, however, may lead to stalemated or "hung" juries, requiring a retrial. To avoid this, many states permit less than unanimity in civil trials.

ii.   Jury Notes; Evidentiary Exhibits

In some jurisdictions jurors are permitted to take notes during trial. Jurors also may have exhibits and testimony in the deliberation room, to aid in jury deliberation.

iii.   Jury Confusion or Lack of Recall

The jury may request that witness testimony or jury instructions be re-read to them, if the jury is uncertain about its recollection of testimony or is confused about the jury instructions.

d.   Forms of Verdicts: Rule 49

There are different methods of submitting the case to the jury. The jury either may render a "general verdict," a "special verdict," or a "general verdict with answers to written questions." The choice of the verdict form is in the judge's discretion, and parties are not entitled to any particular verdict form, or particular interrogatories when this verdict form is used.

i.   The General Verdict

The general verdict is the most common form of verdict in which the jury finds for the plaintiff or defendant, but does not disclose the grounds for its decision. The general verdict is criticized for its "all or nothing" quality. It also is impossible to know the basis for the jury's decision, and whether it was based on passion, emotion, prejudice, popular opinion, etc.

ii. Special Verdicts

The Federal Rules provide for special verdicts. Special verdicts are intended to cure the problems of general verdicts, and to enhance judicial efficiency. The court may require a jury to return only a special verdict in the form of a special written finding on each issue of fact. **Rule 49(a).** Special verdicts allow the judge to control for improper jury sympathy or passion.

iii. General Verdict with Interrogatories: Rule 49(b)

The court requests the jury to render a general verdict, but also requests the jury to answer a series of questions. The answers to these questions assist the court in knowing the jury's basis for its general verdict. Depending on the circumstances, the court also may enter the verdict, order a new trial, or request further deliberation.

e. Findings of Fact and Conclusions of Law in Nonjury Cases

When a case is tried to a judge, the judge is obligated to enter findings of fact and conclusions of law. **Rule 52(a).** In federal court these requirements are mandatory and cannot be waived. States have similar rules for bench trials. This applies even when the judge uses an advisory jury.

i. Purpose

The major purpose for these requirements is to clarify the basis for the judge's decision and to clearly indicate findings to provide a basis for subsequent res judicata effect of the judgment.

ii. Attorney Participation

Some judges invite attorneys from both sides to submit proposed findings of fact and conclusions of law, prior to the decision of the case. Some courts decide the case and then ask the winning attorney to submit proposed findings and conclusions. Some Circuits have rejected this procedure.

iii. Standard of Review

Findings of fact will not be reversed on appeal unless the findings are clearly erroneous. **Rule 52(a)(6).** *See* **Anderson v. City of Bessemer City,** 470 U.S. 564 (1985).

E. CHALLENGING ERRORS—GROUNDS FOR NEW TRIALS: RULES 59 AND 61

A litigant who loses at trial either may request a new trial or contest errors on direct appeal from the judgment. The new trial motion allows the judge to correct any errors that might have occurred at trial, rather than having an appellate court reverse the judge. Also, the judge has first-hand knowledge of what occurred at trial, which an appellate court will not. A judge will not order a new trial for "harmless errors" in the court's admission or exclusion of evidence, or any other ruling. **Rule 61.**

1. Discretion

The judge's discretion to order a new trial is very broad. However, most judges exercise this power cautiously, in deference to the jury's function and the time and expense of conducting a new trial.

2. Timing: Rule 59(b)

New trial motions must be made within 28 days after the judgment is entered. **Rule 59(b).** Courts apply this rule rigidly. The time for making a new trial motion cannot be enlarged. *See* **Rule 6(b).**

3. New Trial Motion Distinguished from Directed Verdicts and JNOVs: Verdicts Against the Weight of the Evidence

"Where there is substantial evidence in support of the plaintiff's case, the judge may not direct a verdict against him, even though he may not believe his evidence or may think that the weight of the evidence is on the other side; for, under the constitutional guaranty of trial by jury, it is for the judge to weigh the evidence and pass on its credibility He may, however, set aside a verdict supported by substantial evidence where in his opinion it is contrary to the clear weight of the evidence, or is based on evidence which is false; for even though the evidence be sufficient to preclude the direction of a verdict, it is still his duty to exercise his power over the proceedings before him to prevent a miscarriage of justice."

4. Grounds for New Trial

Some state rules set out specific grounds for new trials. Where specific grounds are set forth, a judge may not order a new trial "in the interests of justice."

a. New Trial in Federal Court

The Federal Rules permit a judge to order a new trial for any reason "heretofore granted" in actions at law. **Rule 59(a).** Under this broad mandate, judges have ordered new trials because of prejudicial errors in evidentiary rulings, jury instructions, attorney or juror misconduct, newly discovered evidence, the verdict is against the weight of the evidence, or the verdict is legally excessive or inadequate. **Rule 59(a)(1)(A).**

b. Nonjury Trials

A court may grant a new trial after a nonjury trial for any reason for which a rehearing has heretofore been granted in suits in equity. **Rule 59(a)(1)(B).**

c. Incoherent Jury Verdicts

A court may order a new trial when the verdict the jury returns, particularly in multiple claim cases, is incoherent or inconsistent. For example, in a case where the court tendered a single verdict form for multiple liability counts based on separate causes of action, the court could not determine whether the jury's single verdict applied to one or both counts. The court also could not reassemble the jury to clarify its decision. Thus, a new trial was appropriate to clarify the first jury's action. **Magnani v. Trogi,** 70 Ill.App.2d 216, 218 N.E.2d 21 (Ill. App. 1966).

5. Partial and Conditional New Trials

Federal and state judges may order a partial new trial on certain issues. A judge may order a conditional new trial if the judge believes the jury verdict is too small (*see* discussion of remittitur and additur, below). This technique avoids the time and expense of completely retrying the entire case. **Rule 59(a).**

a. Circumstances Not Justifying Partial New Trials

Partial new trials are inappropriate solely on a liability issue if the jury was improperly instructed on the liability standard.

b. Circumstances Justifying Partial and Conditional New Trials: Additur and Remittitur

The most common instance for ordering a partial new trial is on the issue of damages. State judges may order a partial new or conditional new trial, limited to the issue of damages, if the judge believes that the jury verdict is legally inadequate or excessive. Where a verdict is believed inadequate, the new trial is for the purpose of determining whether to enhance the verdict through "additur." If the court believes the verdict excessive, the new trial determines whether to diminish the award, through "remittitur."

i.   Constitutionality of Additur and Remittitur

State courts generally recognize both additur and remittitur. Remittitur is permitted in federal courts, but not additur. **Dimick v. Schiedt,** 293 U.S. 474 (1935). This is because remittitur only decreases a sum already awarded by a jury, but additur determines an amount that the first jury did not.

6.   Constitutionality of New Trial Orders

The judge's ability to order a new trial does not violate the Constitution. This is because the judge effectively is sending the case to a new jury.

F.   POWER TO SET ASIDE JUDGMENTS ON GROUNDS DISCOVERED AFTER IT WAS RENDERED: RULE 60

A litigant may move for relief from the judgment based on a series of grounds set forth in **Rule 60.** A motion for relief from the judgment must be made within a reasonable time, and for some circumstances, no more than a year after the entry of judgment or order or the date of the proceeding. **Rule 60(c).**

1.   Clerical Mistake: Rule 60(a)

A court may correct errors in the judgment that are the result of clerical error, omission, or oversight. This is a ministerial procedure and does not require the case to be reopened or relitigated. This motion may not be used to seek an increase or reduction of a jury award.

2.   Other Grounds—Mistakes, Inadvertence, Excusable Neglect, Newly Discovered Evidence, Fraud, Etc.: Rule 60(b)

a.   Timing: Within One Year

Certain grounds for relief from a judgment must be made within one year from the entry of judgment. These include mistake, excusable neglect, newly discovered evidence, or fraud.

i. Mistake, Inadvertence, Excusable Neglect: Rule 60(b)(1)

These grounds existed at the time the Federal Rules were enacted in 1938. Such relief may be granted only when it is reasonable under the circumstances and the mistake, inadvertence, or neglect is not the result of the attorney's gross negligence.

ii. Newly Discovered Evidence: Rule 60(b)(2)

The party seeking relief on this ground must show that the evidence was in existence at the time of trial but that the attorney was unable to discover it despite due diligence in preparing the case. The attorney may not use this ground to develop a new theory or present some new facts.

iii. Fraud, Misrepresentation or Misconduct of the Other Party: Rule 60(b)(3)

The federal rule abolishes the distinction between extrinsic and intrinsic fraud. Extrinsic fraud relates to party conduct that prevents the other side from developing its case. Intrinsic fraud refers to conduct during trial, such as the presentation of perjured testimony. Some states maintain this distinction and allow a judgment to be reopened only for extrinsic fraud. The movant must establish the fraud by clear and convincing evidence.

b. Timing: "Reasonable Time"

Rule 60(c) sets forth a series of grounds for reopening a judgment within a "reasonable time." These include the ground that the judgment is void (e.g., for lack of jurisdiction), has been satisfied, reversal of the law, or changed circumstances that no longer make it equitable to enforce an injunction. These grounds are very limited in scope.

i. "Any Other Reason"

A litigant also may seek relief from a judgment, within a reasonable time, for "any other reason that justifies relief." This is the broadest possible ground for relief, preserving the court's equitable power to do justice in individual circumstances. Relief has been limited to "extraordinary circumstances."

G. JURY MISCONDUCT

Various errors by the jury or jury misconduct may form the basis for appeal.

1. Deception During Voir Dire

A juror's lying in answer to questions during voir dire may be a ground for overturning a verdict. The court will determine the extent of prejudice caused by the untruthfulness. A juror's honest but mistaken response to a question on voir dire is not a sufficient ground to invalidate a judgment. **McDonough Power Equipment, Inc. v. Greenwood,** 464 U.S. 548 (1984).

2. Misconduct During Deliberation

Juror misconduct includes discussing the case with others (including other jurors) or visiting the site of a claim, when the judge has prohibited such actions. The judge will evaluate the degree of prejudice resulting from improper conversations or viewing. Jurors also may not decide the case from personal knowledge, or decide the case through improper means, such as flipping a coin.

■ XI. APPELLATE REVIEW

A. PERSONS WHO MAY SEEK REVIEW

Typically a losing party may seek appellate review. In certain circumstances, a winning party also may seek appellate review. Finally, in limited circumstances a person or group who was not a party to a litigation may seek to intervene on appeal, although this is highly unusual.

B. THE PROBLEM OF APPEALABILITY: WHEN A DECISION MAY BE REVIEWED

1. The Principal of Finality

In most jurisdictions, litigants (usually the losing party), may only bring an appeal from the entry of a final judgment.

a. Purposes of the Final Judgment Rule

The final judgment rule serves several purposes, most prominently to enhance judicial economy; and reduce delay, expense and harassment.

b.   Difference in State Court Practice

Some states courts, such as New York, are unpersuaded by these rationales supporting the final judgment rule. Instead, these jurisdictions believe that immediate resolution of the validity of interlocutory orders may prevent an unnecessary trial. Also, in absence of appellate guidance, judges may issue inconsistent orders. These jurisdictions, then, permit much more liberal interlocutory appeal than the federal courts provide.

c.   Finality Defined

What constitutes finality for appeal purposes differs from jurisdiction to jurisdiction and usually is defined by statute. Generally, a final judgment is the order that leaves nothing to be done except to execute on the judgment. The final judgment concludes all rights that were the subject of the litigation. Most discovery orders, for example, are not final orders because they are not the subject of the underlying substantive merits of the lawsuit.

d.   The Final Judgment Rule in Federal Practice: Rule 54, 28 U.S.C. § 1291, and 28 U.S.C. § 2072(c)

   i.   Rule 54(a)

   A final judgment in federal practice simply includes any decree or order from which an appeal lies.

   ii.   Jurisdictional Statute: 28 U.S.C. § 1291

   This statute confers jurisdiction on appellate courts of all final decisions of the district courts, except those for which the Supreme Court has direct review. All aspects of whether a federal court may hear an appeal, such as timeliness and finality, are viewed as involving "jurisdiction over the subject matter." *See* **Firestone Tire & Rubber Co. v. Risjord**, 449 U.S. 368 (1981); **Liberty Mutual Insurance Co. v. Wetzel**, 424 U.S. 737 (1976).

   iii.   Judicial Improvements Act of 1990, Added Subsection 28 U.S.C. § 2072(c)

   The Supreme Court may define, by rule, "when a ruling of a district court is final for purposes of appeal under section 1291."

e.   Exceptions to the Final Judgment Rule

Although the final judgment rule is relatively absolute, statutes and doctrine recognize exceptions to the rule whereby an appellate court may have jurisdiction of an interlocutory appeal. Federal statutes recognize four exceptions to the final judgment rule, and state statutes delineate those orders requiring immediate appellate review.

i. Injunctions, Receiverships, Admiralty: 28 U.S.C. § 1292(a)(1)–(3)

This statute provides for immediate jurisdiction of appeals of interlocutory orders relating to injunctions, receiverships, and cases in admiralty.

ii. Interlocutory Appeals under 28 U.S.C. § 1292(b)

Appellate courts also have jurisdiction of those orders a district court judge "certifies" for immediate review. The judge has to certify his or her own order in writing—within 10 days of issuing the order—stating that the order appealed from involves a controlling question of law as to which there is substantial ground for difference of opinion; and that an immediate appeal may materially advance the ultimate termination of the litigation.

iii. The "Collateral Order" Doctrine

The collateral order doctrine is the judicially-created exception to the final judgment rule. Refined through a series of Supreme Court cases, (*see, e.g.,* **Cohen v. Beneficial Indus. Loan Corp.,** 337 U.S. 541 (1949) and **Coopers & Lybrand v. Livesay,** 437 U.S. 463 (1978)), the collateral order doctrine permits immediate review of a trial judge's order that is: (a) final and unrelated to the merits (collateral); (b) involves a right "too important" to be denied review; (c) would result in irreparable harm to the person appealing the order, if immediate review were not available.

iv. The "Death Knell" Doctrine

Several federal circuits developed the "death knell" doctrine as a basis for interlocutory review of orders denying class action certifications, on the ground that such a denial effectively signaled the "death knell" for many small claims holders to pursue relief outside the class action format. *See* **Eisen v. Carlisle & Jacquelin,** 370 F.2d 119 (2d Cir. 1966). This doctrine was extended to orders granting class certification, on an "inverse death knell theory."

v. Repudiation of the Death Knell Doctrine

The Supreme Court repudiated the death knell doctrine in **Coopers & Lybrand v. Livesay,** 437 U.S. 463 (1978). The Court reasoned that the principal vice of the death knell doctrine was that it permitted *indiscriminate* interlocutory review of a trial judge's decisions. The doctrine violates the final judgment rule with an exception encompassing enough to swallow the general rule (i.e., almost every order arguably signals the "death knell" of the litigation).

vi. Irremediable Consequences

A party may obtain immediate review of a judge's order that has irremediable consequences. **Forgay v. Conrad,** 47 U.S. (6 How.) 201 (1848). This exception to the final judgment rule is rarely used in contemporary practice.

2. Mandamus—The Extraordinary Writ: 28 U.S.C. § 1651(a)

A writ of mandamus is an order from a higher court to a lower court judge to perform the judge's duties (usually, to reverse an order or ruling). In federal practice, all courts may "issue writs necessary or appropriate in aid of their respective jurisdictions and agreeable to the usages and principles of law." **28 U.S.C. § 1651(a).**

a. Party Sued

The party who is the object of the mandamus is the trial judge who issues an order. In mandamus actions, either the judge is named in the case caption, or the case is styled "*In the Matter of. . . .* "

b. Extraordinary Nature

The writ of mandamus is an extraordinary remedy, to be used only in instances of extreme or egregious abuse of discretion. The writ is viewed as an intrusive invasion of the trial judge's authority during the course of a trial.

c. Criticism of Mandamus as Alternative Means of Interlocutory Appeal

The writ of mandamus is not intended to provide a "back-door" means of interlocutory review when no other exception applies to permit immediate review of a judge's orders or rulings. It is intended to apply only to exceptional circumstances of judicial abuse. **La Buy v. Howes Leather Co.**

3. Contempt

A contempt order is a final judgment and may be appealed immediately. Contempt, then, may supply a route for interlocutory review of other orders that are not typically final or reviewable until final judgment. Discovery orders, for example, fall into this category. A court may order a party to cooperate in some discovery. The initial discovery request and order is not itself immediately appealable, but the party may obtain review by disobeying the court's order to cooperate, and being found in contempt. The contempt route is risky, however, because if the appellate court affirms the trial judge's discovery order, then the contempt stands.

4. Partial Final Judgments: Rule 54(b)

In multi-party, multi-claim litigation, an order finally determining a claim is immediately appealable—the losing litigant does not have to wait until disposition of the entire case to bring an appeal on the claim that the court has fully determined.

5. Certification Procedure

In a multi-claim case, the court makes an express direction for entry of the judgment on a decided claim and certifies that there is no just reason for delaying an appeal on that claim. **Rule 54(b).**

C. SCOPE OF REVIEW

1. Issues Subject to Review

The scope of appellate review is limited by a series of general rules and principles.

a. Appeals by Losing Parties: Errors on the Trial Record

To be appealable, an error must appear on the trial record. Alleged errors are presented in the litigant's appellate brief, which will include the relevant portions of the trial transcript relating to the alleged error.

b. Appeals by Losing Parties: Prior Objections at Trial

To be appealable, an attorney must have made a prompt objection to the alleged error at trial. This is to give the trial judge an immediate chance to correct or ameliorate any errors at the time they are made during trial. If any attorney does not object at trial, any error is waived.

c. Harmless Errors, to Be Appealable, an Error Must Have Affected Substantial Rights

Appellate courts will not review so-called "harmless errors." **Rule 61.**

d. Appeals by Losing Parties—Grounds to Sustain

If a losing party files an appeal based on a trial error, the opposing party (the appellee) may raise any issue that would sustain its favorable judgment below, whether or not it was decided during the trial. The rules permit a party to file a notice of appeal within 14 days after another party files a notice of appeal. **Federal Rule of Appellate Procedure 4(a)(3).**

e. Appeals by Winning Parties

A winning party may not appeal from a favorable judgment or decree in order to obtain a review of findings the party believes to be erroneous, if those findings are not necessary to the decree. **Electrical Fittings Corp. v. Thomas & Betts Co.,** 307 U.S. 241 (1939); **New York Tel. Co. v. Maltbie,** 291 U.S. 645 (1934).

2. Standards of Review; Harmless Error; Abuse of Discretion

Appellate standards of review are linked to whether the appellate court is asked to review an error of law or fact, and whether the case was tried to a judge or jury.

a. Issues of Law

i. *De Novo* Review

If a case is tried to a jury, then rulings of law receive the fullest scope of appellate review. The appellate court may consider legal rulings *de novo*, or completely fresh.

ii. Abuse of Discretion

Rulings that are within a trial judge's discretion are subject to an "abuse of discretion" standard. An appellate court may reverse a trial judge's rulings on law only for clearly erroneous rulings.

b. Findings of Fact

Appellate courts accord greater deference to findings of fact, especially where a jury is the fact-finder.

i. Jury's Decision Against the Weight of the Evidence

Appellate courts have extremely limited ability to set aside a jury decision as being against the weight of the evidence.

ii. Clearly Erroneous Standard: General Principles

If a case is conducted as a bench trial, an appellate court will only overturn a judge's findings if those findings are clearly erroneous. **Rule 52(a)(6)**.

c. Mixed Questions of Law and Fact

Appellate courts treat mixed questions of law and fact as though they were pure questions of law, and therefore are subject to full *de novo* review. If a jury trial was involved, the appellate court will accord greater deference to protect the jury's factual determinations.

d. Preliminary Injunctions: Abuse of Discretion and Review of Facts

Appellate review of a judge's decision granting a preliminary injunction is governed by an abuse of discretion standard. The appellate court assesses whether the judge exceeded the bounds of permissible choice in the circumstances, not whether the appellate court would have decided differently. This standard is not limited, however, only to cases where the judge may be said to have acted irrationally or fancifully.

e. Declaratory Judgments

Appellate review of declaratory judgment actions is subject to a two-stage inquiry.

i. Abuse of Discretion

The appellate court will first determine whether the trial court abused its discretion by making the choice to hear a claim for declaratory judgment.

ii. *De Novo* Review

The appellate court may then determine, even if a declaratory judgment action was proper, that the trial court's opinion was nonetheless erroneous.

D. APPELLATE PROCEDURE: MECHANICS OF BRINGING AN APPEAL

1. Jurisdictional Nature

A litigant must file an appeal within 30 days of entry of judgment. The time limit for filing appeals is jurisdictional in nature and parties cannot consensually change the time rules. **Torres v. Oakland Scavenger Co.,** 487 U.S. 312

(1988) (**Federal Appellate Rules** 3 and 4 are jurisdictional in nature and their requirements are a mandatory prerequisite to appellate jurisdiction). These time limits are rigidly applied.

2. Timing Considerations: Rules 58, 77, 79; Federal Rules of Appellate Procedure 3–5

a. Entry of Judgment

The time limitations are triggered by the "entry of judgment" in conformity with the requirements of **Rule 58**. *See also* **Rule 79(a).**

i. Notice of Entry of Judgment

The clerk of court is required to mail notice of entry of judgment to the parties. **Rule 77(d).** A party also may elect to serve notice formally on an opponent.

ii. Events Constituting Final Judgments for Appeal

What events or pronouncements constitute an entry of judgment has caused some problems in federal practice.

iii. Relationship to Rule 59 Motions to Amend or Modify

If a party files a timely motion to amend or modify a judgment under **Rule 59** (within 28 days of entry of judgment, *see* discussion *supra*), then the time for appeal runs from the entry of the order granting or denying the **Rule 59** motion. *See* **Federal Rule of Appellate Procedure 4(a)(4).**

b. Extensions

Only the district court—and not the appellate court—may grant extensions of time for filing an appeal.

c. Tolling

The timely filing of certain motions tolls the time clock for filing a motion to appeal. These motions include a motion for a judgment notwithstanding the verdict (**Rule 50(b)**); a motion to amend or make additional findings (**Rule 52(b)**); a motion to alter or amend a judgment (**Rule 59**); or a motion for a new trial (**Rule 59**). Notice of appeal filed before the court has decided any of these motions will not be given effect. Once the court decides the motion, however, a new notice of appeal must be filed. **Federal Rule of Appellate Procedure 4(a)(4).**

E. APPELLATE JURISDICTION OF THE HIGHEST STATE COURTS AND THE UNITED STATES SUPREME COURT

The highest state and federal courts have appellate jurisdiction by constitutional or statutory right, or by discretionary power.

1. Review as of Right

In every state and the federal system, some matters may be directly appealed to the highest court, bypassing intermediate courts of appeal. State and federal courts statutorily define the ability of litigants to bring a direct appeal in the judicial system's highest court, but typically the right of direct review is severely limited—especially in the United States Supreme Court. *See* **28 U.S.C. § 1253.**

a. Direct Appeal from District Court Decisions Where the Supreme Court Would Grant Certiorari

In certain limited situations, the Supreme Court may directly hear an appeal from a district court decision where it also would grant certiorari from an intermediate appellate decision. This review bypasses the review by a court of appeals. *See, e.g.,* **United States v. Nixon,** 418 U.S. 683 (1974).

b. State Court Decisions of Federal Claims

The Supreme Court will directly review a state court decision of a federal claim, but that judgment must necessarily turn on the federal question and cannot rest on an independent state ground. If a decision is based on alternative grounds (i.e., one federal and one state-based), then direct review is unavailable. **Zacchini v. Scripps–Howard Broadcasting Co.,** 433 U.S. 562 (1977).

2. Discretionary Review

Almost the entire Supreme Court docket is now determined by discretionary review, granted through the writ of certiorari. *See* **28 U.S.C. §§ 1254(1); 1257(a); Supreme Court Rule 17(a).**

a. Decisions Involving the Validity of State Laws

Appeals from decisions of state and federal courts involving the validity of state laws under the Constitution, treaties, or laws of the United States receive no special treatment and are reviewed, if at all, through grant of a writ of certiorari. *See* **28 U.S.C. §§ 1254** and **1257.**

b. Rule of Four

At least four Justices of the Supreme Court must agree to grant a writ of certiorari in order for the full Court to review an appeal. *See* **Harris v. Pennsylvania R.R. Co.,** 361 U.S. 15 (1959).

c. Finality for Purposes of Supreme Court Review

The Supreme Court may review only "final judgments of the highest state court in which the decision could be had." **28 U.S.C. § 1257.** There is some suggestion that "final" for the purposes of Supreme Court review is more flexible than the requirement of finality under **28 U.S.C. § 1291.** *See* **Cox Broadcasting Corp. v. Cohn,** 420 U.S. 469 (1975). In general, the Court has suggested that a "technical" definition of finality may give way to a series of pragmatic considerations.

■ XII. THE BINDING, PRECLUSIVE EFFECTS OF JUDGMENTS

A. TERMINOLOGY: ISSUE AND CLAIM PRECLUSION DISTINGUISHED

1. Res Judicata

The term "res judicata" is broadly used by courts to describe two separate doctrines concerning the preclusive effect of prior judgments. Both doctrines are discussed in greater detail, below.

a. Claim Preclusion

Claim preclusion (true res judicata) refers to full relief accorded to the same parties on the same claim or cause of action. Claim preclusion extends to all issues relevant to the claim that were raised, or could have been raised at trial.

i. Merger

When a plaintiff wins, the claim merges in the judgment and the plaintiff cannot seek relief on that claim in a subsequent separate lawsuit. *See, e.g.,* **Rush v. City of Maple Heights,** 167 Ohio St. 221,

147 N.E.2d 599 (1958) (issue of personal injury damages resulting from motorcycle accident could not be litigated in second lawsuit where plaintiff won previous lawsuit arising out of same accident for property damage. Personal injury claim was merged in the prior property damage judgment).

ii. Bar

If a plaintiff loses the first lawsuit and the defendant wins, the plaintiff's claim is extinguished and the defendant's judgment acts as a bar to the plaintiff seeking subsequent relief on that same claim. *See, e.g.,* **Mathews v. New York Racing Association, Inc.,** 193 F.Supp. 293 (S.D.N.Y. 1961) (defendants' prior successful judgment in earlier assault complaint barred subsequent lawsuit by same plaintiff on grounds of assault, kidnapping, false arrest, and false imprisonment, arising from same series of acts and events).

b. Collateral Estoppel or Issue Preclusion

Issue preclusion recognizes that litigation of claims in one lawsuit may resolve issues that are relevant to a subsequent litigation. Issue preclusion bars the relitigation of issues actually adjudicated and essential to the judgment in a prior litigation.

c. Stare Decisis

Stare decisis refers to the policy of courts adhering to precedent, which is given to actual determinations, but not to dicta.

d. Law of the Case

Law of the case refers to the policy whereby an appellate court's rulings on law are binding on the trial court when cases are remanded for further proceedings.

B. PURPOSES SERVED BY PRECLUSION DOCTRINE

1. Avoidance of Redundant Litigation

Preclusion doctrine avoids or eliminates multiple suits on identical rights or obligations between the same parties. Preclusion doctrine also avoids subsequent redetermination of identical issues of duty and breach.

2. Avoidance of "Claim Splitting" and Judicial Economy

Preclusion doctrine prevents so-called "claim-splitting" by requiring that litigants prosecute in one action all claims that could or should be litigated, rather than reserving a portion of the lawsuit for some later litigation. *See* **Rush v. City of Maple Heights** and **Mathews v. New York Racing Association, Inc.**

3. Finality and Avoidance of Harassment

Preclusion doctrine enhances the values of finality to litigation, and avoidance of harassment through the threat of multiple, repeated litigation. Through preclusion doctrine defendants especially may be assured that once a lawsuit is fully and fairly litigated, they will not be subject to relitigation of the same claims in subsequent litigation.

C. CLAIM AND DEFENSE PRECLUSION (RES JUDICATA)

1. Definition

In order to assert claim preclusion, a prior litigation must have occurred. Claim preclusion will then be asserted in a second lawsuit in order to prevent relitigation of claims previously tried to judgment. When a second lawsuit is brought, the judgment in the prior suit is considered conclusive. **Cromwell v. City of Sac,** 94 U.S. (4 Otto) 351, 24 L.Ed. 195 (1876).

a. General Prerequisites

For claim preclusion to operate, the following must exist: (1) a final judgment; (2) the judgment must be valid; (3) the judgment must be "on the merits"; (4) the parties in the subsequent action must be identical to the parties in the first action; and (5) the claim in the subsequent action must include matters properly considered in the first action.

b. Requirement of Final Judgment: Definition of Finality

For the purposes of assertion of res judicata, finality represents the completion of all steps in the adjudication of a claim, short of execution.

i. Appeals

Finality for res judicata purposes is not affected if a litigant brings an appeal from a judgment, unless the appellate court vacates the judgment and orders a new appeal.

c. Requirement of a Valid Judgment

In order to be accorded res judicata effect, the judgment in the prior case must be valid. This means that the court rendering the judgment must have had valid subject matter and personal jurisdiction.

d. Requirement of a Judgment on the Merits

For res judicata to apply, in a subsequent litigation, the common law rule (followed in many federal courts) is judgment in the first litigation must have been "on the merits."

i. Involuntary Pretrial Dismissals

Involuntary dismissals for failure to prosecute or failure to comply with a court rule usually are "with prejudice," meaning that the litigant may not institute a subsequent lawsuit on the same claim and involving the same parties. Typically when a court orders an involuntary dismissal, the court has never considered the merits prior to the dismissal. *See* **Rule 41(b).**

e. Requirement of Identity of Parties

Res judicata applies in a subsequent lawsuit only to persons who were parties, or "in privity" with parties in the first lawsuit. *See* **Mathews v. New York City Racing Association, Inc.**

i. New Parties in Second Action

If new parties are named in the second action, then res judicata will not apply and a separate or new cause of action is presented in the subsequent litigation.

ii. Non-Identity of Parties and Collateral Estoppel

If new parties are named in the second action, issue preclusion or collateral estoppel can operate to prevent relitigation of issues resolved in the prior litigation.

iii. Exception: Class Action Judgments

Class action judgments represent an exception to the "identity-of-parties" requirement for application of res judicata. A valid class action judgment is binding on all class members encompassed by the class description, including both the actual class representatives and the absent class members. *See* **Hansberry v. Lee,** 311 U.S. 32 (1940).

iv. Persons in Privity

A person is in privity with a party if the person acquires an interest in the subject matter of the lawsuit after the lawsuit is brought.

Modern courts have expanded the notion of parties in privity to include a wide range of relationships. Expanded concepts of privity are tied to the substantive law defining or regulating the legal relationship.

2. Requirement of Scope of Matters Litigated

Res judicata applies both to claims actually litigated or that could have or should have been litigated in the first action. Pure *res judicata*, then, (if applicable) works a very harsh effect on litigants to include in the first lawsuit all claims available.

a. Rationale

The major purpose of the "matters litigated" requirement is to prevent claim-splitting and the consequent waste of resources and harassment that attend severing claims into multiple lawsuits. The possibility of a res judicata merger or bar forces litigants to plead and adjudicate all possible claims in one lawsuit, or forego subsequent litigation of those claims.

b. Pleading Strategies

Res judicata principles affect pleading strategies. Thus, the failure to plead an available claim may result in the litigant being precluded from asserting that claim independently in a subsequent lawsuit. In many jurisdictions, this principle extends to the mandatory assertion of compulsory counterclaims.

c. Definition of a Claim for Res Judicata Purposes

Various jurisdictions define what constitutes a "claim" or "cause of action" differently, and use different tests to determine whether res judicata should apply. Some jurisdictions define a claim broadly, to encourage the widest possible joinder of parties and claims and avoid multiple lawsuits. Other courts define a claim narrowly, in order to avoid the harsh consequences of res judicata.

i. Scope of Relief Test

Some courts look to the scope of relief in the first lawsuit, to determine all the explicit and implicit findings supporting that relief. If relief in a subsequent action would be inconsistent with (or contradict) the relief awarded in the prior action, then a court may give preclusive effect to the first judgment. This focus of this test is very narrow.

ii. Primary Rights Test

This test—sometimes called the "primary rights" test, looks to the legal rights or duties involved in the first lawsuit. A second court will apply preclusion doctrine to prevent multiple successive lawsuits on the same grounds for the same wrong or injury. Several rights can be violated by a single act, and such circumstances can give rise to separate causes of action.

iii. Same Evidence Test

This test simply looks to see whether a litigant will produce and rely on the same evidence in the second lawsuit as in a prior litigation. Courts do not widely use this test to ascertain whether preclusion doctrine should apply, because it is difficult to know how much duplicative evidence is needed before claims overlap to such an extent that preclusion doctrine applies.

iv. Transaction Test

The transaction test requires application of preclusion doctrine to any injury or injuries arising out of the same acts, or series of acts constituting a transaction or occurrence. A litigant must present all such claims in a single lawsuit. The transaction test in effect creates a compulsory joinder requirement driven by res judicata. **Rush v. City of Maple Heights,** and **Mathews v. New York City Racing Association.**

3. Quality of the Judgment

Preclusion doctrine usually applies to judgments rendered by judicial tribunals at the conclusion of a litigated trial. Some litigation, however, may be resolved without a litigated proceeding, or by nonjudicial tribunals such as administrative agencies.

a. Settlements or Consent Judgments

"Consent judgments" often present problems for the application of preclusion doctrine. Consent judgments are an agreement between parties settling an underlying dispute and providing for entry of judgment in a pending or contemplated action. Courts often look to the parties' intent to ascertain the preclusive effect to be given a consent judgment.

b. Default Judgments

Default judgments are entitled to the same res judicata effects as any other judgment. Default judgments are always res judicata on the ultimate claim or demand presented in the complaint.

i. Collateral Estoppel Effect

Many courts, however, will not give collateral estoppel effect to issues in a complaint that results in a default judgment, especially if the litigant did not have an incentive to litigate.

c. Judgments of Nonjudicial Tribunals

Whether a court in a subsequent litigation will give preclusive effect to the prior determinations of non-tribunals, such as administrative bodies, depends on the quality, nature, and fairness of the prior hearing.

D. ISSUE PRECLUSION (COLLATERAL ESTOPPEL)

"Collateral estoppel" refers to the preclusion (or relitigation) of an issue (as opposed to a claim) in a subsequent litigation. Collateral estoppel requires that the issue in the first and subsequent litigation are identical, and that the issue was "actually litigated," "necessarily determined," and "essential to the judgment" in the first action. These elements ensure that preclusion will apply only if a litigant had the opportunity to fully and fairly litigate an issue. Most collateral estoppel problems focus on what the court decided in the first action.

1. Identical Issue

Identical issues among successive lawsuits is relatively easy to identify when multiple claims arise from a defendant's single wrongful act, but more complex when claims arise out of different acts at different times (where there usually is no identity of issue). *See, e.g.,* **Jones v. Morris Plan Bank of Portsmouth,** 168 Va. 284, 191 S.E. 608 (1937).

2. Different Burdens of Proof

If the burdens of proof differ in successive cases (for example, if one litigation is a criminal case and the next a civil litigation), then identity of issues usually will be lacking. However, if there is a higher standard of proof on an issue in the first case ("beyond a reasonable doubt" in criminal cases) then a court may give preclusive effect to that issue in a later civil proceeding. The converse is not true: issue preclusion cannot run from a civil case to a criminal proceeding.

3. Actually Litigated

Preclusive effect will not be given to an issue in which a court has not reached a determination of the issue on the merits, as in default or some consent judgments (*see* discussion below). The "actually litigated" requirement ensures that the parties will have engaged a full adversary presentation of the issue. **Cromwell v. County of Sac,** 94 U.S. (4 Otto) 351, 24 L. Ed. 195 (1876).

a. General Verdicts

Jury determinations rendered on general verdicts sometimes make it difficult to ascertain what the jury decided on one or more issues in the case.

i. Majority View: No Collateral Estoppel

Most courts refuse to give preclusive effect where a jury's findings in a general verdict might have been based on more than one issue in the pleadings.

ii. Minority View: Broad Collateral Estoppel Effect

A minority of federal courts give preclusive effect in a second action to all issues actually litigated in the first that comprise the general verdict.

4. Necessarily Determined and Essential to the Judgment

Similar to the "actually litigated" requirement, the "necessarily determined" standard is to ensure that the parties vigorously litigated the issue in the prior litigation and that it is fair to prevent relitigation in a subsequent lawsuit. *See, e.g.,* **Russell v. Place,** 94 U.S. (4 Otto) 606, 24 L. Ed. 214 (1876).

a. Facts: No Collateral Estoppel Effect

Facts found against the prevailing party in the first litigation are deemed unnecessary, largely because the victorious party has no reason or incentive to appeal. Thus, an issue is not given collateral estoppel effect because there is no assurance of vigorous prosecution.

i. Historical Test of Ultimate and Mediate Facts

Many courts determined collateral estoppel effect based on whether facts were "ultimate" or "mediate" facts. *See, e.g.,* **The Evergreens v. Nunan,** 141 F.2d 927 (2d Cir.), *cert, denied,* 323 U.S. 720 (1944). Criticism of the difficulty in distinguishing between mediate and ultimate facts led to its eventual demise as an operative test. This distinction also was eroded by the availability of special verdicts and general verdicts with interrogatories.

ii. Facts: Modern Restatement Approach

Courts in a second suit should determine whether the fact on which collateral estoppel is asserted was necessary and important in the first litigation, rather than merely evidentiary. If the fact was necessary and important and the issue was actually litigated, the court in the second action may fairly preclude relitigation in the second lawsuit.

b. Alternative Holdings: Collateral Estoppel Applied

A second court will give full collateral estoppel effect to alternative holdings and there is no need to determine which finding was necessary to the judgment. Courts assume that one issue is no less necessary than any other.

5. Persons Benefited and Bound

a. The Traditional Model

The traditional rule for assertion of collateral estoppel was the same as for res judicata or claim preclusion: only parties and their privities could benefit from or could be estopped from relitigating an issue adjudicated in a prior litigation. Non-parties, therefore, could not take advantage of the doctrine of collateral estoppel either to defensively or offensively prevent relitigation of an issue in a subsequent litigation.

i. Defensive Collateral Estoppel: Due Process Concerns

Use of collateral estoppel *defensively* (by a prior successful defendant), to prevent relitigation of an issue against a non-party to the first action, was perceived as unfair because the non-party never had an opportunity to be heard in the first action. Thus, due process prevented application of defensive collateral estoppel because the non-party must be given an opportunity to be heard—to have its day in court.

ii. Mutuality Requirement: Offensive Collateral Estoppel

The "mutuality" requirement prevented a non-party to the first lawsuit from offensively asserting collateral estoppel, in a subsequent litigation, on an issue against a party to the first lawsuit. The mutuality requirement was based on fairness considerations, mirroring the rationale that since parties could not assert collateral estoppel against a non-party, neither should non-parties be permitted to assert collateral estoppel against a party.

iii. The Problem of Sideline Sitters

The mutuality requirement also was intended to cope with the problem of potential plaintiffs who could have joined in the first litigation but instead chose to "side on the sidelines," awaiting the first litigation's outcome. Without a mutuality requirement, a sideline sitter could take advantage of the winning plaintiff's judgment if the first plaintiff was successful, but would suffer no detriment if the first plaintiff lost (because the sideline sitter could still sue to have its own day in court).

b. Mutuality Eroded

All federal courts have considerably eroded the doctrine of mutuality, and now recognize both the possibility for defensive and offensive collateral estoppel. Some state courts have not followed the federal lead, and individual state law determines the extent to which the doctrine of mutuality applies, either to assertions of defensive or offensive collateral estoppel.

i. Erosion of Bar Against Defensive Collateral Estoppel

The doctrine of defensive collateral estoppel was first eroded by the California Supreme Court in **Bernhard v. Bank of America Natl. Trust & Sav. Assn.,** 19 Cal.2d 807, 122 P.2d 892 (1942). The Supreme Court endorsed this inroad—thereby permitting assertions of defensive collateral estoppel in federal actions—in **Blonder–Tongue Labs., Inc. v. University of Illinois Foundation,** 402 U.S. 313 (1971).

ii. Rationale for Erosion of the Bar Against Defensive Collateral Estoppel

Defensive collateral estoppel is now recognized as a means of preventing a defendant from being harassed by serial litigation. If a defendant has been sued on an issue and won, then the defendant ought to be able to assert its favorable judgment on that issue to prevent subsequent plaintiffs from suing on the identical issue.

iii. Erosion of Bar Against Offensive Collateral Estoppel

The Supreme Court ultimately abandoned the doctrine of mutuality in situations seeking to invoke offensive collateral estoppel. *See* **Parklane Hosiery Co., Inc. v. Shore,** 439 U.S. 322 (1979).

iv. Fairness Concerns Relative to the Defendant in Assertions of Offensive Collateral Estoppel

In abandoning the mutuality requirement for assertions of offensive collateral estoppel, the Supreme Court requires that the court in the second action determine whether the defendant will be unfairly prejudiced by the non-party plaintiff's offensive use of a prior plaintiff's favorable judgment against the defendant. Considerations include forseeability of the subsequent lawsuit; whether the plaintiff in the second suit could easily have joined in the first; whether the first judgment was typical of or consistent with judgments in similar cases; and whether the second action presented the litigants with procedural options unavailable in the first action.

c. Collateral Estoppel and Non-Parties

i. Multidistrict Litigation

In cases transferred and consolidated pursuant to the multidistrict litigation statute, **28 U.S.C. § 1407,** transferee courts may not, consistent with due process, apply defensive collateral estoppel to bar relitigation of identical liability issues litigated in a prior lawsuit arising from an accident.

ii. Non-Parties Assuming Control over Litigation

If non-parties assume control over a litigation in which they have a direct financial or pecuniary interest, they may be precluded from relitigating issues resolved in the first lawsuit. *See* **Montana v. United States,** 440 U.S. 147 (1979). The relationship among the parties and non-parties need not be a formal legal relationship, such as guardian and child.

iii. Non-Intervenors

Persons who have notice of an action (especially an employment consent decree), a reasonable opportunity to intervene, and who were adequately represented may not subsequently collaterally attack a prior negotiated consent decree to which they were not parties. *See* **Civil Rights Act of 1991 § 108, Pub. L. No. 102–166, tit. I, § 108, 105 Stat. 1071, 1076.** This congressional act was intended to overturn the Supreme Court's holding in **Martin v. Wilks,** 490 U.S. 755 (1989), permitting such collateral attack by non-intervening persons with an interest in the consent decree.

d. Limitations on Collateral Estoppel

i. Seventh Amendment Concerns

Application of offensive collateral estoppel does not violate a litigant's Seventh Amendment right to a jury trial when a second legal action follows a first equitable action. **Parklane Hosiery, Inc. v. Shore.**

ii. Courts of Limited or Exclusive Jurisdiction

Federal courts are split concerning whether they are required to give preclusive effect to state decisions where the substantive law vests exclusive jurisdiction of those claims in the federal courts.

iii. Change of Law

Collateral estoppel will not apply if there is a change of law between the first and second lawsuits, such that it would change the operative facts. *See* **Commissioner of Internal Revenue v. Sunnen,** 333 U.S. 591 (1948).

E. INTERSTATE AND INTERSYSTEM PRECLUSION

1. Interstate Preclusion; Full Faith and Credit Clause

The United States Constitution requires that states give "full faith and credit" to the judgments of sister states. **U.S. Const. Art. IV § 1.** Remember that some states require mutuality for application of preclusion doctrine, while others have abandoned mutuality requirements. State courts disagree, then, whether a sister state must give the same preclusive effect to a judgment as would the state that rendered the judgment. Some states give non-mutual preclusive effect to another state's judgment that the rendering state would not have treated as preclusive.

2. State–Federal Preclusion

The full faith and credit statute, **28 U.S.C. § 1738** imposes the same general principles on federal courts, requiring them to accord full faith and credit to state court decisions. *See* **Matsushita v. Epstein,** 516 U.S. 367 (1996).

a. Exclusive Federal Court Jurisdiction: The *Marrese* Test

In construing statutory full faith and credit, federal courts must apply a two-part test to determine whether to give preclusive effect to a state court determination in a subsequent lawsuit over which federal courts have exclusive jurisdiction (*see* **Marrese v. American Academy of Orthopaedic Surgeons,** 470 U.S. 373 (1985)).

i. Apply State Preclusion Law

The federal court first must determine whether state claim preclusion law would preclude the federal lawsuit. If the state would not bar the federal lawsuit, there is no preclusion.

ii. Exception to 28 U.S.C. § 1738

If the state would bar the federal lawsuit, then the court must ascertain whether the relevant federal law contains an explicit or implicit exception to **28 U.S.C. § 1738** denying preclusive effect to the state judgment.

b. State Adjudication of Fourth Amendment or Habeas Claims

Federal courts will give preclusive effect to state court determinations of alleged constitutional violations or habeas claims in subsequent federal civil rights actions (under **42 U.S.C. § 1983**), provided that the litigant had a full and fair opportunity to litigate the issue in the prior proceeding. *See* **Allen v. McCurry,** 449 U.S. 90 (1980).

i. Failure to Raise Constitutional Issues in Prior Litigation

A federal court may preclude a plaintiff from subsequently raising federal constitutional issues that could have been litigated in the prior state proceeding, but were not. **Migra v. Warren City School District Board of Education,** 465 U.S. 75 (1984) (**Section 1983** civil rights actions do not imply an exception to **28 U.S.C. § 1738**).

c. Decisions of Administrative Agencies

Statutory full faith and credit does not require that federal courts give preclusive effect to prior decisions of state agency findings of fact in Title VII actions. *See* **University of Tennessee v. Elliott,** 478 U.S. 788 (1986).

3. Federal–State Preclusion

Neither constitutional nor statutory full faith and credit rules apply to situations where state courts are asked to give preclusive effect to prior federal judgments. However, no one has seriously challenged the general requirement that state courts give preclusive effect to prior federal judgments. The requirement that state courts are bound by such judgments is variously supported by the Supremacy Clause or the Article III "case and controversy" doctrine.

a. Applicable Preclusion Rules

In general, most commentators and the Restatement Second of Judgments agree that federal law controls the choice of preclusion rules. However, the Restatement also suggests that federal law ought to mandate application of state preclusion rules if such rules are important to effectuate substantive state policies. *Id.*

I

Choosing the Forum: Personal Jurisdiction

■ ANALYSIS

■ CHAPTER OVERVIEW

- This chapter deals with the problems relating to choosing the proper court in which to resolve an adversarial dispute.

- *Jurisdiction* refers to the power or authority of a particular court to render a binding and enforceable judgment in a litigation.

- The United States, as a federal system of government, has a dual or two-tier court system, consisting of state and federal courts. Litigants generally choose to pursue legal relief in either a state court or a federal court. It is possible, however, to litigate in both court systems at the same time (concurrently).

- A litigant's choice of forum will depend on many considerations, some of which are strategic. Among these considerations may be the potential jury pool, the status of the court's docket, a preference for certain judges, or differences in state and federal procedural rules.

- In addition to strategic considerations, a litigant's choice of forum is subject to jurisdictional and venue rules.

- A defendant may object to the plaintiff's choice of forum based on jurisdictional or venue defects. In general, the plaintiff carries the burden of establishing the court's valid jurisdiction and venue.

- There are two types of jurisdiction: personal (territorial) jurisdiction and subject matter jurisdiction.

- *Personal jurisdiction* is a term generally used to describe the territorial reach of a court to issue a binding judgment over a defendant. A defendant may consent to personal jurisdiction. If a defendant appears and does not challenge personal jurisdiction the defendant waives any objections to personal jurisdiction. Personal jurisdiction, then, is a "waivable" defect and it is not absolutely essential that a court have proper personal jurisdiction over a defendant in order to render a binding, valid judgment against the defendant. Territorial theories relating to state sovereignty dominated nineteenth-century concepts of personal jurisdiction. Twentieth-century theories of personal jurisdiction are centered on due process and fairness concerns.

- Modern personal jurisdiction jurisprudence primarily evaluates the nature and quality of a defendant's contacts with the state and whether the assertion of power over the non-resident defendant would offend traditional notions of substantial justice and fair play.

- *Subject matter jurisdiction* refers to the ability of a court to adjudicate a particular claim. State and federal courts determine the permissible subject matters of their courts by constitutional provision or by statute. A court must have valid subject matter jurisdiction in order to render a binding, enforceable judgment. Unlike personal jurisdiction, defects in subject matter jurisdiction cannot be waived. A court either has valid subject matter jurisdiction or it does not. Thus, objections to a court's subject matter jurisdiction may be raised at any time, on direct appeal, or by "collateral" appeal in another court if a litigant seeks to enforce a judgment there. Subject matter jurisdiction is addressed in Chapter II.

- In addition to choosing a forum in which there is valid personal and subject matter jurisdiction, a litigant also must choose a court in an appropriate geographic location or *venue.* A variety of factors contribute to determining appropriate venue, but the chief consideration is convenience. A defendant may consent to a plaintiff's choice of venue and, like personal jurisdiction, defects in venue can be waived. If a particular venue is inappropriate, judges have the ability to transfer cases to a more convenient venue or to dismiss a case altogether. Venue is discussed in Chapter II.

A. JURISDICTION IN ANGLO–AMERICAN LAW

1. Definition of Terms

Jurisdiction refers to the power or authority of a court to hear and determine a case. The term jurisdiction is used to describe a court's territorial reach over its own citizens or citizens of other states. A court must have two types of jurisdiction in order to enter a legally enforceable judgment over a defendant: *personal jurisdiction* over the parties to the dispute, and *subject matter jurisdiction* over the claims presented to the court.

In addition to having the territorial and subject-matter power to decide a dispute, litigants must be afforded adequate notice of a proceeding against them as well as an opportunity to be heard. A court cannot render a valid, binding judgment in absence of territorial power and notice.

a. Jurisdictional Facts

Jurisdictional facts are the information a court must have before it in order to make a determination whether it has the competency and may properly exercise its adjudicatory powers to render a binding judgment. Jurisdictional facts typically include—but are not limited to—the citizenship or residency of the parties to the dispute, the location and nature of the defendant's property, the defendant's affiliating circumstances with the forum, whether and how the defendant was served with process or notice of the action, and the amount in controversy involved in the litigation.

b. Challenges to Jurisdiction

Defendants may raise challenges to jurisdiction in motions to quash service of process, motions to dismiss (under **Federal Rules of Civil Procedure 12(b)(1)** and **(2)**), or on direct appeal to a superior court. A non-resident defendant may make a "special appearance" to challenge a court's jurisdiction without thereby submitting to the court's jurisdiction. If the defendant fails to appear and contest jurisdiction, and suffers a default judgment, that defendant may subsequently collaterally attack the first court's personal jurisdiction determination in another court.

2. Personal Jurisdiction

Courts have basically three territorial bases for asserting jurisdiction: *in personam* jurisdiction, *in rem* jurisdiction, and *quasi in rem* jurisdiction.

a. *In Personam* Jurisdiction

In personam jurisdiction refers to the authority of the court over persons, to render a personally binding judgment against a defendant. Actions brought *in personam* typically are to obtain a judgment against a defendant for monetary or compensatory relief, to be satisfied by the defendant's general assets (legal remedy). In addition, an action *in personam* may be brought to require a defendant to perform some act or to refrain from performing some act (equitable relief).

i. Invoking *In Personam* Jurisdiction—Territorial and Non-Territorial Residents

A court may exercise *in personam* jurisdiction over persons within its territory, and the usual method of obtaining such jurisdiction and providing notice of the action is by personal service of process on the defendant. If a defendant is not within the court's territory, the court's *in personam* jurisdiction may be extended to a non-resident defendant through state "long-arm" statutes. These statutes effectively reach beyond a state's border to subject the non-resident defendant to the court's jurisdiction if the defendant has sufficient connections with the state.

b. *In Rem* Jurisdiction

In rem jurisdiction, or actions *in rem*, refers to adjudication by claimants concerning their respective interests in a specific thing (a *res*), usually a piece of property. The historical basis for a court's *in rem* jurisdiction is the state's absolute authority over all property within its borders, without regard to the location of the defendant. In contrast to *in personam* actions, actions *in rem* typically do not seek to determine a defendant's liability for the defendant's actions. Rather, actions *in rem* seek to determine and affect the interests of persons in the property. Modern examples of actions *in rem* are actions to quiet title to real estate, to foreclose a lien upon property, or to partition a piece of land. *In rem* jurisdiction also extends to certain actions to determine legal status, as in divorce proceedings.

i. Invoking *In Rem* Jurisdiction

A court may assert *in rem* jurisdiction with respect to things within its territory, and this typically is accomplished by seizure or attachment of the property. Attachment or seizure of property usually serves as notice of the *in rem* action. In addition, *in rem* jurisdiction is the basis for assertion of jurisdiction in admiralty, through seizure of the vessel.

c. *Quasi In Rem* Jurisdiction

There are two types of *quasi in rem* actions. In the first instance, a plaintiff may assert *quasi in rem* jurisdiction over a piece of property owned by a defendant, in order to adjudicate personal rights related to the property under the court's control. The property serves as the basis for jurisdiction, and in such *quasi in rem* actions the property itself usually is not involved in the underlying substantive action for relief. An example of this form of *quasi in rem* jurisdiction is an action for specific performance on a contract to convey land.

A second form of *quasi in rem* jurisdiction refers to actions to recover monetary damages totally unrelated to the property and where the court has no personal jurisdiction over the defendant, but does have jurisdiction over an intangible asset such as a debt.

i.   Invoking *Quasi In Rem* Jurisdiction

There are various ways to invoke *quasi in rem* jurisdiction; a plaintiff may do so by seizing the asset, attaching property, or garnishing a debt. If a non-resident defendant appears, defends against the plaintiff's claims and loses, then the defendant is liable to the full extent of the plaintiff's claim. If the non-resident defendant chooses not to appear and defend against the plaintiff's claims, then the court may enter a validly binding default judgment against the non-resident defendant. In such *quasi in rem* actions where the defendant defaults, however, a plaintiff may recover damages only to the extent of the value of the attached property, which may be used to satisfy the claim. In addition, if enforcement of the judgment were sought in another court, that court would be required to give full faith and credit only to the extent of the property's value.

3.   Subject Matter Jurisdiction

In addition to having personal jurisdiction over the parties to the dispute, a court must have valid subject matter jurisdiction. Subject matter jurisdiction refers to whether the court has the competency to adjudicate the particular types of claims or controversies presented to it for resolution. Subject matter jurisdiction is considered more extensively in Chapter II.

a.   State Court Subject Matter Jurisdiction

States determine the jurisdiction of their courts by legislative enactment in their state codes, setting forth the substantive bases for relief and actionable claims. Typically, state statutes set forth the substantive law relating to contracts, property, torts, domestic relations, decedents estates, commercial transactions, and so on. In addition to setting forth the substantive bases for relief, state statutes also will determine court subject matter jurisdiction by the amount in controversy involved in a dispute. Hence, disputes involving relatively small amounts of monetary damages will be assigned to small claims courts; litigation involving increasingly higher compensatory damages will be assigned to other state courts of general jurisdiction. Some state courts handle only particular subject matters, such as surrogates courts or probate courts which deal exclusively with matters relating to probate, estates, wills and trusts.

b.   Federal Court Subject Matter Jurisdiction

Federal court subject matter jurisdiction is constitutionally authorized in **Article III § 2** of the **United States Constitution**. There are two primary statutory bases for federal court jurisdiction: federal question jurisdiction (as provided in **28 U.S.C. § 1331**) and federal diversity jurisdiction (as provided in **28 U.S.C. § 1332**). In addition, **Title 28** of the **United States Code** provides special subject matter jurisdiction for numerous actions of peculiarly federal interest, such as actions involving admiralty, patents, copyright, antitrust, securities, civil rights, and so on.

4.   Other Types of Jurisdiction

In addition to personal (territorial) jurisdiction and subject matter jurisdiction, there are many other types of jurisdiction defining the ability of courts to exercise authority over cases and controversies.

a.   Ancillary Jurisdiction

Ancillary jurisdiction refers to the ability of a court to adjudicate additional party claims that are logically related to the plaintiff's claims. The concept of ancillary jurisdiction is codified in federal court as part of the federal supplemental jurisdiction statute, **28 U.S.C. § 1367.**

b.   Appellate Jurisdiction

Appellate jurisdiction refers to the ability of state or federal court superior tribunals to hear appeals from lower court orders, decisions, or judgments, based on claims of legal error or mistake. Appellate jurisdiction is defined by statutes and rules of appellate procedure.

i.   Types of Appellate Jurisdiction

Appellate courts typically have *mandatory* jurisdiction over certain types of appeals which the legislature has determined have an automatic right of review, and *discretionary jurisdiction* (sometimes referred to as *certiorari* jurisdiction) over other appeals where the court may decline to exercise its appellate jurisdiction. Courts of appeal usually review decisions on direct appeal from final judgments. However, litigants also, under certain circumstances defined by rules and various doctrines, may seek intermediate (*interlocutory*) review of a judge's orders during the course of a litigation.

c.   Concurrent Jurisdiction

Concurrent jurisdiction refers to the ability of two different courts to adjudicate a dispute at the same time, usually within the same territory.

It is possible for state and federal courts simultaneously to adjudicate the same dispute in their concurrent jurisdictions. It is also possible for two or more state or federal courts independently to have jurisdiction over separate actions involving the same parties and claims. When two or more lawsuits are filed in state and federal courts, this is often referred to as parallel, repetitive litigation. When a defendant files an independent lawsuit in another forum involving the same parties and claims, this concurrent litigation is often referred to as a parallel, reactive lawsuit.

i. Problems with Concurrent Jurisdiction

Nothing prohibits litigants from pursuing the same litigation in separate lawsuits in different courts, provided the courts have concurrent jurisdiction and the litigants have the resources to finance such repetitive litigation. However, concurrent litigation generally is viewed as wasteful. Litigants who do not wish to defend concurrent lawsuits, however, have few rules or doctrines to avoid such repetitive litigation. In general, federal courts are prohibited from enjoining or restraining parallel duplicative state court litigation. They are, however, subject to three narrow statutory exceptions to this prohibition. Conversely, state courts have no power or authority to enjoin or restrain parallel federal litigation. Federal courts may invoke abstention doctrine to decline their valid concurrent jurisdiction in deference to a parallel pending state proceeding. Additionally, doctrines exist to ensure that once a matter is fully and finally determined in one court, it cannot be re-litigated in another court. *See* Chapter XII, *infra*.

d. Exclusive Jurisdiction

Some federal statutes provide that federal courts have exclusive jurisdiction over certain types of federal claims or actions, such as the federal antitrust laws. In such instances, if state litigation is filed containing exclusive federal claims, the state court is without power to adjudicate the claims that are within the exclusive jurisdiction of the federal courts.

e. Original Jurisdiction

Original jurisdiction refers to the court where the claim is to be first tried or heard. Federal and state statutes confer original subject matter jurisdiction on federal or state trial level courts, to adjudicate claims and render a judgment. The U.S. Constitution confers original jurisdiction on the Supreme Court. Original jurisdiction is distinguished from appellate jurisdiction.

f. Pendent Claim and Pendent Party Jurisdiction

In federal court, pendent claim jurisdiction refers to the competency of courts to adjudicate additional claims that lack an independent federal subject matter jurisdictional basis—such as a claim based on state law. Pendent party jurisdiction similarly refers to the ability of the court to render a judgment against an additional party for whom there is no independent federal jurisdictional basis. Pendent claim and pendent party jurisdiction are now permitted in federal court subject to the provisions of the supplemental jurisdiction statute, **28 U.S.C. § 1367.**

g. Removal Jurisdiction

Removal jurisdiction refers to the ability of a federal court to assume federal court jurisdiction over a lawsuit originally filed in state court. Federal statutes provide for removal of state cases from state court to the federal system, **28 U.S.C. § 1441** *et seq.* The defendant in the state court litigation petitions for the removal to federal court. The federal court then has jurisdiction to determine whether it has valid federal subject matter jurisdiction. If the case has been improvidently removed because there is no proper federal subject matter jurisdiction, the court will hold that there is no removal jurisdiction and remand the case back to state court.

h. Supplemental Jurisdiction

In federal court, supplemental jurisdiction permits the federal court to adjudicate additional claims and render judgments over additional parties, when the court lacks an independent federal subject matter jurisdictional basis over those claims or parties. Supplemental jurisdiction basically refers to the older doctrines of pendent claim, pendent party, and ancillary jurisdiction. These doctrines have now been codified in the federal supplemental jurisdiction statute, **28 U.S.C. § 1367.**

B. CHOOSING A FORUM IN A DUAL–COURT SYSTEM

1. The Consequences of Federalism

The United States has a federal system of government, consisting of fifty separate state governments and the federal government. One attribute of federalism is the existence of a dual-court system consisting of separate federal and state courts, virtually independent of each other. The Tenth Amendment constrains the federal government from interfering with state court systems. In addition, each state as an independent sovereign has virtually no ability to interfere with a sister state's court system or legal process. However, the **Full Faith and Credit clause** to the **United States Constitution (Article IV § 1** and its enabling statute, **28 U.S.C. § 1738)** requires states to give full faith and credit to the statutes, proceedings, and judgments of other courts.

2. The State Court System

Each of the fifty states, as well as the District of Columbia and the Commonwealth of Puerto Rico, have their own court systems and distinct procedural rules.

a. Structure of State Court Systems

Some state court systems have three tiers consisting of trial courts, intermediate appellate courts, and highest appellate courts (courts of last resort). Other states such as Nebraska have a two-tier court system consisting of trial level and appellate courts. Each state denominates its various courts by different names, so a state's Superior Court may actually be a trial level court, and a state's Supreme Court may actually be an intermediate appellate court. Forty-eight states have "unified" high courts which hear both criminal and civil appeals. Two states have bifurcated supreme courts, one for civil appeals and the other exclusively for criminal appeals.

b. State Court Judges

Each state has its own method for selecting judges. In some states judges may be appointed by the governor or a judicial selection commission; in other states judges run for office in contested or uncontested elections. State judges may sit for varying terms.

c. Relationship of State Courts to Federal Courts

Litigation commenced in a state court generally will remain in the state court system, unless a defendant in the state litigation exercises the right to remove the case to a federal district court. Appeals from adverse state court rulings or judgments must be pursued within the state appellate system. In certain limited circumstances, if a constitutional or federal question is involved, litigants may appeal an adverse decision from the highest state court in which a decision could be had to the United States Supreme Court. **28 U.S.C. § 1257.**

3.   The Federal Court System

The federal court system is a three-tier system of trial level and appellate courts.

a.   United States Federal District Courts

Federal trial courts are called district courts, and the United States is divided into ninety-four federal judicial districts. Some less-populous states, such as Utah and Montana, consist of one federal judicial district. Other more-populous states, such as Texas, New York, and California, have four or five judicial districts (typically denominated as the Northern, Eastern, Western, Southern, and Central districts). Many federal district courts also are divided into divisions, usually the place where a federal judge sits. Federal district courts have a "unified" docket and hear both federal civil and criminal cases.

b.   United States Federal Courts of Appeal

The United States is divided into eleven Judicial Circuits and there are eleven intermediate courts of appeal. In addition, there is a separate Court of Appeals for the District of Columbia and one for the Federal Circuit which hears appeals from certain specialized federal tribunals, such as the Court of Claims. The Circuits have a minimum of four federal appellate judges, who sit in three-judge panels to decide appeals from the district courts within their judicial circuit. Circuit courts hear appeals in both criminal and civil cases.

c.   United States Supreme Court

The United States Supreme Court is the highest court of appeals in the federal system and for certain state-court decisions involving constitutional or federal question issues. The Supreme Court consists of nine justices who hear and decide approximately ninety cases per term (October through June), chiefly on appeal from Circuit Court decisions. The Supreme Court used to have both a mandatory and discretionary docket, but the Court's mandatory docket is very small. Thus, almost the entire current Supreme Court docket is discretionary. The Court hears appeals in both criminal and civil cases.

d.   Appointment and Tenure of Federal Judges

All federal judges are nominated by the President of the United States and appointed with the advice and consent of the United States Senate. If there is a judicial opening for a federal district or circuit judgeship, the

President usually confers with the two Senators from the particular judicial district as a matter of "senatorial courtesy." Judicial nominations are reviewed by the Senate Judiciary Committee, which reports its vote and recommendation to the full Senate. This process is the same for all federal judgeships, including appointments to the Supreme Court. Federal judges have life tenure and may only be removed by impeachment, resignation, or death.

4. Strategic Considerations in Choosing Between State and Federal Court: The Parity Debate

As an initial litigation matter, plaintiffs must decide the forum in which they wish to seek relief. Subject to jurisdictional and venue rules, litigants may sue either in state or federal court. As indicated above, litigants also may pursue relief in both court systems simultaneously, provided there is concurrent jurisdiction in the state and federal courts. In consultation with the client, the attorney will survey various strategic and legal considerations before choosing the forum for litigation. Academic commentators describe the controversy over the comparative strengths and weaknesses of state and federal courts as the "parity debate." Among the strategic factors relating to the choice of forum are:

a. Docket Congestion

State and federal courts within a particular jurisdiction may be more or less current on their civil docket, and parties seeking an expeditious resolution of their litigation may choose the court system with the least crowded docket. Defendants sued in state court may seek to avoid state docket congestion by exercising the right of removal to federal court.

b. Jury Pools

State and federal courts draw their jury pools by different methods and from different geographical locations. Parties seeking more local and sympathetic jury pools typically will prefer state courts. Parties seeking jurors drawn from a broader geographical reach will prefer federal courts.

c. Judges

Some attorneys may be more familiar with local state court judges; other attorneys may be more familiar with federal district judges. Because federal judges have life tenure, in theory they are intended to be more impartial and less subject to political influence. Conversely, elected state court judges are sometimes viewed as less impartial than federal judges. Depending on local legal culture and knowledge of judicial performance on the bench, lawyers either will prefer a state court venue or choose to avoid particular local judges.

d. Procedural Rules

Each state has its own procedural rules. Many states have adopted procedural rules closely based on the Federal Rules of Civil Procedure. Other states have not. The Federal Rules of Civil Procedure tend to be more liberal than comparative state procedural rules. Attorneys will assess whether they wish to litigate in a federal court under liberal federal procedural rules or in state court under more restrictive procedural rules.

e. Location and Convenience of the Courthouse

The physical location of state and federal courts may be in different geographical locations throughout the state, and more or less convenient for litigants and witnesses. In general, plaintiffs' lawyers will choose a courthouse venue most convenient to the plaintiff and plaintiff's witnesses.

5. Legal Considerations in Choosing a Court

In addition to weighing various strategic considerations relating to the possible choice of forum, a litigant's choice of forum also must satisfy the jurisdictional requirements relating to personal jurisdiction, subject matter jurisdiction, and venue. Litigants also may assess the possible substantive law that will apply to the litigation, including statutes of limitations and available remedies.

a. Jurisdictional Requirements

As indicated above, the plaintiff must choose a forum that has valid personal and subject matter jurisdiction and also is an appropriate venue. A defendant may consent to the plaintiff's choice of forum and waive defects in personal jurisdiction and venue. However, the forum must have valid subject matter jurisdiction in order to render a binding, enforceable judgment, and litigants cannot waive defects in a court's subject matter jurisdiction.

b. Applicable Law

In choosing a forum for litigation, plaintiffs frequently will take into account the substantive and procedural law that will apply to the case.

Litigants may attempt to "forum shop" for preferable law. With regard to procedural law, state courts follow their own procedural rules and federal cases are subject to the Federal Rules of Civil Procedure. With regard to substantive law, state courts will apply their own substantive law to disputes involving parties and transactions or events within the state's territorial boundaries. In multi-party lawsuits involving events occurring in multiple states, the forum will apply its choice-of-law rules to determine which state's substantive law applies. Under various standards, a state may determine to apply either its own substantive law or another state's law. This includes the applicable statute of limitations and available remedies. In federal cases within the court's diversity jurisdiction, the federal court will first apply the state's choice-of-law rules to determine which state's substantive law applies to the federal diversity case. In federal cases within the court's federal question jurisdiction, the court will apply applicable federal law and doctrine.

C. PERSONAL JURISDICTION

1. Introductory Notes

a. Personal Jurisdiction over Plaintiffs

Personal jurisdiction concerns the power and authority of a court to render a binding enforceable judgment over the parties to the dispute. There generally are few issues relating to a court's personal jurisdiction over a plaintiff, because the plaintiff chooses the forum, institutes the action, and voluntarily consents to the court's jurisdiction.

- If a plaintiff is counter-sued in a cross-action (counterclaim) by a defendant, the court may issue a valid *in personam* judgment against the plaintiff, who is viewed as having consented to the court's jurisdiction by filing the initial action. "The plaintiff having, by his voluntary act in demanding justice from the defendant, submitted himself to the jurisdiction of the court, there is nothing arbitrary or unreasonable in treating him as being there for purposes for which justice to the defendant requires his presence." **Adam v. Saenger,** 303 U.S. 59, 67–68 (1938).

- However, it is more problematic whether unnamed, absent class members consent to personal jurisdiction by inclusion in a class action. Class members who choose not to exclude themselves from **Rule 23(b)(3)** class actions by exercising a right to opt-out are considered to have validly consented to the court's jurisdiction. (**Phillips Petroleum Co. v. Shutts,** 472 U.S. 797 (1985)). It is unsettled, however, whether the *Shutts* rule applies to mandatory class actions where absent class members do not have a right to opt-out of the class.

b. Personal Jurisdiction over Resident Defendants

There also are relatively few personal jurisdictional problems relating to resident defendants, or defendants owning property within a state. Historically, states have claimed exclusive jurisdiction over persons and property within the state's borders. Almost all problems relating to personal jurisdiction involve the ability to exercise jurisdiction over non-resident defendants. In order to assert jurisdiction over non-resident defendants, various traditional doctrines, such as presence, consent, or territorial sovereignty supported such assertions of jurisdiction. Contemporary notions of personal jurisdiction are determined by statutory provisions and constitutional requirements. Most problems relating to the proper assertion of jurisdiction over defendants relate to corporate entities, whose "presence" in the state for jurisdictional purposes frequently presents more complicated questions than that of individual defendants.

2. Traditional Bases: Territorial Theories

The two most prevalent theories supporting assertions of personal jurisdiction are presence within the state (*in personam* jurisdiction) or ownership of property within the state (*in rem* and *quasi in rem* jurisdiction). The basis for this authority is the sovereign power of each state over persons and property within its borders.

a. Transient Presence within the State

This power extends to persons who are temporarily or transiently within a state. As long as a person is served with process while visiting a state, this presence supports an assertion of personal jurisdiction over the defendant (**Burnham v. Superior Court,** 495 U.S. 604 (1990)). A state has the power to issue an *in personam* judgment against defendants within the state's borders, which judgment must be given full faith and credit by other states under **Article IV § 1** of the Constitution.

i. Jurisdiction over Absent Citizens

Federal courts may assert *in personam* jurisdiction over absent American citizens living abroad by serving process there, without invading the rights of a foreign government. In **Blackmer v. United States,** 284 U.S. 421 (1932) the Supreme Court held that an American citizen's due process rights were not violated by service of process in France, to comply with a subpoena to appear and give testimony in the Teapot Dome Scandal as authorized by federal statute.

ii. State Courts

The *Blackmer* principle applies to state court litigation as well. Domicile within a state alone is sufficient to bring an absent defendant within the reach of a state court's jurisdiction. A state's authority to issue an *in personam* judgment against a state domiciliary is not terminated by the defendant's absence from the state. In **Milliken v. Meyer,** 311 U.S. 457 (1940), Milliken sued Meyer, a Wyoming resident, in Wyoming state court. Meyer was served in Colorado, but did not return to Wyoming, and an *in personam* judgment was entered against him. Four years later Meyer brought an action in Colorado to restrain Milliken's enforcement of the Wyoming judgment. The Supreme Court held that the Wyoming judgment was valid and entitled to full faith and credit because Wyoming had personal jurisdiction over a resident who was not physically present in Wyoming when the action commenced.

b. Property

The presence of property within the state provides a basis for assertion of valid *in rem* jurisdiction. The presence of property within the state, regardless of the location of the defendant, provides a basis for the valid assertion of *quasi in rem* jurisdiction, provided that the property is seized or attached prior to the institution of legal proceedings.

i. Leading Case Authority: Pennoyer v. Neff, 95 U.S. 714 (1877). *Pennoyer v. Neff* Involved Two Lawsuits

Neff was a settler who traveled to Oregon to claim land under the Oregon Donation Act. In 1862 Neff asked Mitchell, a Portland attorney, to handle the paperwork concerning the land patent. Apparently Neff then failed to pay Mitchell. In the first lawsuit, brought in 1865, Mitchell sued Neff in Oregon state court to recover payment for the legal services he performed, an *in personam* action. Neff—who was in California—was not personally served and did not appear and a default judgment was entered against him in 1866. Mitchell next sought a writ of execution on his judgment. Neff's land was sold at a sheriff's auction to Mitchell, who assigned the property to Pennoyer; Mitchell was awarded the proceeds of the sale in satisfaction of his judgment against Neff. Neff brought the second lawsuit—an action in ejectment against Pennoyer—nine years later in 1875 in Oregon federal court. Neff sought to recover the land and claimed ownership based on the Oregon Donation laws. Pennoyer defended based on his ownership from the sheriff's sale. Neff argued that the Oregon state court lacked jurisdiction over him and his property, and the judgment in Mitchell v. Neff was invalid; therefore the conveyance to Pennoyer was invalid.

ii. Supreme Court's Decision in *Pennoyer v. Neff*

The Supreme Court held that the Oregon state court lacked jurisdiction over Neff because he had not been personally served, and the presence of his property alone was insufficient to support the state's assertion of jurisdiction, when the property was not seized or attached prior to the institution of legal proceedings. Therefore the sale of the land and conveyance to Pennoyer was invalid.

iii. Territoriality and State Sovereignty Principles Supporting the Court's Decision: "Twin Principles of Public Law"

The Supreme Court indicated that there were two interrelated "principles of public law" supporting its conclusion that the assertion of jurisdiction over Neff was improper:

- "Every state possesses exclusive jurisdiction and sovereignty over the persons and property within its territory," and

- "No state can exercise direct jurisdiction and authority over persons or property without its territory."

These principles flowed from the nineteenth-century view that states within the United States resembled the independent nation-states in Europe. As a corollary, the Court indicated that a state cannot assert legitimate *in personam* jurisdiction over a non-resident defendant by serving the defendant while in another state.

iv. Strict Rule of Physical Presence

In *Pennoyer*, the Supreme Court laid down a strict and formalistic rule of physical presence within the state for assertions of personal jurisdiction. The Court recognized two kinds of presence. First, a state could assert valid *in personam* jurisdiction over a defendant only by personally serving the defendant within state borders, or by the defendant's voluntary appearance within the state. Second, a court could assert valid *in rem* or *quasi in rem* jurisdiction over a defendant by attaching the defendant's property within the state prior to the institution of legal proceedings.

v. Notice

The Court's notice requirements paralleled its delineation of two bases for assertion of valid personal jurisdiction.

(a) *In personam* **actions—personal service**. In actions based on *in personam* jurisdiction, the Court indicated that only personal service on the resident or non-resident defendant within the state's borders can provide adequate notice of the proceedings.

(b) *In rem* **and** *quasi in rem* **actions**. In actions based on *in rem* or *quasi in rem* jurisdiction, notice by publication is sufficient to provide adequate notice. Attachment of property prior to the institution of proceedings is deemed to provide this notice, and personal service within the jurisdiction is not also required. In *Pennoyer, quasi in rem* jurisdiction was not available because Mitchell failed to attach Neff's property prior to entry of the court's judgment. Had Mitchell attached Neff's property prior to the institution of the proceedings, Mitchell could have satisfied his prior judgment to extent of the value of the property

vi. Constitutional Basis

There is some academic controversy concerning whether the Court's decision in **Pennoyer v. Neff** is constitutionally based in the Fourteenth Amendment's due process requirements. This confusion arises from Justice Field's suggestion, in *dicta*, that the Fourteenth Amendment—which had been recently adopted—provided a due process basis for directly or collaterally attacking judgments of a court lacking valid jurisdiction over the parties. The better view is that the Fourteenth Amendment did not apply directly in **Pennoyer v. Neff**, because the Amendment did not take effect until after Mitchell sold Neff's land. However, the Court's opinion did signal that due process requirements for assertions of personal jurisdiction would be important in subsequent evaluations of such assertions of state power.

vii. Other Qualifications and Exceptions

The Supreme Court qualified its general holdings in *Pennoyer* by recognizing the power of states to assert jurisdiction over non-residents in two other instances:

(a) State's ability to determine status relationships. The Court indicated that every state retained the power to determine the civil status and capacities of its citizens in relation to non-residents and to render binding judgments in such proceedings, even though the non-resident defendants were not personally served or given notice. The Court was principally concerned with the power of states to determine matters relating to marital status even as against non-resident defendants. In contemporary divorce practice, marital status has been treated as a *res* subject to the jurisdiction of the state residence of either spouse. All other incidents of divorce, such as alimony, maintenance, or child support, have been treated as actions *in personam* and subject to ordinary personal jurisdiction rules.

(b) Business associations; consent; appointment of an agent to receive service of process. The Court also recognized that a state legitimately could require a partnership or business association to appoint an agent to receive service of process, or require corporations to be held accountable for their conduct within the state without requiring personal service on officers or members. The Court's articulation of these requirements as pre-conditions for conducting activities within the state was a precursor of twentieth-century doctrines of implied consent.

3. Expanding Bases: Consent

The Supreme Court in **Pennoyer v. Neff** indicated that consent to a state's authority could provide a basis for rendering a binding *in personam* judgment against non-resident defendants. Consent doctrines have assumed increased importance in the twentieth century, as a consequence of the advent of modern means of transportation such as the automobile, and increased interstate commerce. Consent to jurisdiction may be either expressly given or implied by certain actions or waivers.

a. Express Consent

Parties may give express consent to a court's assertion of personal jurisdiction in different ways:

i. Appointment of an In-State Agent

As a condition of doing business within a state, many states require that business associations, corporations, partnerships, and other organizations appoint an agent for service of process. In the early twentieth century, some states even required that out-of-state motorists file a formal instrument appointing an in-state agent to receive process, prior to using the state's highways. In **Kane v. New Jersey,** 242 U.S. 160 (1916), the Supreme Court upheld such a requirement.

ii. Contractual Forum Selection Clauses

Parties contractually may consent to have their disputes litigated in a particular forum, through use of "forum selection clauses." **M/S Bremen v. Zapata Off–Shore Co.,** 407 U.S. 1 (1972); **Carnival Cruise Lines, Inc. v. Shute,** 499 U.S. 585 (1991). Most states and federal courts will uphold these contractual agreements specifying a particular forum, subject to rules relating to contract unconscionability, fraud, and duress. Although litigants may consent to a court's assertion of personal jurisdiction, litigants may not contractually agree to a court's subject matter jurisdiction.

iii. Cognovit Clauses

Cognovit clauses are sometimes included in loan agreements. These provisions allow a creditor to have a judgment entered against a defaulting debtor without personal service of process or notice. Many states uphold cognovit clauses. States that do not recognize cognovit clauses sometimes will give full faith and credit to judgments rendered by states that do recognize such clauses. The Supreme Court has upheld cognovit clauses as not violative of due process, **D.H. Overmyer Co. v. Frick,** 405 U.S. 174 (1972). Like forum selection clauses, cognovit notes are subject to contract doctrines relating to unconscionability and volition.

b. Implied Consent

In addition to giving express consent to a court's assertion of personal jurisdiction over non-resident litigants, modern jurisprudence has developed expanded concepts of implied consent. Thus, there are many circumstances in which parties may impliedly consent to a court's jurisdiction.

i. Non-Resident Motorist Statutes—Inherently Dangerous Activity

With the expanded use of automobiles in interstate travel in the early twentieth century and the increase in accidents involving out-of-state motorists, some states adopted statutes appointing local officials as agents to receive service of process for any actions arising out of travel within the state. These statutes were based on the inherent danger of automobiles and the consequent need for states to protect the health and welfare of their own citizens by allowing them the right to bring a suit in their own state courts for injury caused by non-residents. A non-resident motorist who entered the state, therefore, was deemed to have impliedly consented to the forum's jurisdiction. The Supreme Court validated such a Massachusetts statute in **Hess v. Pawloski,** 274 U.S. 352 (1927) as against a due process challenge. In *Hess* the Court balanced a citizen's due process rights and privileges to travel freely from state-to-state, against the state's police power to protect its own citizens, and upheld the state statute.

ii. Sale of Securities—Inherently Dangerous Business Activity

The doctrine of implied consent was expanded to reach a non-resident defendant selling corporate securities within a state, for controversies arising out of those sales. The Supreme Court validated this use of implied consent in **Henry L. Doherty & Co. v. Goodman,** 294 U.S. 623 (1935), similarly emphasizing the exceptional nature and dangers of securities sales, and the state's interest in regulating such activities to protect its own citizens.

iii. Activities After the Commencement of an Action

Certain activities either by plaintiffs or defendants after the commencement of an action will be deemed to constitute an implied consent to the court's jurisdiction.

(a) **Waiver or consent by failure to object.** A defendant can impliedly consent to a court's jurisdiction by failing to raise any available objections to the court's personal jurisdiction in a timely manner. **Rule 12(h)(1)** provides that a defendant may waive objections to personal jurisdiction by failing to raise those objections either in a **Rule 12** motion or in a responsive pleading or in an amendment allowed by **Rule 15(a)(i)** as a matter of course.

(b) **Waiver or consent by failure to comply with discovery requests regarding jurisdictional facts.** A defendant who contests personal jurisdiction but then fails to comply with court orders to divulge information needed by the plaintiff to support the burden of establishing personal jurisdiction may presumptively be held to have waived objections to personal jurisdiction. The Supreme Court upheld such a waiver as a sanction under federal discovery **Rule 37(b)(2)(A)** in **Insurance Corp. of Ireland v. Compagnie Des Bauxites de Guinee,** 456 U.S. 694 (1982).

(c) **Defendant's "general appearance."** A defendant who wishes to challenge a court's personal jurisdiction may elect to make a special appearance before the court to contest jurisdiction without being subjected to the court's jurisdiction. However, if the defendant appears and presents other defenses or objections, the defendant has made a general appearance and has consented to the exercise of personal jurisdiction.

(d) **Non-resident plaintiffs and counterclaims.** A non-resident plaintiff who enters a forum and institutes a legal proceeding impliedly consents to personal jurisdiction over any cross-actions or counterclaims asserted by a defendant to the action. Consent is implied by the plaintiff's availing itself of the forum in the first instance. **Adam v. Saenger,** 303 U.S. 59 (1938).

4. Modern Constitutional Due Process Approaches

The Supreme Court's decision in **Pennoyer v. Neff** embodied a nineteenth-century approach to thinking about jurisdictional questions, embedded in notions of state sovereignty and strict territoriality. These territoriality concerns would continue well into the twentieth century regarding litigation based on or relating to property: *actions in rem* and *quasi in rem*. However, with the expansion of commercial activities nationally and globally, traditional notions of *in personam* jurisdiction strictly based on presence within the state have been modified to conform to changing notions of due process requirements. Thus, since the Supreme Court's decision in **International Shoe Co. v. Washington,** 326 U.S. 310 (1945), almost all state assertions of *in personam* jurisdiction are now measured against an array of standards assessing the fairness and reasonableness of subjecting a non-resident defendant to a forum state's personal jurisdiction.

a. Defining Constitutional Power: Minimum Contacts and Fairness

The Supreme Court's original formulation of a due process standard for a state's assertion of jurisdiction required a two-part inquiry, asking whether the defendant had sufficient minimum contacts with the forum so as not to violate substantive due process, and also whether such an assertion of jurisdiction would be fair.

i. Leading Case Authority: International Shoe Co. v. Washington, 326 U.S. 310 (1945)

Washington State sued the International Shoe Company to recover the company's unpaid contributions to the state compensation fund. International Shoe was a Delaware corporation with its principal place of business in St. Louis, Missouri. It conducted its shoe manufacturing and sales in many states. It had no office in Washington, made no contracts for the purchase or sale of its merchandise there, and made no deliveries intrastate. It did have eleven to thirteen salesmen who lived in Washington and who rented sample rooms to display shoes. The salesmen had no authority to enter into contracts to or to make collections on orders, which were sent to St. Louis and shipped f.o.b. outside Washington State. The Washington state courts all affirmed the state's jurisdiction over International Shoe. On appeal to the Supreme Court, International Shoe argued that its activities within Washington State were not sufficient to manifest its "presence" and therefore it was a denial of due process to subject it to the court's jurisdiction.

ii. Supreme Court's Decision in *International Shoe Co.*

Recognizing the *Pennoyer* Court's requirement of presence within the state in order to assert jurisdiction over a defendant, the Supreme Court articulated the modern due process standard under the Fourteenth Amendment, for such assertions of state power:

> due process requires only that in order to subject a defendant to a judgment *in personam,* if he be not present within the territory of the forum, he have certain minimum contacts with it such that the maintenance of the suit does not offend "traditional notions of fair play and substantial justice."

iii. Minimum Contacts Defined; Quality and Nature of Contacts

International Shoe itself articulates no criteria for assessing a corporation's contacts or activities within the forum state. Instead, the Court indicated that the operative standard whether due process is satisfied *"must depend rather upon the quality and nature of the activity in relation to the fair and orderly administration of the laws which it is the purpose of the due process clause to ensure."*

iv. No Contacts

A state may not render a binding *in personam* judgment against an individual or corporate defendant that has no contacts, ties, or relations with the forum state. Such a judgment would violate the Fourteenth Amendment Due Process Clause.

v. Single Acts or Contacts

The Supreme Court in *International Shoe* stated the generally recognized principle that "the causal presence of the corporate agent or even his conduct of single or isolated items of activities in a state in the corporation's behalf are not enough to subject it to suit on causes of action unconnected with the activities there." Notwithstanding the Supreme Court's suggestion, however, some states have asserted jurisdiction over non-resident defendants with very few contacts with the forum.

■ EXAMPLES AND ANALYSIS

In **McGee v. International Life Insurance Co.,** 355 U.S. 220 (1957), the Supreme Court upheld California's assertion of jurisdiction over a non-resident insurance company based on an insurance policy issued to a California resident. The Court held that "it is sufficient for purposes of due process that the suit was based on a contract which had substantial connection" with California. The insurance contract had been delivered in California, premiums had been paid from there, and the insured was a California resident when he died. The defendant insurance company had no other contacts with the state. *McGee* offers an extreme example satisfying the *International Shoe* minimum contacts standard; it is sometimes cited as the "single contact"/single contract case. However, the *McGee* decision was additionally supported by a state interest, a factor in the evaluation of the standard's fairness prong, in protecting its citizens in relation to a highly regulated industry (the insurance industry).

Similarly, the Supreme Court upheld Florida's assertion of jurisdiction over a dispute between the Burger King franchise and a

Michigan franchisee, largely based on the franchise contract. **Burger King Corp. v. Rudzewicz,** 471 U.S. 462 (1985). Apart from the contract specifying that Florida law would apply to any disputes between the parties, the Michigan franchisee otherwise had attenuated contacts with the Florida forum.

vi. Systematic and Continuous Business Activities within the State

A state legitimately may assert personal jurisdiction over a non-resident corporation if that business's activities within the state are "systematic and continuous," as opposed to "irregular or casual." The Court in *International Shoe* found that corporation's activities in Washington state sufficient to meet this standard; its operations made it reasonable and just according to "traditional notions of fair play and substantial justice" to permit the state to enforce obligations against the defendant corporation.

Conducting systematic and continuous business within a forum permits a state to assert jurisdiction over a non-resident defendant, but may not compel the state to assume such jurisdiction.

- **Example. In Perkins v. Benguet Consolidated Mining Co.,** 342 U.S. 437 (1952), a Philippine corporation conducted systematic and continuous business activities in Ohio during the Japanese occupation of the Philippines during World War II. A non-resident of Ohio sued the corporation in Ohio for activities that occurred outside the state. The Supreme Court held that while no requirement of due process *prohibited* Ohio from asserting jurisdiction, no due process requirements *compelled* the Ohio courts to assume jurisdiction over the action.

vii. Purposeful Availment of Benefits and Protections of the State

Due process is not violated to the extent that a corporation, in conducting its business activities within a state, benefits from those activities as well as the protection of the state. Conducting business within a state is considered a privilege which may give rise to obligations, including the obligation to answer to a legal proceeding. Among the "benefits" that courts will assess are the profits or revenues a corporation derives from its business within the state.

"Protections" afforded to the defendant may include access to the state's legal system, and well as other health, welfare, and police benefits. In addition, the defendant must have "purposefully" availed itself of these benefits and protections. These standards sometimes are difficult to satisfy.

■ EXAMPLES AND ANALYSIS

The activities of the defendant in the forum state must be *purposeful*, and not random or fortuitous. For example, in **Hanson v. Denckla,** 357 U.S. 235 (1958), an action concerning the validity of a trust under Florida law, the Supreme Court—in reviewing the defendant trust company's contacts with Florida—found that the defendant had not purposefully availed itself of the privilege of conducting business in the state, invoking the benefits and protections of state law. The defendant trust company had no office in Florida, transacted no business there, and had not solicited business in person or by mail. Moreover, none of the trust assets had ever been held or administered in Florida.

In **Kulko v. Superior Court,** 436 U.S. 84 (1978), a father living in New York state sent his children to live with their mother in California. She then filed in California state court seeking a modification of a child support decree and to assert personal jurisdiction over her husband based on the act of sending their children to California. The Supreme Court held that the father's actions in sending the children did not constitute a "purposeful" act since the father was acquiescing in the mother and children's request. Furthermore, the Court held that the father did not derive an economic benefit from the forum state as a result of sending his children there.

Defendants can derive some economic benefit from a forum, but still may not satisfy the purposeful availment test. In **World–Wide Volkswagen Corp. v. Woodson,** 444 U.S. 286 (1980), the Supreme Court held that Oklahoma could not legitimately assert personal jurisdiction over a New York state auto retailer and regional distributor in a tort action arising out of an automobile accident in Oklahoma. The Court held that the defendants had not purposefully attempted to serve the Oklahoma market. The defendants could not be subject to answer in a distant forum because automobiles were mobile and they might derive some revenue from their marketing activities.

viii. "Unilateral Activity" Qualification to the Purposeful Availment Standard

The "minimum contacts" standard cannot be satisfied by the unilateral activities of someone—usually a third party or an outsider to the litigation—who has a relationship to the defendant. The Supreme Court has held that "It is essential in each case that there be some act *by which the defendant* purposefully avails itself of the privilege of conducting activities within the forum State, invoking the benefits and protections of its law. . . . " **Hanson v. Denckla,** 357 U.S. 235 (1958). In addition, the "unilateral activity" of the plaintiff also cannot supply the contacts sufficient to support a defendant's purposeful availment of a forum. **World–Wide Volkswagen Corp. v. Woodson,** 444 U.S. 286 (1980).

■ EXAMPLES AND ANALYSIS

In **Hanson v. Denckla,** 357 U.S. 235 (1958), Donner, a Pennsylvania resident, established a trust with a Delaware bank as trustee. She moved to Florida, executed a will, and left most of her estate to two daughters. Before Donner died she executed a power of appointment and changed her trust beneficiaries to the grandchildren of a third daughter. After Donner's death, her two daughters (named in the will) sought to invalidate the trust appointment in Florida court; the Florida court held it had jurisdiction over the Delaware trustee and declared Donner's power of appointment invalid (causing the trust assets to pass under the will to the two daughters). In a parallel Delaware action involving the same parties and issues, Donner's two daughters argued that the Florida decision was res judicata; the trust beneficiaries argued that Florida had no personal jurisdiction over the Delaware trustee and therefore Delaware was not required to give full faith and credit to the Florida judgment. The Delaware court agreed and subsequently upheld the trust appointment as valid. The Supreme Court, in reaching its conclusion that Florida could not legitimately assert jurisdiction over the Delaware trustee (and therefore Delaware was justified in denying full faith and credit to the Florida judgment), held that the unilateral activities of Donner, in moving to Florida and executing her power of appointment, could not supply the contacts with the state to assert jurisdiction over the non-resident defendant trustee. In other words, the defendant trustee had not, by its own acts or contacts with Florida, purposefully availed itself of the benefits and protections of the state.

In **World–Wide Volkswagen Corp. v. Woodson,** 444 U.S. 286 (1980), the unilateral activity of the plaintiff driving the automobile into Oklahoma could not sustain a finding of the New York retailer or distributor's purposeful availment of the Oklahoma market, or the defendant's deriving benefits from that market.

ix. "Center of Gravity" Qualification to the Purposeful Availment Standard

The fact that a number of events relating to an action cluster within a certain forum will not support an assertion of personal jurisdiction over a non-resident defendant in that forum. Hence, plaintiffs may not successfully urge that a court assert jurisdiction over a non-resident defendant because the forum is the "center of gravity" of the dispute.

■ EXAMPLE AND ANALYSIS

In **Hanson v. Denckla,** 357 U.S. 235 (1958), the Supreme Court rejected the argument that Florida could assert personal jurisdiction over a Delaware trustee because Florida was the "center of gravity" of the dispute among Donner's heirs. Donner's daughters argued that Florida was the center of gravity of the dispute because Donner was domiciled there at her death, had executed her will there, and had executed her final power of appointment over the trust there. In addition, Donner's estate was probated in Florida. The Supreme Court rejected this argument, holding that a court "does not acquire jurisdiction by being the 'center of gravity' of the controversy, or the most convenient location for litigation. . . . "

x. "Reasonable Foreseeability" Qualification to the Purposeful Availment Requirement

For a forum to exercise jurisdiction over a non-resident defendant who purposefully avails itself of the benefits and protections of a forum, the defendant also must reasonably foresee that as a consequence of its activities it may be subject to suit in the state. **World–Wide Volkswagen Corp. v. Woodson,** 444 U.S. 286 (1980). Courts will assess the defendant's conduct or activities outside the state to determine whether that conduct was of such a nature that the non-resident defendant could reasonably have anticipated being "haled into court."

■ EXAMPLES AND ANALYSIS

A non-resident defendant who commits the intentional tort of libel in the plaintiff's state may reasonably foresee being haled into court there. **Calder v. Jones,** 465 U.S. 783 (1984). In *Calder,* the plaintiff entertainer Shirley Jones, a California resident, sued the Florida writer and editor of an article which appeared in the *National Enquirer,* a national magazine with its largest circulation in California. The Supreme Court upheld California's assertion of jurisdiction over the Florida defendants, noting that the intentional libel foreseeably would cause its greatest injury in the plaintiff's community and therefore it was not unreasonable to hold the defendants answerable to a lawsuit there.

A non-resident defendant who negotiates a long-term business contract, including terms requiring payments within the forum and an applicable law provision specifying forum law, can reasonably foresee that it will be required to defend any disputes arising out of the contract in the forum state. **Burger King Corp. v. Rudzewicz,** 471 U.S. 462 (1985).

A corporate or business entity that purposefully enters a national market and derives economic benefit from the sale of its products may reasonably foresee being held subject to lawsuits for defective product actions in those markets. Similarly, an international products manufacturer and a national importer of an allegedly defective product that is marketed and sold in the national market may reasonably anticipate being sued in any state in the market. **World–Wide Volkswagen Corp. v. Woodson,** 444 U.S. 286 (1980) (dicta).

Local retailers of products cannot foresee where the products they sell may wind up, nor do they seek economic benefit from other state's consumers. Therefore such non-resident defendants cannot reasonably anticipate being haled into some distant forum to answer in defective products actions. **World–Wide Volkswagen Corp. v. Woodson,** 444 U.S. 286 (1980).

xi. The "Effects Test" and Purposeful Availment

If a non-resident conducts wrongful activity or commercial transactions outside a state that have injurious effects on residents inside a state, then assertion of personal jurisdiction over the non-resident defendant is not unreasonable under the so-called "effect test." However, merely causing an effect within a forum state is not sufficient to support personal jurisdiction without purposeful availment.

■ EXAMPLES AND ANALYSIS

A divorced parent who voluntarily sends children to another state to live with the other parent cannot be held to that state's personal jurisdiction in a support modification proceeding. The act of sending the children to the distant forum cannot be construed as causing an effect in the forum and does not constitute purposeful availment for minimum contacts standards. **Kulko v. Superior Court,** 436 U.S. 84 (1978).

xii. Applicable Law

The fact that a particular state's law—especially forum law—may apply to a controversy usually is not a factor or "contact" that enters into a due process minimum contact analysis. **Hanson v. Denckla,** 357 U.S. 235 (1958) (*"The issue is personal jurisdiction, not choice of law. . . . "*). However, when parties have contractually stipulated that the forum's law will apply to any future disputes related to the contract, this contract provision will support a finding of reasonable foreseeability of being sued in that forum. **Burger King Corp. v. Rudzewicz,** 471 U.S. 462 (1985).

xiii. Fairness Considerations—Burdens and Inconvenience

In addition to assessing whether the defendant has constitutionally sufficient minimum contacts, the second prong of the *International*

Shoe due process standard requires courts to evaluate the fairness of asserting jurisdiction over the defendant (assuming the defendant has sufficient minimum contacts with the forum). In assessing the reasonableness or fairness of the assertion of jurisdiction against a non resident defendant, the Court indicated that the relevant consideration is *"an 'estimate of the inconveniences' that would result to the corporation from a trial away from its home or principal place of business."* It is considered an unreasonable burden to require a corporation to defend a suit away from the jurisdiction where it carries on more substantial activities than the forum state.

xiv. First Amendment Limitations

A non-resident defendant may not invoke the First Amendment to make invalid an otherwise proper assertion of personal jurisdiction under the Due Process Clause. Writers and publishers have attempted to argue that First Amendment free speech and press concerns should override assertions of personal jurisdiction in distant forums. This is predicated on the theory that if writers and publishers are broadly subjected to litigation in every state where their publications are circulated, the prospect of such litigation will have a chilling effect on free speech and a free press.

■ EXAMPLES AND ANALYSIS

In **Calder v. Jones,** 465 U.S. 783 (1984), the Florida writer and publisher of a libelous article published in the *National Enquirer* sought to quash service of process (another way of challenging personal jurisdiction) in California, arguing that First Amendment chilling of speech concerns outweighed valid assertion of jurisdiction under the Due Process Clause. The Supreme Court refused to consider the First Amendment argument, holding that "We also reject the suggestion that First Amendment concerns enter into jurisdictional analysis. The infusion of such concerns would needlessly complicate an already imprecise inquiry."

The Supreme Court rejected a similar objection raised by Hustler Magazine in **Keeton v. Hustler,** 465 U.S. 770 (1984), concluding "We reject categorically the suggestion that invisible radiations from the First Amendment may defeat jurisdiction otherwise proper under the Due Process Clause."

xv. Commerce Clause Limitations

The potential burden on interstate commerce of a state court's assertion of personal jurisdiction over a non-resident defendant corporation may be taken into account in a court's assessment of *International Shoe* minimum contacts. Such constitutional Commerce Clause objections to state assertions of personal jurisdiction are rare.

■ EXAMPLES AND ANALYSIS

A Kansas corporation sued a Kansas railroad in Minnesota for damages resulting from the loss of grain in a shipment within Kansas. The Supreme Court held that the Commerce Clause barred Minnesota from asserting jurisdiction over the Kansas railroad. **Davis v. Farmers' Co-op Equity Co.,** 262 U.S. 312 (1923).

An Ohio statute permanently tolling the state's statute of limitations for the actions of non-resident corporations that do not consent to the general jurisdiction of the Ohio courts violates the Commerce Clause. **Bendix Autolite Corp. v. Midwesco Enterprises, Inc.,** 486 U.S. 888 (1988).

xvi. General and Specific Jurisdiction

The *International Shoe* decision very broadly suggests the concepts of both general and specific jurisdiction. The Supreme Court would not revisit or discuss the concepts of general and specific jurisdiction for almost thirty years, until its decision in **Helicopteros Nacionales de Colombia, S.A. v. Hall,** 466 U.S. 408 (1984). In *Helicopteros*, the Supreme Court endorsed the concept of general jurisdiction but declined to approve any particular formulation of specific jurisdictional theory. The Supreme Court would revisit the concept of general and specific jurisdiction in **Goodyear Dunlop Tires Operations, S.A. v. Brown,** ___ U.S. ___, 131 S.Ct. 2846 (2011).

(a) **General jurisdiction.** *General jurisdiction* refers to the ability of a state to assert jurisdiction over a non-resident defendant based on the defendant's systematic and continuous business activities in the forum state, which contacts are sufficient to support an assertion of jurisdiction against the defendant for any and all matters, without regard to whether a particular action arises out of or is related to the defendant's activities. Personal jurisdiction in *International Shoe* was predicated on a theory of general jurisdiction. In only two cases post-dating *International Shoe*—*Helicopteros* and *Perkins v. Benguet*, has the Supreme Court validated general jurisdiction. *Goodyear Dunlop Tires*.

(b) **Specific jurisdiction.** *Specific jurisdiction* refers to the ability of a state to assert jurisdiction over a non-resident defendant based on certain contacts with the forum that relate to the action, but which contacts are insufficient to support an assertion of general jurisdiction. States and lower federal courts have recognized various formulations of the standards for assertion of specific jurisdiction. Some states require that the defendant's activities "relate to" or "substantially relate to" the plaintiff's action. Other states require that "but for" the defendant's activities, the plaintiff would not have been harmed. A third variation of specific jurisdiction requires that the plaintiff's claim "arise out of" the defendant's conduct or activities in the state. The Supreme Court declined to endorse any of these specific jurisdiction tests *Nacionales*, but these tests are used by state and lower federal courts. **Goodyear Dunlop Tires Operations, S.A. v. Brown**, ___ U.S. ___, 131 S.Ct. 2846 (2011).

(c) **Specific and general jurisdiction distinguished.** Theories of specific jurisdiction support assertions of jurisdiction over non-resident defendants if a defendant's acts or conduct within the forum relate to the plaintiff's claims (in absence of more systematic and continuous contacts that would support an assertion of general jurisdiction unrelated to those contacts). General jurisdiction, on the other hand, permits an assertion of jurisdiction over a non-resident defendant by virtue of the defendant's systematic and continuous activities in the state, which may be totally unrelated to the plaintiff's claim. In *Goodyear Dunlop Tires, S.A.*, the Supreme Court announced that specific jurisdiction is confined to adjudication of "issue deriving from, or connected with, the very controversy that establishes jurisdiction."

■ EXAMPLES AND ANALYSIS

A Hong Kong ship management company maintained an office in New Orleans from which it conducted operations for five years; its employees performed substantial ship management services; and the office was staffed with two management employees responsible for implementing Hong Kong instructions. A Honduran seaman was killed in an accident off the Oregon coast and his representative brought suit in Louisiana, suing the Hong Kong management company. The Louisiana Supreme Court found sufficient systematic and continuous contacts between the defendant and the forum to support assertion of *in personam* jurisdiction. (**de Reyes v. Marine Management & Consulting Ltd.,** 586 So.2d 103 (La. 1991)).

A Pennsylvania plaintiff brought suit against Walt Disney Company, Walt Disney Productions, and Walt Disney World in Pennsylvania for injuries suffered from a monorail fire at Disney World in Florida. The Disney companies were incorporated in California and Delaware. The Pennsylvania courts upheld jurisdiction in Pennsylvania based on the Disney companies' "substantial and continuous" contacts in Pennsylvania based on its advertising in radio, television, and newspapers; selling Disney products and services in-state; providing a toll-free number for Pennsylvania residents to call; and visiting a junior college to recruit employees. **Cresswell v. Walt Disney Productions,** 677 F.Supp. 284 (M.D. Pa. 1987).

Plaintiffs, residents of North Carolina whose sons died in a bus accident outside Paris, filed a wrongful death action in North Carolina state court, naming Goodyear USA (an Ohio corporation) and Goodyear Dunlop Tires Operations, S.A. as defendants. The defendants were not registered to do business in North Carolina; had no place of business, employees, or bank accounts in the state; did not design, manufacture, or advertise their products in the state; and did not solicit business in the state or sell or ship tires to North Carolina customers. A small percentage of their tires were distributed in North Carolina by Goodyear USA affiliates. The Supreme Court held that because the incident occurred in France and the tire alleged to have caused the accident was manufactured and sold abroad, North Carolina lacked specific jurisdiction to adjudicate the controversy. **Goodyear Dunlop Tires Operations S.A. v. Brown,**___ U.S. ___, 131 S.Ct. 2846 (2011). In addition, North Carolina is not a forum in which it would be permissible to subject the defendants to general jurisdiction.

(d) Leading case authority: Helicopteros Nacionales de Colombia, S.A. v. Hall, 466 U.S. 408 (1984). A helicopter crashed in Peru killing four American citizens who were working on construction of a pipeline for Consorcio, a Peruvian consortium that was part of a joint venture with headquarters in Houston, Texas. None of the decedents were Texas domiciliaries, although all had been hired in Houston. Helicopteros Nacionales de Colombia, S.A. (Helicol) owned the helicopter that crashed; a Helicol officer had negotiated a contract in Houston with Consorcio to supply helicopters for the job. The contract was written in Spanish, signed in Peru, and provided that all controversies relating to the contract would be submitted to the jurisdiction of the Peruvian courts. Consorcio agreed to make payments to Helicol's bank in New York City. During a seven-year period, Helicol purchased approximately 80% of its fleet, spare parts, and accessories for more than $4 million from Bell Helicopters in Fort Worth, Texas. Helicol sent its pilots to Fort Worth for training and to ferry helicopters to South America. Helicol sent management and maintenance personnel to Forth Worth for plant familiarization and technical consultation. Helicol received $5 million from Consorcio drawn on Consorcio's Houston bank. Helicol had no other business contacts with Texas (was not authorized to do business, had never solicited business, signed no contracts, had no employees based there, maintained no office or records, had no real property, and had no shareholders). In Texas wrongful death actions, a jury awarded entered a judgment against Helicol for over $1 million. On appeal, the Texas Supreme Court held that Texas courts had *in personam* jurisdiction under the state's long-arm statute which it interpreted as reaching as far as the Due Process Clause.

- **Supreme Court's holding in *Helicopteros*, recognizing general jurisdiction.** The Supreme Court held that "Even when the cause of action does not arise out of or relate to the foreign corproation's activities in the forum State, due process is not offended by a State's subjecting the corporation to its *in personam* jurisdiction when there are sufficient contacts between the State and the foreign corporation." The Court then reviewed Helicol's contacts with Texas and concluded that these contacts were insufficient to satisfy the requirements of the Due Process Clause (reversing the judgment of the Texas Supreme Court).

- **Supreme Court's holdings in *Helicopteros*, declining to endorse any formulation of specific jurisdiction.** In footnote 10 to its decision, the Supreme Court declined to express any views with regard to whether the plaintiffs' claims "arose out of" or were "related to" Helicol's contacts with Texas because the parties had conceded that the wrongful death claims did not "arise out of" or were not "related to" Helicol's contacts with Texas.

- **Because the issue had not been briefed, the Court declined to reach the questions** (1) whether the terms "arising out of" and "related to" describe different connections between a cause of action and defendant's contacts with the forum, and (2) what sort of tie between a cause of action and a defendant's contacts with a forum is necessary to a determination whether either connection exists. The Court also declined to address the question "whether, if the two types of relationship differ, a forum's exercise of personal jurisdiction in a situation where the cause of action 'relates to,' but does not 'arise out of,' the defendant's contacts with the forum should be analyzed as an assertion of specific jurisdiction."

- **Justice Brennan's dissent in *Helicopteros*.** Justice Brennan would have upheld an assertion of jurisdiction over Helicol because he believed that the plaintiffs' wrongful-death claims were "significantly related to" Helicol's contacts with Texas. Justice Brennan argued that "a court's specific jurisdiction should be applicable whenever the cause of action arises out of *or* relates to the contacts between the defendant and the forum."

(e) **Specific and general jurisdiction after *Helicopteros*.** The Supreme Court had another opportunity in 1991 to revisit the issue of specific jurisdiction in **Carnival Cruise Lines, Inc. v. Shute,** 499 U.S. 585 (1991), but declined to do so. The Ninth Circuit had upheld Washington State's assertion of jurisdiction over the Florida corporation Carnival Cruise Lines, using a "but for" specific jurisdiction test. The validity of this specific jurisdiction formulation on due process grounds was appealed to the Supreme Court, but the Court decided the case on the narrower contract ground looking to the passenger ticket's forum selection clause. As a consequence of the Court's refusal to address the specific jurisdiction issue, various tests for specific jurisdiction are still recognized by many state and lower federal courts.

xvii. Criticisms of the *International Shoe* Due Process Standards

(a) **Emotional appeal.** The Court's broad language describing the due process requirements for assertions of *in personam* jurisdiction over non-resident corporations, couched in terms of "traditional notions of substantial justice and fair play" and "reasonableness" provided little guidance for state and federal courts. Justice Black, in his concurring opinion, noted that these words had "strong emotional appeal," but "they were not chosen by those who wrote the original Constitution or the Fourteenth Amendment as a measuring rod for this Court to use in invalidating State or federal laws passed by elected legislative representatives."

(b) **Vague guidance.** The Court's decision provides only the vaguest guidance concerning what contacts are sufficient to satisfy the "minimum contacts" standard.

(c) **Unanswered questions.** The Court alluded to but left open the question whether a state could assert jurisdiction over a non-resident defendant based on defendant's contacts with the forum related to the action (specific jurisdiction).

(d) **Dubious Fourteenth Amendment basis.** Some academic commentators have challenged the entire due process basis for evaluating assertions of personal jurisdiction, suggesting that the Supreme Court was incorrect in both **Pennoyer v. Neff** and *International Shoe* in locating in the Fourteenth Amendment a defendant's due process right not to be compelled to answer a lawsuit brought in another forum. These commentators reject the entire "minimum contacts" portion of the *International Shoe* jurisprudence, and would assess attempted assertions of personal jurisdiction only against fairness concerns.

b. State Long-Arm Statutes

The Supreme Court's expansive decision in *International Shoe* left the states to elaborate on the requirements of minimum contacts jurisprudence. It prescribes the farthest constitutional limits on personal jurisdiction, but does not require any state to allow its courts to exercise jurisdiction to those limits. Since 1945 almost all states have enacted so-called "long-arm" statutes which permit states to expand their jurisdictional reach beyond state borders and assert jurisdiction over non-resident defendants. Typically these statutes specify the acts or conduct of a defendant both within and outside the state that can subject a defendant to the court's authority.

i. Characteristics of State Long-Arm Statutes

Most state long-arm statutes differ in the degree of detail enumerating the specific acts that can subject a defendant to jurisdiction. Other types of long-arm statutes may subject a defendant to jurisdiction based on the defendant's general activities within the state.

(a) **"Illinois-style" long-arm statutes.** Illinois was the first state to enact a long-arm statute that was intended to reach non-resident defendants to the fullest extent constitutionally permissible under the standards articulated in *International Shoe.* Many states have followed Illinois's example and have enacted textually detailed long-arm statutes. The Illinois long-arm statute includes provisions making both individuals and corporations amenable to jurisdiction in Illinois if the individual or entity transacts business within the state; commits a tort within the state; owns, uses, or possesses property within the state; contracts to ensure any person, property, or risk located in the state; and any claims involving alimony, support, or property division against former residents.

(b) **"California-style" long-arm statutes.** California has a simple one-line long-arm statute that permits the state to assert jurisdiction over non-resident defendants on any basis not inconsistent with the Constitution. This is the broadest possible long-arm statute and this formulation allows states to assert jurisdiction up to the limits allowed by the Constitution. Other states have similarly broad long-arm statutes which permit the state to assert jurisdiction over corporations, non-resident individuals, and partnerships amenable to suit within the state and having the necessary minimum contacts required by the Constitution.

(c) **Other limitations in state long-arm statutes.** Some state long-arm statutes apply only to corporations and do not apply to individuals. In order to subject a business entity to the court's jurisdiction, some states require the doing of business within the state or of an act or omission within the state.

ii. Judicial Construction of State Long-Arm Statutes

Since the enactment of state long-arm statutes, plaintiffs must now satisfy state statutory requirements for the assertion of personal jurisdiction over non-resident defendants. Thus, at the outset of every jurisdictional inquiry, the state court must construe and apply its own long-arm statute (except if the parties have contractually agreed to the forum, or the basis for jurisdiction is transient presence in the state, discussed below).

Jurisdictional analysis now typically requires a two-step process. A court must first examine its own long-arm statute to determine whether a defendant's conduct or activities brings that defendant within the enumerated bases for jurisdiction as determined by the state legislature. If the defendant is subject to the state long-arm statute, then the court will examine whether the state's assertion of jurisdiction comports with the requirements of constitutional due process. **World–Wide Volkswagen Corp. v. Woodson,** 444 U.S. 286 (1980).

(a) **Judicial construction of Illinois-style long-arm statutes.** Long-arm statutes setting forth in great detail the quality and nature of a defendant's activities that may subject the non-resident defendant may not be apparent from the plain language of the statutory provision. Different state courts construing similar or the same statutory language may interpret the state's jurisdictional reach in completely contradictory ways.

■ EXAMPLES AND ANALYSIS

Interpretation of "Commission of Tortious Act Within the State."
Titan Valve Manufacturing Co. manufactured valves that were

incorporated into water heaters sold by American Radiator Co. Titan was sued in Illinois state court by Gray for injuries resulting from an exploding water heater, where Gray resided. Titan's corporate agent was located in Ohio, the valve was manufactured in Ohio, and incorporated into the water heater in Pennsylvania. The Illinois state long-arm statute **§ 17(b)(1)** permitted Illinois to assert jurisdiction over non-resident defendants for tortious acts committed within the state. The Illinois Supreme Court held that Titan's association with the state was sufficient to assert jurisdiction under the Illinois long-arm statute. In construing the statute, the Court held that the tort was committed in Illinois, on two separate rationales. Relying on the **Restatement of Conflict of Law § 377,** the court invoked the rule that the place of a wrong is where the last event takes place necessary to render the actor liable. Second, the Court looked to the statute of limitations which computed from the time when the injury was done. **Gray v. American Radiator & Standard Sanitary Corp.,** 22 Ill.2d 432 (1961).

Contrary Interpretation of "Commission of a Tortious Act Within the State." Plaintiffs were injured in New York by the explosion of a tractor-trailer tank of propane. The tank was manufactured in Kansas and sold to a Missouri corporation, with the knowledge that it would then be mounted on a wheelbase and sold to a Pennsylvania licensed interstate carrier. The New York long-arm statute permitted the state to assert jurisdiction over non-resident defendants who, through agents, committed a tortious act within the state. The New York court refused to assert jurisdiction over the Kansas manufacturer and criticized the Illinois Supreme Court for its conclusion in Gray: "It certainly does not follow that, if the 'place of wrong' for purposes of conflicts of laws is a particular state, the 'place of the commission of a tortious act' is also that same state for the purposes of interpreting a statute conferring jurisdiction, on that basis over non-residents . . . " **Feathers v. McLucas,** 15 N.Y.2d 443, 209 N.E.2d 68 (1965).

In 1966, the New York State legislature amended its long-arm statute to reach defendants such as those in the *Feathers* case.

■ EXAMPLES AND ANALYSIS

"Tortious acts within the state" and remote activities. A Delaware corporation with headquarters in Illinois sought to gain personal jurisdiction over a Texas resident who had served as president of two subsidiaries, for breach of fiduciary duties. All the acts that allegedly injured the corporation were performed outside Illinois, but the plaintiff argued that the consequences of those acts were felt within Illinois and therefore subjected the Texas defendant to jurisdiction under **§ 17(b)(1).** The Illinois Supreme Court disagreed, distinguishing Gray. The Court held that the consequences upon which the plaintiff relied were too remote from the defendant's activities to support a conclusion that the tortious acts were committed in Illinois. **Green v. Advance Ross Electronics Corp.,** 86 Ill.2d 431 (1981).

The Massachusetts long-arm statute provides that the state courts shall have jurisdiction over parties who cause "tortious injury by an act or omission in this commonwealth." The Massachusetts courts have interpreted this provision to apply only when the tortious conduct causing injury occurs within the state.

Causing "injury within the state" and intentional torts. Typically states liberally construe "injury within the state" requirements when the out-of-state defendant commits an intentional (as opposed to an unintentional) tort within the forum state. For example, even under Massachusett's narrowly construed long-arm provision, the commission of an intentional tort across states lines will subject a non-resident defendant to long-arm jurisdiction. A Massachusetts plaintiff successfully asserted jurisdiction over a New York defendant who allegedly had communicated false and misleading representations by mail and telephone. The court held that "sending a libel into a state is indistinguishable from the 'frequently hypothesized but rarely encountered gunman firing across a state line.' . . . We believe this is true of the mailing of a fraudulent misrepresentation into a state." **Murphy v. Erwin–Wasey, Inc.,** 460 F.2d 661 (1st Cir. 1972).

(b) "Specific jurisdiction" tests. Some states have long-arm provisions authorizing the assertion of jurisdiction over a defendant if a cause of action arises from the transaction of any business within the state. In construing these broad provisions, many states and some federal courts have permitted the assertion of jurisdiction over non-resident defendants based on so-called "specific jurisdiction" tests. Some courts have adopted the "but for" causation standard to satisfy "arising from" statutory language. Other states and federal courts have construed the same statutory language to require that a plaintiff show that the plaintiff's cause of action is "related to" or "substantially related to" the defendant's business transacted within the state.

■ EXAMPLES AND ANALYSIS

"But for" specific jurisdiction. French plaintiffs sued in Kansas for damages resulting from an airplane crash in France. The plaintiffs sued the Canadian corporation that sold airplane engines to a Kansas airplane manufacturer. The particular ill-fated engine in the plane that crashed was a replacement installed in Canada. Kansas's long-arm statute authorized jurisdiction over defendants where the cause of action arises from the transaction of any business within the state. Although the engine was installed in Canada and had never been sent to or sold in Kansas, the court nonetheless upheld jurisdiction over the Canadian defendant on a "but for" theory. Hence, "but for" the Canadian corporation's business dealings with the Kansas manufacturer, it would not have had the occasion to install the defective engine in Canada. **Grimandi v. Beech Aircraft Corp.,** 512 F.Supp. 764 (D. Kan. 1981).

Federal Circuit approval of specific jurisdiction tests. The Seventh and Ninth Circuits have adopted and approved "but for" specific jurisdiction tests. In **In re Oil Spill by Amoco Cadiz Off Coast of France,** 699 F.2d 909 (7th Cir. 1983), the court found that but for the negotiation and signing of a contract in Illinois for building an oil tanker, the tanker would not have broken up off the coast of France and caused damage. In **Shute v. Carnival Cruise Lines,** 897 F.2d 377 (9th Cir. 1990), the Ninth Circuit held that but for Carnival Cruise Line's solicitation efforts, the plaintiff Shute never would have taken her cruise and been injured on board. On review of the *Shute* decision, the Supreme Court declined to review the Ninth Circuit's application of the specific jurisdiction test, relying instead on the contractual forum selection clause as the basis for jurisdiction. **Carnival Cruise Lines v. Shute,** 499 U.S. 585 (1991).

(c) **Judicial construction of California-style long-arm statutes.** California-style long-arm statutes authorize states to assert jurisdiction to the full extent of the Constitution. This means that the court must assess the forum's assertion of jurisdiction in relation to due process minimum contacts jurisprudence as elaborated in *International Shoe* and subsequent cases. In states with California-style long-arm statutes, the usual two-stage jurisdictional inquiry effectively is conflated into a constitutional due process inquiry. Furthermore, several states interpret their own detailed long-arm states as authorizing assertion of jurisdiction to the full extent of the Constitution. In these states with long-arm statutes that resemble Illinois-style statutes, the jurisdictional inquiry typically evaluates constitutional due process requirements only.

■ EXAMPLES AND ANALYSIS

The Oklahoma long-arm statute authorizes personal jurisdiction over a "person who acts directly or by an agent, as to a cause of action or claim for relief arising from the person's . . . causing tortious injury in this state by an act or omission outside this state if he regularly does or solicits business or engages in any persistent course of conduct, or derives substantial revenue from goods used or consumed or services rendered, in this state." In the state litigation underlying **World–Wide Volkswagen v. Woodson,** 444 U.S. 286 (1980), the Oklahoma Supreme Court did not construe this statutory provision independently of the constitutional due process inquiry because the Oklahoma long-arm statute had been interpreted as conferring jurisdiction to the limits permitted by the United States Constitution.

c. Stream-of-Commerce Theory

With the transformation of the national economy in the twentieth century and the increased shipment of goods and services across state lines, state courts adapted *International Shoe* due process standards to a "stream of commerce" theory for assertions of personal jurisdiction over businesses that place their products in interstate commerce. Stream-of-commerce theories place less weight on "inconvenience" factors in due process analysis. Current issues concern whether state courts, using "stream-of-commerce" rationales, can extend their reach globally to foreign corporations.

i. Classical Statements of the "Stream-of-Commerce" Theory (Rationales)

- The trend towards expanding state jurisdiction over non-residents is "[i]n part . . . attributable to the fundamental transformation of our national economy over the years. Today many commercial transactions touch two or more States and may involve parties separated by the full continent. With this increasing nationalization of commerce has come a great increase in the amount of business conducted by mail across state lines. At the same time modern transportation and communication have made it much less burdensome for a party sued to defend himself in a State where he engages in economic activity." **McGee v. International Life Insurance Co.,** 355 U.S. 220 (1957).

- "As a general proposition, if a corporation elects to sell its products for ultimate use in another State, it is not unjust to hold it answerable there for any damage caused by defects in those products. Advanced means of distribution and other commercial activity have made possible these modern methods of doing business, and have largely effaced the economic significance of State lines. By the same token, today's facilities for transportation and communication have removed much of the difficulty and inconvenience formerly encountered in defending lawsuits brought in other States." **Gray v. American Radiator & Standard Sanitary Corp.,** 22 Ill.2d 432 (1961).

ii. Stream of Commerce and Foreseeability

Early formulations of the stream-of-commerce theory expansively permitted assertions of jurisdiction over corporations that placed their products into the stream of commerce, even without precise knowledge of where those products eventually might wind up. Jurisdiction also would extend even if a middleman purchased the product or someone other than the defendant shipped the product interstate. **Gray v. American Radiator & Standard Sanitary Corp., 22 Ill.2d 432 (1961).**

- **World–Wide Volkswagen and reasonable expectations.** The Supreme Court in 1980 endorsed the "stream-of-commerce" theory for assertions of personal jurisdiction over non-resident product manufacturers and distributors, but added a requirement that the defendant have some reasonable expectation that its products would wind up in the forum. Thus, the Court stated that a state could constitutionally exercise jurisdiction over "a corporation that delivers its products into the stream of commerce with the expectation that they will be purchased by consumers in the forum State." **World–Wide Volkswagen Corp. v. Woodson,** 444 U.S. 286 (1980). Otherwise, "every seller of chattels would in effect appoint the chattel his agent for service of process." *Id.*

- **Foreseeability test stated:** ". . . the foreseeability that is critical to due process analysis is not the mere likelihood that a product will find its way into the forum State. Rather, it is that the defendant's conduct and connection with the forum State are such that he should reasonably anticipate being haled into court there. . . . " **World–Wide Volkswagen Corp. v. Woodson,** 444 U.S. 286 (1980).

  The Court found that the New York automobile retailer and regional distributor had no reasonable expectation that its product would wind up in Oklahoma and therefore the state's assertion of jurisdiction over them violated due process. The Court indicated, however, that this would not be true for the international manufacturer and national distributor.

- **"Unilateral activity" corollary.** The defendant corporation must place its product in the stream of commerce in order to be held to answer for a lawsuit in a distant forum. It is unfair to make a defendant answerable where the product is brought to the forum by the plaintiff or some other person. **World–Wide Volkswagen v. Woodson,** 444 U.S. 286 (1980), relying on **Hanson v. Denckla,** 357 U.S. 235 (1958).

iii. Stream of Commerce and "Purposeful Availment"

A state legitimately may assert personal jurisdiction over a non-resident manufacturer or distributor if the non-resident defendant makes efforts to directly or indirectly serve a market and purposefully avails itself of the privilege of conducting activities within a state. Absent such purposeful availment, an out-of-state business cannot be held accountable for the random, fortuitous, or isolated possibility that its products might wind up in a particular market.

- In **World–Wide Volkswagen Corp. v. Woodson,** the Supreme Court concluded that the New York automobile retailer and regional distributor could not be subjected to the jurisdiction of the Oklahoma courts because the defendants had not purposefully availed themselves of the benefits and protections of Oklahoma. In addition, the accident fortuitously had occurred in Oklahoma.

iv. Stream of Commerce and "Purposeful Direction" of Products into the Forum

Some courts currently additionally require that a defendant product manufacturer or distributor not only place its product into the stream of commerce, but that the defendant *purposefully direct* the product to the forum state. Absent such purposeful direction a distant forum may not assert jurisdiction over the non-resident defendant consistent with due process.

- **Leading case authority: Asahi Metal Industry Co. v. Superior Court, 480 U.S. 102 (1987).** The plaintiff Zurcher was injured and his wife killed in a motorcycle accident. Zurcher sued a number of defendants including Cheng Shin, the Taiwanese tire tube manufacturer, in California state court. Cheng Shin filed a cross-complaint against Asahi Metal, the Japanese tire valve manufacturer. Zurcher settled his claims with the defendants. The California court assumed jurisdiction over Cheng Shin's indemnity claim against Asahi. Asahi manufactured its tire valve assemblies in Japan, and sold these to Cheng Shin and others for incorporation into finished tires. Asahi had no offices, agents, or property in California, and it solicited no business nor made any direct sales there. It also did not design or control the distribution system for its valve products. A survey indicated that some of Asahi's valve assemblies wound up in Cheng Shin tires in California; Asahi's president claimed that the company never contemplated that its limited sales of valves to Cheng Shin in Taiwan would subject it to lawsuits in

California. Cheng Shin's manager claimed that Asahi knew that some of its valve assemblies would wind up in the United States and California. The California Supreme Court upheld personal jurisdiction over Asahi based on a stream-of-commerce theory. The United States Supreme Court reversed.

(a) **Lack of majority opinion on stream-of-commerce standards.** No group of Justices formed a majority opinion in *Asahi,* although eight Justices agreed that California's assertion of jurisdiction over Asahi was unreasonable given an assessment of Asahi's minimum contacts with the state, under standards set forth in **World–Wide Volkswagen Corp. v. Woodson,** 444 U.S. 286 (1980).

(b) **Purposeful direction standard and "additional conduct" factors (Justice O'Connor's plurality opinion).** Justice O'Connor, writing for a plurality of four Justices, concluded that Asahi's awareness that its valve assemblies would wind up in California was not sufficient to satisfy minimum contacts jurisprudence. She set forth the purposeful direction test, *supra,* requiring that manufacturers or distributors purposefully direct their products at the forum state. In addition, Justice O'Connor listed kinds of "additional conduct" that would indicate an intent or purpose to serve a market:

   (1) Designing a product in the forum state;

   (2) Advertising in the forum state;

   (3) Establishing channels for providing regular advice to customers in the forum state;

   (4) Marketing the product through a distributor who has agreed to serve as the sales agent in the forum state.

(c) **Rejecting purposeful direction standard and "additional conduct" factors (Justice Brennan's concurrence).** Justice Brennan, writing for four Justices, rejected the "purposeful direction" standard and disagreed that the stream-of-commerce theory required "additional conduct" beyond placing a product in the stream of commerce. "The stream of commerce refers not to unpredictable currents or eddies, but to the regular and anticipated flow of products from manufacture to distribution to retail sale. As long as a participant in this process is aware that the final product is being marketed in the forum State, the possibility of a lawsuit there cannot come as a surprise. . . . Accordingly, most courts and commentators have found that jurisdiction premised on the placement of a product into the stream of commerce is consistent with the Due Process Clause, and have not required a showing of additional conduct."

v. Stream-of-Commerce Theory in a Global Economy: International Dimensions

In contemporary minimum contacts analysis, under expanded *World–Wide Volkswagen* standards, *infra,* courts are to take into consideration the interests of the "several states" in the efficient judicial resolution of disputes. The reasonableness of asserting jurisdiction over a foreign corporate defendant must be assessed in the context of federal interests in its foreign-relations policies. The Supreme Court has cautioned that "Great care and reserve should be exercised when extending our notions of personal jurisdiction into the international field." **Asahi Metal Industry Co. v. Superior Court,** 480 U.S. 102 (1987).

vi. Post-*Asahi* Stream-of-Commerce Applications

Some state and federal courts have adopted Justice O'Connor's "purposeful direction" standard in stream-of-commerce cases after *Asahi;* other courts have followed Justice Brennan in repudiating a stream-of-commerce standard that requires "additional conduct." The Supreme Court revisited the *Asahi* decisions in **J. McIntyre Machinery Ltd. v. Nicastro,** ___ U.S. ___, 131 S.Ct. 2780 (2011).

- **Leading case authority: J. McIntyre Machinery Ltd. v. Nicastro, ___ U.S. ___, 131 S.Ct. 2780 (2011).** The plaintiff Nicastro had four fingers sheared off in a metal-shearing machine accident in New Jersey. The shearing machine was manufactured by J. McIntyre Machinery Ltd. in England, its place of incorporation and operation. McIntyre did not markets its goods in New Jersey or ship them there. A U.S. distributor sold McIntyre's machines in the United States; McIntyre officials attended annual scrap recycling conventions to advertise its machines in various states, but never in New Jersey, and no more than four machines, including the one that injured Nicastro, ended up in

New Jersey. The New Jersey Supreme Court held that New Jersey courts could exercise jurisdiction over McIntyre because the injury occurred in New Jersey and because McIntyre knew or reasonably should have known that its products distributed through a nationwide distribution system might lead to those products being sold in any of the fifty states. Also, McIntyre did not take some reasonable step to prevent distribution of its shearing machine in New Jersey. The Supreme Court reversed, holding that the New Jersey Supreme Court's decision and its account of the stream-of-commerce doctrine of jurisdiction were incorrect. In addition, the U.S. Supreme Court indicated that its decision in *Asahi* "may be responsible in part for that court's error regarding the stream of commerce, and this case presents an opportunity to provide greater clarity." The Court held that it was McIntyre's purposeful contacts with New Jersey, and not with the entire United States, that were relevant to the jurisdictional inquiry. Nicastro had failed to establish that McIntyre engaged in conduct purposefully directed at New Jersey.

(a) **Lack of majority opinion on stream of commerce theory.** No group of Justices formed a majority decision. The judgment of the Court was delivered by Justice Kennedy, joined by Justices Roberts, Scalia, and Thomas. Justices Breyer and Alito concurred in the judgment, writing a separate opinion. Justices Ginsburg, Kagan, and Sotomayor dissented.

(b) **Shift of emphasis from fairness to sovereignty of state to exercise jurisdiction**. In revisiting the Court's stream of commerce jurisprudence stemming from **World–Wide Volkswagen Corp.**, the Court noted that the principal inquiry in cases of this sort is whether the defendant's activities manifest an intention to submit to the power of a sovereign. Thus, the Court's precedents make it clear that it is the defendant's actions, not its expectations, that empower a state's courts to subject a defendant to judgment. The Court indicated that jurisdiction is, in the first instance, a question of authority rather than fairness. Whether a judicial judgment is lawful depends on whether the sovereign has authority to render it.

(c) **Rejection of Justice Brennan's foreseeability approach in** *Asahi*. The plurality noted that Justice Brennan's opinion in

Asahi rejected Justice O'Connor's purposeful direction and substantial connection test, discarding the central concept of sovereign authority in favor of considerations of fairness and foreseeability. Justice Brennan's **Asahi** opinion made foreseeability the touchstone of jurisdiction. The plurality held that Justice's Brennan's **Asahi** opinion was inconsistent with the premises of lawful judicial power.

(d) Questioning of Justice O'Connor's opinion in *Asahi*. The McIntyre plurality decision also called into question Justice O'Connor's opinion in **Asahi**, noting that it would not resolve many difficult questions of jurisdiction that arise in particular cases. "The defendant's conduct and the economic realities of the market the defendant seeks to serve will differ across cases, and judicial exposition will, in common-law fashion, clarify the contours of the principle."

(e) Justices Breyer and Alito concurrence. Justices Breyer and Alito concurred in the judgment, opining that the case could be decided based on the Court's own precedents, and that the facts in this case were an unsuitable vehicle for making broad pronouncements that refashioned basic jurisdictional rules.

(f) Justice Ginsburg dissent. Joined by Justices Kagan and Sotomayor, Justice Ginsburg dissented, opining that the plurality opinion was setting the clock back to older jurisdictional principles that would allow a manufacturer to avoid jurisdiction by having independent distributors market the product. In addition, "none of the Court's decisions tug against the judgment made by the New Jersey Supreme Court."

d. Redefined Minimum Contacts Jurisprudence

In 1980, the Supreme Court synthesized existing minimum contacts jurisprudence as it had developed in the state and lower federal courts in the thirty-five years after *International Shoe*. **In World–Wide Volkswagen Corp. v. Woodson,** the Supreme Court reaffirmed some old standards and set forth some new factors to be evaluated in considering the due process dimension of state assertions of personal jurisdiction.

i. Redefined Concept of Minimum Contacts (Purposes)

Minimum contacts jurisprudence "performs two related, but distinguishable functions":

- The protection of states as co-equal sovereigns (the so-called "sovereignty branch" of jurisdictional analysis);

- The protection of defendants against the burdens of litigating in a distant or inconvenient forum (the so-called "convenience branch" of jurisdictional analysis, also described in terms of "reasonableness" or "fairness").

ii. Additional Factors in Determining the Reasonableness of a Forum's Assertion of Personal Jurisdiction over a Non-Resident Defendant ("Affiliating Circumstances" Test)

- the burden on the defendant;

- the forum state's interest in adjudicating the dispute;

- the plaintiff's interest in obtaining convenient and effective relief;

- the interstate judicial system's interest in obtaining the most efficient resolution of controversies;

- the shared interests of the several states in furthering fundamental substantive social policies.

iii. Minimum Contacts Analysis Post-*World–Wide Volkswagen*

(a) **Two-part analysis.** The Supreme Court reiterated that an appropriate personal jurisdiction analysis requires a two-part inquiry, evaluating the assertion of jurisdiction against both a state's long-arm statute as well as independent constitutional due process requirements.

(b) **Sovereignty concerns.** The reasonableness of an assertion of personal jurisdiction over a non-resident defendant must be assessed "in the context of our federal system of government," taking into account the sovereignty and interests of sister states [the "sovereignty branch"];

(c) **Affiliating circumstances.** Minimum contacts now must be evaluated against an expanded set of factors and affiliating circumstances, indicated *supra.*

iv. Significance of *World–Wide Volkswagen's* Reformulated Minimum Contacts Jurisprudence

The Court's decision in **World–Wide Volkswagen** broadened minimum contacts jurisprudence by shifting analysis to other considerations beyond the defendant's contacts with the forum. On the other hand, the Court's definition of a foreseeability standard narrowed application of jurisdiction possibilities.

5. Property as a Basis for Jurisdiction, Revisited

State assertions of jurisdiction based on the presence of property in the state, except for purely *in rem* actions, must be assessed against *International Shoe* minimum contacts due process jurisprudence. Assertions of jurisdiction either *in personam* and *quasi in rem* must be measured by the same due process requirements.

a. Leading Case Authority: *Shaffer v. Heitner*, 433 U.S. 186 (1977)

A shareholder owning one share of stock in Greyhound Corp. brought a shareholder's derivative lawsuit against the Greyhound Corporation, its subsidiary Greyhound Lines, as well as various officers and directors of the company. Greyhound was incorporated in Delaware and had its principal place of business in Arizona. The individual defendants were scattered around the country; none lived in Delaware. The lawsuit was instituted under a Delaware sequestration order, by placing "stop transfer" orders on the company's books. None of the certificates representing the seized property were located in Delaware. The Delaware Chancery Court and Delaware Supreme Court upheld personal jurisdiction based on the sequestration statute. The Supreme Court reversed, holding that the sequestration of the defendant's property alone was insufficient to confer jurisdiction in absence of other minimum contacts with Delaware.

i. Supreme Court's Holdings in *Shaffer v. Heitner*

The Court held that "all state assertions of state-court jurisdiction must be evaluated according to the standards set forth in *International Shoe* and its progeny."

(a) Rationales for extending the same test of "fair play and substantial justice" to *quasi in rem* actions

- The phrase embodying *in rem* jurisdiction ("judicial jurisdiction over a thing") is a customary elliptical way of referring to jurisdiction over the interests of a person in a thing. "This recognition leads to the conclusion that in order to justify an exercise of jurisdiction *in rem*, the basis for that jurisdiction must be sufficient to justify exercising 'jurisdiction over the interests of persons in a thing.' The standard for determining whether an exercise of jurisdiction over the interests of persons is consistent with the Due Process Clause is the minimum-contacts standard elucidated in *International Shoe*."

- ". . . jurisdiction based solely on the presence of property satisfies the demands of due process . . . , but it is not decisive. . . . The fiction that an assertion of jurisdiction over property is anything but an assertion of jurisdiction over the owner of the property supports an ancient form without substantial modern justification. Its continued acceptance would serve only to allow state-court jurisdiction that is fundamentally unfair to the defendant."

(b) Justice Brennan's dissent in *Shaffer v. Heitner*. Justice Brennan dissented in *Shaffer* on two primary grounds. First, he argued that the Court's majority opinion amounted to an advisory opinion because the plaintiffs did not know that the Supreme Court was going to change long-standing doctrine and apply the *International Shoe* minimum contacts to its shareholder suit. Therefore, the plaintiffs never made a record of the defendant's contacts with Delaware. Second, Justice Brennan argued that sufficient minimum contacts existed to support an assertion of personal jurisdiction over the defendant under due process standards.

b. Impact of *Shaffer v. Heitner* on *In Rem* and *Quasi In Rem* Jurisdiction

Shaffer v. Heitner does not affect actions purely in a court's *in rem* jurisdiction, but it has affected *quasi in rem* actions. The rules relating to assertions of jurisdiction based on the presence of property within the state are as follows:

i. Pure *In Rem* Actions

Jurisdiction is permissible where the presence of property within the state is itself the subject matter of the dispute—whether tangible or intangible—and is directly related to the plaintiff's cause of action. The presence of property within the state supplies the contacts necessary and sufficient to permit the exercise of jurisdiction.

- **Admiralty actions.** Pure *in rem* jurisdiction continues to be upheld in cases in the federal court's admiralty jurisdiction, derived from **Article III § 2.**

ii. *Quasi In Rem* Actions

Jurisdiction is permissible where the plaintiff's claims relate to rights and obligations arising out of the defendant's ownership of property within the state, provided the defendant meets *International Shoe* minimum contacts requirements. An example would be a plaintiff's claim for tortious injury suffered on the defendant's property. In these kinds of actions, however, jurisdiction typically will be provided for under modern state long-arm statutes; but assertions of jurisdiction are nonetheless subject to minimum contacts jurisprudence. The *Shaffer* rule has its greatest impact on assertions of *quasi in rem* jurisdiction where the plaintiff's cause of action is completely unrelated to the defendant's property.

■ EXAMPLES AND ANALYSIS

Debtor obligations (intangible property). The existence of a debtor obligation no longer can provide a basis for an assertion of *quasi in rem* jurisdiction. The *Shaffer* decision was intended to modify the Supreme Court's holding in **Harris v. Balk,** 198 U.S. 215 (1905), where a North Carolina debtor's traveling debt provided the valid *quasi in rem* jurisdiction of a Maryland state court. In that case, the Supreme Court had declared that "the obligation of the debtor to pay his debt clings to him and accompanies him wherever he goes." In *Shaffer,* the Supreme Court declared that under its new rule requiring evaluation of due process concerns, "[f]or the type of *quasi in rem* action typified by **Harris v. Balk** . . . , accepting the proposed analysis would result in significant change."

Insurance contracts (intangible obligations). A court's attachment of an insurance policy to effect *quasi in rem* jurisdiction is unconstitutional in absence of other defendant's minimum contacts with the forum state. (**Rush v. Savchuk,** 444 U.S. 320 (1980)). The Supreme Court's holding in *Savchuk* effectively overruled a contrary New York state post-*Shaffer* decision holding that an insurance company's contractual obligation was a debt subject to attachment and sufficient to support the state court's assertion of personal jurisdiction. **Seider v. Roth,** 17 N.Y.2d 111, 216 N.E.2d 312 (1966).

6. Personal Service Within the Jurisdiction: Transient or "Tag" Jurisdiction

A state legitimately may assert jurisdiction over a non-resident defendant who is temporarily within the state and who is served with process while within the state. This is called "transient" or "tag" jurisdiction and is one of the oldest forms of assertion of personal jurisdiction. The Supreme Court in **Pennoyer v. Neff** recognized transient jurisdiction as one of the legitimate bases for a state's assertion of personal jurisdiction. The Supreme Court's decision in **Shaffer v. Heitner** has not modified the doctrine of transient jurisdiction. Assertions of transient jurisdiction, then, do not have to satisfy *International Shoe* minimum contacts jurisprudence. **Burnham v. Superior Court,** 495 U.S. 604 (1990).

a. Leading Case Authority: Burnham v. Superior Court, 495 U.S. 604 (1990)

Mrs. Burnham, a California resident, brought a suit for divorce against her husband, a New Jersey resident. While Mr. Burnham was in southern California on business, he visited his children in the San Francisco area for a weekend. Upon returning the children to his wife, he was served in California with process in the divorce. He returned to New Jersey and then subsequently made a special appearance in California to quash service and contest the state's assertion of jurisdiction. The California courts upheld personal jurisdiction and the Supreme Court affirmed on appeal.

b. Justice Scalia's Majority Opinion in *Burnham*

(1) Among the most firmly established principles of personal jurisdiction in the American tradition is that the courts of a State have jurisdiction over non-residents who are physically present in the State.

(2) This principle may be traced to Roman origins, has antecedents in English common law practice, and was shared by American courts in 1868 at the time of the adoption of the Fourteenth Amendment. The principle historically was so well-settled that it went largely unlitigated in American courts. The American jurisdictional practice is not only merely old; it is continuing.

(3) Jurisdiction based on physical presence alone constitutes due process because it is one of the continuing traditions of our legal system

that define the due process standard of "traditional notions of fair play and substantial justice."

(4) "Contemporary notions of due process" applicable to personal jurisdiction are the enduring "*traditional* notions of fair play and substantial justice," of which transitory jurisdiction is such a traditional notion.

c. Justice Brennan's Concurring Opinion in *Burnham*

Justice Brennan, for four Justices, argued that even assertions of transient jurisdiction must be subject to minimum contacts jurisprudence after **Shaffer v. Heitner.** Justice Brennan failed to command a majority of Justices in this view, however.

- The critical insight of **Shaffer v. Heitner** is that all rules of jurisdiction, even ancient ones, must satisfy contemporary notions of due process. While the Court's holding in *Shaffer* may have been limited to assertions of *quasi in rem* jurisdiction, the mode of analysis required in jurisdictional inquiries was not limited to such actions.

7. Modern Consent: Choice-of-Forum and Choice-of-Law Clauses

Assertions of transient jurisdiction continue to fall outside the *International Shoe* due process requirements. So too do assertions of jurisdiction based on contractual agreements to litigate in a particular forum.

a. Choice-of-Forum Clauses

The presence of a choice-of-forum clause ("forum selection clause") is binding on the parties. Such agreements are presumably valid and courts will enforce such agreements unless it would be unreasonable. **M/S Bremen v. Zapata Off–Shore Co.,** 407 U.S. 1 (1972), **Carnival Cruise Lines, Inc. v. Shute,** 499 U.S. 585 (1991).

i. Leading Case Authorities: M/S Bremen v. Zapata Off–Shore Co., 407 U.S. 1 (1972) and Carnival Cruise Lines, Inc. v. Shute, 499 U.S. 585 (1991)

In *The Bremen,* the Supreme Court upheld a forum selection clause designating the London Court of Justice as the forum for resolving any disputes arising out of a commercial towing contract between an American corporation and a German corporation for the towing of a drilling rig from Louisiana to Italy. The rig was damaged in a storm off Florida and towed to Tampa; the Houston corporation sued in federal court in Florida but the court dismissed the case, upholding the forum selection clause. Finding the forum selection clause to be a freely negotiated agreement between sophisticated businessmen, the Court noted that "[t]he expansion of American business and industry will hardly be encouraged if, notwithstanding solemn contracts, we insist on a parochial concept that all disputes must be resolved under our laws and in our courts . . . We cannot have trade and commerce in world markets and international waters exclusively on our terms, governed by our laws, and resolved in our courts."

ii. Expansion to Consumer Contracts

In **Carnival Cruise Lines, Inc. v. Shute,** 499 U.S. 585 (1991), the Supreme Court reaffirmed the *Bremen* decision and upheld a forum selection clause in a passenger ticket designating Florida courts as the forum for resolution of any disputes arising out of passage on the cruise line's ships. Mrs. Shute, a resident of Washington State, was injured on a Carnival Cruise Line ship while vacationing off the coast of Mexico and she attempted to sue the cruise line in Washington State. Although the state courts and the Ninth Circuit upheld this assertion of jurisdiction under the specific "but for" jurisdictional test, the Supreme Court invalidated Washington state jurisdiction based on the forum selection clause. In *Carnival Cruise Lines,* the Supreme Court expanded the enforceability of forum selection clauses to consumer contracts.

iii. Rationales Supporting Enforceability of Contractual Forum Selection Clauses

- Forum selection clauses eliminate confusion over the place of litigation and thereby reduce satellite litigation and costs related to litigating jurisdictional motions;

- Forum selection clauses conserve judicial resources that otherwise might be devoted to resolving such motions;

- Forum selection clauses enhance international trade and commerce by ensuring in advance of litigation the forum for resolution of disputes;

- Forum selection clauses benefit consumers by lowering costs through limiting the possible places in which litigation may occur.

iv. *The Bremen* and *Carnival Cruise Lines* "Reasonableness Factors" for Evaluating the Reasonableness of a Forum Selection Clause

- Whether the forum selection clause was freely negotiated and unaffected by fraud, undue influence, or overweening bargaining power;

- The business sophistication of the bargaining parties;

- The serious difficulty or inconvenience of the contractual forum to one or both of the parties;

- whether in light of commercial realities and expanding international trade the forum selection clause should control;

- whether enforcement of the forum selection clause would contravene a strong public policy of the state in which the suit was brought.

- In addition to these factors, lower federal courts have evaluated the reasonableness of forum selection clauses applying other factors such as: (1) mistake, (2) injustice, (3) lack of consideration, (4) unconscionability, (5) availability of remedies in the chosen forum, (6) governing law, (7) conduct of the parties, (8) identity of the law governing construction of the contract, (9) place of execution of the contract, (10) place where the transactions have been or are about to be performed, (11) location of the parties, (12) convenience of the prospective witnesses, and (13) accessibility of evidence.

v. Criticisms of Forum Selection Clauses in the Consumer Context

The *Carnival Cruise Lines* decision has been heavily criticized for extending the "presumptively valid" forum selection clause doctrine to consumer cases. Critics suggest that the Court's majority failed to recognize problems relating to fine-print unconscionable provisions in consumer contracts such as the Carnival Cruise Lines passenger ticket.

vi. Lack of Notice of the Forum Selection Provision

In general failure to read a contract or lack of knowledge of a contract provision will not render a contract provision unenforceable, and courts construing forum selection clauses have applied these contract doctrines to forum selection clauses. However, an issue left open by the *Carnival Cruise* decision is whether complete lack of notice of such a provision—such as the failure to receive the passenger ticket with the forum selection clause—renders the provision unenforceable.

b. Choice-of-Law Provisions

A contractual provision specifying that a forum's law is to apply to disputes arising from a contract may support an assertion of that forum's jurisdiction, even in the absence of a forum selection clause.

i. Leading Case Authority: Burger King Corp. v. Rudzewicz, 471 U.S. 462 (1985)

In *Burger King,* a Michigan franchisee entered into a franchise agreement with Burger King, a Florida corporation which contained a provision specifying that Florida law would apply to any disputes arising under the franchise agreement. The agreement did not contain a forum selection clause, however. The Supreme Court upheld Florida's assertion of jurisdiction over the Michigan franchisee, in part based on the choice-of-law provision.

(a) **Purposeful availment theory.** A choice-of-law provision supports the minimum contacts standard of "purposeful availment" in that a defendant may be said to have purposefully availed itself of the benefits and protections of the forum's law by entering into a contract that expressly provides that those laws will govern contract disputes.

(b) **Foreseeability theory.** A choice-of-law provision supports the minimum contacts foreseeability theory in that a defendant who has contractually agreed in advance to the application of a particular forum's laws to any disputes arising from the contract cannot be surprised that the defendant will be answerable to disputes in that forum.

8. Jurisdictional Reach of Federal Courts

The jurisdictional reach of federal courts over defendants located both inside and outside a federal judicial district are governed by a complicated, interrelated set of Federal Rules provisions as well as independent federal statutory authority. The primary authority for federal assertions of personal jurisdiction are located in **Rule 4 (Summons).** In general, the jurisdictional reach of the federal courts is no broader than the states in which those district courts sit. However, some federal statutes explicitly provide for nationwide jurisdiction over defendants in particular actions and in such instances the defendants need only have "minimum contacts" with the United States. Moreover, in 1993 **Rule 4** was amended to permit federal court to assert jurisdiction over defendants in claims arising under federal law when the defendant would not otherwise be subject to a state's personal jurisdiction.

a. Actions *In Personam*

i. Defendants Located within the Federal Judicial District

Defendants who are located within the federal judicial district are subject to the federal court's personal jurisdiction by reference to the state's jurisdiction statutes and interpretations of those statutes. **Rule 4(k)(1)(A)** provides that the federal court may establish jurisdiction over a defendant who could be subjected to the jurisdiction of a court of general jurisdiction in the state in which the district court is located.

(a) **Additional authority. Rule 4(e)(1)** provides that service may be effected in any judicial district pursuant to the law of the state in which the district court is located . . . for the service of a summons upon the defendant in an action brought in the courts of general jurisdiction of the state.

ii. Defendants Located within 100 Miles of the Federal District Courthouse: The 100–Mile Bulge Rule

Federal courts may exert personal jurisdiction over certain defendants who may be located within 100 miles of the federal courthouse, but are in another state. **Rule 4(k)(1)(B).** This "100–mile bulge" rule applies only to third parties who are impleaded in an action under **Rule 14,** or parties who are needed for a just adjudication under **Rule 19.**

iii. Federal Interpleader Actions

Federal courts may assert personal jurisdiction over any parties who are joined in a federal interpleader action under **28 U.S.C. § 1335 Rule 4(k)(1)(C).**

iv. Federal Statutory Authorization

Federal courts may assert personal jurisdiction over defendants in a federal action wherever they may be located, if authorized by federal statute. In federal actions brought against federal officials and United States agencies, **28 U.S.C. § 1391(e)** authorizes service by certified mail anywhere in the country. Similarly, the **Federal Interpleader Act, 28 U.S.C. § 2361,** also authorizes nationwide service of process. The federal court's personal jurisdictional reach, then, extends fully and the defendants need only have minimum contacts with the United States.

v. Federal Question Cases Involving Foreign Defendants Not Subject to Any State's Law

Federal courts may assert personal jurisdiction over defendants if the action involves a federal question and the defendant is not otherwise subject to the jurisdiction of the courts of general jurisdiction of any state. **Rule 4(k)(2).**

(a) Import of Rule 4(k)(2). The Advisory Committee on Civil Rules added this particular provision as part of its 1993 amendment of **Rule 4** which is intended to solve the problem identified by the Supreme Court in **Omni Capital International Ltd. v. Wolff & Co.,** 484 U.S. 97 (1987). In that case an American plaintiff sued in Louisiana under the federal Commodities Exchange Act and attempted to implead two English defendants. The Commodities Act does not contain a provision for nationwide service of process. The defendants had minimum contacts with the United States, but not with Louisiana. The Supreme Court invalidated personal jurisdiction over the foreign defendants because the Court would not authorize nationwide jurisdiction where Congress had not done so by statute, and the state's jurisdictional reach would not subject the defendants to state court jurisdiction.

(b) Limitations of new Rule 4(k)(2). This provision applies only to claims in the federal court's federal question jurisdiction, not to cases in the courts' diversity jurisdiction. The defendant also must have minimum contacts with the United States as a whole, but insufficient minimum contacts to support a state's assertion of personal jurisdiction. In general, **Rule 4(k)(2)** is most likely to apply to foreign defendants.

b. Actions *In Rem*

Federal courts may assert jurisdiction in actions *in rem* in two different manners:

- By seizure of property as provided by federal statute. **Rule 4(n)(1).**

- By seizure of a defendant's assets found within the district under the circumstances and manner as provided by the law of the state in which the district court is located. **Rule 4(n)(2). (Note:** It may be possible to challenge such seizures under the principles of **Shaffer v. Heitner.**)

9. Challenging Assertions of Personal Jurisdiction

Parties may challenge a court's assertion of personal jurisdiction either directly in a first action, or—in limited circumstances—collaterally in a subsequent action to enforce a prior judgment.

a. Direct Attacks on Personal Jurisdiction

i. State Court Litigation: Special Appearance

Challenges to a state court's assertion of personal jurisdiction typically are brought on a motion to dismiss or a motion to quash service of process. A non-resident defendant may appear specially to contest the sole issue of the court's personal jurisdiction without thereby subjecting to the court's jurisdiction. However, if the defendant appears and presents other claims or defenses, the defendant will be deemed to have made a general appearance and to have consented to the court's jurisdiction.

ii. Federal Court Litigation: How Asserted—Rules 12(b)(2), 12(g), and 12(h)(1)

(a) **Prior to responsive pleading.** A federal defendant may challenge the court's personal jurisdiction in a motion prior to the filing of a responsive pleading such as the defendant's answer, **Rule 12(b)(2),** although if the objection is not raised by motion it may still be made in the defendant's answer (or an amendment permitted by **Rule 15(a)). Rule 12(h).**

(b) **Consolidation of motions.** If the defendant intends to raise a number of grounds for dismissal, the jurisdictional challenge must be consolidated with all other **Rule 12** grounds, and such objections cannot be raised *seriatim.* **Rule 12(g).**

(c) **Waivable defect.** Finally, the failure to object to a federal court's assertion of personal jurisdiction is a waivable defect, and it will be lost if it is not asserted in a timely fashion. **Rule 12(h)(1).**

iii. Burdens of Proof on Motions to Dismiss for Lack of Personal Jurisdiction

The mode of determination of a motion to dismiss for lack of personal jurisdiction is left to the trial court, which may either consider the motion on written affidavits, or request a fuller evidentiary hearing. The trial court also may defer consideration of the jurisdictional issue until trial, in which instance the jurisdictional inquiry may become intertwined with the merits of the litigation. In general, however, pretrial determinations of personal jurisdiction are not supposed to involve a consideration of the litigation's merits. **Data Disc, Inc. v. Systems Technology Assoc. Inc.,** 557 F.2d 1280 (9th Cir. 1977).

(a) **Determinations on written affidavits.** The plaintiff must make only a prima facie showing of jurisdictional facts in order to avoid dismissal.

(b) **Evidentiary hearings—issues of credibility or disputed facts.** If the written materials present issues of credibility or disputed facts, the court has the discretion to hold an evidentiary hearing to resolve these questions. The plaintiff will then be put to full proof and must establish jurisdictional facts by a preponderance of the evidence.

(c) **Discovery of jurisdictional facts—failure to comply.** A defendant who contests jurisdiction and then fails to cooperate with court-ordered discovery to obtain jurisdictional facts may suffer a sanction of a presumptive finding of jurisdiction. (**Insurance Corp. of Ireland, Ltd. v. Compagnie des Bauxites de Guinee,** 456 U.S. 694 (1982).)

b. Default

A defendant who believes that a court lacks jurisdiction may elect not to appear at all either to contest jurisdiction or to defend on the merits of the lawsuit. A defendant who fails to appear will suffer a default judgment. In federal courts, defaults are governed by **Rule 55.** A defaulting defendant may subsequently "collaterally" attack the court's jurisdiction if the plaintiff seeks to enforce that judgment in another forum. The defendant may argue that the second court does not have to give full faith and credit to a judgment rendered by a court that lacked personal jurisdiction over the defendant.

c. Direct Appeal

If a defendant makes a special appearance and litigates the jurisdictional issue and loses, the defendant may renew the issue on direct appeal to a higher court.

d. Collateral Attacks on Personal Jurisdiction

Defendants may or may not be able to collaterally attack a first court's judgment on personal jurisdiction grounds in a subsequent enforcement action in another forum.

i. Defendants Not Specially Appearing—Default

A defendant who does not specially appear to challenge jurisdiction and who suffers a default may collaterally attack the first court's judgment in a subsequent enforcement action.

ii. Defendants Defending on Merits without Raising Objections to Personal Jurisdiction—Waiver

A defendant who appears generally in an action, defends on the merits, and loses, may not subsequently collaterally attack the first court's personal jurisdiction in a subsequent enforcement action. The failure to timely raise an objection to the first court's jurisdiction constitutes a waiver of any objections to personal jurisdiction.

■ CHAPTER REVIEW CHECKLIST

Almost all civil procedure exams will contain a problem or problems relating to personal jurisdiction. You should read the fact pattern carefully first, attempting to identify those personal jurisdiction cases which the facts presented in the problem most closely resemble. Many personal jurisdiction problems fall into categories of cases—for example, "stream-of-commerce" cases. You should be able to quickly identify the "type" of personal jurisdiction problem presented by the facts.

You also should preliminarily examine the facts to determine whether there are any time bars or other limits to pursuing a challenge based on personal jurisdiction. If there are not, you should then determine whether the facts require an analysis of *International Shoe* minimum contacts jurisprudence, or fall outside those constitutional requirements. If the problem will require an analysis of affiliating circumstances, you should make a quick list of the pertinent "jurisdictional facts."

The following is a checklist of questions to guide your response to a personal jurisdiction exam problem.

1. **Do the facts present any time bars or other limitations to asserting a challenge to personal jurisdiction?**

   - Is the case in state or federal court? If the case is in federal court, is the defendant raising the challenge to personal jurisdiction properly in a **Rule 12(b)(2)** motion?

   - Is the challenge being raised in the defendant's answer or an amended pleading? Is the challenge being raised at trial, on direct appeal, or in a collateral attack?

      — If the defendant is collaterally attacking personal jurisdiction in another court in an enforcement proceeding, did the defendant appear and contest jurisdiction in the first proceeding?

      — Is the second forum required to give full faith and credit to the first court's jurisdictional determination?

   - Has the defendant waived the right to challenge personal jurisdiction because the defendant has not consolidated all **Rule 12** motions pursuant to **Rule 12(g)?**

   - Has the defendant waived the right to challenge personal jurisdiction in any other manner, such as failing to cooperate in court-ordered discovery relating to jurisdictional facts?

2. **Do the facts present a case in federal or state court? If the case is in federal court, for personal jurisdiction purposes, ask:**

   - What is the basis of the federal court action? Is the action *in personam* or *in rem?*

   - Who are the defendants and where are they located? Are they located in the federal district? If the defendants include third parties, are they located within 100 miles of the federal district? Are the defendants foreign nationals?

   - Is there a federal statute providing for nationwide service of process?

   - Is the case within the court's federal question jurisdiction?

3. **Do the facts present a personal jurisdiction problem not subject to due process constraints? Ask:**

   - Has the defendant expressly or impliedly consented to the court's jurisdiction?

   - Is the defendant present or domiciled in the state?

   - Does the defendant have property within the state that is the basis for the plaintiff's claim and is directly related to the claim (*i.e.*, does the problem involve a pure *in rem* assertion of jurisdiction?). Is the case within the federal court's *in rem* admiralty jurisdiction?

   - Do the facts include a forum selection clause or a choice-of-law clause?

     — If the basis for jurisdiction is a forum selection or choice-of-law clause, you must assess whether such provisions are "reasonable" under the ***Bremen*** and ***Carnival Cruise Lines*** standards (*see supra*).

   - Has the defendant been served with process while within the state? Is there a basis for transient or "tag" jurisdiction?

4. **If none of the above bases for jurisdiction exist, you must then conduct a two-part jurisdictional analysis. Ask:**

   - Is there a state long-arm statute? [statutory basis for jurisdiction]

   - Would assertion of personal jurisdiction comport with constitutional due process requirements? [constitutional basis for jurisdiction]

5. **Evaluating assertions of jurisdiction under state long-arm statutes: Ask:**

   - What type long-arm statute is involved? Is it a California-style long-arm statute or an Illinois-style long-arm statute?

   - How do state courts interpret their own long-arm statute? If the long-arm statute is a textually-detailed statute, do the state courts nonetheless interpret it to apply to the full extent of the Constitution?

— If the state long-arm statute is a textually detailed Illinois-style statute, do the facts presented in the problem come within the provisions of the long-arm statute? Come within the state's interpretation of the applicability or reach of its provisions?

— If the state long-arm statute is a California-style statute, how fully have state courts expanded their constitutional reach? (Note that California-style long-arm statutes typically only require an analysis of minimum contacts jurisprudence.)

• Does the state long-arm statute provide a basis either for assertion of specific jurisdiction or general jurisdiction over non-resident defendants?

6. Evaluating constitutional due process requirements—minimum contacts jurisprudence:

• The test for assessing a defendant's minimum contacts with a forum cannot be simply mechanical or quantitative. It depends on the quality and nature of the defendant's activities in relation to the fair and orderly administration of the laws.

Assess:

• Whether the defendant has sufficient minimum contacts with the forum such that the maintenance of the lawsuit does not offend traditional notions of fair play and substantial justice;

• The burdens or inconvenience to the defendant of defending in a distant forum;

• The forum state's interest in obtaining convenient and effective relief;

• the interstate judicial system's interest in obtaining the most efficient resolution of controversies;

• the shared interest of the several states in furthering fundamental substantive social policies.

Also Assess:

• Does the defendant conduct systematic and continuous business activities within the forum state?

- Has the defendant purposefully availed itself of the benefits and protections of the forum state?

- Does the case involve a "stream-of-commerce" problem? If so:

- Are the defendant's activities covered by the state's long-arm statute? In tortious liability cases, is the defendant being asked to answer for actions occurring outside the state but causing consequences or effects inside the state?

- How did the product causing injury arrive in the forum state? Did the defendant purposefully direct its product to the forum state? Did a consumer bring the product to the state? Did some third party bring the product into the state? ["unilateral activity" test]

- Are foreign (international) corporations involved that might implicate foreign policy concerns?

- Could the defendant reasonably have foreseen being haled into court as a result of its activities in the forum state?

7. **Unavailing Theories:**

- Do the facts implicate either a *"center of gravity"* theory of personal jurisdiction or a *First Amendment defense?* "Center of gravity" arguments will not support minimum contacts requirements; First Amendment objections will not defeat otherwise proper assertions of jurisdiction.

II

Choosing the Forum: Subject Matter Jurisdiction

■ **ANALYSIS**

■ CHAPTER OVERVIEW

- This chapter concerns the subject matter jurisdiction of courts, and restraints on judicial power imposed by venue requirements. The focus primarily is on federal subject matter and venue requirements.

- *Subject matter jurisdiction* refers to courts' authority to adjudicate the subject or types of claims presented for relief.

- State courts are courts of *general jurisdiction* and are able to adjudicate all types of claims, subject only to certain monetary limitations among different courts.

- Federal courts are courts of *limited jurisdiction.* There are two primary bases for federal court subject matter jurisdiction: *diversity jurisdiction* and *federal question* jurisdiction.

- A court must have valid subject matter jurisdiction in order to render an enforceable, binding judgment. Objections to subject matter jurisdiction may not be waived and challenges to subject matter jurisdiction may be asserted at any time. Parties may not consent to a court's subject matter jurisdiction.

- For cases to be within federal diversity jurisdiction, all plaintiffs to the lawsuit must be citizens of different states than all the defendants. In addition, the lawsuit must involve more than $75,000 in relief.

- For cases to be within federal question jurisdiction, the cases or controversy must arise under the Constitution, laws, or treaties of the United States.

- In order to assume valid federal subject matter jurisdiction, the federal grounds for relief must appear in the plaintiff's complaint. The court may not look to the defendant's answer to supply the federal jurisdictional base. This is called the "well-pleaded complaint" rule.

- A plaintiff may not assign a contract right or otherwise join parties in order to collusively create federal court jurisdiction. There is no corollary rule prohibiting collusive destruction of federal court jurisdiction.

- A state court case may be *removed* to federal court by the defendant if a basis for federal jurisdiction exists. If there is no basis for federal jurisdiction then the federal court will *remand* the case back to state court.

- A federal court may exercise jurisdiction over state claims and additional parties which lack an independent federal jurisdictional basis if the additional claims and parties form part of the same case or controversy under Article III. The federal *supplemental jurisdiction* statute permits the joinder of pendent claims and pendent parties.

- Federal court supplemental jurisdiction is *discretionary* and federal courts need not hear state-based claims or join additional parties under the statute.

- Venue indicates the most appropriate or convenient forum or courtroom for the parties and witnesses in which a lawsuit should be heard. Venue in federal courts is governed by statutes that designate the appropriate venue for different kinds of cases and parties.

- Improper venue is a waivable defect.

- Improper venue may be cured by transfer to a more appropriate venue, where such transfer is for the convenience of the parties and witnesses and in the interests of justice. A venue transfer may be accomplished either on a motion of the parties, or by the court.

- A court also may dismiss a case altogether if the forum is not convenient. This type of dismissal is called a *forum non conveniens* dismissal. Usually federal courts will dismiss on *forum non conveniens* grounds only if there is an alternative forum in which the litigants may sue, but this is not absolutely necessary.

A. THE CONCEPT OF SUBJECT MATTER JURISDICTION: COMPETENCY OF THE COURTS

1. Subject Matter Jurisdiction Defined

Subject matter jurisdiction concerns the power or authority of a court to adjudicate the case or controversy presented to the court for resolution. It is also referred to as the court's competency to hear a particular case. The subject matter of both state and federal courts is based in the Constitution and statutes setting forth the subject matter jurisdiction of the courts.

a. Requisite for Binding Judgment

Subject matter jurisdiction must exist in order for a court to render a binding, enforceable judgment. Sister states are under no obligation to give full faith and credit to state court judgments rendered by courts lacking subject matter jurisdiction. Courts have the power to make a binding determination of their own jurisdiction and sister courts must give *res judicata* effect to that determination. Thus, if a state court fully and fairly considers the question of subject matter jurisdiction and determines that it validly exists, then a sister state must give full faith and credit to that jurisdictional determination.

b. Not Waivable

Subject matter either exists or it does not exist. Subject matter jurisdiction is not a waivable defect and parties may not consent to a court's subject matter jurisdiction. Challenges to subject matter jurisdiction may be raised at any point during legal proceedings. A trial court or appellate court may question its own subject matter jurisdiction even if the issue is not raised by the parties. **Capron v. Van Noorden**, 6 U.S. (2 Cranch) 126 (1804).

c. Jurisdiction to Determine Jurisdiction

Courts have jurisdiction to determine the validity of their own subject matter jurisdiction.

2. Distinguished from Personal or Territorial Jurisdiction

Personal or territorial jurisdiction refers to the territorial sovereign authority of the courts over *parties* to the litigation. It is specifically concerned with the authority of courts to render binding judgments against defendants not found within the borders of the state. Unlike subject matter jurisdiction, personal jurisdiction is a waivable defect. Personal jurisdiction chiefly is governed by statutory provisions, subject to constitutional due process constraints. *See* Chapter I.

3. Distinguished from *Justiciability* or *Prudential Doctrines*

Courts must have subject matter jurisdiction to render an enforceable judgment binding the parties. In addition, the parties must present the court with a "justiciable" case or controversy. Justiciability refers to the competence or feasibility of a court hearing a particular matter—some disputes present "non-justiciable" controversies that a court may decline to adjudicate even though the court has subject matter jurisdiction to render a decision. The doctrines relating to justiciability usually are studied in either constitutional law or federal courts. Justiciability doctrines include:

a. Standing

Parties must have the legal right to challenge the conduct of others in a court of law. They must directly have suffered an actual injury for which the law provides a remedy.

b. Real Case or Controversy

The dispute among the parties must present a "real case or controversy." The litigants may not present an abstract, pretended, or hypothetical case to the court. The parties must have real or adverse interests, and not have collusively created the lawsuit in order to obtain relief from the court.

c. Advisory Opinions

Courts will not render advisory opinions, that is ask the court to indicate how it might rule on a legal question that the court has not previously considered in past litigation. The bar against seeking an advisory opinion is related to the "real case and controversy" requirement.

d. Political Questions

Courts will not resolve disputes raising issues that are committed to the exclusive jurisdiction of the legislature. For many years, courts would not decide questions relating to legislative districting because these questions were "political questions" best determined by the federal and state legislature. This, however, is no longer embraced by the political question doctrine and contemporary courts do adjudicate legislative redistricting disputes.

e. Ripeness and Mootness

The doctrine of "ripeness" is a doctrine of judicial self-restraint in which a court makes the discretionary determination not to decide a claim or issue "in advance of the necessity of deciding it." A related doctrine of self-restraint is "mootness," where a court declines to decide a case which, because of the passage of time or events, no longer presents a real case or controversy to the court. In such instances, the court's decision essentially would be an advisory opinion that would have no practical effects upon a controversy that once existed.

B. SUBJECT MATTER JURISDICTION IN STATE COURTS

1. General Jurisdiction

States courts are courts of general jurisdiction. This mean that state courts have the ability to adjudicate any and all types of cases as provided in state statutory provisions. State codes provide for the substantive rights of action in state courts. In many states, the jurisdiction of various courts is established by amount-in-controversy requirements, so disputes involving small claims will be assigned to municipal or small claims courts.

2. Specialized Jurisdiction

Many states have created courts with specialized subject matter jurisdiction, such as courts handling criminal matters, probate matters, domestic relations issues, etc. Some specialized courts also may have their subject matter jurisdiction circumscribed by amount-in-controversy requirements, such as small claims courts.

3. Federalism Concerns

The existence of a federal system raises issues about the power of state courts to adjudicate claims based on the laws of other states. In addition, the dual court system raises issues about the ability of state courts to adjudicate claims within the federal courts' jurisdiction.

a. Interstate Subject Matter Jurisdiction

Courts of one state may open its courts—and may be constitutionally required to do so—to claims based on the laws of another state.

- **Example.** Under the **Full Faith and Credit Clause, Article IV § 1,** a Wisconsin state court is required to open its courts to a claim under the Illinois wrongful-death statute, in absence of a valid Wisconsin policy against adjudicating such an action. **Hughes v. Fetter,** 341 U.S. 609 (1951). "[A state] . . . cannot escape [its] constitutional obligation to enforce the rights and duties validly created under the laws of other states by the simple device of removing jurisdiction from courts otherwise competent."

b. Limitation on Intersystem Claim Assertion: Valid State Policies

Although a state must open its courts to claims based on other state's laws, a state may apply its own law to vindicate policies related to the conduct of litigation in its own courts, such as statutes of limitation or tolling provisions.

- **Examples. Statutes of limitations.** A state may apply its own limitations period to bar a claim that would otherwise be timely in the forum in which the claim arose. **Wells v. Simonds Abrasive Co.,** 345 U.S. 514 (1953). Conversely a state may apply its own longer statute of limitations even though the claim would have been time-barred in the forum in which the claim arose. **Sun Oil Co. v. Wortman,** 486 U.S. 717 (1988).

c. Concurrent Federal-State Subject Matter Jurisdiction

State courts are competent to adjudicate claims within the federal courts' subject matter jurisdiction, except for claims with the federal court's exclusive jurisdiction. However, even where some claims are within the federal court's exclusive jurisdiction, in some instances both federal and state courts can exercise concurrent jurisdiction over the same conduct.

i. Presumption of Concurrent Subject Matter Jurisdiction—Rationale

". . . [U]nder our federal system, the States possess sovereignty concurrent with that of the federal Government, subject only to limitations imposed by the Supremacy Clause. Under this system of dual sovereignty, we have consistently held that the state courts have inherent authority, and are presumptively competent, to adjudicate claims arising under the laws of the United States." **Tafflin v. Levitt,** 493 U.S. 455 (1990).

ii. Presumption of Concurrent Jurisdiction Rebutted—Exclusive Federal Jurisdiction

"This deeply rooted presumption in favor of concurrent state court jurisdiction is, of course, rebutted if Congress affirmatively ousts the state courts of the jurisdiction over a particular claim. . . . Thus, the presumption of concurrent jurisdiction can be rebutted by an explicit statutory directive, by unmistakable implication from legislative history, or by a clear incompatibility between state-court jurisdiction and federal interests." **Tafflin v. Levitt,** 493 U.S. 455 (1990).

iii. Exclusive Federal Subject Matter Jurisdiction with Concurrent State Jurisdiction over Common Law Claims

Although federal courts may have been conferred exclusive jurisdiction over some subject matters by statute, this does not prohibit a state court from having concurrent jurisdiction over state law claims related to the federal claim within the federal court's exclusive jurisdiction.

■ ILLUSTRATIONS

Federal patent, copyright, and trademark jurisdiction, 28 U.S.C. § 1338. Federal courts have exclusive jurisdiction to hear cases arising under the federal copyright, patent, and trademark laws. However, state courts may exercise concurrent jurisdiction to adjudicate state claims based on unfair competition, or breach of contract of the license or patent.

Federal antitrust jurisdiction. Actions arising under the federal antitrust laws have been construed to be within the exclusive jurisdiction of the federal courts. However, litigants may also pursue relief under parallel, concurrent state antitrust provisions.

Federal securities jurisdiction, 15 U.S.C. § 78a. Federal courts have exclusive jurisdiction over claims arising under the federal **Securities Exchange Act of 1934** for fraudulent or manipulative conduct relating to the purchase or sale of securities. However, litigants also may pursue relief under state court under common law fraud theories for the same conduct.

iv. Requirement that State Courts Hear Federal Claims— Supremacy Clause Concerns

The refusal of a state court to hear a claim arising under federal law may violate the Supremacy Clause.

■ ILLUSTRATION

A student brought a civil rights action in Florida state court under the federal civil rights statute, **42 U.S.C. § 1983**, against a local school board for violations of federal constitutional rights resulting from a car search and suspension from school. The Florida state court dismissed the lawsuit holding that sovereign immunity remained in effect with respect to federal civil rights actions brought in state court (although the state had waived its sovereign immunity for state court tort actions). The Supreme Court held that there was no valid or neutral excuse for the Florida court's refusal to hear the **§ 1983** action, and the court's decision to decline jurisdiction "whether presented in terms of direct disagreement with substantive federal law or simple refusal to take cognizance of the federal cause of action, flatly violates the Supremacy Clause." **Howlett v. Rose,** 496 U.S. 356 (1990).

C. SUBJECT MATTER JURISDICTION IN FEDERAL COURTS

1. Introductory Notes

The subject matter jurisdiction of federal courts is based both in constitutional and statutory provisions. Unresolved questions remain whether the statutory reach of federal court jurisdiction is as broad as the federal courts' constitutional reach.

a. Constitutional Bases for Federal Court Jurisdiction

i. Congressional Power to Create Federal Courts

Article III § 1 of the Constitution vests judicial power "in one supreme Court, and in such inferior Courts as the Congress may from time to time ordain and establish." Thus, the Constitution provides only for the United States Supreme Court. All other federal courts have been created by Congress, which has the power to create new federal courts and to determine the size of the federal judiciary. In theory, Congress could reduce the size of the federal judiciary and eliminate federal courts if it chose to do so.

ii. Constitutional Scope of Federal Court Jurisdiction

Article III § 2 sets forth the scope of federal court subject matter jurisdiction, providing for both federal question jurisdiction and federal diversity jurisdiction (*see* detailed discussion infra).

b. Congressional Statutory Bases for Federal Court Jurisdiction

Congress must by statute provide federal subject matter jurisdiction to the inferior federal courts that it creates. Until 1875, Congress only provided the federal courts with diversity jurisdiction. In 1875 Congress statutorily enacted federal question jurisdiction (current **28 U.S.C. § 1331**). Congress also has statutorily provided for federal court removal jurisdiction (**28 U.S.C. § 1441** *et seq.*) and, in 1990, for federal court supplemental jurisdiction (**28 U.S.C. § 1367**).

c. Limited Jurisdiction

Unlike state courts, federal courts are viewed as courts of limited jurisdiction, able to hear only cases within their constitutional or statutory authority. Federal courts may not hear any and all cases presented to them.

2. Federal Diversity Jurisdiction

Federal court diversity jurisdiction is based both in the Constitution and federal statutory provisions. Congress could, if it wished, abolish this federal statutory basis for federal court jurisdiction and has, from time to time, modified the diversity statute. For example, Congress has increased the jurisdictional amount-in-controversy requirement from its original level of $500 to its present level of more than $75,000. There is a long-standing and continuing debate whether federal courts ought to continue to have diversity jurisdiction and to hear diversity cases.

a. Constitutional Basis for Diversity Jurisdiction

Article I § 2 of the Constitution provides that "[t]he judicial power [of the United States] shall extend . . . to controversies . . . between Citizens of different States, . . . and between a State, or Citizens thereof and foreign States, Citizens or Subjects."

b. Congressional Statutory Basis for Diversity Jurisdiction

28 U.S.C. § 1332 provides that district courts shall have original jurisdiction of all civil actions where the matter in controversy exceeds the sum or value of $75,000 (exclusive of interests and costs) and the controversy is among the four following possibilities of diverse parties:

(1) citizens of different states;

(2) citizens of a state and citizens or subjects of a foreign state;

(3) citizens of different states and in which citizens or subjects of a foreign state are additional parties;

(4) a foreign state (as plaintiff) and citizens of a state or different states.

c. Rationales for Diversity Jurisdiction

The rationales underlying diversity subject matter jurisdiction in federal court have been controversial and continue to play a part in the ongoing debate whether to eliminate or modify federal diversity jurisdiction. At least two rationales have been suggested in support of diversity jurisdiction.

i. Protection Against Local Bias or Prejudice

"However true the fact may be, that the tribunals of the states will administer justice as impartially as those of the nation, . . . it is not less true that the constitution itself either entertains apprehensions on this subject, or views with such indulgence the possible fears and apprehensions of suitors, that it has established national tribunals for the decision of controversies . . . between citizens of different states." **Bank of the United States v. Deveaux,** 9 U.S. (Cranch) 61, 3 L.Ed. 38 (1809) (Justice Marshall). Empirical data relating to actual or perceived bias against out-of-state defendants is sparse and inconclusive.

ii. Security to Investors in Nineteenth Century

An additional rationale offered in support of the federal court's diversity jurisdiction was to afford protection and security to investors in the southern and western portions of the country during the early nineteenth century.

d. Policy Debate over Continued Existence of Federal Diversity Jurisdiction

Critics of diversity jurisdiction have advanced a number of arguments for eliminating or curtailing the federal court's diversity jurisdiction. Among these arguments:

i. Docket Congestion

Diversity cases cause congestion in federal courts with essentially state-based claims. Diversity cases account for approximately twenty-five percent of the federal docket.

ii. Applicable Law

In federal diversity cases, federal courts must apply state substantive law pursuant to *Erie* doctrine (*see infra*). This is thought to waste federal judges' time and efforts, and a task better accomplished by state judges presumably more knowledgeable about substantive state law.

iii. Interference with State Autonomy

For federal courts to decide cases arising under state law is an encroachment on state autonomy.

iv. Development of State Law

The diversion of cases based in state substantive claims impairs the ability of state courts to develop their own law. States courts are sometimes viewed as "laboratories" for legal change and common law development.

v. Disincentive for State Court Reform

Federal diversity jurisdiction creates a disincentive for state court reform when, by virtue of diversity jurisdiction, litigants may avoid state courts altogether.

e. Judicial Exceptions to Federal Diversity Jurisdiction

In some areas of law, federal courts have carved out long-standing exceptions to their own diversity jurisdiction. The two most prominent exceptions to permissible federal diversity jurisdiction concern probate matters and cases involving domestic relations.

i. Historical Basis for the Probate and Domestic Relations Exceptions

The original diversity statute granted federal courts jurisdiction over "suits of a civil nature in law or equity." Cases involving probate and domestic relations matters were not viewed as "suits of a civil nature" but rather claims that would have been heard in the ecclesiastical courts. Hence, federal courts early construed the federal diversity jurisdiction as not including probate and domestic relations matters.

ii. The Probate Exception

In general, federal courts will not hear cases involving issues relating to wills, trusts, estates, and other probate matters, leaving the resolution of these issues to state courts. However, the probate exception is not absolute and federal courts may hear cases where there is diversity between an estate's legal representative (an executor or administrator) and the estate. **28 U.S.C. § 1332(c)(2).** The federal courts may determine the rights of claimants, but the federal court cannot order the distribution of estate property or execute on its judgment.

iii.   The Domestic Relations Exception

Federal courts will not hear cases relating to domestic relations issues such as divorce, alimony, property claims, maintenance, support, or child custody. The domestic relations exception is a long-standing judicially created exception to a federal court's diversity jurisdiction, which the Supreme Court reaffirmed in **Ankenbrandt v. Richards,** 504 U.S. 689 (1992). However, similar to the probate exception, the "domestic relations" exception is itself riddled with numerous exceptions provided in various federal statutes regulating spousal property and child custody rights. In addition, federal courts may assume diversity jurisdiction over family disputes based on claims other than divorce, alimony, and child custody.

- **Example.** A Louisiana plaintiff brought suit in federal court against her former husband and his companion, citizens of Illinois, based on tort law claims of child abuse. The Supreme Court upheld the federal district court's jurisdiction over this diversity action. **Ankenbrandt v. Richards,** 504 U.S. 689 (1992).

f.   Complete Diversity Rule

- **Leading case authority—Strawbridge v. Curtiss, 7 U.S. (3 Cranch) 267, 2 L. Ed. 435 (1806).** Federal diversity jurisdiction requires "complete" diversity between all plaintiffs and all defendants: that is, no plaintiff may be *from* the same state as any defendant (but plaintiffs and defendants need not be diverse among themselves). The complete diversity rule has a long lineage. Although Chief Justice John Marshall announced the complete-diversity rule in 1806, historical research has suggested that the Chief Justice may not have intended it as a constitutional limitation on federal court jurisdiction.

- **Exceptions to the complete diversity rule.** Congress may provide for exceptions to the complete diversity rule by statute, or the federal courts may create such exceptions by judicial construction.

- **Example. "minimal diversity requirement" in the federal interpleader statute, 28 U.S.C. § 1335.** The federal interpleader statute provides that district courts shall have original jurisdiction over interpleader actions if there are two or more adverse claimants of diverse citizenship. This statute is an example of a statutory provision requiring only "minimal diversity" among parties to a dispute; not all plaintiffs must be diverse from all defendants.

- **Class action litigation.** Historically, in class action litigation, only the named class representatives must be completely diverse from the defendants; not every class member must be diverse from every defendant. **Supreme Tribe of Ben Hur v. Cauble,** 255 U.S. 356 (1921). The rationale for this exception is that it would be virtually impossible to establish a diversity class action in absence of the exception, since it would be impossible to create a class of completely diverse plaintiffs and defendants. In 2005, Congress enacted **28 U.S.C. § 1332(d),** which created special diversity jurisdiction for class actions. Class actions require only minimal diversity between adversarial parties. **28 U.S.C. § 1332(d)(2).**

g. Establishing Citizenship for the Purposes of the Diversity Rule

The basic diversity statute requires diversity of citizenship, but **28 U.S.C. § 1332** does not itself define "citizenship" for the purposes of diversity jurisdiction. In contrast, federal venue provisions are based on a party's residence. **28 U.S.C. § 1391** *et seq.,* discussed *infra.* In general, citizenship for diversity purposes is the same as a party's domicile—as distinguished from a party's residence. Moreover, diversity of citizenship requirements depend on party status.

(1) Citizenship Defined

Citizenship for federal diversity purposes means a party's domicile. A domicile is a person's fixed place of abode, coupled with an intention to remain. A person has only one domicile; a person may have more than one residence.

■ EXAMPLES AND ANALYSIS

Leading case authority—Mas v. Perry, 489 F.2d 1396 (5th Cir. 1974).
Mr. Mas, a citizen of France, and his wife attended graduate school

at Louisiana State for approximately two years and then moved to Illinois. While in Baton Rouge their landlord Perry observed them through two-way mirrors. The Mases sued in Louisiana federal court for damages. The court found two different bases of diversity jurisdiction for each spouse in the litigation. The court held that federal diversity jurisdiction existed between Mr. Mas, a citizen of France, and Perry, a citizen of Louisiana. The court further determined that valid diversity jurisdiction existed between Mrs. Mas and Perry because at the time of her marriage she was a domiciliary of Mississippi, and that this domicile was unaffected by her time spent in Louisiana because she lacked the requisite intention to remain there (even though she also had no intention of returning to Mississippi). The court further held that Mrs. Mas's citizenship was not changed by her marriage to a foreign alien (and therefore she was not putatively a citizen of France).

---

(2) Citizenship Requirements Based on Status

The federal diversity statute has different requirements based on the status of the parties to the dispute. Some the diversity requirements have been created through judicial construction of the diversity statute:

(a) **Individuals.** As indicated above, an individual's citizenship for diversity purposes is determined by the individual's legal domicile.

(b) **Aliens, 28 U.S.C. § 1332(a).** Since 1988, aliens who are lawfully admitted to the United States with permanent resident status are deemed to be citizens of the state in which the alien is domiciled.

(c) **"Stateless" persons.** An alien who cannot satisfy either foreign state or American citizenship and is therefore a "stateless" person cannot meet federal diversity requirements. **Blair Holdings Corp. v. Rubinstein,** 133 F.Supp. 496 (S.D.N.Y. 1955).

(d) **Foreign states, 28 U.S.C. § 1332(a)(4) and 28 U.S.C. § 1603(a).** Foreign states, for the purpose of diversity jurisdiction, are defined with reference to United States Code provisions relating to the sovereign immunity of foreign states. A foreign state is defined to include political subdivisions or agencies or instrumentalities of a foreign state.

(e) Corporations, 28 U.S.C. § 1332(c)(1). A corporation has "dual citizenship" and is deemed a citizen of:

- any state which has incorporated the corporation; *and*

- the state where the corporation has its principal place of business.

A corporation may have only one "principal place of business." Historically, the problem of identifying a corporation's principal place of business gave rise to difficult interpretation problems, and federal appellate courts have applied at least three different tests:

- **"Nerve center" test.** This test looked to the locus of corporate decision-making authority and overall control.

- **"Corporate activities" or "operating assets" test.** This test looked to the location of a corporation's production or service activities.

- **"Total activity" test.** This test considered all circumstances surrounding a corporation's business activities, balancing all relevant factors.

In 2010, the Supreme Court ended the confusion over the test for corporate citizenship, holding that a corporation was a citizen of the location of its corporate headquarters. The Court rejected all other lower court tests to determine corporate citizenship. **The Hertz Corp. v. Friend,** 559 U.S. 77 (2010).

(f) Insurance companies, 28 U.S.C. § 1332(c)(1). In direct actions against insurance companies where the insured party is not joined as a defendant, the insurance company is deemed a citizen of:

- the state in which the insured person is a citizen;

- the state which has incorporated the insurance company;

- the state where the insurance company has its principal place of business.

(g) Partnerships. A partnership is not viewed as a single legal entity for the purpose of diversity citizenship and therefore the citizenship of each and every member of both general and limited partnerships must be considered in establishing diversity jurisdiction. **Carden v. Arkoma Assoc.,** 494 U.S. 185 (1990).

(h) Unincorporated associations. Unincorporated associations (such as labor unions) are not treated as single entities for the purpose of diversity jurisdiction and therefore the citizenship of each member must be considered in establishing diversity jurisdiction. **United Steel Workers of America v. R.H. Bouligny, Inc.,** 382 U.S. 145 (1965).

(i) Legal representatives of decedents' estates, 28 U.S.C. § 1332(c)(2). The legal representative of a decedent's estate is deemed to be a citizen of the same state as the decedent for diversity purposes. Congress added this provision to the diversity statute in 1988 in order to remedy a problem that had developed concerning the collusive appointment of estate executors and administrators for the purpose of creating or destroying diversity jurisdiction. **Mecom v. Fitzsimmons Drilling Co.,** 284 U.S. 183 (1931); **Vaughan v. Southern Ry. Co.,** 542 F.2d 641 (4th Cir. 1976).

(j) Legal representatives of infants or incompetents, 28 U.S.C. § 1332(c)(2). The legal representative of an infant or incompetent is deemed to be a citizen only of the same state as the infant or incompetent. Congress added this provision to the diversity statute in 1988.

(k) Fictitious "Doe" defendants, 28 U.S.C. § 1441(b). Congress amended the federal removal statute to provide that the citizenship of defendants sued under fictitious names (so-called "Doe" defendants) shall be disregarded for the purposes of removal jurisdiction. The designation of Doe defendants, then, may not be used in order to destroy federal court diversity jurisdiction.

h. Collusive Creation or Destruction of Diversity Jurisdiction

Some plaintiffs may prefer to have their case heard in federal court and may attempt, through various devices, to "create" federal court jurisdiction in order to gain access to the federal courts. Conversely, some plaintiffs may wish to have their cases heard exclusively in state courts, and may attempt to frustrate a defendant's right to remove the case to federal court by ensuring that the litigation involves no basis for federal jurisdiction. There is a federal statutory prohibition against manipulative efforts to create federal diversity jurisdiction. However, that statute does not per se prohibit efforts to destroy federal diversity jurisdiction. Some federal courts will nonetheless repudiate blatant manipulative efforts to evade or destroy federal diversity jurisdiction.

i. Collusive Joinder, 28 U.S.C. § 1359

Federal courts may not assume jurisdiction in two instances:

(a) Collusive joinder. Federal courts may not assume jurisdiction when parties to the litigation have collusively or improperly joined other parties for the purpose of creating federal jurisdiction, or,

(b) Assignment of rights. When parties to the litigation have improperly assigned a right (usually a contract right) for the purpose of creating federal jurisdiction.

■ ILLUSTRATION

Leading case authority: Kramer v. Caribbean Mills, Inc., 394 U.S. 823 (1969). In *Kramer,* a Panamanian corporation assigned its contract with a Haitian corporation to a Texas lawyer, Kramer, for $1 consideration. In a separate agreement Kramer reassigned ninety-five percent of any recovery he might receive back to the Panamanian corporation. Kramer sued the Haitian corporation based on diversity jurisdiction. The Supreme Court upheld dismissal of the action because the contract had been assigned for the improper and collusive purpose of creating diversity jurisdiction where none otherwise would exist. The Court held that, "If federal jurisdiction could be created by assignments of this kind, which are easy to arrange and involve few disadvantages for the assignor, then a vast quantity of ordinary contract and tort litigation could be channeled into the federal courts at the will of the parties. Such 'manufacture of federal jurisdiction' was the very thing which Congress intended to prevent when it enacted § 1359 and its predecessors."

ii. Manipulative Defeat of Diversity Jurisdiction

In **Rose v. Giamatti,** 721 F.Supp. 906 (S.D. Ohio 1989), the baseball player Pete Rose, an Ohio citizen, sued in Ohio state court seeking a temporary restraining order against a pending disciplinary action. In order to circumvent removal to federal court, Rose named Bart Giamatti (the baseball commissioner and a citizen of New York), Major League Baseball (an unincorporated association) and the Cincinnati Reds as defendants. When Giamatti sought removal to federal court, Rose argued there was no diversity because the Cincinnati Reds and Major League Baseball were citizens of Ohio. The district court upheld the removal, holding that its diversity jurisdiction would be based on the citizenship of the real parties in interest to the lawsuit and that the Cincinnati Reds and Major League Baseball were only nominal parties to the dispute—whose citizenship could be disregarded for diversity purposes.

i. The Amount-In-Controversy Requirement: 28 U.S.C. § 1332(a)

In order to satisfy federal diversity jurisdiction requirements, the controversy also must "exceed the sum of value of $75,000, exclusive of interests or costs."

(a) Rationale and Historical Background

The basic purpose of the amount-in-controversy requirement is to keep small-claim cases out of federal courts. Congress periodically raises the requisite amount-in-controversy requirement which has the effect of reducing the federal court's diversity caseload. In 1988 Congress amended the diversity statute to raise the amount-in-controversy from $10,000 to $50,000; it was raised to $75,000 in 1996. Until 1980, federal question cases brought under **28 U.S.C. § 1331** also had to satisfy an amount-in-controversy requirement. Congress eliminated this requirement for almost all federal question cases, in large measure because of the difficulty of ascertaining the value of some federally-created rights. In a few instances, certain federal statutes still expressly require pleading of an amount-in-controversy (such as actions brought under the Consumer Product Safety Act).

(b) The Good Faith Pleading and "Legal Certainty" Standard

The amount claimed by a plaintiff in the plaintiff's complaint controls "if the claim is apparently made in good faith. It must appear *to a legal certainty* that the claim is really for less than the jurisdictional amount to justify a dismissal." **St. Paul Mercury Indemnity Co. v. Red Cab Co.,** 303 U.S. 283 (1938).

- **The legal certainty standard and injunctive or declaratory relief.** Determining the amount-in-controversy in cases seeking injunctive or declaratory relief presents special problems because of the intangible rights involved. Federal courts have developed different approaches for determining whether the requirement is met:

    - **Value to the plaintiff (plaintiff's point of view).** The amount-in-controversy requirement is assessed with reference to the right that the plaintiff seeks to protect measured by the extent of the impairment to be prevented by the injunction.

■ ILLUSTRATION

A travel agency sought an injunction against a former employee to enjoin use of confidential agency information in soliciting future tour clients, pleading damages that were "in an amount which is not presently ascertainable, but which is believed to exceed the sum of $50,000." The complaint also sought punitive damages of "no less than $250,000." Although the agency was not afforded an opportunity to make a proper evidentiary record on the value of its claims, the court could not conclude to a legal certainty that the value of the agency's claims (measured against its potential losses if the injunction was not granted against the former employee) did not exceed the jurisdictional minimum. In addition, the request for punitive damages might provide a basis for satisfying the amount-in-controversy **A.F.A. Tours, Inc. v. Whitchurch,** 937 F.2d 82 (2d Cir. 1991).

- **Viewpoint of the party seeking to invoke the federal court's jurisdiction.** The amount-in-controversy is assessed from the plaintiff's point of view (or valuation) if the plaintiff invokes federal jurisdiction, or from the defendant's point of view if the defendant invokes federal jurisdiction by removing the case to federal court. Some courts will evaluate the cost to a defendant to comply with a proposed injunction and the burden is placed on the defendant to show that the minimum amount is not involved.

- **"Either viewpoint" rule.** The test for determining the amount-in-controversy is the pecuniary result to either party which the judgment would directly produce.

(c) Multiple Parties and Claims: Special Aggregation Problems

Under the Federal Rules of Civil Procedure, plaintiffs may liberally join multiple claims and parties in a single, unified complaint. The presence of multiple claims and parties raises issues as to whether parties' claims may be aggregated to meet the amount-in-controversy requirement. The federal courts have developed the following general rules:

- **Class actions. 28 U.S.C. § 1332(d)** permits the aggregation of class members' claims to satisfy the $5 million amount-in-controversy requirement. This provision overrules **Zahn v. International Paper Co.,** 414 U.S. 291 (1973).

- **Single plaintiff with multiple claims arising from same event.** A single plaintiff may aggregate all related and unrelated claims the plaintiff has against the defendant arising out of the same transaction or occurrence.

■ ILLUSTRATION

A plaintiff sues a defendant for property damage of $30,000 and $55,000 for personal injuries resulting from an auto accident. These two claims may be aggregated to meet the jurisdictional amount.

- **Plaintiff's claim and defendant's counterclaim.** The plaintiff will not be permitted to aggregate its own claims with any amount the defendant asserts in a permissive counterclaim.

■ ILLUSTRATION

A plaintiff asserts a $50,000 property damage claim and the defendant asserts a $25,000 counterclaim. The claim and counterclaim amounts may not be aggregated to meet the jurisdictional minimum. To do so would in effect permit the litigants to consent to the court's subject matter jurisdiction, which is prohibited. If both claims are valid, one will be set off against the other and the plaintiff will only recover $25,000. In addition, looking to the defendant's counterclaim to satisfy the amount-in-controversy requirement would violate the "well-pleaded complaint rule."

- **Compulsory counterclaim exception. In Horton v. Liberty Mutual Insurance Co.,** 367 U.S. 348 (1961), the Supreme Court in a 5–4 decision involving state worker's compensation claim permitted a defendant's compulsory counterclaim to supply the requisite amount in controversy where the plaintiff's claim failed to met the minimum requirement. Other federal courts have limited the holding in this case.

- **Removal to federal court with compulsory counterclaims in excess of the jurisdictional amount.** Federal courts are split on whether a defendant may remove a case to federal court where the plaintiff has pleaded claims for less than the jurisdictional amount but the defendant has responded with counterclaims in excess of the jurisdictional amount. Some federal courts permit this; others do not.

- **Single plaintiff with unrelated claims not arising out of the same event.** A plaintiff may aggregate two unrelated claims asserted against a single defendant not arising out of the same event.

  - **Example.** A plaintiff sues a defendant on two unrelated claims, a $25,000 breach of contract claim and a $50,000 personal injury claim. These two claims may be aggregated to meet the jurisdictional amount.

- **Single plaintiff suing multiple defendants on separate and distinct claims.** If the plaintiff's claims against each of the defendants is separate and distinct, then aggregation of the plaintiff's claims is not permitted.

- **Example.** A plaintiff sues two defendants for $40,000 each as a result of an auto accident. The plaintiff may not aggregate these claims.

- **Multiple plaintiffs with "separate and distinct" claims.** Two or more plaintiffs with separate and distinct claims cannot aggregate those claims to meet the jurisdictional amount.

  - **Example.** Two plaintiffs are injured in the same auto accident by a defendant. Each has a claim for $40,000. The plaintiffs may not aggregate their claims to meet the amount-in-controversy requirement.

- **Multiple plaintiffs and defendants: The "joint and common interest" rule and "single indivisible harm" rule.** Two or more plaintiffs may aggregate their claims against a defendant if the plaintiffs have a "joint and common interest" in the subject matter of the action, or if they have suffered a "single indivisible harm." Courts will similarly uphold jurisdiction if multiple defendants have a "joint and common interest" in the subject matter of the dispute. This rule applies where the substantive law has determined that the various interests of parties are to be treated as one: for example, joint ownership of property under community property laws or joint ownership of partnership assets.

  - **Example.** Two partners sue to recover a $80,000 debt. Even though each partner technically has only a $40,000 interest in the claim, aggregation of the claims is permitted because each partner has an undivided interest in the partnership assets.

(d) Failure to Meet Amount-In-Controversy Requirements at Trial

If during trial or at judgment the plaintiff does not recover the minimum amount-in-controversy required by the diversity statute, this will not cause a dismissal for lack of subject matter jurisdiction. Instead, the court may impose costs on the plaintiff (and deny costs to the plaintiff). This will be calculated without regard to any setoffs or counterclaim amounts due to the defendant. **28 U.S.C. § 1332(b).** This provision is rarely used in most federal diversity cases.

j. Timing Requirements for Determining Diversity Jurisdiction

The requirements for diversity jurisdiction must exist at the time of the commencement or filing of the action in federal court. Before filing a lawsuit, individuals may change their domicile or corporations may reincorporate in another state in order to create diversity jurisdiction. Any events occurring after the commencement of the suit, such as a change in the parties' domicile, will not effect the court's subject matter jurisdiction. A post-filing change in a party's citizenship cannot serve to cure defects in diversity jurisdiction. **Grupo Dataflux v. Atlas Global Group,** 541 U.S. 567 (2004) (affirming longstanding "time-of-filing" rule).

k. Realignment of Parties—Involuntary Plaintiffs and Defendants

In some rare instances, courts may "realign" the parties to a lawsuit in order to determine whether diversity requirements are satisfied. If a defendant is realigned on the plaintiff's side of the suit, the defendant is called an "involuntary plaintiff"; conversely, a realigned plaintiff is called an "involuntary defendant." The court will realign the parties to correspond to their real interests in the litigation, which may be tied to substantive law.

- **Example. Shareholder derivative lawsuits.** In shareholder derivative lawsuits, the corporation usually is named as a plaintiff along with the shareholder plaintiffs who bring the litigation. However, if the corporation is controlled by persons antagonistic to the interests of the shareholders, then the courts will realign the corporation as a defendant because the ultimate interests of the controlled corporation are adversarial to those of the shareholder-plaintiffs.

l. Diversity Class Actions

Congress enacted the **Class Action Fairness Act** in 2005 which created a new diversity provision especially for class actions. **28 U.S.C. § 1332(d).** In order to establish a diversity class action the proponents must show (1) minimal diversity of citizenship between class members and the opposing party; (2) at least 100 members in the class, and (3) $5 million as an amount-in-controversy. Damages may be aggregated to satisfy this requirement. The provision includes several exceptions and exemptions for local state controversies. Congress simultaneously enacted a new removal provision for state class actions. **28 U.S.C. § 1453**.

3. Federal Question Jurisdiction

Federal question jurisdiction is based on both the Constitution and various statutory provisions. In general, the scope of federal courts' constitutional jurisdiction is viewed as more expansive than the courts' statutory reach, but difficult interpretation problems exist for both constitutional and statutory federal question jurisdiction.

a. Constitutional Federal Question Jurisdiction

Article III § 2 of the Constitution provides for federal question jurisdiction over the following kinds of cases:

i. Cases Arising under the Constitution; The Laws of the United States, and Treaties (discussed below)

ii. Cases Affecting Ambassadors, Other Public Ministers, and Consuls

iii. Cases Involving Admiralty and Maritime Jurisdiction

The federal courts' admiralty jurisdiction extends both to the procedure for adjudicating the case as well as the substantive admiralty law governing the dispute. Admiralty law extends to torts that occur on navigable waters and contracts relating to maritime matters. There are special federal admiralty rules. State law may govern some maritime transactions.

iv. Cases in Which the United States Is a Party

(a) Suits involving the government as a party in federal court. The United States or any of its agencies authorized by statute to bring an action in federal court may bring suit in federal courts. **28 U.S.C. § 1345**. The United States is immune from suit under doctrines of sovereign immunity, unless the United States consents to be sued by statutory provision.

■ ILLUSTRATIONS

The United States government may be sued in federal court for tax refunds (**28 U.S.C. § 1346(a)(1)**); for contract claims of $10,000 or less (**28 U.S.C. § 1346(a)(2)**); or under the **Federal Torts Claim Act** for "a negligent or wrongful act or omission" if a private person "would be liable to a claimant." **28 U.S.C. § 1346(b).**

The United States may be sued in federal court for claims against the United States based on the Constitution, any Act of Congress, or regulation or executive order, or for any express or implied contract with the United States. **28 U.S.C. § 1491(a)(1).** Claims for more than $10,000 must be brought in the United States Claims Court.

(b) **Suits involving the government as a party in state court.** In general, state courts may not exercise jurisdiction over a suit against the United States government, except for actions affecting property on which the United States has a lien. **28 U.S.C. § 2410(a).** The United States may appear, however, as a plaintiff in state courts.

b. Other Constitutional Provisions: Bankruptcy Matters

Article III § 2 of the United States Constitution is the primary constitutional basis for the federal courts' constitutional reach. In addition, **Article I § 8** of the Constitution authorizes Congress to "establish uniform Laws on the subject of Bankruptcies." Congress has created federal bankruptcy courts as adjuncts to federal district courts, to handle bankruptcy matters. Bankruptcy courts, however, are not **Article III** courts and the Supreme Court has held unconstitutional the broad delegation of jurisdiction in bankruptcy matters under **28 U.S.C. § 1471(c). Northern Pipeline Construction Co. v. Marathon Pipeline Co.,** 458 U.S. 50 (1982).

c. Constitutional "Arising Under" Jurisdiction: Interpretation Problems

The "arising under" language in **Article III § 2** is repeated in the statutory enabling legislation, **28 U.S.C. § 1331** first enacted by Congress in 1875. The Supreme Court and federal courts generally have construed the **Article III** provision as conferring more expansive jurisdiction than **§ 1331.** Both the constitutional and statutory bases for federal question jurisdiction have presented difficult interpretation problems for the courts.

i. "Original Ingredient Theory"

This theory posits that federal courts have jurisdiction over a plaintiff's cause of action ("the original cause") if it is based in part on federal law.

(a) **Leading case authority: Osborn v. Bank of the United States, 22 U.S. (9 Wheat) 738, 6 L. Ed. 204 (1824).** By congressional act, Congress created the bank of the United States and authorized it "to sue and be sued . . . in any Circuit Court of the United States." The Bank brought an action in federal court to restrain an Ohio state auditor from collecting a tax it believed was unconstitutional. The court granted an injunction, but the state auditor forcibly entered the bank and took the money he believed the state was owed. The federal court ordered the money returned; the state auditor argued that the federal court lacked subject matter jurisdiction over the case. Chief Justice John Marshall narrowly held that the congressional charter had authorized federal court jurisdiction in all cases in which the bank was a party (and that the action originated in and was sustained by that charter).

(b) **Expansive *Osborn* dicta.** In more expansive dicta, Justice Marshall seemingly suggested that the constitutional **Article III § 2** "arising under" language supported the validity of federal court jurisdiction in all cases to which the bank was a party: "We think, then, that when a question to which the judicial power of the Union is extended by the constitution, forms an ingredient of the original cause, it is in the power of Congress to give the circuit courts jurisdiction of that cause, although other questions of fact or law may be involved."

(c) **Interpretation problems relating to *Osborn* and the "original ingredient" theory.** It is not clear what Justice Marshall meant by his "original ingredient" theory, combined with other statements in the *Osborn* opinion. In general, however, *Osborn* has been interpreted as embodying Justice Marshall's intent that Article III "arising under jurisdiction" be given expansive scope. This was true in the *Osborn* case itself, because the only federal element in the litigation was the fact that the Bank was congressionally chartered; no other federal law was involved in the plaintiff's claim, the defendant's defense, or the evidence in the action.

(d) **Expansive *Osborn* interpretation reaffirmed.** The expansive reach of federal courts under its constitutional "arising under" authority was similarly affirmed in **Bank of the United States v. Planters' Bank of Georgia,** 22 U.S. (9 Wheat) 904, 6 L. Ed. 244 (1824) in which the Supreme Court upheld federal jurisdiction in a suit brought by the Bank in federal court for payment on notes issued by a state bank.

(e) ***Osborn* and congressionally-chartered entities.** The Supreme Court reaffirmed the narrow *Osborn* holding relating to congressionally-chartered entities 168 years after *Osborn.* In **American Red Cross v. S.G.,** 505 U.S. 247 (1992), the Court held that the "sue or be sued" language in the American Red Cross's congressional charter was a grant of federal court subject matter jurisdiction "separate and independent" from jurisdiction based on **28 U.S.C. § 1331.** There are hundreds of associations and entities that are congressionally chartered with "sue or be sued" in the federal courts language.

ii. Other Expansive Constitutional Theories of "Arising Under" Jurisdiction (Extensions of the *Osborn* Theory)

The most extreme view of *Osborn* is that there is federal question jurisdiction whenever there is a potential federal question in the case. Justice Frankfurter expressed this view in his dissent in **Textile Workers Union v. Lincoln Mills,** 353 U.S. 448 (1957), suggesting that such an interpretation of *Osborn* would authorize federal court jurisdiction "whenever there exists in the background some federal proposition that might be challenged, despite the remoteness of the likelihood of actual presentation of such a federal question."

(a) **Federal labor relations law.** In *Lincoln Mills,* the Supreme Court, taking an expansive view of *Osborn,* interpreted the **Federal Labor Relations Act** as authorizing federal courts to develop a federal common law of labor relations. **Section 301** of the **Taft Hartley Act** gave the district courts jurisdiction of actions involving labor contracts affecting interstate commerce. The Supreme Court held this provision as implicitly also giving federal courts the power to create a federal substantive law governing such contracts, and that actions based on that law "arose under federal law" in the traditional sense.

(b) Foreign Sovereign Immunities Act. This act provides federal court jurisdiction for actions involving foreign sovereigns as well as the substantive law governing the scope of their sovereign immunity from suit under international law. In **Verlinden B.V. v. Central Bank of Nigeria,** 461 U.S. 480 (1983), an action between a Dutch corporation and the government bank of Nigeria, the Supreme Court upheld exercise of federal jurisdiction under an expansive constitutional theory.

d. Statutory Bases for Federal Court Jurisdiction

The general federal question jurisdiction of the federal courts is provided for in **28 U.S.C. § 1331.** In addition, numerous federal statutes also provide for "special federal question" jurisdiction.

i. Special Federal Question Jurisdiction; Concurrent and Exclusive Jurisdiction

Special federal question jurisdiction simply means original jurisdiction conferred on the federal district courts by some provision other than the general statute **28 U.S.C. § 1331.**

- **Examples.** Federal statutes provide for original jurisdiction of the federal courts over actions involving commerce and antitrust regulations (**28 U.S.C. § 1337**); patents, copyright, and trademarks (**28 U.S.C. § 1338**); civil rights and elective franchise (**28 U.S.C. § 1343**). There are many other such statutory provisions. State courts may exercise concurrent jurisdiction over the same subject matters unless the federal jurisdictional statute explicitly indicates that the federal courts are to exercise exclusive jurisdiction. If the federal statute provides for exclusive federal court jurisdiction, the matter may only be heard in federal court.

ii. Statutory "Arising under" Jurisdiction: 28 U.S.C. § 1331

The general federal question jurisdictional statute provides that federal courts shall have original jurisdiction of all civil actions "arising under the Constitution, laws, or treaties of the United States." Although the statute repeats the language of **Article III,** federal courts have interpreted the scope of statutory federal question jurisdiction as narrower than the federal court's constitutional reach. **T.B. Harms Co. v. Eliscu,** 339 F.2d 823 (2d Cir. 1964) (rejecting Justice Marshall's broad "original ingredient" standard for the statutory jurisdictional grant in **28 U.S.C. § 1331**).

The general requirements for asserting statutory federal question jurisdiction are as follows:

(a) **Plaintiff's claim must rest on federal law: Express rights of action.** The plaintiff's cause of action must be expressly conferred by the Constitution, a federal statute, or a treaty provision.

- **Justice Holmes's "creation test."** Justice Holmes defined the standard for statutory "arising under" jurisdiction: "[a] suit arises under the law that creates the cause of action." **American Well Works Co. v. Layne & Bowler Co.,** 241 U.S. 257 (1916).

- **State actions involving the construction or interpretation of federal law: Smith v. Kansas City Title & Trust Co.,** 255 U.S. 180 (1921). A shareholder brought suit against a Missouri trust company to enjoin the company from investing in federal bonds as a violation of state laws relating to the purchase of securities and the *ultra vires* actions of corporate officers. The plaintiff argued that the congressional act authorizing the issuance of the bonds was unconstitutional. The Supreme Court held that the action "arose under" federal law (even though the action was state-created): "The general rule is that where it appears from the bill or statement of the plaintiff that the right to relief depends upon the construction of application of the Constitution or laws of the United States, and that such federal claim is not merely colorable, and rests upon a reasonable foundation, the District Court has jurisdiction."

■ EXAMPLES AND ANALYSIS

Patent jurisdiction: T.B. Harms v. Eliscu, 339 F.2d 823 (2d Cir. 1964). Judge Friendly, applying Justice Holmes's "creation test," held that an action brought in federal court to determine whether to enforce or rescind a copyright assignment did not "arise" under the federal copyright jurisdiction of federal courts. Resolution of this lawsuit involved application of state-based contract principles and would not require any interpretation of the Copyright Act or any construction of federal law.

Moore v. Chesapeake & Ohio Ry. Co., 291 U.S. 205 (1934). A plaintiff brought an action under the Kentucky Employer's Liability Act, alleging his injury was due to the defendant's failure to comply with the Federal Safety Appliance Act. The plaintiff's action was state-created. Although the plaintiff implicated a federal regulatory statute, the Supreme Court refused to find federal "arising under" jurisdiction: "a suit brought under the state statute which defines liability to employees who are injured while engaged in interstate commerce, and brings within the purview of the statute a breach of duty imposed by the federal statute, should [not] be regarded as a suit arising under the laws of the United States and cognizable in the federal court in absence of diversity of citizenship."

Current vitality of the *Smith* and *Moore* decisions. A five-Justice majority of the Supreme Court has suggested that it may be possible to reconcile the seemingly conflicting decisions in *Smith* and *Moore* by focusing on the nature of the federal interest involved in each case. **Merrell Dow Pharmaceuticals Inc. v. Thompson,** 478 U.S. 804 (1986). Hence, a federal interest was paramount in the *Smith* case because the litigation turned on the constitutionality of a federal statute. In *Moore,* however, the litigation essentially involved a state tort action which incidentally involved whether a federal standard had been violated as an element of the state tort. The federal interest in *Moore,* then, was slight. Four dissenting Justices, however, argued that the results in *Smith* and *Moore* were irreconcilable; that the *Moore* decision had long been "in a state of desuetude," was "moribund," had not "survived the test of time," and ought to be overruled. The dissenters thought the *Smith* decision articulated the better result and that the decision's "continuing vitality . . . is beyond challenge."

(b) **Plaintiff's claim must rest on federal law: Implied rights of action.** Alternatively, the plaintiff's action must be implied from a constitutional provision or federal statute creating a benefit or duty in the plaintiff's favor. If the plaintiff's claim is based on an implied right, the plaintiff must show that Congress intended to supply a private right of action in federal court to an injured plaintiff for breach of a federally-created duty. Although implied rights of action were accepted in federal courts in the 1960s and 1970s, implied rights of action currently are disfavored in federal courts.

- **Statutorily-implied rights of action. Cort v. Ash, 422 U.S. 66 (1975).** The Supreme Court has articulated a four-part test to determine whether a private right of action should be implied from a federal statute that does expressly provide for a private remedy:

- Is the plaintiff one of a class for whose especial benefit the statute was enacted? Does the statute create a federal right in favor of the plaintiff?

- Is there any indication of legislative intent, explicit or implicit, either to create such a remedy or to deny one?

- Is it consistent with the underlying purposes of the legislative scheme to imply a remedy for the plaintiff?

- Is the cause of action one traditionally relegated to state law, in an area basically the concern of states, so that it would be inappropriate to infer a cause of action based solely on federal law?

- **Constitutionally-implied rights of action. Bivens v. Six Unknown Named Agents of the Federal Bureau of Narcotics, 403 U.S. 388 (1971).** The Supreme Court held that the Fourth Amendment impliedly provides a right of action against federal agents for damages resulting from illegal searches and seizures. The theory supporting this finding of an implied constitutional right of action is that the Fourth Amendment guarantee against unreasonable searches and seizures would be an empty guarantee in absence of the ability to enforce it.

(c) **Statutory "arising under" jurisdiction revisited: Justice Frankfurter's "litigation-provoking" problem**

- **Leading case authority: Merrell Dow Pharmaceuticals Inc. v. Thompson, 478 U.S. 804 (1986).** In *Merrell Dow*, Scottish and Canadian plaintiffs sued the Merrell Dow company in Ohio state court on six state-based claims to recover for children's birth defects resulting from their mother's ingestion of the drug Bendectin. The plaintiffs stated various claims based in state theories of negligence, breach of warranty, strict liability, fraud and gross negligence. One count included an allegation that the drug had been misbranded in violation of the federal Food, Drug, and Cosmetic Act (FDCA). Merrell Dow removed the case to federal court, which upheld jurisdiction based on the *Smith* decision. The federal district court then dismissed the case on *forum non conveniens* grounds (*see* discussion of removal and *forum non conveniens, infra*). The Sixth Circuit Court of Appeals reversed, holding that the FDCA did not create or imply a private right of action.

  On appeal to the Supreme Court, the parties all agreed that no implied right of action existed under the FDCA. Therefore, the only issue before the Court was whether the federal courts possessed "arising under" jurisdiction because the federal statute was an element of the state claims. The Court characterized the problem as involving what Justice Frankfurter previously called a "litigation-provoking" problem: that is, a case involving *the presence of a federal issue in a state-created cause of action.*

- **Holding: No "arising under" jurisdiction.** The Supreme Court concluded "that a complaint alleging a violation of a federal statute as an element of a state cause of action, when Congress has determined that there should be no private, federal cause of action for the violation, does not state a claim 'arising under the Constitution, laws, or treaties of the United States.'"

- **Justice Brennan's dissent.** Justice Brennan, writing for four Justices, contended that the *Smith* decision was of continuing vitality and controlled to confer federal jurisdiction in this case because the plaintiff's right to relief depended upon a construction of a federal law—the FDCA. In addition, numerous policy reasons supported this result, such as the federal courts' interest in uniformity of decisions pertaining to federal matters; federal expertise in construing federal statutes, and the complexity of the federal legislation.

(d) Post-*Merrell Dow* decisions upholding federal court jurisdiction. In two major post-*Merrell Dow* decisions, the Supreme Court has upheld federal question jurisdiction, reconciling or distinguishing the Court's holdings in *Merrell Dow*.

- **Grable & Sons Metal Prods., Inc. v. Darue, 545 U.S. 308 (2005).** The IRS sold Grable's property in Michigan to satisfy a tax delinquency. The IRS failed to notify Grable of the seizure of the property in the exact manner required by **Title 26 U.S.C. § 6335**, which requires that notice be left at the property owner's usual place of abode or business. Grable brought a quiet title action in state court and Darue, as the new property owner, removed the case to federal court as presenting a federal question concerning application of the federal notice provision. The district court accepted jurisdiction and rendered summary judgment for Darue; the Sixth Circuit Court of Appeal reversed. The Supreme Court granted review to resolve a split on the Circuits concerning application of Merrell Dow. The Supreme Court affirmed the lower federal courts, holding that the national interest in providing a federal forum for tax litigation is sufficiently substantial to support the exercise of federal-question jurisdiction over the disputed issue on removal.

  i. **Restated test for federal question jurisdiction.** The Court held that the test for federal question jurisdiction is: "does a state-law claim necessarily raise a stated federal issue, actually disputed and substantial, which a federal forum may entertain without disturbing any congressionally approved balance of federal and state responsibilities."

  ii. **Merrell Dow not to the contrary.** The Court held that its decision was not contrary to its holdings in *Merrell Dow*, because in that case, after carefully examining the strength of the federal interest at stake and the implications of opening a federal forum, the Court held that federal jurisdiction was unavailable. The Merrell Dow decision needs to be read in its entirety as treating the absence of a federal private right of action as evidence relevant to, but not dispositive of, the sensitive judgments about congressional intent that § 1131 requires.

- **Mims v. Arrow Financial Services, LLC**, ___ U.S. ___, 132 S.Ct. 740 (2012). The plaintiff Mims instituted legal action against Arrow Financial Services in Florida federal district court, invoking federal question jurisdiction, alleging multiple violations of the **Telephone Consumer Protection Act of 1991 (TCPA)**. The district court and Eleventh Circuit dismissed the case for lack of subject matter jurisdiction. The TCPA vested exclusive jurisdiction of private suits in federal court, but also contained language stating that a private person could seek redress for violations of the Act "in an appropriate court of a State," "if [such an action is] otherwise permitted by the laws or rules of [that] State." The Supreme Court held that it could find no convincing reason to read the TCPA's permissive grant of jurisdiction to state courts any barrier to the U.S. district courts' exercise of federal question jurisdiction. The district court retains jurisdiction under **§ 1331** unless the TCPA, expressly or by fair implication, excludes federal court jurisdiction. Thus, federal and state courts have concurrent jurisdiction over private suits arising under the TCPA.

  i. **Test for concurrent jurisdiction.** The Court held that there is a deeply rooted presumption favoring concurrent state court jurisdiction, which is rebuttable and may be overcome if Congress affirmatively ousts the state court of jurisdiction over a particular claim. In the absence of strong direction from Congress, courts should apply the default rule that federal courts have **§ 1331** jurisdiction over claims that arise under federal law.

(e) The "well-pleaded" complaint rule. The federal cause of action must appear in the plaintiff's complaint and may not be found or supplied by the defendant's answer, or by an anticipated defense.

- **Leading case authority: Louisville & Nashville R. Co. v. Mottley, 211 U.S. 149 (1908).** The plaintiffs received free lifetime railroad passes on the railroad as settlement of claims against the railroad for damages. The railroad subsequently declined to renew the passes in reliance on an act of Congress prohibiting such passes. The plaintiffs brought suit in federal district court, anticipating that the railroad would contend that it did not violate the plaintiffs' due process rights because the railroad had relied on the congressional act in denying renewal of the passes. The Supreme Court held that there was no valid federal question jurisdiction: "It is not enough that the plaintiff alleges some anticipated defense to his cause of action, and asserts that the defense is invalidated by some provision of the Constitution of the United States. . . . A suggestion of one party, that the other will or may set up a claim under the Constitution or laws of the United States, does not make the suit one arising under that Constitution or those laws."

- **The well-pleaded complaint rule and federal declaratory judgment actions—the *Skelly Oil* rule.** Actions brought seeking a declaratory judgment in federal court present special problems under the well-pleaded complaint rule. It is important to understand the usual procedural posture of a declaratory judgment action. Typically, declaratory judgment actions are "anticipatory" actions. The party seeking a declaratory judgment does so in anticipation of being a defendant in a litigated action and hopes that the favorable determination of rights or duties will foreclose such litigation. Federal courts, however, will not permit declaratory judgment actions that essentially violate the well-pleaded complaint rule and will look beyond the pleadings to ascertain the true adverse interests of the parties if those interests were presented in a real litigation. **Skelly Oil Co. v. Phillips Petroleum Co.,** 339 U.S. 667 (1950):

- "To sanction suits for declaratory relief as within the jurisdiction of the District Courts merely because . . . artful pleading anticipates a defense based on federal law would contravene the whole trend of jurisdictional legislation by Congress, disregard the effective functioning of the federal judicial system and distort the limited procedural purposes of the Declaratory Judgment Act." **Skelly Oil Co. v. Phillips Petroleum Co.**

- The *Skelly Oil* rule applies to state declaratory judgments that a defendant removes to federal court. **Franchise Tax Board v. Construction Laborers Vacation Trust,** 463 U.S. 1 (1983).

(f) Artful pleading to avoid federal jurisdiction. Usually, a plaintiff is considered to be "the master of his [or her] own complaint" and courts will not interfere with a plaintiff's statement or characterization of the grounds for relief. Concerns about possible manipulation of federal subject matter jurisdiction permeate jurisdictional rulings. Federal courts will exert jurisdiction if the defendant convinces the court that the plaintiff has "artfully pleaded" the complaint to mask claims truly based in federal law for the purpose of avoiding federal jurisdiction.

- **Example.** A plaintiff brought suit against his employer in state court for breach of contract for failure to compensate him based on contractual requirements, because the employer withheld state and federal taxes. The Ninth Circuit held that a plaintiff is not permitted to conceal the true nature of a complaint through artful pleading, which in this case essentially involved a challenge to the employer's compliance with federal withholding laws. **Bright v. Bechtel Petroleum, Inc.,** 780 F.2d 766 (9th Cir. 1986).

4. Supplemental Jurisdiction

In addition to diversity and federal question jurisdiction, federal courts have expanded their jurisdictional reach through the doctrine of "supplemental" jurisdiction. The doctrine of supplemental jurisdiction allows a federal court, in its discretion, to add parties to a dispute who otherwise would not have a valid jurisdictional basis to be in federal court, or to add claims that independently lack a federal jurisdictional basis (such as state-based claims). Until 1990, the principles permitting federal court supplemental jurisdiction were judicially-created doctrines—pendent claim, pendent party, and ancillary jurisdiction. In 1990 Congress enacted **28 U.S.C. § 1367,** which is the current supplemental jurisdiction statute. Now, all assertions of supplemental jurisdiction in federal court are governed by the statute. However, it is useful to understand the major cases defining the scope of supplemental jurisdiction, as an aid to understanding the extent to which the supplemental jurisdiction codifies the common-law rules.

a. Types of Supplemental Jurisdiction

The supplemental jurisdiction statute basically codifies three possible types of supplemental jurisdiction. Prior to 1990, these forms of supplemental jurisdiction were defined and limited by judicially-created principles:

i. Pendent Claim Jurisdiction

Pendent claim jurisdiction usually is the easiest form of supplemental jurisdiction to recognize. This typically involves a situation where a plaintiff in federal court asserts a federal claim for relief, but also includes a claim or claims for state-based relief that otherwise—standing alone—would not be permitted to be pursued in federal court. Federal courts lack subject matter jurisdiction over the state-based claims. Under the theory of pendent claim jurisdiction, the general rule was that if the federal claim had a valid federal jurisdictional basis, then the federal court also could exercise jurisdiction over the state-based claim as long as the federal and state claims "arose from a common nucleus of operative facts." In this sense, then, the state-based claim was "appended" to the federal claim.

■ EXAMPLES AND ANALYSIS

Leading case authority: United Mine Workers v. Gibbs, 383 U.S. 715 (1966). Gibbs was a worker who refused to join a labor strike in the Tennessee coal mines and entered into a contract to haul coal for a mining company. During the strike there was violence at the picket site; Gibbs lost his job and never performed on the haulage contract. He brought an action in federal district court against the United Mine Workers International under § 303 of the **Federal Labor Management Relations Act,** and for state law claims based in theories of unlawful conspiracy, unlawful boycott, and wanton, willful and malicious interference with a business contract. After a trial awarding Gibbs damages, the court set aside the judgment based on the federal claim, but upheld the jury's award for his state-based claims. The Sixth Circuit affirmed; the Supreme Court also upheld the district court's exercise of pendent claim jurisdiction over Gibb's state-based claims, even after dismissal of the federal claim.

Rationales Supporting Pendent Claim Jurisdiction.

- **"One constitutional case."** The Supreme Court suggested that the power to exercise jurisdiction over pendent state claims derived from the federal court's **Article III** jurisdiction over claims arising under the Constitution, federal laws, and treaties and where the relationship of the federal claim to a state claim was such that the "entire action before the court comprises but one constitutional 'case'."

- **Judicial efficiency and fairness to litigants.** The justification for pendent claim jurisdiction lies in the values of judicial economy, efficiency, and fairness to litigants (avoidance of duplicative litigation in federal and state courts).

- **Other** *Gibbs* **principles**

  — The federal claim must have "sufficient substance" to confer jurisdiction on the federal court.

  — The federal and state claims must arise out of a common nucleus of operative facts.

  — The federal court's power to exercise pendent claim jurisdiction is discretionary.

  — If the federal claims are dismissed before trial, then the state claims should be dismissed as well.

  — In situations where a state claim is strongly tied to federal policy, the federal courts may retain state-based claims even after dismissal of the federal claim.

  — If a state claim "constitutes the real body of the case to which the federal claim is only an appendage," then the state claim should be dismissed.

ii. Pendent Claim Jurisdiction Codified at 28 U.S.C. § 1367(a) and (c)

The supplemental jurisdiction statute in subsection (a) states that "district courts shall have supplemental jurisdiction over all other claims that are so related to claims in the action within such original jurisdiction that they form part of the same case or controversy under **Article III** of the United States Constitution."

(a) **Relationship of § 1367(a) to the *Gibbs* decision.** The legislative history to the supplemental jurisdiction statute and its drafters have indicated that subsection (a) of the decision was intended to codify the *Gibbs* decision permitting pendent claim jurisdiction. The statute, however, does not set forth the "common nucleus of operative facts" test. Instead, the provision uses the *Gibbs* formulation of "one constitutional case." Some lower federal courts, in applying statutory pendent claim jurisdiction, have looked to the *Gibbs* "common nucleus of operative facts" test to determine whether to exercise pendent claim jurisdiction.

(b) **Discretionary jurisdiction. Subsection (c)** of the supplemental jurisdiction statute provides federal courts the discretion to decline to exercise supplemental claim jurisdiction under **subsection (a)** if:

- the claim raises a novel or complex issue of state law;

- the claim substantially predominates over the claim or claims over which the district court has original jurisdiction;

- the district court has dismissed all claims over which it has original jurisdiction, or

- in exceptional circumstances, there are other compelling reasons for declining jurisdiction.

(c) **Relationship of § 1367(c) to the *Gibbs* decision. Subsection (c)** of the supplemental jurisdiction statute basically codifies the discretionary ability of federal courts to decline to exercise supplemental claim jurisdiction on the same grounds delineated in *Gibbs.* The fourth "exceptional circumstances" ground is a new standard, however.

iii. Pendent Party Jurisdiction

Pendent party jurisdiction refers to the ability of a federal court to exercise jurisdiction over an additional party brought into a lawsuit under various joinder rules, for whom there is no independent federal jurisdictional basis, but whose joinder is logically related to the plaintiff and defendant's case-in-chief.

(a) Pendent party jurisdiction in lower federal courts prior to 1989. Prior to 1989, lower federal courts were split in their decisions concerning whether pendent party jurisdiction was permitted, even though the Supreme Court had repudiated the doctrine of pendent party jurisdiction. The Supreme Court had rejected an extension of the *Gibbs* doctrine to pendent parties in **Aldinger v. Howard,** 427 U.S. 1 (1976), suggesting that the analogy between pendent claim and pendent parties was inapt: "it is quite another thing to permit a plaintiff, who has asserted a claim against one defendant with respect to which there is federal jurisdiction, to join an entirely different defendant on the basis of a state-law claim over which there is no independent basis of federal jurisdiction." The Court did acknowledge that pendent party jurisdiction might be appropriate when the independent claim is based on exclusive federal subject matter jurisdiction; the Court rejected this suggestion, however, in **Finley v. United States,** *infra.*

(b) Pendent party jurisdiction rejected—leading case authority: Finley v. United States, 490 U.S. 545 (1989). The Supreme Court again rejected pendent party jurisdiction in *Finley,* where a plaintiff, domiciled in California, suing in federal court under the Federal Tort Claims Act (which gives federal courts exclusive jurisdiction) attempted to amend her complaint to add the City of San Diego and a local utility company, both non-diverse from the plaintiff, as defendants. In an opinion by Justice Scalia, the Court "retained the line" against pendent party jurisdiction set forth in *Aldinger;* Scalia's opinion also suggested that Congress could change the scope of the federal court's jurisdiction by statute, if it so desired.

iv. Pendent Party Jurisdiction Codified at § 1367(a) and (b)

In 1990, in direct response to the *Finley* decision and Justice Scalia's invitation to Congress to codify the doctrine of pendent party jurisdiction by statute, the second sentence of **28 U.S.C. § 1367(a)** specifically provides for supplemental jurisdiction over claims adding pendent parties: "Such supplemental jurisdiction shall include claims that involve the joinder or intervention of additional parties." The intention of this subsection was to overrule *Finley* and cases like *Finley* where lower federal courts had repudiated pendent party jurisdiction.

v. Common Law Limitations on Party Joinder in Diversity Supplemental Jurisdiction

(a) **Ancillary jurisdiction.** The judicially-created doctrine of ancillary jurisdiction permitted federal courts to exercise jurisdiction over additional claims or parties brought into a lawsuit as a result of impleader (**Rule 14**), permissive joinder of parties (**Rule 20**), intervention (**Rule 24**), or parties joined because their presence in the lawsuit was necessary for a just adjudication (**Rule 24**).

- Ancillary jurisdiction traditionally was available to support a court's assertion of jurisdiction over counterclaims, cross-claims, and third-party complaints that lacked an independent federal jurisdictional basis, but which were "logically related" to the case-in-chief between the plaintiff and the defendant. Similar to the rationales supporting pendent claim jurisdiction, the doctrine of ancillary jurisdiction rests on considerations of judicial economy and convenience to the parties.

(b) **Limitations on ancillary jurisdiction in diversity cases: Leading case authority—Owen Equipment & Erection Co. v. Kroger, 437 U.S. 365 (1978).** In *Owen Equipment* the Supreme Court endorsed the doctrine of ancillary jurisdiction for its traditional uses, but indicated that ancillary jurisdiction could not be used to support a plaintiff's attempted assertion of federal court jurisdiction over an impleaded defendant, where the plaintiff originally could not have sued that defendant because no diversity existed between the original plaintiff and the impleaded defendant. Here, claims against the defendant over whom there was independent subject matter jurisdiction were dismissed, leaving two non-diverse parties. The Court held that to allow the requirement of complete diversity to be circumvented in such a fashion "would simply flout the congressional command." This limitation on diversity supplemental jurisdiction is called the *Owen Equipment* rule.

vi. Statutory Codification of the *Owen Equipment* Rule in § 1367(b)

The 1990 supplemental jurisdiction statute attempted to codify the *Owen Equipment* rule in **§ 1367(b).** This subsection of the statute basically provides that in federal actions brought in diversity jurisdiction, the federal court may not exercise supplemental jurisdiction over claims by plaintiffs against parties joined under **Rules 14, 19, 20,** or **24** if to do so would violate the requirements of diversity jurisdiction.

(a) **Other limitations.** In addition, courts also may not exercise supplemental jurisdiction over *persons proposed to be joined as plaintiffs* under **Rule 19** (as a necessary party), or **Rule 24** (an intervenor), if the addition of these parties similarly would be inconsistent with the requirements of federal diversity jurisdiction.

(b) **Change in ancillary jurisdiction for intervenors of right.** This particular requirement effects a change in existing doctrine relating to "intervenors of right." Prior to the enactment of § 1367(b), there was automatic ancillary jurisdiction over intervenors of right who qualified under **Rule 24(a).**

vii. Tolling Provisions: § 1367(d)

The supplemental jurisdiction statute includes a tolling provision which effectively stops or "tolls" the running of the statute of limitations for claims that may not properly be within the federal court's supplemental jurisdiction, or for supplemental claims that are voluntarily dismissed at the same time as an original federal claim is dismissed. Limitations periods are tolled while the federal claim is pending. Any limitations periods are also tolled for thirty days after a claim is dismissed from federal court. The reason for the tolling provisions is to protect the ability of litigants to pursue their claims in state court if the attempted assertion of federal supplemental jurisdiction either is mistaken or the court in its discretion declines to hear the supplemental claim.

b. Interpretation Problems under the New Supplemental Jurisdiction Statute

The lower federal courts have encountered significant problems interpreting and applying the supplemental jurisdiction statute.

i. Did the Supplemental Jurisdiction Statute Overrule *Zahn v. International Paper Co.*, 414 U.S. 291 (1973)?

The Supreme Court in **Zahn** had ruled that in class action litigation multiple plaintiffs with separate and distinct claims each had to satisfy the amount in controversy requirement for federal diversity jurisdiction. The legislative history to the supplemental jurisdiction statute indicated that the statute was not intended to overrule the **Zahn** requirement. In the aftermath of the statute's enactment, the lower federal courts split concerning whether the supplemental statute overruled **Zahn**. The Supreme Court ultimately addressed this issue in its first decision construing the supplemental jurisdiction statute. **Exxon Mobil Corp. v. Allapattah**, 545 U.S. 546 (2005).

- **Leading case authority: Exxon Mobil Corp. v. Allapattah, 545 U.S. 546 (2005).** The Allapattah decision actually embraced two consolidated cases on appeal. In Exxon Mobil, 10,000 Exxon dealers filed a diversity class action lawsuit in Florida federal court alleging that they were overcharged for fuel. After a unanimous jury verdict in favor of the plaintiffs, the district court certified the case for interlocutory review asking if it had properly exercised supplemental jurisdiction over the claims of class members who did not meet the $75,000 amount-in-controversy requirement. The Eleventh Circuit upheld the exercise of supplemental jurisdiction. In the second consolidated case, an appeal form the district court in Puerto Rico, the court had dismissed the claims of parents joined in a diversity tort suit against Star–Kist for damages arising from a slicing injury from a tune fish can. Although the daughter met the amount in controversy, her parents did not. In this case, the First Circuit declined to exercise supplemental jurisdiction over the parents' joined claims. The Supreme Court, in a split 5–4 decision in consideration of both cases, held that supplemental jurisdiction under **28 U.S.C. § 1367** could be exerted over the additional parties' claims that did not independently satisfy the amount-in-controversy requirement.

(a) **Majority's holdings under § 1367(a).** Section 1367 is a broad grant of supplemental jurisdiction over claims within the same case or controversy and extends to claims involving joinder or intervention of additional parties. If the court has jurisdiction over a single claim in the complaint, it has jurisdiction over a "civil action" within the meaning of § 1367(a).

(b) **No applicable exceptions under § 1367(b).** Nothing in the text of § 1367(b) withholds jurisdiction over plaintiffs permissively joined under **Rule 20** or certified in a class action pursuant to **Rule 23**. The natural and necessary inference is that § 1367 confers supplemental jurisdiction over claims by **Rule 20** and **Rule 23** plaintiffs.

(c) **Zahn overruled.** The majority held that § 1367 by its plain text overruled **Zahn.** If the threshold requirement of § 1367(a) is satisfied, where some, but not all, of the plaintiffs in a diversity action satisfy the amount in controversy, then a court can exert supplemental jurisdiction over all parties' claims not meeting the threshold amount-in-controversy.

(d) **Supplemental jurisdiction statute not ambiguous.** The majority held that § 1367 was not ambiguous and therefore there is no need to look to other interpretive tools, including legislative history, to conclude that Congress did not intend to overrule **Zahn.** At any rate, the legislative history of § 1367 is murky and a footnote to the House Report (derived from a Subcommittee Working Paper) suggested that overruling **Zahn** would be a good idea. In addition, three law professors who assisted in the drafting agree that § 1367, on its face, overrules **Zahn.**

(e) **Justices Stevens and Breyer dissent.** Justices Stevens and Breyer dissenting, noting that statutory ambiguity "is in the eye of the beholder." Believing the statute to be ambiguous, and making recourse to the legislative history, these dissenters argued that the House Report specifically said that § 1367 was not intended to overrule **Zahn.**

(f) **Justice Ginsburg dissent** (joined by J. Stevens, O'Connor, and Breyer). The dissenters would read § 1367 more narrowly than the majority; a narrower reading better comports with historical and legal context of Congress's enactment of the supplemental jurisdiction statute, and established limits on pendent and ancillary jurisdiction.

ii. Plaintiff's Compulsory Counterclaims

Does § 1367(b) eliminate automatic ancillary jurisdiction of a plaintiff's compulsory counterclaim against a third-party defendant?

(a) **Problem relating to plaintiff counterclaims.** Under prior law a plaintiff was required to assert a compulsory counterclaim against an impleaded third-party defendant, and this claim automatically came within the court's ancillary jurisdiction. It is unclear whether this ancillary jurisdiction now survives § 1367(b), which prohibition extends to claims by plaintiffs against such parties. However, the general legislative history to the statute indicates that the statute was not intended to modify pre-existing rules. This argument may not be sustainable if other federal courts follow the Fifth Circuit's lead in **Free v. Abbott Laboratories,** 51 F.3d 524 (5th Cir. 1995), in disregarding the statute's legislative history. Also, arguably a plaintiff's compulsory counterclaim is not a "claim by a plaintiff" but instead is a counterclaim by a "party opposing" a claim by a third-party defendant. *See* discussion of **Rule 13(a),** *infra.*

iii. Defendant's Counterclaims for Set-Offs

Does the supplemental jurisdiction statute authorize supplemental jurisdiction for set-offs?

(a) **Problem relating to set-offs.** A defendant may assert a counterclaim for a set-off as against a plaintiff's judgment. Often such set-off claims are unrelated to the plaintiff's claims. If § 1367(a) authorizes supplemental jurisdiction only for claims that arise out of a "common nucleus of operative facts" under the *Gibbs* test, then federal courts may lack a statutory basis for asserting supplemental jurisdiction over such set-off claims.

5. Removal Jurisdiction

Removal refers to the ability of a defendant to jurisdiction move or shift a case that the plaintiff originally filed in state court to a federal district court.

a. Scope and Basis of Removal Right

i. Defendant's Right

The right to remove a case from state court to federal court is a defendant's right, not a plaintiff's right. **Shamrock Oil & Gas Corp. v. Sheets,** 313 U.S. 100 (1941). This makes sense because the plaintiff is viewed as being "the master of his [or her] complaint" and if the plaintiff wanted to sue in federal court, the plaintiff could have made that decision initially.

(a) Historical basis. Removal is a very old right and was provided for by **Section 12** of the **Judiciary Act of 1789. Shamrock Oil & Gas Corp. v. Sheets,** 313 U.S. 100 (1941). Removal is not a constitutionally based right.

(b) Modern statutory basis. The removal statute, **28 U.S.C. § 1441** and subsequent provisions, has been amended several times. The basic removal statute at **§ 1441(a)** provides that any civil action brought in a state court "may be removed by the defendant or defendants."

(c) Defendant's federal defense or counterclaim

- **Federal defenses.** A state case may not be removed to federal court merely because the defendant asserts a federal defense. The "well-pleaded complaint rule" (*see supra*) applies to bar removal in this situation. **Oklahoma Tax Commission v. Graham,** 489 U.S. 838 (1989).

- **Federal counterclaims.** If the defendant interposes a counterclaim based in federal law, the plaintiff may not remove the case to federal court, because removal is a defendant's right. **Shamrock Oil & Gas Corp. v. Sheets,** 313 U.S. 100 (1941). In addition, the "well-pleaded complaint rule" applies.

ii. No Reverse-Removal Right

Removal is a procedure that is only available to state court defendants to move a case from state court into the federal court system. Currently, there is no parallel right of federal court litigants to move a case out of the federal court system into the state court system.

However, a federal litigant, in appropriate circumstances, may ask the federal court to invoke an abstention doctrine and decline to exercise its validly conferred jurisdiction in deference to a state court's jurisdiction. Abstention doctrines typically are outside the scope of first year civil procedure courses and are taught in constitutional law or federal courts courses.

b. Removable Actions; Parties Who May Remove: Statutory Provisions

The general removal statute is **28 U.S.C. § 1441. Sections 1442–1444** delineates the removal power of specific defendants in specific kinds of cases.

i. Removal Power in Relation to Types of Cases

(a) Federal question removal. If the defendant's basis for removal is that the case is within the federal court's federal question jurisdiction, the case is removable without reference to the citizenship or residence of the parties to the litigation. **28 U.S.C. § 1441(a).**

- **Omitted federal claim.** If the state plaintiff has a possible federal question claim but chooses not to assert it, the defendant may not attempt to remove the case by relying on the unasserted federal claim. But if the state plaintiff subsequently amends its pleading to assert the federal claim, the defendant may, at that point, remove the case to federal court.

- **Dismissed federal claim.** Federal courts retain the ability to remand cases back to state court after a plaintiff drops a federal claim that provided the basis for the removal in the first instance. **Carnegie–Mellon University v. Cohill,** 484 U.S. 343 (1988).

(b) **Diversity removal: Out-of-state limitation.** In diversity removal cases, the defendant may remove only if none of the defendants are in-state citizens. **28 U.S.C. § 1441(b).** Hence, diversity removal is only available to out-of-state citizens.

- **Rationale.** Diversity jurisdiction exists primarily to protect out-of-state citizens from local bias. As such, federal diversity removal should only be available to protect defendants who are out-of-state citizens, not in-state defendants. However, prior versions of the removal statute that made reference to the removal of actions because of the inability to obtain justice because of prejudice or local influence have been deleted from the statute itself. The Advisory Committee Notes to the statute indicate: "Indeed, the practice of removal for prejudice or local influence has not been employed much in recent years."

- **Fraudulent joinder of defendants to defeat diversity removal.** If a plaintiff attempts to fraudulently join a nondiverse defendant for the purpose of manipulating or otherwise defeating removal, the court may look to the real parties in interest to determine whether federal jurisdiction and removal are appropriate and disregard the presence of the nondiverse defendants. **Rose v. Giamatti,** 721 F.Supp. 906 (S.D. Ohio 1989). The presence of such nondiverse defendants will not defeat removal.

- **Subsequent actions affecting federal diversity jurisdiction, 28 U.S.C. § 1447(e) (added by Congress in 1988).** If a state plaintiff, after removal, attempts to add defendants whose presence in the lawsuit would destroy diversity jurisdiction, in this instance the federal court may either deny joinder of the additional defendants, or permit the joinder of the additional defendants and then remand the case back to state court.

(c) **Civil rights cases.** Any state civil or criminal action brought in state court involving a denial or deprivation of a person's civil or equal protection rights may be removed to the federal district court (or division) where the state action is pending. **28 U.S.C. § 1443.**

(d) **Foreclosure actions against the United States.** Foreclosure actions brought against the United States in state court may be removed to the federal district court (and division) where the state action is pending. **28 U.S.C. § 1444.**

ii. **Removal Power Based on Party Status**

(a) **Defendants generally.** A defendant who is sued in state court may remove the case to the federal district court (and the division of that district court) where the state action is pending. **28 U.S.C. § 1441(a).** The case must be one in which the plaintiff originally could have sued in federal court, but chose not to do so. Thus, the case must have federal jurisdictional grounds for removal, either in the federal court's diversity or federal question jurisdiction.

(b) Fictitious or Doe defendants. If the defendant seeks removal on diversity grounds, then the citizenship of any named fictitious or "Doe" defendants is disregarded in determining whether the federal court has diversity jurisdiction. **28 U.S.C. § 1441(b)(1).**

(c) Foreign states. A foreign state named as defendant in a state court action may remove the action to the federal district court (and division) where the state action is pending. Such removed actions involving foreign defendants are tried without a jury or in a so-called "bench trial" solely to a federal district judge. **28 U.S.C. § 1441(d).** Time limitations relating to removal by a foreign state may be extended at any time for good cause.

(d) Federal officers. Various federal officers, including federal property owners, federal court officers, and congressional members who are named as defendants in any state civil or criminal action may remove the case to the federal district court (and division) where the action is pending. **28 U.S.C. § 1442.** This removal right includes actions brought by aliens against government officers. **28 U.S.C. § 1442(b).** Members of the armed forces enjoy a more expansive removal right than other defendants, and may remove an act from state court to federal court at any time during the trial or final hearing. **28 U.S.C. § 1442a.**

c. Non-Removable Actions

Defendants may not remove four types of actions from state court to federal court. **28 U.S.C. § 1445.** These non-removable actions involve:

i. Railroads

Actions against railroad or its trustees are not removable, **§ 1445(a);**

ii. Common Carriers

Actions against a common carrier or its receivers or trustees to recover less than $10,000 in damages for delay, loss, or injury to shipments, are not removable, **§ 1445(b);**

iii. State Worker's Compensation

Actions based on state worker's compensation laws are not removable, § 1445(c).

iv. Violence Against Women Act

Actions based on § 40302 of the **Violence Against Women Act** are not removable.

d. Removal Procedure: 28 U.S.C. § 1446

In general, a defendant seeking to remove a case from state court files a *notice or petition for removal* in the appropriate federal district court. The state court no longer has any jurisdiction over the action; the federal district court has physical possession of any pleadings, papers, or motions relating to the case. Removal procedure is subject to certain technical requirements:

i. Removal Petition: "Notice of Removal"

A defendant seeking to remove a case from state court to federal court must file a notice of removal containing "a short and plain statement of the grounds for removal," which must be signed and is subject to **Rule 11** (signing of pleadings and other papers in federal court) **§ 1446(a).** This defendant's statement of grounds will be that the case is within the federal court's diversity or federal question subject matter jurisdiction. The notice of removal is filed in the federal district court along with the state court complaint, service of process, and any other orders.

ii. Timing of Removal

A defendant must file a notice of removal within the shorter of two possible time periods (**§ 1446(b)**):

- Within *thirty days* after receiving a copy of the plaintiff's state court complaint; or,

- Within *thirty days* after receiving the service of summons if the plaintiff's complaint was filed in state court and not required to be served on the defendant.

- **Amended pleadings.** In addition, defendants may file a notice of removal within *thirty days* of receiving any amended complaints if it later becomes apparent that a state case that was not originally removable has become removable by virtue of an amended pleading.

- **Removal time limitation on diversity actions.** Defendants may not remove a state action for which there is valid federal diversity jurisdiction more than *one year* after commencement of the state court action, unless the plaintiff has acted in bad faith to prevent a defendant from removing the case. § 1446(c).

iii. Notice to Adverse Parties of the Removal Petition

Promptly after filing a notice of removal the defendant must give written notice of the removal petition to all adverse parties (usually the state court plaintiff) and to the clerk of the federal district court. § 1446(d).

iv. Effect of the Removal Petition: No State Authority

When a defendant files a notice of removal with the federal district court, the filing of the notice effects the removal and "the State court shall proceed no further unless the case is remanded." § 1446(d).

e. Procedure After Removal: 28 U.S.C. § 1447

i. Federal Court Authority

After removal the federal district court may issue all necessary orders and process to bring the parties to the dispute before the court. § 1447(a). The federal court also may order that all state court papers be filed with the federal court. § 1447(b). Once a case has been removed to federal court it is governed by federal procedure.

ii. State Plaintiff's Petition for Remand

The former state plaintiff who opposes the removal must seek to have the case *remanded* by the federal district court and will file a *motion or petition for remand.* § 1447(c).

(a) **Timing.** The motion to remand must be filed within *thirty days* of the defendant's filing the notice of removal. § 1447(c).

(b) **Grounds for remand.** The federal district court (not the state court) will determine whether appropriate grounds for removal exist to permit federal court assertion of jurisdiction over the litigation. The standard for assessing proper removal is: "If at any time before final judgment it appears that the district court lacks subject matter jurisdiction, the case shall be remanded." § 1447(c). The federal district court will decide this either on the written papers or after a hearing on the motion. If the federal court determines that it is without removal jurisdiction, it will order a *remand* of the case back to state court.

- **Impermissible remand grounds: Federal docket congestion.** A federal district judge may not remand a removed case that is validly within the federal court's jurisdiction because the judge's docket is overcrowded. **Thermtron Prods., Inc. v. Hermansdorfer,** 423 U.S. 336 (1976).

(c) **Costs and expenses.** If the federal court decides to remand the case to state court, it may order the defendant who attempted the removal to pay the state plaintiff's expenses and attorney's fees in opposing the removal in federal court. § 1447(c).

(d) **Appellate review.** Federal court orders remanding cases to state court are not reviewable (except for civil rights cases). § 1447(d).

- **Current trends relating to non-reviewability of remand orders.** The doctrine of non-reviewability of remand orders is under attack in some federal courts, which find ways to circumvent the prohibition against appellate review of remand orders. However, most federal courts continue to deny review to federal remand orders.

- **Non-reviewability doctrine upheld: Liberty Mutual Insurance Co. v. Ward Trucking Corp., 48 F.3d 742 (3d Cir. 1995).** After discovery a defendant learned that a plaintiff's claim was for more than $150,000 and removed the case to federal court. The district court remanded the case to state court without allowing the defendant an opportunity to respond to the plaintiff's remand motion. The Third Circuit held the remand order non-reviewable.

- **Contrary authority—non-reviewability doctrine circumvented: Carlsbad Technology Inc. v. HIF BIO Inc., 556 U.S. 635 (2009).** HIF BIO Inc. filed suit in California state court against Carlsbad Technology Inc. alleging that Carlsbad had violated state and federal law in connection with a patent dispute. Carlsbad removed the case to the federal district court for the Central District of California under § 1441(c), which allows removal of an entire case when it includes at least one claim over which the federal court has original jurisdiction. Carlsbad then moved to dismiss the only federal claim in the lawsuit (a RICO claim), which the district court granted. The court then declined to exercise supplemental jurisdiction over the remaining state law claims pursuant to 28 U.S.C. § 1367(c)(3). The district court then remanded the case to state court. On appeal, the appellate court dismissed the appeal, finding that the remand could colorably be characterized as a remand based on lack of subject matter jurisdiction and therefore not reviewable under §§ 1447(c) and (d). The Supreme Court held that remand orders to state court after declining to exercise supplemental jurisdiction are not based on lack of subject matter jurisdiction for the purposes of §§ 1447(c) and (d). The decision declining to exercise the statutory authority over supplemental jurisdiction was not based on a jurisdictional defect but on a discretionary choice not to hear the claims despite its subject matter jurisdiction over them. § 1447 permits appellate courts to review a district court decision of this kind, even if only for abuse of discretion.

iii. Subsequent Actions Affecting Federal Jurisdiction: 28 U.S.C. § 1447(e) (Added by Congress in 1988)

If a plaintiff, after removal, attempts to add defendants whose presence in the lawsuit would destroy diversity jurisdiction, in this instance the federal court may either:

- Deny joinder of the additional defendants, or

- Permit the joinder of the additional defendants and then remand the case back to state court.

f. Removal of Complaints That Contain Both State and Federal Claims: 28 U.S.C. § 1441(c)

If a plaintiff files a complaint that contains a federal question in the court's § 1331 arising under jurisdiction and the complaint contains

claims that are not within the court's original or supplemental jurisdiction, the entire case may be removed if the action would be removable
without the claim. After removal, the court should sever from the action
all non-removable claims and remand the severed claims back to state
court. Only defendants against whom the federal claim is asserted are
required to join in or consent to the removal. **§ 1441(c)** was amended to
remove language describing "separate and independent claims" that
had caused significant problems of interpretation for federal courts. The
current statute no longer contains the requirement or language of
separate and independent claims as the basis for removal of a combined
complaint.

D. LOCATING THE LAWSUIT—RESTRAINTS ON JURISDICTIONAL POWER

1. Venue Provisions

Venue refers to the place or geographical location of a litigation and it usually
is determined with reference to the possible burdens or inconvenience on the
defendants of litigating in a particular place. Both federal and state court
have venue rules, which are typically defined in intricate detail in statutory
provisions. A plaintiff's choice of forum must satisfy venue rules in addition
to establishing valid personal and subject matter jurisdiction. However,
venue is a waivable defect and if a plaintiff selects a court that is in an
improper venue, the court can either dismiss the case or—in the federal
system—transfer the case to the proper venue. **Hoffman v. Blaski,** 363 U.S.
335 (1960).

a. Local and Transitory Actions Distinguished

Historically, state courts have distinguished venue based on the concepts
of "local" and "transitory" actions. The federal venue statutes are not
couched in the terminology of "local" and "transitory" actions. However, many state common law decisions still rely on these distinctions,
and some federal authorities make reference to these concepts.

i. Local Actions and the "Local Action Rule"

Local actions typically involved litigation concerning real property
such as suits to gain access to land, quiet title, or foreclose a lien.
Under the so-called "local action rule," venue of such actions could
only be in the court where the property was located. In this sense,
local actions resembled the concept of *in rem* jurisdiction. The local

action rule was justified on various grounds. Among these was the notion that a court was not qualified to render a judgment on land outside its geographical boundaries. Another rationale was to encourage plaintiffs to pursue any remedies relating to property where the property was located, rather than waiting to do so in some other place. **Reasor–Hill Corp. v. Harrison,** 220 Ark. 521, 249 S.W.2d 994 (1952).

ii. Transitory Actions

Transitory actions essentially are actions that might have arisen anywhere, such as torts or contract claims. Venue for transitory actions generally is appropriate wherever the plaintiff can assert personal jurisdiction over the defendant, and in this sense transitory actions sometimes have been analogized to *in personam* actions in the jurisdictional sense.

b. Venue in Federal Court

Venue in federal court is determined by reference to a highly detailed statutory scheme that delineates appropriate venue for federal cases depending on the subject matter jurisdiction of the case, the status of the parties, or the nature of the claim. The "general venue statute" is **28 U.S.C. § 1391.** Similar to the removal provisions, the venue statutes contain a number of separate, additional venue provisions for specialized cases or controversies.

i. Federal Question or Diversity Actions: § 1391(b)

Federal venue refers to the appropriate federal judicial district court in which a plaintiff may bring a civil action. There are ninety-four federal district courts, so venue must be established with reference to one or more of these federal judicial districts. In actions based either in federal question or diversity jurisdiction, appropriate venue for a civil action could be in:

(a) A judicial district where any defendant resides, if all the defendants reside in the same state (§ 1391(b)(1))

- **Individual defendants.** "Residence" for venue purposes generally is construed as an individual's domicile, and therefore is the same as citizenship for diversity purposes. However, some federal courts recognize more than one residence for venue purposes (whereas a person is a citizen of only one state for diversity purposes in determining subject matter jurisdiction).

- **Defendant corporations.** A corporation is a citizen, for venue purposes, of any judicial district in which it is subject to personal jurisdiction at the time the action is commenced. **§ 1391(d).** Congress added this provision with the intent of making corporate venue rules congruent with personal jurisdiction doctrine. In a state with more than one federal judicial district, a corporation is deemed to reside in any judicial district with which it has sufficient minimum contacts to support personal jurisdiction. Hence, federal judicial districts are treated like separate states for venue purposes.

- **Defendant unincorporated associations.** Unincorporated associations such as labor unions are treated as entities and therefore deemed to "reside" in any state where it is "doing business." **Denver & R.G.W.R. Co. v. Brotherhood of Railroad Trainmen,** 387 U.S. 556 (1967).

- **Partnerships.** Partnerships generally are treated like unincorporated associations for venue purposes, although some federal courts will look to the residence of individual partners to establish possible venue.

(b) **A judicial district in which a substantial part of the events or omissions giving rise to the claim occurred, or a substantial part of the property that is the subject of the action is situated, (§ 1391(b)(2)), or**

- Congress added this provision in 1990 and eliminated language permitting venue in a judicial district "where the claim arose," which gave rise to a variety of conflicting interpretations. Under the prior statutory language, it was generally held that venue could be had in only one judicial district. **Leroy v. Great Western United Corp.,** 443 U.S. 173 (1979). The amended language is intended to permit venue in multiple possible venues.

- It is uncertain whether the revised language, however, providing for venue in any district where a "substantial part of the events or omissions giving rise to the claim occurred," gives any clearer guidance to locating the proper venue than the prior standard.

- **Example.** A debtor living in the western district of New York brought a federal action under the Fair Debt Collection Practices Act against a collection agency which transacted no regular business in New York. The debtor had incurred the debt while living in Pennsylvania. The collection agency sought payment by sending a demand letter to Pennsylvania, which was then forwarded to the debtor in New York. The court held that there was venue in the western district of New York under § 1391(b)(2) because a "substantial part of the events" giving rise to the claim had occurred there: receipt of the forwarded collection letter. The court reasoned that if the collection agency wished to avoid being subject to the New York venue, it could have marked its letter as not forwardable. **Bates v. C & S Adjusters, Inc.,** 980 F.2d 865 (2d Cir. 1992).

(c) **A judicial district in which any defendant is subject to the court's personal jurisdiction, if there is no district in which the action may otherwise be brought**

ii. Special Venue Based on Case Types: Additional and Exclusive Venues

Various provisions of the federal venue statutes provide special venue rules for certain types of cases. In some instances, these provisions permit venue in courts other than the venue indicated by the general venue statute. In other instances, the special venue statutes require that certain kinds of cases be brought in only one particular venue.

(a) **Tax cases.** These actions may be brought in the district where the liability for the tax accrues, the taxpayer's residence, or the district where the return was filed. **28 U.S.C § 1396.**

(b) **Interpleader actions.** Interpleader actions may be brought only in one of the judicial districts where the claimants to the interpleader fund reside. **28 U.S.C. § 1397.**

(c) **Patents and copyright.** Actions relating to copyright may be brought in the district where the defendant or his agent resides.

Patent infringement actions may be brought in the judicial district where the defendant resides, or has committed the infringing acts, or has a place of regular established business. **28 U.S.C. § 1400.**

iii. Venue Based on Party Status: Additional Rules

(a) **Defendants not resident in the United States, 28 U.S.C. § 1391(c).** A defendant not resident in the United States may be sued in any judicial district.

(b) **The United States Government, 28 U.S.C § 1391(e).** The United States government or any of its agencies or officials may be sued in any judicial district in which: (1) the defendant resides; (2) a substantial part of the events or omissions giving rise to the claim occurred; or (3) the plaintiff resides if no property is involved.

(c) **Foreign states, 28 U.S.C. § 1391(f).** Foreign states or their political subdivisions may be sued in any judicial district in which: (1) a substantial part of the events or omissions giving rise to the claim occurred; or a substantial part of the property that is the subject of the action is situated; (2) a vessel or cargo of the foreign state is located; (3) where an agency or instrumentality of the foreign state is licensed to do business or is doing business; or (4) in the District Court for the District of Columbia if the action is brought against a foreign state or political subdivision.

c. Venue in State Court

Venue in state is similarly defined by state statutory provisions. Venue in state court is typically defined by the appropriate county in which to pursue relief. Each state varies in the grounds for determining venue. All states permit change-of-venue or transfer to another location within the state to mitigate problems of local bias and other convenience reasons. In general, state venue rules are more stringently applied to in-state defendants and more liberally applied to non-resident defendants.

d. Challenging Venue: Method and Timing of a Challenge

In federal cases, defects in venue typically are raised in federal court by a **Rule 12(b)(3)** motion or in a responsive pleading (or to an amended pleading) such as the defendant's answer. If the defendant fails to raise defects relating to venue in either circumstance, then the defendant is deemed to have consented to the venue and waives any objections to that venue. **Rule 12(h)(1).** *See also* **28 U.S.C. § 1406(b):** "Nothing in this chapter shall impair the jurisdiction of a district court of any matter involving a party who does not interpose timely and sufficient objection to venue."

e. Transfer of Venue

Actions filed in federal court may be transferred to another judicial district either upon the request of the parties, or *sua sponte* (i.e., by the court itself). Venue transfers are subject to a set of statutory provisions and judicially-created rules.

i. Convenience Transfers

In addition, a federal judge may, "for the convenience of parties and witnesses, in the interests of justice," either dismiss the action or, (as is more usual) transfer the case to "any district or division in which it could have been brought." **28 U.S.C. § 1404(a).**

(a) **"Where it could have been brought."** This refers to the judicial district where the plaintiff originally could have brought the lawsuit. This rule is true even if a defendant requests a transfer to another district court and consents to venue in that court. **Hoffman v. Blaski,** 363 U.S. 335 (1960).

(b) **Legislative history and relationship to *forum non conveniens.*** Congress added **§ 1404(a)** in 1948, the year after the Supreme Court handed down its decision in **Gulf Oil Corp. v. Gilbert,** 330 U.S. 501 (1947), the Court's leading decision on the doctrine of *forum non conveniens*. Although this statutory provision has its legislative roots in the *Gilbert* decision, it is not a complete codification of the *forum non conveniens* doctrine. Federal courts have generally held that venue transfers under **§ 1404(a)** may be made upon a lesser showing of inconvenience than is necessary for a *forum non conveniens* dismissal. Federal *forum non conveniens* determinations are subject to the common law precepts set forth in the *Gilbert* decision, discussed below.

ii. Improper Venue

If a plaintiff "lays venue" in the wrong district court (or division of a district court), then the judge may either dismiss the case or transfer it to any other district where the case could have been brought. **28 U.S.C. § 1406(a).** This provision is distinguished from transfers under **§ 1404(a),** which presume that the first forum had proper venue.

(a) **Venue transfers where original district lacked jurisdiction.** The Supreme Court has held that a federal district court may transfer a case pursuant to **§ 1406(a)** even where the first court lacked personal jurisdiction over the action. **Goldlawr Inc. v. Heiman,** 369 U.S. 463 (1962). The *Goldlawr* decision has been highly criticized on many grounds, including the anomaly that a court theoretically can offer relief to a plaintiff who files a case lacking in both proper venue and personal jurisdiction, but not to a similar plaintiff who selects a district having proper venue, but lacking personal jurisdiction.

iii. Multidistrict Litigation, 28 U.S.C. § 1407

Federal courts have the power to transfer cases already filed in the federal judicial system to one particular federal district court for consolidated pretrial proceedings. This is commonly called an "MDL transfer" and the case becomes an "MDL" proceeding. In order to create an MDL proceeding, the separate federal cases must be pending in different judicial districts and must involve "one or more common questions of fact." **28 U.S.C. § 1407(a).**

- A special panel of federal judges, called the "Multidistrict Litigation Panel," determines whether such transfer will be for the convenience of the witnesses and parties, and will promote the just and efficient conduct of such action. Cases transferred to the MDL district are supervised by a federal district judge who coordinates pretrial discovery and limited motion practice. If the MDL case does not settle—and a very high percentage of MDL cases do settle—then the cases are remanded back to their original districts for trial. A consolidated MDL cases may be tried in the MDL district if the parties consent. If the parties do not consent, then the MDL court has no authority to try cases that are consolidated for MDL purposes. **Lexecon, Inc. v. Milberg Weiss Bershad Hynes & Lerach,** 523 U.S. 26 (1998).

iv. Transfer Procedure

(a) Who may request. Usually defendants request a change of venue. **Van Dusen v. Barrack,** 376 U.S. 612 (1964). Plaintiffs, however, may request a transfer. **Ferens v. John Deere Co.,** 494 U.S. 516 (1990). Plaintiff-initiated venue changes are rare because the plaintiff makes the original choice of forum. In addition, a court on its own initiative may transfer a case to another venue.

(b) **Effects of transfer: Applicable law in diversity cases.** In diversity cases transferred under **§ 1404(a),** the federal transferee court is obligated to apply the law of the transferor court; in other words, applicable law transfers with the case. The general rule is that "[a] change of venue under **§ 1404(a)** generally should be, with respect to state law, but a change of courtrooms." **Van Dusen v. Barrack,** 376 U.S. 612 (1964). This rule applies to plaintiff-initiated transfers, as well. **Ferens v. John Deere Co.,** 494 U.S. 516 (1990). The *Ferens* rule has been highly criticized, however, because in that litigation the plaintiff exploited the rule to take advantage of another state's longer statute of limitations, and to have that longer period applied after transfer.

(c) **Federal question cases.** Federal courts are less likely to apply the *Van Dusen* rule in cases based on federal claims. At least two federal circuits have indicated that the transferee forum's law should be given some consideration in transferred federal claim cases, but the law of another circuit is not *stare decisis* or binding on the transferor court. **In re Korean Airlines Disaster of Sept. 1, 1983,** 829 F.2d 1171 (D.C. Cir. 1987), aff'd. on other grounds sub nom. **Chan v. Korean Airlines, Ltd.,** 490 U.S. 122 (1989); **In re Pan American Corp.,** 950 F.2d 839 (2d Cir. 1991); **Menowitz v. Brown,** 991 F.2d 36 (2d Cir. 1993).

f. Contractual Venue

Parties contractually may stipulate to a particular court's venue.

2. Discretionary Decline of Jurisdiction: *Forum Non Conveniens*

Federal courts may decline to exercise their jurisdiction under the judicially-created doctrine of *forum non conveniens.* In general, a greater showing of "inconvenience" is required for a *forum non conveniens* dismissal than for a "convenience" transfer under **28 U.S.C. § 1404(a).** The two leading Supreme Court cases setting forth the factors to be evaluated in determining whether to dismiss a case on a *forum non conveniens* motion are **Gulf Oil Corp. v. Gilbert,** 330 U.S. 501 (1947), and **Piper Aircraft Co. v. Reyno,** 454 U.S. 235 (1981).

a. Factors Relevant to a *Forum Non Conveniens* Determination

i. The Private Interests of the Litigants in:

- ease of access to available sources of proof;

- availability of compulsory process for attendance of unwilling witnesses;

- costs of obtaining attendance of willing witnesses;

- possibility of view of the premises, if appropriate for the action;

- all other practical problems relating to ease, speed, and expense;

- enforceability of a judgment if obtained;

- relative advantages and obstacle to a fair trial;

- the existence of an alternative forum that will provide adequate relief.

ii. The Public Interest in:

- administrative difficulties for courts;

- burdens of jury duty on a community which may have little or no relationship to the litigation;

- interest of the local community in having a trial touching on the community's interest tried locally, rather than in a distant forum where citizens can learn of it only by report;

- interest in diversity cases in having the litigation tried in the home forum with the state law that must govern the case, rather than having some distant forum interpret the state's laws;

- interest in avoiding having courts interpret other state's laws or foreign law.

b. Standard for Granting an Appellate Review

A *forum non conveniens* determination is within a federal judge's discretion and may be reversed only for a clear abuse of discretion. **Piper Aircraft v. Reyno**, 454 U.S. 235 (1981).

c. Alternative Forum

A requirement for a *forum non conveniens* dismissal is that there must be another more convenient forum where the plaintiff may obtain adequate relief. Some courts condition *forum non conveniens* dismissals on stipulations from the defendant waiving defendant's objections to personal jurisdiction and statutes of limitations in the alternative forum. **In re Union Carbide Corp. Gas Plant Disaster at Bhopal, India in Dec. 1984,** 809 F.2d 195 (2d Cir. 1987). However, in *forum non conveniens* dismissals to an alternative foreign state's court, the federal courts lack the ability to impose such conditions as adherence to federal discovery rules. **In re Union Carbide Corp. Gas Plant Disaster at Bhopal.**

- **Contrary authority. In Islamic Republic of Iran v. Pahlavi,** 62 N.Y.2d 474, 467 N.E.2d 245 (1984), a New York state court dismissed an action on *forum non conveniens* grounds brought by the Islamic Republic of Iran against the former Shah in New York state courts, although there was no alternative available forum because of the revolutionary political situation in Iran. The court dismissed the "alternative forum" requirement of *Gulf Oil* as dicta, and considered it merely a "most important factor" to be considered.

d. Applicable Law

The possibility that a *forum non conveniens* dismissal will preclude the plaintiff from being able to take advantage of a forum's more favorable law is not a dispositive factor in a *forum non conveniens* determination. **Piper Aircraft Co. v. Reyno,** 454 U.S. 235 (1981). Some lower federal courts take possible applicable law into consideration in assessing whether to grant or deny a *forum non conveniens* dismissal.

e. Pre-Emption of State Law

Federal *forum non conveniens* doctrine does not pre-empt state law in a state court suit between domestic parties. **American Dredging Co. v. Miller,** 510 U.S. 443 (1994).

■ CHAPTER REVIEW CHECKLIST

Civil procedure examinations frequently include a problem relating to federal subject matter jurisdiction or venue. Be certain to distinguish this from any problem or question asking whether the court may assert *personal jurisdiction* over the defendants. Carefully read the facts presented. Pay special attention to jurisdictional facts that bear on whether the court has subject matter jurisdiction, as well as those that bear on selecting the appropriate forums for venue. Most likely the problem will present issues relating to subject matter jurisdiction or venue in *federal court*. In order to answer a question relating to state subject matter jurisdiction or venue, you would need to be supplied with relevant state statutory provisions governing jurisdiction and venue.

To answer a problem relating to subject matter jurisdiction, ask:

1. Do the facts present a problem that comes with the federal court's diversity jurisdiction? (28 U.S.C. § 1332)

- What is the status of the parties to the dispute? Are they individuals, partnerships, corporations, unincorporated associations, aliens, a governmental entity?

- What is the citizenship of each of these parties? Where are the individuals domiciled? Where is the corporation incorporated or has its principal place of business?

- What is the nature of the dispute? Does the litigation involve a class action, which provides an exception to diversity rules?

- Are the parties to the dispute completely diverse from each other? That is, are all the plaintiffs from different states than each of the defendants?

- Has the plaintiff *in good faith* pleaded an amount in controversy that is to a *legal certainty* in excess of $75,000? Does the problem involve multiple parties or claims so that you must assess aggregation rules?

  — Do the facts involve an individual plaintiff with multiple claims each for less than $75,000? Are these claims related or unrelated to each other?

  — Do the facts involve multiple plaintiffs or defendants who are claiming less than the jurisdictional amount? Do the parties have a collective right or have they suffered an indivisible harm, so that their claims may be aggregated to meet the jurisdiction amount?

  — Do the facts involve a class action? Do the facts permit aggregation of claims under a theory of supplemental jurisdiction (*see infra*)?.

  — Has the plaintiff attempted to collusively manipulate federal diversity jurisdiction by assigning a contract right for token consideration, or improperly designating another party as a legal representative for the purpose of creating diversity where it otherwise might not exist (in violation of the collusive joinder statute, **28 U.S.C. § 1359)?**

2. **Do the facts present a problem within the federal court's federal question jurisdiction (Article III § 2 of the Constitution or 28 U.S.C. § 1331)?**

    •   Do the facts present a problem arising directly under Article III? Does the federal question form "an *original ingredient*" of the plaintiff's claim?

    •   Does the problem involve an entity that has been congressionally chartered and the charter contains a provision specifying that the entity *"may sue or be sued in federal court"*?

    •   Is there a federal statute *explicitly* conferring federal jurisdiction on the courts for claims arising under the statute?

    •   Does the claim arise under the statute creating the federal right to relief?

    •   Is there a constitutional or statutory basis for *implying* a right of action in federal court?

    •   Does the resolution of a state claim turn on the construction or interpretation of a federal statute? (i.e., do the facts present a *"litigation-provoking problem"*?)

3. **Do the facts present a problem within the federal court's supplemental jurisdiction? (28 U.S.C. § 1367)**

    •   Has the plaintiff joined state-based claims with a federal claim? Do the federal and state claims form *"one constitutional case"* such that the federal court should decide the state and federal claims in one proceeding? Under the older *Gibbs* test, do the federal and state claims share a *"common nucleus of operative facts"*?

    •   Has the plaintiff joined additional parties for whom there is no independent federal jurisdictional basis? What is the basis for joinder of the additional party?

— Has the additional party been joined under **Rules 14, 19, 20,** or **24**? If the additional party has been joined under one of these rules, would the plaintiff originally have been able to sue the defendant?

— Do the facts involve a class action? Has the plaintiff joined additional claims in a class action? Is the class action based in diversity jurisdiction? Do the claims satisfy or fail to satisfy the amount-in-controversy requirement?

- Do the facts present grounds for the federal court to decline to exercise supplemental jurisdiction in its discretion?

— Has the federal claim been dismissed?

— Do the state-based claims predominate? Do the state-based claims present novel issues better resolved by state courts?

— Are there exceptional circumstances favoring remand?

4. **Do the facts present grounds for removing the case from state to federal court? (28 U.S.C. § 1441)**

- Who is seeking to remove the case?

- Does the defendant have valid federal court jurisdictional grounds for seeking the removal?

- Has the defendant complied with the technical rules for removal, including notice?

- Has the case been improvidently removed? Has the court ordered a remand? Has the federal court retained the case?

- Does the removed case contain both federal and state claims?

— Do the federal and state claims come within the federal court's supplemental jurisdiction on removal?

5. **Do the facts present a problem relating to the federal court's venue, transfer, or** *forum non conveniens?*

- For venue purposes: (**28 U.S.C. § 1391** *et seq.*)

— Have the parties contractually or consensually agreed to the venue?

— Has the defendant waived any objections to venue by failing to raise them in a timely fashion?

— What is the status of the parties and what is the type of case involved? Do the facts implicate one of the specialized venues for particular federal claims?

— What is the residence of the parties?

— Where did a substantial portion of the events or omissions relating to the claim occur?

— Where is property relating to the claim located?

- For transfer purposes: (**28 U.S.C. §§ 1404 and 1406**)

    — Who is initiating the transfer? For what reasons?

    — Would it be more convenient for the parties and witnesses to litigate the dispute in another venue?

    — Would it serve the interests of justice to litigate the dispute in another forum?

    — Has the plaintiff selected the improper venue by mistake?

- For *forum non conveniens* purposes: (***Gulf Oil Co. and Piper Aircraft***)

    — Does the court have valid venue?

    — Would it serve the private and public interests to dismiss the case in favor of an alternative forum? Do the facts satisfy the ***Gulf Oil*** and ***Piper Aircraft*** factors for a *forum non conveniens* dismissal?

    — Is there an alternative forum in which the plaintiff may receive adequate relief?

    — Has the court conditioned its *forum non conveniens* dismissal on the defendant's agreement to certain conditions? Are those conditions permissible?

III

Ascertaining Applicable Law

E.   Federal Common Law
    1.   Traditional Bases for Federal Common Law
    2.   Interstitial Federal Common Law

■ CHAPTER OVERVIEW

- This chapter concerns how state and federal courts determine what law to apply in a civil litigation.

- State and federal courts use different methods to determine what law applies in a lawsuit.

- If a lawsuit is filed in a state court, then the court will apply its own laws (*forum law*), or, using *choice-of-law rules,* apply the law of some other state that has some relationship to the litigation such that the application of the other state's law would be fair.

  — In general, states apply their own procedural rules to govern the conduct of the litigation and their substantive law to decide substantive claims.

- State courts also may apply federal substantive law in state cases that include federal claims.

- If a lawsuit is in federal court, what law applies depends in great part on the basis for the federal court's subject matter jurisdiction.

  — If the lawsuit is based on the United States Constitution, a federal statute, or a treaty, then the federal court will apply the federal substantive law Congress has enacted, or federal common law developed for the federal claim.

  — If the lawsuit is based on the federal court's diversity jurisdiction, then the federal court will apply the substantive law of a state, and the federal procedural rules for the conduct of the proceedings. These rules are called the *"Erie* doctrine."

  — Federal courts apply state substantive law in compliance with the **Rules of Decision Act.**

  — The federal court will first determine the choice-of-law rules used in the state in which the district court is located.

  — Applying these choice-of-law rules, the federal court will determine which state's substantive law to apply in the federal diversity lawsuit.

— Federal courts determine applicable state law by first looking at the decisions of the state's highest courts, and next to intermediate courts or other decisional bodies.

— If a state has not determined an applicable question of law, the federal court may in some instances "certify" that question for determination by the state court. In the alternative, the federal court may anticipate what the state high court might decide if presented with the question.

— In federal diversity cases, the court will apply federal procedural rules to govern the conduct of the litigation.

— Federal courts may apply federal procedural rules through power vested in the federal judiciary through the Rules Enabling Act, which permits federal courts to enact their own procedural rules, as long as those rules do not abridge, amend, enlarge, or alter substantive rights.

• Prior to the Supreme Court's declaration of the *Erie* doctrine in 1938, federal courts applied notions of "federal substantive common law" to resolve state-based diversity claims. In the *Erie* case, the Court repudiated this notion and held that there is no general federal common law.

• Federal common law still is applied in certain limited circumstances, however, including certain disputes between states and where Congress has specifically authorized the federal courts to create the substantive law under a statutory scheme.

A. DEFINING THE PROBLEM OF APPLICABLE LAW

Both state and federal courts must determine what substantive and procedural law applies to the case. The question of what law applies arises as a consequence of the American federal system of government, and the two-tier or dual-court system. Students should be aware that there is not "one law," but the possibility of multiple states' laws, or federal law. The problem of determining what applicable law applies to resolve a dispute is called "choice of law" or "conflict of law." "Conflicts" typically is taught as a separate upper-level course in most law school curriculums.

1. The Applicable Law Problem in State Courts: "Horizontal" Choice of Law

State courts may choose to apply the forum state's law, the law of some other state, or federal law. Federal law is sometimes required. What law applies will depend on the parties to the lawsuit, the claims, and the events or transactions giving rise to the claims.

a. Apply Forum Substantive Law

States will almost universally choose to apply their own, or *forum* law to completely localized disputes where the parties, claims, and events giving rise to the litigation all are contained within the state's jurisdiction. The court will apply both the state's substantive legal principles (i.e., tort, contract, property, etc.) as well as the state's procedural rules for the conduct of the action.

b. Apply Some Other State's Substantive Law

If a litigation involves out-of-state parties, or if the claims arise from events with contacts in other states (such as a dispersed tort), then a state may determine to apply some other state's law, rather than forum law. This choice-of-law determination is called "horizontal" choice of law, because it requires states to look "horizontally" across sister states for the appropriate choice of law. This is distinguished from a "vertical" choice of law, or choice of law between the federal and state court systems (*see Erie* discussion, *infra*).

i. Choice-of-Law Principles

The method by which a state court decides what other state's law to apply is through application of the state's own choice-of-law rules. Most states have adopted a specific set of choice-of-law rules, either by statute or common law. There are a number of different analytical methods for determining applicable law, including principles set forth in the First and Second Restatement of Conflicts; government interest analysis; or choice-influencing factors.

ii. Due Process Concerns

A state may choose to apply any other state's law, provided the application of another state's law does not violate the party's due process rights. **Allstate Company v. Hague,** 449 U.S. 302 (1981).

c. Apply Federal Law

State courts are competent to interpret and apply federal law in a state case that contains federal claims. A state's application of federal law is called a "reverse *Erie*" problem (*see* discussion *infra*).

d. Procedural Law

In all instances, whether a state court applies forum law, some other state's law, or federal law, the state court will apply its own procedural rules to the conduct of the litigation.

i. Special Limitations Problems

Whether a state's statute of limitations (and related concepts such as tolling) are part of procedural or substantive law has caused great difficulties in both horizontal and vertical choice-of-law problems. Some states and federal courts "borrow" another state's limitations periods; other states do not and apply forum limitations to foreign substantive law.

2. The Applicable Law Problem in Federal Courts

Determining applicable law in federal court chiefly (but not always) is tied to the jurisdictional basis for the lawsuit—either federal question jurisdiction or diversity jurisdiction.

a. Applicable Law in Federal Question Cases

In federal cases based on federal question jurisdiction—raising a claim under the United States Constitution, or a treaty—federal courts apply federal law. Constitutional questions are determined by federal constitutional law principles. For other federal claims, Congress either may statutorily supply federal substantive law or may authorize the federal courts to create federal common law to give content to newly created substantive rights.

b. Applicable Law in Federal Diversity Cases: Vertical Choice of Law

By definition, cases within the federal court's diversity jurisdiction involve at least two adverse parties from different states, and the claims in the lawsuit are state-based claims. In federal cases based on the federal court's diversity jurisdiction, federal courts will apply state substantive law and federal procedural law. These two principles comprise the so-called "*Erie* doctrine", discussed at length *infra*.

c. Applicable Procedural Law

In all federal cases, federal courts apply the Federal Rules of Civil Procedure. Federal courts will apply state statutes of limitation, however, if the federal court determines that the state statute of limitations is substantive in effect. *See* **Guaranty Trust Co. v. York,** 326 U.S. 99 (1945) (discussed *infra*).

B. STATE LAW IN FEDERAL COURTS: THE *ERIE* PROBLEM

Until 1938, federal courts freely applied notions of "federal common law" to all federal cases, including cases within the court's diversity jurisdiction. The reign of federal common law was repudiated by the Supreme Court's 1938 decision in **Erie R.R. Co. v. Tompkins,** 304 U.S. 64 (1938).

1. The Rule of *Swift v. Tyson*

The long-standing reign of federal common law derived from the Supreme Court's interpretation, in **Swift v. Tyson,** 41 U.S. 1, 16 Pet. 1, 10 L.Ed. 865 (1842), of the **Rules of Decision Act of 1789,** now **28 U.S.C. § 1652.** This Act requires that federal courts apply "the laws of the several states" as their rules of decision, except when the Constitution, federal law, or a treaty provides otherwise.

a. Construction of "Laws" in Section 34 of the Judiciary Act of 1789 and the Rules of Decision Act

In *Swift,* the Supreme Court, in a decision written by Justice Story, interpreted "laws" to mean only state statutes or state common law on issues that were peculiarly local in character. "Laws" did not apply to the decisions of state judicial tribunals, or to issues of broader national character, such as issues involving commercial paper.

b. General Federal Common Law

In litigation involving non-localized issues, federal judges were free to make recourse to "general principles" of "federal common law" to resolve a dispute. Over the ninety-plus years between *Swift* and *Erie,* the areas in which federal courts applied federal common law expanded considerably.

2. *Erie* Doctrine

In 1938 the Supreme Court in **Erie Railroad Co. v. Tompkins** repudiated the earlier Court's interpretation of **Section 34** and the **Rules of Decision Act** and overruled **Swift v. Tyson.** The important practical import of the *Erie* decision was its rejection of the concept that federal judges were empowered to ascertain and apply principles of "general federal common law" in federal diversity cases. Perhaps the most famous statement in the *Erie* decision is the Court's declaration that there is "no general federal common law."

a. "Laws" and Section 34 and the Rules of Decision Act

The Supreme Court, based on "newly discovered evidence" in a law review article written by Charles Warren concerning the intent of the drafters of **Section 34** of the **Judiciary Act of 1789,** determined that "laws" in the Act included judge-made law.

i. Effect of *Erie* Interpretation of What Constitutes "Law"

The *Erie* decision basically requires federal judges to look to both statutory and judge-made (that is, judicial development of common law precedent) and to apply that law under the **Rules of Decision Act.**

b. Rationales Underlying *Erie* Decisions: The "Twin Aims of *Erie*"

The *Erie* decision was intended to remedy the "mischievous" practices that had developed under the reign of *Swift*-based federal common law.

i. Forum-Shopping, Inequitable Discrimination, and Lack of Equal Protection of the Law

The *Swift* rule encouraged litigants to forum-shop for a better choice of law, usually by seeking federal diversity jurisdiction in order to benefit from a federal court willing to apply federal common law. *See, e.g.,* **Black & White Taxicab & Transfer Co. v. Brown & Yellow Taxicab & Transfer Co.,** 276 U.S. 518 (1928). In extreme instances, such as the *Black & White Taxi* case, a corporation would reincorporate in another state to benefit from diversity jurisdiction and more favorable federal common law.

ii. Rejection of Fallacy of Transcendental Body of Federal Common Law

The *Erie* Court also suggested that the *Swift* decision rested on the erroneous assumption that there is a "transcendental body of law outside of any particular State but obligatory within it unless and until changed by statute." In another famous statement, Justice Brandeis explained that law is not a brooding omnipresence in the sky—rejecting the existence of a transcendental body of general federal common law "discoverable" by federal judges.

c. Constitutional Basis for the *Erie* Decision

The Court in *Erie* did not hold **Section 34** of the **Judiciary Act of 1789** unconstitutional. However, the Court suggested that in applying the *Swift* doctrine, the federal courts "h[ad] invaded rights which in our opinion are reserved by the Constitution to the several states."

i. Academic Debate Concerning Constitutional Basis for the *Erie* Decision

A major academic debate has long centered on the issue whether the *Erie* decision is constitutionally based. Many consider the *Erie* decision's discussion of its constitutional basis as dicta.

(a) **Proponents** of the constitutionally based theory argue the *Swift* doctrine invaded states' rights to create their own common law, an aspect of state sovereignty guaranteed by the Tenth Amendment.

(b) **Opponents** of the constitutional theory contend, along with Justice Butler's dissent, that the Court did not need to reach a constitutional question to determine the validity of applicable state law. Justice Reed's concurrence also suggested that the Court did not need to address any constitutional issue in resolving the *Erie* case, because the Court simply could construe the term "laws" more broadly than under the prevailing *Swift* interpretation.

3. Modes of *Erie* Analysis

Although the *Erie* decision overruled *Swift* and effectively ended the reign of general federal common law, the *Erie* decision itself provided very little guidance to federal courts concerning what state law to apply, and how to ascertain that state law. This methodology for ascertaining applicable state law in federal cases has developed over a series of Supreme Court decisions since 1938, and this group of cases provides the modes of analysis collectively known as "*Erie* doctrine."

- **Two branches of *Erie* analysis.** *Erie* analysis has developed two major branches, known as the **"Rules of Decision"** branch and the "Rules Enabling Act" branch. Almost all *Erie* problems may be classified as a problem of applicable law falling within one mode of analysis or the other.

a. *Erie* Analysis under the Rules of Decision Act

After *Erie*, federal courts have no power to create federal substantive common law, but rather must follow the substantive statutory or common law of the states. Although the *Erie* decision instructed federal courts to apply state substantive law, that decision did not indicate how to classify the law or issues involved as substantive or procedural. Subsequent Supreme Court cases have attempted to offer some analytical guidance to the lower federal courts.

i. No Conflict between State and Federal Law

In federal diversity cases, if there is no conflict between possible applicable state and federal law, then there is no *Erie* problem and the federal court is not confronted with the need to choose between conflicting law. However, if a conflict does exist between possible applicable state and federal law, then the court is confronted with an *Erie* problem.

(a) **No applicable federal law on point.** If there is no federal applicable law on point in contrast to a state law or rule, then federal courts will apply state law.

(b) **Federal law generally regulating an area; specific state statutes.** If federal statutes generally regulate an area but state law provides a very specific rule not inconsistent with the federal government's regulatory scheme, then federal courts will apply the state law without violating federal regulatory provisions. (This presents a variation of the no-conflict rule). **Cohen v. Beneficial Industrial Loan Corp.,** 337 U.S. 541 (1949) (applying New Jersey state security-for-expenses bond in shareholder derivative suit, even though **Rule 23.1** does not require this).

ii. The "Outcome Determination" Test—Leading Case Authority: Guaranty Trust Co. v. York, 326 U.S. 99 (1945)

Shortly after the *Erie* decision, the Supreme Court issued a clarifying decision to assist federal courts in distinguishing between substantive and procedural issues. *Guaranty Trust* involved a diversity equity action for breach of fiduciary supervision of a trust. The *Erie* problem was whether the federal court should have applied the New York state statute of limitations, which would have barred the lawsuit, or federal law, which did not. Although there was no federal statute of limitations—that is, an absence of federal law on point—the federal court permitted the action.

(a) **The *Erie* inquiry.** In *Guaranty Trust,* the Supreme Court suggested principles to govern the *Erie* inquiry to assess whether an issue is substantive or procedural for *Erie* purposes:

- Is the issue one which is tightly or loosely bound up with the creation of the rights being sued on?

- Would application of a different rule in federal court *determine the outcome* of the litigation differently (and more favorably) than application of the state rule?

- Would the application of the federal rule be *outcome determinative* because it would induce forum shopping in favor of the federal courts and result in unequal administration of the laws (recall, these are the "twin evils" of the *Swift* doctrine).

(b) Application of outcome determination test in *Guaranty Trust.* Applying these principles in **Guaranty Trust,** the Supreme Court decided that New York state's statute of limitations was substantive for *Erie* purposes and that the federal court was obliged to apply the state limitations period.

(c) Other examples:

- **Tolling statutes. Rule 3** is not intended to govern questions concerning the tolling of statutes of limitation, and therefore in diversity cases state rules determine when limitations statutes are tolled. **Ragan v. Merchants Transfer & Warehouse Co.,** 337 U.S. 530 (1949).

- **State door-closing statutes.** Federal courts will apply state statutes that foreclose litigation by corporations that are not qualified to do business in the state. **Woods v. Interstate Realty Co.,** 337 U.S. 535 (1949).

- **State limitations on damages.** Federal courts should apply state statutes limiting damages in civil actions. *See* **Gasperini v. Center for Humanities, Inc.,** 518 U.S. 415 (1996). Such state legislatively enacted damage caps are substantive for *Erie* purposes. Denials of new trial motions for remittitur may only be reviewed by appellate courts under an abuse of discretion standard.

iii. The *Byrd* "Balancing Test": Leading Case Authority—Byrd v. Blue Ridge Rural Electric Cooperative, Inc., 356 U.S. 525 (1958)

In *Byrd,* the Supreme Court had to resolve a conflict between a South Carolina practice which permitted the question of whether a person was a statutory employee (under the South Carolina Workman's Compensation Act) to be decided by a judge, and federal law which would have entitled the petitioner to a jury resolution of that question.

(a) **Balancing test.** In *Byrd,* the Supreme Court articulated a test requiring federal courts to balance the relative federal and state interests in application of their respective rules, asking:

- What is the federal interest in avoiding state law or the federal policy to be fostered by applying state law?

- Would the use of a federal standard have an adverse impact on federalism? Would application of the federal rule intrude on a state's ability to regulate a legitimate area of state interest?

(b) **Application of *Byrd* balancing test.** The Court held that the federal court's interest in providing federal litigants with a Seventh Amendment jury trial guarantee outweighed South Carolina's weak interest in having its "policy" of referring the issue of a statutory employee to a judge. *Byrd, id.*

(c) **Deference to state interests.** Unless a very important federal interest—such as a Seventh Amendment jury trial right—is implicated, in close cases the *Byrd* balancing test will tip in favor of federal courts deferring to strongly articulated state rules.

- **Federal constitutional rights subsequent to Byrd.** No *Erie* decision subsequent to *Byrd* has required a federal court to balance a federally guaranteed constitutional right versus a state rule or policy. Hence, the *Byrd* facts presented the most extreme and clear application of the *Byrd* balancing test.

- **Bases for establishing a strong state interest in enforcement of its rule.** Subsequent to *Byrd,* in applying the *Byrd* balancing test, federal courts attempt to ascertain whether a state has manifested a strong interest in having its rule or policy enforced. Often such intent may be shown by explicit statutory reference or through legislative history.

b. *Erie* **Analysis under the Rules Enabling Act: Federal Procedural Rulemaking Power**

The **Rules of Decision Act** does not apply to determine governing law when federal and state procedural rules are in conflict. Such conflicts, instead, implicate the procedural rulemaking power and federal courts analyze these problems using analysis derived from the **Rules Enabling Act. 28 U.S.C. §§ 2071, 2072** (discussed *infra*).

i. Constitutional Authorization for the Federal Courts

Article III § 2 of the **United States Constitution** creates one Supreme Court and such inferior courts as the Congress chooses to establish. Pursuant to this authority, Congress created the lower federal courts. Inherent in the power to create federal courts is the power to prescribe rules of procedure governing procedures in those courts.

ii. Constitutional Basis for Federal Rulemaking Authority

Congress, under the authority to make all laws "necessary and proper" to carry out the functions of a federal government, enacted the Rules Enabling Act to authorize Congress and the federal judiciary to create federal rules of civil procedure. *See* **U.S. Const. Art. I § 8; 28 U.S.C. §§ 2071, 2072.** Congress and the federal judiciary share rulemaking power to create and revise federal rules of procedure.

iii. The Rules Enabling Act and the Federal Rules of Civil Procedure

In 1934 Congress enacted the Rules Enabling Act, which provided the statutory authority for the Federal Judicial Conference, working through an advisory committee, to promulgate the original Federal Rules of Civil Procedure in 1938. The Rules Enabling Act provides that the Supreme Court may promulgate rules of procedure for the federal courts so long as those rules do not enlarge, abridge, or modify substantive rights. **28 U.S.C. § 2072(b)**.

iv. Presumptively Valid Federal Rules of Civil Procedure

If the Supreme Court and Congress approve a Federal Rule of Civil Procedure (or a subsequent amendment to a rule), the Federal Rule is virtually presumptively valid. *See* **Sibbach v. Wilson & Co.,** 312 U.S. 1 (1941) (concluding that promulgation of **Rule 35** on mental and physical exams was within congressional power); **Schlagenhauf v. Holder,** 379 U.S. 104 (1964) (same).

v. *Erie* Conflicts between a State Rule of Procedure and a Federal Rule of Civil Procedure

If a question presents a conflict between a state rule of procedure and a Federal Rule of Civil Procedure that is exactly on point, then

Erie doctrine requires that the federal court apply the Federal Rule of Procedure over any conflicting state rule of procedure. **Hanna v. Plumer,** 380 U.S. 460 (1965) (applying more liberal provisions of **Rule 4** relating to service of process, over conflicting and more narrow Massachusetts state law service requirements).

- Compare **Marshall v. Mulrenin,** 508 F.2d 39 (1st Cir. 1974) (holding that Massachusetts statute for amendments changing a party against whom a claim is asserted should be applied rather than the provisions of **Rule 15(c)**).

- **Federal Rule of Appellate Procedure 38,** which permits assessment of penalties for frivolous appeals, applies rather than any contrary state provision mandating penalties for all unsuccessful appeals of money damages. *See* **Burlington Northern R.R. Co. v. Woods,** 480 U.S. 1 (1987) (conflict between discretionary Federal Rule and mandatory state rule).

vi. Rationale for Application of Federal Procedural Rules

The federal judiciary has a legitimate interest in establishing and maintaining a uniform system of procedural rules within the federal court system. As long as Congress and the judiciary validly promulgated the rule, and it does not contravene the Rules Enabling Act by enlarging, abridging, or modifying substantive rights, then federal courts are entitled to apply the federal rule pursuant to the Supremacy Clause. **U.S. Const. Art. VI.**

(a) Note. To date no Federal Rule of Civil Procedure has ever been found to be invalidly promulgated under the Rules Enabling Act, and the presumption of constitutional validity has prevailed in cases involving the Federal Rules.

(b) Practical effect—always apply Federal Rule. The practical effect of courts' never holding a Federal Rule unconstitutional is that when there is a conflict between a Federal Rule and a contrary state rule, courts will always apply the Federal Rule.

vii. No Direct Conflict between Federal Rule and State Rule: Tolling Statutes

If a federal rule and state statute appear to conflict but actually are designed for different purposes, then *Hanna* analysis does not apply and the federal court may comfortably apply both rules. *See, e.g.,* **Walker v. Armco Steel Corp.,** 446 U.S. 740 (1980) (**Rule 3** governs timing consideration in federal actions, but not tolling of state limitations periods; Oklahoma tolling statute applied. There was no direct conflict between the Federal Rule and the state law; *Hanna* analysis did not apply).

viii. Conflicts between Federal Statutes and State Law

If a conflict exists between a federal statute (as opposed to a Federal Rule of Civil Procedure) and a state law, *Hanna* analysis applies and the federal statute governs under the Supremacy Clause, **U.S. Const. Art. VI.** *See* **Stewart Organization, Inc. v. Ricoh Corp.,** 487 U.S. 22 (1988) (federal venue transfer statute, **28 U.S.C. § 1404(a)** applies rather than state law denying enforceability of contractual forum selection clauses).

C. DETERMINING STATE LAW FOR *ERIE* PURPOSES

Erie analysis presumes that federal courts can determine existing state law on a contested issue. Sometimes state law is not evident, especially if state law is in flux. Additionally, complex problems of ascertaining applicable law arise when state courts have not considered an issue (or there is no governing statute).

1. Determining Which State's Law Governs: *Erie* and Conflicts Principles

If a federal court determines that it must apply state substantive law, then the threshold question arises: "which state's law?" The Supreme Court answered this basic problem in **Klaxon Co. v. Stentor Electric Mfg. Co.,** 313 U.S. 487 (1941).

a. The *"Klaxon"* Rule

Federal courts in diversity cases must apply the conflict-of-law rules of the state in which the district court sits. For example, in federal diversity cases, the District Court for the Southern District of Texas must apply Texas state choice-of-law rules.

i. Rationale for the *Klaxon* Rule

The *Klaxon* rule is intended to promote the uniform application of substantive law within a state.

ii. Practical Implications of the *Klaxon* Rule

In practice, a federal judge in a diversity case sits as though he or she were a state court judge. The judge's first inquiry is to determine the state's choice-of-law regime (*see* discussion *supra*), and then to determine whether, under the state's choice of law principles, the court should apply forum state law or some other state's law.

- **Note.** It is possible, in a federal diversity case for a federal court to apply forum state law, or to apply some other state's law (if so directed by the forum's choice-of-law rules).

b.   Transferred Cases within the Federal System: The *Van Dusen* and *Ferens* Rules

If litigants file a federal diversity lawsuit and then transfer the case to another judicial district, the law of the transferor court applies in the transferee court. This rule applies whether the transfer is initiated by either the defendant or the plaintiff under **28 U.S.C. § 1404(a)**. *See* **Van Dusen v. Barrack,** 376 U.S. 612 (1964) (defendant-initiated transfers) and **Ferens v. John Deere Co., Inc.,** 494 U.S. 516 (1990).

i.   Rationale for the *Van Dusen* and *Ferens* Rules

The basic rationale underlying these rules is to prevent forum-shopping. Thus, if the law of the transferor court did not follow the case, litigants would have a great incentive to file a lawsuit in one federal forum and then transfer it to another in order to take advantage of federal law. In order to defeat such forum-shopping opportunities, the rules require that the applicable state law (including the state conflicts rules) travel with the case. All the transfer changes is the courtroom, not the applicable law.

ii.   Practical Implications of the *Van Dusen* and *Ferens* Rules

A federal judge in the Southern District of Texas may receive a federal diversity case transferred from a New York district court. In this instance, the Texas federal judge is required to think like a New York state judge and first ascertain New York state choice-of-law principles. The Texas judge may then determine to apply New York state law, or the law of some other state (if that is the result mandated by New York choice-of-law principles).

2.   Ascertaining State Law

Once a federal judge determines which state's law applies, the judge must then ascertain the sources of authority for and content of that law.

a.   Hierarchy of Authority

Federal courts look to state statutes and state common law decisions as the authoritative basis for ascertaining state law. The federal judge will first look to decisions of the state's highest court, and if there is no decision on point, then to decisions of intermediate state courts.

i. Decisions of Lower State Courts

Although decisions of lower state courts are entitled to some weight in *Erie* determinations, lower state court decisions do not necessarily control a federal court's reading of state law in diversity cases. *See* **Commissioner v. Bosch's Estate,** 387 U.S. 456 (1967).

b. State Law in Flux

In some federal diversity cases, federal judges may be presented with a legal question where the state law is in flux because lower state courts have repudiated older doctrine, but the highest state court has not yet definitively overturned existing precedent. Alternatively, a case may simply present an issue on which the highest state court has not yet ruled.

i. Federal Court Predictions of State Law

Federal courts may, in situations where state law is in flux (or where a state high court has not yet considered the issue), forecast what the state's highest courts might do if confronted with the legal issue. *See, e.g.,* **McKenna v. Ortho Pharmaceutical Corp.,** 622 F.2d 657 (3d Cir.), *cert. denied,* 449 U.S. 976 (1980); **Mason v. American Emery Wheel Works,** 241 F.2d 906 (1st Cir. 1957). Obviously, the power of federal judges to predict what state high courts might do is fairly controversial.

- **Predictive bases.** To predict how the state court might rule, federal courts may look to the state's disposition of issues or claims in analogous areas to determine a state's "probable disposition" of a novel legal question. *See* **McKenna v. Ortho Pharmaceutical Corp.,** *supra.*

ii. State Certification Procedures

Many states have adopted "certification" procedures that permit a federal court to petition a state's highest court for a decision on how that state court might rule on an issue of law on which the court has not yet spoken. *See, e.g.,* **Ill. Sup. Ct. Rule 20.**

D. FEDERAL LAW IN STATE COURTS: THE "REVERSE *ERIE*" PROBLEM

Many federal statutes create concurrent jurisdiction with state courts and permit litigants to pursue relief for federal law violations in state court. In such instances, the Supremacy Clause, **U.S. Const. Art. VI** requires that state courts apply federal law. This situation is called a "reverse *Erie*" problem, but as a practical matter this presents a rare situation.

1. Federally Created Claims

When a state case involves a federally created claim, state courts must apply federal substantive law. *See* **Dice v. Akron, Canton & Youngstown R.R. Co.,** 342 U.S. 359 (1952) (Federal Employers' Liability Act concerning validity of releases raises federal question to be determined by federal, and not state, law); **Testa v. Katt,** 330 U.S. 386 (1947); **Ward v. Love County,** 253 U.S. 17 (1920).

2. Federally Conferred Right to Jury Trial

If a federal statute creating rights also supplies a right to a jury trial on an issue, states are duty-bound to supply a jury trial even though state law would not permit this. *See* **Dice v. Akron, Canton & Youngstown,** *supra.*

3. Federal Defenses

When a plaintiff asserts a state-based claim, a defendant may interpose a federal defense. For example, in a state contract action for recovery of royalties under a patent, the defendant may assert as a defense the invalidity of the patent, or that it has been used in violation of federal antitrust laws. The application of these defenses requires the state court to apply federal law. *See, e.g.,* **Sola Elec. Co. v. Jefferson Elec. Co.,** 317 U.S. 173 (1942).

4. Federal Rules of Procedure in State Courts

Congress may require that state courts use the federal procedural rules when litigants seek to enforce certain statutory rights in state court (effectively displacing state procedures). *See* **Federal Energy Regulatory Commission v. Mississippi,** 456 U.S. 742 (1982) (upholding provisions of the **Public Utilities Regulatory Policies Act of 1978** requiring state public utility commissions to observe federal procedures in regulating energy use).

E. FEDERAL COMMON LAW

Even though the Supreme Court declared in *Erie* that there is no "general federal common law," that limitation applies only to federal courts sitting in their diversity jurisdiction. Thus, federal courts have continued to apply notions of federal common law in certain limited circumstances.

1. Traditional Bases for Federal Common Law

Federal courts have most typically applied federal common law in cases implicating important federal interests.

a. **Interstate Disputes**

A classic arena in which federal courts have articulated and applied federal common law is in the resolution of interstate disputes, such as over water rights, where it would be unfair to apply the law of a particular state. *See, e.g.,* **Hinderlider v. La Plata River & Cherry Creek Ditch Co.,** 304 U.S. 92 (1938).

b. **Admiralty and Maritime Cases**

The Constitution vests jurisdiction over admiralty cases in the federal courts, and federal courts have long created federal common law to develop a uniform body of admiralty law in these cases. *See, e.g.,* **Kossick v. United Fruit Co.,** 365 U.S. 731 (1961).

c. **International Relations**

In order to "speak with one voice," federal courts frequently resolve cases involving international disputes—including commercial disputes between United States citizens and foreign nationals, according to principles of federal common law. *See, e.g.,* **Banco Nacional de Cuba v. Sabbatino,** 376 U.S. 398 (1964).

d. **Legal Activities of the United States: Commercial Paper**

The rights and duties of the United States government on commercial paper are issues governed by federal common law, rather than by local law. **Clearfield Trust Co. v. United States,** 318 U.S. 363 (1943). The application of state law in this area would subject the rights and duties of the United States to "exceptional uncertainty."

  i. **Test for Determining Federal Common Law under *Clearfield Trust***

  See **United States v. Kimbell Foods, Inc.,** 440 U.S. 715 (1979):

  - Does the question involve a right of the United States arising under the operation of a nationwide program?

  - Is there a need for a national body of uniform law? Would the application of state law frustrate the specific objectives of the federal program?

  ii. **Cases Not within the *Clearfield* Doctrine: Litigation between Private Parties Not Involving Federal Interests**

■ ILLUSTRATIONS

Bank of America National Trust & Savings Association v. Parnell, 352 U.S. 29 (1956) (issue of whether defendants took bonds in good faith was a matter of state law, and such litigation between purely private parties does not touch on the interests of the United States government).

Miree v. DeKalb County, 433 U.S. 25 (1977) (state law applied whether petitioners as third-party beneficiaries under FAA contracts had standing to sue. The application of federal common law to resolve this issue would promote no federal interest. Only the rights of private litigants are involved in determining applicable contract principles).

But cf. **Kohr v. Allegheny Airlines, Inc.,** 504 F.2d 400 (7th Cir. 1974), *cert. denied sub nom.* **Forth Corp. v. Allegheny Airlines, Inc.,** 421 U.S. 978 (1975) (federal law of contribution and indemnity applied to predominant, almost exclusive interest of the federal government in regulating the nation's airways).

2. Interstitial Federal Common Law

Federal courts are empowered to create federal common law when there is a "statutory gap" that does not supply applicable substantive law to enforce a congressionally created right. This type of federal common law is called "interstitial federal common law."

a. Implied Congressional Directive: Labor Law

The federal courts have been able to fashion federal common law in the labor area, based on an implied congressional directive authorizing the federal courts to develop a uniform, national body of collective bargaining law. *See* **Textile Workers Union v. Lincoln Mills,** 353 U.S. 448 (1957) (federal common law governs the decision whether federal court had jurisdiction to enforce collective bargaining agreement under the **Labor Management Relations Act of 1947).**

b. Statutes of Limitations

In instances where a federal statute is silent and does not supply an applicable statute of limitations, federal courts may draw timeliness rules from federal law (either express limitation periods from related federal statutes, or alternatives such as laches). *See* **DelCostello v. International Bhd. of Teamsters,** 462 U.S. 151 (1983). This is especially true where state statutes of limitation are unsatisfactory vehicles for the enforcement of federal law.

c. Exceptions

When a federal statute is silent, federal courts will not always create federal common law to fill the gap. *See, e.g.,* **Texas Industries, Inc. v. Radcliff Materials, Inc.,** 451 U.S. 630 (1981) (federal court not permitted to fashion federal common law of contribution among antitrust violators; presumption is strong that Congress deliberately omitted remedy when it enacts a comprehensive, integrated scheme of enforcement procedures).

■ CHAPTER REVIEW CHECKLIST

A problem relating to how to determine applicable law—especially *Erie* doctrine—is a standard first-year civil procedure exam topic. First-year students tend to become overly concerned about *Erie* analysis, but an *Erie* problem can be simply approached by asking a series of questions and to first determine what type of *Erie* problem the facts present.

Some professors may not be interested in the actual application of *Erie* rules to facts, but may instead be more interested in the constitutional underpinnings for the *Erie* doctrine. If this was your law professor's focus, then you should review the federalism concerns implicated by applicable law problem.

It is highly unlikely that your law professor will test you on state choice-of-law issues, since you will not have studied the various means of determining choice of law in the state context (remember, this is called the "horizontal" choice-of-law problem). You should, however, be conversant with the *Klaxon, Van Dusen,* and *Ferens* rules, which provide the basis for federal judges determining state law based on state conflicts principles, and in transferred cases. Your law professor can quickly create a seemingly complicated *Erie* problem by moving a case around the federal system.

To answer a problem relating to applicable law, first ask:

1. **Where has the lawsuit been filed?**

    *   Is the lawsuit filed in state court so that applicable law must be determined by state choice-of-law rules? (horizontal choice of law). Do the facts indicate what methodology the state has adopted to determine applicable law?

        — If the lawsuit is in state court, are all the parties, claims, issues, and events relating to the state local, (i.e., have affiliating contacts with the state) such that the application of forum state law does not offend due process?

— If the lawsuit is in state court, are the parties, claims, and events giving rise to the lawsuit dispersed such that the court might apply the law of some other state?

• Is the lawsuit filed in federal court? What is the basis for the federal court's jurisdiction?

— Is the case within the federal court's federal question jurisdiction? (*See* 2, *infra*)

— Is the case within the federal court's diversity jurisdiction? (*See* 3, *infra*)

2. Is the case within the federal court's federal question jurisdiction?

• Does federal law supply the applicable body of law to determine the rights or claims?

— Does the litigation involve a constitutional question?

— Does the litigation involve a treaty?

— Does the litigation involve enforcement of federal rights under a federal statute?

— Does the federal statute explicitly also create the substantive law to enforce rights created by the statute?

— Does the federal statute authorize the federal courts to create and develop federal common law?

— Does the litigation involve a uniquely or predominantly federal interest such that the federal courts are empowered to apply federal common law? (e.g., interstate disputes, international relations, commercial paper, admiralty and maritime claims).

3. Is the case within the federal court's diversity jurisdiction?

• Do the facts involve a Federal Rule of Civil Procedure?

— Is the Rule in conflict with a state rule directly on point?

— Was the Rule validly promulgated by Congress and the Federal Judiciary pursuant to the Rules Enabling Act?

— Does the Rule in any way enlarge, abridge, or modify substantive rights?

- If the facts do not involve a Rule, is the issue substantive (so that the federal court must apply state law), or procedural (so that the federal court may apply federal law)? (The following analysis combines factors articulated in the *Guaranty Trust* "outcome determination" test and the *Byrd* balancing test):

  — Is the issue one which is tightly or loosely bound up with the creation of the rights being sued upon? If so, then the issue should be viewed as substantive, requiring application of state law.

  — Would the application of the federal rule be outcome determinative of the litigation so that it would induce forum-shopping by a litigant to benefit from application of a more favorable rule?

  — Would the application of the federal rule, in derogation of the state rule, result in the unequal administration of the laws?

  — What is the federal interest in avoiding the state law?

  — What is the federal policy to be fostered by applying federal law? Is the rule or policy of constitutional dimension, similar to a Seventh Amendment right to trial by jury?

  — Would use of the federal rule or standard have an adverse impact on federalism? Would application of the federal rule undermine a state's interest in legitimately regulating an area of state interest?

- How strong is the state's interest in its rule? Is the rule codified by practice? Is there legislative history indicating the importance of the rule in effectuating state substantive law? Is the state rule merely a "policy," rather than a codified rule?

Commencing the Action: Notice and Service of Process

■ ANALYSIS

■ CHAPTER OVERVIEW

- This chapter concerns the legal requirements and the technical means for commencing an action in state or federal court, including filing a complaint and service of process. The formal commencement of an action is important for timing considerations relating to the course of civil litigation, such as the filing of responsive pleadings or motions. The proper commencement of an action also relates to statute of limitations deadlines. From a constitutional perspective, proper commencement of an action is necessary to satisfy the requirements of procedural due process.

- Procedural due process under the Fifth and Fourteenth Amendments requires that parties receive notice of an action as well as an opportunity to be heard in response to an action that might deprive the parties of life, liberty, or property.

- The notice required by due process is notice *reasonably calculated,* under all the circumstances, to apprise interested parties of the pendency of the action and to afford them an opportunity to present their objections.

- In general, notice of a lawsuit is given by serving process on the defendant. State courts have their own rules relating to the appropriate and proper manner of service of process in a state court action. In general, most state court civil litigation is commenced by filing a complaint in the appropriate state court, followed by personal delivery of a copy of the complaint and summons on the named defendants.

- There are basically three forms of service of process: *actual service, substituted service, and constructive service. Actual service* of process typically involves the personal delivery of the complaint and summons to the parties named in the lawsuit, or in the case of businesses or corporations, their designated agents. Some states require actual service of process. *Substituted service* refers to other means of notifying parties than through in-person notice, such as service by mail. *Constructive service* generally refers to notice given by publication in a newspaper or other media.

- In state practice, an action may be "commenced" either by the filing of the complaint or when service of process is effectuated on the parties to the suit. In states where an action is commenced only when service of process is accomplished, a plaintiff may encounter statute of limitations problems if the complaint is filed close to the limitations date.

- In federal practice, formal commencement of a civil action is governed by **Rule 3.** A suit is commenced when a copy of the complaint is filed in federal district court. **Rule 6** governs timing requirements relating to the filing of motions and papers in a federal action, including requests for extensions of time.

- In federal practice, the rules governing service of process are delineated in **Rule 4. Rule 4** has been amended several times since the promulgation of the Federal Rules in 1938, to change the various means by which service of process may be effectuated in a civil action.

- **Rule 4** provides for various means of serving process, including the form and issuance of the summons, and waiver of the service requirement. Since amendment of **Rule 4** in 1993, federal rules now favor defendants' waiver of service in order to reduce and avoid the costs of serving process.

- **Rule 4** provides for various specific means of serving process on individuals in foreign countries, infants and incompetent persons, corporations and associations, and the federal government and its agencies. **Rule 4** also includes geographical and territorial limits to the reach of federal service.

- In federal practice, service of process is a waivable defect. If a party has been improperly served or the form of the notice is defective, then that party may move to dismiss the action on defective process grounds. However, if a party does not make a timely motion concerning defective process, then any objections relating to defective process are subsequently waived. In addition, since 1993, parties may waive the requirement of formal service if they are otherwise notified by the plaintiff(s) of the filing of the complaint.

- Service of process may not be effectuated by fraud, force, artifice, or inducement into a state for the purpose of serving process.

- In general, parties making a special appearance in a jurisdiction to respond to a particular litigation are immune—during the course of the pending litigation—from service of process in another litigation.

- In actions involving *provisional remedies* such as temporary restraining orders, preliminary injunctions, and prejudgment attachments of property, constitutional due process requires notice of the prejudgment seizure, as well as a meaningful opportunity to be heard before a neutral court officer prior to the attachment. Such prejudgment property seizures cannot be made upon conclusory affidavits or in an *ex parte* hearing that does not involve the person whose property is being seized. Due process is enhanced if the state law also requires the posting of a security bond in advance of the seizure.

A. THE REQUIREMENT OF REASONABLE NOTICE

1. Introductory Note on Notice and Service of Process

State and federal courts require that parties be given notice of an action against them. Notice has both constitutional and nonconstitutional (statutory) dimensions. The constitutional dimensions of notice concern the requirements of due process in order to bind parties to a judgment. In addition, constitutional due process is especially concerned with protecting the interests of property-holders whose property might be seized in advance of a judgment. The nonconstitutional dimensions of notice concern the mechanical statutory requirements for properly serving process on parties.

2. Constitutional Notice and Due Process

The Fifth and Fourteenth Amendments to the Constitution provide that no person may be deprived of life, liberty, or property without due process of law. The Fifth Amendment applies to federal actions and the Fourteenth Amendment to state actions. The Supreme Court has held: "An elementary and fundamental requirement of due process in any proceeding which is to be accorded finality is notice reasonably calculated, under all the circumstances, to apprise interested parties of the pendency of the action and to afford them an opportunity to present their objections." **Mullane v. Central Hanover Bank & Trust Co.,** 339 U.S. 306 (1950).

a. Leading Case Authority—Mullane v. Central Hanover Bank & Trust Co., 339 U.S. 306 (1950)

In 1946 the Central Hanover Bank & Trust Company set up a "common trust fund" to invest and administer a pool of 113 small trust funds, consisting of both testamentary trusts and *inter vivos* (or live) trusts. In 1947 the bank petitioned for judicial approval of the first settlement of the accounts, and gave notice of this settlement by publication in a local newspaper during four successive weeks. This was the only notice required under relevant New York statutes. The court appointed Mullane as the special guardian and attorney for persons known and unknown who might have any present or future interest in the income of the common fund. Another guardian, Vaughan, was appointed to represent the interests of claimants in the trust principal. Mullane objected to the notice by publication, arguing that it was inadequate to afford due process to the beneficiaries and therefore the court lacked jurisdiction to render a binding judicial settlement of the trust account. The Supreme Court held that notice by publication was sufficient for the unknown beneficiaries, but inadequate for known beneficiaries.

3. *Mullane* Notice Requirements

a. General *Mullane* Standards

(1) Notice must be reasonably calculated, under all the circumstances, to apprise interested parties of the pendency of the action and afford them an opportunity to present their objections.

(2) The notice must be of such nature as reasonably to convey the required information (concerning the nature of the action).

(3) The notice must afford a reasonable time for those interested to make their appearance.

(4) The court should have "due regard" for the "practicalities and peculiarities" of the case.

b. Notice and Actions Involving Real Property

Attachment of a chattel or real estate, together with publication, may provide adequate notice.

i. Rationale

Attachment plus publication confers adequate notice because property owners theoretically are usually aware and concerned about the status of their property. (Compare the similar notice theory articulated in **Pennoyer v. Neff,** 95 U.S. (5 Otto) 714 (1877).)

(a) **Known property owners—condemnation proceedings.** Where the names and addresses of property owners are known, then publication alone may be insufficient to provide property owners of notice in condemnation proceedings, *see, e.g.,* **Walker v. City of Hutchinson,** 352 U.S. 112 (1956), or when coupled with notices posted on trees, *see, e.g.,* **Schroeder v. City of New York,** 371 U.S. 208 (1962).

(b) Property mortgagees. Notice by publication and posting was insufficient to provide a real property mortgagee with adequate notice of a proceeding to foreclose on the mortgaged property for nonpayment of taxes. The constructive notice by publication must be supplemented either by personal service or by notice mailed to the mortgagee's last known address. **Mennonite Board of Missions v. Adams,** 462 U.S. 791 (1983).

c. Notice Requirements for Known Parties

Mullane requires that known parties be given notice in a manner *reasonably calculated* to reach them directly, such as by personal or mail service. Personal service, however, is not absolutely required. Where the names and post office addresses of parties are known, newspaper publication is constitutionally *inadequate* to provide notice to known parties.

i. Example

Notice by publication of the settlement of the trust accounts in *Mullane* was constitutionally insufficient to reach the known beneficiaries of the Central Hanover Bank common trust fund. The Central Hanover Bank trustee had the names and addresses of the income beneficiaries, and they were entitled to personal or mail notice of the settlement action.

ii. Exception: Courts Will Not Require the Impracticable

Hence, in *Mullane,* the Supreme Court conceded that Central Hanover Bank, as trustee, was not required to conduct extensive searches to ascertain the current addresses of the trust's current or contingent beneficiaries.

iii. Probate Proceedings

Publication notice only of the commencement of probate proceedings under state law is constitutionally insufficient to give adequate notice to a known or reasonably ascertainable creditor. On balance, satisfying a creditor's substantial practical need for actual notice is not so cumbersome or impracticable as to unduly burden the state's need for expeditious resolution of decedents' estates. Mail service of process is inexpensive, efficient, and reasonably calculated to provide actual notice. **Tulsa Professional Collection Services, Inc. v. Pope,** 485 U.S. 478 (1988).

iv. Non-Resident Motorist Statutes

A New Jersey non-resident motorist statute that designated the Secretary of State as the defendant's agent for service of process was constitutionally insufficient to provide adequate notice because the statute did not expressly require the Secretary of State to communicate notice of the commencement of an action against the non-resident. The statute was invalid even where the Secretary of State actually had notified the defendant of the action. **Wuchter v. Pizzutti,** 276 U.S. 13 (1928). Such non-resident motorist statutes should require the plaintiff's summons to list the address of the defendant and should impose a duty of notifying the defendant by mail.

d. Notice Requirements for Unknown Parties: Publication or Constructive Notice

Mullane indicates that notice by publication is constitutionally sufficient for unknown parties or missing parties.

i. Disfavored Method

Notice by publication alone is a disfavored method of providing notice. However, resort to publication as a substitute for other means of actual or constructive notice is permissible in certain cases where it is not reasonably practicable or possible to provide more adequate warning of a lawsuit. Such cases typically involve unknown or missing persons.

- **Example. Sufficient notice by publication.** Notice by publication was sufficient for the unknown, contingent beneficiaries of the Central Hanover Trust in *Mullane.*

- **Example. Insufficient notice by publication.** Notice by local newspaper publication is insufficient to give notice to a resident who has departed a state to establish a domiciliary elsewhere, even though his family remains in the state. **McDonald v. Mabee,** 243 U.S. 90 (1917).

e. **Notice by the "Best Methods Reasonably Practicable"— Applications**

- **Example. Sufficient notice by substitute mail service.** In an automobile accident where the tort-feasor failed to furnish the injured plaintiff with a correct address at the scene of the accident, court-ordered substitute service by ordinary mail to the defendant's last known address, and publication in a local newspaper, was constitutionally sufficient notice. **Dobkin v. Chapman,** 21 N.Y.2d 490, 289 N.Y.S.2d 161, 236 N.E.2d 451 (1968).

- **Example. Insufficient notice by posting.** In a forcible entry and detainer action prior to an eviction, the posting of a summons on an apartment door in a public housing project was insufficient to provide adequate notice. Merely posting the notice on an apartment door did not satisfy minimum standards of due process, where service by mail would be a superior method of giving notice. Under the conditions prevalent in the public housing projects where notices were frequently removed by children and tenants, notice by posting could not be considered a "reliable means of acquainting interested parties of the fact that their rights are before the courts." **Greene v. Lindsey,** 456 U.S. 444 (1982).

B. THE MECHANICS OF GIVING NOTICE: SERVICE OF PROCESS

1. Introductory Notes on Commencement of an Action

a. Commencement of an Action under State Law

State law provides different methods for determining the official commencement of an action. The date of the commencement of an action is important because this date typically triggers the filing requirements for responsive pleadings—such as the defendant's answer—or other pretrial motions, such as motions to dismiss or demurrers. Fixing the official date of the commencement of an action also is important because actions must be commenced prior to the running of any applicable statutes of limitations. In some states, a civil action is officially commenced when a complaint is filed in court. In other states, an action is commenced only when the complaint has been filed in court and the defendant has been properly served. In the latter instance, a plaintiff who files a complaint very close to a statute of limitations deadline may run into problems if the defendant cannot be properly served prior to the running of the statute of limitations.

b. Commencement of an Action in Federal Court

In federal court, "a civil action is commenced by filing a complaint with the court." **Rule 3.**

i. Timing Requirements from Service

In federal court, the timing requirements for many of the defendant's responsive pleadings and motions typically run from the service of process of the complaint and summons, rather than filing of the complaint. For example, a defendant's answer or motions to dismiss must be served within 21 days of the defendant's being served with the summons and complaint, unless the defendant waived service of the summons (in which case the defendant has 60 days to respond or 90 days if the defendant is outside the U.S.). Thus, if the defendant waives service the defendant enjoys a "bonus" of additional time to respond. This procedure saves time, expense, and improves efficiency.

2. Service of Process Provisions: Rule 4

a. Historical Note on Revisions of the Federal Service of Process Rule

The federal service of process rule, **Rule 4,** has been one of the most frequently amended rules. The Rule has grown lengthier and more detailed with each successive amendment. Prior to 1983, the primary means for accomplishing service in federal court was through the United States Marshal's Service. In 1983 **Rule 4** was extensively amended to provide for service of process by first-class mail with the return of an acknowledgment form. After a decade of problems with this mail procedure, the Advisory Committee on Civil Rules largely abandoned the mail-service-and-acknowledgment form in a 1993 revision of **Rule 4. Rule 4** was amended again in 2000, in provisions in subsection 4(i) relating to actions involving United States employees.

b. The 1993 Amendments to Rule 4 Service of Process

Rule 4 was completely rewritten as of 1993, and significant provisions of the old Rule were revised, eliminated, or renumbered. Thus, case law prior to 1993 may refer to **Rule 4** provisions that have been eliminated or moved to another place within the Rule. *Amended Rule 4 addresses both the manner and form of service of process and the assertion of personal* (in personam*) jurisdiction over defendants.*

i. Minor Changes and Renumbering

Several 1993 changes in **Rule 4** relate to the form and issuance of the summons; proof of service; and time limits for service, found in **Rule 4(a)–(c)** (described below). The manner of service provisions are now set forth at new paragraphs **Rule 4(e)–(j)** (described *infra*). The territorial limits on service are now described at **Rule 4(k)** (described *infra*).

ii. Major Change: Waiver of Service

The most significant 1993 change to **Rule 4** concerns the provisions for a defendant's waiver of service, contained in **Rule 4(d)** and described *infra.*

c. Complaint; Form and Issuance of the Summons

As indicated above, a federal civil action is commenced by the filing of a complaint. **Rule 3.** The defendant must be served with a copy of the complaint and a summons. After filing the complaint, a plaintiff presents a summons to the court clerk for signing. The summons must indicate the name of the parties, the court, the plaintiff's attorney (or the name of the plaintiff, if the plaintiff does not have a lawyer). The summons also must indicate the time in which the defendant must appear or suffer a default judgment for failure to respond within that time. A court clerk must sign the summons, which should bear the court's seal. If there are multiple defendants in the action, a summons must be issued to each. **Rule 4(a), (b).**

i. Obligation to Make Service

The plaintiff is responsible for serving the defendant with copies of the complaint and summons within the time limits sets forth in **Rule 4(m)** (*see infra*).

ii. Persons Who May Make Service

A party to the action may not make service of process on the defendant. The following persons may make service (**Rule 4(c)(2)**):

- Any person who is at least 18 years old;

- A United States marshal or deputy United States marshal, at the plaintiff's request;

- Any court-appointed person or officer;

- Any court-appointed person to serve process for a pauper, under **28 U.S.C. § 1915;**

- Any court-appointed person to serve process in a seaman's action authorized under **28 U.S.C. § 1916.**

d. Proof of Service

Under the 1993 amendments to **Rule 4,** a defendant may waive service of process altogether. *See* **Rule 4(d)** (discussed *infra*). However, if a defendant does not waive service, then the plaintiff must effect service of process and provide proof of that service to the court. **Rule 4(l).** This proof may be furnished by an affidavit sworn by the person who has served the process on the defendant. If the defendant is outside the United States, proof of service may be furnished according to any means agreed to by treaty, or by a receipt signed by the addressee (or other evidence of delivery to the addressee). A plaintiff's failure to make proof of service of process does not affect the validity of the process, and proof of service may be amended. **Rule 4(l).**

e. Time Limits for Service; Consequences for Failure to Meet Time Limits: Rule 4(m)

i. In General

A defendant must be served within **120 days** after the filing of the complaint.

ii. Failure to Effect Service within 120 Days

If a plaintiff fails to make service within 120 days, the court may do one of two things:

- Dismiss the action against the defendant, without prejudice to the plaintiff's ability to refile the action (provided that any relevant statutes of limitation have not run); or,

- If the plaintiff can show *good cause* for the failure to accomplish service, the court may extend the time for making service for an appropriate period.

- A federal court, in its discretion, may extend the 120 day period for service even if good cause is not shown. *See* **Espinoza v. United States,** 52 F.3d 838 (10th Cir. 1995); **Petrucelli v. Bohringer & Ratzinger, GMBH,** 46 F.3d 1298 (3d Cir. 1995).

iii. Time Limits: Waiver (Rule 4(d)(1)(F))

If a plaintiff notifies a defendant of commencement of an action and requests a waiver of service, the defendant is entitled to a "reasonable time" to return the waiver. "Reasonable time" is defined as:

- At least 30 days from the date on which the plaintiff sends the request for waiver, if the defendant is located in the United States; or,

- At least 60 days from the date on which the plaintiff sends the request for waiver, if the defendant is located outside the United States.

f. Manner of Service on Individuals and Entities

The federal rules provide for different methods of service on individuals and entities such as corporations or associations. Service rules also relate to whether the named party is located in the United States, or abroad. An individual or entity may waive service of process under **Rule 4(d).** If the defendant does not waive service, then the following rules apply:

i. Service on Individuals Located within a Judicial District of the United States: Rule 4(e)

Individuals located in the United States may be served in the following ways:

- Pursuant to the state law in which the district court is located;

- Personal service of the complaint and summons on the individual;

- Leaving copies of the complaint and summons at the individual's "dwelling house or usual place of abode with some person of suitable age and discretion then residing therein;"

- **Leading authority: Rovinski v. Rowe,** 131 F.2d 687 (6th Cir. 1942). In construing the "usual place of abode" provision of

Rule 4, federal courts have given liberal and flexible construction to what constitutes a defendant's usual place of abode. In *Rovinski,* the federal court upheld service delivered to Rovinski's mother's home in Michigan, a place Rovinski visited from Minnesota but where he had not resided for two years.

- Delivery of the complaint and summons to an authorized agent.

- **Leading case authority: National Equipment Rental, Ltd. v. Szukhent, 375 U.S. 311 (1964).** The Supreme Court upheld a contractual provision designating an agent to receive service of process, even though the agent was not personally known to the party and there was no express provision for the agent to convey the notice to the party. While the contract set forth a method of notification, it also established personal jurisdiction over Michigan residents in New York through consent. Parties to a lawsuit may agree in advance to submit to a court's jurisdiction, to permit notice to be served to an opposing party, or to even waive notice altogether.

ii. Service on Individuals Located in a Foreign Country: Rule 4(f)

Service on individuals located abroad may be accomplished in the following ways:

- By any internationally agreed means reasonably calculated to give notice (such as means authorized by the **Hague Convention on the Service Abroad of Judicial and Extrajudicial Documents**);

- By any means prescribed by the foreign country's law for service of process in its own courts;

- By means directed by a foreign authority in response to a request letter;

- By personal delivery or mail service with a signed receipt (unless the foreign country prohibits such methods of service);

- By any other means not prohibited by international agreement as may be directed by the court.

iii. Service on Infants or Incompetents: Rule 4(g)

Service on infants and incompetents may be accomplished in any manner prescribed by state law. If an infant or incompetent is located abroad, service may be accomplished according to the foreign country's service provisions, or in a manner directed by the foreign authority.

iv. Service on Corporations, Partnerships, or Associations: Rule 4(h)(1)

Unless some federal statute provides for a different means of service, a corporation, partnership, or unincorporated association located in the United States may be served:

- By the state service rules for corporations;

- By delivery to a managing or general agent, or agent authorized by appointment or law to receive service;

- By delivery to an authorized agent and if required by statute, also by mail to the defendant.

If the defendant corporation, partnership, or unincorporated association is located outside the United States, then service may be accomplished under any of the methods for serving individuals, except if personal delivery is prohibited by the foreign country's law. **Rule 4(h)(2).**

v. Service on the United States Government: Rule 4(i)

(a) The United States may be served: Rule 4(i)(1)

- By delivery to a U.S. attorney for the district in which the action is brought;

- By delivery to an assistant U.S. attorney or clerical employee who has been designated in writing by the U.S. attorney (to receive process);

- By registered or certified mail to the civil process clerk at the U.S. attorney's office;

- By also sending process by registered or certified mail to the U.S. Attorney General in Washington, D.C.

(b) Federal officers, agencies, or corporations: Rule 4(i)(2). Officers, agencies, or corporations of the United States may be served:

- By any of the methods for serving the United States as a party; or

- By sending process by registered or certified mail to the officer, agency, or corporation.

vi. Service on Foreign, State, or Local Governments: Rule 4(j)

- Service on foreign states or their political subdivisions may be effected pursuant to the provisions of **28 U.S.C. § 1608. Rule 4(j)(1).**

- Service on states, municipal corporations, or other governmental organizations may be effected by delivery of process to the entity's chief executive officer or in a manner prescribed by state law. **Rule 4(j)(2).**

g. Property Seizure as the Basis for Jurisdiction and Notice: Rule 4(n)

i. Authorized by United States Statute

A court may assert jurisdiction over property if it is authorized by federal statute. Once the federal government has seized such property, notice must be given to claimants of that property either as the federal seizure statute provides, or by the regular service provisions in **Rule 4. Rule 4(n)(1).**

ii. Seizure of Assets under State Law

If a court cannot obtain personal jurisdiction over a defendant by reasonable efforts to serve process, then a court may assert jurisdiction over any of the defendant's assets found within the jurisdiction as provided for by state seizure laws (the state laws in which the federal district court is located). **Rule 4(n)(2).**

h. Territorial Limits: Rule 4(k)

i. Jurisdictional Effects of Service of Process: In General

In a federal action, service of process or the filing of a waiver of service is effective to establish personal jurisdiction, which of course must meet constitutional due process requirements. Provided constitutional requirements are satisfied, service of process may establish assertion of personal jurisdiction over:

- party defendants if the defendant could be subject to personal jurisdiction in the state where the district court is located (**Rule 4(k)(1)(A)**);

- additional parties—the "100 mile bulge rule"—who are impleaded under **Rule 14,** or who are needed for a just adjudication of the dispute under **Rule 19,** provided service is within 100 miles from the federal courthouse issuing the summons (**Rule 4(k)(1)(B)**);

- parties when authorized by federal statute (**Rule 4(k)(1)(C)**).

ii.   Jurisdictional Effects of Service of Process: Federal Claims

In actions based on federal claims, service of process (or waiver of service of process) is effective to establish personal jurisdiction over a defendant who is not subject to the jurisdiction of any state—provided that exercise of jurisdiction comports with constitutional due process requirements. **Rule 4(k)(2).**

i.   Waiver of Service: Rule 4(d)

The centerpiece of the 1993 amendment of **Rule 4** was the addition of provisions for waiver of service of process by the defendant in an action. If the defendant waives service and the plaintiff files the waiver with the court, the plaintiff is not required to furnish proof of service. **Rule 4(d)(4).**

i.   Shift in Notice Philosophy; Duty to Avoid Unnecessary Costs; Burden on Plaintiff to Request Waiver

The 1993 amendment reflects a shift in the relative obligations of the parties with regard to notice; the new waiver provisions place an *affirmative duty* "to avoid the unnecessary costs of serving the summons." To avoid costs, a plaintiff must notify the defendant(s) of the filing of a complaint, and provide the defendant with an opportunity to waive service. **Rule 4(d)(2).**

ii.   Duty to Avoid Unnecessary Costs; Burden on Defendant to Grant Waiver

A defendant who fails to comply with a request for waiver is required to pay the plaintiff's costs in effecting service on the defendant, unless the defendant can show *good cause* for failing to comply with the plaintiff's request for a waiver. **Rule 4(d)(2).**

- Costs for failure to comply with a request for waiver include costs of the service, and any reasonable attorney's fees as a consequence of a motion to collect the costs of service. **Rule 4(d)(2)(B).**

iii. Implementation Provisions

A plaintiff is obligated to send a notice of the action, a copy of the complaint, and a request for waiver to the defendant (or the defendant's agent) by first-class mail or other reliable means. The defendant has to be informed of the consequences of failure to comply with the request for waiver, and the time period in which to comply. **Rule 4(d)(1)(A)–(G).**

- **Form 1A** sets forth the federal form for the plaintiff to give notice of the lawsuit and request for a waiver of the service of summons.

- **Form 1B** sets forth a federal form for a defendant to waive service and the summons.

iv. Time Limits: Return of Waiver (Rule 4(d)(3))

If a plaintiff notifies a defendant of commencement of an action and requests a waiver of service, the defendant is entitled to a *reasonable time* to return the waiver. *Reasonable time* is defined as:

- At least 30 days from the date on which the plaintiff sends the request for waiver, if the defendant is located in the United States; or,

- At least 60 days from the date on which the plaintiff sends the request for waiver, if the defendant is located outside the United States.

v. Waiver and Time Limits for Responsive Pleadings

A defendant who returns a waiver is not required to serve an answer until 60 days after the date on which the plaintiff sent the request for the waiver, or 90 days if the defendant is outside the country. *See also* **Rule 12(a)(1)(B)** (same timing provision).

(a) **Contrasting timing rule for service of process.** If the defendant does not comply with the request for waiver, then the plaintiff must effect service of process under other provisions of **Rule 4.** When service of process is made on the defendant, the defendant then has 21 days after being served with the summons and complaint to file an answer. **Rule 12(a)(1)(A).**

3. Service of Process and Statutes of Limitations

a. Timing Considerations: Limitations, Accrual, and Tolling Distinguished

i. Statutes of Limitations

States have statutes of limitations that describe or limit the period in which an action may be brought. Different substantive claims, such as contract, tort or property actions, typically have different limitations periods. The failure to bring an action within the statutory limitation period bars the action and the defendant may raise the statute of limitations as an affirmative defense. *See* **Rule 8(c)** (affirmative defenses). In many federal actions based on federal statutes that lack a specific limitation period, federal courts will "borrow" a limitations period from the closest analogous state or common law form of action.

ii. Accrual

Accrual refers to the time when an action begins to run for statute of limitations period. State and federal law determine when a particular claim or action begins to accrue. This may depend on the substantive nature of the claim. For example, in some states certain personal-injury tort claims accrue from the date of the *discovery* of the injury, rather than the date of the injury.

iii. Tolling

Tolling refers to the suspension of the running of the statute-of-limitations period. State and federal law determine under what circumstances tolling may occur. Tolling usually is contemplated when a plaintiff, for some reason, is unable to assert his or her claim in a timely fashion.

b. Service of Process and Timing Provisions

i. State Law—Commencement of an Action and Statutes of Limitation

(a) **Commencement and service.** In some states, an action is not deemed commenced until the plaintiff has effected service of process. Hence, a defect in either the process or service of process can be fatal to the plaintiff's lawsuit if service is not validly effected prior to the running of the statute of limitations.

(b) **Commencement and filing.** In other states, an action is commenced with the filing of the complaint. Filing relates to any applicable statute-of-limitations periods.

C. IMMUNITY FROM PROCESS AND FRAUDULENT INDUCEMENT

1. General Immunity Rule

Non-resident attorneys, parties, and witnesses are immune from service of process in an unrelated action during the period they are traveling to appear at, or are appearing at, a criminal or civil action within a state.

a. Settlements Discussions Included

Immunity from service extends to litigation participants who appear in a jurisdiction for the purpose of negotiating a settlement.

b. Special Statutory Immunity

Representatives of foreign governments and their families are entitled to immunity from service of process by federal statute. *See* **22 U.S.C. §§ 254a–d and 288(d)(b).** Other federal statutes similarly afford immunity from process to specially designated persons.

c. Exceptions to General Immunity Rule

i. Counterclaims Against Non-Resident Plaintiff

If a non-resident plaintiff brings a lawsuit in a state, then that non-resident plaintiff is not immune from service of a counterclaim asserted by the defendant. The rationale is that the non-resident plaintiff has consented to the jurisdiction of the court by availing itself of the opportunity to sue within the state.

ii. Defendants Entering Jurisdiction Prior to Commencement of an Action

Immunity from process will not extend to a defendant who enters a jurisdiction prior to the commencement of a legal action against that defendant, and who is involuntarily detained and then served with process.

- **Leading case authority: State ex rel. Sivnksty v. Duffield, 137 W.Va. 112 (W. Va. 1952).** Sivnksty traveled to Gilmer County, West Virginia to go fishing and was subsequently jailed on criminal charges after an accident. While in jail, he was served with process in a civil action based on the same facts as the criminal prosecution. The court held—over a dissent—that Sivnksty was not entitled to immunity from process in the civil case because he had voluntarily entered the county and was not originally brought there under criminal process.

iii. Non-Resident Defendants Subject to Long-Arm Jurisdiction

Immunity from process also does not apply to non-resident defendants who otherwise are subject to a state valid long-arm jurisdiction. In other words, a non-resident defendant cannot avoid service of process simply by staying outside a state's borders.

2. Rationale for Immunity Rule

Immunity from service under such circumstances is granted to non-residents in order to encourage active participation in legal proceedings.

a. Original Purpose

The original purpose of the process immunity rule was as a privilege of the court to secure the administration of justice free from outside interference or influence. **State ex rel. Sivnksty v. Duffield,** 137 W.Va. 112 (W. Va. 1952).

b. Modern Rationale

In absence of immunity, lawyers, parties, and witnesses might refuse to attend legal proceedings if they feared being subject to service in an unrelated matter. **State ex rel. Sivnksty v. Duffield,** 137 W.Va. 112 (W. Va. 1952).

3. Fraudulent Inducement

A plaintiff may not effect service of process on a defendant by fraudulently inducing the defendant into the jurisdiction for the purpose of serving process and conferring jurisdiction.

a. Rationale

A judgment procured fraudulently lacks jurisdiction and is null and void. A fraud affecting jurisdiction is the equivalent of a lack of jurisdiction. **Wyman v. Newhouse,** 93 F.2d 313 (2d Cir. 1937).

- **Leading case authority: Wyman v. Newhouse, 93 F.2d 313 (2d Cir. 1937).** A Florida woman sought to recover money she loaned a boyfriend, as well as for seduction under a promise of marriage. She encouraged the New York boyfriend to travel to Florida to visit her. She encouraged this by sending a letter indicating that her mother was sick, she was leaving the country, and she needed to talk to him about their affairs—followed by subsequent letters and phone calls expressing love and affection. When the defendant came to Florida, he was served with a summons. He immediately returned to New York, where his lawyer advised him to ignore the summons. After he suffered a default judgment in the Florida action, he brought a collateral attack in New York. The New York court held the judgment invalid for lack of jurisdiction because of the fraudulently induced appearance in Florida.

D. CHALLENGING DEFECTIVE OR IMPROPER SERVICE OF PROCESS

1. Two Types of Challenges

Under **Rule 12,** there are two available grounds for challenging improper service of process: insufficiency of process, **Rule 12(b)(4),** and insufficiency of service of process, **Rule 12(b)(5).** *These two challenges are distinct, and have distinct consequences.*

a. Insufficiency of Process: Rule 12(b)(4)

Insufficiency of process refers to a defect in the form or content of the summons.

i. Misnomer

A summons is facially defective if it misnames a party to the dispute. *See* **Schiavone v. Fortune,** 477 U.S. 21 (1986), where notice was held insufficient because the complaint and summons named "Fortune" rather than "Time, Inc.," even though an agent for Time received the complaint and knew that Time published Fortune.

ii. Doe Defendants

Where state rules permit, a plaintiff may designate a "Doe defendant" where the defendant is unknown and then subsequently amend the complaint and summons to substitute the proper defendant's name when the defendant becomes known.

iii. Improper Completion

A summons also is defective if it is not properly completed, for example, if it is not signed by a clerk of the court.

iv. Consequences of Insufficiency of Process

If the form or content of the summons is defective, the court will invalidate the process and dismiss the action *without prejudice* to the plaintiff's ability to re-file the action and re-serve the defendant.

b. Insufficiency of Service of Process: Rule 12(b)(5)

Insufficiency of service of process refers to the improper *manner of service* on the defendant(s).

i. Consequences of Insufficient Service of Process

If a plaintiff fails to accomplish sufficient service of process, the defendant has not received proper notice of the action and the court lacks jurisdiction over the improperly served defendant. Consequently:

- The action will be dismissed for insufficiency of service of process; and,

- If a relevant statute of limitations has run, the action *will be dismissed with prejudice* (that is, the plaintiff is unable to refile the action).

- A default judgment entered in a defendant's absence based on insufficient service of process also lacks valid jurisdiction and will be set aside.

2. Methods for Asserting Challenges to Service of Process

Insufficient process or insufficient service of process may be challenged in the following ways:

- *Motion to quash* or set aside service (usually state-based relief);

- *Plea in abatement* (at common law, for circumstances such as fraudulent inducement into the forum);

- *Motion to dismiss* (**Rule 12(b)(4), (5)**)

E. PROVISIONAL REMEDIES AND DUE PROCESS REQUIREMENTS

1. Due Process Notice Requirements Revisited

Constitutional due process requires that a defendant must have adequate notice of an action as well as a meaningful opportunity to be heard in response to that action. *See* **Mullane v. Central Hanover Bank & Trust Company,** discussed at A.2., *supra.*

2. Provisional Remedies Defined

"Provisional remedies" are forms of relief that a court affords a plaintiff prior to an actual adjudicated trial of the merits asserted by a plaintiff against a defendant. The most common form of relief prior to trial involves seizure or attachment of the defendant's property, or other restraints enjoining the defendant from using, wasting, or alienating the property. Provisional remedies include:

- Temporary restraining orders;

- Preliminary injunctions;

- Prejudgment attachments, seizures, or sequestrations.

3. Provisional Remedies and Due Process: The Constitutional Issue

Many provisional remedies are equitable, and are obtained on an expedited or emergency basis. Since most provisional remedies involve prejudgment attachment or seizure of the defendant's property, the constitutional issue concerns what due process is required to protect the defendant's property interests, particularly where the state law defines the manner of effecting the prejudgment seizure.

a. Constitutional Basis

In actions where state law defines the availability and manner of prejudgment seizure (or other provisional relief), such statutes are subject to the **Fourteenth Amendment to the United States Constitution:** "No state shall make any law . . . depriving any person of life, liberty, or property without due process of law. . . . "

b. Property Interests Protected under the Fourteenth Amendment in Provisional Remedies Situations

i. What Constitutes a "Taking"

A person's property interests are protected by the Fourteenth Amendment without regard to the length of a possible deprivation. Hence, even a temporary seizure of property through a provisional remedy must meet constitutional standards. The Fourteenth Amendment does not distinguish between temporary or permanent deprivations of property. **Fuentes v. Shevin,** 407 U.S. 67 (1972).

ii. What Constitutes "Property"

The Fourteenth Amendment extends protection to any significant property interest and has never been interpreted to protect only the rights of undisputed ownership of property. Hence, the Fourteenth Amendment protection extends to conditional sales contracts where a person may not yet possess full legal title to goods. **Fuentes v. Shevin,** 407 U.S. 67 (1972).

4. Governmental Deprivations of Property: Due Process Requirements

a. General Constitutional Principles—Leading Case Authority: Fuentes v. Shevin, 407 U.S. 67 (1972)

Constitutional due process in prejudgment provisional remedies cases requires:

(1) the right to notice and an opportunity to be heard at a meaningful time and in a meaningful manner;

(2) notice and an opportunity to be heard *before* the seizure; meaning a time when the deprivation can still be prevented;

(3) informed evaluation of the claims to the property by a neutral official.

b. *Mathews v. Eldridge* Analytical Framework

See **Mathews v. Eldridge,** 424 U.S. 319 (1976). When a government seeks to deprive a defendant of property on its own initiative, a court is required to evaluate:

(1) the private interest that will be affected by the official action;

    (2)   the risk of an erroneous deprivation of such interest through the procedures used;

    (3)   the probable value, if any, of additional or substitute safeguards; and

    (4)   the "government's interest, including the function involved and the fiscal and administrative burdens that the additional or substitute procedural requirement would entail."

■ ILLUSTRATION

A car owner illegally parked his car on seven separate occasions before it was immobilized by attachment of a Denver boot. The owner argued that the city's failure to provide a hearing before immobilizing the auto violated due process. Applying the *Mathews* factors, the court held that a prior hearing was not constitutionally required where the city had an important governmental interest in enforcing its parking ordinances. **Patterson v. Cronin,** 650 P.2d 531 (Colo. 1982).

■ ILLUSTRATION

In the case based on the same facts, the city did not provide the owner with a post-deprivation hearing. The court held that the failure to provide a post-deprivation hearing violated the owner's constitutional due process rights. **Patterson v. Cronin,** 650 P.2d 531 (Colo. 1982).

c.   Garnishment Statutes—Leading Case Authority: Sniadach v. Family Finance Corp., 395 U.S. 337 (1969)

The Supreme Court struck down a Wisconsin prejudgment wage garnishment procedure as violative of due process; the statute did not provide for notice or an opportunity to be heard prior to the garnishment.

d.   "Extraordinary Situations" Exception

Certain situations may justify an exception to the due process requirements for prejudgment notice and a hearing. These situations, however, "must be truly unusual." **Boddie v. Connecticut,** 401 U.S. 371 (1971). Such seizures must:

(1) be directly necessary to secure an important governmental or general public interest;

(2) be a special need for very prompt action;

(3) be kept under strict control by the government possessing a monopoly of legitimate force;

(4) be initiated by a government official responsible for determining under the standards of a narrowly drawn statute that such an emergency seizure was necessary or justified in the particular instance.

Examples of "extraordinary situation" exceptions include:

(1) summary seizure of property to collect the internal revenue of the United States;

(2) to meet the needs of a national war effort;

(3) to protect against the economic disaster of a bank failure;

(4) to protect the public from misbranded drugs and contaminated food.

5. Private–Party Disputes and Prejudgment Seizures

Mathews v. Eldridge supplies the analytical framework for assessing due process requirements of prejudgment seizures in disputes between individuals and the government (*see supra*).

a. Different Focus in Private Disputes

The Supreme Court has suggested that the prejudgment seizure due process inquiry has a *different focus* in disputes between private parties. **Connecticut v. Doehr,** 501 U.S. 1 (1991). In disputes involving private parties, the appropriate analytical framework for evaluating the due process sufficiency of prejudgment seizure statutes involves consideration of:

(1) the private interest that will be affected by the prejudgment measure;

(2)   the risk of erroneous deprivation through the procedures under attack;

(3)   the probable value of additional or alternative safeguards;

(4)   principal attention to the interest of the party seeking the prejudgment remedy;

(5)   due regard to the ancillary interest the government may have in providing the procedure or foregoing the added burden of providing greater protections.

6.   *Mathews* and *Doehr* Standards Compared

The *Mathews* analytical framework is properly used in prejudgment seizure cases where the government itself initiates the seizure or attachment of property, such as garnishment of an employee's wages. The *Doehr* standards apply in disputes between private parties, where the government is not the party seizing the property The focus of the *Doehr* standards is on the interests of the private party seeking the prejudgment remedy; under the *Doehr* standards, the government's interests are *ancillary* to that of the parties.

7.   Specific Applications of the *Fuentes/Mathews/Doehr* Standards

a.   *Fuentes v. Shevin*, 407 U.S. 67 (1972)—General Holdings

The Supreme Court, in a 4–3 decision, with two Justices not participating, invalidated two state replevin statutes under constitutional due process standards for provisional remedies:

i.   Florida Replevin Statute

The Supreme Court held unconstitutional a Florida prejudgment replevin statute which permitted the seizure of property based on an applicant's filing of a *conclusory complaint and a security bond*. The defendant was entitled to a hearing only after the property was seized. The officer who seized the property was required to hold it for three days, during which time the defendant could reclaim it by posting a security bond for double the property's value. If the defendant did not post this security bond, the property was transferred to the party who sought writ of replevin pending a final judgment in the underlying litigation.

ii.   Pennsylvania Replevin Statute

The Supreme Court also invalidated as constitutionally deficient a Pennsylvania statute which allowed a prejudgment writ of replevin through a *summary ex parte application*. The party seeking the writ was required to post a *security bond* for double the value of the property, although the person whose property was seized could post a *counter-bond* within three days to gain repossession. The statute provided *no opportunity for prior notice or a prior hearing* before the property was seized. The party seeking the replevin was not required to institute an action for repossession of the property. The statute did not require that there ever be a hearing on the merits of the disputed claims to the property. A person whose property was seized through the replevin statute had to initiate a lawsuit in order to obtain a post-seizure hearing.

iii. Qualifications to *Fuentes* Holdings

(a) **Narrow holding.** The Supreme Court indicated that its *Fuentes* holding was narrow. The Court did not question the power of states to seize goods prior to a final judgment in order to protect the security interests of creditors, provided that those creditors tested their claim to the goods through a fair prior hearing.

(b) **Exceptional situations exception.** The Court also indicated that its general holdings did not apply to the "exceptional situations" where a prior hearing might not be possible or feasible (*see* discussion *supra*).

iv. *Fuentes* Dissent

Three Justices dissented in *Fuentes,* arguing that creditors had a property interest as deserving of protection as the debtor. In addition, the dissenters argued that the decision would encourage creditors to more explicitly state repossession rights in installment sales contracts, or might lead to diminishing the availability of credit altogether.

b. *Mitchell v. W.T. Grant Co.*, 416 U.S. 600 (1974)

In *Mitchell,* the Supreme Court upheld a Louisiana sequestration statute to seize goods in anticipation of an action to enforce a vendor's lien. The creditor had an installment sales contract and alleged that the debtor was in delinquency on the contract. The *Mitchell* opinion was authored by Justice White, who dissented in *Fuentes.*

i. Provisions of the Louisiana Sequestration Statute

The sequestration statute required a *verified petition or affidavit alleging specific facts* to be made to a judge. The creditor seeking the writ had to post bond to protect the debtor against damages if the sequestration was shown to be improvident. The writ could be obtained on the creditor's *ex parte* application, without notice to the debtor or an opportunity for a hearing, but the debtor could seek immediate dissolution of the writ. If the creditor could not prove the grounds on which the writ was sought, the court could order return of the property, damages, and attorney's fees.

ii. *Mitchell* Rationale

In upholding the Louisiana statute, the Court held that "we are convinced that *Fuentes* was decided against a factual and legal background sufficiently different from that now before us that it does not require the invalidation of the Louisiana sequestration statute, either on its face or as applied." The Court concluded that there was "far less danger" of a mistaken seizure and a corresponding decrease in the utility of an adversary hearing, which would be made immediately available in any event.

iii. Relationship of *Mitchell to Fuentes*

There is some dispute whether the *Mitchell* decision can be reconciled with *Fuentes.* Three Justices (Stewart, who wrote the majority opinion in *Fuentes,* Douglas, and Marshall) dissented arguing that the factual issues were no different than in *Fuentes* and that the majority had disregarded *stare decisis* in overruling *Fuentes.* They also suggested that the Louisiana requirement of an affidavit in reality was merely a *pro forma* requirement, and that replacing a court clerk with a judge would have little or no effect on assessment of the affidavit.

c. *North Georgia Finishing, Inc. v. Di–Chem, Inc.*, 419 U.S. 601 (1975)

The Supreme Court invalidated as unconstitutional a Georgia garnishment statute. Di–Chem filed a suit against North Georgia Fishing for recovery of $52,279 in goods it had sold and delivered. Before North Georgia responded to the complaint, Di–Chem filed an affidavit and bond in order to garnish North Georgia's bank account.

i. Provisions of the Georgia Garnishment Statute

A garnishment writ could issue on an affidavit by the creditor or the creditor's attorney and could contain *conclusory allegations.* The writ could be *issued by a court clerk* without supervision of a judge. Upon issuance of the writ, the debtor's bank account was frozen; the only method to dissolve the garnishment was for the debtor to *file a bond* to protect the creditor. The statute had *no provision for an early hearing* at which the creditor would have to show probable cause for the garnishment. Without the debtor's filing a bond, there would be no means to challenge the garnishment. The creditor had to post a double bond in the eventuality that garnishment proved unjustified.

ii. *Di–Chem* Rationale

The Court held that the Georgia garnishment statute failed under *Fuentes* standards, and was not "saved" by the previous year's decision in *Mitchell.* The Court further refused to distinguish between deprivations of property involving consumer installment contracts and deprivations of property in commercial settings: "We are no more inclined now than in the past to distinguish among different kinds of property in applying the due process clause."

d. *Connecticut v. Doehr*, 501 U.S. 1 (1991)

The Supreme Court held that a Connecticut statute authorizing the prejudgment attachment of real estate without a prior notice or hearing, without a showing of extraordinary circumstances, and without a requirement that the person seeking the attachment post a bond, did not satisfy the due process requirements of the Fourteenth Amendment.

i. Refinement of Due Process Requirements in Private Disputes

The Court in *Doehr* refined the **Mathews v. Eldridge** analytical framework for disputes between private parties. (*see* discussion *supra*). The *Doehr* standards shift the focus of concern to the interests of the party seeking the provisional remedy, making the government's interests an ancillary consideration. On the facts, the Court concluded that the plaintiff's interest in Doehr's real estate was minimal, and no governmental interest affected the analysis.

ii. Nature of the Property Interest

Prejudgment attachment of a property owner's real estate (unrelated to the underlying assault and battery claim) is a protectable interest under the Fourteenth Amendment.

(a) **Clouding title.** Such attachment clouds title and impairs an owner's ability to sell or otherwise alienate the property, taints the owner's credit rating, and reduces the owner's chances of obtaining additional or other mortgage financing.

(b) Other property impairment. Temporary or impartial impairments to property rights such as attachments, liens, and encumbrances are sufficient to merit due process protection.

iii. Remaining Due Process Issue—Bond Requirement

(a) Majority state practice. Most states now require that the plaintiff post a bond even if the statute also provides for a hearing before or soon after an attachment occurs.

(b) Supreme Court plurality opinion on bond requirement. Four justices suggested that due process also requires that the plaintiff post a bond before a property attachment occurs. Such a bond requirement does not, however, excuse the need for a hearing or other safeguards. Justices Rehnquist and Blackmun, concurring in the judgment, thought it unwise for the Court to have discussed the additional due process requirement of a bond, an issue that they argued was not before the Court.

■ CHAPTER REVIEW CHECKLIST

Civil procedure examinations may include a problem relating to the constitutional dimensions of notice, particularly a fact pattern involving a provisional remedy or other prejudgment seizure of property. Your procedure professor is less likely to ask a question relating to the mechanical aspects of service of process, but you should be aware of the difference between *defects in the form of the process* (insufficiency of process), and *defects in the manner of service* (insufficient service of process), as well as the different consequences for each. Read the facts presented carefully. If the facts present a problem relating to constitutional notice, first determine whether the notice problem deals generally with an adversary proceeding, or involves a prejudgment seizure statute. List any statutory requirements and also note procedures or safeguards that the statute does not provide.

To answer a problem relating to notice in an adversary proceeding, ask:

1. **Do the facts present a problem relating to the plaintiff's provision of notice to the defendant? Has the defendant's due process right to adequate notice been violated?**

   - Are the means of providing notice delineated in a state or federal statute? What does the statute provide?

- Who are the defendants in the action? Are there known defendants? Unknown defendants? In what manner did the plaintiff comply with providing the defendants with notice?

- Was the notice that the plaintiff afforded the defendant *"reasonably calculated, under all the circumstances, to apprise interested parties of the pendency of the action and to afford them an opportunity to present their objections?"*

  — For known parties, was notice personally served or mailed to the party's last known address?

  — For unknown parties, was notice afforded by constructive service such as through newspaper or other media publication?

- Are there any special circumstances bearing on the practicality of providing notice?

To answer a problem concerning notice in a provisional remedies case, ask:

1. **Do the facts involve a provisional remedy such as a preliminary injunction or prejudgment attachment?**

   - Is there a federal or state statute delineating the requirements for prejudgment seizures? What does the statute provide? Does the statute require:

     — notice of the attachment prior to the seizure?

     — a pre-deprivation hearing? Is the pre-deprivation hearing between the parties, or *ex parte*?

     — a post-deprivation hearing? How soon after the seizure is the defendant afforded a hearing? Who must initiate the post-deprivation hearing?

     — an evidentiary basis for the prejudgment attachment? Can the plaintiff have the defendant's property seized based on a conclusory allegation of facts?

     — a hearing before a judge? A neutral court officer? Who has the power to order the prejudgment seizure? Can the defendant's property be seized by order of a court clerk?

     — posting of a security bond? Who is required to post a security bond, when, and in what amount?

2. **Do the facts involve a dispute between the government and an individual?**

- If so, first ask whether any exceptional circumstances exist requiring an immediate seizure of property without notice or a hearing:

   — Is the property seizure necessary to secure an important governmental or general public interest?

   — Is there a special need for very prompt action?

   — Has the property seizure been kept under strict control by the government?

   — Has the seizure been initiated by a government official responsible under the standards of a narrowly drawn statute justifying an emergency seizure in the particular instance?

- If no exceptional circumstances exist, then use the **Mathews v. Eldridge** analytical framework to evaluate whether the deprivation violates due process. Balance:

- the private interest that will be affected by the official action;

- the risk of an erroneous deprivation of such interest through the procedures used;

- the probable value, if any, of additional or substitute safeguards; and

- the government's interest, including the function involved and the fiscal and administrative burdens that the additional or substitute procedural requirement would entail.

3. **Do the facts involve a dispute between private parties? If so, then apply the Connecticut v. Doehr analytical framework. Balance:**

- the private interest that will be affected by the prejudgment measure;

- the risk of erroneous deprivation through the procedures under attack;

- the probable value of additional or alternative safeguards;

- principal attention to the interest of the party seeking the prejudgment remedy;

- due regard to the ancillary interest the government may have in providing the procedure or foregoing the added burden of providing greater protections.

V

Pleadings

■ ANALYSIS

■ CHAPTER OVERVIEW

- This chapter concerns history, philosophy, and rules relating to pleading in American state and federal courts. The primary focus is on federal pleading rules, although various state pleading rules will be compared to the Federal Rules.

- Pleading refers to the form and manner of stating claims and defenses in an action. In its narrowest meaning, a "pleading" is the paper a litigant files to present claims or defenses.

- American state and federal systems of pleading are derived from, and often in reaction to, ancient English forms of pleading. However, many older forms of English pleading, as well as this language and terminology, is still used in some state pleading systems. Moreover, federal pleading rules often embody practices that have the same purpose or effect of older English pleading rules.

- In general, modern American state and federal pleading rules have developed as a reaction to the restrictive system of common law pleading in England, dating back to the thirteenth century. The English common law system of pleading was aimed at arriving at a single issue and therefore prohibited raising more than one issue in a pleading. Pleading at common law was intended to serve four basic purposes:

  — providing notice of a claim or defense;

  — identifying baseless claims;

  — presenting each party's view of the facts; and

  — narrowing issues.

- The English common law system of pleading was based on particular *"forms of action"* for each cognizable claim. For each form of action, the complainant had to swear out a particular "writ." Thus, the English system of common law pleading was tied to distinct forms of action and writs.

  — The failure of a complainant to assert the appropriate form of action or swear out the appropriate writ was fatal to the ability to state a claim and secure a remedy from the legal system.

— Over time, the English system of common law pleading became increasingly difficult and characterized by "traps for the unwary" pleader.

— At the end of the thirteenth century, in order to supply relief which the king's court could not, English law developed the chancery courts, or courts of equity. Equity developed as a separate branch of law, with its own procedural rules, doctrines, and courts.

— The increasing complexity of English common law pleading and the length of time to plead and respond to a complaint led to reform of the English pleading system in the nineteenth century, in the period between 1825–1843. These reforms led to a modernization and simplification of English pleading procedures.

• In the American colonies in the seventeenth and eighteenth centuries, the English forms of action were not as rigidly adhered to as in England. However, by the first half of the nineteenth century American lawyers followed the same rigid technicalities of English common-law pleading, as legal texts such as Blackstone's treatise became increasingly available to American lawyers.

• The first major reform of American pleading occurred in New York State in 1847–1848, with the promulgation of the so-called "Field Code."

— The New York Field Code modernized American pleading rules and served as the model for modernization of many other state pleading systems. States that adopted modern versions of pleading based on the New York Field Code are called *"code pleading" states.* The Field Code also is widely viewed as a precursor for the Federal Rules of Civil Procedure, which Congress enacted in 1938.

— Notwithstanding the improvements of code pleading, various problems still persisted in pleading.

• In 1938, Congress enacted the Federal Rules of Civil Procedure, pursuant to authority granted under the 1934 Rules Enabling Act. The enactment of the Federal Rules of Civil Procedure culminated a four-year process of civil rulemaking within the federal judiciary.

• The Federal Rules of Civil Procedure *merged law and equity.* Under modern federal procedure, a litigant may seek both legal and equitable relief from the unified federal courts.

- Unlike English pleading at common law, modern pleading under the Federal Rules of Civil Procedure is intended primarily to provide litigants of notice of the nature of claims and defenses. Federal pleading is not intended to serve the other purposes of common law pleading, such as narrowing of issues or identifying baseless claims.

- Modern federal pleading rules are intended to expedite and facilitate a plaintiff's assertion of claims, and to avoid "traps for the unwary" pleader.

- The Federal Rules of Civil Procedure shifted to other procedural devices, such as motions to dismiss and summary judgment, the functions of narrowing issues and screening baseless claims.

- The liberalized pleading rules were intended to be used in tandem with a newly created liberal discovery system, which would allow the pleader to "discover" additional information about the facts of the claim, subsequent to filing the complaint. Unlike common law pleading, a pleader under the Federal Rules is not expected to know the entire factual basis for the plaintiff's claims at the time of filing a complaint.

- The Federal Rules of Civil Procedure have greatly simplified the form and manner of pleading—in contrast to common law pleading. Hence, there are only *three forms of pleadings* available under the Federal Rules of Civil Procedure: *a complaint, an answer, and the reply.* A plaintiff initially asserts any claims against the defendant in a *complaint.* The defendant may respond either by filing various motions to dismiss the complaint, under **Rule 12,** or file an answer. The only other pleading permitted by the Federal Rules is a reply, which the plaintiff may file if the defendant asserts a counterclaim to the plaintiff's complaint.

  — A pleader is required only to file "a short and plain statement of the claim showing that the pleader is entitled to relief." **Rule 8(c).** Federal Rules do not require a great deal of specific fact pleading, except for a few special kinds of cases, such as cases involving fraud or libel.

  — Every pleading, motion, or other paper in federal court must be signed by an attorney or, if the party is not represented by an attorney, then by the party. The person who signs any pleading, motion, or paper must certify that the allegations or contentions contained in the paper have been made "to the best of that person's knowledge, information, and belief, formed after an inquiry reasonable under the circumstances." **Rule 11.**

— A defendant may seek sanctions for any pleading, motion, or paper filed in violation of this rule. However, a person who has filed the defective pleading or paper has 21 days to cure any defect in that pleading.

— Some federal circuit courts require "heightened" fact pleading for other substantive claims, such as securities or civil rights actions. The Supreme Court has articulated a standard of plausibility in pleading claims to withstand a motion to dismiss under **Rule 12(b)(6)**.

— Under the Federal Rules, a pleader may assert alternate or inconsistent theories for relief, which was not permitted at common law. A pleader also may plead legal and equitable theories.

— A defendant may respond to a complaint either through various motions to dismiss under **Rule 12,** or by filing an answer.

— Some objections to the plaintiff's complaint must be raised in a timely fashion or they will be waived. Other objections to a plaintiff's complaint are not waivable and may be raised at any time.

— A defendant may not serially raise objections to the plaintiff's complaint. All the defendant's objections must be consolidated into one motion, or raised in the defendant's answer.

— If the defendant's motions to dismiss are unsuccessful, the defendant must file an answer. In the answer, the defendant may respond to the plaintiff's claims (admit or deny), assert affirmative defenses, or allege any counterclaims that the defendant may have against the plaintiff. A defendant may *generally deny* the plaintiff's entire claims, but federal practice does not favor *general denials.*

— Litigants may amend their pleadings in three different circumstances: (1) relatively soon after filing a complaint, without having to ask the court's permission; (2) during or after trial, to "conform" the pleadings to proof that has been offered at trial; and (3) after the statute of limitations has run, if a party mistakenly has been mis-named and there would be no prejudice to that mis-named party. **Rule 15.**

— Amendments after statutes of limitations have run are permitted only in extremely rare instances.

— A litigant may make *supplemental pleadings* to aid claims that have already been made in a complaint, but not to add new or additional material to an existing pleading.

A. THE DEVELOPMENT OF MODERN PLEADING— HISTORICAL CONTEXT

1. Importance of Historical Pleading Rules to Understanding Modern Federal Pleading Rules

The philosophy underlying the 1938 Federal Rules of Civil Procedure represents a marked departure from the English common law system of pleading and state "code" pleading regimes. Modern federal pleading reforms were enacted in response to perceived problems with existing common law or code pleading systems. Hence, it is important to understand English common law and code pleading because:

a. Relief from Common Law Pleading

The "liberal" pleading regime under the Federal Rules of Civil Procedure is intended to relieve the narrow, restrictive requirements of English common law pleading and the problems under the codes, and to permit a complainant's claims to be heard on the merits, rather than dismissed because of defective pleading;

b. Common Law Analogs

Many modern procedural devices have common law analogs or antecedents, and some states still retain common law forms of pleading and terminology.

c. Modern Causes of Action

English common law pleading was tied to and responsible for the development of most modern substantive causes of action.

2. Common Law Pleading and Divided Power

a. Introductory Notes on the Early Development of Common Law Pleading in England

i. Oral Pleading

The first development of a studied science of pleadings occurred in the thirteenth century, during the reign of Edward I. Pleadings were made orally and centered on verbal descriptions of relevant facts in dispute. The purpose of these statements was to assist in developing the precise legal question or issue.

(a) Modes of decision or proof at early common law. The various modes of decision for issues of fact during this period included *"trial" by ordeal, combat, or by oath.* These were not trials as we understand today; requiring proof undertaken by one or both of the parties (as in combat).

ii. Shift to Written Pleadings

The development of a system of written pleadings began in the late fourteenth century and extended into the sixteenth century

iii. Distinction between Local (Communal) Courts and Royal Courts

(a) Local or communal courts. For at least a century after the Norman conquest in 1066, most disputes were heard in local or communal courts, or to feudal courts in which a lord heard cases involving tenants.

(b) Royal courts. These courts heard offenses against the king's laws and cases involving feudal lords as tenants-in-chief. Gradually royal courts absorbed cases brought before the local or communal courts.

b. The Writ, Forms of Action, and Substantive Law in the Royal Courts

i. The Writ System

The writ was the document or paper by which an action was commenced. The modern analog of the English writ is the summons. Technically, a person with a grievance sought justice from the king; the king issued the writ which ordered a sheriff to bring the defendant before the king's judges to answer the complaint.

(a) Relationship of writs to forms of action. Over time, English common law developed a particular writ for each distinctive *"form of action."* The failure of the plaintiff's lawyer to swear out the appropriate writ for the particular cause of action was fatally defective to the case and would result in a dismissal.

(b) No writ available. If there was no writ that fit the particular case, a plaintiff could not obtain relief in the royal courts.

ii. Forms of Action

Under English common law pleading, the "form of action" governed:

- the method of commencing the litigation (that is, the form of action was tied to a particular writ);

- the substantive requirements of the case, including burdens of proof and persuasion;

- the manner of trial; and

- the remedy, relief or sanction for a judgment.

c. Basic Structure of Common Law Pleading

i. Purpose of Common Law Pleading Requirements

The basic purpose of common law pleading was to reduce the dispute to a single issue of law or fact. Common law pleading did not permit multiple parties or multiple claims to be present in an action.

ii. Possible Substantive Responses to a Claim

Under the common law system of pleading, a party had one of three possible ways to respond to a claim:

- deny that the alleged facts gave the claimant any legal right, even if the facts were true (an issue of law);

- deny that the alleged facts were true (an issue of fact); or,

- assert that additional facts negated the asserted right (requiring further responsive pleading to resolve).

d. Detailed Structure of Successive Rounds of Common Law Pleading

Pleading at English common law was characterized by multiple, successive rounds of responsive pleading. Many of these pleading forms have analogs under modern pleading systems.

i. The Declaration

A civil action at common law was instituted with a declaration which set forth the plaintiff's claim. The *complaint* is the modern analog of the common law declaration.

ii. Defendant's Responses: Demurrer or Plea

In response to the plaintiff's declaration, the defendant either had to *demur* to the declaration, or respond in a *plea.*

(a) **The demurrer.** The *demurrer* challenged the legal sufficiency of the declaration. A demurrer also was granted if the plaintiff chose the wrong writ or form of action. If the court granted the defendant's demurrer the plaintiff lost, but the plaintiff could begin again by suing for the correct form of action. If the demurrer was not granted by the court (or quashed), then the plaintiff won and judgment was entered for the plaintiff.

- **The demurrer in modern practice.** Some state codes have retained the common law demurrer. The demurrer has been abolished in the Federal Rules of Civil Procedure, but this form of objection is available in **Rule 12(b)(6),** the motion to dismiss for failure to state a claim upon which relief can be granted.

- **Special demurrer.** Another form of objection to the plaintiff's declaration was the *special demurrer,* which challenged various technical defects in the complaint. If the defendant did not raise these technical defects, these objections were waived.

(b) **Pleas.** If the defendant did not demur to the declaration, the defendant could respond with a plea. There were two types of pleas: *dilatory pleas* and *peremptory pleas.*

- **Dilatory pleas.** Dilatory pleas challenged the court's right to hear the case. These pleas included objections to the court's jurisdiction, variances between the declaration and the writ, and pleas that the case must be suspended for some technical reason, such as the minority of one of the parties. Dilatory pleas did not challenge the merits of the plaintiff's claims.

- **Dilatory pleas in modern practice.** The Federal Rules of Civil Procedure have abolished the various common law pleas. However, some of the dilatory pleas may be found in **Rule 12** motions, such as the challenges to the court's jurisdiction. Objections to the capacity of the parties may be raised under **Rule 17(b)** and **(c),** which deals with the capacity of parties to the lawsuit.

- **Peremptory pleas (or plea in bar).** A *peremptory plea* or *plea in bar* was a denial on the merits. If the defendant denied the plaintiff's allegations, this was called a *traverse.* A traverse squarely placed the facts in issue and a trial would resolve the competing claims. Another form of peremptory plea was the *confession and avoidance.* If the defendant elected this response, the defendant would admit to the plaintiff's allegations ("the confession"), but assert some grounds for "avoiding" culpability, such as the defendant's minority. If the defendant entered a peremptory plea of confession and avoidance, no issue would be reached and the plaintiff would have to respond in another round of pleadings.

- **Peremptory pleas in modern practice.** Peremptory pleas have been abolished in the Federal Rules of Civil Procedure. The traverse has its modern analog in the defendant's *denial* of the plaintiff's claims on the merits. **Rules 7(a), 8(b).** The modern analog of the confession-and-avoidance is found in the ability of defendants to assert *affirmative defenses.* **Rule 8(c).**

iii. Plaintiff's Responses to the Defendant's Plea

If the defendant entered a plea, then the plaintiff had to respond in another pleading. The plaintiff had two possible methods for responding to the defendant's confession-and-avoidance.

(a) Demurrer. The plaintiff could respond to the defendant's plea with a demurrer challenging whether the particular defense was legally available to the plaintiff's action.

(b) Replication. The plaintiff could respond to the defendant's plea in a *replication,* meaning that the plaintiff could *traverse* (or deny) the defendant's allegations, or enter a *confession-and-avoidance* to the plea. If the plaintiff pleaded a confession-and-avoidance in response to the defendant's confession-and-avoidance, then the defendant would be required to respond again.

iv. Defendant's Response to Plaintiff's Replication Pleading a Confession-and-Avoidance

If the plaintiff pleaded a confession-and-avoidance in response, the defendant could respond with either:

- A demurrer to the plaintiff's confession-and-avoidance; or,

- A rejoinder to the confession-and-avoidance.

v. Successive Rounds of Pleading

Since at each round of pleading either party could assert a confession-and-avoidance by way of defense, in theory, common law pleading could go on indefinitely. Such successive pleadings were denominated as *surrejoinders, rebutters,* and *surrebutters.*

e. Problems with English Common Law Pleading

i. "Traps for the Unwary Pleader"

A plaintiff was required to choose the appropriate writ for each substantive claim, and failure to swear out the appropriate writ for a particular form of action was a fatal defect and subject to dismissal on demurrer.

ii. Delay

The multiple, successive rounds of permissible pleading led to lengthy periods for pleading the claim.

iii. Inability to Hear Claims on the Merits

Under common law pleading, the process of pleading became an end in itself, and the technical requirements plus the length of time for responsive pleading frustrated the ability of the courts to hear claims on the merits.

iv. Limitations on Joinder of Parties and Claims

One of the major purposes of common law pleading was to produce a single issue; therefore, it was necessary to prohibit duplication in pleading. A person was prohibited from raising more than one issue of fact or law in a pleading, or joining multiple parties.

f. Chancery and the Rise of Equity Procedure

Equity courts and procedure began to develop at the end of the thirteenth century, in the king's Chancery. Equity developed as a parallel, alternative system to afford relief to petitioners unable to obtain justice or a remedy at law. Such petitions were referred by the king to the Chancellor, and by the end of the fourteenth century, directly to the Chancellor. Equity developed its own distinctive characteristics:

i. Common Law Jurisdiction Distinguished

The Chancellor was not empowered to hear claims that were cognizable at common law in the ordinary law courts, which could provide legal relief for a claimant. Thus, equity would not lie for actions involving claims relating to property, torts, or contracts. Actions at law were entitled to a trial by jury. A judgment at law declared a legal relationship between the parties; if the plaintiff prevailed, the plaintiff was entitled to relief from the defendant, but the judgment did not order the defendant to do anything. If the defendant *refused* to pay, the plaintiff needed to enforce the judgment.

ii. Equity Jurisdiction

Other disputes were considered highly appropriate for handling in the equity courts, such as matters involving wills and trusts, fraud or breach of trust, or injunctive relief. Actions in equity were tried to a judge and not a jury. A decree in equity (unlike a judgment at law) was directed at the defendant, and an equity court could order imprisonment or fines to enforce compliance. The maxim describing this relationship states that "equity acts *in personam* and not *in rem.*" The primary means of equitable relief was the *injunction:* an order directing a defendant to perform (or to cease performing) certain conduct.

iii. Equity Procedure

Over time, equity developed its own separate court system and procedural rules.

- An equity proceeding was initiated by a "bill in Chancery."

- The petitioner had to allege that compensatory relief would be inadequate to provide relief.

- Equity would not direct a party to take action outside the equity court's territorial reach.

- Criminal activity was outside the scope of equitable jurisdiction and equity could not enjoin criminal conduct.

- Equity could not order specific performance of building or personal services contracts.

- The availability of equitable relief—to accomplish justice where a legal remedy could not—was itself circumscribed by doctrines of fairness and justice. For example, equitable maxims required that "he who seeks equity must do equity"; that a petitioner seeking equitable relief had to have "clean hands" in the relationship; that equity abhors a forfeiture; and that equity will not protect a petitioner who has slept on his rights (been dilatory in seeking relief—the doctrine of *laches*).

- Equity permitted for discovery in cases at common law. A litigant in a common law litigation could file a *bill of discovery* in equity to obtain documents or information about the case from the defendant. The bill of discovery in equity was a precursor of modern discovery practices under the Federal Rules of Civil Procedure.

iv. Equity in Colonial America

Generally, Northern courts did not retain the English distinction between law and equity courts. Many Southern states, however, did retain the distinctive two-court system, recognizing separate actions at law and in equity, as well as the distinctive procedural prerequisites and remedies for each system.

v. Modern Equity Practice

The Federal Rules of Civil Procedure have merged law and equity into one unified civil action. Both legal and equitable relief may be sought in a federal civil action in the same court. **Rules 1** and **2.** Requests for equitable relief, however, still retain their distinctive procedural and substantive prerequisites. A few states still retain separate equity courts and procedure.

3.   Reform: New Pleading, Abolition of Forms of Action, and Merger of Law and Equity

a.   Reforms in Nineteenth-Century England

The **Common Law Procedure Acts of 1852, 1854,** and **1860** were the major statutory bills that reformed English pleading. These statutes liberalized pleading rules, weakened the forms of action, and expanded joinder possibilities. English legal reform culminated in the **Judicature Acts of 1873** and **1875,** which merged the common law courts and Chancery into the Supreme Court of Judicature. These acts merged law and equity and abolished the forms of action.

b.   American Reforms in the Nineteenth Century: The Field Code, and the Merger of Law and Equity

New York state led the nineteenth-century American reform of procedure. In 1846 a new state constitution abolished the Chancery court, and the legislature authorized a commission to reform civil procedure. As a result of the commission's report, the legislature enacted a Code of Civil Procedure, commonly called the *Field Code* (after David Dudley Field, the most prominent of the commission's members).

i.   Feature of the Field Code

The most prominent features of the Field Code included:

- abolition of the distinction of actions at law and suits in equity;

- creation of one form of action—the civil action;

- abolition of all prior forms of pleading.

ii.   Pleading Innovations of the Field Code

The Field Code:

- abolished all pleadings, except for a complaint, answer, reply, and demurrers;

- permitted a complaint requiring simply "a statement of facts constituting the cause of action, in ordinary and concise language, and in such a manner as to enable a person of common understanding to know what is intended";

- In 1851 the New York legislature amended the complaint rule to require that a complaint consist of "A plain and concise statement of the facts constituting a cause of action without unnecessary repetition." This language is substantially duplicated in modern **Rule 8(a).**

- required a demand for relief, stating the amount of money damages if requested;

- encouraged the liberal construction of allegations in the pleadings, "with a view to substantial justice between the parties";

- suggested that defects and errors in pleadings which did not adversely affect the substantial rights of the opponent be disregarded; and

- that errors or defects in pleadings not be a ground for reversing a judgment.

c. Code Pleading and Persistent Problems

Many states followed New York's model and enacted "code pleading" regimes similar to the Field Code. Although the intent of code pleading was to effect a clean break with the problems of common law pleading, many state courts persisted in interpreting code pleadings in light of common law rules and restrictions.

B. MODERN PLEADING UNDER THE FEDERAL RULES OF CIVIL PROCEDURE

1. Introductory Notes on the Federal Rules and Rulemaking Authority

In 1934 Congress enacted the **Rules Enabling Act, 28 U.S.C. § 2071,** authorizing the Supreme Court to promulgate rules of procedure for the federal district courts. After a four-year rulemaking process, Congress enacted the Federal Rules of Civil Procedure in 1938. Since 1938 the Federal Rules have been amended and revised several times, although the underlying philosophy of the federal rules has remained constant since 1938.

a. Theory of Transsubstantive Rules

The Federal Rules of Civil Procedure are intended to be *transsubstantive*— that is, to apply uniformly to all substantive claims and actions. With very few exceptions (such as shareholder derivative lawsuits (*see* **Rule 23.1**)), the Federal Rules are not case-specific. Federal pleading rules are the antithesis of common law forms of action and writs, a substance-specific pleading regime.

b. Goals of the Federal Rules

Federal Rule of Civil Procedure 1 sets forth the declared purpose of the federal rules, to secure the "just, speedy, and inexpensive determination of every action." Federal judges are to construe the rules to ensure these purposes. **Rule 1** was amended in 1993 to add the phrase "and administered," indicating an intent that federal judges actively manage federal cases to ensure these goals of judicial economy.

c. General Reforms

The Federal Rules were patterned after the Field Code and nineteenth-century procedural reforms, merging law and equity, simplifying pleading, and abolishing forms of action as well as multiple rounds of pleading.

d. Limitations on Pleadings

The Federal Rules permit only three types of pleadings: *a complaint, an answer,* and a plaintiff's *reply* to defendant's counterclaim. **Rule 7(a).** If the defendant does not assert a counterclaim, then the plaintiff is not permitted to file a reply.

e. Policy Favoring Merits Resolution

The Federal Rules were intended to permit a resolution of claims on the merits, without pleadings serving as a barrier to reaching the merits. Dismissals based on technical pleadings defects were discouraged, and pleaders were not expected to know all the facts at the time of pleading.

f. Creation of Liberal Discovery Regime

The Federal Rules created a system of liberal discovery provisions to assist in fact development after filing the complaint.

g. Fostering Liberal Joinder

The Federal Rules permitted and encouraged liberal joinder of parties and claims.

h. Intent of Liberal Construction

The Federal Rules were intended to be liberally construed, including amendments to pleadings and joinder of parties and claims.

i. Postponed Claim Screening

Federal Rules 11, 12, and **56** were intended to filter out baseless claims through pretrial motions to dismiss factually or legally deficient claims.

2. The Complaint

a. Statement of Claims: General Principles and the Problem of Specificity

The major function of pleading under the Federal Rules is to provide parties notice of the nature of claims or defenses.

i. Notice Pleading

The Federal Rules require a complaint to contain simply "a short and plain statement of the claim showing that the pleader is entitled to relief." **Rule 8(a)(2).** The pleader also must state the grounds for the court's jurisdiction, **Rule 8(a)(1),** and a demand for relief, **Rule 8(a)(3).**

(a) **Standard.** The Federal Rules also provide that "each allegation must be simple, concise, and direct," and that "no technical form is required." **Rule 8(d).**

■ EXAMPLES AND ANALYSIS

- **Dioguardi v. Durning,** 139 F.2d 774 (2d Cir. 1944). Dioguardi, an immigrant with limited English skills, filed a complaint written by himself in federal court imperfectly alleging that bottles of tonic imported from Italy had somehow been illegally or improperly seized and sold at public auction by customs authorities, and he demanded a refund for this merchandise. He subsequently filed an amended complaint, again in imperfect and unclear English, alleging disparities in the auction bidding price and the disappearance of two cases of tonic. The district court dismissed the complaint on defendant's motion. The appellate court reversed, concluding that however "inartistically" Dioguardi had stated his case, under **Rule 8** he had made out claims for improper conversion as well as possibly for an improper government auction. The Second Circuit also concluded that on remand the district court could possibly make out other cognizable claims, strongly urging that Dioguardi retain legal counsel to assist with filing an amended complaint.

- *Conley v. Gibson* **and the "no set of facts" standard.** Consistent with *Dioguardi*, the Supreme Court affirmed that federal pleading rules do not require a plaintiff to set out in great detail the facts upon which the claim is based. **Conley v. Gibson**, 355 U.S. 41 (1957), citing *Dioguardi. Conley* involved a class action lawsuit in federal district court in Texas by African–American members of a local railway union against the union, when it failed to represent them in negotiations with the railroad when they were discharged or their jobs were abolished. The defendant union moved to dismiss on various grounds, including that the complaint failed to state a claim upon which relief could be granted. The district court granted the motion, which the Fifth Circuit affirmed. The Supreme Court reversed, holding that the plaintiffs' complaint adequately set forth a claim upon which relief could be granted.

  i.   **The *Conley* pleading standard.** The Supreme Court held that the Federal Rules of Procedure do not require a claimant to set out in detail the facts upon which the claimant bases its claim. The Court famously held that: *"A complaint should not be dismissed for the failure to state a claim unless it appears beyond doubt that the plaintiff can prove no set of facts in support of his claim which would entitle him to relief."*

  ii. **Purpose of liberal notice pleading: pleading is not a game of skill**. The Court noted that the Federal Rules reject the approach that pleading is a game of skill in which one misstep by counsel may be decisive to the outcome and accept the principle that the purpose of pleading is to facilitate a proper decision on the merits. Instead:

    - the rules require a short and plain statement of the claim that will give the defendant fair notice of what the plaintiff's claim is and the grounds upon which it rests;

    - the illustrative forms appended to the rules illustrate this;

- simplified notice pleading is made possible by liberal discovery and other pretrial procedures established by the rules to disclose more precisely the basis of the claims and defenses, and to define more narrowly the disputed facts and issues, such as **Federal Rules 12(c), (e)**, and **(f)**; **Rule 15** (amendment of pleadings), **Rule 16** (pre-trial procedure); **Rules 26–37** (discovery); and **Rule 56** (summary judgment).

ii. Repudiation of *Conley v. Gibson* and the "No Set of Facts" Pleading Standard

The Supreme Court's ruling upholding a broadly liberal pleading standard under which a federal complaint could not be dismissed unless it appeared beyond a doubt that the plaintiff could prove no set of facts in support of his claim, remained the prevailing federal standard for more than fifty years, and in spite of repeated challenges to this liberal standard. In two landmark decisions 2007 and 2009, the Supreme Court reversed this prevailing test and repudiated the **Conley** standard.

- **Leading case authority: Bell Atlantic Corp. v. Twombly, 550 U.S. 544 (2007).** Two plaintiffs, Twombly and Marcus, subscribers to local telephone and high speed internet services, brought a federal class action against various so-called "Baby Bell" companies after the federally-ordered divestiture of AT & T. The complaint alleged violations of **§ 1** of the Sherman Act, complaining that the defendants conspired to restrain trade (which resulted in overcharging and providing inferior service). In addition, the complaint alleged that the local Baby Bells, in violation of federal antitrust law, agreed to refrain from competing with one another. The defendants moved to dismiss the case pursuant to **Fed. R. Civ. 12(b)(6)** for failure to state a claim upon which relief could be granted. The district court granted the dismissal, holding that in order to withstand dismissal, the plaintiffs needed to allege additional facts that tended to exclude independent self-interested conduct as an explanation for the defendants' parallel behavior. The Second Circuit reversed, holding that the district court had tested the complaint by the wrong standard. The appellate court held that plus factors were not required to be pleaded to permit an antitrust claim based on parallel conduct to survive dismissal.

- **Supreme Court holdings in *Twombly*** (7–2 decision; Justices Stevens and Ginsburg dissenting): The Supreme Court reversed the decision of the Second Circuit, repudiating the **Conley v. Gibson** liberal pleading standard. Applying a new "plausibility" standard, the Court held that the plaintiff's claim of conspiracy in restraint of trade failed to assert a set of facts that could plausibly support such a claim. "Because the plaintiffs here have not nudged their claims across the line from conceivable to plausible, their complaint must be dismissed."

  i. **Pleader's obligation under Rule 8(a)(2)**: a complaint attacked by a **Rule 12(b)(6)** motion does not need detailed factual allegations. However, a pleader's obligation to provide the grounds of entitlement to relief requires:

     — More than labels and conclusions;

     — More than a formulaic recitation of the elements of a cause of action;

     — Factual allegations enough to raise a right to relief above the speculative level

  ii. **The "plausibility" standard.** A plaintiff must allege sufficient facts, taken as true, to assert a plausible grounds (in this case) to infer an agreement to restrain trade.

     — The requirement of plausible grounds to raise an inference does not impose a probability requirement at the pleading stage;

     — The requirement of plausible grounds simply calls for enough fact to raise a reasonable expectation that discovery will reveal evidence (in this case) of an illegal agreement

     — A well-pleaded complaint may proceed even if it strikes a savvy judge that actual proof of those facts is improbable, and that recovery is remote and unlikely

     — The plausibility standard reflects the threshold requirement that a pleader's plain statement of its complaints possess "enough heft to show that the pleader is entitled to relief."

iii. **Rationale for plausibility standard**. A pleader should be required to show something beyond a mere possibility of a legal claim in order that plaintiffs with largely groundless claims take up the time of defending parties and the courts, or induce an increased *in terrorem* settlement value to a baseless claim. In addition, under the facts in this case, antitrust litigation and antitrust discovery is highly expensive and to impose this burden in absence of a plausible claim to relief places an unfair burden on defendants.

iv. **Rationale for repudiating *Conley* "no set of facts" standard.** The *Conley* standard has puzzled the profession for over 50 years; the "no set of facts" language has been questioned, criticized, and explained away long enough and has earned its retirement.

— In addition, the majority rejected the dissenters' contention that a problem with a complaint just shy of plausibility could be remedied by careful case management.

v. **Justice Stevens' dissent (joined by Justice Ginsburg).** The dissenting Justices argued that the *Conley* standard had prevailed for more than fifty years and the Court had reaffirmed its basic understanding in numerous cases. Conley, therefore, deserved a more decent burial. The majority's economic concern over excessive costs in antitrust litigation could be handled by judicious case management techniques. A transparent policy concern favoring antitrust defendants drives the majority's decision.

vi. **Interpretive problems after *Twombly*.** The Court's decision in *Twombly* was immediately attacked and criticized for both repudiating the Conley liberal pleading standard and substituting an opaque "plausibility" standard. Two questions in the wake of Twombly asked whether the Court had imposed a new regime of heightened fact pleading into federal procedure, and whether the Twombly decision was limited only to complex and expensive antitrust cases. The court addressed these questions in **Ashcroft v. Iqbal,** 556 U.S. 662 (2009).

- **Leading case authority:** *Ashcroft v. Iqbal,* **556 U.S. 662 (2009).** After September 22, 2001, Iqbal, a Muslim citizen of Pakistan was arrested on criminal charges and detained by federal officials. He subsequently brought suit in federal court in New York claiming deprivations of various constitutional rights while he was detained. He sued various federal officials, including John Ashcroft, the former Attorney General of the United States, and Robert Mueller, the Director of the FBI. Iqbal's 21 count complaint alleged that the defendants had adopted an unconstitutional policy that subjected Iqbal to harsh conditions of confinement on account of his race, religion, or national origin. The district court declined to dismiss Iqbal's complaint, applying *Conley's* "no set of facts" standard. On appeal, the Second Circuit held that the district court had incorrectly applied the Conley standard, which *Twombly* had retired. However, the Second Circuit construed the Twombly decision as mandating a "flexible plausibility standard," which obliges a pleader to amplify a claim with some factual allegations in those contexts where such amplification is needed to render the claim plausible. The Second Circuit then held that Iqbal's appeal did not present one of those contexts requiring amplification, and therefore denial of the defendants' motion to dismiss was proper. In a concurrence, Judge Cabranes urged the Supreme Court to provide further clarity to the *Twombly* plausibility standard.

- **Supreme Court holdings in *Iqbal*.** The Supreme Court reversed the Second Circuit decision. The Court split 5–4 (with Justices Souter, Stevens, Ginsburg, and Breyer dissenting). Applying *Twombly* plausibility principles, the Court concluded that Iqbal had not nudged his claims of invidious discrimination "across the line from conceivable to plausible."

  i. **Plausibility standard clarified**. The Court held that "A claim has facial plausibility when the plaintiff pleads factual content that allows the court to draw the reasonable inference that the defendant is liable for the misconduct alleged."

— the plausibility requirement is not akin to a probability requirement.

ii. **Reaffirming *Twombly* principles**:

— court must accept all allegations in a complaint as true;

— threadbare recitals of elements of a cause of action, supported by conclusory statements, are insufficient;

— formulaic recitations of the elements of a (constitutional discrimination) claim are not sufficient to withstand a motion to dismiss;

— determining whether a complaint states a plausible claim for relief is a context-specific task that requires a reviewing court to draw on its judicial experience and common sense

— where well-pleaded facts do not permit a court to infer more than a mere possibility of misconduct, it has not been shown that the pleader is entitled to relief

iii. *Twombly* **not limited to antitrust cases**. The Court held that its decision in *Twombly* applies to antitrust and discrimination cases alike.

iv. **Rejection of case-management approach**. The Court reiterated that its rejection of the careful case management approach suggested by *Twombly's* dissenters; suggesting that this rejection was especially important in cases where government officials were named as defendants.

v. **Justice Souter dissent (joined by Justices Stevens, Ginsburg, and Breyer).** The dissenting Justices' contended that Iqbal's lengthy complaint were sufficient to satisfy the *Twombly* standards, and were more than mere naked legal conclusions nor consistent with legal conduct. The factual allegations sufficiently linked the defendants to the discriminatory conduct of their subordinates. The fallacy of the majority's position lay in their looking at relevant assertions in isolation.

iii. Insufficient Facts: Motion for More Definite Statement (Rule 12(e))

A plaintiff must state a claim with a level of specificity sufficient for the defendant to frame a response. If a plaintiff's complaint is factually too vague, a defendant, in a *motion for a more definite statement,* may request the plaintiff to state more facts specifically detailing the claim. **Rule 12(e).**

- **Example.** A motion for a more definite statement was granted to a defendant-employer in a lawsuit under the Labor Management Relations Act, ordering the plaintiff to specifically identify which of 2,000 strikers had not been recalled to jobs for which they were qualified. The employer claimed it had no information concerning to which strikers the alleged violations applied, and that it could not prepare a proper defense without the names of the strikers. **Lodge 743, International Assn. of Machinists v. United Aircraft Corp.,** 30 F.R.D. 142 (D. Conn. 1962).

(a) **Proper purpose of Rule 12(e) motion.** "The motion for a more definite statement 'is designed to strike at unintelligibility rather than simple want of detail,' and the motion will be granted only when the complaint is so vague and ambiguous that the defendant cannot frame a responsive pleading." **Frederick v. Koziol,** 727 F.Supp. 1019 (E.D. Va. 1990).

- **Contrast—sufficiency under the forms.** A complaint generally alleging negligence in the improper extraction and post-operative care of a tooth was sufficient under the **Form 9,** without a need for the plaintiff to state more definitely the acts constituting the negligence. **Webb v. Webb,** 32 F.R.D. 615 (W.D. Mo. 1963).

(b) **Rule 12(e) motions disfavored.** The **Rule 12(e)** motion for a more definite statement is a disfavored motion. Under liberal-pleading theory, a pleader should be required to provide an enhanced, more definite statement of the pleader's claims. In addition, **Rule 12(e)** is not intended to be a substitute for discovery. *See* Chapter VII, Obtaining Information Prior to Trial—Discovery.

iv. Illustrative Pleading Forms

The pleading forms contained in the Appendix to the rules are presumptively sufficient to state a claim in federal court. **Rule 84.** The forms "are intended to indicate the simplicity and brevity of statement which the rules contemplate." **Rule 84.**

v. Heightened Pleading Requirements—Specific Cases

Some lower federal courts require more specific or *heightened pleading* in certain types of cases. However, the Supreme Court has generally repudiated heightened pleading in federal complaints. **Leatherman v. Tarrant County Narcotics Intelligence & Coordination Unit,** 507 U.S. 163 (1993). The types of cases in which federal courts have required more specific fact pleading include:

(a) Securities fraud. Some federal courts, particularly the Second Circuit, require "slightly more" detail than **Rule 8(a)(2)** for claims alleging securities fraud. This heightened pleading requirement is viewed as consistent with the **Rule 9** requirement for specific pleading in fraud allegations. These courts also are greatly concerned with conclusory allegations of the defendants' knowledge or intent. *See, e.g.,* **Ross v. A.H. Robins Co.,** 607 F.2d 545 (2d Cir. 1979), holding a complaint inadequate for its failure to specifically plead the events which gave rise to a strong inference of the defendants' knowledge of the facts of the health risks caused by the Dalkon Shield intrauterine device.

- **Example. Tellabs, Inc. v. Makor Issues & Rights, Ltd.,** 551 U.S. 308 (2007). In an action brought under the **Private Securities Litigation Reform Act of 1995 (PSLRA),** the Supreme Court held that in pleading a securities fraud violation including the element of the defendant's scienter, the pleading of scienter must be more than plausible or reasonable: it must be cogent and at least as compelling as any opposing inference of non-fraudlent intent.

  i. **Beyond Twombly/Iqbal.** In **Tellabs,** the Court imposed a higher pleading standard for PSLRA cases than in **Twombly** and **Iqbal.** The Court indicated that Congress imposed heightened pleading requirements in securities' cases.

(b) Civil rights cases. Some federal courts, most notably in the Third Circuit, have required heightened fact pleading in civil rights cases. This has been justified by the increase in claims brought under the **Civil Rights Act**, and is intended to weed out frivolous and insubstantial cases at an early stage of the proceedings.

- **Example.** The United States Department of Justice brought a suit against the Philadelphia police department, alleging systematic violation of minorities' civil rights by physical abuse. The district court dismissed the case, citing that such claims could be vexatious to local officials. The Third Circuit upheld the dismissal on the ground that the complaint did not satisfy specificity requirements for civil rights cases. **United States v. City of Philadelphia**, 644 F.2d 187 (3d Cir. 1980).

- **Criticism.** The Third Circuit's approach to enhanced pleading requirements in civil rights cases has been criticized by the plaintiffs' civil rights bar as not appropriate or authorized by **Rule 8(a)(2).**

- **Contrast: leading case authority—Leatherman v. Tarrant County Narcotics Intelligence & Coordination Unit, 507 U.S. 163 (1993):** The Supreme Court held that a federal court may not use heightened pleading requirements in civil rights cases alleging municipal liability under **42 U.S.C. § 1983,** relying on **Conley.** The Court reaffirmed that the federal rules do not require a claimant to set out in detail the facts upon which the plaintiff bases its claim. Although **Rule 9(b)** requires greater specificity for certain claims (such as fraud), it does not include among the enumerated actions any reference to complaints alleging municipal liability under **§ 1983. Leatherman** is an older precedent and, as such, might be questionable under **Twombly/Iqbal** standards.

b. Consistency and Honesty in Pleading

i. Alternative and Inconsistent Allegations: Rule 8(d)(2)

(a) At common law. At common law, a pleader was prohibited from setting forth alternative or inconsistent allegations in a declaration because the common-law pleading system was designed to reduce every case to a single issue of law or fact. The Federal Rules permit such pleading.

(b) **Under the Federal Rules.** Under the Federal Rules, a pleader (either the plaintiff or the defendant) may state alternative or hypothetical allegations, if made in good faith, either in the complaint or a responsive pleading, such as a defense. **Rule 8(d)(2).** Many states also permit the assertion of inconsistent allegations.

(c) **Separate statement of allegations: Rule 10(b).** Federal pleaders are urged to set forth claims based on different transactions in separate paragraphs whenever this facilitates the clear presentation of claims and defenses. **Rule 10(b).** However, the separate paragraph suggestion is not a requirement of the rule. Some states that permit pleading of alternative facts or law require these allegations be set forth in separate paragraphs.

ii. **Signature and Certification Requirements: Rule 11**

Every pleading, motion, and paper filed in federal court must be signed by an attorney of record or, if a party is not represented by a lawyer, then by the party. In general, pleadings do not need to be verified (that is, by sworn oath before a notary—under penalty of perjury) or accompanied by an affidavit. **Rule 11(a).** A few exceptions require verified pleadings, such as shareholder derivative complaints. *See* **Rule 23.1** (discussed *infra*).

(a) **Historical Notes on Rule 11. Rule 11,** the so-called federal sanctioning provision, was a largely moribund provision from 1938 through the late 1970s and early 1980s. Only a few dozen cases reported sanctions under old **Rule 11.**

(b) **1983 Rule 11 amendment.** In 1983, the Advisory Committee on Civil Rules amended **Rule 11** to "put teeth" into the rule and empower federal judges to more actively impose sanctions for frivolous and inadequately investigated complaints. The major doctrinal shift in the courts was away from a *subjective standard* for what constituted a reasonable inquiry prior to filing, to an *objective standard.* The 1983 amendment of **Rule 11** led to a decade of aggressive enforcement and imposition of **Rule 11** sanctions, with hundreds of reported decisions in the lower federal and appellate courts. Many of these cases set forth conflicting interpretations of amended **Rule 11,** and sanctions varied widely.

(c) **Supreme Court Rule 11 decisions, 1989–1992.** Between 1989 and 1992, the Supreme Court decided four major Supreme Court cases construing the 1983 amended **Rule 11.** In these cases the Court narrowly and literally construed the punitive and deterrent purposes of the 1983 amended rule, upholding the imposition of sanctions. In one case *(Pavelic)*, the Supreme Court held that a law firm might not vicariously be sanctioned for the conduct of one of its attorneys. *See* **Pavelic & Leflore v. Marvel Entertainment Group,** 493 U.S. 120 (1989); **Cooter & Gell v. Hartmarx Corp.,** 496 U.S. 384 (1990); **Business Guides, Inc. v. Chromatic Communications Enterprises, Inc.,** 498 U.S. 533 (1991); and **Willy v. Coastal Corp.,** 503 U.S. 131 (1992).

(d) **1993 Rule 11 amendments.** During the decade spanning 1983–1993, abuse of the **Rule 11** sanctioning provision led to another round of rule reform, culminating in a revision of **Rule 11** in 1993. The intended purpose of the 1993 rule revision was to lessen the harsh impact of the 1983 amendments on the practicing bar. The two major revisions of **Rule 11** changed the imposition of sanctions from *mandatory to discretionary,* and included a *"safe harbor"* provision to allow a pleader to correct or withdraw a challenged pleading or paper. The most significant amendments of the 1993 revisions are indicated *infra.*

iii. Purpose of the Signature Requirement

The purpose of the signature requirement is to make the attorney or party pleader responsible for truthfulness of the allegations contained in the complaint.

iv. Reasonable Inquiry Standard

A pleader certifies that the allegations made in the complaint were formed after "an inquiry reasonable under the circumstances." In addition, the pleader certifies that, to the person's best knowledge, information, and belief:

- the complaint is not being presented for any improper purpose, such as to harass or cause unnecessary delay or needless increase in the cost of litigation;

- the claims, defenses, and other legal contentions are warranted by existing law or by a nonfrivolous argument for the extension, modification, or reversal of existing law, or the establishment of new law;

- the allegations or other factual contentions have evidentiary support or are likely to have evidentiary support after a reasonable opportunity for further investigation or discovery;

- denials of factual contentions are warranted on the evidence, or are reasonably based on a lack of information or belief.

v. **Sanctions for Rule 11 Violations**

The 1993 revisions changed several significant provisions relating to the imposition of sanctions for violation of the rule.

(a) **Who may be sanctioned.** A *party, lawyer, or law firm* may be sanctioned for violations of **Rule 11.** *See* **Rule 11(c).**

(b) **1993 amendment of "signer."** The 1993 rule amendment changed the sanction provision from "signer," specifically adding that law firms could be sanctioned under **Rule 11.** A law firm is jointly responsible for the actions of its partners, associates, and employees under **Rule 11.**

(c) **Repudiation of *Pavelic* holding.** This change effectively repealed the Supreme Court's contrary conclusion in **Pavelic & LeFlore v. Marvel Entertainment Group,** 493 U.S. 120 (1989), where the Court held that **Rule 11** did not permit sanctions to be imposed on a law firm for an individual attorney's signature of court papers.

(d) **Party liability.** The 1993 amendment affirmed the Court's holding in **Business Guides, Inc. v. Chromatic Communications Enterprises, Inc.,** 498 U.S. 533 (1991), that a party who signs a court paper may be independently subject to **Rule 11** sanctions.

(e) **Who may seek sanctions.** Any person, party, or the court on its own initiative, may seek **Rule 11** sanctions.

(f) **Procedure for seeking Rule 11 sanctions.** A person seeking **Rule 11** sanctions must present the request in a motion that is separate from other motions or requests. This 1993 reform was intended to eliminate the prior practice of routinely seeking **Rule 11** sanctions along with **Rule 12** and **Rule 56** summary judgment motions.

(g) **Notice; safe harbor provision; opportunity to be heard.** A person seeking sanctions for a **Rule 11** violation is required to serve notice on the person who has filed the challenged paper. That person then has 21 days (a "safe harbor") either to withdraw or correct the challenged claim, defense, contention, or allegation. If the challenged paper is not corrected or withdrawn within 21 days, then the person seeking sanctions may file the request for sanctions with the court.

- **Example.** After a police stop-and-search of a vehicle in Colorado, two plaintiffs arrested and charged on narcotics violations subsequently sued the officers under **42 U.S.C. § 1483**, alleging violation of their civil rights. The defendants filed motions for sanctions and fees under **28 U.S.C. § 1927**. The two plaintiffs filed **Rule 11** motions for sanctions against the defense attorneys on the grounds that they did not meet and confer with the plaintiffs or their attorneys prior to filing their sanction motion. Although the defendants had sent a letter to plaintiffs' counsel informing them of the proposed sanctions, the court held that this letter did not suffice to satisfy the safe harbor requirements under **Rule 11(c)(1)(A)**. The court remanded for further consideration of sanctions under **§ 1927**. **Roth v. Green**, 466 F.3d 1179 (10th Cir. 2006).

(h) **Purpose of the safe harbor provision.** The 21 day safe harbor provision was added as part of the 1993 reforms in order to permit the pleader to correct any challenged defects prior to being sanctioned by the court. The safe harbor provision was intended as a common-sense reform to alleviate the very large number of **Rule 11** sanctions that were sought and imposed for technical defects under **Rule 11** from 1983 to 1993. Thus, the safe harbor provision is intended to support and enhance the goal of **Rule 11** to secure the just, speedy, and inexpensive resolution of civil actions.

(i) **Sanctions available.** Prior to the amendment of **Rule 11** in 1993, a court was *required* to impose a monetary sanction against a **Rule 11** violator. The 1993 amendments of **Rule 11** substantially modified the available array of sanctions under the rule and additionally provided that sanctions may be imposed in the court's *discretion.*

- Among the available sanctions, a court may issue a nonmonetary directive against a person who has violated **Rule 11.** A court also may order the violator to pay a monetary penalty to the court that is necessary to deter a repetition of the offending conduct. A violator may be required to pay some or all of the attorney's fees incurred in seeking the sanction.

(j) **Limitations on sanctions.** Monetary sanctions cannot be awarded for persons who attempted to state novel claims or defenses. Additionally, a court may not order money sanctions against a party voluntarily dismissing or settling a claim, unless the court issues a show cause order relating to the sanctions prior to the dismissal. This particular provision is intended to alleviate the harshness of the Supreme Court's ruling in **Cooter & Gell v. Hartmarx Corp.,** 496 U.S. 384 (1990) in which a unanimous Court held that an attorney could not avoid **Rule 11** sanctions by voluntarily dismissing the complaint under **Rule 41(a)(1).**

(k) **Jurisdiction to impose Rule 11 sanctions**

- **Lack of federal court subject matter jurisdiction.** A federal court may impose **Rule 11** sanctions *even if it is subsequently determined that the court lacked subject matter jurisdiction over the claims asserted in the case.* A federal court has an interest in obedience to the federal rules, even though a final determination precludes litigation of the claims in federal court. **Willy v. Coastal Corp.,** 503 U.S. 131 (1992).

- **Inapplicability to discovery abuses. Rule 11** does not apply to any papers filed requesting or responding to discovery matters. **Rule 11(d). Rule 37** provides the basis and sanctions for discovery abuses.

(l) Other sanctioning provisions:

- **28 U.S.C. § 1927.** An attorney may be sanctioned for unreasonably and vexatiously multiplying proceedings. The attorney may personally be assessed excess costs, expenses, and attorney fees.

- **Fed. R. App. Pro. 38.** A circuit court may award damages and single or double costs if it is determined that an appeal is frivolous.

- **Inherent powers of the court.** Federal judges may sanction attorneys as part of the inherent powers of the Court. **Chambers v. Nasco, Inc.,** 501 U.S. 32 (1991).

iii. Certification Requirements: Other Provisions—Shareholder's Derivative Suits under Rule 23.1

Although the Federal Rules do not require a pleader to verify the pleadings by notarization or affidavit, certain actions require verification. The leading example is the shareholder's derivative suit, which requires the plaintiff to sign a verified complaint. **Rule 23.1(b).** A verified signature subjects the signer to penalty of perjury for false statements. A falsely verified complaint may also result in dismissal of the action as a *sham pleading.*

(a) Purpose of verification requirement. The purpose of the verification requirement in shareholder derivative suits is to protect defendants against frivolous *strike suits.* A strike suit is an action brought by a person with no bona fide claim. The theory of the action is to harass the adversary (typically a corporation) by burdensome pretrial procedures into a remunerative settlement.

(b) 1995 federal securities litigation legislation. In 1995, Congress enacted the **Securities Litigation Reform Act,** which included several provisions relating to the assertion of frivolous shareholder derivative class action lawsuits. The **Rule 23.1** verification requirement remains an independent requirement in shareholder derivative suits.

(c) Leading case authority—Surowitz v. Hilton Hotels Corp., 383 U.S. 363 (1966). Mrs. Surowitz, a Polish immigrant with limited English abilities, brought a shareholder's derivative lawsuit against the Hilton Hotels Corporation on behalf of herself and other shareholders against the officers and directors of the corporation, alleging fraud and illegal schemes to cheat the corporation and enrich the individual defendants. Her lawyer signed the complaint in conformity with **Rule 11,** and Mrs. Surowitz signed and verified the complaint in compliance with **Rule 23.1** (the shareholder's derivative lawsuit rule). In depositions, Mrs. Surowitz indicated that she did not understand the complaint and had little knowledge concerning what the lawsuit was about. The defendants moved to dismiss the complaint on the grounds that the pleading was a sham pleading; the district court granted the motion and the appellate court affirmed. On appeal, the Supreme Court held that the dismissal of the case was erroneous and remanded for a trial. The court held that Mrs. Surowitz had signed and verified the complaint not based on her own knowledge and understanding, but on her faith in her lawyer's (who also was her son-in-law) advice that the statements in the complaint were true. The Court further indicated that **Rule 23** was not intended to bar shareholder derivative suits, but to discourage strike suits. In light of this purpose, Surowitz's suit was not a strike suit.

iv. State Verification Requirements

Some states require certain types of pleadings to be verified, such as petitions for divorce, state petitions to enjoin a nuisance, or complaints to obtain support of an illegitimate child.

c. Pleading Special Matters: Rule 9

Rule 9 requires that certain matters have to be pleaded with greater specificity or particularity.

i. Fraud or Mistake

The circumstances constituting fraud or mistake need to be pleaded with particularity. **Rule 9(b).**

(a) Policies underlying the particularity requirement for fraud or mistake allegations. The particularity requirement for fraud or mistake allegations is justified because of the potential harm to the defendant's reputation as a consequence of the allegations, or to deter the possibility of nuisance or "strike" suits.

(b) Qualification: Pleading conditions of the mind. Pleading so-called "conditions of the mind," such as malice, intent, or knowledge may be alleged generally. **Rule 9(b).**

ii. Special Damages

Special damages also must be specifically stated and claimed, or they will be forfeited. Special damages are those that are "a proximate result of the defendant's conduct but that occur only because of the specific situation of the plaintiff." *See* discussion *infra*, on pleading damages.

iii. Denial of Performance or Occurrence of Conditions Precedent

A pleader is required to plead specifically and particularly the denial of performance or occurrence of conditions precedent. **Rule 9(c).** However, a pleader may generally state the performance or occurrence of conditions precedent.

d. Pleading Damages; Prayer for Relief

i. The Demand for Relief

The concluding paragraphs of the complaint typically contain the "prayer for relief" setting forth the legal or equitable remedies the pleader seeks for the claims set forth in the complaint. The paragraph requesting monetary damages is called an *ad damnum* clause.

(a) State practice. State procedural rules typically require pleaders to state a request for relief, but some states have eliminated the prayer for relief in medical malpractice cases (although the complaint must allege that the claim meets or exceeds the amount-in-controversy jurisdictional requirement). Some state courts prohibit pleaders from requesting an amount in all personal injury cases.

- **Rationale for elimination of the *ad damnum* clause.** In some states the *ad damnum* clause is viewed as anachronistic and unnecessary. In states that permit the jury to view the pleadings, *ad damnum* clauses are feared to cause potential prejudice to the defendant.

(b) Federal practice. In federal court a pleader must set forth "a demand for the relief sought." A pleader may seek alternative relief, or several different types of relief (such as a combination of legal and equitable remedies). **Rule 8(a)(3).** There is some sentiment that the *ad damnum* clause also is anachronistic in federal practice, but it is still a requirement of the rules. *See* **Bail v. Cunningham,** 452 F.2d 182 (7th Cir. 1971).

ii. Judgment Exceeding the Demand: Permissible Recovery of Damages

A federal pleader is entitled to recover an amount exceeding what was demanded in the complaint. **Rule 54(c); Bail v. Cunningham,** 452 F.2d 182 (7th Cir. 1971). Most states follow the federal rule with regard to the recovery of excessive damages.

(a) **Default exception.** In cases where the defendant suffers a default judgment, then damages are capped by the amount requested in the *ad damnum* clause. **Rule 54(c).**

iii. Amending the Prayer for Relief

Some states that do not follow **Rule 54(c)** (damages in excess of the *ad damnum* clause) instead allow the plaintiff to amend the complaint to increase the amount of damages, in order to permit full recovery. *See, e.g.,* **Haney v. Burgin,** 106 N.H. 213, 208 A.2d 448 (1965) (permitting plaintiff to successively amend complaint four times, increasing amount of damages with each amendment).

(a) **Possible prejudice to defendants.** Amendments of *ad damnum* clauses increasing damage requests usually are granted, provided the amendment does not prejudice the defendant's presentation of its case.

iv. Damages in Excess of Jurisdictional Amount

State court jurisdiction often is circumscribed by amount-controversy limitations, but plaintiffs may plead damages in excess of the court's jurisdiction.

v. Pleading Special Damages: Rule 9(g)

Special damages must be specifically stated in a federal complaint. **Rule 9(g).** Many states also require that special damages be specially pleaded. *See, e.g.,* **Ziervogel v. Royal Packing Co.,** 225 S.W.2d 798 (Mo. App. 1949).

(a) **Special damages defined.** Special damages are damages which a defendant cannot reasonably expect to follow from an injury or breach alleged by the plaintiff. No allegation of special damages is required where damages are a logical and necessary result of the injuries claimed.

- **Example.** A plaintiff in an automobile accident requested damages for injuries sustained to her neck, back, spine, and nervous system. At trial, she sought to introduce evidence and collect damages for increased blood pressure and a shoulder injury. The court held it was an error to admit evidence of those other injuries, as the plaintiff had failed to include a request for these special damages, nor had requested leave to amend the complaint to include such special damages. **Ziervogel v. Royal Packing Co.,** 225 S.W.2d 798 (Mo. App. 1949).

- **Contrast.** A woman injured in an auto accident alleged injury and lacerations to her head, body, and limbs, but sought and was permitted to collect damages for a required abortion. The court held that the abortion augmented the physical injury and pain and suffering of the accident. **Ephrem v. Phillips,** 99 So.2d 257 (Fla. App. 1st Dist. 1957).

(b) **Consequences of failure to plead special damages**

- A pleader who fails to specifically allege special damages in the complaint will not be permitted to enter proof of those damages at trial.

- In some state courts, where special damages are an integral part of the claim, a pleader's failure to allege the special damages may result in a *dismissal by demurrer* or other motion to dismiss.

(c) **Medical bills as a result of personal injury.** *Cases are split* concerning whether medical bills as a result of personal injury need to be specially pleaded. Some courts hold that a general allegation of injury and damages is sufficient to permit proof of medical bills, and that it is unnecessary to specially plead medical expenses. Other courts hold directly to the contrary and require special pleading of medical expenses.

   (d) **Contract actions.** In contract actions, a pleader must allege any special damages that would not normally be foreseen as a consequence of the defendant's breach of the contract.

3. Responding to the Complaint: Responsive Motions and Pleadings

a. General Considerations

Defendants have two possible ways of responding to a complaint. The defendant may either challenge the complaint by a motion prior to answering (*see* discussion *infra*), or if not by a motion, then by filing an answer to the complaint (discussed *infra*).

i. Timing of the Response

   (a) **Defenses and objections made pursuant to Rule 12.** Rule 12 motions must be asserted within the time period in which a defendant has to answer a complaint (or in which a plaintiff must respond to a defendant's counterclaim). Thus, a defendant who wishes to raise any defenses or objections permitted in **Rule 12** must do so before filing an answer. Similarly, a plaintiff who wishes to raise **Rule 12** objections or defenses to a counterclaim must do so prior to filing a reply to the counterclaim. **Rule 12(b).**

   (b) **Answer.** A defendant has a different amount of time to file an answer, depending on whether the defendant waived service of process, or declined to waive process and was actually served:

   - **Defendant waiving service:** A defendant who waives service of process under **Rule 4(d)** must file an answer within 60 days of when the request for waiver was sent (90 days if the defendant is outside the United States). **Rule 12(a)(1)(B).**

   - **Defendant actually served.** A defendant who declines to waive service and is actually served must file an answer within 21 days after being served with the summons and complaint. **Rule 12(a)(1)(A)(ii).**

   - **Counterclaims and cross-claims.** Parties served with counterclaims or cross-claims have 21 days to respond after being served.

ii. Effect of Rule 12 Motions on Timing of Responsive Pleadings

In general, a **Rule 12** motion extends the time for filing a responsive pleading such as an answer for 14 days after notice of the court's action. **Rule 12(a)(4)(A), (B).**

iii. Extensions of Time

Attorneys frequently request extensions of time in which to file responsive pleadings, which is permitted under the rules. *See* **Rule 6(b)—"Enlargement of Time."** In general, the parties mutually agree to extensions of time. Judges also may order extensions of time by written stipulation (*i.e.,* agreement) of the parties.

b. Pre-Answer Motions: Motions to Dismiss—Rule 12

i. Historical Antecedents of the Motion to Dismiss

(a) Motion to dismiss for failure to state a claim. The modern motion to dismiss for failure to state a claim upon which relief can be granted has its historical antecedents in the *common law demurrer* (*see* discussion *supra*). The concept of the demurrer was incorporated into state code pleading systems, which permitted a complaint to be dismissed for a failure to state facts sufficient to constitute a cause of action, for deficiencies in the form of pleading, or for lack of subject matter jurisdiction.

(b) Other jurisdictional defects: Common law analogs. Federal motions to dismiss based on technical defects in jurisdiction, venue, process, and failure to join necessary parties (contained in **Rule 12(b)(1)** through **12(b)(5)** and **12(b)(7)**) are modern counterparts to common law *pleas in abatement* (*see* discussion *supra*).

- "Speaking motions." Federal practice permits extraneous materials to be introduced in support or opposition to these motions, since the validity of these challenges is rarely apparent on the face of the pleadings. This practice was recognized at common law. An example of "extraneous material" would be a copy of the contract, referred to in a plaintiff's complaint for breach of contract.

- **Rule 12(b)(6) and extraneous materials. Rule 12** was amended in 1948 to specifically permit the introduction of outside materials in support of the **Rule 12(b)(6)** motion to dismiss for failure to state a claim (*see* discussion *infra*).

ii. Rule 12 Motions to Dismiss: Available Challenges and Defenses

Rule 12 provides for seven separate grounds for dismissing a complaint:

- lack of subject matter jurisdiction (**Rule 12(b)(1)**);

- lack of personal jurisdiction (**Rule 12(b)(2)**);

- improper venue (**Rule 12(b)(3)**);

- insufficient process (**Rule 12(b)(4)**);

- insufficient service of process (**Rule 12(b)(5)**);

- failure to state a claim upon which relief can be granted (**Rule 12(b)(6)**);

- failure to join a party needed for a just adjudication (under **Rule 19—Rule 12(b)(7)**).

(a) **Consolidation requirement.** A defendant who wishes to raise more than one **Rule 12** objection or defense—or any other motion available under the rule (*see* discussion *infra*)—must join all those objections into one consolidated motion.

- **Purpose of the consolidation requirement.** The purpose of the consolidation requirement is to prevent the defendant from serially presenting different defenses and objections to the court, which increase the cost and delay of litigation and may serve to harass the plaintiff.

- **Exceptions to the consolidation rule.** The consolidation rule does not apply to the defense of failure to state a claim upon which relief can be granted; failure to join a party under **Rule 19;** or failure to state a legal defense to a claim.

  - These defenses may be raised in any pleading, or on a motion for a judgment on the pleadings under **Rule 12(c),** or at trial on the merits.

(b) Procedure for Rule 12 motions. Rule 12(b) motions to dismiss, and **Rule 12(c)** motions to dismiss on the pleadings, are heard by the court and decided before trial. The court also may defer ruling on a motion until trial. **Rule 12(i).**

(c) Waiver of defenses. Four defenses must be timely asserted either in a **Rule 12** motion, the answer, or an amended pleading (permitted under **Rule 15**). These are: lack of personal jurisdiction, improper venue, insufficient process, or insufficient service of process. The failure to raise these defenses constitutes a waiver of these objections. **Rule 12(h)(1).**

- **Subject matter jurisdiction non-waivable defense.** Objections to the court's subject matter jurisdiction are not waivable and are never lost. Objections to the court's subject matter jurisdiction may be raised prior to, during, and after trial. If the court finds that it lacks subject matter jurisdiction, it must dismiss the case. **Rule 12(h)(3).**

iii. Motion to Dismiss for Failure to State a Claim: Rule 12(b)(6)

The Federal Rules permit a defendant to challenge the factual sufficiency of a complaint in a motion to dismiss for failure to state a claim upon which relief can be granted. **Rule 12(b)(6).**

(a) Standard. Courts evaluate **Rule 12(b)(6)** motions to dismiss based on the plausibility standard articulated in **Twombly** and **Iqbal**. *See supra.*

(b) Conversion into summary judgment motion

- **The "speaking demurrer."** At common law, a person seeking a demurrer was not permitted to introduce materials outside the pleadings. This remains the technical rule in many states.

- **Federal practice—introduction of materials outside the pleadings.** The motion to dismiss is based on the allegations stated in plaintiff's complaint only, and is a challenge to the sufficiency of the plaintiff's pleading. The court does not construe any other papers or materials on the motion.

- If materials outside the pleading are introduced in support of its sufficiency, then the **Rule 12(b)(6)** motion or **Rule**

12(c) motion is converted into a **Rule 56** motion for summary judgment, and the defendant is given an opportunity to respond to the summary judgment motion. *See* **Rule 12(d).**

- **Distinction between a Rule 12(b)(6) challenge and summary judgment. Rule 12** was amended in 1948 to permit a **Rule 12(b)(6)** motion to be treated as a summary judgment motion if matters were introduced outside the pleadings. **Rule 12(b)(6)** challenges the sufficiency of a legal claim or defense; a summary judgment recognizes the facial legal sufficiency of the claims, but attacks the factual basis of the pleading.

(c) Pleading construed in light most favorable to pleader. The court is required to construe the complaint in a light most favorable to the plaintiff, with all doubts resolved in the pleader's favor and the allegations taken as true.

(d) Defenses need not be anticipated or negated. A plaintiff generally is not required in the complaint either to anticipate or negate a possible defense that might be raised by the opposing party. Some courts, however, hold that where a defense can be anticipated, it must be effectively avoided or the complaint will be dismissed. **Baggett v. Chavous,** 107 Ga.App. 642, 131 S.E.2d 109 (1963).

(e) Consequences of a successful Rule 12(b)(6) motion to dismiss for failure to state a claim. In most federal courts, the grant of a **Rule 12(b)(6)** motion serves as an adjudication on the merits and further actions based on the same claim are barred by the principles of res judicata.

- **Criticism:** Other courts believe this result is too harsh, and that a pleader should be permitted to modify or amend the complaint and re-serve it on the defendant, provided applicable statutes of limitation have not expired. *See* **American Nurses Assn. v. Illinois,** 783 F.2d 716 (7th Cir. 1986).

(f) Relationship to frivolous pauper complaints. A plaintiff who files as a pauper (*in forma pauperis*) may not have the complaint dismissed under **28 U.S.C. § 1915(d)** (which authorizes federal courts to dismiss such cases if the action "is malicious or frivolous"), if the complaint raises an arguable question of law. The Supreme Court has indicated that **§ 1915(d)** and **Rule 12(b)(6)** do not encompass each other: "When a complaint raises an arguable question of law which the district court ultimately finds is correctly resolved against the plaintiff, dismissal on **Rule 12(b)(6)** grounds is appropriate, but dismissal on the basis of frivolousness is not." **Neitzke v. Williams,** 490 U.S. 319 (1989).

iv. Motion for a Judgment on the Pleadings: Rule 12(c)

This motion is the means for challenging the substantive sufficiency of the opposing party's pleadings once all the pleadings have been completed.

(a) **Timing.** A motion for a judgment on the pleadings may be made after all the pleadings (complaint, answer, and reply) have been filed and the pleadings are "closed."

(b) **Standard.** The motion for judgment on the pleadings is treated in the same fashion as other motions under **Rule 12(b)** (*see* discussion *supra*).

(c) **Conversion into summary judgment motion.** A motion for a judgment on the pleadings is converted into a **Rule 56** summary judgment motion if a party introduces extraneous materials in support of the motion. When such outside materials are allowed by the court, the opposing party must be given an opportunity to respond to the summary judgment motion. **Rule 12(d)**.

v. Motion to Strike: Rule 12(f)

The motion to strike is the means by which a party challenges the substantive sufficiency of defenses raised in an answer (or in a plaintiff's reply).

(a) **Common law and code pleading analogs.** The common law and code pleading analogs to the federal motion to strike were motions to strike allegations as sham, frivolous, irrelevant, redundant, repetitious, unnecessary, immaterial, or impertinent. Almost all these grounds have been eliminated in modern **Rule 12(f),** in order to reduce unnecessary delays caused by disputes over the formal propriety of the allegations.

(b) **Timing.** A party may file a motion to strike material from an opposing party's pleading before responding to that pleading. If no other responsive pleading is allowed, then a party may move to strike material within 21 days after service of that pleading. Material also may be stricken on the court's own initiative, at any time.

(c) **Standard.** Only the following may be ordered stricken from a pleading:

- an insufficient defense;

- redundant, immaterial, or scandalous matter.

Material will not be stricken from a pleading unless its presence will prejudice the adverse party. The question whether allegations are prejudicial turns on whether the contents of the pleadings will be made available to the jury.

- In some instances the pleadings themselves become part of the evidence and may be shown to the jury. This usage is limited by evidence rules, and irrelevant or prejudicial matters independently may be excluded under the evidence rules.

To strike material as scandalous "it must be obviously false and unrelated to the subject matter of the action." **Gateway Bottling, Inc. v. Dad's Rootbeer Co.,** 53 F.R.D. 585 (W.D. Pa. 1971).

(d) **Disfavored motion.** Motions to strike materials from an opposing party's pleading are disfavored and rarely granted. Motions to strike are often viewed as a dilatory tactic.

c. Other Pretrial Motions

i. Motion for a More Definite Statement

A party may request a more definite statement from a pleader if the party is unable to frame a responsive pleading. **Rule 12(e).**

(a) **Timing.** A party may move for a more definite statement prior to filing its responsive pleading. If the court grants the motion, the pleader has 14 days to clarify the challenged allegations or statements.

(b) **Standard.** The motion for a more definite statement is granted if a pleading is "so vague or ambiguous that a party cannot reasonably prepare a response."

- **Example.** A complaint based on a slander claim fails to set out the utterance constituting the alleged slander, or the facts to establish its publication. The omission of these facts constitutes vagueness sufficient to grant a motion for a more definite statement within the contemplation of **Rule 12(e). Garcia v. Hilton Hotels Intl., Inc.,** 97 F.Supp. 5 (D. Puerto Rico 1951).

(c) **Consequences of failure to clarify.** If the court orders a pleader to submit a more definite statement and the pleader fails to comply, then the court may order the pleading stricken, or make any other order it deems just concerning the vague or ambiguous statement.

ii. **Affirmative Defenses**

Preliminary motion practice in federal courts is not restricted to the objections and defenses enumerated in **Rule 12.** Many federal courts also permit affirmative defenses (available in **Rule 8(c)**) to be raised in a pretrial motion, although these defenses probably were intended to be raised solely in the answer.

- **Example.** A *statute of limitations* defense may appear on the face of the complaint, and presents a common situation where federal court will permit a pretrial assertion of this affirmative defense in a motion (rather than requiring that it be asserted in the answer).

- **Rationale.** Dispositive affirmative defenses, if asserted and granted prior to an answer, save the time and expense of filing the responsive pleading.

iii. **Summary Judgment**

Defendants may move for a summary judgment dismissal prior to filing a responsive pleading. **Rule 56(a).** In addition, **Rule 12** motions may be converted into summary judgment motions if material outside the pleadings is introduced in support of those **Rule 12** motions (*see* discussion *supra*).

4. The Answer

a. Timing

An answer must be filed by the defendant either 21, 60, or 90 days after waiver of process or actual service of process, depending on whether the defendant is located in the United States or outside the United States. This time period is extended if the defendant instead chooses to file a **Rule 12** motion, or other motions (such as a summary judgment motion) (*see* discussion of timing rules *supra*).

b. Signing and Verification

An answer under the Federal Rules must be signed by the pleader and is subject to **Rule 11** requirements. Answers *do not need to be verified* or accompanied by an affidavit. Some states require that answers be verified.

c. Defendant's Possible Responses in the Answer under Rule 8(b)

Rule 8(b) requires that a defendant make one of three possible responses to the averments or allegations in the plaintiff's complaint. These three possible responses are to:

(1) admit each allegation;

(2) deny each allegation; or,

(3) plead that the defendant lacks knowledge or information to form a belief as to the truth of an allegation.

d. The General Denial

A federal pleader may "generally deny" all the allegations contained in a complaint, including the jurisdictional allegations. **Rule 8(b)(3).** Some states permit general denials; other states do not permit a defendant to generally deny the entire complaint. In California, for example, an answer cannot contain a general denial and must also be verified.

i. Effect of the General Denial

The effect of a general denial is to place each and every allegation stated in the complaint in issue, as a contested fact. This means that the plaintiff at trial must offer proof as to every allegation in the complaint.

ii. General Denials Disfavored

General denials are disfavored on the theory that at least some allegations in the complaint are truthful and incontrovertible, such as statements of the court's jurisdiction. **Biggs v. Public Serv. Coordinated Transp.**, 280 F.2d 311 (3d Cir. 1960) (jurisdictional allegations deemed admitted where defendant generally denied plaintiff's diversity-of-citizenship allegations, including the express claim that the defendant was a New Jersey corporation).

- General denials are additionally disfavored as they tend to defeat the purpose of allowing the pleadings to narrow the issues in controversy.

iii. Compliance with Rule 11 Requirements

A federal defendant who generally denies all the averments in a complaint is subject to the requirements for truthfulness and reasonable inquiry set forth in **Rule 11**. A general denial in federal court must be made in good faith and only where everything in the complaint may legitimately be denied.

iv. Risk Involved with General Denials

The Federal Rules require that a defendant's denials "must fairly respond to the substance of the allegation." **Rule 8(b)(1)(B).** If a court decides that a general denial does not meet this standard, it may deem the defendant to have admitted the plaintiff's specific averments. For this reason, general denials are rarely alleged in federal practice.

- **Example.** A complaint in a personal injury action against the plaintiff's employer alleged that the fork-lift driven by the plaintiff was "owned, operated, and controlled by the defendant, . . . and that the same . . . did come into contact with the plaintiff causing him to sustain the injuries [stated in the complaint]." Approximately a year before the accident, the company had been sold to another owner. The named defendant generally denied this allegation. The court held that the general denial under the circumstances was improper and that the defendant should specifically have admitted the allegations in part (relating to the occurrence of the accident), but specifically denied in part (the allegations relating to ownership). The partial, specific denial would have alerted the pleader to the incorrectly named defendant. **Zielinski v. Philadelphia Piers, Inc.,** 139 F.Supp. 408 (E.D. Pa. 1956).

- **Equitable estoppel and statutes of limitations problems.** Some courts apply the doctrine of *equitable estoppel* to prevent a party from taking advantage of the statute of limitations where the plaintiff has been mislead by the defendant's conduct in responding with a general denial. In such instances, the court will deem admitted the misleading allegations that were generally denied by the defendant. **Zielinski v. Philadelphia Piers, Inc.,** *supra.*

e. Evasive Denials

A defendant may respond to allegations in a complaint by stating that the pleader *"neither admits or denies"* the plaintiff's allegations. **Rule 8(b)** does not particularly prohibit evasive denials, but such a response may fail to comport with the requirement that denials fairly meet the substance of the allegations denied. Some states specifically prohibit such evasive denials.

i. Denials Constituting a "Negative Pregnant"

The doctrine of the so-called "negative pregnant" is a form of evasive denial. A negative pregnant is a form of response in which the defendant's denial effectively includes an affirmative implication that is favorable to the adversary.

- **Example.** A plaintiff's complaint for recovery on a series of notes contained the allegation that as for each note, "the sum of $150.00 is a reasonable sum to be allowed the plaintiff" for its attorney's fees. The defendant denied this allegation. On a favorable summary judgment for the plaintiff, the court awarded $100 in attorney's fees, which the defendant appealed contending that its answer put the issue in contention. On appeal to uphold the fee award, the plaintiffs argued that the defendants' general denial contained a negative pregnant supporting the fee award. The state supreme court agreed, holding that the defendants had only denied that $150.00 was a reasonable fee, but that the defendant had not denied that any lesser fee would be a reasonable amount. If the defendant wished to contest any other amount, then the defendant had to state in its responsive pleadings what they considered the maximum amount to be. **Wingfoot California Homes Co. v. Valley Natl. Bank,** 80 Ariz. 133, 294 P.2d 370 (1956).

f. Specific Denials; Form of Denials

If a defendant does not make a general denial, then the answer typically will contain numbered paragraphs corresponding to the complaint which specifically admits some allegations and denies others. A defendant may partially admit and deny statements contained within a plaintiff's paragraphs. *See* **Zielinski v. Philadelphia Piers, Inc.,** 139 F.Supp. 408 (E.D. Pa. 1956).

i. Consequences of Specific Denials

A specific denial places the particular allegation in issue and the plaintiff must offer proof in support of the contested allegation at trial. In contrast, allegations that the defendant admits are not in issue and the plaintiff need not prove these facts at trial.

ii. Denials Based on Lack of Knowledge or Information (The "Nonpositive Denial")

A party also may state that the pleader lacks knowledge or sufficient information upon which to form a belief as to the truth of the allegation.

(a) **Consequence of denial based on lack of knowledge of information.** A response based on lack of knowledge or information has the same effect as an outright denial.

(b) **Facts presumptively within the defendant's knowledge.** Some facts are deemed to be presumptively within a defendant's knowledge and therefore in such instances the defendant cannot respond by asserting this form of denial.

- **Example.** A defendant's response that it lacked knowledge or information concerning whether it was an unincorporated business association constituted a defective denial because this is a fact that is presumptively within the defendant's knowledge and frequently is a matter of public record. **Oliver v. Swiss Club Tell,** 222 Cal.App.2d 528, 35 Cal.Rptr. 324 (1963).

g. Consequence of Failure to Deny

All averments to which a defendant does not specifically respond are deemed admitted. This means that the plaintiff will not be required to present evidence in support of the allegation, and the defendant will not be able to contest the claims at trial.

- **Pleading tactic to avoid deemed admissions.** In order to accidentally avoid having allegations deemed admitted for a failure to specifically deny, many defendants routinely add an all-inclusive paragraph denying each and every allegation unless otherwise admitted.

h. Affirmative Defenses: Rule 8(c)

Affirmative defenses are available under both state procedural rules and **Rule 8(c).** In federal diversity cases, the federal court usually will look to state law to determine the availability of an affirmative defense, but not always. *See, e.g.,* **Taylor v. United States,** 821 F.2d 1428 (9th Cir. 1987), *cert. denied,* 485 U.S. 992 (1988) (declining to give effect to California affirmative defense of limitation of liability on noneconomic damages).

i. When Raised

An affirmative defense must be raised if it is a defense that does not flow logically from the plaintiff's claim or claims.

ii. Purpose

The purpose of requiring the assertion of affirmative defenses is to put the plaintiff on notice of the existence of the defense (the same is true for defendants if the plaintiff files a reply to a counterclaim), and to avoid unfair surprise.

- "A defendant should not be permitted to hide behind a log and ambush the plaintiff with an unexpected defense." **Ingraham v. United States,** 808 F.2d 1075 (5th Cir. 1987).

iii. Types of Affirmative Defenses Available

Rule 8(c) lists **affirmative defenses** that a party may set forth in a responsive pleading: accord and satisfaction; arbitration and award;

assumption of risk; contributory negligence; duress; estoppel; failure of consideration; fraud; illegality; injury by fellow servant; laches; license; payment; release; res judicata; statute of frauds; statute of limitations; and waiver.

- **Other affirmative defenses.** The list of available affirmative defenses in **Rule 8(c)** is not exhaustive.

iv. Mistaken Denomination of an Affirmative Defense

If a pleader mistakenly labels a defense as a counterclaim or a counterclaim as a defense, a court may treat the allegations as if they were properly designated ("if justice so requires"). The purpose of this rule is to alleviate the harshness of common law technical pleading defects as a resulting of mis-naming claims or defenses. **Rule 8(c)(2).**

v. Failure to Timely Plead an Affirmative Defense: Waiver

A pleader who fails to assert an affirmative defense in a timely fashion waives the defense.

i. Counterclaims

A defendant in the answer or a plaintiff in a reply may assert any counterclaims that are available to the pleader. In some instances the pleader is *required* to assert certain *compulsory* counterclaims. *See* **Rule 13(a), (b)** (discussed in Chapter VI, *infra*).

j. Cross-Claims

A defendant in the answer may assert any cross-claims it has against co-defendants in the lawsuit. *See* **Rule 13(g).** Similarly, a plaintiff in its reply to a counterclaim also may assert any claims the plaintiff has against co-plaintiffs, although this is more unusual. Cross-claims are discussed in Chapter VI, *infra*.

5. The Reply: Rule 7(a)

A reply is one of the three forms of pleading permitted under federal pleading rules.

a. Relationship to Common Law Pleading

The reply in federal practice (and most states) is the last permissible responsive pleading. This reflects a reaction to common law pleading, which permitted multiple successive rounds of pleading until disputed issues were identified.

b. When Available

i. Federal Practice

A plaintiff may file a reply if the defendant asserts a counterclaim. A court may order a reply to an answer. A third-party plaintiff also may file a reply to a third-party answer. *See* third-party practice and **Rule 14** generally (discussed in Chapter VI, *infra*).

(a) **Court-ordered replies.** A federal court may order a reply to allegations other than a counterclaim, but is reluctant to do so unless there is "a clear and convincing factual showing of necessity or other extraordinary circumstances of a compelling nature." **Moviecolor Ltd. v. Eastman Kodak Co.,** 24 F.R.D. 325 (S.D.N.Y. 1959).

ii. State Practice

In some states, the failure to deny the allegations of a defendant's affirmative defenses in a responsive reply results in those affirmative defenses being deemed admitted.

c. Replies and Jury Demands

Rule 38(b) provides, in relevant part, that a pleader may demand a jury trial "no later than 14 days after the last pleading directed to the issue is served."

i. Tactical Implications

If a plaintiff initially fails to make a jury demand in its answer, the plaintiff may have a second opportunity to make a jury demand if the plaintiff subsequently files a reply, since this is the "last responsive pleading" under **Rule 38(b).** However, if the plaintiff must request leave to amend and it is denied, then the plaintiff's demand for a jury trial will be forfeited because the defendant's answer would be the last pleading directed to the issue. **Beckstrom v. Coastwise Line,** 13 F.R.D. 480 (D. Alaska 1953).

d. Consequences of Failure to Reply

If a reply is not filed then any allegations requiring a responsive pleading are deemed admitted. Any matter not denied in a reply also is deemed admitted.

- **Reply not permitted.** If a plaintiff is not permitted to file a reply, or a reply is not necessary, then any allegations to which the plaintiff has not responded are considered to be denied or avoided, and are contested issues at trial.

6. Amendments to the Pleadings: Rule 15

a. Liberal Amendment Philosophy

In general, amendments of pleadings under the Federal Rules are liberally permitted in the early stages of a litigation, especially before responsive pleadings are served. This liberal amendment philosophy supports many of the goals and purposes of federal notice pleading:

i. Avoidance of Unnecessary Cost and Delay

Liberal amendment permits a pleader to correct any discovered defects in the litigant's own pleadings, which avoid unnecessary cost and delay caused by mistaken or defective pleadings.

ii. Consistent with Notice Pleading

Liberal amendment is consistent with the notice pleading philosophy underlying the rules—that a federal pleader may not have all fact information at the time of the initial filing of a complaint or responsive pleading.

iii. Consistent with Trial on Merits

Liberal amendment also is consistent with the federal philosophy that litigants ought to have an opportunity to test their claims on the merits, rather than be defeated for pleading defects.

iv. Qualification of the Liberal Amendment Approach

Although most federal courts endorse a liberal approach to permitting amendments to pleadings, courts will balance the desirability of allowing the amendment against the potential burdens of the opposing party as well as prejudice as a result of the amendment (*see* discussion *infra*).

b. Scope

The amendment provisions apply to all pleadings: the plaintiff's complaint, the defendant's answer, and the plaintiff's reply (if filed); as well as all pleadings filed relating to cross-claims and third-party claims.

c. Timing Considerations: When Amendments May Be Sought

Technically, a federal pleader may seek to amend its pleadings at any time after filing a pleading, as well as during or after trial (although this is most unusual). The earlier a pleader seeks to amend the pleadings, the more likely a court will grant a request to amend (if court permission is required). Generally, requests to amend pleadings may occur at four different times during the progress of a litigation (**Rule 15(a)**):

i. Before a Responsive Pleading Is Served

A party may amend its pleadings once "as a matter of course," within 21 days of serving the pleading, or 21 days after a responsive pleading.

- This early amendment rule allows pleaders to correct defects in their own pleadings at the soonest possible time without causing any burden on or prejudice to the opposing party.

ii. Amendment at All Other Times

If a party does not amend its pleadings within these early windows for amend party may amend either by:

- Leave of court (i.e., with the court's permission), or

- Written consent of the adverse parties.

iii. Leave to Amend "Freely Given"

Rule 15(a) states that "the court should freely give leave when justice so requires." Reasons that will defeat liberal leave to amend include:

- undue delay;

- bad faith;

- dilatory motive;

- repeated failure to cure deficiencies by previous amendments;

- undue prejudice to the opposing party; or

- futility of the amendment.

■ ILLUSTRATION

A defendant manufacturer of pool slides answered a complaint in a personal injury action. In framing its answer, the named defendant relied on the report of its own insurance investigators. Subsequently the company's president visited the accident site and discovered that the company had not manufactured the equipment. By this time, the statute of limitations had run on the plaintiff's claims. The defendant moved to amend its answer, denying manufacture, which the court granted. The appellate court upheld this ruling, finding no bad faith, prejudice, or undue delay sufficient to overcome **Rule 15(a)'s** mandate to give leave to amend "freely." The defendant had not lacked diligence in investigating the circumstances surrounding the accident, and should not be denied its right to litigate the factual issue of the equipment's manufacture. **Beeck v. Aquaslide 'n' Dive Corp.,** 562 F.2d 537 (8th Cir. 1977).

iv. Responding to Amended Pleadings

If a party serves an amended pleading on the opposing party, the opposing party may respond to the amended pleading within any time that remains for answering the original pleading. Alternatively, the opposing party may respond within 14 days after service of the amended pleading—whichever period is longer.

- **Time extensions by court order.** A court may order that a party has a longer period in which to respond to an amended pleading.

d. Amendments to Conform the Pleadings: Rule 15(b)

i. When Used

A party may at any time during or after trial ask the court for permission to amend the party's pleadings to "conform" those pleadings to the proof offered at trial. This situation arises when a party has not pleaded certain issues in their complaint or answer but raises these issues at trial, and offers proof in support.

- **Relationship to common law variance.** At common law, the situation where the proof offered at trial did not conform to the pleadings was called a *variance.* Modern federal pleading rules have abolished the variance, but the concept is embodied in the ability of a party to conform the pleader's pleadings to its proof.

ii. Who May Raise; Timing

Any party, at any time (even after trial) may assert a motion to conform the pleadings to the proof, even after a judgment. **Rule 15(b)(2).**

- **Failure to request conformity amendment.** A party's failure to move to amend the pleadings to conform to the proof does not affect the trial of those issues. **Rule 15(b).**

iii. Failure to Plead Issues: Express and Implied Consent

If a party fails to plead certain issues in the case, those issues may be tried either by express or implied consent. **Rule 15(b).**

(a) Express consent. A party who has not raised issues in its pleadings but subsequently places evidence in support of those issues at trial may do so if the opposing party *expressly consents* to having the additional issues presented. Such unpleaded issues tried by consent are treated the same as if they had been raised in the pleadings. If a party objects at trial, the court may grant a continuance to enable the objecting party to meet the evidence. **Rule 15(b)(1).**

(b) Implied consent. A party who has not raised issues in its pleadings but subsequently introduces evidence in support of those issues at trial may do so through the implied consent of the opposing party. Consent will be implied if the opposing party does not object to the introduction of evidence in support of unpleaded issues. Unpleaded issues tried by implied consent are treated the same as if they had been raised in the pleadings. **Rule 15(b)(2).**

- **Standard for implied consent.** Courts will determine whether the objecting party had actual notice of the unpleaded matters by a fair reading of the pleadings and trial presentation, as well as an adequate opportunity to litigate the matters and cure any surprise from their introduction. **Moore v. Moore,** 391 A.2d 762 (D.C. App. 1978).

■ ILLUSTRATION

A father brought an action to obtain custody of his child. During trial, his ex-wife's lawyer introduced evidence supporting the ex-wife's claim that it would be in the best interests of the child to be in the wife's custody; of the financial needs of the child; of counsel's fees, and of the wife's financial needs. The husband's lawyer did not object to the introduction of this evidence. After trial the wife moved to amend her answer to assert counterclaims against her husband for custody, child support, separate maintenance, and counsel fees. The court granted the motion to amend for custody, child support, visitation and bond, and attorney's fees, holding that these issues either were fairly contemplated by the husband's original custody action, or by implied consent for failure to object at trial. The court denied the motion to amend to state a counterclaim for separate spousal maintenance, as this was not uniquely pertinent to a custody action and the husband did not have timely notice or an adequate opportunity to respond. **Moore v. Moore,** 391 A.2d 762 (D.C. App. 1978).

- **Overcoming implied consent: Objections to evidence of unpleaded issues.** In order to avoid implied consent to the trial of an unpleaded issue, an opposing party must object to the introduction of evidence in support of the unpleaded issue. If such an objection is raised, then the pleader will be given the opportunity to amend the pleadings. **Moore v. Moore,** *supra.*

- **Standards for amendment at trial.** Federal courts are to grant leave to amend "freely" if the presentation of the merits of the action would be served by permitting the amendment.

- **Prejudice to objecting party.** Liberal amendment is to be denied if the objecting party fails to convince the court that the admission of evidence on the unpleaded issues would prejudice the party in its action or defense. *The burden is on the defendant to convince the court of the unfairness of permitting trial amendments of the pleadings to conform to the proof.*

- **Continuance.** Federal courts may grant the objecting party a continuance if it grants amendment of the pleadings during trial. The continuance is to afford the opposing party the opportunity to investigate and respond to the amended issues. **Rule 15(b)(1).**

- **Tactical dilemma for opposing party.** At trial if a party attempts to introduce evidence of an unpleaded issue, the opposing party is faced with the tactical dilemma of either remaining silent and impliedly consenting to the trial of the issue, or objecting and thereby causing the court to permit the pleader to amend its pleadings. **Moore v. Moore,** *supra.*

- **Better course to object.** In this situation, the better course is for the opposing party to object to the presentation of evidence on the unpleaded issue, which at least allows the objector to convince the court of the prejudice as a result of allowing proof of the unpleaded issue.

e. Permissive Amendments and Statute of Limitations: The Relation-Back Doctrine—Rule 15(c)

i. Statute of Limitations Problems

In general, a party may amend its pleadings at any time, subject to the limitations indicated above. However, if a statute of limitations has expired on a claim, then a party may not be able to amend a pleading.

- **Relation-back doctrine.** In certain special circumstances, a party may be permitted to amend a pleading after a statute of limitations has run, and then the amended pleading "relates back" to the date of the original pleading. The relation-back doctrine then is a saving doctrine that permits otherwise expired claims to be asserted, or mistaken parties to be changed or added to the litigation.

ii. Circumstances Permitting Relation-Back of Amendments

A party may amend a pleading to relate-back in three separate circumstances:

(a) Where permitted by law. If the statute supplying the limitations permits the relation-back of an amendment, then a federal pleader may amend. **Rule 15(c)(1).**

- **More restrictive state statutes.** Some states have more restrictive provisions for joinder of defendants after the limitations period has run.

- **More liberal state statutes.** Some states have more liberal joinder and amendment provisions, such as California, which permits a pleader to replace the actual names of defendants for originally designated "Doe defendants." (*see* discussion *infra*).

- *Erie* **implications of Rule 15(c)(1).** Federal courts disagree whether **Rule 15(c)** is "substantive" or "procedural" for *Erie* purposes. *See* **Marshall v. Mulrenin,** 508 F.2d 39 (1st Cir. 1974) and **Davis v. Piper Aircraft Corp.,** 615 F.2d 606 (4th Cir.), *cert. dismissed,* 448 U.S. 911 (1980). *See* discussion of *Erie* doctrine, Chapter III, *supra.*

- Pursuant to the *Erie* doctrine, if a federal statute does not supply a statute of limitations period, then the federal courts will follow or borrow a state limitations period. If, however, **Rule 15(c)** supplies a limitations rule, then it will supersede any conflicting state provision.

- **Example.** At least one federal court has held that, in diversity cases, **Rule 15(c)** is "procedural" for *Erie* purposes, and that with regard to unknown defendants, **Rule 15(c)** trumps any conflicting state statutes. **Worthington v. Wilson,** 790 F.Supp. 829 (1992).

(b) Amendment of claims—same conduct, transaction, and occurrence. A federal pleader may amend if the allegations in the amended pleading arose out of the same conduct, transaction or occurrence set forth in the original pleading; (or was attempted to be set forth in the original pleading). **Rule 15(c)(1)(B).**

- Some courts are less likely to permit amendments that add substantially different facts to the original allegations or change the focus of a litigation.

- **Example.** In a lawsuit based on negligent manufacture and breach of implied warranties of merchantability, a court would not permit an amendment to failure-to-warn of an inherently dangerous condition. **Tarbert v. Ingraham Co.,** 190 F.Supp. 402 (D. Conn. 1960). This decision, however, is more restrictive than usual and most federal courts probably would permit amendment based on the theory that the underlying transaction was the purchase and use of the product that injured the plaintiff.

(c) Amendment of parties: General standards. A federal pleader may amend to change the name of a party if:

- the amended pleading arose out of the same conduct, transaction, or occurrence set forth (or attempted to be set forth) in the original pleading, and

- within the period specified in **Rule 4(m)** for service of the summons and complaint the party to be brought in by the amendment:

- has received notice of the institution of the action such that the party will not be prejudiced in maintaining a defense on the merits; and

- knew or should have known that, but for a mistake concerning the identity of the proper party, the action would not have been brought against the party.

All these conditions must be satisfied to permit an amendment to change a party that will relate-back to the original statute of limitations.

(d) 1991 Rule 15(c) amendment relating to notice requirement. Current **Rule 15(c)** requires that a party to be changed in an amendment must have had notice of the institution of the lawsuit within 120 days of filing the complaint (*see* discussion *infra*). Congress enacted this rule change in 1991 to effectively overturn the Supreme Court's decision in **Schiavone v. Fortune,** 477 U.S. 21 (1986).

- *Schiavone* **holding.** In *Schiavone,* the Supreme Court held that a party to be changed by amendment had to have had actual notice of the action and that it was a proper party, before the statute of limitations period expired. It was not sufficient that notice was given within the time for service.

- *Schiavone* **criticized.** The *Schiavone* decision was widely criticized for imposing too rigid a construction of **Rule 15(c),** especially in innocent cases involving a misnomer or mistaken identification of a party. This restrictive reading of the rule foreclosed the trial of meritorious claims because of a technical procedural error.

- **Purpose of the 1991 amendment.** The purpose of the 1991 rule revision was to overturn *Schiavone* and to prevent parties against whom claims are asserted from taking unjust advantage of inconsequential pleading errors such as misnomer.

(e) **Amendment of parties: Calculating the time in which to amend. Rule 15(c)** ties timing of its notice provision to the **Rule 4(m)** time period for effecting service of process, which is 120 days after filing the complaint. In order for a plaintiff to be permitted to amend to change a party, that party would have had to have known of the institution of the action within that 120 day period.

(f) **Amendment of parties: Purpose of notice provisions. Rule 15(c)** has additional requirements for amendments that seek to change parties in order to avoid unfair surprise or prejudice to the party who is added through the amended pleading. Unfair surprise is eliminated because the rule requires that the changed party have had notice of the action within 120 days of its institution.

(g) **Amendment of parties: Misnomers and new parties.** Most federal courts will liberally permit an amendment to correct a party's name that is a *misnomer* or *spelling defect*. Federal courts are split, however, concerning whether amendment is available to *add a new party altogether* who was not originally named in the complaint.

- **Doe defendants.** Some federal courts hold that a request to substitute actual names for fictitious "Doe" defendants designated in the original complaint does not involve a "mistake" and therefore is not entitled to relation-back under **Rule 15(c)**. *See* **Rylewicz v. Beaton Services, Ltd., 888 F.2d 1175 (7th Cir. 1989).**

- **Contrary authority.** The Ninth Circuit, following California law, permits amendment to substitute the true name of a Doe defendant and allow relation-back.

(h) **Leading case authority. Krupski v. Costa Crociere S.p.A., 560 U.S. 538, 130 S.Ct. 2485 (2010).** The plaintiff Krupski tripped and injured herself on a cruise, the Costa Magica. On return home she filed a negligence action against Costa Cruise, three weeks before the one-year statute of limitations had expired. Her passenger ticket indicated that the ship was owned by Costa Crociere S.p.A, but went on to indicate that Costa Cruise Lines N.V. was the sales and marketing agent for Costa Lines. In the next several months and after the statute of limitations had expired, Costa Cruise notified Krupski and her attorney three times of Costa Crociere's existence. Costa Cruise and Costa Crociere shared legal counsel. Costa Cruise answered that it was not the proper defendant and subsequently moved for summary judgment, stating that Costa Crociere was the proper defendant. The district court denied Costa Cruise's motion and permitted Krupski to amend her complaint, which she served on Costa Crociere. Costa Cruise was dismissed from the case and Costa Crociere moved to dismiss contending that Krupski's amendment did not relate back under **Rule 15(c)** and was therefore untimely. The district court and Eleventh Circuit agreed. The Supreme Court reversed, holding that Krupski had satisfied all the requirements for the relation-back doctrine to apply, including the requirement under **Rule 15(c)(1)(C)(ii)**.

- **Supreme Court holdings in *Krupski v. Costa Crociere*:**

  — in order for a complaint naming a party to relate back to the date of its original filing, the plaintiff must satisfy the conditions set out in **Rule 15(c)(1)** with regard to the newly named party, within the time period specified by **Rule 4(m)**

  — the party must have such received notice of the action that it will not be prejudiced in defending on the merits; and

— the party knew or should have known that the action would have been brought against it, but for a mistake concerning the proper party's identity (**Rule 15(c)(1)(C)(ii)**)

— the key issue in assessing the **Rule 15(c)(1)(C)(ii)** requirement is not whether the plaintiff made a deliberate choice to sue one party over another

— **Key issue in applying Rule 15(c)(1)(C)(ii): what did the defendant know? Rule 15(c)(1)(C)(ii)** asks what the prospective defendant knew or should have known during the **Rule 4(m)** period, not what the plaintiff knew or should have known at the time of the filing of her complaint

— Costa Crociere had constructive notice of Krupski's complaint during the **Rule 4(m)** period and should have known that Krupski's failure to make it as a defendant in her original complaint was due to a mistake concerning the proper party's identity.

f.   New or Substituted Plaintiffs

Rule 15(c) does not deal with new or substituted plaintiffs after a statute of limitations has run. There is no need for a rule relating to change of plaintiffs since the defendant will already be on notice of the suit and it is not inconsistent with statutes of limitations to permit a new plaintiff to be substituted for an original one after the complaint has been filed.

g.   Rule 25

Rule 25 (substitution of parties) provides an additional (and different) basis for substituting a new legal representative when the original plaintiff is for some reason, such as death or incapacity, unable to prosecute the lawsuit.

7.   Supplemental Pleadings: Rules 7(a) and 15(d)

a.   State Practice

Some states prohibit pleaders from asserting a new cause of action in a supplemental pleading. Other states, however, very liberally permit a pleader to add new claims or issues filed as supplemental pleadings even if the pleader had no cause of action at the time of filing the original complaint.

• **Example**

Under the New York State rules permitting liberal filing of supplemental pleadings, a New York court permitted a wife suing her husband for separation to supplementally add a cause of action for divorce, on the ground that her husband had developed into an adulterer. **Herzog v. Herzog,** 43 Misc.2d 1062, 252 N.Y.S.2d 704 (Sup. Ct. 1964).

- **Contrary New York Authority**

  Another New York court refused to permit supplemental pleadings that alleged new theories of liability based on facts not previously alleged; three years had elapsed since the original complaint and discovery proceeded on the original legal theories; and the plaintiff failed to file an affidavit establishing the merits of the proposed supplemental claims or asserting a reasonable excuse for the plaintiff's delay in seeking leave to serve the supplemental pleadings. **Hypertronics Inc. v. Digital Equip. Corp.,** 159 A.D.2d 607, 552 N.Y.S.2d 662 (1990).

b. Federal Practice: Rule 15(d)

i. When Available and How Made

A party must seek permission of the court to serve supplemental pleadings. The supplemental pleadings must satisfy three requirements:

(1) reasonable notice to the opposing party of the supplemental pleadings;

(2) under "just term"; and

(3) setting forth transactions, occurrences, or events that have happened after the date of the pleading that is being supplemented.

ii. New Claims

There is substantial authority in lower federal courts that a plaintiff (or other pleader) is permitted to bring new claims in a supplemental pleading. *See, e.g.,* **Keith v. Volpe,** 858 F.2d 467 (9th Cir. 1988). This is based on the rationale that allowing such supplemental pleadings promotes the economical and speedy disposition of the controversy. A minority of federal courts take the position that newly arising claims can only be asserted in a new action.

iii. Defendant's Response to Supplemental Pleadings

A defendant is permitted to assert counterclaims to a supplemental pleading, even after the defendant has filed an answer. **Rule 13(e).**

iv. Curative Supplemental Pleadings

A plaintiff may correct a factually deficient pleading through supplemental pleadings (a supplemental pleading is allowed "even though the original pleading is defective in stating of a claim for relief or defense"). This provision was added to the Rule in 1963, to correct a split in the lower federal courts concerning whether a party could use supplemental pleadings to cure defective original pleadings.

■ CHAPTER REVIEW CHECKLIST

Civil procedure examinations usually do not include a question relating to technical pleading requirements at common law or the history of the development of modern pleading. You may be expected, however, to know and understand the historical common law and code antecedents to modern federal pleading rules. You also may be expected to know and understand some state variations on federal pleading rules. Your procedure professor is most likely to test on the sufficiency of a federal complaint or responsive pleading, such as a **Rule 12** motion, or the defendant's answer. Another favorite topic for civil procedure exams concerns amendments to pleadings. You are less likely to be tested on replies or supplemental pleadings, although you should know when these are available and for what purposes. Read the facts presented carefully and determine whether the facts present a problem relating to a complaint, a responsive pleading, or amendments.

To answer a problem relating to a federal complaint, ask:

1. **Do the facts present a problem relating to technical defects in the complaint? Does the complaint contain all the necessary components?**

    - Does the complaint contain a statement of the claims for relief?

    - Have claims been set out in separate numbered and captioned paragraphs?

    - Does the complaint set forth the basis for the court's jurisdiction?

    - Does the complaint contain a prayer for relief? What type of relief is requested?

        — Remember that the Federal Rules have merged law and equity and mixed prayers for relief are acceptable under the Federal Rules.

— Do the claims involve any special damages? Has the plaintiff specially pleaded special damages?

2. Are the plaintiff's allegations sufficient under the Federal Rules?

- Is the plaintiff's complaint based on a Form in the Appendix of Forms?

- Is the plaintiff's statement of the claim made in a "short and plain statement" showing that the pleader is entitled to relief?

- Has the plaintiff pleaded sufficient facts to withstand a motion to dismiss for failure to state a claim upon which relief can be granted? Do the facts constitute a cognizable legal claim?

- Are the allegations vague or ambiguous? Do the allegations contain any redundant, immaterial, impertinent or scandalous matter?

- Has the plaintiff alleged any facts relating to fraud or mistake? Are these facts pleaded with sufficient particularity?

3. Has the plaintiff complied with Rule 11 provisions to ensure truthfulness in pleading?

- Is the complaint one of the few that needs to be signed and verified under oath? Who must sign the complaint? Who did sign the complaint?

- Did the plaintiff's attorney conduct a reasonable inquiry under the circumstances prior to filing the complaint?

  — What kind of investigation did the plaintiff's attorney conduct? On whom did the plaintiff rely for information?

  — Did the plaintiff's attorney independently conduct an investigation of facts in support of the factual and legal basis of the claims?

- Is the plaintiff asserting a novel theory of law, or a request for an extension or modification of existing law?

- Has the defendant filed a sanction motion?

  — Was the plaintiff's lawyer given a period to correct the defective pleading? Did the plaintiff's lawyer correct the pleading within that period?

- Has a **Rule 11** sanction been imposed?

  — What is the basis for the sanction?

  — What is the nature of the sanction?

- Is there any other basis for imposing sanctions apart from **Rule 11**?

To answer an examination problem relating to **Rule 12** motions, ask:

1. **Do the facts present a situation where the defendant is challenging the complaint in a** Rule 12 **motion prior to filing an answer?**

   - Has the defendant filed a **Rule 12** motion?

     — Does the **Rule 12** motion consolidate all the available objections and challenges into one motion?

     — Has the **Rule 12** motion been filed in a timely fashion? Have any **Rule 12** challenges or objections been waived?

     — Does the **Rule 12** motion challenge the technical sufficiency of the complaint (jurisdiction, venue, process or joinder), or the legal sufficiency of the complaint (motion to dismiss for failure to state a claim)?

     — Is the defendant moving under **Rule 12** to strike portions of the plaintiff's allegations? Do those allegations contain matter that is redundant, immaterial, impertinent, or scandalous?

     — Is the defendant moving under **Rule 12** for a more definite statement from the plaintiff? Are the plaintiff's allegations deficiently vague or ambiguous?

To answer an examination problem relating to the defendant's answer, ask:

1. **What does the defendant's answer contain?**

   - Has the defendant generally denied the plaintiff's allegations?

   - Has the defendant specifically denied the plaintiff's allegations?

   - What is the form of the defendant's denials? Do the denials sufficiently meet the plaintiff's averments?

     — Has the defendant partially admitted and partially denied some allegations?

— Has defendant asserted a lack of knowledge or sufficient information to form a belief concerning the truth of the allegations?

- Does the defendant have any available affirmative defenses? Has the defendant pleaded those affirmative defenses?

- Has the defendant asserted any counterclaims? Gross-claims?

- Do the facts suggest any compulsory counterclaims that the defendant must assert or lose?

2. **Does the defendant's answer comply with Rule 11 requirements to ensure truthfulness in pleading? (See above analysis for plaintiff's Rule 11 requirements)**

To answer an examination question relating to the amendment of pleadings, ask:

1. **What type of amendment is sought, and when?**

   - Is the pleader seeking to amend prior to the filing of a responsive pleading?

   - Is the pleader seeking to amend after a responsive pleading has been filed?

   - Is the pleader seeking to amend at trial, or after trial?

   - Is the pleader seeking to amend when the relevant statute of limitations has already run?

2. **Is the pleader seeking to amend to conform the pleading to the proof?**

   - Did the opposing party have fair notice of the unpleaded claim presented at trial?

   - Will the opposing party be prejudiced by an amendment of the pleadings at trial, or post-trial?

   - Did the opposing party object to the introduction of evidence of impleaded claims at trial? Did the opposing party remain silent and thereby impliedly consent to the trial of the unpleaded issues?

   - If the court granted the motion to conform the pleadings, was the opposing party given a continuance to defend against the amended issues?

3. **Is the pleader seeking an amendment after a statute of limitations has expired?**

- Is there a state statute of limitations applicable? Does it conflict with **Rule 15(c)?**

- Is the pleader seeking to amend to change or add claims? Are the amended allegations transactionally related to the original claims?

- Is the pleader seeking to amend to change a party?

  — Why is the pleader seeking to change a party? Does the original pleading involve a misnomer or other technical defect, such as a misspelling?

  — Does the pleading name a Doe defendant who subsequently has become known?

- If the pleader is seeking to change a party, then ask whether:

  — the amended pleading arose out of the same conduct, transaction, or occurrence set forth (or attempted to be set forth) in the original pleading, and

  — within the period specified in **Rule 4(m)** for service of the summons and complaint (120 days) the party to be brought in by the amendment:

    (1) has received notice of the institution of the action such that the party will not be prejudiced in maintaining a defense on the merits; and

    (2) knew or should have known that, but for a mistake concerning the identity of the proper party, the action would not have been brought against the party

VI

Joinder

■ ANALYSIS

■ CHAPTER OVERVIEW

- This chapter deals with the ability to expand the scope of a civil action by joining additional claims and parties in the action, either at the inception of the lawsuit or while the suit is proceeding to trial.

- Historically at common law—and under many current state code pleading systems—the joinder of additional claims and parties in a civil action was severely limited by the writ system and forms of action.

- The Federal Rules favor and encourage liberal joinder of claims and parties in the interests of economical and efficient resolution of disputes.

- Under the Federal Rules of Civil Procedure there are several means by which parties to the litigation may add additional claims.

    - **Counterclaims.** A counterclaim is a claim which a party has against an adversary pleader. Defendants usually assert counterclaims in response to a plaintiff's complaint, but a plaintiff may assert a counterclaim against a defendant in the plaintiff's reply. Other pleaders, such as cross-claimants, may also assert counterclaims in responsive pleadings. **Rule 13.**

    - **Types of counterclaims.** There are two types of counterclaims available under the Federal Rules: permissive counterclaims (**Rule 13(b)**) and compulsory counterclaims (**Rule 13(a)**).

    - **Cross-claims.** Parties may assert cross-claims against co-parties. **Rule 13(g).** Usually, defendants assert cross-claims against other defendants, but it is possible for a plaintiff to assert a cross-claim against a co-plaintiff if this is justified by a defendant's assertion of a counterclaim.

- **Real party in interest.** The real party in interest must assert the claims in a lawsuit. **Rule 17.** The complaining party also must have *legal capacity* to bring the lawsuit and constitutional standing.

- In general, parties may be permissively joined under the Federal Rules. **Rule 20.**

- Certain parties must be joined for a just adjudication. **Rule 19.** If these parties are unable to be joined for jurisdictional or other reasons, then the court either must dismiss the lawsuit, or allow it to go forward in the absence of the party who has not been joined.

- **Third-party practice: Impleader.** A person who has not been joined in the lawsuit may be made a party to the litigation if that person is or may be liable to a party already named in the lawsuit. This form of party joinder is called *impleader,* and the means of bringing the person into the litigation is called "third-party" practice. **Rule 14.** Typically, a defendant *impleads* the non-joined person, by filing a third-party complaint against the person who may be liable to the defendant.

- **Interpleader.** Under federal statute (**28 U.S.C. § 1335**) and rule provisions (**Rule 22**), a party may seek to join all persons interested in a financial stake. In this form of action, the court becomes the stakeholder and seeks to resolve the competing claims to that stake. Interpleader is a frequently used joinder method in insurance litigation.

- **Intervention.** Persons who have not been named as parties in a lawsuit may seek to become parties to the litigation by asking the court's permission to intervene under **Rule 24.** There are two types of intervention: intervention as of right (**Rule 24(a)**), and permissive intervention (**Rule 24(b)**). Persons who are permitted to intervene become parties to the litigation, although their participation may be circumscribed by the court.

- If a litigation becomes too complex because of the joinder of multiple claims or the addition of multiple parties, the court may *sever* claims or issues for separate trial in order to enhance jury comprehension. **Rule 20(b); Rule 42(b).**

- **Class actions.** Class actions, authorized by **Rules 23, 23.1,** and **23.2,** and represent the largest aggregation device under the Federal Rules. Although not technically a form of joinder of claims, it is a means for "aggregating" claims in a representational litigation.

  — The single most important concept relating to the class action is that it is a representational litigation. Because a class action is a representational litigation, class action procedure is circumscribed by numerous due process protections for so-called "absent class members."

— In order to be certified as a class action, the class must meet four threshold requirements: numerosity, commonality, typicality, and adequacy of representation. **Rule 23(a)(1)–(4).**

— A class action also must meet the definitional requirements of three possible functional categories of class action. **Rule 23(b)(1)–(3).** Two of these class actions are mandatory and binding on all class members (**Rule 23(b)(1)** and **(b)(2)**); the third is a non-binding "opt-out" class (**Rule 23(b)(3)**).

— Class actions entail many difficult problems of professional ethics relating to conflicts-of-interest, fee arrangements, and settlement.

— Litigants may not compromise or settle a class action without the court's approval after a "fairness hearing." **Rule 23(e).**

• Each and every claim and party in a federal lawsuit must have a valid jurisdictional basis, including personal jurisdiction, subject matter jurisdiction, and proper venue. The subject matter jurisdictional basis may be supplied by theories of supplemental jurisdiction under **28 U.S.C. § 1367;** *see* discussion of supplemental jurisdiction at Chapter II, *supra.* The ability to join parties and claims is subject to jurisdictional limitations, particularly diversity requirements in federal court.

• Jurisdictional requirements under **§ 1367(b)** may limit the ability of a plaintiff to assert claims against a third-party defendant who the plaintiff did not originally sue in the plaintiff's complaint.

A. JOINDER OF CLAIMS

1. Historical Background and Modern Federal Rules Approach

a. Common Law Joinder Rules

At common law the ability to join distinct causes of action was limited by the forms of action and writ system.

• Different forms of action could not be pleaded in one action.

• However, if the same form of action could be adopted for several injuries, then these could be united in one case.

• This was true even if each injury arose out of a different transaction, at a different time, and in a different place.

i. Example of Common Law Joinder Rules

A man publicly accused another of being a thief and stealing a horse. He took the horse, arrested the man, and jailed him for a few days. The accused man subsequently sued for false imprisonment and slander. The defendant demurred, alleging that the several causes of action were improperly joined.

(a) **Joinder permitted.** If the accused man was arrested on a warrant, the causes of action for false imprisonment, slander, and conversion of the horse could have been united in one action, because these actions were each actions on the case. **Harris v. Avery,** 5 Kan. 146 (1869).

(b) **Joinder restricted.** If the accused was arrested without process, the causes of action for false imprisonment and slander could not have been united in one action, because the first would have to be sued as *an action of trespass* and the other as *an action on the case.* In addition, it would make no difference that the two claims arose out of the same transaction. **Harris v. Avery,** *id.*

(c) **Consequences of joinder restrictions.** The joinder restrictions at common law forced a pleader to state different causes of action in a multiplicity of lawsuits, even if the claims arose from the same events.

• The joinder restrictions also made the pleader vulnerable to dismissal by demurrer for improper joinder of causes of action.

b. Joinder Rules under Code Pleading Systems

Code pleading systems abolished the common law forms of action and consequently liberalized joinder rules. Code pleading also merged law and equity and made it possible to state claims seeking both types of relief.

i. Same Transaction Standard

Code pleading systems introduced the concept that claims could be joined if they constituted *the same transaction or transactions connected with the same subject of action.* **Harris v. Avery,** *id.*

ii. Purpose of the Code Reforms Relating to Joinder

The purpose of the joinder reforms effectuated in code pleading systems was to avoid multiplicity of lawsuits and to settle in one action the entire subject matter of the controversy.

- **Example.** In the above lawsuit in which the accused's asserted claims for false imprisonment and slander, the court overruled the demurrer and permitted joinder under the state's code pleading rules. **Harris v. Avery,** *id.* The court could find no reason not to unite the claims "when both do arise out of the same transaction."

iii. Formalistic Code Pleading Joinder Rules

In many states that adopted code pleading regimes, parties could join claims if the claims fell into certain categories. Typical categories included:

- Express or implied contracts;

- Injuries to the person;

- Injuries to character;

- Injuries to property;

- Actions to recover real property;

- Actions to recover chattels;

- Actions arising out of the same transaction or transactions connected with the same subject of the action.

In this regard, code pleading joinder rules often were as formalistic and restrictive as common law joinder rules.

2. Methods of Claim Joinder and Severability

a. Liberal Joinder of Claims: Rule 18(a)

Rule 18(a) sets forth the basic liberal joinder-of-claims provision in the Federal Rules. Under this rule a pleader may join:

- as many claims as the party has against an opposing party; and

- all legal and equitable claims.

i. Permissive Joinder: Not Compulsory

A federal plaintiff may join any and all claims in one action against a defendant, but is not compelled to do so. The rule is not mandatory.

(a) *Res judicata* **implications against splitting a cause of action.** Although the joinder rule is permissive, principles of *res judicata* that prohibit a pleader from "splitting claims" may effectively require a pleader to assert all available claims or be subject to subsequent merger doctrines. *See* discussion of *res judicata* principles in Chapter XII, *infra*.

(b) **Contrary state authority.** Some states, however, such as Michigan require compulsory joinder of all available claims.

ii. Jurisdictional Limitations

Permissible joinder of claims is limited by the requirements of personal jurisdiction, subject matter jurisdiction, and venue. (*See* Chapters I and II, *supra*, for discussions of these requirements.) Thus, every claim and party in a litigation must have an independent jurisdictional basis, as well as meet personal jurisdiction and venue requirements (*see* discussions *infra*).

iii. Rationale for Federal Liberal Joinder Rule

Similar to the code pleading reforms of common law joinder rules, the major purpose of **Rule 18(a)** is to avoid a multiplicity of lawsuits.

iv. Contrary State Authority: Example

A New York state court refused to allow a plaintiff to join four causes of action for negligence with one cause of action for malicious prosecution. The court rejected this joinder because of a fear of jury confusion and potential prejudice to the defendant of trying the different claims together. **Sporn v. Hudson Transit Lines,** 265 App. Div. 360, 38 N.Y.S.2d 512 (1942).

- **Severance under Rule 42.** The problems of jury confusion and prejudice may be remedied in federal practice by severing the claims under **Rule 42(b)** (*see* discussion *infra*).

b. Counterclaims and Cross-Claims: Rule 13

i. Counterclaims at Common Law

The modern counterclaim did not exist at common law.

(a) **Set-off and recoupment in equity.** The concepts of *set-off* and *recoupment*, however, did exist in equity practice and are precursors of the modern counterclaim.

- The theory underlying the set-off or recoupment was that it made little sense to require a defendant to pay a plaintiff what the defendant would be entitled to recover back.

- Over time, recoupment developed as a means to reduce the plaintiff's recovery by the amount that might be due a defendant for a defendant's claim against the plaintiff arising out of the same transaction that the plaintiff sued upon.

- Where claims arose out of a different transaction, common law recoupment was not permitted and the defendant had to bring a separate suit to recover from the plaintiff.

- Equity relieved this by allowing a set-off of claims arising out of a different transaction than the plaintiff's claim.

(b) The English Judicature Act of 1873. Provisions of this statute eliminated limitations on a defendant's ability to assert claims against a plaintiff.

ii. Counterclaims in Code Pleading Systems

(a) The Field Code. The 1848 original **Field Code** made no mention of counterclaims. Amendment of the **Field Code** in 1852 permitted counterclaims for:

- a cause of action arising out of the contract or transaction set forth in the complaint, as the foundation of the plaintiff's claim, or connected with the subject of the action; and

- in an action arising on contract, any other cause of action arising on contract, and existing at the commencement of the action.

(b) Early twentieth-century code practice. At the beginning of the twentieth century, many states amended their codes to follow the English practice and eliminate all barriers to the defendant's ability to assert claims against the plaintiff.

iii. Counterclaims under Federal Rules 13(a)–(e)

The modern Federal Rules of Civil Procedure are even more expansive concerning counterclaims than English or code pleading practice. Under the Federal rules, not only are counterclaims *permissive,* but some other counterclaims are *compulsory* and *must be raised* or they will be lost forever, barred by preclusion rules.

(a) Compulsory counterclaims: Rule 13(a). A pleader must assert a compulsory counterclaim against the opposing party which exists at the time of service. The counterclaim is compulsory if it is:

- **Transactionally related.** That is, arises out of the same transaction or occurrence that is the subject matter of the opposing party's claim; and

- **No jurisdictional bar.** Does not require the joinder of third parties over whom the court cannot acquire jurisdiction.

(b) "Transactionally related" standard. The requirement that a compulsory counterclaim be transactionally related is a criterion repeated throughout the joinder rules. Courts have variously defined what circumstances satisfy this requirement:

- Some courts require only a "logical relationship" between the plaintiff's claim and the defendant's counterclaim. **Moore v. New York Cotton Exchange,** 270 U.S. 593 (1926).

- The term "transaction" is a word of flexible meaning, given broad interpretation. **Moore v. New York Cotton Exchange,** *id.*

- The "transaction" criterion does not require the two claims to share an "absolute identity of factual backgrounds." **Lesnik v. Public Industrials Corp.,** 144 F.2d 968 (2d Cir.).

- Four tests may be used to assess the "transaction" criterion:

  - Are the issues of fact and law raised by the claim and counterclaim largely the same?

  - Would *res judicata* bar a subsequent lawsuit brought by the defendant if there were no compulsory counterclaim rule? (*see* discussion of *res judicata* in Chapter XII, *infra*).

- Will substantially the same evidence be used in support of the plaintiff's claim and defendant's counterclaim?

- Is there a logical relationship between the claim and the counterclaim?

(c) Jurisdictional basis for compulsory counterclaims:

- **Ancillary jurisdiction.** Prior to the promulgation of the supplemental jurisdiction statute as part of the **Judicial Improvements Act of 1990,** compulsory counterclaims were by definition *ancillary* to the plaintiff's complaint and therefore required no independent basis for federal subject matter jurisdiction (*see* discussion of federal subject matter jurisdiction in Chapter II, *supra*). "Ancillary" jurisdiction was subsumed in 1990 by creation of federal statutory "supplemental" jurisdiction.

- **Supplemental jurisdiction.** Since 1990, compulsory counterclaims find jurisdictional support in **28 U.S.C. § 1367(a)** that provides jurisdiction over claims that are part of "the same case or controversy under Art. III of the Constitution." (*see* discussion of federal supplemental jurisdiction in Chapter II, *supra*).

- There is some academic debate whether the "same case or controversy" standard in **§ 1367(a)** is broader than the same "transaction or occurrence" standard in **Rule 13(a).**

(d) Applications of transactional standard for compulsory counterclaims.

■ EXAMPLES AND ANALYSIS

Example 1. An excavating contractor brought a lawsuit against a prime contractor to recover payments for work on two jobs, one at a federal Navy base and the other at a non-government site. The prime contractor denied liability on the Navy job and counterclaimed for overpayments to the excavating company for both jobs. The excavating company then filed a reply denying liability on the defendant's overpayment counterclaims, and asserting its own reply counterclaim to recover on the non-governmental job. The court held that the counterclaims were compulsory under **Rule 13(a)** because there was a close and logical relationship between the Navy job and the non-governmental job. Both claims arose out of the "same transaction or occurrence" broadly defined, because the contracts were entered into by the same parties for the same type of work and carried on during substantially the same period. **United States v. Heyward–Robinson Co.,** 430 F.2d 1077 (2d Cir. 1970).

Jurisdictional concerns. The non-governmental claims, as compulsory counterclaims under **Rule 13(a),** were within the *ancillary jurisdiction* of the federal court (which had valid subject matter jurisdiction over the Navy claim based on the federal **Miller Act**). **United States v. Heyward Robinson,** *id.* (*Note:* the same jurisdictional conclusion would result under **28 U.S.C. § 1367(a).**)

Concurrence. Judge Friendly disagreed with the majority's holdings that the counterclaims were compulsory, arguing that even on the broadest and most liberal notion of "logical relation" it was difficult to perceive how the two separate contracts arose out of the same transaction and occurrence. However, Judge Friendly also argued that they should not be dismissed because permissive counterclaims should not be required to have an independent jurisdictional base (*see* discussion of permissive counterclaims, *infra*). **United States v. Heyward–Robinson Co.,** *id.*

Example 2. An employee left his job at a rubber-tubing manufacture company and founded his own company, using information gained at his former job. The new business obtained customers of the former employer. The employer then sued based on theories of (a) unfair competition and unfair business practices, (b) engaging in business as an "unlicensed patent infringer," and (c) making false representations about the employer's products that damaged or threatened the employer's business operations. The former employee filed an answer that included counterclaims based on violations of the federal **Sherman Antitrust Act, 15 U.S.C. §§ 1** and **2** for conspiracy to restrain and monopolize interstate commerce. The counterclaim also alleged bad faith prosecution by the former employer in bringing its original complaint. On defendant's motion, the court dismissed the case for lack of diversity jurisdiction, but retained jurisdiction over the former employee's counterclaims because the counterclaim had an independent basis in federal question jurisdiction. In response, the former employer (whose complaint had been dismissed) filed an answer to the defendant's counterclaim and its own new counterclaim, which substantially repeated the allegations contained in the original complaint. The court held that the employer's counterclaims were transactionally related, compulsory within **Rule 13(a),** and supported by ancillary jurisdiction. **Great Lakes Rubber Corp. v. Herbert Cooper Co.,** 286 F.2d 631 (3d Cir. 1961).

(e) Consequences of failing to plead a compulsory counterclaim:

- **No rule provision. Rule 13(a)** does not indicate the consequences of filing to assert a compulsory counterclaim.

- **Bar in subsequent federal suit.** A pleader who fails to assert a compulsory counterclaim in a federal action will be barred from asserting the claim in a subsequent federal suit. **Twin Disc, Inc. v. Lowell,** 69 F.R.D. 64 (E.D. Wis. 1975).

- **Competing rationales.** Courts disagree on the theory for barring subsequent litigation of an unpleaded compulsory counterclaim, applying three possible theories: *res judicata,* waiver, and estoppel.

- **Effect on subsequent state action.** Although federal courts may prevent litigation of a previously unasserted compulsory counterclaim, it is less likely that the federal courts have any power to enjoin a subsequent state action if a person seeks to assert a claim not previously asserted as a compulsory counterclaim in a federal action. **Fantecchi v. Gross,** 158 F.Supp. 684 (E.D. Pa. 1957).

(f) Exceptions to the compulsory counterclaim rule. A compulsory counterclaim need not be asserted if:

- it is the subject of another action pending at the time the plaintiff's action is filed. **Rule 13(a)(2)(A)** and **Union**

Paving Co. v. Downer Corp., 276 F.2d 468 (9th Cir. 1960) (no waiver effected by failure to assert such a compulsory counterclaim under these circumstances).

- the opposing party sued on its claim by attachment or other process that did not establish personal jurisdiction over the pleader on that claim, and the pleader does not assert a counterclaim. **Rule 13(a)(2)(B)**.

(g) **Compulsory counterclaims in state practice.** States have widely different rules and approaches to compulsory counterclaims. For example, Minnesota's compulsory counterclaim rule omits the word "occurrence" and that provision has been construed more narrowly than **Rule 13(a)**. *See* **House v. Hanson,** 245 Minn. 466, 72 N.W.2d 874 (1955) (omission of "occurrence" from statute to ensure that tort counterclaims would not be compulsory).

(h) **Permissive counterclaims.** A pleader may assert any counterclaim against the opposing party that is not compulsory. **Rule 13(b)**.

- **Most liberal formulation.** This is the most liberal counterclaim provision and it overcomes any common law or code pleading restrictions based on transactional-relatedness of counterclaims and the opposing party's claims.

- **Jurisdictional implications.** Prior to the enactment of the supplemental jurisdiction statute, permissive counterclaims needed to be supported by an independent jurisdictional base and did not come within the court's *ancillary* jurisdiction. *See* **United States v. Heyward–Robinson Co.,** 430 F.2d 1077 (2d Cir. 1970).

- **Supplemental jurisdiction statute.** There is some support for the theory that permissive counterclaims now come within the supplemental jurisdiction standard of **28 U.S.C. § 1367(a)** of "same case or controversy under **Art. III**."

(i) **Later-maturing counterclaims.** A federal pleader may use supplemental pleadings, with the court's permission, under **Rule 15(d)** (*see* discussion *supra*) to assert any counterclaim which matures or is acquired after service of process. **Rule 13(e).**

(j) **Cross-claims against co-parties: Rule 13(g).** Cross-claims are permitted under the Federal Rules and may be asserted by a party against a co-party:

- arising out of the transaction or occurrence that is the subject matter of the original action; or

- arising out of the transaction or occurrence that is the subject matter of a counterclaim; or

- relates to any property that is the subject matter of the original action.

(k) **Joinder of additional parties to answer for cross-claims and counterclaims.** Additional persons may be added or joined in a federal lawsuit (under **Rules 19** and **20**) to be made parties to asserted cross-claims or counterclaims. **Rule 13(h).**

■ ILLUSTRATION

Liberal construction of claim-joinder rules. Construing Rules 13(g) and (h), a federal appellate court upheld a complex construction litigation involving claims, counterclaims, cross-claims and third-party complaints involving the project prime contractor, subcontractors, sureties, and the architect based on various tort and contractor theories. Over a dissent, the court held that although several different contracts were involved in the complex web of claims, all related to the same project and problems arising out of the marble used in the construction of the city hall. **LASA Per L'Industria Del Marmo Societa Per Azioni v. Alexander,** 414 F.2d 143 (6th Cir. 1969). A dissenting judge urged that proofs in the various cross-claims would be entirely different and the same issues of fact would not determine both the original contract action and the subsequent cross-claims.

- Joinder under **Rule 14** (impleader) distinguished:

  - **Rule 14** is used to bring someone into a litigation who has not been named as a party. **Rule 14** requires derivative liability, whereas **Rule 13** does not.

- **Rule 13(h)** also is used to add parties not already in the lawsuit. However, in this instance a party in the lawsuit must be asserting a permissive or compulsory counterclaim, or a cross-claim, against someone who is already in the lawsuit.

c. Consolidation: Rule 42(a)

i. Consolidation Defined and Distinguished from Other Joinder Devices

Consolidation refers to combining separate actions in one federal court. Typically, the individual actions retain their separate nature and individual counsel, but the common issues may be tried together in a joint trial.

(a) **Creating a consolidated action: Standards.** A court may order a consolidated action if there are actions before the court that involve common questions of law or fact.

- **"Before the court."** The actions that will form a consolidated case must be pending before the court in order to create the consolidated litigation. Therefore, separate actions that are dispersed throughout the federal system sometimes are transferred to a federal court, using the transfer provisions (**28 U.S.C. §§ 1404, 1406, 1407**), prior to a consolidation order.

- **Circumstances permitting consolidation.** A court may order consolidation without the parties' consent; where all the parties are not exactly identical; for pre-trial purposes only; or for a joint trial on common issues.

- **Balancing convenience.** Before ordering a consolidation, the judge will balance the convenience and savings against any delay or expense entailed in a consolidated proceeding.

(b) **Consequences of consolidation: Joint hearing, separate judgments.** The court may order a joint hearing of any or all matters in issue in the separate cases. The court also may make any other orders "to avoid unnecessary costs or delay." However, in the typical consolidation each action retains its distinct character and requires a separate judgment.

d. Separate Trials: Rule 42(b)

i. Standards for Ordering Separate Trials

A court may order separate trials of any claims or issues in an action in the interests of convenience, to avoid prejudice, or to expedite and economize. Under **Rule 42(b),** a court also may sever claims for separate resolution from an action involving multiple parties and claims. A court will balance convenience, prejudice, and expense in deciding whether to order separate trials of issues, or the severance of claims.

ii. Separation and Severance Distinguished

Technically, there is a distinction between the separate trial of issues and the "severance" of claims, but many courts interchangeably refer to separation and severance.

(a) **Example of separate trial of issues: Bifurcated or trifurcated trial plans.** The most common use of **Rule 42(b)** is to create bifurcated or trifurcated actions. In a bifurcated trial plan, the court tries the liability issue separate from damages. Only if the plaintiff prevails on the liability issue will the court then try the damage issue. In a trifurcated trial plan, the court separately tries the issues of causation, liability, and damages. The plaintiff must win on causation and liability before the trial will proceed to the damage issue.

- **Criticism of bifurcated trial plans: "Sterile laboratory" theory.** Some courts and critics have objected to bifurcated and trifurcated trial plans, arguing that the separation of liability and damage issues detrimentally presents the plaintiff's case in a "sterile laboratory" atmosphere (*see* **In re Beverly Hills Fire Litigation,** 695 F.2d 207 (6th Cir. 1982)). Empirical studies confirm that bifurcated trial plans do affect a plaintiff's outcome in personal injury litigation, when plaintiffs are unable as effectively to exploit a jury's sympathy.

(b) **Severance of claims.** A court will sever claims where the joint trial of such claims would be inefficient, prejudicial, or contribute to jury confusion.

- Examples of appropriate circumstances for severance:

- A defendant properly joined in an action involving multiple defendants objects to the court's venue. If venue over the objecting defendant is improper, the court may sever the claim against the objecting defendant and transfer it to a more proper venue.

- A court may sever the claim of a properly joined plaintiff in an action involving multiple plaintiffs, to permit a defendant to implead that plaintiff under **Rule 14.**

ii. Purpose of Separate Trials and Severance

The separate trial of issues or severance of claims allows more efficient processing of a complicated case. Separate trial of issues may expedite resolution of an entire case. Severance of claims may facilitate other procedural techniques, or may reduce jury confusion.

iii. Seventh Amendment Trial by Jury Concerns

A judge may order severance or separate trial of issues or claims. When ordering a separate trial, the court must preserve any federal right to jury trial.

- **Legal and equitable claims.** In cases involving both legal and equitable claims, the court must try all common legal issues to a jury first, and then any equitable issues (*see infra* Chapter X, Trial, for a discussion of the Seventh Amendment right to jury).

B. JOINDER OF PARTIES

1. Identifying Parties Who May Sue and Be Sued

Whether a party may sue and be sued involves three different concerns: (1) *standing* to sue, (2) *capacity,* and (3) *real party in interest.* A litigant must be the real party in interest, have the requisite capacity to sue or be sued, and have standing. It is possible for a litigant to be the real party in interest, but to lack capacity or standing.

a. Standing to Sue

Standing refers to a doctrine federal courts have derived from Article III to ensure that only adverse litigants with actual injury sue in federal court. This doctrine primarily protects the judicial system's interest in hearing only real cases and controversies. Standing is related to other justiciability doctrines prohibiting collusive lawsuits, advisory opinions, and political questions. State courts employ various standing concepts similar to federal doctrine. Standing doctrine is studied in detail in constitutional law and federal courts.

i.   Standing Requirements

Federal courts have variously defined standing requirements. The core standing test derives from the Article III requirement that federal courts adjudicate only actual cases or controversies. In addition, federal courts have developed other policy-based prudential standing considerations.

(a) **Constitutional standards for determining standing.** Generally, standing requires that:

- the litigant must have suffered an injury;

- the injury must arise out of or relate to the litigation;

- the litigant must have a personal stake in the outcome of the litigation; and

- the law must offer some remedy for the injury.

(b) **Policy considerations: Prudential aspects of standing.** In litigation challenging federal regulatory and executive decisions, federal courts also consider:

- whether the plaintiff has been injured in fact by the challenged agency conduct; and

- whether the interest the plaintiff seeks to protect is within the zone of interests protected (or regulated) by a statutory or constitutional guarantee (the "zone of protection" standard).

- **Example.** The Sierra Club challenged a licensing agreement between Walt Disney Enterprises and the Department of the Interior to develop part of the Sequoia National Park into a ski resort. The Supreme Court held that the Sierra Club did not have standing because it was not personally injured and the alleged injury was not a legally protected right. **Sierra Club v. Morton,** 405 U.S. 727 (1972).

- **Capacity.** Capacity refers to the ability of a person or an entity to enforce rights (or to be sued by someone else). Capacity is specially defined for "artificial persons" such as corporations, partnerships, and unincorporated associations. Special capacity rules apply for children and incompetents. Generally, capacity is determined by state law, and federal courts follow state capacity rules. **Rules 17(b)** and **(c).**

  i. **Individuals**

     An individual's capacity is determined by the law of the individual's domicile. **Rule 17(b)(1).**

  ii. **Corporations**

     The capacity of a corporation is determined by the state law under which the corporation is organized. **Rule 17(b)(2).**

  iii. **Partnerships and Unincorporated Associations**

     If state law does confer capacity, a partnership or unincorporated association nonetheless may sue or be sued to enforce a federal or constitutional right. **Rule 17(b)(3)(A).**

  iv. **Receivers**

     The capacity of federally appointed receivers is governed by **28 U.S.C. §§ 754** and **959(a). Rule 17(b)(3)(B).**

  v. **Infants and Incompetents**

     In federal court, infants and incompetents may be represented by a guardian, committee, conservator, or other fiduciary. If an infant or incompetent does not have a representative, the court may appoint a *guardian ad litem* to represent the infant or incompetent. **Rule 17(c).**

b. The Real Party in Interest

In addition to having standing and capacity, the person who sues (or is sued) must be the "real party in interest." This rule applies to every party asserting a claim in an action. **Rule 17(a).**

i. **Determining the Real Party in Interest**

The real party in interest generally is the person who, under substantive law, possesses the right to be enforced.

(a) **Historical practice.** Historically, the real-party-in-interest concept was strictly applied to actions at law. In equity proceedings, anyone with an equitable or beneficial interest could sue.

(b) **Modern practice.** In modern practice, courts look to the nature of the substantive right to determine if the person asserting the right is the real party in interest. A person who might benefit from a litigation may not always be the real party in interest.

- **Example.** Under some state law, the real party in interest in wrongful death actions must be a person who suffers a loss of support as a result of the death. The real party is limited only to husbands, widows, children, or parents of the deceased. No other relatives qualify as the real party in interest, although they might financially benefit from such an action.

(c) **Assignments of interest.** A party who has an assigned claim or is otherwise an assignee may sue or be sued as the real party in interest. State law determines the validity of the assigned claim.

- **Assignments in federal court.** In federal practice, executors, administrators, guardians, bailees, trustees, and parties to contracts made for the benefit of others may sue in their own names. There is no need to also name the person for whose benefit the action is brought. **Rule 17(a).**

(d) **Special problems: Insurance recovery.** Many states require that insurance companies, as the real party in interest to recover for loss, must sue in their own names, rather than the insured's. **Ellis Canning Co. v. International Harvester Co.,** 174 Kan. 357, 255 P.2d 658 (1953). Other states, however, allow only the insured to enforce claims against a tortfeasor, even after payment by the insurance company. *See* **R.J. Reynolds Tobacco Co. v. Laney & Duke Storage Warehouse Co.,** 39 F.R.D. 607 (M.D. Fla. 1966).

- **Tactical considerations:** In insurance litigation the real-party-in-interest rule is important because of tactical considerations in presenting a case to the jury. Insurance companies prefer to have injured claimants as the plaintiff because juries typically are more sympathetic to the claimant rather than the insurance company.

(e) **Federal and state real-party conflicts: *Erie* implications.** Where there is a conflict between federal and state real-party rules and those rules are determined to be procedural, then **Rule 17(a)** prevails. If the rights to be enforced are substantive and the real party is determined to be a substantive designation, then state rules will prevail. *See* **R.J. Reynolds Tobacco Co.,** *supra.* (*see* Chapter III on *Erie* doctrine, *supra*).

(f) **Federal diversity of citizenship.** Federal diversity of citizenship is determined by the real party in interest to the lawsuit. (*see* federal diversity of citizenship, Chapter II, *supra*). Persons may not assign interests or appoint representatives in order to create diversity jurisdiction, which is prohibited by the so-called "collusive joinder statute," **28 U.S.C. § 1359** (*see* Chapter II, *supra*). Persons may defeat diversity jurisdiction by assignment or appointment, because there is no parallel federal statute prohibiting such devices to defeat federal diversity jurisdiction. However, some courts have used the real-party-in-interest concept to repudiate such manipulative attempts to defeat diversity jurisdiction. *See, e.g.,* **Rose v. Giamatti,** 721 F.Supp. 906 (S.D. Ohio 1989) (*see* Chapter II, *supra*).

(g) **Failure to name real party in interest.** A federal court will not dismiss a lawsuit for the failure to designate the real party in interest as the plaintiff. Rather, the parties have a reasonable time to substitute the real party. **Rule 17(a)(3).** A court will dismiss an action if the real party is not substituted, but this is not a dismissal on the merits. The real party in interest may later bring an action on the same claim, provided that any relevant statute of limitations has not expired.

- **Statute of limitations implications.** The amendment of a complaint to substitute the name of the real party in interest generally will be allowed to relate-back to the date of the original filing of the complaint, to avoid any statute of limitations bar. See **Rule 15(c)(1)(C).**

ii. When Determined; Waiver

The real-party-in-interest rule is a threshold defense and usually is raised in a preliminary motion or the answer. In some courts, the failure to raise this objection as soon as possible constitutes a waiver of this objection. If a defendant delays in raising this objection, some courts assess the prejudice to the opposing party as a consequence of the delay The trend is to allow courts broad discretion in handling challenges based on the real-party-in-interest rule.

iii. Abolition of the Real-Party-in-Interest Concept

Some commentators have urged that the real-party-in-interest rule is antiquated, superfluous, and unnecessary because state substantive law defines the real party, and the law would be the same without any express rule. New York State, the originator of the real-party rule, has abolished it.

2. Claims Involving Multiple Parties

a. Permissive Joinder of Parties: Rules 20 and 21

i. Historical Practice and Common Law Rules

At common law the ability to join parties in a legal action depended on whether the parties' rights were jointly or severally held. If rights were jointly held, then parties could be joined in one action. If rights were severally held, then parties could not be joined. Problems in determining the nature and scope of joint and several rights led to the development of modern liberal party joinder rules.

(a) **Example.** A husband and wife occupying the same berth in a railroad sleeping car could not bring a joint action if both were physically injured in the same train wreck. The rights of each spouse are several, not joint.

- Hotel employees rudely awakened a husband and wife staying at the hotel and required they move to other accommodations. The couple subsequently sued for injury to their reputations, credit, and business. Under South Carolina law the husband and wife could not join their claims in one action, as the torts were several. Even though there was a close relationship between the husband and wife, there was no joint cause of action. **Ryder v. Jefferson Hotel Co.,** 121 S.C. 72, 113 S.E. 474 (1922).

- *Ryder* **approach rejected:** A substantial number of state courts have rejected the very restrictive *Ryder* approach to party joinder

(b) Equitable actions. Equitable actions permitted more flexible party joinder in order to render complete justice among all people with an interest in an action.

ii. Modern Permissive Party Joinder Practice

Modern party joinder rules are considerably more flexible than common law practice, requiring some loose overlap of interest. Parties may be joined if their interests are joint, several, or in the alternative. In federal court, parties to be joined must satisfy both a transaction and occurrence standard and common question test.

(a) Elimination of joint and several criteria. Rule 20(a) (and many states) permit permissive joinder of parties who assert any right to relief either jointly or severally. In addition, federal courts permit a plaintiff to sue defendants in the alternative.

- **Example.** A widow of a deceased railroad worker brings an action under the Federal Employers Liability Act. She is not sure which of several possible employers her husband worked for when he died. She may join and sue the companies, in the alternative, in one action.

(b) Transaction or occurrence standard. Parties may be joined if they assert some right to relief arising out of the same transaction or occurrence that comprises the subject of the action. **Rule 20(a).** Courts generally ask whether there is a *logical relationship* between the case and the claim of the party to be joined, *see* **Moore v. New York Cotton Exchange,** 270 U.S. 593 (1926), and whether it is *efficient* to have the parties litigate together. Courts often flexibly interpret and apply this standard.

- **Examples.** A person injured in a car accident had those injuries further aggravated during an ambulance trip to the hospital eighteen days later. The court permitted joinder of the two negligence defendants since the ambulance trip was necessitated by the original accident. **Lucas v. City of Juneau,** 15 Alaska 413, 127 F.Supp. 730 (1955).

- A person whose car was struck twice in one day—once on the way to work and again on the way home—could permissibly join both defendants in one action. **Watts v. Smith,** 375 Mich. 120, 134 N.W.2d 194 (1965).

(c) **Common questions.** Parties may be joined if there is a question of law or fact common to them that will arise in the action. **Rule 20(a).**

- **Example.** Victims of an airplane crash may join together in one action, arising out of their common factual relationship to the single disaster.

- **Example.** One hundred and ninety-three plaintiffs permissibly joined in an action alleging fraudulent inducement to purchase corporate stock. The fraud question was common to all the plaintiffs, even though individual reliance questions were present in the litigation. **Akely v. Kinnicutt,** 238 N.Y. 466, 144 N.E. 682 (1924).

iii. Separate Trials: Rule 20(b)

Federal courts flexibly balance the interests of efficiency against possible prejudice in allowing party joinder. If party joinder will result in embarrassment, delay, or additional expense, a court may order separate trials to prevent or mitigate delay or prejudice.

iv. Misjoinder or Non-Joinder of Parties: Rule 21

A court may not dismiss an action for misjoinded parties. At any stage of a litigation and just terms a court may order that parties be added or dropped on a motion by any party or on the court's own initiative.

v. Relationship to Joinder of Claims

Courts evaluate the joinder of parties independently of joinder of claims. Even if claim joinder rules are satisfied, party joinder rules must also be satisfied before parties can be added with regard to new claims.

- **Example.** A plaintiff who desires to sue multiple defendants in a single action can do so only if there is at least one claim arising out of the same transaction and occurrence that applies to all the defendants *and* if there is a common question of law or fact common to all.

b. Compulsory Joinder of Parties: Rule 19

Permissive joinder of parties deals with who may be present in a lawsuit and the expansive outer limits of the size of a litigation. Compulsory joinder, on the other hand, specifies not who may be present in the litigation, but *who must be present* in the lawsuit. Hence, compulsory joinder of parties is governed by more restrictive rules than permissive joinder.

i. Historical Background: Necessary and Indispensable Parties

Compulsory joinder principles traditionally distinguished between two types of parties: those who are *necessary* to the litigation, and those who were *indispensable.*

(a) **Federal practice: Leading case authority—Shields v. Barrow, 58 U.S. (17 How.) 130, 15 L. Ed 158 (1854).** The Supreme Court determined that parties could be classified as necessary or indispensable based on whether their substantive rights were joint or severable. If a party was indispensable and joinder destroyed diversity jurisdiction, then the action had to be dismissed. To circumvent the harshness of this rule, some federal courts applied strained interpretations to determine whether substantive rights were joint or several.

- **Historical note on terminology:** Until 1966, the federal compulsory joinder rule (**Rule 19**) was entitled: "Necessary Joinder of Parties." In 1966 **Rule 19** was amended to read "Joinder of Persons Needed for a Just Adjudication." This change reflected the Advisory Committee on Civil Rule's decision to eliminate references to "necessary" and "indispensable" parties, which terms had caused interpretation difficulties in the lower federal courts. After the Rules styling project, **Rule 19** was re-denominated as "Required Joinder of Parties."

(b) **Necessary parties.** Necessary parties are those who are so interested in a controversy that they must be joined if it is feasible to do so, but if these parties cannot be joined, the lawsuit can still proceed and the court does not have to dismiss it. *See* **Bank of California Natl. Assn. v. Superior Court,** 16 Cal.2d 516, 106 P.2d 879 (1940).

(c) **Indispensable parties.** Indispensable parties are those parties who must be joined in the lawsuit and, if they cannot be joined for any reason, the lawsuit cannot proceed without them and the court must dismiss the action. *See Bank of California,* id.

■ ILLUSTRATION

Leading case authority: Bank of California v. Superior Court, 16 Cal.2d 516, 106 P.2d 879 (1940). A woman died leaving her estate to numerous beneficiaries living in various states and foreign countries. She designated the Bank of California as executor and a hospital as residuary legatee. A niece challenged the probate proceedings (through an action to enforce an alleged contract to leave the estate to her). Some beneficiaries were not served or did not appear in the action. The Bank of California, as executor, moved to bring in these defendants on the ground that they were necessary and indispensable parties. The California Supreme Court held that the absent beneficiaries were only necessary parties, but were not indispensable and that the niece could litigate her case against the defendants who did appear. The court further held that the court's decree would only bind the defendants who appeared, but would not bind the absent defendants.

(d) **Policy dilemmas raised by the indispensable party rule.** The older indispensable party rule, in particular, led to a conflict between the judicial system's desire to resolve disputes before the court, and the requirement that actions involving indispensable, non-joinable parties be dismissed. These classifications often encouraged courts to creatively deem absent parties as necessary rather than indispensable, or to refuse to order clearly indispensable parties joined if their presence would require dismissal of an action.

ii. **Modern Federal Practice: Amended Rule 19**

(a) Pragmatic approach to absent parties. Rule 19 was amended in 1966 to provide a pragmatic basis for resolving the policy dilemmas raised by the older necessary and indispensable party classifications. The amended rule requires courts to analyze factors balancing various considerations relating to absent parties.

(b) **How invoked.** A defendant typically challenges a person's absence in the lawsuit through a motion based on **Rule 12(b)(7):** a "failure to join a party under **Rule 19.**" This objection also may be raised in the answer, and in some states, through a demurrer.

- **Timing and non-waiver.** A defense of failure to join a party indispensable under **Rule 19** is serious enough that it is not waived by a delay in raising the challenge. A party may raise this objection in any pre-answer motions, pleadings, judgment on the pleadings, or at the trial on the merits. **Rule 12(h)(2).**

- **Court's own initiative.** Even if parties to the litigation do not raise an objection to a missing party, the court may order joinder of an absentee on its own initiative. This may occur at the trial or appellate level. *See, e.g.,* **Provident Tradesmens Bank & Trust Co. v. Patterson,** 390 U.S. 102 (1968).

(c) **Persons to be joined if feasible: Rule 19(a).** If an absent person is subject to service of process and that person will not deprive the court of its jurisdiction (for example, by destroying diversity jurisdiction), then the court must determine whether to join the absent party This portion of amended **Rule 19** parallels the older concept of "necessary" parties.

1. **Standard.** In making this evaluation, the court will consider the absent party's interest in the litigation, asking if:

    - in the person's absence complete relief cannot be accorded among those already parties;

    - the person claims an interest relating to the subject of the action and is so situated that the disposition of the action may:

      - as a practical matter impair or impede the person's ability to protect that interest, or

      - leave any of the persons already parties subject to a substantial risk of incurring double, multiple, or inconsistent obligations by reason of the claimed interest.

2. **Consequences: Alignment of parties under Rule 19(a).** If an absent party satisfies any of the **Rule 19(a)** criteria, then

the non-party must be joined if feasible. The action will not be dismissed for non-joinder.

- If the person should be joined as a plaintiff and refuses to do so, the court may order the absent party to be joined as a defendant. This person may later be realigned as a plaintiff.

- The court also may order an absent person to be joined as an involuntary plaintiff.

(d) Joinder not feasible: Rule 19(b). In certain circumstances an absent party may satisfy **Rule 19(a)** criteria, but it may not be feasible to join them. Among the possible reasons are:

- joinder will defeat diversity jurisdiction;

- the court cannot obtain personal jurisdiction over the absent party; or

- the absent party has a valid venue objection.

(e) Equitable Assessment. When joinder is not feasible, the court must determine whether it can proceed "in equity and good conscience," or whether it must dismiss the action altogether, evaluating the possible prejudice to those already parties as well as the absent person.

(f) Relationship to indispensable party concept. Rule 19(b) has its roots in the concept of the indispensable party. In making this determination, the court evaluates four factors:

1. **Potential prejudice:** whether a judgment rendered in the person's absence might be prejudicial to the absent person or those already parties.

   - Courts assess possible "prejudice" practically and pragmatically, including whether there is a likelihood of subsequent litigation.

2. **Shaping relief:** whether the court can reduce or eliminate any possible prejudice to the litigants by shaping relief or other measures to mitigate the absence of the non-joined person.

- For example, courts may make orders delaying payment of final judgments until all claims against a fund are resolved, or providing legal relief instead of a requested equitable remedy.

3. **Adequacy of judgment:** whether a judgment entered in the person's absence will be adequate.

   - Court assesses the impact of its decision on the parties before the court and whether it can frame a judgment to minimize the need for additional litigation.

4. **Costs to plaintiff:** whether the plaintiff will have an adequate remedy if the court dismisses the action for failure to join the absent party.

   - If the plaintiff's federal case is dismissed for nonjoinder of an absent party, the plaintiff may still bring a state court action. The federal court must determine whether this is a practical possibility, or whether practical impediments might bar or frustrate such a state action, such as the running of a statute of limitations.

   - **Consequences:** If a court determines under **Rule 19(b)** that it must dismiss the case for non-joinder, this dismissal is without prejudice to the plaintiff's ability to institute a subsequent action. Non-joinder defects are not jurisdictional.

■ EXAMPLES AND ANALYSIS

Leading case authority: Provident Tradesmens Bank & Trust v. Patterson, 390 U.S. 102 (1968). A car with two passengers collided with a truck. Dutcher, the car's owner, had given the keys to Cionci, the driver. Cionci was killed in the accident, along with a passenger (Lynch) and the truck driver. Another passenger was severely injured. The decedents' estates brought various state and federal (diversity) tort actions. Lynch's estate also brought a federal declaratory judgment action to clarify an insurance coverage issue, asking whether Cionci's use of the car had been with

Dutcher's permission. Lynch named the insurance company and Cionci as defendants, but did not join Dutcher, whose presence in the suit would have destroyed diversity. The district court directed verdicts in favor of the decedents' estates and a jury awarded favorable plaintiffs' verdicts. The Third Circuit, on *en banc* appeal, reversed the holding that Dutcher was a non-joined indispensable party. On appeal, the Supreme Court reversed, relying on the then recently amended **Rule 19.**

The Court emphasized that the amended rule was intended to depart from the rigid classifications of necessary and indispensable parties, and to implement a *flexible, pragmatic* approach to evaluating whether a lawsuit could proceed in the absence of a non-joined party.

- **Rule 19(a) analysis: Necessary parties.** The Supreme Court held that Dutcher was a necessary party under the **Rule 19(a)** factors, as he had an interest in preserving the insurance fund to cover the potential liability from all the tort claimants. When the case went to trial, there was a possibility that a judgment might impair or impede Dutcher's ability to protect this interest.

- **Not feasible to join.** The Court also acknowledged that it was not feasible to join Dutcher, because his presence in the suit would have destroyed diversity jurisdiction.

- **Rule 19(b) analysis: Equity and good conscience factors.** The Court analyzed the prejudice to Dutcher and those already parties, plus the other **Rule 19(b)** factors and determined that in equity and good conscience the case could have gone forward in Dutcher's absence. In arriving at this conclusion, the Court was additionally motivated by the fact that the case had reached the appellate level without the parties having been prejudiced by Dutcher's absence, and that a reversal at this stage would undo the results of a jury trial.

3. Impleader: Third–Party Practice under Rule 14

a. Terminology

Impleader is the procedural means by which a defendant may bring into the lawsuit another party who the defendant believes is or may be liable to the defendant as a consequence of the plaintiff's claim. When the defendant asserts such a claim and brings a new party into the lawsuit, this is called "third-party practice." Impleader practice in federal court is governed by **Rule 14;** state courts have identical or similar impleader rules.

i. The Third-Party Plaintiff

The original defendant who asserts a claim against a person who is not already a party to the lawsuit is called the "third-party plaintiff." The original defendant (the third-party plaintiff) is said to implead the third-party defendant. **Rule 14(a)(1).**

ii. The Third-Party Defendant

The person whom the original defendant brings into the lawsuit is called the third-party defendant. This defendant is *impleaded* into the lawsuit. **Rule 14(a)(2).**

b. Who May Implead Third Parties

i. Defendant Impleader

Typically, defendants implead or bring other persons into the lawsuit, based on various theories of liability and/or contribution (*see* discussion below). **Rule 14(a)(5).**

ii. Plaintiff Impleader

Plaintiffs also may implead persons who are not already in the lawsuit, in the same fashion as a defendant may under the rules. **Rule 14(b).** This is logical, because the defendant's counterclaim essentially transforms the defendant into a plaintiff, and the plaintiff into a defendant.

c. Principles Supporting Impleader of Third Parties

i. Derivative Liability

Rule 14(a) provides that a third-party plaintiff may implead any nonparty who is or may be liable to it for all or part of the claim against it. **Rule 14(a)(1).** Principles supporting impleader include:

- indemnity

- subrogation

- contribution

- breach of warranty

- other theories of derivative liability

ii. Recognized by Relevant Substantive Law

The relevant substantive law must recognize the concept of derivative liability. **Rule 14** cannot be used to create any form of derivative liability, because this would violate the **Rules Enabling Act, 28 U.S.C. § 2072,** which prohibits federal procedural rules from abridging, enlarging, or modifying substantive rights.

d. Timing Considerations, Complaint and Service

i. Impleader without Leave of Court

Anytime after the commencement of an action, a defendant may bring a nonparty into the lawsuit, without the court's permission, if the defendant serves a third-party complaint not later than 14 days after the defendant serves its original answer on the original plaintiff. **Rule 14(a)(1).**

ii. Impleader with Leave of Court

If more than 14 days have elapsed since the defendant served its answer in the original action, then the defendant must obtain "leave" or permission from the court to implead a third party. **Rule 14(a)(1).**

iii. Complaint and Service

A defendant who seeks to implead a third-party defendant accomplishes this by serving a third-party complaint and summons, which are subject to the federal pleading and service rules.

iv. Acceleration Effect

Rule 14(a) permits impleader of a nonparty who "is or may be liable to" the defendant. Consequently, federal impleader allows a defendant to bring in a third party against whom the original defendant's claim has not yet accrued unless and until the plaintiff wins the lawsuit. The effect of permitting impleader in these circumstances is to accelerate determination of the defendant's contingent claim against the impleaded party. *See, e.g.,* **Jeub v. B/G Foods, Inc.,** 2 F.R.D. 238 (D. Minn. 1942).

e. Rationale for Impleader; Discretionary Procedure

i. Efficiency Rationale

Similar to many of the joinder rules, one of the underlying purposes of impleader is to serve the interests of judicial efficiency and economy. This is accomplished by joining all transactionally related parties and claims in one litigation, and avoiding splitting parties and claims into several successive lawsuits.

ii. Discretionary Joinder

Impleader is not a matter of litigant rights. Even though the requisites for impleader may be satisfied, the court has the discretion to permit or deny the joinder. The court weighs the efficiency of permitting the impleader balanced against the possibility of prejudice to the existing parties by complicating the lawsuit with additional parties.

f. Status of Impleaded Parties; Consequences of Impleader

i. Persons Not Party to the Action

Only persons who are not parties to the original action may be impleaded or brought into the action. It is technically impossible to implead an existing defendant. A person who is impleaded into a litigation then has the status of a party to the action.

ii. Rule 12 Defenses

Once a person is impleaded into a litigation as a third-party defendant, that third-party defendant may assert any **Rule 12** defenses against the original defendant (that is, the third-party plaintiff who filed the third-party complaint against the third-party defendant). **Rule 14(a)(2)(A).** (*See* discussion of **Rule 12** defenses, *supra.*)

iii. Counterclaims

A third-party defendant also may assert any counterclaims it may have against the third-party plaintiff. If there are other defendants in the lawsuit, the third-party defendant may assert any cross-claims against those defendants. **Rule 14(a)(2)(B);** (*see also* **Rule 13,** *supra*).

iv. Relationship of Impleaded Third-Party Defendant to the Original Plaintiff

(a) Defenses. The third-party defendant may assert any defenses against the original plaintiff which the original defendant has to the plaintiff's original claim. **Rule 14(a)(2)(C).**

- If the original plaintiff asserts any claims against the impleaded defendant (*see* discussion below), the impleaded defendant has the right to assert any available **Rule 12** defenses, or **Rule 13** counterclaims or cross-claims. **Rule 14(a)(3).**

(b) Claims

- The third-party defendant may assert any claims it has against the plaintiff that *arise out of the same transaction or occurrence that is the subject matter* of the plaintiff's claim against the original defendant. **Rule 14(a)(2)(D).**

- The original plaintiff may assert any claim against the impleaded defendant that *arises out of the same transaction or occurrence that is the subject matter* of the original claim against the original defendant. **Rule 14(a)(3).**

g. Severance or Separate Trial

Any party may move to strike a third-party claim, or to move for its severance or separate trial. **Rule 14(a)(4).**

h. Jurisdiction over Impleaded Parties

Courts must have appropriate subject matter and personal jurisdiction over impleaded parties.

i. Subject Matter Jurisdiction

Jurisdiction over impleaded parties is governed by the supplemental jurisdiction statute, **28 U.S.C. § 1367,** which provides such supplemental jurisdiction over additional claims so long as they are part of the same case or controversy as the action over which the court has original jurisdiction.

(a) **Scope of supplemental jurisdiction.** The supplemental jurisdiction statute encompasses:

- impleader claims, and

- additional claims by the third-party plaintiff against the third-party defendant.

(b) **Jurisdictional limitations.** If the federal court's jurisdiction is based on diversity, then plaintiff's ability to assert claims against impleaded parties is limited by diversity requirements. *See* 28 **U.S.C. § 1367(b).** That provision of the supplemental jurisdiction statute is intended to codify the principle of **Owen Equipment & Erection Co. v. Kroger.**

ii. Personal Jurisdiction

Although the supplemental jurisdiction expansively provides a subject matter jurisdiction basis for impleaded parties, federal courts have not relaxed personal jurisdiction requirements for impleaded parties. These requirements still must be independently satisfied for the court to have good jurisdiction over impleaded parties.

4. Interpleader: Rule 22 and 28 U.S.C. § 1335

a. Definition; Equitable Basis

Interpleader is an equitable device that permits multiple claimants to money or property to resolve their competing claims in one lawsuit. The person who has the obligation to pay, or who holds the property, is known as the stakeholder.

- Both state and federal courts provide for interpleader actions, but state interpleader is severely limited by state jurisdictional rules. Most interpleader actions are therefore in federal court (*see* discussion *infra*).

b. Concept of the Stakeholder

In interpleader actions, the stakeholder is the person who has some obligation to others, but is uncertain which claims are legitimate and how to satisfy the competing claims. The stakeholder deposits the "stake" (money or property) with the court. The court serves notice on the competing claimants and resolves those claims.

c. Historical Standards

Historically, a person seeking an interpleader action had to show:

(1)   a stakeholder with an obligation to multiple claimants;

(2)   claimants with adverse interests in the same stake;

(3)   the stakeholder was not independently liable to any claimant on some other claims;

(4)   the stakeholder was disinterested in the stake; and

(5)   the stakeholder does not assert any claim or defense with regard to the stake.

- **Modern practice.** In modern practice the person seeking an interpleader action need only show a stake with competing claimants that gives rise to the possibility of multiple vexatious litigation.

d. Two-Stage Proceeding

Interpleader actions typically occur in two stages:

i.   First Stage

The court determines whether an interpleader action is proper (a controversy between a stakeholder and competing claimants). If granted, the stakeholder deposits the property with the court and withdraws from the litigation.

ii.   Second Stage

The court determines the competing claims to the stake or the fund.

e. Limitations on Interpleader Actions

i.   Equitable Limitations

Equitable principles apply and may limit or prevent an interpleader. For example, the doctrine of laches applies if the stakeholder has delayed in seeking a resolution of the claims.

ii.   Jurisdictional Limitations: State Court

Interpleader actions are *in personam* and state courts must have valid personal jurisdiction over the claimants to render a valid binding judgment. **New York Life Insur. Co. v. Dunlevy,** 241 U.S. 518 (1916). (*See* discussion of *in personam* actions and personal jurisdiction requirements, *supra.*)

f. Federal Statutory and Rule Interpleader

There are two possible bases for interpleader in federal court, pursuant either under **Rule 22** or through a series of statutory provisions (discussed below). The former is called "rule interpleader" and the latter is called "statutory interpleader." In general, **Rule 22** serves as a mere joinder device and is more limited than statutory interpleader.

i. Characteristics of Rule 22 Interpleader

(a) Subject matter jurisdiction. Interpleader actions require only minimal diversity among the claimants. The diversity of the stakeholder is irrelevant. The amount-in-controversy must exceed $75,000.

(b) **Personal jurisdiction.** Personal jurisdiction is governed by the state law in which the district court sits. Most state long-arm statutes do not permit assertion of personal jurisdiction over non-resident claimants to a stake. **Rule 22** interpleader, therefore, typically is limited to claimants who reside within the state.

(c) **Venue.** Venue is proper in any judicial district in which a claimant resides. **28 U.S.C. § 1397.**

(d) **Deposit requirements.** A stakeholder is not required to deposit the stake or fund with the court, although the stakeholder may do so. **Rule 67** ("Deposit into Court"). When the stakeholder desires to maintain control over the stake for as long as possible, **Rule 22** interpleader is the better means to do this.

(e) **Injunctive power.** The power of a federal court to enjoin the prosecution of other lawsuits against the stakeholder is limited under **Rule 22.** The **Anti–Injunction Act** prohibits federal courts from enjoining parallel state proceedings, unless the injunction "is in aid of its jurisdiction." *See* **28 U.S.C. § 2283.** Federal courts have narrowly construed this exception to apply to parallel *in rem* actions.

ii. Statutory Interpleader

Statutory interpleader is governed by a series of related statutes at **28 U.S.C. §§ 1335, 1397,** and **2361.** In general, statutory interpleader requirements are more liberal than **Rule 22** interpleader.

- Sections **1335, 1337,** and **2361** are successor statutes to the original **Federal Interpleader Act** enacted in 1917, in response to the *Dunlevy* decision, *supra,* to resolve the jurisdictional limitations on multi-state interpleader actions.

(a) **Subject matter jurisdiction.** Only minimal diversity is required among parties and only $500 need be in controversy. The stakeholder's citizenship is irrelevant. **28 U.S.C. § 1335; State Farm Fire & Cas. Co. v. Tashire,** 386 U.S. 523 (1967).

(b) **Personal jurisdiction.** Nationwide service of process is available and therefore personal jurisdiction is co-extensive with contacts with the United States. **28 U.S.C. § 2361.**

(c) **Venue.** Venue may be in any district where any claimant resides. **28 U.S.C. § 1397.**

(d) **Deposit requirements.** The stakeholder must deposit the property with the court or post a bond for its value. **28 U.S.C. § 1335.**

(e) **Injunctive power.** Federal courts may enjoin claimants from prosecuting lawsuits against the stakeholder in other courts. **28 U.S.C. § 2361.** This power does not violate the federal **Anti–Injunction Act** (*supra*), because the Act does not apply when Congress expressly authorizes injunctive power by statute.

5. Intervention: Rule 24

a. Definition and Statutory Basis

Intervention is the means by which a person (or groups) who are not named in a lawsuit may join the litigation if they have an interest they seek to protect. Intervention is largely a modern statutory invention (*see* **Brune v. McDonald,** 158 Or. 364, 75 P.2d 10 (1938)).

- **Other party joinder rules distinguished.** Other rules relating to party joinder provide means for persons *already in the lawsuit* to join additional parties. Intervention is different in that a person *completely outside the litigation* seeks to join the action. Thus, it is possible for the original plaintiff or defendant to oppose the intervention of someone outside the lawsuit because if they desired that person to be a part of the litigation, they would originally have named the intervenor as a party This is especially true for the plaintiff, who traditionally is regarded as in control of the litigation.

b. Purposes of Intervention

Intervention serves three basic purposes:

(1) Protection of non-parties to the litigation;

(2) Efficient judicial administration and trial convenience;

(3) Protection of the original parties to the litigation.

c. General Grounds for Intervention

State standards for intervention vary, but focus on the similar principle that an intervenor's right or interest must be of a direct or immediate character such that the intervenor will either gain or lose by the direct legal operation of the judgment. *See* **Brune v. McDonald,** *supra.*

- **Example.** An insurance company sought to intervene in a tort action, believing that the plaintiff and defendant fraudulently colluded to deceive the insurance company concerning the driver's intoxicated state at the time of the accident. The insurance company sought an injunction against prosecution of the plaintiff's case until the court could determine whether the insurance company was liable to the defendant under the policy terms. The court refused to permit the insurance company to intervene because the company's complaint raised an entirely new and different issue than that in the tort case. **Brune v. McDonald,** *supra.*

- **Contrary authority:** *Compare* **Knapp v. Hankins,** 106 F.Supp. 43 (E.D. Ill. 1952) where a federal court permitted an insurance company to intervene to determine the validity of policy coverage on the ground that it would be unfair to the insurance company to defend a litigant if the policy were void.

d. Competing Policy Concerns

Intervention embodies conflicting policy concerns. On the one hand, intervention supports the judicial system's interest in efficient adjudication through the joinder of all interested parties in one litigation. On the other hand, intervention may undermine judicial efficiency by increasing complexity and possible jury confusion.

e. Federal Intervention

There are two types of intervention in federal court: intervention of right and permissive intervention.

i. Timing Considerations

A person seeking to intervene, either permissively or by right, may do so at any time on timely motion. **Rule 24(a)** and **(b).** The earlier a person seeks to intervene, the less the possible prejudicial effects of the intervention. As a litigation progresses toward trial, many courts are less sympathetic towards permitting new parties to join the lawsuit. However, courts have permitted intervention even as late as on appeal. *See, e.g.,* **Smuck v. Hobson,** 408 F.2d 175 (D.C. Cir. 1969), although such intervention will be permitted only in very few unique situations where the intervention will not prejudice the rights of existing parties or interfere with the "orderly processes of the court." *See* **McDonald v. E.J. Lavino Co.,** 430 F.2d 1065 (5th Cir. 1970).

ii. Procedure for Initiating Intervention

A person who seeks to intervene files a motion which must be served on the parties already in the lawsuit. **Rules 24(c)** and **Rule 5.** The motion to intervene must state the grounds that are the basis for the intervention and be accompanied by a pleading that sets out the claim or defense for which intervention is sought.

iii. Standards for Intervention of Right: Rule 24(a)

There are two grounds that provide a person a right to intervene:

(a) **Statutory basis.** A person has a right to intervene when a federal statute confers an unconditional right to intervene. **Rule 24(a)(1).**

- **Examples. Section 902** of the **Civil Rights Act of 1964, 42 U.S.C. § 2000h–2** confers an unconditional right on the United States to intervene in actions alleging denial of Fourteenth Amendment equal protection.

- **Example. Section 2403** of the **Judicial Code** confers an unconditional right on the United States to intervene in actions challenging the constitutionality of a congressional act. **Section 2403(b)** confers an unconditional right to intervene on states in actions challenging the constitutionality of state statutes.

(b) Interest impairment. A person also has a right to intervene when the applicant:

- claims an interest relating to the property or transaction that is the subject of the action, and

- the disposition of the action may as a practical matter impair or impede the applicant's ability to protect that interest, unless:

  - the applicant's interest is adequately represented by the existing parties.

  - **What constitutes an "interest."** "Interest" is broadly defined for intervention purposes. An interest sufficient to support intervention need not be an economic interest. *See, e.g.,* **Smuck v. Hobson,** *supra* (parental interest in school administration sufficient to support a right of intervention). Public interest and environmental groups frequently seek intervention to protect non-economic interests, such as clean air.

  - **Interest impairment.** A prospective intervenor need not show that the applicant will be prejudiced by being bound by a judgment if not joined. Modern intervention principles do not require that the applicant meet *res judicata* standards. Instead, courts look to whether the applicant's interest will be impaired "as a practical matter." The adverse impact of *stare decisis* has been held sufficient to support a right to intervene. *See, e.g.,* **Atlantis Development Corp. v. United States,** 379 F.2d 818 (5th Cir. 1967).

  - **Inadequate representation.** The prospective intervenor need not show an actual conflict between the existing litigants and itself (although this is the strongest ground for supporting inadequate representation). The intervenor may show that no party already in the action will vigorously pursue the intervenor's interest.

iv. Standards for Permissive Intervention: Rule 24(b)

An applicant permissively may intervene when:

(1) A federal statute confers a conditional right to intervene, or,

(2) The applicant's claim or defense and the main action share a common question of law or fact.

- **Discretionary standard.** In contrast to intervention of right, permissive intervention is discretionary with the court.

- **Balancing test.** The court will balance the advantages of permitting the intervention against the potential delay or prejudice to the existing parties.

v. Example

A group of students at the University of Michigan appealed denial of their motion to intervene in a lawsuit brought to challenge race-conscious admissions policy at the university. The Sixth Circuit reversed and remanded for entry of an order permitting intervention of right under **Rule 24(a)**. The court held that the proposed intervenors satisfied the tests showing that they had a substantial legal right in gaining admission to the university; that right would be impaired if the university was precluded from considering race in admissions; and that there was a potential that the university would not adequately represent their interests. **Grutter v. Bollinger**, 188 F.3d 394 (6th Cir. 1999). The court further held that its decision mooted the question of permissive intervention under **Rule 24(b)**.

f. Consequences of Intervention: Status of the Intervenor

Applicants granted intervention become parties to the lawsuit and, in general, have all the rights of other parties to the suit, including service of pleadings, motions, and papers in the litigation. However, courts may limit the nature or scope of the intervenor's involvement in the litigation, in the interests of sound judicial case management. If the court denies intervention, it may suggest that the applicant file a "friend of the court" brief *(amicus curiae)* in lieu of intervention, to apprise the court of the person's interests.

g. Jurisdictional Considerations: Supplemental Jurisdiction

i. Intervention of Right

If an applicant satisfies the prerequisites for intervention of right, the court must grant this, provided that the presence of the intervenor does not destroy diversity jurisdiction.

- **1990 legislative change:** Prior to 1990, intervenors of right automatically came within the court's ancillary jurisdiction. The 1990 supplemental jurisdiction statute, **28 U.S.C. § 1367(b)** specifically excludes intervenors from supplemental jurisdiction if their presence would destroy diversity jurisdiction under circumstances similar to **Owen v. Kroger**. *See* discussion of supplemental jurisdiction, *supra.*

ii. Permissive Intervention

Permissive intervenors must satisfy subject matter jurisdictional requirements. This is true for both pre-1990 intervention and post-1990 intervention.

h. Relationship to Indispensable Party Requirements and Rule 19(a)

The "impairment" requirement for intervention of right under **Rule 24(a)(2)** repeats the same language of **Rule 19(a)(1)(B)(i).** There is some suggestion that a person who satisfies the requirements to intervene as of right should have been joined as an indispensable party under **Rule 19.** *See* **Atlantis Development Corp. v. United States,** 379 F.2d 818 (5th Cir. 1967).

i. Relationship to *Amicus Curiae* Participation

Some courts that deny intervention will instead recommend that persons file a friend of the court brief to apprise the court of the applicant's special interests in the litigation. *Amicus curiae* status is perceived as a less-desirable alternative to intervention, because it is questionable whether *amicus curiae* briefs have the same influence on a litigation as intervention in the proceedings.

j. Appellate Review of Intervention Decisions

i. Grant of Intervention

In general, an order granting intervention is not final and not appealable. Parties opposing intervention must await until the conclusion of trial to bring a direct appeal.

ii. Denial of Intervention: Split of Authority

Lower federal courts are split concerning whether the denial of a motion to intervene is immediately appealable. The Supreme Court has held that an order denying intervention of right, but permitting permissive intervention, is non-appealable under the final judgment rule. **Stringfellow v. Concerned Neighbors in Action,** 480 U.S. 370 (1987). Many courts have held that denial of intervention of right is appealable under the so-called collateral order doctrine, but that denial of permissive intervention is only appealable for abuse of discretion. At least one federal court has held that all orders denying intervention are final for purposes of immediate review. **Ionian Shipping Co. v. British Law Ins. Co.,** 426 F.2d 186 (2d Cir. 1970). (*See* discussion of interlocutory appeal, *supra.*)

C. CLASS ACTIONS: RULE 23

1. History and Philosophy of Class Actions

a. Equitable Origins

The concept of group or aggregative litigation originated in medieval English equity procedure in the "bill of peace." Chancery courts permitted a representative action when (1) many people were involved who were too numerous to permit joinder, (2) the group members possessed a joint interest, and (3) the named parties would adequately represent the group. A judgment bound all members of the represented group. Professor Stephen Yeazell documents the history of aggregate litigation in *From Medieval Group Litigation to the Modern Class Action* (1987).

b. State Codes

In the nineteenth and early twentieth centuries, many states adopting code procedure included precursors of the modern class action rule.

c. Federal Equity Rules

Prior to the enactment of the Federal Rules of Civil Procedure in 1938, the **Federal Equity Rules** provided for class action procedure.

d. Rule 23

The Federal Rules enacted in 1938 contained the original modern class action rule. With the merger of law and equity, class actions could be pursued in actions at law and equity.

i. Original Class Action Rule 23; Categories and Consequences

(a) Types of class actions. The 1938 class action rule provided for three highly specific categories of class actions, rigidly defined by the nature of the right asserted.

- **"True" class actions.** A "true" class action existed when class members possessed a joint and common interest in the subject matter of the action.

- **"Hybrid" class actions.** A "hybrid" class action existed when several claims to the same property were at issue.

- **"Spurious" class actions.** A "spurious" class action existed when persons having independent interests joined together in one lawsuit.

(b) **Consequences.** Each type of class action was subject to different rules relating to jurisdiction, statutes of limitations, and *res judicata*. The original categories proved difficult to apply, and some courts would manipulate the categories to avoid harsh results relating to the classifications.

ii. 1966 Amendment of Rule 23

The Advisory Committee on Civil Rules extensively revised **Rule 23** in 1966 to eliminate the existing rigid class action categories. The major purpose of the 1966 revision of the class action rule was to create functional tests for types of class actions. The 1996 amendments to **Rule 23** created the three **Rule 23(b)** categories (*see* discussion below). In addition, the 1966 amendments invented the so-called **(b)(3)** "opt-out" damage class, a device that had not existed under the original class action rule.

(a) **Underlying purposes and rationales for modern class action procedure.** The central rationale for class action procedure is that class members are similarly situated in some way and the interests of judicial economy are served by adjudicating all party claims in one action. Class litigation eliminates multiple, repetitive litigation and enhances the ability of multiple plaintiffs to recover from defendants whose funds might be exhausted by repetitive individual litigation.

(b) **Joinder device versus representational litigation.** There are at least two possible views of the class action procedure. One is that the class action is merely another joinder device, permitting the largest aggregation of claimants. Another view is that class actions are a representational device permitting the prosecution of claims on behalf of people who would not or could not have otherwise sued independently on their own.

iii. Effect of 1966 Amendments

Since the 1966 amendments, use of the class action rule has varied considerably, reflecting a "pendulum effect" of rule revision:

(a) **Mid–1960s to early 1970s.** Plaintiffs' lawyers aggressively exploited the new functional class action categories to pursue group litigation and class relief. The enactment of new federal causes of action relating to civil rights, voting rights, employment law, equal protection, and other areas of domestic social policy provided a substantive basis for group claims. The late 1960s were the heyday of public institutional reform litigation addressing problems in prison systems, schools, mental health facilities, and the workplace. The chief form of class action during this period was the **(b)(2)** injunctive class.

(b) **Doctrinal limitations on class actions.** Between 1969 and 1974, partially in response to the explosion of class action litigation, the Supreme Court issued major decisions restricting class action procedure. Collectively, these decisions caused a retreat from aggressive use of the class action device:

- **Amount-in-controversy requirements.** The Court held that class action members could not aggregate their claims to meet the amount-in-controversy requirement in diversity class actions, and that each claim independently had to satisfy the amount requirement. These rulings did not affect class actions brought under federal laws or constitutional claims, but it did have an impact on so-called "small claims" class action. **Snyder v. Harris,** 394 U.S. 332 (1969); **Zahn v. International Paper Co.,** 414 U.S. 291 (1973). The Supreme Court overruled **Zahn** in **Exxon Mobil Corp. v. Allapattah**.

- **Cost of notice.** The Court held that named class members must pay the cost of individual notice to all members of a

(b)(3) opt-out class. **Eisen v. Carlisle & Jacquelin,** 417 U.S. 156 (1974).

(c) **Mid–1970s through mid–1980s.** This era was marked by the first attempts to use the class action rule to aggregate mass tort claims. Through the mid–1980s, federal courts consistently resisted attempts to use the class action rule in mass tort cases (*see* discussion *infra),* on the grounds that the Advisory Committee Note to the 1966 amendments prohibited use of the class action device for mass accident cases. A few notable cases in this period, however, such as the *Agent Orange* and *Dalkon Shield* litigations, were resolved through class action settlements.

(d) **Mid–1980s through mid–1990s.** Some federal courts reversed the federal trend and permitted mass torts to be certified as class actions. *See, e.g.,* **Jenkins v. Raymark Industries,** 782 F.2d 468 (5th Cir. 1986); **In re School Asbestos Litig.,** 789 F.2d 996 (3d Cir. 1986). Various experiments under class action procedure were used in this period to litigate or settle mass tort cases. *See, e.g.,* **Cimino v. Raymark Industries,** 739 F. Supp. 649 (E.D. Tex. 1990).

(e) **Mid–1990s to present.** Federal courts again reversed course and manifested renewed resistance to mass tort litigation and heightened scrutiny of settlement classes. *See, e.g.,* **Castano v. The American Tobacco Co.,** 84 F.3d 734 (5th Cir. 1996) (litigation class decertified); **In re American Medical Systems, Inc.,** 75 F.3d 1069 (6th Cir. 1996) (litigation class decertified); **In re Rhone–Poulenc Rorer Inc.,** 51 F.3d 1293 (7th Cir. 1995) (litigation class decertified); **Georgine v. AmChem Prods., Inc.,** 83 F.3d 610 (3d Cir. 1996) (settlement class reversed); **In re General Motors Corp. Pick–Up Truck Fuel Tank Prods. Liab. Litig.,** 55 F.3d 768 (3d Cir. 1995) (settlement class reversed).

- **Settlement classes.** In the mid–1990s the creation and use of "settlement classes" became the focus of controversy in federal class action litigation, and the object of proposed reform of the class action rule (*see* discussion of settlement classes, below).

iv. The 1998 and 2003 Revisions to Rule 23

In 1993, the Advisory Committee on Civil Rules began consideration of revision of **Rule 23. Rule 23** was amended in 1998 as well as 2003. In 1998, a new subsection **(f)** was added to **Rule 23,** to provide an avenue for appellate review of court orders either granting or denying class certification. In December 2003, a more expansive set of **Rule 23** revisions became effective. These revisions changed existing provisions of **Rule 23(c)** and **(e),** and added new subsections **(g)** and **(h),** dealing with the appointment of class counsel and attorney fees.

v. Major Supreme Court Decisions

In the late 1990s, the Supreme Court decided two major appeals concerning class action settlements, in **Amchem Prods, Inc. v. Windsor,** 521 U.S. 591 (1997) and **Ortiz v. Fibreboard Corp.,** 527 U.S. 815 (1999).

vi. Class Action Fairness Act of 2005

Congress enacted the **Class Action Fairness Act (CAFA)** to create new federal diversity subject matter jurisdiction over diversity class actions. **28 U.S.C. § 1332(d).** The statute also created new removal jurisdiction for state class actions. **28 U.S.C. § 1453.** The diversity statute delineates numerous exceptions for local state controversies. In general, to establish a federal class action, proponents must establish (1) minimal diversity between class member and defendants; (2) at least 100 members in the class; and (3) in excess of $5 million in controversy.

- As a consequence of **CAFA**, numerous state class actions are removed to federal court.

2. Modern Class Action Procedure: Due Process Considerations

a. Class Actions as Representational Litigation

The distinguishing feature of the class action is that it is a *representational litigation.* Most class members are not actually present and do not individually litigate their claims. Instead, a designated plaintiff (the "class representative") and class counsel virtually represent the interests of class members. Many class actions include more than one named class plaintiff (*see* discussion *infra*). Class members other than the class representatives are called "absent" or "unnamed" class members.

b. Consequences of Representational Litigation

Class members (especially absent class members) do not have a traditional relationship with the class lawyer or the prosecution of their individual claims. Class action litigation has the potential for conflicts of interest between the class representatives, class members, and class counsel.

- To protect the interests of class members, class action procedure requires enhanced due process protections for class litigants that are not required or available in traditional simple litigation. Due process requires that class procedures adopted "fairly insure[] the interests of absent parties who are to be bound by [the judgment]." **Hansberry v. Lee,** 311 U.S. 32 (1940).

- Three entities theoretically are entrusted with protecting the class interests: (1) the class representative, (2) class counsel, and (3) the court. However, financial disincentives or a lack of information may prevent protection of class interests.

c. Binding Effects of Judgments

In general, a person cannot be bound to an *in personam* judgment unless that person has been designated as a party, is properly served, and is subject to the court's jurisdiction.

- Class action suits are an exception to this rule. The judgment in a class action suit binds the named parties and all the class members identified in the class description. **Hansberry v. Lee,** *supra.*

- **Full faith and credit.** A class action judgment that comports with due process is binding on all class members, and the **Full Faith and Credit Clause** requires that sister states recognize the valid judgment against all class claimants. Class members may not collaterally attack a valid class judgment in another state or federal court. This rule applies to class settlements, as well. *See* **Matsushita Electrical Indus. Co. v. Epstein,** 516 U.S. 367 (1996) (upholding a Delaware class settlement against a collateral attack in federal court); *see also* **Hansberry v. Lee,** *supra.*

i. Adequacy of Representation

Procedural due process requires that the class representative must fairly and adequately represent the interests of absent class members. Due process is lacking if the class representative and class members have actual or potentially conflicting interests. **Hansberry v. Lee,** 311 U.S. 32 (1940); *see also* **Amchem Prods. Inc. v. Windsor,**

521 U.S. 591 (1997) and **Ortiz v. Fibreboard Corp.,** 527 U.S. 815 (1999).

- **Leading case authority: Hansberry v. Lee, 311 U.S. 32 (1940).** Litigants brought suit in Illinois state court to enforce a racially restrictive property covenant, relying on the binding effect of an earlier state court action allegedly establishing the validity of the covenant. The Illinois Supreme Court affirmed, holding that the earlier action was a class action binding on successor land owners. The United States Supreme Court reversed, holding that the plaintiffs in the first action did not and could not represent the interests of landowners wishing to resist the restrictive covenant. The dual and conflicting interests of the parties—in enforcing or resisting the covenant—prevented the landowners from pursuing a representational class bound by a judgment.

- **Examples.** Class representatives may not adequately represent a class of claimants that includes claimants who are currently injured as a consequence of exposure to asbestos products ("present claimants"), as well as claimants who have only been exposed, but have not yet manifested any physical injury ("future claimants"). These claimants have conflicting interests, and one representative cannot adequately represent these different types of claims. This problem might be solved through the use of subclasses with independent representatives, or other "structural assurances" of due process. **Amchem Prods. Inc. v. Windsor,** 521 U.S. 591 (1997). Similarly, class representatives cannot simultaneously represent a class of asbestos claimants that includes person insured under policy terms that existed before 1959, and claimants with policy coverage under terms after 1959. This situation presents a similar type of conflict present in the **Amchem** asbestos settlement class. **Ortiz v. Fibreboard Corp.,** 527 U.S. 815 (1999).

  - **When determined.** The adequacy of class representation may be assessed at three separate junctures:

    - at the time of class certification (*see* discussion of **Rule 23(a)** requirements, *infra);*

    - at a settlement fairness hearing (*see* discussion *infra* of **Rule 23(e)** settlement and fairness hearing); or

- at a subsequent collateral attack on the *res judicata* effect of a prior class action judgment (as in *Hansberry*); *see also* **In re Agent Orange Prods. Liab. Litig., Dow Chemical Co. v. Stephenson,** 539 U.S. 111 (2003); **Stephenson v. Dow Chemical Co.,** 273 F.3d 249 (2d Cir. 2001).

ii. Notice

Due process requires that members of a **Rule 23(b)(3)** opt-out class receive notice of the class action. **Eisen v. Carlisle & Jacquelin,** 417 U.S. 156 (1974). Effective December 1, 2003, an amendment to **Rule 23(c)(2)(A)** permits judges to order notice in the mandatory **Rule 23(b)(1)** and **(b)(2)** classes, but does not require such notice.

iii. Personal Jurisdictional over Absent Class Members

A state court may render a binding judgment over absent class members who do not opt-out of a **(b)(3)** class action, even though they lack minimum contacts with the forum state. **Phillips Petroleum Co. v. Shutts,** 472 U.S. 797 (1985).

(a) **Consent basis for due process.** The ability of absent **(b)(3)** class members to opt-out of the class satisfies due process requirements. The failure to opt-out of a **(b)(3)** class signifies consent to the court's jurisdiction. **Rule 23** does not affirmatively require class members to "opt-in" to the action. **Phillips Petroleum Co. v. Shutts,** *id.*

(b) **Unresolved *Shutts* due process issue: Applicability to mandatory class actions.** The *Shutts* holding applies to class actions concerning claims "wholly or predominantly for money judgments." The Supreme Court has not yet resolved whether the *Shutts* holding applies to mandatory **(b)(1)** or equitable **(b)(2)** class actions. The Supreme Court had the opportunity to address this issue, but declined to do so twice, in two cases where the Court improvidently granted certiorari. This remains an undecided issue, with conflicting lower court decisions.

- **Split of authority on *Shutts* issue:** Lower federal courts are split on whether mandatory class judgments violate the due process rights of absent members lacking contacts with the forum. *See, e.g.,* **In re Real Estate Title & Settlement**

Servs. Antitrust Litig., 815 F.2d 695 (3d Cir. 1987); **Brown v. Ticor Title Ins. Co.,** 982 F.2d 386 (9th Cir. 1992); cf. **Grimes v. Vitalink Communications Corp.,** 17 F.3d 1553 (3d Cir. 1994).

(c) **Applicability of *Shutts* to federal class actions.** There is disagreement whether the *Shutts* holding, based on a Kansas *state* class action statute, applies to federal class actions under **Rule 23.**

d. Class Settlements

A class action may not be settled, compromised, or dismissed unless a federal judge reviews and approves the settlement. **Rule 23(e).** Effective December 1, 2003, **Rule 23(e)** has been extensively revised and requires that a judge now hold a fairness hearing prior to approving a proposed class action settlement to determine whether the proposed class settlement is *fair, adequate, and reasonable.* In non-class litigation, by contrast, the court does not review a settlement agreed to by the parties and their lawyers. In class action litigation, the requirement of court approval is a further due process protection to ensure that absent class members' interests are not compromised by fellow class members or class counsel.

- Proposed settlement classes are subject to the same certification requirements as litigation classes, except for **Rule 23(b)(3)** classes, which do not need to satisfy the "manageability" requirement for certification. **Amchem Prods., Inc. v. Windsor,** 521 U.S. 591 (1997) and **Ortiz v. Fibreboard Corp.,** 527 U.S. 815 (1999).

- **Rule 23(e)** was extensively amended effective December 1, 2003 to add provisions governing how and when settlements may be effectuated and approved by a court. **Rule 23(e)** now specifies that notice must be given of the proposed settlement, and makes provision for objectors to the settlement.

3. Operation of the Class Action Device

a. Initiation of Class Action

A court may initiate a class action on its own (*sua sponte*) although this is very rare. A single plaintiff may initiate a class action. Plaintiffs' lawyers typically initiate class actions. In such instances, the plaintiff's lawyer initiates the class action by filing a class complaint on behalf of a named plaintiff and other similarly situated claimants.

- **Professional responsibility: Solicitation concerns.** The ability of plaintiffs' lawyers to create class action litigation is circumscribed by professional responsibility rules relating to client solicitation. *See, e.g.,* **Ohralik v. Ohio State Bar Association,** 436 U.S. 447 (1978) (in-person solicitation prohibited) (*see* discussion of ethical problems, *infra*).

i. **Class Complaint**

The class complaint is designated as a class action. The complaint names the class representatives as plaintiffs. Frequently counsel will name more than one class representative. Only the class representatives are parties to the litigation. For most purposes, absent class members are not parties to the class action.

(a) **Multiple class representatives.** Multiple class representatives often are designated to ensure the representativeness of the named plaintiffs across the class membership. Also, multiple class representatives ensure against the potential problem of a "headless" class action. Thus, if one or more class representatives either lack capacity, are dropped from the case, or settle with defendants, the remaining class plaintiffs continue representing the class.

(b) **Class definition.** The class complaint also will contain a definition of the class membership. The class definition is particularly important for certification requirements (*see* discussion *infra*). The class definition describes the claimants in the class who will be bound by the judgment. A class definition must be stated with reference to objective criteria, and may not be vague or overbroad.

ii. **Consent of Class Members: Notification**

A plaintiff or class counsel may file a class complaint without first seeking the consent or permission of unnamed class members. Some potential class members may not desire the class action and may oppose class certification at a certification hearing.

(a) **Federal opt-classes.** Absent class members must be given notice of the certification of a **(b)(3)** opt-out class and the opportunity to exclude themselves from the class.

(b) **Notice in mandatory classes.** Effective December 1, 2003, federal judges may permit notice be given in the mandatory

Rule 23(b)(1) and (b)(2) classes, although such notice is not required. **Rule 23(c)(2)(A).** Prior to 2003, no notice was provided for mandatory classes.

(c) **State practice: Opt-in requirements.** Some states require that class members receive notice of the class and affirmatively opt-in to the class action. Individuals who do not are not considered part of the class.

b. Certification Requirements

Unlike simple litigation, a court must certify an action that is to be resolved as a class action. **Rule 23(c)(1).** The certification requirement is another due process protection for absent class members, providing court scrutiny of the proposed class action.

i. Timing of Class Certification

A court must determine whether a proposed action may be maintained as a class action "at any early practicable time" after parties sue or are sued in a class complaint. Rule **23(c)(1)(A).** The rule does not specify when this certification must occur.

(a) **Typical certification.** Some federal courts certify class actions soon after a class complaint is filed. However, courts may certify a class after the litigation and discovery is underway. Some courts may order limited discovery to ascertain facts pertinent to establishing the requirements for class certification.

(b) **Settlement certification.** Courts also may certify a class a part of a negotiated settlement. **Amchem Prods. Inc. v. Windsor,** 521 U.S. 591 (1997); **Ortiz v. Fibreboard Corp.,** 527 U.S. 815 (1999). Settlement classes must satisfy all the same requirements for class certification as litigation classes, except that (b)(3) settlement classes need not satisfy the "manageability" requirement. *Id.*

(c) **Altering or amending class certification.** The court may alter or amend its original certification order before final judgment. **Rule 23(c)(1)(C).** The 2003 amendments to **Rule 23** eliminated the possibility for courts to conditionally or provisionally certify class actions.

ii. Certification Hearing

To determine whether a class action may be maintained, a court may review class certification requirements based on the complaint and other papers the lawyers submit on the certification motion. Opponents to the class action may retain counsel and oppose the class certification. In other instances, judges hold a certification hearing at which the parties supporting and opposing the class certification present their arguments.

(a) **Burdens.** The class proponents carry the burdens of persuasion and proof that the proposed action satisfies class requirements. The defendants carry no burden to disprove that class action requirements are not satisfied.

(b) **Standard; preview of the merits.** The decision to certify a class action is within the judge's discretion. In determining whether to certify an action, the judge is not permitted to assess the plaintiff's likelihood of success on the merits of their claims. *See* **Eisen v. Carlisle & Jacquelin,** *supra.* However, a judge is required to conduct a "rigorous analysis" of class certification requirements, which requires the judge to probe beyond the pleadings and examine the underlying relevant facts, claims, defenses, and applicable substantive law. *See, e.g.,* **Castano v. The American Tobacco Co.,** 84 F.3d 734 (5th Cir. 1996).

iii. Threshold Requirements

A proposed class action must satisfy two general threshold requirements not codified in the class action rule. There must be a class, and the class representative must be a member of the class.

(a) **Necessity of a class: Importance of class description.** The court must determine that a class exists that fits the plaintiff's proposed class description. Vague or overbroad class descriptions (*e.g.,* "all poor people") do not satisfy this requirement. The 2003 amendments to **Rule 23** now require the court to define the class and to identify, in its certification order, the claims, issues, or defenses involved in the class litigation. **Rule 23(c)(1)(B).** The court also must appoint counsel under **Rule 23(g)**.

(b) **Class representative: Mootness concerns.** The class representative must be a member of the class. If the representative's claim is dismissed or settled, the court may dismiss the class action as moot. *See* **Bradley v. Housing Authority,** 512 F.2d 626

(8th Cir. 1975). In situations where prospective class representative's claims will repetitively expire prior to a class certification decision, a court may certify the class despite the mootness of the plaintiff's claim. *See* **Gerstein v. Pugh,** 420 U.S. 103 (1975).

iv. Class Action Prerequisites: Rule 23(a)

A proposed class must satisfy four prerequisites: numerosity, commonality, typicality, and adequacy. Only if the proposed class satisfies these prerequisites will a court then determine whether the action may be maintained as a particular type of class (*see* discussion below, concerning the types of class actions maintainable under the rule).

(a) **Numerosity.** A class must have so many members that their joinder is "impracticable." Proposed classes with fewer than 25 members usually will not be certified; proposed classes between 25 and 40 members may be; and proposed classes with 40 or more classes generally will satisfy the numerosity requirement. The "impracticable" criterion is highly relevant to federally-created "small claims" class actions, where each claimant has only a small monetary stake and lacks a sufficient incentive to sue individually. **Rule 23(a)(1).**

(b) **Commonality.** The proposed class must raise questions of law or fact common to the class. To satisfy commonality, the plaintiffs' claims must depend upon a common contention of such a nature that it is capable of classwide resolution. This means that its determination of its truth or falsity will resolve an issue that is central to the validity of each class members' claim in one stroke. **Wal–Mart Stores, Inc. v. Dukes,** ___ U.S. ___, 131 S.Ct. 2541 (2011).

(c) **Typicality.** The claims of the class representative must be typical of the class members; that is, some nexus between the class representative's claims and those of other class members. Typicality does not require an absolute identity of the representative's claim with each and every class member, however. *See, e.g.,* **Wetzel v. Liberty Mutual Ins. Co.,** 508 F.2d 239 (3d Cir. 1975). Courts will not certify proposed classes, however, where the class representative's claims are completely dissimilar and distinct from other class members. **Rule 23(a)(3).**

- **Example.** A proposed employment discrimination class under Title VII of the Civil Rights Act was not properly certified where the class plaintiff asserted claims based on discrimination in promotion, but the proposed class included members with claims based on discrimination in hiring. **General Tel. Co. v. Falcon,** 457 U.S. 147 (1982).

- **Overlap with commonality inquiry.** In practice, courts frequently construe the typicality and commonality requirements together, as facets of the same inquiry. **Amchem Prods., Inc. v. Windsor,** 521 U.S. 591 (1997).

(d) **Adequacy.** A proposed class must satisfy at least three different adequacy requirements. **Rule 23(a)(4).**

- **Class representative.** The class representative(s) must be adequate. Most importantly, the court will assess whether the class plaintiff is free of actual or potential conflicts with class members or counsel. This standard derives from the due process requirements in **Hansberry v. Lee,** *supra.* In addition, the court will assess whether the class representative will aggressively prosecute the class claims on behalf of absent class members.

- **Examples.** Class representatives may not adequately represent a class of claimants that includes claimants who are currently injured as a consequence of exposure to asbestos products ("present claimants"), as well as claimants who have only been exposed, but have not yet manifested any physical injury ("future claimants"). These claimants have conflicting interests, and one representative cannot adequately represent these different types of claims. This problem might be solved through the use of subclasses with independent representatives, or other "structural assurances" of due process. **Amchem Prods. Inc. v. Windsor,** 521 U.S. 591 (1997). Similarly, class representatives cannot simultaneously represent a class of asbestos claimants that includes person insured under policy terms that existed before 1959, and claimants with policy coverage under terms after 1959. This situation presents a similar type of conflict present in the Amchem asbestos settlement class. **Ortiz v. Fibreboard Corp.,** 527 U.S. 815 (1999).

- **Class counsel: New Rule 23(g) provision. Rule 23** was amended effective December 1, 2003 to add a new subsection **(g)** setting forth standards and procedures for appointment of class counsel. Prospective class counsel must now submit a petition to the court requesting consideration for appointment as class counsel. The court is directed to evaluate various considerations, including the experience of counsel, resources, and possible conflicts of interest, among other factors. The court may appoint interim counsel while it is making a final determination of appointment of class counsel. Prior to 2003, class counsel were evaluated as part of the **Rule 23(a)(4)** adequacy inquiry. **Rule 23(g)** was intended to codify case law relating to the adequacy of counsel.

- **Internal class conflicts.** The court will evaluate the proposed class to ascertain whether class members have any actual or potential class conflicts among class members. *See* **Hansberry v. Lee,** *supra.*

v. Types of Class Actions

The current class action rule provides for three different types of class actions, the so-called **"Rule 23(b)"** actions. In general, **(b)(1)** and **(b)(2)** class actions are *mandatory classes;* the **(b)(3)** class is a *non-mandatory opt-out* class. The contemporary mandatory classes existed under the original 1938 version of the class action rule; the **(b)(3)** class was newly created as part of the 1966 rule revisions and had no analog in the older class action rule.

(a) **Mandatory "prejudice" class actions. Rule 23(b)(1)** provides for two different types of "prejudice" class actions.

- **Prejudice to defendants.** Courts may certify a class action if the possibility of individual lawsuits by individual claimants would create a risk that defendants might be subject to inconsistent adjudications that would establish "incompatible standards of conduct" for the defendants. **Rule 23(b)(1)(A).**

  - **Examples.** A class action would be a suitable and desirable means to resolve riparian rights among property owners around a lake, or property owners complaining against a common nuisance.

- The mere possibility, however, that a defendant might be subject to different compensatory damage verdicts does not satisfy the "inconsistent adjudications" standard. A minority of federal courts permit monetary recovery in **Rule 23(b)(1)(A)** class actions.

- **Prejudice to plaintiffs.** Courts may certify a mandatory class action if the possibility of separate lawsuits creates a risk that such an individual lawsuit might dispose of their interest or substantially impair or impede their ability to protect those interests. **Rule 23(b)(1)(B).**

  - **Example.** Multiple claimants to a defendant's limited fund might not be able to recover any damages from the defendant if a prior lawsuit exhausted the defendant's resources. This is called the "limited fund" theory and class actions pursued under this provision are called "limited fund class actions." The plaintiffs must prove to the court the existence of a limited fund.

(b) **Mandatory injunctive or declaratory judgment classes.** Courts may certify a class action that seeks injunctive relief or a declaratory judgment. **Rule 23(b)(2).** Such a class certification is appropriate when:

- **Scope:** the defendants has acted or refused to act on "grounds that generally apply to the class." There is no requirement that the defendant's conduct apply to every member of the class.

- **Predominantly equitable relief.** Courts will certify a **(b)(2)** class where the predominant form of relief is based in equity—either an injunction or declaratory judgment. Some courts permit a class to be certified as a **(b)(2)** class action where the plaintiff incidentally seeks some form of legal relief, such as back wages in injunctive employment discrimination cases. *See* **Wetzel v. Liberty Mutual Ins. Co.,** *supra.* Generally, however, **(b)(2)** class actions may not be pursued to recover monetary damages. **Wal–Mart Stores, Inc. v. Dukes,** *supra.*

- **Plaintiffs' classes only.** Some federal courts have held that only plaintiffs' classes may be certified under **(b)(2)**, and not defendants' classes.

(c) **Non-mandatory compensatory damage class actions. Rule 23(b)(3)** authorizes the so-called "damages" class action. In addition to the other class action requirements, a **(b)(3)** class must satisfy two additional requirements. These requirements are designed to ensure that a class action is truly a more efficient means of resolving multiple individual claims. These requirements also embody a conceptual preference for individual litigation, when possible.

- **Predominance requirement.** The questions of law or fact in a **(b)(3)** damages class must "predominate" over the claims of individual class members. Some courts evaluate whether a majority of issues are common; other courts assess whether the most important issues are common. Court also will balance the efficiency of resolving the claims in the aggregate against the interest of each class member in having its claim resolved individually.

- **Superiority requirement.** The **(b)(3)** class action must be shown to be a "superior" means of resolving the litigation as opposed to any other method of joinder (such as permissive joinder, consolidation, MDL treatment, or other forms of alternative dispute resolution).

- **Other factors. Rule 23(b)(3)** also supplies four additional factors courts may take into account as part of the finding of *pre-dominance* and *superiority*. These factors include:

  - the interests of class members in individually prosecuting or defending their own actions;

  - any other litigation already in progress that involves the same controversy and litigants;

  - the desirability of concentrating the litigation in one forum; and

  - the difficulties likely to be encountered in the management of the class (the **"manageability"** factor).

Whether a class action is manageable often turns on the related questions of whether class claimants satisfy the "common question" and typicality requirements, as well as the predominance and superiority requirements. Problems relating to applicable law in multi-state diversity class actions also may undermine the manageability of a proposed class action.

- **Example.** A proposed nationwide class action of some fifty million cigarette smokers addicted to nicotine, based on various fraud and deception theories, presents a prospectively unmanageable class action. The existence of fifty differing state tort laws defeats the commonality requirement. Varying reliance defenses also defeat the commonality and typicality requirements. *See* **Castano v. The American Tobacco Co.,** 84 F.3d 734 (5th Cir. 1996).

c. Appellate Review of Class Certification Decisions

i. Pre-1998: Lack of Interlocutory Review and the Final Judgment Rule

Prior to 1998, it was somewhat difficult for litigants to obtain review of a judge's order either granting or denying class certification. This was because a judge's order granting or denying class certification was not immediately appealable to a higher court. Such orders were not a final judgment under **28 U.S.C. § 1291** (*see* discussion of appellate jurisdiction, *infra*), because class certification orders could be decertified, amended, or altered by the court prior to the litigation's conclusion. *See* **Cooper & Lybrand v. Livesay,** 437 U.S. 463 (1978).

(a) **Demise of the death knell doctrine.** Prior to 1978, some federal courts permitted an immediate appeal of a *class certification denial,* on the ground that such a denial effectively signaled the "death knell" of the ability of small claimants to pursue judicial relief. In *Cooper & Lybrand,* the Supreme Court rejected the so-called death knell doctrine. Certification denials, therefore, are not an exception to the final judgment rule.

ii. Judicial Certification for Appellate Review

Prior to the 1998 amendment of **Rule 23,** a judge's class certification order was immediately appealable if the judge certified that order for immediate review by an appellate court under **28 U.S.C. § 1292(b).** In such instances the judge had to certify that the certification decision involved "a controlling question of law as to which there is a substantial ground for difference of opinion and an immediate appeal from the order may materially advance the ultimate termination of the litigation." *See, e.g.,* **Jenkins v. Raymark Indus.,** 782 F.2d 468 (5th Cir. 1986); **In re Northern Dist. of Calif., Dalkon Shield IUD Prods. Liab. Litig.,** 693 F.2d 847 (9th Cir. 1982).

iii. Pre-1998 Alternative Means of Appeal: Mandamus

If the trial judge did not certify the class order for review under **28 U.S.C. § 1292(b),** then litigants could appeal a court's certification order through a *writ of mandamus* proceeding pursuant to **28 U.S.C. § 1651** on the grounds of judicial abuse of discretion in granting or denying the class certification. Mandamus is a disfavored means for supplying appellate jurisdiction of class certification decisions, but it is nonetheless recognized as a legitimate method for seeking interlocutory review. *See* **In the Matter of Rhone–Poulenc Rorer, Inc.,** 51 F.3d 1293 (7th Cir. 1995).

iv. Rule 23(f) Appeals

In 1998, **Rule 23** was amended to add a new provision **(f)** to provide for interlocutory appeals of class certification orders. This provision was added to ameliorate the problems relating to difficulties in seeking review of class certification orders. **Rule 23(f)** now authorizes immediate appellate review (within 14 days after the entry of order) of class certification decisions. Jurisdiction of such appeals is within the discretion of the appellate court, which may consider the opinions and recommendations of the lower court judge who certified (or denied certification) of a proposed class. An appeal does not stay proceedings in the district court unless the judge or court of appeals orders such a stay.

d. Class Notice Requirements

i. When Required: Non-Mandatory Opt-Out Classes

Members of damage classes certified under **Rule 23(b)(3)** must receive "the best notice that is practicable under the circumstances." **Rule 23(c)(2)(B).** This notice language tracks the due process standard the Supreme Court articulated in **Mullane v. Central**

Hanover Bank & Trust, 339 U.S. 306 (1950). In December 2003, a new **Rule 23(c)(2)(A)** provision was added to the rule to provide that a court may direct appropriate notice to classes certified under subsections **Rule 23(b)(1)** and **(b)(2).** Prior to 2003, classes certified under the **(b)(1)** and **(b)(2)** subsections did not direct or require notice.

(a) **Mandatory class actions: discretionary notice.** Courts may now order notice be given in mandatory **(b)(1)** and **(b)(2)** classes, but this is not required in all such classes. **Rule 23(c)(2)(A).**

ii. Who Must Provide Notice

The wording of the class action rule is ambiguous concerning who is responsible for supplying notice—the court or the litigants. *See* **Rule 23(c)(2)** ("the court must direct to class members the best notice . . . ").

(a) **Plaintiff-prepared notice.** Conventionally, the plaintiffs' lawyers prepare and serve notice on class members, especially because plaintiffs are responsible for the cost of notice. *See* **Eisen v. Carlisle & Jacquelin,** 417 U.S. 156 (1974).

- **Improper solicitation.** A problem inherent in plaintiff-prepared class notice is that such notice might be used for improper purposes, such as client-solicitation. In reality, class defense lawyers review the proposed class notice, and the court also reviews the proposed notice.

(b) **Court-prepared notice.** It is possible for a court to prepare the class notice, but this might involve the court in improper communications with the class, or mislead potential class members concerning the litigation. Courts usually do not prepare class notice, but rather review proposed notice of the litigants' choosing.

iii. Content of Notice: Damages Classes

In Rule 23(b)(3) class actions, the notice to class members must advise the class member of:

(a) the nature of the action;

(b) the definition of the certified class;

(c) the class claims, issues, and defenses;

(d) the right to enter an appearance with an attorney;

(e) the right to exclude one's self from the class;

(f) the time and manner for requesting exclusion; and

(g) the binding effect of a Rule 23(b)(3) class judgment.

- Class members virtually never request to make an appearance with counsel in the class action, but instead rely on class counsel to represent their interests in the litigation.

e. Orders Regulating Pretrial and Trial Proceedings

In addition to certification and notice orders, judges are authorized to issue any other case management orders that will assist in the conduct of the proceedings. **Rule 23(d).** Frequently, class action procedure will be governed by procedures and recommendations set forth in the *Manual for Complex Litigation* (Federal Judicial Center 4th ed. 2004). Orders in class actions may include:

i. Discovery Orders

Judges may issue orders regulating the time, place, and manner of discovery

(a) **Discovery in class actions.** Typically, only the named parties are subject to discovery in class actions. However, courts may require that absent class members also respond to discovery requests. *See* **Dellums v. Powell**, 566 F.2d 167 (D.C. Cir. 1977) (nominal parties must respond to discovery requests); *contra,* **Wainwright v. Kraftco Corp.**, 54 F.R.D. 532 (N.D. Ga. 1972) (absent class members need not comply with discovery requests).

ii. Lawyers' Committees

The court may set up lawyer's committees to conduct discovery, motion practice, and trial presentation. The court may appoint a lead counsel to present all oral motions to the court, and a liaison counsel to coordinate communications among attorneys in the litigation. The court may create or approve other committee structures among class counsel. The purpose of lawyers' committees is to coordinate and streamline presentation of motions and filings to the court.

iii. Trial Plans and Time Limitations

The court may issue orders setting forth a trial plan for the presentation of issues and evidence. The plan may include multiple trial phases of issues, including **bifurcation, trifurcation,** or **polyfurcation** of issues (*see* discussion *infra*).

iv. Appointment of Special Masters and Experts

The court may appoint a special master, pursuant to **Rule 53,** to assist the court with various aspects of the litigation, such as performing an accounting or formulating a trial plan. The court also may appoint its own expert witnesses, pursuant to **Federal Rule of Evidence 706.**

v. Other Orders

Judges also may issue orders approving or rejecting *class action settlements* (*see* **Rule 23(e),** discussed below), and approving or disapproving of requests for attorney's fees. *See, e.g.,* **In re Agent Orange Prod. Liab. Litig. (Appeal of David Dean),** 818 F.2d 216 (2d Cir. 1987) (reversing Judge Weinstein's approval of attorney-fee arrangement in Agent Orange litigation).

f. Proving Class Claims and Administering Class Relief

Judges may have options for structuring class action trials and relief. Again, courts will make recourse to the *Manual for Complex Litigation,* for recommendations relating to these complex procedures.

i. Unitary Trial and Class Relief

The unitary trial of a class action will try the class representative's case to determine the defendant's liability and damages. If liability is determined, the court will then determine how to distribute the award to class members.

ii. Multi-Phase Trial Plans

Judges have great discretion in ordering multi-phase trial plans in complex class actions.

(a) Bifurcated trial plan. In a bifurcated trial, liability is tried first. Only if the plaintiff wins will the case proceed to try the damage issue.

(b) Reverse bifurcated trial plan. A reverse bifurcated trial plan will try a damage issue first, such as punitive damages. A reverse bifurcated trial plan also might try a causation issue prior to liability or damages.

(c) Trifurcated trial plan. In tort litigation, a trifurcated trial plan tries the causation issue first; then liability, and then damages. The failure of the plaintiff to prevail on any issue ends the trial.

(d) Reverse trifurcated trial plans. Reverse trifurcated trial plans scramble the usual order of issue presentation.

(e) Damages in multi-phase trial plans. Damages in multi-phase trials may be determined in various ways, either by individual damage trials, or small group mini-trials, or by statistical extrapolation, or by classwide damages.

iii. Fluid or Cy Pres Relief

A court may order a "fluid recovery" in different circumstances. One instance is where it is impossible to identify individually all the claimants in the class, and the recovery exceeds the number of claimants. Another instance is where the class distribution does not exhaust the recovery, leaving a fund remaining. In such instances courts may order some remedy that provides a general benefit to all class members (rather than individual compensation). Alternatively, courts may invoke a cy pres remedy to distribute class funds to a charitable or research entity, or some other cause or endeavor.

- **Examples:**

  - A court orders taxi cab drivers to reduce charges for a certain period as relief for a class of overcharged taxi riders who cannot all be identified to receive individual compensation.

  - A court orders excess funds from a products liability class action to be paid into a research fund for research on related illnesses and disease.

g. Class Settlement

Class actions differ from simple litigation in that the class action may not be "compromised" or dismissed unless the court approves. In practice, this means that the court reviews the terms of the proposed class settlement. Court scrutiny of proposed settlements is another due process protection for absent class members, to ensure that the terms of the settlement do not compromise or prejudice their rights. *See* **Amchem Prods., Inc. v. Windsor,** 521 U.S. 591 (1997) and **Ortiz v. Fibreboard Corp.,** 527 U.S. 815 (1999).

i. Manner of Review

Rule 23(e) was amended effective December 1, 2003 to require that a judge hold an evidentiary hearing before approving a proposed settlement. This is known as a "fairness hearing." The court will hear testimony and receive evidence from the proponents and opponents of the settlement. **Rule 23(e). Rule 23(e)** was extensively amended effective December 1, 2003 to provide additional guidance to courts, litigants, and objectors concerning applicable procedures for submitting evidence and approving class action settlements.

ii. Standard of Review

The judge must determine whether the proposed settlement is fair, adequate, and reasonable. Circuit courts have delineated detailed factors to determine whether the general standards are met by the settlement. It is not necessary that all members of the class agree to the settlement, and the court may approve a settlement even when some class members do not want the settlement. Settlements also may be approved over the objections of the class representatives. **Rule 23(e)** was amended effective December 1, 2003 to provide an opportunity for objectors to appear and object to proposed class settlements.

iii. Burdens

The proponents of the settlement carry the burden of demonstrating that the settlement is fair, adequate, and reasonable.

iv. Ability to Modify

The court had no power to change or modify the terms of a class action settlement. The court must approve or reject the settlement in its entirety.

v. Timing Considerations—"Settlement Classes"

Class settlements may occur at any time during proceedings. In the usual instance, a class is certified at the outset of the litigation and the court reviews the settlement of the pre-existing certified class. In recent years, however, some federal courts have reviewed class certification simultaneous with the court's review of the terms of a negotiated settlement. Hence, class certification is part of the settlement agreement, with no pre-existing certification prior to the settlement. *See, e.g.,* **In re A.H. Robins Co.,** 880 F.2d 709 (4th Cir. 1989). This mechanism or procedure is called a "settlement class."

(a) **Controversy over settlement classes.** In the 1990s, a substantial controversy existed concerning whether **Rule 23** authorized the use of the settlement class device. Some courts and commentators believed that judges cannot make informed settlement decisions without previously having determined the existence of a legitimate class action. Other commentators argued that the judicial system should encourage and support settlement of disputes. *See* **In re General Motors Corporation Pick–Up Truck Fuel Tank Products Liability Litigation,** 55 F.3d 768 (3d Cir. 1995); **Georgine v. Amchem Prods., Inc.,** 83 F.3d 610 (3d Cir. 1996). Controversial issues included:

- whether the standards for certification of settlement classes are the same as for certification of litigation classes (*see* **Georgine v. Amchem Prods., Inc,** *supra,* holding that the standards are and should be the same);

- the existence and nature of the attorney-client relationship when a settlement is negotiated first and the class is then certified as part of the deal;

- due process protections for class members in the absence of a prior certification determination; and

- inherent pressures to approve negotiated settlements, particularly in long-running complex cases.

(b) **Proposed Rule 23 revision relating to settlement classes.** In the late 1990s and prior to the Supreme Court's decisions in **Amchem** and **Ortiz,** the Advisory Committee on Civil Rules proposed an amendment to **Rule 23** to specifically provide for settlement classes. This proposal subsequently was withdrawn and was never acted on by the Advisory Committee. The proposal for a settlement class provision has inspired renewed interest in the twenty-first century.

(c) **Supreme Court resolves settlement class debate.** In the late 1990s, in two landmark eases, the Supreme Court resolved the debate over settlement classes by upholding and recognizing the possibility of such classes under **Rule 23.** The Court held that when class certification is sought along with approval of a proposed settlement, the proposed class must satisfy all the same requirements for certification as litigation classes, except for the "manageability" factor. *See* **Amchem Prods., Inc. v. Windsor,** 521 U.S. 591 and **Ortiz v. Fibreboard Corp.,** 527 U.S. 815 (1999).

h. Special Problems: Role of Attorneys; Ethical Issues; Attorney's Fees

Class action litigation, as representational litigation, departs from the traditional model of the attorney-client relationship in simple litigation.

i. Role of the Attorneys

Class action litigation often involves more than one class lawyer and in extremely complex cases, the court may organize plaintiffs' and defense lawyers into committees (*see* discussion *supra*).

(a) **Determining the client.** Unlike simple litigation with a readily identifiable client, sprawling class litigation may make it difficult to determine who the client is, or what the client's interests are. The indeterminancy of the class client exacerbates other issues inherent in the attorney-client relationship, such as applicable privileges and immunities.

(b) **Client communications.** Massive class actions also present difficult problems of communicating with the class clients— particularly absent class members. A frequent complaint in complex mass tort litigation—for example the **Agent Orange and Silicone Gel Breast Implant Litigation**—is the failure of class counsel to keep the class claimants informed about the progress of the litigation, or the resolution of their claims.

ii. Ethical Issues

Class action litigation raises significant ethical issues that are heightened by the representational nature of the litigation. The most pressing ethical dilemmas include:

(a) **Improper solicitation.** The often lucrative recoveries in successful class actions can serve as an inducement to improper solicitation of class representatives and class clients.

(b) **Conflicts-of-interest.** The relationship of class counsel to class members often is fraught with potential conflicts-of-interest, particularly concerning quick settlement of class claims to enhance the attorney fee recovery and diminish class counsel's labors (*see* discussion of attorney's fees, *infra*).

(c) **Secrecy; client confidence and secrets.** Class actions, particularly those invested with a public interest, raise ethical tensions between the attorney's duty to protect client confidences and secrets and the public's right to disclosure of information that is actually or potentially harmful.

iii. Attorney's Fees; Cost and Expenses

Attorneys may subsidize the ongoing costs and expenses of class litigation, which costs and expenses are chargeable to and recoverable from the class. **Rule 23** was amended effective December 1, 2003 to add a new subsection **(h)** which provides for attorney fees. **Rule 23(h).**

(a) **New Rule 23(h) provision for judicial determination of attorney fees. Rule 23(h)** provides standards and guidance for judicial determination of attorney fees in class action litigation. **Rule 23(h)** provides for a motion for the award of attorney fees, objections to the motion, a hearing and findings on fees, and the possibility for referral of fee issues to a special master or magistrate.

(b) **Methods for determining attorney fees.** The Advisory Committee Note to **Rule 23(h)** suggests various methods by which courts may determine and set attorney fee awards in class actions. These suggestions collect various methodologies that existed before codification of **Rule 23(h).** Attorney fees in class actions may be determined in a number of different manners. In many class actions, the attorneys fee awards are subject to court scrutiny under **Rule 23(e).** Attorney's fees may be determined by the following methods:

- **Statutory provisions.** Some federal and state statutes provide for the award of attorneys' fees to successful plaintiffs' counsel; the purpose is to encourage "private attorneys general" in pursuing relief for injured claimants.

- **Fee-shifting statutes.** Some federal statutes provide for fee-shifting, that is, requiring defendants to pay the costs of plaintiffs' attorneys. This type of provision enhances the ability of plaintiffs to find lawyers willing to pursue relief under federal law. *See, e.g.,* **Civil Rights Attorney's Fees Awards Act, 42 U.S.C. § 1988.**

- **Contingency fee arrangements.** Class counsel receive a percentage of the class recovery. If the plaintiffs are not successful, class counsel receives no compensation. Generally, attorney's fees in large complex class actions are not determined by this method.

- **Common benefit fund.** Where class counsel have prevailed and a settlement generates a fund of money for the class, attorney fees are determined in the aggregate as a percentage of that common benefit fund. In most cases using this method, attorney fees will be in the range of 25–30% of the fund. In so-called "mega-cases," the percentage of attorney fees will be lower, in the range of 10–15% of the fund.

- **Hourly billable rate.** Some class counsel determine fees by an hourly billable rate.

- **Lodestar formula.** Some federal courts review attorney's fees in class actions according to a version of a "lodestar" formula. The lodestar formula assesses, among other factors:

  - the time and normal billing rate of each attorney's work on the case;

- a multiplier for each function performed;

- a contingency or risk factor in pursing the particular claims or relief;

- the quality of each lawyer's performance.

- **Combined percentage and lodestar approach.** Most federal courts have abandoned lodestar determination of attorney fees as too time consuming, and have adopted the common benefit fund methodology. However, several Circuits courts use the lodestar formula as a check on common benefit fund awards.

- **Other fee arrangements; fee-sharing; auctions.** Class counsel sometimes may negotiate fee arrangements among themselves, based on capital-investment in the litigation and work performed. Such fee arrangements raise ethical questions concerning the propriety of fee-splitting among lawyers from different firms. The Second Circuit struck down such an agreement in the *Agent Orange* litigation. *See* **In re Agent Orange Prod. Liab. Litig.,** 818 F.2d 216 (2d Cir. 1987).

- The Second Circuit and some academic commentators have proposed auctioning off class action representation.

i. Defendant Classes

Most class actions are structured as plaintiffs' class actions. However, **Rule 23(a)** permits certification of a defendant class: "one or more members of a class *may sue or be sued* as representative parties . . . "

i. Rarity of Defendant Classes

Defendant classes are very rare. A defendant class must meet the same **Rule 23** requirements as a plaintiff's class. Reasons for the rarity of defendant classes include:

(a) Lack of numerosity. Class actions typically do not involve a sufficient number of defendants to satisfy the threshold numerosity requirement.

(b) Lack of commonality and typicality. Even when the numerosity requirement is met, multiple defendants frequently fail to satisfy the **Rule 23(a)** commonality and typicality requirements. More often, defendants desire to present individual defenses or counterclaims.

    (c) **Inadequacy of representation.** Finally, individual defendants and their lawyers may not be interested in presenting a joint or common defense to a plaintiff's class, so adequacy of representation may be a bar to class certification.

j. Intervention into Class Actions

It is possible for a person who is not captured by the class description to intervene in the class to protect that non-party's interests in the litigation.

i. Criteria for Intervention in a Class Action

Intervention in a class action litigation is governed by the criteria of **Rule 24** (*see* discussion of Intervention, *supra*). The consensus is that intervention in class actions is governed by the same principles as in any other proceeding.

    (a) **Impair or impede standard.** The criteria for intervention of right under **Rule 24(a)(2)** parallels the standard for certification of a **Rule 23(b)(1)(B)** class ("adjudications with respect to individual members of the class . . . would as a practical matter be dispositive of the interests of other members not parties to the adjudications or substantially impair or impede their ability to protect their interests").

    (b) **Adequacy of representation.** Both **Rule 24(a)** and **Rule 23(a)** require a showing of adequacy of representation. At least one federal court has suggested that an order to deny intervention under **Rule 24(a)** requires a higher showing of adequacy than to satisfy the requirements of **Rule 23(a)**. *See* **Woolen v. Surtran Taxicabs, Inc.,** 684 F.2d 324 (5th Cir. 1982).

ii. Orders Relating to Intervenors

A judge may issue any orders "imposing conditions . . . on intervenors." **Rule 23(d)(1)(C).**

iii. Relationship of Intervention to Objectors

The Supreme Court has ruled that nonnamed class members who have objected in a timely manner to a proposed class settlement, at a fairness hearing, have a subsequent right to appeal the court's judgment approving the settlement, without formally intervening in the action. **Devlin v. Scardelletti,** 536 U.S. 1 (2002).

k. "Limited Issues" Classes and Subclasses

i. "Limited Issues" Classes

A judge has the ability to authorize or create class actions that are limited to the trial of specific issues, rather than the entire claim. **Rule 23(c)(4)** ("an action may be brought or maintained as a class action with respect to particular issues"). For example, a judge may authorize a class action limited to a trial of the causation issue, or state of the art defense. *See* **In re Bendectin Litig.,** 857 F.2d 290 (6th Cir. 1988); **Jenkins v. Raymark,** *supra.*

- **Objections to limited-issues classes.** Although authorized by the class action rule, limited-issues classes frequently inspire heated challenges based on due process and Seventh Amendment jury trial objections.

ii. Sub-Classes

Judges and the litigants also may structure a class action to include sub-classes. **Rule 23(c)(5).** Each subclass is treated the same as any other class action, and must satisfy all class requirements. Sub-classes are one means of resolving lack of commonality and typicality problems in heterogeneous damage class action under **Rule 23(b)(3).** Similar claimants may then be grouped together in subclasses.

l. Class Actions and Mass Tort Litigation

i. Unsuitability for Aggregate Tort Litigation: 1966 Advisory Committee Note

In the late 1970s and early 1980s, federal courts were resistant to certifying mass tort cases as class actions. This refusal was based largely on the 1966 Advisory Committee Note stating that "mass accident" cases resulting in injuries to numerous persons was not appropriate for class action treatment. Additionally, federal courts held that such class actions failed to satisfy threshold commonality, typicality, and adequacy requirements, and that attempted **(b)(3)** classes also failed the predominance and superiority tests. *See, e.g.,* **In re Northern Dist. Cal. Dalkon Shield IUD Prods. Liab. Litig.,** 693 F.2d 847 (9th Cir. 1982); **Yandle v. PPG Indus., Inc.,** 65 RR.D. 566 (E.D. Tex. 1974) (refusal to certify asbestos class action).

ii. **Mass Tort Litigation Class Actions Authorized**

Although the general trend was to refuse to certify mass tort class actions, in the early 1980s courts in the Second, Third, and Fifth Circuits upheld class actions in significant mass tort litigations.

(a) **The *Agent Orange* litigation.** The district court for the Eastern District of New York and the Second Circuit upheld class certification of a **(b)(3)** opt-out class of Agent Orange claimants. *See* **In re Agent Orange Prod. Liab. Litig.,** 506 F.Supp. 762 (E.D.N.Y. 1980), affd., 818 F.2d 145 (2d Cir. 1987).

(b) **DES litigation.** The district court in Massachusetts upheld a class of claimants exposed to DES who were born and domiciled in Massachusetts. **Payton v. Abbott Labs.,** 83 F.R.D. 382 (D. Mass. 1979).

(c) **Asbestos personal injury claims.** The Fifth Circuit upheld certification of a limited-issues **(b)(3)** personal injury asbestos class. **Jenkins v. Raymark Indus.,** 782 F.2d 468 (5th Cir. 1986). The certification was limited to the issue of the "state of the art" defense, and applied only to claims within the Eastern District of Texas.

(d) **Asbestos property damage claims.** The Third Circuit upheld certification of a *nationwide* **(b)(3)** opt-out limited issues class, relating to property and contract claims arising from the abatement of asbestos in school buildings. **In re School Asbestos Litig.,** 789 F.2d 996 (3d Cir. 1986).

iii. **Mass Tort Litigation Class Actions Repudiated**

Receptivity to use of the class action rule to adjudicate mass torts has been mixed. In the 1990s, federal courts renewed their rejection of proposed mass tort class actions in a series of decisions. *See, e.g.,* **In re Fibreboard Corp.,** 893 F.2d 706 (5th Cir. 1990) (reversing proposed four-phase **Rule 23(b)(3)** class action trial plan of asbestos personal injury claims); **In re Keene Corp.,** 14 F.3d 726 (2d Cir. 1993) (repudiating attempted **Rule 23(b)(1)(B)** *limited fund* class action involving present and future asbestos claimants); **In the Matter of Rhone–Poulenc Rorer, Inc.,** 51 F.3d 1293 (7th Cir. 1995) (reversing nationwide class certification in contaminated blood products litigation); **In re American Medical Sys., Inc.,** 75 F.3d 1069 (6th Cir. 1996) (reversing certification of **Rule 23(b)(3)** *nationwide class* of defective penile implants claimants); **Castano v. American Tobacco Co.,** 84 F.3d 734 (5th Cir. 1996) (reversing certification of a **Rule 23(b)(3)** nationwide class of all smokers addicted to tobacco products).

iv. Mass Tort Settlement Classes

Proposed settlement classes are subject to the same certification requirements as litigation classes, except for **Rule 23(b)(3)** classes, which do not need to satisfy the "manageability" requirement for certification. **Amchem Prods., Inc. v. Windsor,** 521 U.S. 591 (1997) and **Ortiz v. Fibreboard Corp.,** 527 U.S. 815 (1999). Federal courts have upheld some mass tort settlement classes, *see, e.g.,* **In re A.H. Robins Co.,** 880 F.2d 709 (4th Cir. 1989) (Dalkon Shield settlement class), but repudiated others. *See e.g.,* **In re General Motors Corp. Pick–Up Truck Fuel Tank Products Liab. Litig.,** 55 F.3d 768 (3d Cir. 1995) (proposed settlement not fair, adequate, and reasonable; questioning whether settlement classes permissible under **Rule 23**).

■ CHAPTER REVIEW CHECKLIST

Civil procedure examinations may contain a problem relating to the joinder of claims or the addition of parties to the lawsuit. Your procedure professor is most likely to test on joinder problems with overlapping jurisdictional issues (such as permissive or compulsory counterclaims, impleader, or intervention). Therefore it is useful to review jurisdictional concepts in tandem with joinder issues. Some first year procedure courses do not cover consolidation or class action procedure and it is unlikely that you will be tested on the concept of consolidation. However, if you have studied class actions, this area is a good testable topic. Your professor is likely to focus either on class certification issues, or the due process concerns entailed in class action procedure. Read the facts presented carefully and determine whether the facts present a problem relating to party or claim joinder. Identify the particular type of claim joinder or party joinder involved, and review the rule basis for that joinder first.

To answer a problem relating to joinder of claims, ask:

1. **Do the facts present a problem relating to the permissive joinder of claims?**

   - Is the plaintiff or the defendant seeking to permissively join a claim?

     — Do the facts involve multiple claims the plaintiff or plaintiffs are seeking to assert? **Rule 18(a).**

     — Do the facts involve a counterclaim the defendant is permissively seeking to assert? **Rule 13(b).**

   Remember that the Federal Rules have merged law and equity and a person may join in one action all legal and equitable claims.

   - What is the nature of the additional claim? Against whom is the claim asserted?

     — Is the plaintiff asserting multiple claims against the defendant? **Rule 18.**

     — Is the additional claim a counterclaim by the defendant against the plaintiff? **Rules 13(a)** and **(b).**

     — Is the additional claim a cross-claim against a co-party, such as a co-defendant? **Rule 13(g).** If the additional claim is a cross-claim, then does the cross-claim:

       (1) arise out of the transaction or occurrence that is the subject matter of the original action; or

       (2) arise out of the transaction or occurrence that is the subject matter of a counterclaim; or

       (3) relate to any property that is the subject matter of the original action?

     — Is the additional claim against a third party impleaded into the litigation? **Rule 14(a).**

   - What is the jurisdictional basis of the additional permissive claim?

     — Does the claim have an independent basis in the court's federal question or diversity jurisdiction?

     — Does the claim come within the court's supplemental jurisdiction?

2. **Do the facts present problems relating to the compulsory joinder of claims?**

- Is the additional claim a compulsory counterclaim? **Rule 13(a).**

  — What is the factual and legal basis for the defendant's counterclaim?

  — Is the defendant's counterclaim the subject matter of some other pending lawsuit at the time the plaintiff filed this lawsuit?

  — Does the defendant's claim arise out of the same transaction or occurrence that is the subject matter of the plaintiff's claim?

  — Does the counterclaim require the presence of some third party over whom the court cannot acquire jurisdiction?

- What is the jurisdictional basis of the compulsory claim? Does the claim have an independent basis in the court's federal question or diversity jurisdiction? Does the claim come within the court's supplemental jurisdiction?

3. **Do the facts involve a consolidation of separate cases into one litigation? Rule 42(a).**

   - Do the facts indicate that multiple separate lawsuits have been filed?

   - Where are those actions located?

     — Are all the lawsuits pending before one district court?

     — Are the lawsuits dispersed throughout the federal system?

     — Do the separate actions need to be transferred to one district before a consolidation may be considered?

   - Do the separate actions have a common question of law or fact?

     — Will consolidation of the actions avoid unnecessary costs or delay?

4. **Do the facts present a situation appropriate for separate trials or severance of claims or issues? Rule 42(b).**

   - Will separate trials of claims or issues:

     — enhance convenience;

     — enhance the expeditious resolution of the litigation,

— serve the interests of judicial economy, and

— avoid prejudice?

- Will the separate trial of claims or issues violate the Seventh Amendment right to trial by jury? Have Seventh Amendment rights been considered and protected in the trial plan?

To answer an examination problem relating to joinder of parties, ask:

1. **Who are the parties to the lawsuit?**

   - Is the named plaintiff the *real party in interest* in the litigation? **Rule 17(a).**

     — What is the nature of the right or claim asserted, and whose right or claim is it?

   - Do the parties have standing to sue (or be sued) and do they have the capacity required by law? **Rule 17(b)** and **(c).**

2. **Can the parties permissively be joined in the action? Rule 20(a).**

   - What is the relationship of the parties?

     — Do the parties jointly or severally possess any right to relief?

     — Do the parties have rights that arise out of the same transaction, occurrence, or series of transactions and occurrences, *and* have questions of law or fact common to all?

   - Will the permissive joinder of a party cause embarrassment, delay, or unnecessary costs because no claim is asserted by or against that party?

   - Will the permissive joinder of parties cause delay or prejudice? Should the court order separate trials under **Federal Rule 20(b)** or **42(b)?**

   - Does the court have valid personal and subject matter jurisdiction over each party who is permissively joined in the action?

     — Are the parties to be joined pendent parties? Does supplemental jurisdiction support their joinder under **28 U.S.C. § 1367(a)?**

     — Is the basis for the court's jurisdiction diversity jurisdiction? Would the permissive joinder of the party under **Rule 20** violate the complete diversity rule? (which is prohibited by **28 U.S.C. § 1367(b)**).

3. Are the parties necessary to be joined for a just adjudication? Rule 19.

- Has a person who should be in the litigation been left out (not named in the complaint) by the plaintiff?

- Has the defendant filed a **Rule 12(b)(7)** motion to dismiss the case for the plaintiff's failure to join a person under **Rule 19**?

- Why has that person not been named by the plaintiff? Is it *feasible* to join the person who has not been joined by the plaintiff? **Rule 19(a):**
  — Would the presence of the unnamed person destroy the court's diversity jurisdiction?
  — Is it impossible to serve the unnamed person, or are there venue problems?

- Will the court be unable to afford complete relief to all the parties already in the lawsuit if the absent person is not joined?

- Does the absent person have an interest in the litigation such that if the court affords relief in that party's absence:
  — as a practical matter the court's disposition of the case will impair or impede the absent person's ability to protect the interest, or
  — the persons already party to the lawsuit may be subject to a substantial risk of multiple or inconsistent obligations.

- If it is *not feasible* to join the absent party, then may the court proceed in *equity and good conscience* with the action among the parties before it, or should the court dismiss the action? **Rule 19(b):**
  — To what extent would a judgment rendered in the person's absence be prejudicial to those already parties to the action?
  — To what extent can the court lessen possible prejudice by fashioning protective provisions in the judgment?
  — To what extent will a judgment rendered in the party's absence be adequate?
  — To what extent will the plaintiff have an adequate remedy if the court dismisses the action for the failure to join the absent

party? Does the plaintiff have the ability to bring another lawsuit in state court?

- Is the basis for the court's jurisdiction diversity jurisdiction? Would the compulsory joinder of the party under **Rule 24** violate the complete diversity rule? (which is prohibited by **28 U.S.C. § 1367(b)**).

4. Are the parties to be joined through impleader? Rule 14.

- Is there a person who is not part of the lawsuit—whom the plaintiff did not name a party—that the defendant seeks to join into the lawsuit?

  — In what way is the person liable to the defendant?

- Is the basis for the court's jurisdiction diversity jurisdiction? Would the compulsory joinder of the party under **Rule 14** violate the complete diversity rule? (which is prohibited by **28 U.S.C. § 1367(b)**).

- Does the person so joined (as the third-party defendant) assert any claims or defenses against the original defendant?

- Does the third-party defendant have claims against the original plaintiff, arising out of the same transactions and occurrences forming the subject matter of the original complaint?

- Does the original plaintiff have claims against the third-party defendant? Could the plaintiff have sued the third-party defendant originally (but failed to do so)?

- Has the defendant asserted a counterclaim? Does the plaintiff now have claims against someone not named in the lawsuit, who is or might be liable to the plaintiff for the counterclaim?

5. Do the facts involve an action in interpleader? Rule 22 and 28 U.S.C. §§ 1335, 1397, 2361.

- Has a "stakeholder" requested that the court resolve competing claims to the stake or fund? That is, has a litigant requested an action in interpleader?

- Has the interpleader action been invoked under **Rule 22** ("rule interpleader")?

— Does the court have valid subject matter and personal jurisdiction over all the parties to the interpleader? Is there complete diversity among the parties?

- Has the interpleader action been invoked under the federal statutory interpleader provisions?

- Is there minimal diversity among the parties?

6. **Are persons seeking to intervene into the lawsuit? Rule 24.**

- Is there a person or persons who are not part of the lawsuit but who wish to join the lawsuit? Why?

- At what point in the litigation is the person seeking to intervene? Has the person made a "timely" application to the court for intervention?

- Does the person have a right to intervene? **Rule 24(a).**

  — Does a federal statute confer an unconditional right to intervene?

  — Does the prospective intervenor have an interest relating to the property or transaction that is the subject of the lawsuit?

    (1) If the person is not permitted to intervene, will the prospective intervenor's ability to protect that interest as a practical matter be impaired or impeded?

    (2) Is the prospective intervenor's interest already adequately protected by the parties already in the lawsuit?

- May the court permissively allow the person to intervene? **Rule 24(b).**

  — Has the applicant made a "timely application" to permissively intervene?

  — Does a federal statute confer a conditional right to intervene?

  — Does the prospective intervenor's claim (or defense) have a question of law or fact in common with the existing lawsuit?

  — Will discretionary permissive intervention by the applicant cause undue delay or prejudice to the parties already in the lawsuit?

- Should the court limit the nature and scope of the intervenor's participation in the lawsuit?

- Can the court's and the prospective intervenor's interests be adequately served through friend-of-the-court (*amicus curiae*) participation?

- Is the person seeking to intervene on the plaintiff's side of the litigation, or the defendant's side? Are there jurisdictional problems with joinder of the prospective intervenor?

    — If the action is based in the federal court's diversity jurisdiction, will the joinder of the intervenor violate the complete diversity rule?

    — Does **28 U.S.C. § 1367(b)** limit or prohibit joinder of the proposed intervenor?

To answer an examination problem relating to class actions (**Rule 23**), ask:

1. **What type of class action do the facts implicate or suggest?**

    - Is the class action being pursued under constitutional claims or based on federal law?

    - Is the class action based on state-law claims? Is the class based in the federal court's diversity jurisdiction?

2. **Are the plaintiffs (or the litigants) seeking certification of a litigation class?**

    - When is class certification sought?

    - Is there a definable class?

        — Is the class description too vague or overbroad?

    - Is there a real class representative whose claims are not moot?

    - Does the class meet the threshold requirements for certification?

        — Is the class of claimants *numerous* enough?

        — Do the class members' claims share a *common question* of law or fact?

— Are the claims of the class representatives *typical* of the class members?

— Will the class representative *adequately represent* the interests of class members? Are there any conflicts-of-interest between the class representative and other class members? Is class counsel also adequate? Does class counsel have the experience and resources to represent the class? Are there any conflicts between class counsel, the class representatives, and class members?

• May the class action be maintained as one or more of particular types of class actions permitted under **Rule 23(b)?**

• Do the facts suggest that a class action is desirable because if the claims proceeded as individual lawsuits, either the defendants or the plaintiffs might be prejudiced by the individual lawsuits? **Rule 23(b)(1)(A)** and **(B):**

— Do the facts suggest the possibility of inconsistent adjudications or standards of conduct for the defendant?

— Do the facts suggest that in absence of a class action, the ability of plaintiffs to protect their interests might be impaired or impeded?

— Do the defendants have a *limited fund* that might be exhausted before all plaintiffs could recover in successive individual lawsuits? Have the plaintiffs demonstrated the existence of that limited fund?

• Are the plaintiffs seeking equitable relief in the form of an injunction or declaratory judgment? **Rule 23(b)(2).**

• Are the plaintiffs seeking compensatory damages? **Rule 23(b)(3):**

— Do common questions of law or fact *predominate* over any questions affecting only individual members of the class?

— Is a class action superior to any other means of resolving the dispute?

— Do the class members each have a very considerable interest in controlling the prosecution or defense of their claims in individual actions?

— Is there already existing litigation in other courts by or against the class members?

— Is it desirable to concentrate the litigation all in one forum?

— Will the class action be manageable?

3. **Does the class action satisfy due process requirements?**

- Has adequate notice been provided to **(b)(3)** class members? Does the content of the notice conform to the requirements of **Rule 23(c)(2)?**

- In **Rule 23(b)(3)** damages actions, have absent class members been given the chance to exclude themselves from the class?

- Are the class representatives and class counsel adequately protecting the interests of absent class members? Are there any conflicts of interest between the class representatives, class counsel, and absent class members?

- Have the parties submitted a proposed class settlement to the court for approval? **Rule 23(e):**

— Was the class certified prior to the negotiation and settlement agreement?

- If the settlement includes a provision requesting class certification as part of the settlement, would the "settlement class" meet the same standards for certification as a litigation class?

- Who negotiated the settlement and how was the settlement accomplished? Was there any collusive behavior on the part of the negotiating lawyers? Were the interests of the absent class members fairly and adequately protected in the settlement negotiations?

- Are the substantive terms of the class settlement fair, adequate and reasonable?

- How have attorney's fees been determined? Is the award of attorney's fees fair and reasonable?

4. **Are there any jurisdictional problems with the class action?**

- Is the class action based in the court's diversity jurisdiction? Does it satisfy the requirements of **28 U.S.C. § 133(d)?**

- Do any exceptions apply to keep the proposed class action out of federal court?

Remember: class actions are an exception to the complete diversity rule, so that **28 U.S.C. § 1332(d)** requires only minimal diversity among parties & class members.

- Is the class a mandatory **(b)(1)** or **(b)(2)** class action? Does the plaintiffs' class include members from other states who lack minimum contacts with the forum state?

- *Note:* This is the so-called ***Shutts*** problem—arguably, a court cannot bind absent plaintiffs who lack minimum contacts with the forum state and are not permitted to opt-out. But this is an open question left unresolved by ***Shutts.***

VII

Obtaining Information Prior to Trial: Discovery

■ ANALYSIS

■ CHAPTER OVERVIEW

- This chapter deals with the ability of parties to a lawsuit to obtain information about their claims and defenses prior to trial. Discovery also is important because it frequently provides the basis for one of the parties—usually the defendant, to move for summary judgment. However, plaintiffs also may move for summary judgment after discovery, as well.

- Historically, the practice of pretrial discovery of information was extremely limited and available only in equity. Even today in English and many continental legal systems, discovery is virtually unknown.

- Modern discovery is a creation of the Federal Rules of Civil Procedure. The discovery provisions are collected in **Rules 26** through **37.**

- Modern discovery is the hand-maiden of the liberal pleading permitted under modern federal procedural rules. (*see* Chapter V on pleading, *supra*). Liberal discovery provisions enable the pleader to learn information about the case subsequent to filing the action.

- Modern federal discovery serves three major purposes:

  — The preservation of relevant information.

  — The ascertainment and isolation of issues in controversy.

  — The ascertainment of evidence and judging its strengths and weaknesses relating to disputed factual issues.

- The scope of discovery is very broad. A party to the litigation may discover any information that is *relevant to claims or defenses of any party,*

  — The information sought through discovery need not be admissible at trial. The information sought only has to be *"reasonably calculated to lead to the discovery of admissible evidence."*

- Parties may seek information relating to any claim or defense.

- Parties may not obtain any information that is covered by an *attorney-client privilege, attorney work product immunity,* or other privilege (e.g., doctor-patient, clergy-congregant, etc.).

—   The nature and scope of the *attorney-client privilege* is defined by federal and state law. The privilege primarily protects the attorney-client relationship and protects from disclosure client confidences and secrets revealed in that relationship that is not otherwise discoverable. Within the corporate setting, the privilege extends to lower-level employees.

—   *Attorney work product immunity* protects a lawyer's trial preparation materials prepared in anticipation of litigation. There are two major types of attorney work product; ordinary work product and opinion work product. Ordinary work product enjoys a limited immunity and it can be overridden on a showing of substantial need and the inability to obtain the information through other means. Opinion work product—a lawyer's mental impressions, thought processes, legal strategies—is more absolutely protected.

•   Parties may seek discovery from expert witnesses. In seeking such discovery, the Federal Rules distinguish among the purposes for which a party has retained the expert witness.

•   Parties to a litigation may protect information from disclosure by seeking a protective order from the court. The party seeking a protective order has to demonstrate *"good cause"* for protecting the material from disclosure.

•   The parties typically conduct their discovery without much involvement from the court.

•   Parties are required to exchange certain information at the outset of the litigation without having to make a formal request. These are called *"mandatory initial disclosures."*

—   The new mandatory informal discovery provision, **Rule 26(a)(1),** was the centerpiece of the 1993 revisions of the discovery rules. This provision was amended again in 2000 to impose national uniformity on initial disclosure requirements.

—   Parties also are required to confer on discovery matters and to agree to a discovery schedule prior to the first pretrial conference with the court, if the court requires such a conference under **Rule 16** and local rules.

— Parties also are obligated to meet and confer attempt to resolve discovery disputes in good faith before seeking resolution in court. Only if the parties cannot resolve their own discovery disputes will a court then become involved in the discovery process.

- There are five formal means of conducting discovery in federal court.

  — **Interrogatories.** Parties may send a set of questions to the opposing party (and not to non-party witnesses). Interrogatories are frequently the discovery device first used to obtain information in a litigation. The permissible number of interrogatories (including subparts) is limited by federal and local rules.

  — **Depositions.** Depositions are a trial-like method of examining a person involved in the litigation and preserving that testimony for use at trial, either as the deponent's testimony or for cross-examination purposes. Parties, non-parties, and expert witnesses all may be deposed. Depositions are taken under oath, on the record, and may subject the deponent to perjury for untruthful statement given at deposition.

  — **Document production and inspection of premises.** The discovery rules permit parties to obtain documents relating to the litigation. When relevant, parties also may inspect premises.

  — **Physical and mental examinations.** A court may order a party to submit to a physical or mental exam when there is "good cause" and the party's physical or mental condition is *in controversy.* Such an order does not violate the person's constitutional rights.

  — **Requests for admissions.** A party may request that an opposing party either admit or deny allegations involved in the litigation. A party admission is then binding at trial, and is not a contested issue.

- Discovery requests must be signed by the attorney seeking disclosure and must contain an attestation that the discovery request is consistent with the rules and not made for any improper purpose such as to harass or delay the proceedings. Violation of the signature requirements will subject the attorney to discovery sanctions under **Rule 37.**

- Parties are under a continuing duty to supplement their discovery responses.

- Discovery may be used in support of a summary judgment motion, or used at trial. Discovery materials may be used as direct testimony, evidence, or to impeach a witness.

- Failure to comply with a valid and legitimate discovery request can result in various sanctions under **Rule 37,** ranging from contempt citation to dismissal of the offending party's claim or defense.

- Discovery in international private litigation is governed by treaty provisions and the **Hague Convention.**

A. MODERN DISCOVERY: HISTORICAL CONTEXT

1. At Common Law and Equity

The ability to obtain information about the opponent's or one's own case was not an integral part of the litigation process at common law. The American concept of "discovery" was largely unknown in the English courts, a tradition that continues into modern times. Many other legal systems also do not recognize the modern American concept of discovery.

a. At Common Law

At common law a defendant could obtain information about the plaintiff's case through a *bill of particulars.* The defendant could only require the plaintiff to set forth in detail the items of account that the plaintiff was suing on.

b. In Equity

A litigant could file an equitable action asking for a *bill of discovery.* This procedure, however, only allowed a litigant to uncover facts to support the litigant's own case. The bill of discovery could not be used to learn about the evidence and information the opposing parties had for trial.

- **Private investigation.** Prior to the creation of formal discovery rules, litigants could use their own private investigators to learn as much as possible about their own and their opponent's case. Even after the advent of modern discovery, private investigation is still an important part of a lawyer's pretrial investigation and development of the case.

2. Discovery under the Federal Rules of Civil Procedure

In American practice, discovery techniques existed prior to the promulgation of the Federal Rules of Civil Procedure in 1938. The 1938 rules, however, set forth a detailed system for broad discovery of information relating to the litigation.

a. Relationship of Modern Federal Discovery Rules to Modern Pleading

The modern federal discovery rules are a hand-maiden to the liberal pleading philosophy embodied in the 1938 rules (*see* Chapter III, Pleading, *supra*). Because the new Federal Rules permitted notice pleading, there was no expectation that a pleader would know all the facts underlying the claims at the time the person filed the lawsuit. The new federal discovery rules, then, were conceived as the means by which litigants could obtain more information about their own and their opponent's case even after commencement of the action.

b. Impact of the Modern Federal Discovery Rules

i. Local Federal District Court Rules

Although many federal district courts follow the general federal discovery rules, local federal district courts have modified discovery procedures by local rule (**Rule 83**). In addition, almost all federal district courts have modified discovery procedures as a consequence of the reforms mandated by the **1990 Civil Justice Reform Act** (*see* discussion *infra* in Chapter VIII).

ii. State Practice

The modern federal discovery rules provide a model for many state courts. However, some states, such as Arizona, New Jersey, and Texas have been in the vanguard in modifying discovery rules to cope with increasing problems of discovery abuse. In general, these state reforms have required increased mandatory disclosure and have restricted non-disclosure based on various privileges and immunities.

3. Purposes of Discovery

The modern discovery rules greatly expanded the nature and scope of the information that litigants may obtain during an ongoing litigation. The expansive nature of discovery has, in some instances, led to abuse of the discovery system, raising questions relating to harassment and privacy (discussed *infra*). In general modern discovery is intended to serve three purposes:

a. Preservation of Evidence

One of the primary functions of discovery is to preserve relevant evidence that might not be available at trial. *See* **Rule 27** and **Rule 32(a)(4).**

i. The earliest discovery devices in federal court were designed to serve this obvious and necessary purpose.

ii. The classic examples of unavailability are age, death, illness, travel, or imprisonment. A witness who is more than 100 miles from the place of trial also may not have to appear. **Rule 32(a)(4)(B).**

iii. In such instances, the court will accept the person's deposition testimony in lieu of the actual appearance of the witness.

b. Ascertainment of Issues in Controversy

Another purpose of discovery is to ascertain and isolate those issues that are in controversy and disputed. Often pleadings in federal court contain many facts that are not in dispute. If the pleadings have put a claim in issue, it is legitimate to ask whether the pleader contests the facts underlying that issue. If certain facts are not contested, then trial time does not have to be wasted proving these facts. This goes far beyond the function intended by the complaint and answer.

i. Admissions of Facts

The primary discovery device for narrowing contested facts is the "Request for Admissions." This discovery technique requires the pleader to admit or deny factual allegations in the pleadings. *See* **Rule 36.** Any factual matter admitted is not subject to subsequent proof or dispute. Matters that are not admitted may be disputed and must be proven at trial.

ii. Prelude to Summary Judgment

Discovery also serves as a prelude and basis for a summary judgment motion (*see* **Rule 56** discussed in Chapter VIII, *infra*). Information that a litigant obtains during discovery may be used to support a motion to dismiss the action because there is no genuine issue as to a material fact, and the party moving for the summary judgment is entitled to a judgment as a matter of law.

c. Evidence on Issues in Dispute: Prelude to Trial

Discovery also is used to ascertain relevant evidence to disputed factual issues that will be contested at trial.

i. Necessity for Pretrial Formal Discovery Devices

The discovery devices provide a coercive means to obtain information from people who might not otherwise cooperate in supplying needed information. For example, certain witnesses might not want to become involved in a litigation, or to provide documents. The discovery rules enable parties to require that witnesses submit to depositions and provide whatever knowledge or information they have relating to the litigation. Similarly, the discovery devices enable one party to obtain documents from another.

4. Tension in Modern Discovery Practice: Competing Concerns

Modern discovery practice, particularly in federal court, has sometimes been characterized as either a game of "show and tell," or "hide and seek." Both models capture a tension inherent in modern discovery that has inspired an on-going debate about the scope and limits of modern discovery.

a. Broad-Discovery Proponents

Some litigants favor broad discovery based on a model of "show and tell." The underlying rationale is that voluntary disclosure of as much information as possible, without formal request or coercion, supports and accomplishes the goal of **Rule 1** to ensure the *"just, speedy, and inexpensive"* resolution of disputes. These supporters of the liberal discovery provisions believe that eliciting fact information should not be reduced to a game of "hide and seek." A related reason for permitting widespread liberal fact discovery is to *reduce or eliminate surprise* at trial. Attorneys can evaluate the relative strengths or weaknesses of their respective cases and often settle the dispute.

b. Limited-Discovery Proponents

The prime concern of opponents of liberal discovery relates to the sweeping scope of permissible discovery (*see* discussion *infra*). Hence, the concern is that the Federal Rules permit (and encourage) "fishing expeditions" into an opposing party's personal life or corporate affairs. Second, opponents contend that liberal discovery invades privacy rights. Third, opponents argue that liberal discovery costs very little to the party seeking discovery and therefore encourages abusive behavior such as expansive, burdensome, or potentially embarrassing discovery requests. Fourth, opponents contend that liberal discovery encourages some litigants to sit back and do very little, instead living off the "borrowed wits" of their opponents. Fifth, open discovery is antithetical to the adversary process.

B. SCOPE AND DISCRETIONARY LIMITS ON DISCOVERY

1. The Scope of Discovery

The scope of discovery under the Federal Rules and analogous state practice is very broad.

a. General Problem

The purpose of discovery is to permit the litigants to discover as much factual information as possible about both their own claims as well as the opposing party's defenses. In this sense, discovery enhances the "truth-seeking" function of the judicial process. However, the concept of liberal discovery is in tension with the idea that each litigant should prepare his or her own case, and not sit back and allow the opponent to do all the work.

b. Standard

The standard for discovery under **Rule 26(b)(1)** has five parts:

i. "Any Non-Privileged Matter"

This is the broadest formulation concerning the scope of permissible discovery. Discovery extends both to:

- Information relating to one's own case, and

- Information relating to the opposing party's case.

- **Example.** Litigants may depose the adversary's witnesses for possible impeachment at trial.

ii. "Relevant to the Claim or Defense of Any Party"

Courts interpret relevance broadly

- **Example.** A lawyer may obtain the names of eyewitnesses to an accident. A lawyer also may obtain the names of people who talked to or saw those witnesses.

iii. "Whether Admissible (or Not) at Trial"

Lawyers may obtain discovery of information that might not be admissible at trial. At a deposition, a lawyer may ask questions that might be objectionable if asked at trial.

- **Example.** A lawyer may request, in interrogatories, whether the defendant product manufacturer has made any subsequent changes in a product after the accident giving rise to litigation. Although evidence of such subsequent changes would not be admissible at trial, it is permissible to request this information during discovery because it "may lead to the discovery of admissible evidence." **Lindberger v. General Motors Corp.,** 56 F.R.D. 433 (W.D. Wisc. 1972).

- **Example: hearsay.** A lawyer may obtain hearsay statements (that would not be admissible at trial) as long as those statements may supply information to the lawyer about the case, or help the lawyer in ascertaining other information about the case. The attorney should object to the hearsay for the record at trial, but still allow the witness to answer.

- **Insurance coverage.** Parties are required to furnish, without awaiting a discovery request, copies of any insurance agreements that exist to satisfy all or part of a judgment. **Rule 23(a)(1)(A)(iv).** Normally this would not lead to the discovery of admissible evidence, but in contemporary litigation practice the disclosure of insurance coverage supports the policy favoring settlement (parties are more likely to settle if they have insurance coverage of the claims).

iv. "Reasonably Calculated to Lead to the Discovery of Admissible Evidence"

Discovery must be justified, in some way, as assisting the litigant in finding information that will be admissible at trial. This standard is very broadly construed and most lawyers are able to justify a discovery request as somehow "reasonably calculated" to lead to admissible evidence. However, this standard may limit some discovery requests.

- **Example: information about trial tactics.** Lawyers cannot probe into the trial strategy or tactics of the opposing party. Not only is this information not reasonably calculated to lead to admissible evidence, but it also is non-discoverable as attorney work product (*see* discussion below).

- **Example: defendant's assets.** Lawyers are restrained from obtaining general discovery of a defendant's assets if the party's finances are not in issue. This information is not relevant and entails a serious invasion of privacy. However, such information is discoverable if relevant to the claim or remedy, such as punitive damages.

v. "Not Privileged"

Litigants may liberally discover a wide range of information, but that information cannot be covered by a privilege or immunity (*see* discussion *infra*).

2. Timing and Sequence of Discovery

a. Discovery Prior to the Commencement of an Action

The Federal Rules and state practice provide for very limited discovery prior to the formal commencement of an action. (*see* Chapter IV, *supra,* on Commencement of an Action).

i. Depositions before Action: Rule 27(a)

Before filing a complaint, a person who intends to file a lawsuit may *"perpetuate testimony"* about any cognizable matter, by taking that party's deposition. The person seeking to take this deposition must file a verified petition in a district court where the deponent resides, stating that the person intends to file an action but is presently unable to do so (without violating **Rule 11**). The petition also has to state the subject matter of the forthcoming litigation, the testimony to be elicited, and the reasons for wishing to perpetuate that testimony.

- **Preservation of testimony.** Pre-commencement depositions are desirable and make sense when a witness may not be available due to illness or death.

ii. Fact Elicitation before Filing

Courts disagree whether litigants may use discovery before filing a lawsuit merely in order to discover facts. Courts generally agree that discovery may not be used to learn if one has a case at all.

- **Assistance in drafting complaint.** Some states statutorily permit litigants to discover facts to assist in drafting a complaint.

b. Initial Discovery Scheduling and Conferences: Rules 26(d), (f) and 16(c)

i. General Prohibition

Parties generally may not seek discovery from any source before they have met and conferred as required by **Rule 26(f)** (*see* discussion *infra*).

ii. Local Rules Exemption (Rule 83)

Rules 26(d), (f) and **Rule 16(c)** prescribe when parties must meet, discuss, and plan discovery. Federal district courts, however, may exempt themselves from this Federal Rule and specify any other discovery timing rule for the district.

iii. Discovery Meeting and Agreement

Attorneys of record and all unrepresented parties must meet at least 21 days prior to a scheduling conference with a federal district judge magistrate. **Rule 26(f).** At this meeting, the parties must, *in good faith:*

- Discuss their claims and defenses and possible settlement;

- Arrange for informal exchange of the information required under **Rule 26(a)(1)** (*see infra*);

- Discuss any issues about claims of privilege or work product immunity;

- Discuss any issues relating to discovery and disclosure of electronically-stored information; and

- Develop a proposed formal discovery plan.

Within 14 days after this meeting, the parties must submit to the court a written report of the meeting's results.

iv. Court-Mandated Scheduling Order: Rule 16(c)

When the federal court receives the parties' **Rule 26(f)** written report, the court will confer with the attorneys by phone, mail, or in person and issue a scheduling order.

(a) **Timing of scheduling order.** The court must issue a scheduling order:

- "as soon as practicable," or

- within 90 days of the defendant's appearance (meaning the filing of a responsive motion, pleading, or answer), or

- within 120 days after the plaintiff serves the complaint on the defendant.

(b) Modifications of discovery schedule; Rule 16(b)(4). A discovery schedule may be modified only for good cause and with the judge's consent.

(c) Contents of the discovery order. Rule 16(b)(3). The scheduling order will limit the time for discovery; provide for disclosure or discovery of electronically-stored information; agreements or privilege; and set dates for pretrial conferences and trial.

c. Mandatory Informal Exchange of Information: Rule 26(a)(1)

The centerpiece of the 1993 amendment of the Federal Rules was the addition of the new **Rule 26(a)(1),** mandating early informal exchange of information. In 2000, **Rule 26(a)(1)** was again amended to establish a nationally uniform practice with regard to initial disclosures required in federal actions.

i. Background to the 1993 Rule Revision

The addition of **Rule 26(a)(1)** to the federal discovery provisions was part of a civil justice reform initiative in state and federal courts. The Federal Rule was patterned after a similar rule in Arizona and a few federal district courts (Southern District of Florida and the Central District of California). Congress also recommended that local district courts adopt informal discovery exchanges as part of the **Civil Justice Reform Act of 1990.**

(a) Discovery abuse. The central purpose of the mandatory informal disdovery rule is to curtail various discovery abuses by requiring litigants to voluntarily turn over routine information to the opposing side without having to await formal and expensive discovery requests. The informal discovery provisions are to assist courts in carrying out the mandate of **Rule 1,** to ensure the *just, speedy, and inexpensive* resolution of disputes.

(b) Controversy over informal discovery procedure. Interest groups hotly debated and resisted the proposed amendment to require mandatory early exchange of information. Initially, plaintiffs' lawyers supported and defense counsel opposed the proposal, because the plaintiffs' bar alleged that defense lawyers often use the discovery process to "wear down" their opponents. By 1993, however, almost all segments of the practicing bar opposed the reform. During the period when the Advisory Committee on Civil Rules was considering the draft proposal, Congress independently attempted to pass legislation that did not include a mandatory disclosure provision. The Supreme Court approved **Rule 26(a)(1)** in 1993, but Justices Scalia, Thomas, and Souter dissented from this amendment. The congressional discovery legislation did not pass through both legislative chambers.

ii.   Required Disclosures

Without awaiting a discovery request parties must now disclose:

(1)   Names, addresses, and telephone numbers of individuals likely to have discoverable information that the disclosing party may use to support its claims or defenses, unless solely for impeachment, identifying the subjects of the information;

(2)   Descriptions and locations of documents, data compilations, and tangible things in the possession, custody or control of a party that the disclosing party may use to support its claims or defenses, unless solely for impeachment;

(3)   A computation of damages the disclosing party claims, as well as documents or other evidence supporting the calculation of those damages (and including materials bearing on the nature and extent of injuries); and

- **Exception for privileged materials.** Parties need not disclose any materials relating to damages that are privileged or immunized.

(4)   Any insurance agreement which may satisfy or indemnify all or part of a judgment.

- **Exemptions from initial disclosure.** The 2000 amendment to **Rule 26(a)(1)** also included, for the first time, a list of materials and information that are exempted from the initial disclosure requirement.

iii. Timing of Informal Information Exchange

Parties are required to exchange **Rule 26(a)(1)** information at or within 14 days after they meet to discuss the litigation required in **Rule 26(f)** (*see supra*). **Rule 26(f)** requires the attorneys to meet at least 21 days before the **Rule 16** scheduling conference, and to submit a written report no later than 14 days after their meeting. The **Rule 16** scheduling conference, at the latest, will occur either 90 or 120 days after the defendant makes an appearance or the plaintiff serves the complaint.

- The practical implication of these timing rules is that the parties will likely begin information exchange prior to the **Rule 16** scheduling conference, although the court may modify the deadline for **Rule 26(a)(1)** mandatory disclosure in its scheduling order.

iv. No Excuses

Parties must make the required disclosure of the information listed in **Rule 26(a)(1)** *"based on the information then reasonably available to it."* A party is not excused from making the required disclosures because:

- the party has not completed its investigation, or

- the party challenges the sufficiency of the opposing party's disclosures, or

- another party has not made its disclosures.

d. Expert Witnesses: Rule 26(a)(2)

The amended discovery rules require parties to disclose the identity of any expert witness to be used at trial to present evidence under **Federal Rules of Evidence 702, 703,** or **705.**

i. Expert Witness Report and Opinions

Parties must supply expert witness reports of retained, testifying expert witnesses. The report must state the expert's opinions, the basis for those opinions, exhibits, the expert's qualifications, publications, and other cases in which the expert has testified within four years.

ii. Timing of Expert Witness Disclosure

Expert witness disclosure may be made at various times:

- At times or in sequences as directed by the court;

- by party stipulation;

- at least 90 days before trial or the date the case is to be ready for trial.

iii. Rebuttal Expert Witness Testimony

If a party wishes to retain a rebuttal expert witness, then disclosure of the rebuttal expert witness must occur within 30 days after the disclosure that prompted the need for rebuttal testimony.

- **Example.** During a deposition an expert witness testifies that the only method consistent with due process to litigate personal injury asbestos claims is through individual trials. Opposing counsel now desires to call a rebuttal expert witness to testify that it is consistent with due process to adjudicate such claims in an aggregate fashion. The opponents have 30 days to meet the disclosure requirements for the newly-retained rebuttal expert witness.

e. Pretrial Disclosures: Rule 26(a)(3)

Prior to trial, in addition to early disclosure and expert witness information, parties also must disclose certain evidentiary material that will be used for other than impeachment purposes.

i. Nature of the Information That Must Be Disclosed

- Names, addresses, and phone numbers of witnesses who will be called to testify at trial, and those who may be called if the need arises;

- Designation of witnesses whose testimony will be furnished by deposition, including a transcript of portions of the deposition;

- Designation of documents, exhibits, and summaries of evidence which the party will offer, or may offer if the need arises.

ii. Timing of Disclosures

Final pretrial disclosures must be made within 30 days of trial.

iii. Objections

Parties may, within 14 days of the final pretrial disclosures, object to the designation of portions of deposition testimony, or to the admissibility of documents or exhibits.

(a) **Waiver of objections.** Parties who do not object prior to trial waive their objections unless the court excuses the failure *for good cause.*

f. Discovery in Other Special Circumstances

i. Class Certification

Some federal courts may order discovery limited to ascertainment of facts in support of class certification.

ii. Summary Judgment

Courts may order additional discovery in support of a summary judgment motion, particularly after a responding party has satisfied its burden of production and the burden of proof shifts to the moving party (*see* Chapter XIII on summary judgment, *infra*). **Rule 56(e)(1).**

3. Discretionary Limits on Scope of Discovery in Adversary System

There are three primary ways of protecting information from disclosure during discovery: through invocation of a valid privilege, immunity, or protective order.

a. Means of Protecting Information from Disclosure

The concept of "privileged" information, in discovery, also encompasses the immunity that attaches to information prepared by lawyers and their associates in anticipation of litigation. This second form of protection is called the *attorney work product immunity.* While attorney-client privilege and attorney work product immunity have many similarities, they are conceptually different and apply differently (*see* comparative discussion *infra*). The third discretionary method of protecting information from disclosure is through a court-mandated "protective order" (*see* discussion *infra*).

b. Privileges in General

Federal Rule 26(b)(1) permits discovery of matter that is "not privileged." In general, the same rules of privilege that apply at trial also apply during discovery, and the "reasonably calculated to lead to discovery of admissible evidence" standard does not circumvent privilege. When a person invokes a validly held privilege, that person does not have to disclose the requested information; the privilege usually attaches to a communication.

i. Privileges at Common Law

The common law has long recognized various testimonial privileges, including communications between attorney and client, doctor and patient, clergy and congregant, and husband and wife. State law determines the existence and scope of these privileges. Some states have limited spousal immunity. In addition, almost no jurisdiction recognizes a privilege for reporter and source, although federal legislation would seek to create such a reportorial privilege.

(a) Purpose of the privileges. Testimonial privileges protect the privacy and secrecy of persons in certain relationships. Public policy encourages confidence in these special relationships as against the competing value in information for litigation purposes.

ii. Testimonial Privileges

Testimonial privileges include the privilege against self-incrimination, testifying against a spouse, and revealing the identity of confidential police informants. These privileges protect the individuals involved from harm, as against the possible benefit from disclosure. Protection of informants assists police in obtaining information. In recent years, spousal immunity and protection of informants has eroded in certain circumstances.

c. Attorney-Client Privilege

All American state and federal courts recognize attorney-client privilege. The attorney-client privilege is the oldest common law principle protecting confidential communications.

i. Attorney-Client Privilege in Federal Court: Source of Authority

In purely federal claims, attorney-client privilege is a matter of federal law. In federal diversity cases, attorney-client privilege is governed by state common law principles. *See* **Federal Rule of Evidence 501** ("the privilege of a witness . . . shall be governed by the principles of the common law as they may be interpreted by the courts of the United States").

ii. Rationale or Purpose of the Attorney-Client Privilege

The purpose of the attorney-client privilege is to encourage the full and frank communication between the attorney and client. "The privilege recognizes that sound legal advice or advocacy serves public ends and that such advice or advocacy depends upon the lawyer's being fully informed by the client." **Upjohn v. United States,** 449 U.S. 383 (1981).

iii. Scope of the Attorney-Client Privilege and Standards for Invoking the Privilege

If the attorney-client privilege is validly invoked, it attaches to all communications between the client and the client's attorney.

- the person holding the privilege must be a client;

- the person to whom the communication was made must be:

  — a bar member, or a bar member's subordinate (e.g., secretary, paralegal, investigator, etc.), and,

  — acting as a lawyer (or lawyer's agent) in connection with the communication;

- the attorney must have received the communication:

  — from the client,

  — not in the presence of strangers or third parties,

  — for the purpose of securing either a legal opinion, legal services, or legal assistance in some proceeding, and

  — not for the purpose of committing a crime, fraud, or tort;

  — nor can privilege be created by giving an attorney an otherwise discoverable document (or keeping documents hidden by the attorney).

- the client has not in some manner waived the privilege (*see* discussion below).

iv. How Invoked; Burdens of Proof

The person claiming the attorney-client privilege must invoke it at the time of the **Rule 26(f)** and **Rule 16** conferences, or in response to a discovery request. The party invoking the privilege carries the burden of establishing the existence of the privilege.

(a) **1993 amendment.** The 1993 amendments to the federal discovery provisions added a specific provision requiring parties to expressly claim the privilege in response to a discovery request. **Rule 26(b)(5).** In addition, the party also must describe the nature of the documents, communications, or things that are not produced in a manner that will enable other parties to assess the applicability of the privilege, without revealing information that is itself privileged.

(b) **Purpose of 1993 amendment.** When a party invokes a privilege and withholds documents, the party seeking discovery frequently lacks the basis to refute the privilege. The 1993 amendment attempts to strike a balance between the privilege holder's right to protect truly privileged information and the requesting party's access to sufficient information to refute the existence of the privilege.

v. Possessor of the Privilege

The client possesses the privilege and must invoke it. As a practical matter, the attorney invokes the privilege on the client's behalf.

(a) **Corporations and attorney-client privilege.** Attorney-client privilege extends to all corporate employees who seek or secure legal advice from counsel. **Upjohn Co. v. United States,** 449 U.S. 383 (1981). The protection is not limited to a "control group" or upper-echelon management, but applies as well to middle-level and lower-level employees. *Id.*

vi. Nature of the Privilege

Attorney-client privilege is *absolute,* except for limited qualifications, waivers, and exceptions indicated below. If the privilege exists, it bars disclosure of the protected information. It is not a qualified privilege, and cannot be overcome on a showing of need for the information by the party requesting disclosure (compare work product doctrine, which is a *qualified immunity*).

vii. Qualifications, Waivers, and Exceptions

Attorney-client privilege is subject to certain qualifications, exceptions, and waivers. The following information is not protected by attorney-client privilege:

(a) **Facts.** The attorney-client privilege does not protect factual information, which is always discoverable.

(b) **Consent.** A client may consent to disclosure of information that otherwise might be protected by the attorney-client privilege.

(c) **Disclosure.** Similar to consent, a client voluntarily may disclose otherwise privileged information. Disclosure is a form of both waiver and consent.

(d) **Voluntary disclosure.** A party may voluntarily disclose information if it is communicated in the presence of third persons. Disclosure to non-parties effectively destroys the privilege.

(e) **Involuntary or inadvertent disclosure.** Sometimes in litigation a party may inadvertently disclose privileged information, for example in response to a massive document production request. The burden is on the producing party to review documents prior to disclosure, especially to ascertain any material that might be privileged or immunized. Many courts are unsympathetic to inadvertent disclosure of protected materials, on the theory that it is impossible to put the genie back in the bottle once it has escaped. Other courts permit retrieval of the privileged information.

(f) **Partial waivers through disclosure.** Courts disfavor partial waivers once information has been disclosed. A party may be forced to disclose all information relating to a matter when partial disclosure occurs. *See* **Duplan Corp. v. Deering Milliken, Inc.,** 397 F.Supp. 1146 (D.S.C. 1974).

(g) **Crime, fraud, or tort.** The attorney-client privilege does not protect an ongoing or future crime, fraud, or tort. A client who proposes an ongoing or future crime to the attorney may not subsequently use the privilege to prevent disclosure of the crime, fraud, or tort. The attorney may be under a professional duty to disclose the crime, fraud, or tort.

- *This rule does not apply to past crimes, fraud, or tortious conduct.* In such circumstances the lawyer is under an affirmative professional duty not to disclose the client's revelation of a past crime, fraud, or tort.

(h) Waiver. A client may be informed of the existence of the privilege, but agree to waive it. Waiver is a form of consent.

d. Attorney Work Product Doctrine

Unlike attorney-client privilege, which has a long heritage at common law, attorney work product immunity is a relatively recent twentieth-century American invention in federal practice. Work product immunity is primarily a protection of the lawyer, rather than the client. Although established by doctrine and rule, there is no reason why work product immunity could not be abolished altogether, as at least one academic commentator has suggested.

i. Attorney Work Product Doctrine in Federal Court: Sources of Authority

The two major authoritative sources for work product doctrine in federal court are the Supreme Court's 1947 decision in **Hickman v. Taylor,** 329 U.S. 495 (1947) and the Advisory Committee's 1970 codification of the doctrine in **Rule 26(b)(3)** ("Trial Preparation: Materials").

■ EXAMPLES AND ANALYSIS

Leading case authority: Hickman v. Taylor, 329 U.S. 495 (1947). A tugboat sank in the Delaware River, and five crew members drowned. The tugboat's owner retained a law firm to defend against litigation. A lawyer took statements from survivors and other persons believed to have information relating to the accident. Subsequently, one of the decedent's estates brought a Jones Act federal lawsuit and filed interrogatories seeking these statements. In addition to the written statements, the interrogatories also requested the defense lawyers to supply detailed reports of oral statements made to the lawyer. The lawyers refused, claiming that the material was privileged matter obtained in preparation for the litigation.

Improper discovery method. The Supreme Court first noted that use of interrogatories to obtain statements was not the proper method to secure documentary information, which must be requested through **Rule 34.** The Court also noted that the statements, memoranda, and attorney's mental impressions were not protected by attorney-client privilege.

Holding. The Court held, however, that the requested materials were protected attorney work product. These materials were prepared by the lawyer in anticipation of litigation, and disclosure would amount to an unwarranted intrusion into the attorney's files and mental impressions. Absent any showing of necessity, hardship, or undue prejudice, the opposing counsel was not entitled to secure these materials.

Limitations. The Court indicated that non-privileged facts were not protected by the work product doctrine and are subject to discovery.

Qualified immunity for ordinary work product. The burden rests on the party seeking work product to justify the invasion of the opposing lawyer's privacy. The party seeking disclosure must show necessity for production of the materials, or that the failure to obtain the materials would cause undue prejudice, hardship, or injustice.

---

ii. **Rule 26(b)(3)**

In 1970, the Advisory Committee on Civil Rules partially codified the principles of **Hickman v. Taylor in Rule 26(b)(3).** The federal work product rule distinguishes between discovery of "ordinary" work product and "opinion" work product.

(a) **Ordinary work product. Rule 26(b)(3)** permits discovery of:

- Documents and tangible things

- Prepared in anticipation of litigation or for trial;

- By or for another party, or,

- By or for that other party's representative (including the other party's attorney, surety, consultant, indemnitor, insurer, or agent).

- *See* discussion of these standards, *infra.*

(b) Ordinary work product: Showing necessary. Ordinary work product is a qualified immunity, meaning that a party seeking discovery may overcome the immunity upon a proper showing of need for the materials. The rule requires a showing that:

- The party seeking discovery has a substantial need of the materials in preparation of the party's case, and

- The party is unable without undue hardship to obtain the substantial equivalent of the materials by other means.

- The party seeking discovery of ordinary work product must make a reasonable effort to obtain the substantial equivalent of the materials prior to asking the court to override the immunity (*see* discussion *infra*). This rule is justified on the ground that courts do not wish to reward "lazy attorneys" who would rely on their opponent's work product or investigation.

(c) Opinion work product. Opinion work product consists of an attorney's "mental impressions, conclusions, opinions, or legal theories." The protection extends to the opinion work product of other party representatives. **Rule 26(b)(3)(B)** requires courts to protect opinion work product from disclosure. Required disclosure of opinion work product would be too much of an intrusion on the adversary process.

- **Scope of protection for opinion work product:** In general, the majority of federal courts hold that opinion work product is absolutely protected from disclosure and may not be compelled, even upon a showing of substantial need. *See, e.g.,* **Duplan Corp. v. Moulinage et Retorderie de Chavanoz,** 509 F.2d 730 (4th Cir. 1974), *cert. denied,* 420 U.S. 997 (1975). A minority of federal courts engage in a balancing test to determine whether even opinion work product may be ordered to be disclosed. *See, e.g.,* **Xerox Corp. v. International Business Machs. Corp.,** 64 F.R.D. 367 (S.D.N.Y. 1974) (ordering production of lawyer's notes of interviews with defendant's employees who could not recall crucial information at depositions; parties cannot conceal information by imparting it to a lawyer and then hiding behind work product immunity).

— **Compare Rules 33(a)(2) and 36(a)(1)(A)** which permit interrogatories and requests for admission involving opinions or contentions that relate to fact or the application of law to fact.

- **Party statements.** A party's own statement is not protected work product. Thus, a party is entitled to obtain his or her own statement previously given. A person who is not a party also may obtain their own statement, without having to make a showing of need. If the request is refused, the person may seek a court order and receive expenses entailed in making the motion. *See* **Rule 26(b)(3)(C), Rule 37(a)(5).**

iii. *Hickman* and Rule 23(b)(3) Compared

The federal work product rule is considered to be a partial codification of the Supreme Court's holding in *Hickman.* For example, the Federal Rule covers only "documents and tangible things," but *Hickman* extends work product protection to intangible work product, such as oral statements. Federal courts typically refer to both the Supreme Court's holding in *Hickman* and **Rule 23(b)(3)** as authoritative sources for the work product doctrine.

iv. Rationale or Purpose of the Attorney Work Product Immunity

The attorney work product immunity is based on a number of supporting rationales:

(a) **"Zone of privacy."** It is essential that lawyers be able to perform their duties "with a certain degree of privacy, free from the unnecessary intrusion by opposing parties and their counsel." **Hickman v. Taylor,** *supra.*

(b) **Potential for sharp practices.** In absence of work product immunity, lawyers fearing disclosure might cease certain practices, such as note-taking. "An attorney's thoughts, heretofore inviolate, would not be his own. Inefficiency, unfairness and sharp practices would inevitably develop" in giving legal advice and preparing cases for trial. **Hickman v. Taylor,** *supra.*

(c) **Demoralization of the profession.** Forcing a lawyer to supply detailed accounts of oral statements gives rise to the dangers of inaccuracy and untrustworthiness. In extreme instances, a lawyer might be called to testify to his knowledge of these statements at trial, which information could then be used for impeachment purposes. **Hickman v. Taylor,** *supra.* This possibility places the lawyer in an untenable position. A lawyer cannot serve as a witness in the client's case, and in such circumstances would have to be disqualified.

(d) "Borrowed wits." The adversary system relies on each lawyer to prepare his or her own case and not to exploit the opposing counsel's efforts to prepare for litigation. Work product immunity, therefore, prevents one lawyer from living off the "borrowed wits" of opposing counsel. **Hickman v. Taylor,** *supra.*

v. How Invoked; Burdens of Proof

The person claiming attorney work product must invoke it in response to a discovery request, and carries the burden of establishing the existence of the immunity. **Rule 26(b)(5)** also applies to work product immunity.

(a) 1993 amendment. The 1993 amendments to the federal discovery provisions added a specific provision requiring parties to expressly claim the immunity in response to a discovery request. **Rule 26(b)(5).** In addition, the party also must:

- describe the nature of the documents, communications, or things that are not produced in a manner that will enable other parties to assess the applicability of the immunity, without revealing information that is itself immunized.

(b) Overcoming the immunity. Once the party invoking the immunity states the grounds for the immunity's existence, the party seeking disclosure carries the burden of overcoming the immunity by showing substantial need for the requested materials and an inability to obtain a substantial equivalent by other means.

(c) "Anticipation of litigation" standard. Federal courts variously construe what constitutes "anticipation of litigation." In its broadest sense, almost everything a lawyer does is in anticipation of litigation. Some courts interpret this standard broadly as meaning "with an eye towards litigation," or "in contemplation of litigation." Other courts construe this standard more narrowly:

- **Investigations prior to initiation of litigation: The ordinary course of business exception.** If documents or things are normally prepared in the "ordinary course of business," and not specifically for litigation, these materials generally will not be protected by work product immunity. *See* **Thomas Organ Co. v. Jadranska Slobodna Plovidba,** 54 F.R.D. 367 (N.D. Ill. 1972) (insurance company's investigative reports of loss, recorded months before hiring lawyer and institution of litigation, not protected work product). *But cf.* **Almaguer v. Chicago, R.I. & P.R. Co.,** 55 F.R.D. 147 (D. Neb. 1972) (claims agent's report and statement of injured railroad worker taken two months before the worker retained a lawyer was protected work product; there was a reasonable assumption of the expectation of litigation.)

vi. Possessor of the Immunity

Attorney work product immunity primarily exists to protect the lawyer's trial preparation materials and thought processes, and thus chiefly is the lawyer's immunity. **Rule 26(b)(3)** extends the protection to any materials prepared by or for the party's representatives, including all agents working for the lawyer or the client, such as paralegals, investigators, and the like. Although attorneys usually invoke the protection, the client also may invoke the work product immunity if the lawyer does not wish to seek this protection.

vii. Qualifications, Waivers, and Exceptions

Attorney work product immunity is subject to the same qualifications, waivers, and exceptions as attorney-client privilege (*see* discussion in sections relating to attorney-client privilege, *supra*). In addition to this list of exceptions, work product immunity also *excludes party statements from work product protection* (*see* discussion *supra*).

e. Protective Orders: Rule 26(c)

Although the Federal Rules enable liberal discovery, the manner and scope of discovery may be tailored to protect against embarrassment, harassment, or release of certain proprietary information (such as trade secrets). Parties may shield such information through a "protective order."

i.   Stipulated Agreements

Parties may negotiate protective orders or confidentiality agreements, and may *stipulate* to the terms of such agreements. If the parties cannot agree, then a person seeking to shield information may file a motion for a protective order (*see* discussion *infra*).

ii.   Umbrella Protective Orders

Lawyers in complex litigation sometimes agree to an "umbrella" protective order at the outset of the litigation, that covers entire categories of materials that the producing party designates as confidential. This arrangement avoids the necessity of having a court determine whether to issue a protective order on a document by document basis. *See, e.g.,* **Zenith Radio Corp. v. Matsushita Elec. Indus. Co.,** 529 F.Supp. 866 (E.D. Pa. 1981).

iii.   Court-Mandated Protective Orders: Who May Seek

A party or any person from whom discovery is sought may seek a protective order to shield information an opposing party seeks through a discovery request.

(a)   Attorney conference. Prior to seeking a protective order, the attorneys must confer (or attempt to confer) to resolve the dispute relating to disclosure of the requested material. If the lawyers are unable to agree, then the party seeking a protective order must furnish the court with a certificate that the lawyers have conferred in good faith and attempted to resolve the discovery dispute. **Rule 26(c)(1).**

(b)   Third-party intervenors. Courts are split concerning whether third-party intervenors have *standing* to intervene for the purpose of obtaining access to discovery information of parties to an existing litigation. *Compare* **Public Citizen v. Liggett Group, Inc.,** 858 F.2d 775 (1st Cir. 1988) (upholding third-party intervention) *with* **Oklahoma Hospital Assn. v. Oklahoma Publishing Co.,** 748 F.2d 1421 (10th Cir. 1984), *cert. denied,* 473 U.S. 905 (1985) (third-party intervenor lacked standing to attack protective order).

iv. Motion for Protective Order: Where Made

A party who seeks a protective order may do so either in the court in which the action is pending, or if the protective order seeks to shield possible deposition testimony, in the district where a deposition is to be taken. **Rule 26(c).**

v. Standards

In its *discretion,* a court may issue an order *"to protect a party or person from annoyance, embarrassment, oppression, or undue burden or expense."* **Rule 26(c)(1).**

(a) **"For good cause shown."** The party or person seeking the protective order must demonstrate "good cause" for issuance of the order. Courts generally have held that the party seeking the order must demonstrate that disclosure "will work a clearly defined and very serious injury." **Citicorp v. Interbank Card Assn.,** 478 F.Supp. 756 (S.D.N.Y. 1979). The movant may not meet this requirement with conclusory statements, but must make a showing of specific and particular facts. **General Dynamics Corp. v. Selb Mfg. Co.,** 481 F.2d 1204 (8th Cir. 1973).

(b) **Balancing of hardships.** Courts typically will compare the hardship to the party against whom discovery is sought, if discovery is allowed, with the hardship to the party seeking discovery if discovery is denied. *See* **Marrese v. American Academy of Orthopaedic Surgeons,** 726 F.2d 1150, *revd. on other grounds,* 470 U.S. 373 (1985).

- **Example.** Discovery was denied where the plaintiff in a medical malpractice action involving abortion sought to discover the names of women who previously had abortions at the defendant's hospital. The stated purpose was to gather impeachment testimony. The court concluded that the possible injurious consequences of allowing revelation of other women's names outweighed the plaintiff's need for possible impeachment testimony. **Williams v. Thomas Jefferson Univ.,** 343 F.Supp. 1131 (E.D. Pa. 1972).

- **Example.** Similarly, state courts have denied discovery of blood donors' names to persons claiming to have received HIV-infected blood during blood transfusions. *See* **Rasmus-**

sen v. South Florida Blood Service, Inc., 500 So.2d 533 (Fla. 1987) and Snyder v. Mekhjian, 125 N.J. 328, 593 A.2d 318 (1991).

vi. *In Camera* Inspection

When a party seeks a protective order relating to information contained in documents, courts frequently examine the documents in an *in camera ex parte* proceeding. This means a judge reviews the materials in chambers, without the presence of the party seeking discovery. *See, e.g.,* Marrese v. American Academy of Orthopaedic Surgeons, *supra.*

(a) Purpose of *in camera* inspection. The purpose of the *in camera* inspection is to permit a neutral judge to assess whether the requested material ought to be shielded, disclosed, or partially protected through such techniques as redaction (editing of protected materials).

vii. Scope of the Protective Order

A judge has wide latitude in fashioning a protective order. In most instances, the judge will not totally deny discovery. Instead, the judge will structure a protective order to permit access to as much information as the requesting party needs, without invading the privacy of the objecting party. *See* Marrese v. American Academy of Orthopaedic Surgeons, *supra;* Guerra v. Board of Trustees of California State Universities & Colleges, 567 F.2d 352 (9th Cir. 1977). The judge may order that:

- the person need not make disclosure;

- disclosure be made on certain terms and conditions, including a designation of time and place;

- discovery be made by some other method than the one requested;

- the scope of discovery be limited, or certain matters not asked;

- discovery be conducted with no one else present except persons the court designates;

- sealed depositions be opened only by court order;

- that trade secrets of confidential research not be revealed, or be revealed only in a designated way;

- parties simultaneously file specified documents or information in sealed envelopes to be opened as the court directs.

viii. Denial of Protective Orders: Expenses

If a court denies a motion for a protective order, the court may order discovery. The court also may award expenses incurred in relation to the motion. **Rule 37(a)(5); Rule 26(c)(3).**

ix. Modification of Protective Orders

Whether to lift or modify a protective order is committed to the sound discretion of the court. **Krause v. Rhodes,** 671 F.2d 212 (6th Cir.), *cert denied,* 459 U.S. 823 (1982). Most courts generally will not modify a protective order once granted. A party seeking to modify a protective order must show that the protective order was improvidently granted or must demonstrate some extraordinary compelling need for disclosure of the information. **Palmieri v. New York,** 779 F.2d 861 (2d Cir. 1985).

x. Duration of Protective Orders; Public Purpose Exception

Lawyers may stipulate that material covered by a protective order remains shielded even after a litigation is concluded. Courts disagree, however, whether a judge may rescind a protective order and unseal protected documents if the judge concludes that the underlying litigation was imbued with a public purpose, and disclosure of documents or information would prevent future harm. *See, e.g.,* **In re Agent Orange Prod. Liab. Litig.,** 821 F.2d 139 (2d Cir. 1987) (upholding order by Judge Weinstein unsealing materials produced during Agent Orange litigation and protected by settlement agreement); *cf.* **Mirak v. McGhan Medical Corp.,** 142 F.R.D. 34 (D. Mass. 1992) (denying intervenor's motion to vacate protective order concerning confidential documents in the Silicone Breast Implant litigation).

- **Proposed change to Rule 26(c).** During the early 1990s the Advisory Committee on Civil Rules endorsed a proposal to codify a "public purpose" exception to the protective order provision. This proposed amendment has not yet been promulgated through the rulemaking process.

xi. First Amendment Concerns

There is no First Amendment right to obtain or disseminate information obtained through discovery. *See* **Seattle Times Co. v. Rhinehart,** 467 U.S. 20 (1984) (upholding as constitutional a protective order prohibiting a newspaper from publishing donor's list of a religious foundation).

4. Formal Discovery Devices: 1993 Amendments

The 1993 amendments to the discovery provisions added a number of provisions permitting federal judges greater latitude in managing formal discovery and controlling potential and actual discovery abuse.

a. Timing and Sequencing: Rules 26(d) and (f)

Parties may not seek to conduct formal discovery until they have met as soon as practicable to discuss and plan discovery. After the initial discovery conference, parties may use formal discovery methods in any sequence. The fact that one person is conducting discovery shall not operate to delay another party's discovery. These requirements may be modified either by local rule or by court order.

b. Limits on Formal Discovery: Rule 26(b)(2) (1993 Amendment to Curb Discovery Abuse)

Federal judges, either on their own initiative or on a motion by a party, may limit the frequency or extent of discovery methods if the court determines that:

i.   the discovery sought is unreasonably cumulative or duplicative, or it is obtainable from some other source that is more convenient, less burdensome, or less expensive;

ii. the party seeking discovery has had ample opportunity by discovery in the action to obtain the information sought;

iii. the burden or expense of the proposed discovery outweighs its likely benefit, taking into account the needs of the case, the amount in controversy, the parties' resources, the importance of the issues at stake in the litigation, and the importance of the proposed discovery in resolving the issues.

- **Discovery of electronically stored information.** Parties need not provide discovery of electronically stored information from sources that the parties identify as not reasonably accessible because of undue burden or expense.

c. Interrogatories: Rule 33

Interrogatories are a series of questions directed at the opposing party. Interrogatories typically are one of the first methods of formal discovery, often used to obtain leads to other information helpful in depositions or requests for documents.

i. Advantages

Interrogatories are especially useful because they are a relatively inexpensive means of obtaining information, and require the responding party to investigate available information from employees and agents.

ii. Disadvantage

The major disadvantage of interrogatories is that the party responses are not spontaneous, but typically are formulated with careful attorney supervision.

iii. Procedure

No court order is required to request or obtain interrogatories; interrogatories typically are served by mail.

(a) **Parties.** Interrogatories may only be served on parties; they may not be sent to any person who might have information about the litigation. Although the party must answer and sign the interrogatories, the party's lawyer typically assists and oversees the formal party responses. An attorney who objects must sign the objections.

- Non-parties are not usually represented by counsel and it would be unfair to burden such persons with questions that might inadvertently produce misleading responses.

(b) **Artificial persons; government entities.** Corporations, partnerships, associations, and government agencies may respond to interrogatories through an officer or agent. **Rule 33(b)(1)(B)**.

iv. Responses

A party must respond within 30 days after service of the interrogatories. The court may direct a longer or shorter period, or the parties agree in writing to modify this period. **Rule 33(b)(2).** The responding party is required to answer each interrogatory separately and fully in writing, under oath. The person answering the interrogatories must sign them. **Rule 33(b)(3), (5).**

(a) **Basis for responses: personal knowledge.** A party must respond to interrogatories based on personal knowledge, but also information that can be reasonably obtained from other people (such as the attorney, employees, or agents) through investigation.

(b) **Contention interrogatories.** Federal courts and many state court jurisdictions require that a party respond to contention interrogatories by stating their opinions or contentions as to facts involved in the litigation.

- **Example.** It is permissible to ask, and a party must respond with an opinion, whether a defendant was negligently driving a vehicle at the time of an accident. The defendant may answer no, but may not refuse to respond on the ground that the interrogatory was inappropriate. The defendant is not obliged to state a legal conclusion, only facts.

v. Number of Permissible Interrogatories

A party is limited to 25 interrogatories including all subparts. **Rule 33(a)(1).** This rule also applies to cases that are removed from state court, which may allow larger numbers of interrogatories. A federal court may grant leave to serve additional interrogatories.

vi. Objections

A party may respond to an interrogatory by stating an objection and the reasons for the objection. Objections must be stated with specificity **Rule 33(b)(4).** The attorney who makes objections must sign for the objections. **Rule 33(b)(5).** If possible, the party shall answer to the extent that the interrogatory is not objectionable. **Rule 33(b)(3).** Any grounds for objection that are not stated are waived, unless the failure to object is excused on a showing of good cause.

- **Burdensome interrogatories.** The fact that interrogatories may force a party to expend considerable time, effort, and expense or interfere with business operations is not a ground for disallowing the interrogatories, if the opposing party seeks relevant information. **Roesberg v. Johns–Manville Corp.,** 85 F.R.D. 292 (E.D. Pa. 1980). However, a party cannot be compelled to prepare the opponent's case by making extensive investigations, compiling data or summaries, and the like. *See* **Kainz v. Anheuser–Busch, Inc.,** 15 F.R.D. 242 (N.D. Ill. 1954); **Haider v. International Tel. & Tel. Co.,** 75 F.R.D. 657 (E.D.N.Y. 1977).

vii. Option to Produce Business Records

A party may respond to an interrogatory by designating business records that will supply the answer to the interrogatory. A party may do this only if the burden on the requesting party, in ascertaining this information, is substantially the same as it would be for the responding party. **Rule 33(d).** If the burden in ascertaining the information would be greater on the requesting party, then the responding party must supply the information in an answer. **American Rockwool, Inc. v. Owens–Corning Fiberglas Corp.,** 109 F.R.D. 263 (E.D.N.C. 1985).

- **Specificity requirement.** The party invoking the business records option must designate specifically what documents satisfy the interrogatory request. **Rainbow Pioneer No. 44–18–04A v. Hawaii–Nevada Inv. Corp.,** 711 F.2d 902 (9th Cir. 1983); **In re Master Key Antitrust Litig.,** 53 F.R.D. 87 (D. Conn. 1971).

d. Depositions: Rules 28, 30, and 31

Depositions are a discovery method where a party may summons a party or a non-party and ask that person questions regarding the subject matter of the case while under oath. The person who is questioned is called the "deponent."

i. Advantages

Depositions are perhaps the most frequently used discovery method. The prime advantage of taking a deposition is that the lawyers are able to elicit and observe the in-person testimony of a potential witness—to assess the possible strengths or weaknesses of calling that person at trial. Depositions also enable lawyers to elicit fact information and to memorialize inconsistencies that may be exploited during cross-examination at trial. Depositions are superior to interrogatories because they elicit spontaneous responses and permit the examining lawyer to develop questions based on the deponent's answers.

ii. Disadvantages

Depositions are typically very time consuming and expensive. Each party must pay the expenses of conducting a deposition, including any witness fees and travel expenses, the stenographer's fee (or other recordation method), and transcription of the deposition. Sometimes deposition costs may be recovered as part of a judgment, but if the parties settle, deposition costs will be absorbed in the negotiated settlement.

iii. Procedure: Who May Be Deposed and Attend; Methods for Compelling Attendance

Unlike interrogatories, which may only be directed to parties, a party may take a deposition of any person. **Rule 30(a)(1).** Depositions are arranged among the lawyers, and are typically arranged without the leave of court, unless the lawyers wish to take more than ten depositions. A party initiates a deposition by notifying the opposing counsel of the time and place where a deposition will occur. A non-party witness must be subpoenaed under **Rule 45,** unless the deposing party wishes to take the chance that the deponent will not show up for the deposition (*see* discussion at subsection **(b)**, *infra*).

(a) **1993 amendments to curb abusive deposition practice.** The Advisory Committee in 1993 added a number of provisions to the deposition provisions to curb abusive deposition practice.

- **Limits on number of depositions.** Plaintiffs, defendants, or third-party defendants may take only ten depositions without the court's permission. The court must approve depositions beyond this number. **Rule 30(a)(2)(A)(i).**

- **Repetitive depositions.** A party also must obtain the court's approval to depose a person who already has been deposed in the litigation. **Rule 30(a)(2)(A)(ii).**

(b) **Parties.** A party deponent need not be served with a subpoena. A party is required to attend the deposition and bring any documents demanded in the deposition notice. **Rule 30(b).**

(c) **Non-parties.** Non-parties do not have to be subpoenaed to appear for deposition, and there are no sanctions for failure to appear Therefore, in order to compel the appearance of a non-party witness at a deposition, lawyers frequently subpoena the witness. If the non-party then fails to appear, the court may cite the non-appearing person for contempt. **Rule 45(e).** *See* **Less v. Taber Instrument Corp.,** 53 F.R.D. 645 (W.D.N.Y. 1971).

- *Subpoena duces tecum:* If the deposing party wishes the non-party witness to produce documents and bring them to the deposition, these documents must be requested by *a subpoena duces tecum.* **Rule 30(b)(2).**

(d) **Artificial persons; government entities.** A party may take the deposition of a corporation, association, or governmental agency. The party seeking information, in the notice of deposition, must specify the issues to be explored, so that the organization can ascertain which personnel have relevant knowledge. A subpoena is needed to advise non-party organizations of the duty to designate a person to give the deposition testimony on behalf of the organization. **Rule 30(b)(6).** *See also* **Less v. Taber Instrument Corp.,** *supra.*

(e) **Failure to attend own noticed deposition.** If a party gives notice of a deposition and then fails to attend, the court may order the party to pay the other attorney's expenses incurred in attending the deposition that was not held, including reasonable attorney's fees. **Rule 30(g).**

(f) **Who may attend a deposition.** Depositions usually occur in the presence of the opposing counsel, the deponent, and a stenographer or other person recording the testimony. In theory, however, almost anyone may attend a deposition because there is no specific provision excluding any person's attendance.

iv. Objections

A deposition proceeds like examination and cross-examination at trial. The deponent's lawyer may interpose objections to questions asked by opposing counsel. **Rule 30(c)(2)** was amended in 2000 to add specific guidance concerning permissible and impermissible objections during depositions. *See* **Rule 30(c)(2).**

(a) **Manner of objections.** Objections must be "stated concisely and in a non-argumentative and non-suggestive manner." **Rule 30(c)(2).**

(b) **To preserve an objection for trial.** A lawyer may instruct the deponent not to answer a question in order to preserve a privilege or immunity, but privileged questions do not have to be answered, even in a deposition. **Rule 30(c)(2).**

(c) **To enforce a court limitation on evidence.** If the court has ordered a limitation on evidence, the deponent's lawyer may interpose an objection to enforce the court's limitation.

(d) **Objections interposed for improper purposes.** The Advisory Committee added provisions in 1993 to reduce obstructionist objections during depositions. Therefore, lawyers must now state their objections "concisely" and in a "non-argumentative" and "non-suggestive" fashion. **Rule 30(c)(2).**

- **Deponent-leading objections.** A lawyer may not, in objecting to a question, attempt to coach the deponent's testimony through a lengthy, suggestive statement. A lawyer who makes such objections may be subject to sanctions.

(e) **Harassing or bad faith examination.** A lawyer may not conduct a deposition in a bullying fashion. If a lawyer conducts a deposition in an unreasonable manner, the deponent's lawyer may ask to suspend the deposition to seek a court order to cease the deposition. In some federal districts, judges permit lawyers to call the court in order to cease abusive deposition tactics. **Rule 30(d)(3).**

- **Standard.** A deposition may not be conducted "in bad faith or in a manner that unreasonably annoys, embarrasses, or oppresses the deponent or party."

- **Award of attorney's fees.** If the deponent's lawyer succeeds in suspending or terminating the deposition, the lawyer may be awarded attorney's fees in seeking the motion. **Rule 37(a)(5); Rule 30(d)(3)(C).**

v. Recordation, Transcription, and Signature Requirements

The party noticing the deposition may arrange for a stenographer, or specify any other non-stenographic means of recording the deposition (without the leave of court). In many circumstances lawyers now videotape depositions. **Rule 30(b)(3).**

(a) **Stenographic transcripts.** The stenographer who records the deposition testimony creates a transcript. A deponent or party may review and sign the transcript only if they request. When the transcript is available, deponents have 30 days to review the transcript and make any changes. Substantive changes must be accompanied with a signed statement giving the reasons for making the change.

(b) **Video depositions.** Lawyers must ensure the integrity of video depositions, and are prohibited from distorting the appearance, demeanor, or audio presentation of deponents appearing on tape. *See* **Carson v. Burlington Northern Inc.,** 52 F.R.D. 492 (D. Neb. 1971) (plaintiff could not be required to engage in a staged, unnatural reproduction of accident giving rise to the litigation).

(c) **Telephonic or remote electronic means.** Lawyers may conduct depositions by telephone or remote electronic means, in the district where the deponent is to answer questions. **Rule 30(b)(4).**

vi. Depositions on Written Interrogatories: Rule 31

A deposition on written questions operates the same way as an oral deposition, except the attorneys are not present. Questions are sent to an officer who reads the question aloud to the deponent, whose answers are recorded.

(a) **Use of depositions on written interrogatories.** Depositions on written questions are an infrequently used discovery device. Lawyers use this to obtain undisputed information. Since the attorneys typically are not present, this method saves attorney costs. But deposition testimony taken in this fashion lacks spontaneity and the ability to shape questions in light of the deponent's answers. Thus, depositions on written interrogatories are not much better than interrogatories, which are even less expensive.

(b) **1993 amendments limiting depositions on written questions.** The same provisions limiting the number of depositions, repetitive depositions, and premature depositions that were added to **Rule 30,** are incorporated into **Rule 31.** *See* **Rule 31(a)(2).** In addition, amended **Rule 31** shortens the time periods for serving cross, redirect, and records questions. *See* **Rule 31(a)(5).**

e. Document Production and Inspection of Things: Scope of Rule 34

A party may compel an opposing party to produce documents or other tangible things for inspection. A party may also compel the opposing party to allow them to come onto property to inspect, measure, survey, photograph, test or sample the property, or to observe an operation taking place on the property. **Rule 34(a).**

i. Procedure for Production of Documents or Things in the Possession of Parties

A party seeking production or inspection serves notice on the opponent stating what the opponent wants to see, and when, where and how they would like to see it. **Rule 34(b).** Without leave of court, such a request may not be made before the time specified in **Rule 26(d)** (*see* discussion *supra*).

(a) **"Reasonable particularity" standard.** The request for production of documents or things must describe the items with "reasonable particularity." This is a flexible standard and courts permit descriptions of general categories of items (example: "all written communications" between certain dates).

(b) **"Possession, custody, or control" standard.** A party may inspect and copy only documents and tangible things which are in the "possession, custody, or control" of the opposing party. *See* **Hart v. Wolff,** 489 P.2d 114 (Alaska 1971).

- Parties may not evade discovery by placing documents with others, and "control" does not mean legal control. Parties may not plead lack of possession or control to avoid discovery. *See* **Societe Internationale v. Rogers,** 357 U.S. 197 (1958) (defendant required to deliver documents even though this would subject the defendant to criminal penalty under Swiss law).

- **Combined interrogatory request.** Lawyers frequently use a **Rule 33** interrogatory to request an opposing party to identify documents, coupled with a **Rule 34** request to produce those documents. In lawsuits involving corporate or governmental entities, lawyers frequently use interrogatories to ascertain who has "possession, custody, and control" of documents.

(c) **No good cause showing.** A party seeking production of documents or an inspection of property does not have to seek a court order or to show good cause (these were requirements before 1970). If a responding party does not wish to comply with a request, the responding party must object or seek a protective order (*see* discussion of protective orders, *supra*).

(d) **Time for response.** A responding party has 30 days to produce documents after the service of a request. **Rule 34(b).** Lawyers usually negotiate the time, place, and manner of document production or inspection of premises.

ii. Documents or Things in the Possession of Non-Parties; Inspection of Premises

A person who is not a party to the action may be compelled to produce documents or submit to an inspection, through a subpoena. **Rules 34(c), 45.**

(a) **Lawyer subpoenas.** Lawyers, as officers of the court, may issue the subpoena for documents in limited circumstances. *See* **Rule 45(a)(3).** However, a lawyer may be sanctioned for imposing undue burden or expense on a non-party in producing documents. **Rule 45(c)(1).**

(b) **State practice.** Many states do not permit production of documents from non-parties, or limit such production to depositions of non-parties.

iii. Form of Production

A lawyer may not produce documents in a jumbled mess, hoping that the opposing party will not be able to locate useful or damaging information. A responding lawyer must turn over requested documents "as they are kept in the usual course of business or must organize them and label them to correspond with the categories in the request." **Rule 34(b)(2)(E).** The requesting party may have to pay for the cost for organizing documents in special categories.

iv. Objections

An opposing lawyer must state the reasons for any objection to a request for production of documents or inspection of premises. **Rule 34(b)(2)(C).**

(a) **Partial objections.** A lawyer may object to part of a request for documents or inspection of premises. If a lawyer makes a partial objection, discovery proceeds as to the remaining parts of the unobjectionable request. **Rule 34(b)(2)(C).**

f. Physical and Mental Examinations: Rule 35

A person whose physical or mental condition is in controversy in a litigation may be compelled to submit to a medical examination.

i. Physical and Mental Examination by Agreement

In practice, attorneys often consensually agree by stipulation to conduct a physical or mental exam. In such instances, no court order is necessary to compel such an examination.

ii. Court-Ordered Examinations: Competing Values and Concerns

Individuals and their physicians have access to their own medical records, which generally are privileged (*see* discussion of common law privileges, *supra*). Requests for medical records are made under **Rule 34.** A party may request a court-compelled medical examination, under the authority of **Rule 35.** Such a request may invade an individual's privacy and is highly intrusive. However, if a person's condition is in issue in a litigation—particularly in personal injury actions—the opposing party needs access to information about the plaintiff's condition in order to prepare for trial.

(a) **Constitutional privacy concerns. Rule 35,** permitting court-ordered examinations, is constitutional despite challenges that the rule is unconstitutional because it abridges the examined party's right to privacy. *See* **Sibbach v. Wilson,** 312 U.S. 1 (1941) and **Schlagenhauf v. Holder,** 379 U.S. 104 (1964). The Supreme Court also has twice ruled that **Rule 35** does not impermissibly violate the **Rules Enabling Act, 28 U.S.C. §§ 2071–2072,** by creating substantive law. *Id.* (*See also* discussion of the Rules Enabling Act in Chapter III on applicable law.)

iii. Order for Examination: Standards

When the mental or physical condition (including the blood group) of a party is *in controversy,* the court in which the action is pending may order the party to submit to a physical or mental examination by a suitably licensed or certified examiner. **Rule 35(a); Schlagenhauf v. Holder,** 379 U.S. 104 (1964).

(a) **Person in party's custody or legal control.** A court may order that a party "produce for examination a person who is in its custody or under its legal control." *Id.*

- **Good faith efforts: practical effects.** Children or others who are subject to legal guardianship, conservatorship, or the like have to be "produced" by their parents or guardians for an examination. A party can only be required to make a *good faith effort* to produce the person to be examined. If a party fails to comply with an order under **Rule 35(a),** the court can issue various orders under **Rule 37(b)(2)(B).**

(b) **Condition in controversy.** A person's physical or mental condition is in controversy if it is directly in issue in the litigation. A person's condition also may be in controversy if it has substantial bearing on facts in issue.

- **Examples. Medical conditions in controversy.** In personal injury cases, the plaintiff's condition is in controversy. In a contract case relating to a plaintiff's recovery of disability payments, the plaintiff's condition is in controversy. In a breach of contract case excusing breach of performance for illness or injury, the non-performing party's condition is in controversy. A defendant's condition and skills (or lack thereof) in operating a vehicle are in issue in a case arising from an accident. *See, e.g.,* **Schlagenhauf v. Holder,** *supra.*

- **Counter-example: medical condition not in controversy.** Not every mental or physical condition is "in controversy" because such evidence might be used at trial. The condition of an eyewitness's eyesight is not "in controversy" for **Rule 35** purposes and the witness could not be compelled to be subject to a medical examination.

(c) **Showing of good cause.** No party may obtain a court order for a physical or mental examination unless the party has shown good cause for the request. A defendant demonstrates good cause by showing that the defendant has not had an opportunity to make an independent analysis of the plaintiff's condition.

- **Information from other sources.** If the defendant is able to obtain information about the plaintiff's condition from other sources, then good cause is not shown. **Crider v. Sneider,** 243 Ga. 642, 256 S.E.2d 335 (1979).

(d) **Time, place, and manner restrictions.** A court may tailor its order for an examination with particular time, place, and manner restrictions. **Rule 35(a).**

iv. Exchange of Records: Waiver of Confidentiality Privilege

A person who is examined pursuant to **Rule 35** may obtain a copy of the results of that examination. Once the examinee has received this record, however, the examinee must turn over to the opposing party all prior reports regarding the same condition. **Rule 35(b)(1).** By making the request for the report the examinee waives any doctor-patient privilege. **Rule 35(b)(4).**

- A person who divulges a prior medical report pursuant to a court order but not as a result of personal request, is not required to furnish this prior report to the opposing lawyer. **Benning v. Phelps,** 249 F.2d 47 (2d Cir. 1957).

g. Requests for Admission: Rule 36

A party may serve on another party a written request to admit the truth of certain matters of fact, or the application of law to fact, or the genuineness of a document or other evidence.

i. Status as a Discovery Device

Requests for admissions are the least frequently used discovery technique. In a technical sense, this is not a discovery device at all, because it does not seek to discover new information. Instead, it narrows the issues for trial.

ii. Purpose: Trial Expedition

The major purpose of admissions is that such statements help to expedite trial by eliminating uncontested facts from proof at trial.

Admitted facts need not be proved at trial and therefore the lawyer does not have to adduce evidence in support of the admitted facts. **Rule 36(b).** Unlike other discovery responses, a responding party cannot contradict an admission at trial or explain it away.

iii. Procedure

(a) **Timing considerations.** A party may serve requests for admission at any time without the necessity of a court order, except that requests for admission may not be served prior to the time period specified in **Rule 26(d)** (*see* discussion of **Rule 26(d),** *supra*). Requests for admissions are self-executing, and if the responding party does not respond within 30 days (*see infra*), then the matters in the request are deemed admitted without the party having to seek additional discovery.

(b) **Forms of responses.** The responding party must answer each request for admission separately, and indicate whether the responding party admits, denies, or cannot truthfully admit or deny the matter. **Rule 36(a)(4).** *See* similarity to **Rule 8** (forms of responses in answer).

- **Denials.** Denials must specifically deny the matter or set forth in detail why the responding party cannot truthfully admit or deny the matter. A denial has to fairly meet the substance of the requested admission. *Id.*

- **Good faith qualified responses.** If good faith requires, a party may qualify an answer or deny only part of the matter; in such instances the party must specify which parts are true and which parts are not true.

- **Lack of information.** A party may not respond to a request for an admission by asserting a lack of knowledge or information, unless the party states that he or she has made a *reasonable inquiry* and that the information known or readily available to the responding party is insufficient to enable the party to admit or deny. *Id.*

(c) **Objections.** A responding party must state any objections to the requested admissions. If the responding party does not raise any objections, the matters asserted in the requests are deemed admitted. The party must not object solely on the ground that the request presents a genuine issue for trial.

- **Party seeking requests for admissions.** The party seeking the admissions may, after receiving the opposing party's responses, move to determine the sufficiency of those answers or objections. **Rule 36(a)(6).** If a party seeking admissions prevails, the party may be entitled to attorney's fees in bringing the motion. *See* **Rule 37(a)(4), (5).**

- **Unjustified objections.** If the court determines that an objection is not justified, it can order an answer.

- **Non-complying answer.** If the court determines that an answer is not in compliance with the rule, the court may order the matter admitted.

(d) **Postponement of court determination.** In lieu of issuing any orders relating to disputed requests for admissions, the court may postpone such a determination until pretrial conference or some other designated time before trial.

5. The Duty to Supplement Responses: Rule 26(e)

In federal court and many state courts, parties have a duty to update or supplement material they disclose during discovery. The Federal Rule relating to the duty to supplement discovery responses was substantially rewritten as part of the 1993 amendments to the discovery rules, chiefly to eliminate confusing language in the earlier rule.

a. Duty to Supplement Information Disclosed as Part of Initial Mandatory Disclosure

The 1993 amendments added a new provision requiring early mandatory informal exchange of information at the outset of the litigation. *See* discussion of **Rule 26(a)**, *supra*. A party is under a duty to supplement these initial disclosures, or to correct the disclosure, if the party acquires information after the disclosure. The amended rule does not specify any particular form of supplementation.

i. Standard for Duty to Supplement

A party must supplement or correct a response if the party "learns that in some *material respect* the information disclosed is *incomplete or incorrect* and if the additional or corrective information has not been made known to the other parties during the discovery process or in writing." **Rule 26(e)(1).** This eliminates the need for parties to keep resubmitting the same discovery requests to make sure nothing has changed since the last response.

b. Formal Discovery Methods: Duty to Supplement

A party is under the same duty to supplement or correct information disclosed through formal discovery procedures.

i. Expert Witnesses

The duty to supplement extends to information in an expert's report, or an expert's deposition. **Rule 26(e)(2).**

ii. Interrogatories, Requests for Document Production, and Requests for Admissions

A party is under a duty to *"seasonably"* amend a prior response to an interrogatory or a request for admission if the party learns that the prior response was in *some material respect incomplete or incorrect*, and if the additional or corrective information has not already been made known to the parties, or in writing. **Rule 26(e)(1).**

c. Sanctions for Failure to Supplement

Prior to the 1993 amendments to the discovery provision, there was no specific sanction for the failure to supplement. The 1993 **Rule 37** amendments include a sanction for a failure to supplement responses as required in **Rule 26(e)**. *See* **Rule 37(c)(1)**, barring the use of any witness or information the responding party did not supplement or correct.

6. The Use of Discovery at Trial: Rules 32, 33(c), 36(b)

The discovery rules contain specific provisions indicating when parties may use discovery materials at trial. **Rule 32** indicates the appropriate uses of deposition testimony at trial, and **Rule 33(c)** indicates the permissible use of interrogatory answers at trial. Use of discovery materials at trial also is governed by state and federal evidence rules.

a. Relevant Party Statements

Evidence rules permit a party to introduce any relevant statement of an opposing party, even if the opposing party does testify. **Federal Rule of Evidence 801(d)(2).**

- Any answer to a deposition question or an interrogatory qualifies; these also are statements made under oath.

b. Statements of Party Agents or Employees

Parties also may use at trial the statements of managing agents or persons authorized to speak for the party, as well as an employee statement about his or her duties.

c. Impeachment Purposes

The classic use of discovery materials at trial is to impeach a witness with former inconsistent statements made under oath in an earlier deposition or discovery response, or to refresh recollection. *See* **Rule 32(a)(2); Federal Rule of Evidence 613.**

d. Hearsay Statements

The discovery rules permit reading deposition testimony at trial if the deponent is dead, ill, incompetent, or beyond the subpoena power of the court. **Rule 32(a)(4).** In this respect, the discovery rules provide an exception to the evidentiary rule barring hearsay or out-of-court statements from being introduced at trial.

e. Limitations on Use of Discovery at Trial

i. Deposition Testimony

A party may use deposition testimony at trial.

(a) Depositions on short notice. A deposition cannot be used against a party who received less than 14 days notice and who at the time of the deposition had a pending motion for a protective order requesting that the deposition not be held, or be held subject to restrictions. **Rule 32(a)(5).**

ii. Interrogatory Answers

A party may not introduce the party's own answers to interrogatories. This rule is intended to eliminate a party from supplying long and self-serving answers to interrogatories. *See* **Callaway v. Perdue,** 238 Ark. 652, 385 S.W.2d 4 (1964) (plaintiff's answers to interrogatories were "self-serving declarations" and inadmissible under evidence rules).

iii. Admissions

Admissions are conclusive for the purposes of a pending trial, unless the court permits the responding party to withdraw or amend the answer to the request for the admission. **Rule 36(b).**

7. Judicial Supervision of Discovery and Sanctions: Rules 26 and 37

The general sanctioning provisions for failure to cooperate or respond to discovery requests is contained in **Rule 37,** which provides an array of possible sanctions a court may impose for discovery abuse. Prior to the 1993 amendment of the discovery rules, litigants did not often seek discovery sanctions and courts did not frequently impose them.

a. Availability of Discovery Sanctions, in General

Discovery typically is conducted by the parties, without court orders implementing the discovery requests. Sanctions are available, then, only when the discovery process breaks down and an aggrieved party seeks a court order requiring a person to attend a deposition, answer interrogatories, or produce requested documents. **Rule 37(a). Rule 11** sanctions are inapplicable to discovery disputes.

i. Contempt

Contempt sanctions usually cannot be issued for failure to comply with discovery requests, because the initial discovery request typically is not made under compulsion of a court order.

ii. Jurisdictional Issues

Only a court with personal jurisdiction over a witness may issue an order compelling the witness to make responses to discovery requests. The court in which an action is pending, therefore, may not be able to compel or sanction a witness outside the court's territorial reach. **Rule 37(a)(2).**

- **Jurisdiction as a discovery sanction.** However, as a sanction for failure to respond to a discovery request, a federal court may deem personal jurisdiction to exist, *See* **Insurance Corp. of Ireland, Ltd. v. Compagnie des Bauxites de Guinee,** 456 U.S. 694 (1982) (permissible sanction to take as established personal jurisdiction over the defendants—as to which discovery information was sought but evaded).

b. Signature Requirements: 1993 Amendments to Rule 26(g)

The 1993 amendments to the discovery provisions added extensive provisions to **subsection (g)** relating to the attorney's duties to sign all discovery requests, as well as responses to discovery requests.

i. Signature Requirements for Early Mandatory Exchange of Information: Rule 26(g)(1)

Lawyers who disclose information as part of the new mandatory informal discovery provisions (*see* **Rules 26(a)(1)** and **(3)**) must sign those disclosures. Unrepresented parties also must sign such disclosures. The signature serves as a certification that to the best of the signer's knowledge, information, and belief formed after a reasonable inquiry, the disclosure is complete and correct as of the time it is made.

ii. Signature Requirements for Discovery Requests and Responses: Rule 26(g)(1)

The signature requirement for discovery requests was modified to parallel the language of **Rule 11** relating to truth-in-pleading (*see* discussion of **Rule 11** in Chapter V, *supra*), although **Rule 11** does not itself apply to discovery requests. The attorney's signature constitutes the lawyer's certification that to the best of the signer's knowledge, information, and belief, formed after a reasonable inquiry, that a request, response or objection is:

- Consistent with the discovery rules and warranted by existing law or a good faith argument for the extension, modification, or reversal of existing law;

- Not interposed for any improper purpose, such as to harass or cause unnecessary delay or needless increase in the cost of litigation; and

- Not unreasonable or unduly burdensome or expensive, given the needs of the case, the discovery already had in the case, the amount in controversy, and the importance of the issues at stake in the litigation.

iii. Sanctions for Non-Compliance with Signature Requirements: Rule 26(g)

(a) **Failure to sign.** If an attorney or unrepresented party fails to sign discovery requests, responses, or objections, it shall be stricken unless it is signed promptly after the omission has been called to the attention of the party. **Rule 26(g)(2).**

(b) **Certifications in violation of the rule.** If a certification violates the rule without substantial justification, the court either on its own initiative or on a motion may impose any appropriate sanction against the offending party. The sanction may include reasonable attorney's fees incurred because of the violation. **Rule 26(g)(3).**

c. Court-Ordered Discovery: Possible Sanctions

Even where discovery is court-ordered, federal courts have been reluctant to sanction non-complying parties, and generally will do so only if there is willful non-compliance. However, when a party fails to comply, courts have an array of possible sanctions. **Rules 37(b)–(f).**

i. Severity of Sanctions

Sanctions must be tailored to the conduct of the non-responding party and must not be overly harsh or violate the party's due process rights. "Considerations of fair play may dictate that courts eschew the harshest sanctions provided by **Rule 37** where failure to comply is due to a mere oversight of counsel amounting to no more than simple negligence." **Cine Forty–Second Street Theatre Corp. v. Allied Artists Pictures Corp.,** 602 F.2d 1062 (2d Cir. 1979).

(a) Judicial discretion. The trial judge has wide discretion to determine what sanction is appropriate and reasonable given the discovery sought and the responding party's reasons for non-disclosure. **National Hockey League v. Metropolitan Hockey Club, Inc.,** 427 U.S. 639 (1976).

(b) Due process requirements. Due process requires that a party be given notice and an opportunity to be heard before the court imposes a discovery sanction. *See* **Roadway Express, Inc. v. Piper,** 447 U.S. 752 (1980).

(c) Flagrant misconduct or gross professional negligence. Judges typically reserve the most severe sanctions for cases of flagrant abuse. *See, e.g.,* **Insurance Corp. of Ireland, Ltd. v. Compagnie des Bauxites de Guinee,** 456 U.S. 694 (1982) (permissible sanction to take as established personal jurisdiction over the defendants—as to which discovery information was sought but evaded).

ii. Contempt

Once a court has issued a discovery order, a non-responding party may be held in contempt for failure to comply with the court order.

A party held in contempt may be fined or jailed until such time as he or she complies with the discovery request. **Rule 37(b)(2)(A)(vii).**

- **Failure to submit to a physical or mental examination.** A person may not be jailed for a refusal to submit to a physical or mental examination. **Sibbach v. Wilson & Co.,** 312 U.S. 1 (1941). Other sanctions are available under **Rule 37(b)(2)(B).**

iii. Attorney's Fees

A party that has been unreasonable in refusing to comply with a discovery request may be assessed the opposing counsel's attorney's fees incurred in seeking the motion. *See e.g.,* **Rules 37(a)(5); (b)(2)(C).**

iv. Striking Portions of Claims or Defenses

A court may sanction a party who receives notice of a deposition and fails to appear, or fails to answer interrogatories, by striking all or a portion of a claim or defense. **Rule 37(d)(3).**

v. Other Possible Sanctions: Default, Dismissal, Limiting Trial Testimony

In addition to contempt and striking portions of claims and defenses, courts may issue an array of sanctions for discovery abuse, including granting a default judgment, dismissing the action, or limiting the testimony available at trial. **Rule 37(b)(2)(A).**

vi. Admissions

Technically, if a party fails to respond to a request for admissions, then the matter is deemed admitted and the requesting party does not have to offer proof of the matter at trial. **Rule 36(a)** (*see* discussion *supra*).

A party who responds to a request for admissions with a knowingly false denial may be assessed the opposing counsel's attorney's fees in proving the matter. **Rule 37(c)(2).**

d. Other 1993 Amendments to Rule 37

Rule 37 was substantially amended in 1993. The Advisory Committee added several provisions requiring attorneys seeking relief to have in good faith conferred or attempted to confer with the party against whom relief is sought.

i. In General

Rule 37 was amended at several points to include sanctions for failure to provide early mandatory disclosure information required under new **Rule 26(a)(1)** (*see* discussion *supra*), or to supplement responses as required in **Rule 26(e)**.

ii. Sanctions for Failure to Provide Mandatory Exchange of Information under Rule 26(a)(1)

A lawyer who fails to comply and disclose information listed in **Rule 26(a)(1)** may not offer as evidence at trial information that, without substantial justification, was not included in the attorney's initial disclosures or by supplemental disclosure. **Rule 37(c)(1).**

- **Criticism of remedy:** This is not an especially effective remedy for non-compliance, because the party that desires not to disclose evidence doesn't want it to be used at trial, anyway. Therefore the non-complying party is not penalized if the party cannot use the information at trial.

iii. Additional or Supplemental Sanctions

For failure to comply with **Rules 26(a)(1)** or **26(e),** the court may impose any substitute or additional sanctions. **Rule 37(c)(1).**

iv. Informing Jury

The court also may inform the jury of a party's failure to make required disclosures. **Rule 37(c)(1).**

8. Discovery Problems in International Litigation

a. Discovery Located Abroad

General problem. Frequently litigation involves parties or documentary evidence located abroad. The fundamental problems relating to such discovery concern the territorial reach of the Federal Rules of Civil Procedure, as well as international comity concerns.

- **More restrictive discovery practice.** Most other legal systems do not have provisions similar to American discovery rules and would not permit the same access to information that American federal courts liberally permit.

b. Hague Convention on the Taking of Evidence Abroad

This convention provides procedures on requesting evidence that is located in foreign countries. **Hague Convention on the Taking of**

Evidence Abroad in Civil or Commercial Matters, 23 U.S.T. 2555 (text of Convention located at **28 U.S.C. § 1781).**

- The United States has been a signatory to this convention since 1972.

c. Relationship of Federal Discovery Rules to the Hague Convention

The Hague Convention provisions do not replace the Federal Rules of Discovery, but are rather a supplemental consideration that a court may take into account when a litigation entails discovery abroad. **Societe Nationale Industrielle Aerospatiale v. U.S. District Court,** 482 U.S. 522 (1987).

■ CHAPTER REVIEW CHECKLIST

Your civil procedure examination may contain a problem relating to discovery. Your procedure professor is least likely to test on the technical requirements of the formal discovery devices. However, it is wise to review which discovery methods may be used on parties and non-parties, and any special rules relating to discovery from artificial entities such as corporations or government agencies. Also take note of territorial limitations and discovery methods requiring subpoena power. Your professor is more likely to set forth a discovery problem relating to the scope of discovery, or the applicability of attorney-client privilege or attorney work product immunity. Another possible topic for an exam question concerns the availability and scope of a protective order. Finally, a comprehensive discovery question might raise issues relating to suitable sanctions for abusive or non-cooperative discovery practices.

To answer a problem relating to the scope of discovery, ask:

1. **What is the nature of the discovery request? What is the subject matter of the lawsuit? To whom is it directed? Is the request to a party, non-party, or artificial entity such as a corporation, business association, or governmental agency?**

    - What kind of material or information is sought? Is the request attempting to ascertain the existence, description, nature, custody, condition, or location of books, documents, electronically stored information, or tangible things?

        — Is the discovery seeking the identity and location of persons who have knowledge of any discoverable matter?

- Is material or information requested *relevant to claims and defenses* involved in the pending action? Is it sought to be used solely for impeachment purposes?

- Would the material or information requested be admissible at trial? If not, is the information *"reasonably calculated to lead to the discovery of admissible evidence?"*

- Is the material or information requested protected by an attorney-client or other common law privilege? Is the material or information protected by attorney work product immunity? (*see infra*).

2. **To answer a question relating to the form of discovery ask:**

- Have the attorneys met in a timely fashion and agreed to exchange information as under **Rule 26(f)?**

- Have the attorneys agreed to a discovery plan and schedule? Have the lawyers agreed to any stipulated discovery?

- Have the lawyers complied with the signature requirements both for mandatory informal disclosures and for formal discovery methods?

- Is the discovery method directed appropriately to a party or non-party? If a discovery request is directed to a non-party, where is that person located? Are the persons from whom discovery is sought within the territorial jurisdiction of the court where the action is pending?

  — Is it necessary or advisable to use a subpoena to compel a person's presence at a deposition? To obtain documentary evidence?

- If discovery is directed towards a corporation, does the notice of discovery identify the categories of information sought and the persons most likely to have custody and control over documents?

- Has the discovery request been made for any *improper purpose,* such as to harass the opposing party or to cause unnecessary delay or needless increase in the costs of the litigation? Is the discovery request unduly burdensome or expensive (balancing the needs of the case, discovery already accomplished, the amount in controversy, and the importance of the issues at stake)?

3. **To answer a question relating to responses to discovery requests, ask:**

- Have the discovery responses been signed in conformity with the requirements of **Rule 26(g)?** Has a response or objection been interposed for any improper purpose? (*see supra*).

- If the responses are answers to requests for admissions, do the answers fully admit, deny, or partially respond to the questions? Has the respondent indicated a lack of information or belief upon which to admit or deny?

- Have documents been produced (or made available for inspection) in some reasonably usable form?

- Has the respondent raised an objection or a privilege in a timely fashion?

4. To answer a question relating to attorney-client privilege, ask:

- Has the objection to discovery based on attorney-client privilege been raised in a timely fashion?

- Who is invoking the privilege? Is there an attorney-client relationship?

  — Is the person holding the privilege a client;

  — Was the person to whom the communication was made a bar member, or a bar member's subordinate and, acting as a lawyer in connection with the communication;

  — Did the attorney receive the communication from the client, not in the presence of strangers or third parties, for the purpose of securing either a legal opinion, legal services, or legal assistance in some proceeding?

- Has the privilege been overcome by an exception, qualification, or waiver to the privilege, such as consent, voluntary or involuntary disclosure, crime, fraud, or tort?

5. **To answer a question relating to attorney work product, ask:**

- Has the attorney raised an objection to the discovery based on work product in a timely fashion?

- Who is invoking the immunity? A lawyer, client, or third party?

- Does the requested material qualify as work product? Was the material:

  — Documents and tangible things;

  — Prepared in anticipation of litigation or for trial;

  — By or for another party, or,

  — By or for that other party's representative (including the other party's attorney, surety, consultant, indemnitor, insurer, or agent)?

- Is the requested material ordinary work product? Can the requesting party overcome the immunity by showing:

  — the party seeking discovery has a substantial need of the materials in preparation of the party's case, and

  — the party is unable without undue hardship to obtain the substantial equivalent of the materials by other means?

- Is the requested material opinion work product (does it consist of the mental impressions, conclusions, or legal theories of the attorney or other party representative)?

- Has the immunity been overcome by an exception, qualification, or waiver to the immunity, such as consent, voluntary or involuntary disclosure, crime, fraud, or tort?

6. **To answer a question relating to protective orders, ask:**

- Who is seeking the protective order? Can the party show *good cause* for issuance of a protective order, to protect the party from annoyance, embarrassment, oppression, undue burden or expense?

  — Is the person seeking a protective order to shield trade secrets or proprietary information?

  — Is it possible for the court to tailor or craft a protective order to accommodate the needs of the requesting party while protecting the legitimate interests or concerns of the party seeking protection?

- Is it appropriate for the court to hold an *in camera* hearing on the requested materials or information?

- Is it possible for the court to order redaction of documents to shield certain information from disclosure?

- Does the subject matter of the dispute entail First Amendment concerns, such as the public's right to know? Is the litigation "imbued with a public purpose"?

VIII

Resolution Without Trial

■ ANALYSIS

■ CHAPTER OVERVIEW

This chapter deals with the ability of parties to a lawsuit to resolve the litigation prior to trial, without the necessity of going to trial.

Voluntary dismissal. One method for ending a litigation prior to trial occurs if the plaintiff voluntarily withdraws the lawsuit. In general, a plaintiff usually may do this without "prejudice" to the ability of the plaintiff to institute a subsequent lawsuit at a later time. If parties settle, they enter a joint voluntary dismissal to conclude the case.

- A plaintiff may be unable to file a subsequent lawsuit, however, if a relevant statute of limitations has run on the action.

Involuntary dismissal. A second means by which a lawsuit may be terminated prior to trial is if the court involuntarily dismisses the litigation. The most common form of involuntary dismissal occurs when a plaintiff fails to prosecute the case in a timely fashion, but a court also may order dismissal for failure to comply with court rules or orders.

Default. A third means by which a lawsuit may be terminated prior to trial is if the defendant fails to appear to defend in the action. In this instance, the defendant suffers a default judgment, which the court may enter against the non-appearing defendant. Default judgments are binding as if the defendant had appeared in the action and defended against the plaintiff's claims.

- A plaintiff must subsequently execute the judgment against the defaulting defendant.

- In some instances, a defendant may collaterally attack the default judgment in an enforcement action or other proceeding. For example, the defendant may collaterally attack the first judgment for a lack of personal jurisdiction (*see* Chapter I, *supra*, for a discussion of personal jurisdiction).

Summary judgment. A fourth—and major—means of terminating a litigation prior to trial is through the grant of a summary judgment motion.

- A court will grant a summary judgment and dismiss the case if a moving party demonstrates that there is no genuine issue as to a material fact in the litigation, and therefore the moving party is entitled to a judgment as a matter of law.

- Summary judgment motions used to be disfavored motions in federal courts, and many federal judges preferred to allow the case to go to the jury to determine whether a factual dispute existed.

- After a 1986 Supreme Court trilogy of decisions relating to the appropriate use of summary judgment, federal courts have been encouraged to use summary judgment more liberally to terminate litigation that ought not to go to trial.

- The purpose of summary judgment is to serve the interests of judicial efficiency and economy. There is little sense in going through an empty ritual of a trial if there is nothing for the jury to determine, because the facts are not in dispute.

- Summary judgment motions typically occur during discovery, or after discovery has been completed, when a party determines that no factual dispute exists as to an issue or issues in the litigation. Discovery materials are used in support of the motion to carry the movant's burden of demonstrating that there is no genuine issue of fact.

  — Either the plaintiff or the defendant may move for summary judgment.

  — A plaintiff may move for summary judgment either on its own claims, or in relation to counterclaims asserted by the defendant against the plaintiff. Similarly, any additional parties to the litigation may move for summary judgment in relation to claims asserted by or against them in the litigation.

- The same evidentiary standards that would apply at trial apply to the court's determination whether the party seeking summary judgment has satisfied its burden of proof on the motion.

- A court may permit a responding party additional time in which to conduct discovery in response to a summary judgment motion.

- A court may grant partial summary judgment, in order to remove certain issues or claims from the litigation (if there is no genuine issue as to a material fact and the movant is entitled to a judgment as a matter of law).

  — If the court grants a partial summary judgment in a litigation with multiple claims, the party against whom the summary judgment was granted may bring a direct appeal of that determination under the final judgment rule.

- Summary judgment has long been considered to be inappropriate in certain circumstances, such as where the credibility of a witness is in issue, or in certain kinds of complex litigation, such as antitrust lawsuits. The federal courts' resistance to issuing summary judgments in antitrust litigation, however, has been eroded in recent years.

A. VOLUNTARY DISMISSAL, DEFAULT, AND INVOLUNTARY DISMISSAL

1. Voluntary Dismissal: Common Law

At common law a plaintiff was viewed as the master of the case until a judgment was rendered, and therefore permitted to withdraw the lawsuit voluntarily and without prejudice at any time prior to a judgment. Modern state and federal rules limit the period in which a plaintiff voluntarily may withdraw a lawsuit without consequences, and have rejected the common law approach.

2. Voluntary Dismissal: Rule 41(a)

In general, a plaintiff is permitted to withdraw a lawsuit so long as the defendant is not unduly burdened by the plaintiff's actions. In most jurisdictions, this is usually codified as some time before "trial" or the "commencement" of trial (which is a matter of judicial construction). In federal court, a plaintiff may voluntarily dismiss the action without a court order in one of two ways:

a. Before Service of Process

By filing a notice of dismissal at any time before service by the opposing party of an answer or a motion for summary judgment, whichever occurs first.

- **Purpose.** Allowing the plaintiff to freely withdraw a lawsuit at such an early juncture is based on the notion that the defendant has not suffered any time or expense in responding to the litigation.

b. After Appearance of Parties

By filing a stipulation of dismissal signed by all the parties who appeared in the action.

- **Purpose.** The stipulation by all the parties manifests their consent to the dismissal; if no one who has appeared in the litigation objects, the court will honor the agreement.

c. Effect of Voluntary Dismissal

A voluntary dismissal either by notice or stipulation is *"without prejudice,"* meaning that the plaintiff may institute another action at a later time, provided the action is not barred by an applicable statute of limitations. **Rule 41(a)(1)(B).**

- **The two dismissal rule—repetitive dismissals.** A plaintiff may dismiss an action as a matter of right only once. If, however, the plaintiff already has previously filed and dismissed the same claim in a state or federal court, then the subsequent voluntarily dismissal will operate as an *adjudication on the merits* and is a dismissal "with prejudice." **Rule 41(a)(1)(B).**

- **Costs of previously dismissed action.** If a plaintiff previously has dismissed an action and then commences an action based on the same claim against the same defendant, the court may make any order for payment of costs of the previously dismissed action. The court also may stay the pending proceeding until the plaintiff complies with the order to pay costs for the previously dismissed action. **Rule 41(d).**

- **Protection against harassment.** This provision protects defendants from the expense of having to defend against claims brought and repetitively dismissed by plaintiffs.

d. Court-Ordered Voluntary Dismissals: Rule 41(a)(2)

Unless a plaintiff moves to voluntarily withdraw a litigation as indicated above, a plaintiff may not voluntarily withdraw the case without a court order. Judges often will hold a hearing to determine if a party will be prejudiced by the voluntary dismissal. The grant or denial of the request to dismiss is in the court's discretion.

i. Counterclaims

If the defendant pleads a counterclaim prior to the plaintiff's motion to dismiss the complaint, the action cannot be dismissed against the defendant's objection unless the counterclaim remains pending for independent adjudication by the court. A dismissal under these circumstances is also without prejudice to the plaintiff's ability to re-institute a subsequent lawsuit on the same claim or issues. **Rule 41(a)(2).**

- **Strategic implications.** As a practical matter, it is possible for a plaintiff to have its complaint dismissed, but have to defend against a counterclaim.

e. Purpose

A plaintiff may dismiss a case in order to maintain a relationship with the defendant or if the plaintiff wishes to conduct more research before refiling the lawsuit.

3. Involuntary Dismissals: Rule 41(b)

A court, in its discretion, may dismiss a lawsuit under three circumstances:

a. Failure to Prosecute the Case

A plaintiff is expected to go forward with its case with "due diligence." **Messenger v. United States,** 231 F.2d 328 (2d Cir. 1956). If the plaintiff fails to prosecute its own litigation, the court has the authority to dismiss the case with prejudice. This power is derived from the judiciary's inherent powers to manage its affairs and ensure the orderly disposition of cases.

i. Timing

Some states set time limits before which an involuntary dismissal cannot occur; other jurisdictions set time limits beyond which such a dismissal is mandatory. In most jurisdictions, including federal courts, the timing of an involuntary dismissal is entirely within the court's discretion.

ii. Standards

There is a general disinclination to involuntarily dismiss a lawsuit because the law favors deciding cases on the merits. However, courts will look to the entire factual circumstances involved in the failure to prosecute the case. The defendant does not have to show prejudice because it is presumed from the delay. **Link v. Wabash R.R. Co.,** 370 U.S. 626 (1962); **Messenger v. United States,** *supra.*

A court generally will not order a dismissal when:

- there has been no prejudice to the defendant, **Citizens Utilities Co. v. American Tel. & Tel. Co.,** 595 F.2d 1171 (9th Cir. 1979), *cert. denied,* 444 U.S. 931;

- the defendant is at least partially responsible for the delay;

- the delay is due to the lawyer's malfeasance, rather than the client, *see e.g.,* **Donnelly v. Johns–Manville Sales Corp.,** 677 F.2d 339 (3d Cir. 1982).

b. Failure to Comply with the Federal Rules

Under the inherent powers of the court, a judge may dismiss a case for failure to comply with the Federal Rules of Civil Procedure. Such a sanction is an extreme penalty and is used only for the most egregious and willful disregard of the rules. *See, e.g.,* **Link v. Wabash R.R. Co.,** 370 U.S. 626 (1962) (dismissal for failure to conduct discovery and failure to appear at pretrial conference as mandated under the Federal Rules). Frequently such dismissals are with prejudice.

c. Failure to Comply with a Court Order

Under the inherent powers of the court, a judge also may dismiss a case for a party's failure to comply with a court order. This is an extremely harsh sanction for noncompliance, however, and is used only rarely in extreme cases of noncompliance. *See, e.g.,* **Calvert Fire Ins. Co. v. Cropper,** 141 Cal.App.3d 901, 190 Cal.Rptr. 593 (1983) (dismissal for willful failure to admit as requested in discovery). Frequently such dismissals are with prejudice.

d. Effect of Involuntary Dismissal: Rule 41(b)

A court-ordered dismissal operates as an *adjudication on the merits*. This does not apply to dismissals based on a lack of jurisdiction, improper venue, or failure to join a party needed for a just adjudication under **Rule 19.**

i. Subsequent State Action

In some jurisdictions it may be possible to institute an action based on the same claim involuntarily dismissed from federal court, even though it would be barred in federal court.

4. Defaults: Rule 55

There are two types of defaults—an "entry of default" which is simply the court clerk's notation of the defendant's failure to appear and defend, and a court-ordered "default judgment." An "entry of default" is not itself a judgment, it is merely a docket notation.

a. Occasions for Default

A defendant may suffer a default in three circumstances:

(1) failure to appear or answer the plaintiff's complaint;

(2) appear in the action, but then fail to file an answer or appear at trial;

(3) failure to comply with a procedural requirement or court order during pretrial proceedings (default serves as a sanction).

b. Entry of Default

If a party does not appear in the litigation and plead or present defenses, then the court may enter a default against the non-appearing party. **Rule 55(a).** The default rules apply to all plaintiffs, counterclaimants, and cross-claimants in a litigation. Default is considered a drastic remedy because it runs counter to the judicial system's preference for an adjudication of a dispute on the merits.

i. Hearing on the Default Application: Notice

If a party has previously appeared in the case, then the party must be given written notice 7 days prior to the court's hearing on the application for a default judgment. **Rule 55(b)(2).** The failure to provide notice justifies reversal or setting aside a default. **Marshall v. Boyd,** 658 F.2d 552 (8th Cir. 1981).

ii. Appearance

The notice requirement only applies to those defendants who have previously "appeared" and taken an interest in the litigation. What constitutes an "appearance" for notice purposes differs from jurisdiction to jurisdiction. In some courts, appearing to attack personal jurisdiction is sufficient. Other courts take an even more flexible approach, allowing even less formal activity to constitute an "appearance" (such as an exchange of settlement letters).

c. Calculation of Damages

The party that has brought the suit may request the court to enter a default judgment in the amount of damages, plus costs, if it is clear from the complaint that a certain sum is due. **Rule 55(b)(1).** No hearing is necessary, but the court may hold a hearing to assess those damages. **Rule 55(b)(2).**

- A claimant may not subsequently recover more than the amount demanded or the type of relief requested in the complaint.

d. Exceptions for Infants, Incompetents

Default judgments may not be entered against infants or incompetents unless they have been represented by a guardian, conservator, or other representative. **Rule 55(b)(2).**

e. Setting Aside Defaults

A court may set aside an "entry of default" (the docket notation) for good cause. **Rule 55(c).** A default judgment may be set aside under the more stringent conditions specified for relief from a final judgment, including mistake, inadvertence, excusable neglect, newly discovered evidence, or fraud. *See* **Rule 60(b).**

B. SUMMARY JUDGMENT: FEDERAL RULE 56

1. Purpose of Summary Judgment

The purpose of summary judgment is to end a litigation where there is no disputed factual issues to be determined at trial and therefore one of the parties is entitled to a judgment as a matter of law. In these circumstances, a summary judgment eliminates the need for a trial. This serves the goal of judicial efficiency and economy because it avoids unnecessary trials and permits the court to process more cases with actual factual disputes.

a. Practical Effect of Granting a Summary Judgment

The practical effect of a court's granting a summary judgment is that the case does not go to trial and is not decided by a jury. If a summary judgment motion is denied, then the case will go to trial. If the court grants a partial summary judgment (*see* discussion *infra*) as to certain issues or claims, then the case proceeds to trial, but the issues for which summary judgment has been granted are not tried to the jury. *See* **Rule 56(g).**

b. Disfavored Motion until 1986

From 1938 through 1986, the summary judgment was a disfavored motion and rarely granted in many federal courts, and especially in some circuits, such as the Second Circuit. Judges generally favored allowing cases to be tried to juries, rather than disposing of the litigation on paper motions. In 1986, in a trilogy of decisions interpreting the nature and scope of summary judgment procedure, the Supreme Court signaled its desire that the lower federal courts more aggressively employ summary judgment as a tool to eliminate cases where it is clear that a trial is unnecessary. *See* **Celotex Corp. v. Catrett,** 477 U.S. 317 (1986); **Anderson v. Liberty Lobby, Inc.,** 477 U.S. 242 (1986), and **Matsushita Electric Industrial Corp. v. Zenith Radio Corp.,** 475 U.S. 574 (1986).

2. Terminology

Either a plaintiff or defendant, or any party added who asserts claims, counterclaims, or cross-claims, may ask the court for a summary judgment. The summary judgment rule is not organized with reference to plaintiffs or defendants.

a. Movants

Because either a plaintiff or defendant or third party may move for summary judgment, it is conceptually more helpful to characterize the party requesting the summary judgment as the "movant," and party responding to the summary judgment as the "adverse party," the "non-movant," or "party opposing the motion."

b. Cross-Motions for Summary Judgment

Both parties may file summary judgment motions against the opposing party, simultaneously. The parties agree there is no factual dispute but disagree concerning who should prevail as a matter of law. In this circumstance, the motions are called "cross-motions" for summary judgment.

3. Timing: When a Party May Seek a Summary Judgment

When a party may seek a summary judgment depends on whether the party is a claimant or defending party. Parties may seek a summary judgment relatively early in the proceedings, but typically parties do not seek summary judgment until discovery is conducted and further fact information is elicited to support or refute disputed issues.

a. Who May File

A party may file a motion for summary judgment at any time until 30 days after the close of discovery (unless a local rule sets a different time, or a court orders a different time).

b. Relationship to Rule 12(c): Motion for a Judgment on the Pleadings

If, after the close of pleadings, a party moves for a judgment on the pleadings and supports that motion with materials outside the pleadings, such as affidavits or other documentary evidence, then the **Rule 12(c)** motion is "converted" in a summary judgment motion and will be evaluated according to the standards required for a summary judgment motion made under **Rule 56.** *See* Chapter V, *supra,* for a discussion of **Rule 12** motions. **Rule 12(d).**

4. Procedure for Seeking Summary Judgment

a. How Presented

A motion for summary judgment is presented to the court, along with a supporting memoranda of law and materials attached in support of the summary judgment. Such materials may be pleadings, depositions, portions of depositions, electronically stored information, answers to interrogatories, answers to admissions, affidavits, declarations, or stipulations. In addition, parties may submit various documents, such as a copy of a contract or a will.

i. Initial Burden on Movant

The party seeking a summary judgment—either a claimant or defending party—may move for a summary judgment by providing supporting materials. There is, however, no affirmative requirement that the moving party support its motion with any materials in support of the motion. **Celotex Corp. v. Catrett,** 477 U.S. 317 (1986). Usually, however, moving parties do supply the court with more information than what is alleged in the party's pleadings.

(a) **Affidavit requirements: Federal Rule 56(c)(4).** Affidavits submitted in support of a summary judgment must:

- be made on personal knowledge;

- set forth facts that would be admissible in evidence; and

- show that the affiant is competent to testify to the matters in the affidavit.

(b) **Supplementation.** Affidavits may be supplemented with sworn and certified copies of other discovery materials.

b. Standard

A court is required to grant a summary judgment if the pleadings and other supporting materials *"show that there is no genuine issue as to any material fact and that the moving party is entitled to a judgment as a matter of law."*

i. Relationship to Directed Verdicts

The standard for summary judgment generally mirrors the standard for a directed verdict under **Rule 50(a).** (*see* Chapter X, *infra,* for a discussion of directed verdicts.) In fact, **Rule 50** motions were renamed motions for "judgment as a matter of law" to mirror summary judgment standards. A trial judge must "direct a verdict if, under governing law, there can be but one reasonable conclusion as to the verdict . . . if reasonable minds could differ as to the import of the evidence, a verdict should not be directed. . . . " **Anderson v. Liberty Lobby,** *supra.* The difference between the two motions is a timing consideration; summary judgment occurs prior to trial, and directed verdict occurs at trial.

ii. Inferences and Credibility Issues: Burden of Production

When a party is unable to establish the existence of a central act or event directly through affidavits, documents, or other evidence, courts generally may not allow inferences to be taken into account on summary judgment. *See, e.g.* **Cross v. United States,** 336 F.2d 431 (2d Cir. 1964). Similarly, as discussed below, where issues of witness credibility or demeanor are involved, courts are reluctant to grant summary judgment. *Cross, id.; see also* **Lundeen v. Cordner,** 354 F.2d 401 (8th Cir. 1966).

iii. Recent Trend: Inferences

Although courts have been reluctant to draw inferences on summary judgment, in 1986 the Supreme Court affirmed a summary judgment where the lower court had decided the motion based on its assessment of competing inferences. *See* **Matsushita Elec. Indus. Co. v. Zenith Radio Corp.,** 475 U.S. 574 (1986) (*see* discussion *infra*).

c. Shifting Burdens of Production, Persuasion, and Proof

Until 1986, there was a great deal of confusion in the lower federal courts concerning the appropriate allocation of burdens of production, persuasion, and proof on a summary judgment motion. In a 1986 trilogy of cases addressed to this issue, the Supreme Court attempted to clarify the burdens on the movant and adverse party in a summary judgment proceeding. *See* **Celotex Corp. v. Catrett,** 477 U.S. 317 (1986); **Anderson v. Liberty Lobby, Inc.,** 477 U.S. 242 (1986), and **Matsushita Electric Industrial Corp. v. Zenith Radio Corp.,** 475 U.S. 574 (1986). The major insight of the *Celotex* decision is to relate burdens of production and proof on the summary judgment motion to the party that carries those burdens at trial.

■ TABLE 8–1 BURDENS OF PRODUCTION AND PERSUASION ON SUMMARY JUDGMENT*

See Mullenix, *Summary Judgment: Taming the Beast of Burdens,* 10 Am. J. Trial Advoc. 433 (1987), discussing the "trilogy."

A. Party Moving for Summary Judgment:

Initial Burden of Production

Movant carries burden of persuasion at trial	Nonmovant carries burden of persuasion at trial
Must show:	Must show:
(1) Credible evidence to support directed verdict at trial	(1) Affirmative evidence negating essential element of non-moving party's claim *or* (2) Nonmoving party's evidence is absent or insufficient to establish essential element of nonmoving party's claim

B. Party Opposing Summary Judgment:

Shifted Burden of Production

Movant carries burden of persuasion at trial	Nonmovant carries burden of persuasion at trial

Must show:	Must show:
(1) Evidentiary materials demonstrating existence of genuine issue for trial	(1) Sufficient evidence to make out its claim
	or
	(2) Affidavit requesting additional time for discovery

C. Party Moving for Summary Judgment:

Ultimate Burden of Persuasion

Evaluate:

(1) Entire setting of case; entire record and summary judgment materials.

(2) Whether it is clear that trial is unnecessary.

(3) Whether there is any doubt as to existence of genuine issue for trial (to be resolved against moving party).

i. Initial Burden of Production: The *Celotex* Decision

The party seeking a summary judgment—either a claimant or defending party—may move for a summary judgment. There is, however, no affirmative requirement that the moving party support its motion with any materials in support of the motion. *Celotex,* supra. **Usually, however, moving parties do supply the court with more information than what is alleged in the party's pleadings. In addition, the nature of the showing depends on who bears the burden of persuasion at trial, and what standard of proof is required (*see* discussion *infra*).**

(a) Clarification of misinterpretation of the *Adickes* decision. One of the central points of the Court's *Celotex* decision was to rectify a misapplication of a prior Court holding in **Adickes v. S.H. Kress & Co.,** 398 U.S. 144 (1970). The civil rights action, which included conspiracy claims, arose from the denial of service to blacks in a Kress restaurant. The Supreme Court reversed a grant of summary judgment in Kress's favor, on the ground that Kress, as the movant, had failed to adduce evidence to demonstrate the absence of police from the restaurant. Because Kress had not met its initial burden of establishing the absence of a policeman in the store, *Adickes* was not required to produce counter-affidavits.

(b) **Movant need not negate opponent's claim.** In *Celotex,* Justice Rehnquist writing for the Court's majority, held that the Court could find "no express or implied requirement in **Rule 56** that the moving party support its motion with affidavits or other similar materials *negating* the opponents claim."

- **Lessening of initial burden: Impact.** The Supreme Court's lessening of the initial burden in *Celotex* was intended to facilitate more frequent use (and approval) of summary judgment procedure.

(c) **Nature of showing in support: Justice Brennan's dissent.** Writing for three dissenting Justices, Justice Brennan attempted to clarify the nature of the parties' burdens of production by relating that to the burden of persuasion each party carries at trial. Thus, the initial showing and shifted burdens vary in relation to whether the movant or the adverse party carries the burden of persuasion on the issue at trial.

- **Initial summary judgment burdens, as related to trial burdens (***see*** Table 8–1):**

- **Movant carries burden of persuasion at trial.** If the party moving for summary judgment also carries the burden of persuasion at trial, then the movant's initial burden on summary judgment is to show credible evidence to support a directed verdict at trial.

- **Non-movant carries the burden of persuasion at trial.** If the non-movant carries the burden of persuasion at trial, then the party moving for summary judgment may satisfy its initial burden by showing affirmative evidence negating an essential element of the non-moving party's claim, or that the non-moving party's evidence is either absent or insufficient to establish an essential element of the non-moving party's claim.

(d) **Disagreement over initial burden after *Celotex:* Justice White's concurrence.** Justice Rehnquist's majority opinion in *Celotex* clearly states that a party moving for summary judgment may request the summary judgment "with or without affidavits," and imposes no requirement that the movant come forward with anything else. **Rule 56** also refers to *"affidavits, if any."* Justice White's concurrence, however, disagrees that a movant may discharge its initial burden without adducing anything other than its motion: "But the movant must discharge the burden the rules place upon him: It is not enough to move for summary judgment without supporting the motion in any way or with a conclusory assertion that the plaintiff has not evidence to prove his case."

ii.   **Shifted Burden of Production and Persuasion: Burden on the Party Opposing the Motion**

Once the movant has satisfied its initial burden of production on the motion, then the burden of production shifts to the party opposing the motion—the adverse party. Again, the nature of the shifted burden depends on who bears the burden of persuasion at trial.

(a)   **Burden of production on adverse party: Supporting materials.** The party opposing the summary judgment must set forth specific facts, either through affidavits or other materials, that there is a genuine issue for trial. *Celotex,* supra. **In contrast to the moving party's initial burden, the party opposing the motion has an affirmative duty to produce some facts demonstrating the existence of a factual dispute.**

   - In satisfying this burden, the adverse party may *not rest upon its allegations or denials in its pleadings.*

(b)   **Nature of the shifted burden of production, as related to trial burdens:**

   - **Movant carries the burden of persuasion at trial.** If the movant carries the burden of persuasion at trial, then the party opposing the summary judgment must show evidentiary materials demonstrating the existence of a genuine issue for trial, or, submit an affidavit requesting additional time for discovery (*see infra*).

   - **Continuance for additional discovery.** If the adverse party cannot present by affidavit facts essential to justify its opposition to the summary judgment motion, the court may either refuse the application for judgment or may order a continuance to allow the adverse party to make additional discovery in support of its opposition. **Rule 26(e).**

- **Non-movant carries burden of persuasion at trial.** If the non-movant carries the burden of persuasion at trial, then the party opposing the summary judgment must show sufficient evidence to make out its claim.

- **Example.** Plaintiff sued defendant on the grounds of slander. The defendant moved for summary judgment, supported by affidavits of all witnesses to the alleged defamation, each denying it occurred. The court appropriately granted summary judgment for the defendant, because even if the plaintiff could impeach the witnesses at trial, the plaintiff would have no competent evidence to discharge its burden at trial of proving the defamation. **Dyer v. MacDougall,** 201 F.2d 265 (2d Cir. 1952).

(c) **Failure to respond.** If a adverse party fails to respond with supporting materials raising a genuine issue as to a material fact, then the court may enter a summary judgment against the party. **Rule 56(e)(3).**

iii. Ultimate Burden of Persuasion on the Motion

If the adverse party satisfies its shifted burden of production and adduces materials suggesting a genuine issue as to the material fact, then the movant carries the ultimate burden of proof and persuasion on the motion. *Celotex,* supra. **The court must evaluate:**

- the entire setting of the case, the entire record, and the materials submitted on the summary judgment motion;

- whether it is clear that trial is unnecessary; and

- whether there is any doubt as to the existence of a genuine issue for trial (to be resolved against the moving party).

iv. Evidentiary Standards on the Motion: *Anderson v. Liberty Lobby*

A court must evaluate the summary judgment materials in light of the applicable substantive standards of proof required at trial. **Anderson v. Liberty Lobby, Inc.,** 477 U.S. 242 (1986).

(a) *Anderson* **decision.** The Supreme Court's *Anderson* decision formed part of the 1986 trilogy of cases dealing with different aspects of summary judgment procedure. In this defamation suit, the Court held that the existence of malice had to be established at summary judgment by clear and convincing evidence (the trial standard), rather than a preponderance of the evidence.

(b) **Impact of the** *Anderson* **decision.** The Court essentially read the directed verdict standard back into the summary judgment standard, effectively increasing the non-moving party's burden to withstand a summary judgment against it.

(c) **Justice Brennan's dissent.** Justice Brennan's dissented, suggesting that the *Anderson* rule would effectively turn summary judgment into a full-blown paper "trial before trial" on the merits, thereby defeating the efficiency and economy of summary judgment procedure. He also objected that the *Anderson* rule forces judges to impermissibly weigh, evaluate, and assess the quantum and caliber of evidence on the motion, a jury function which he believed summary judgment procedure did not allow to judges.

5. Special Problems Relating to Summary Judgment

a. Credibility and Demeanor Issues

Summary judgment traditionally is considered inappropriate in cases that require assessment or evaluation of a witness's credibility or demeanor. This is especially true because summary judgment, if granted, effectively forecloses the non-movant's ability to cross-examine a witness at trial. *See, e.g.,* **Cross v. United States,** 336 F.2d 431 (2d Cir. 1964) (summary judgment improvidently granted where Internal Revenue Service should have opportunity to call at trial a taxpayer claiming travel deductions; government should have benefit of jury determination of taxpayer's credibility for claimed deductions). *Cf.* **Lundeen v. Cordner,** 354 F.2d 401 (8th Cir. 1966) (no need for cross-examination where there is no indication that affiant is biased, dishonest, or unaware or unsure of facts). If a non-moving party with the burden of proof at trial fails to produce any evidence and instead wishes only to cross-examine affiants hoping to expose them at trial as untruthful, this is not sufficient to defeat the motion and proceed to trial.

b. State of Mind

Some jurisdictions prohibit summary judgment when a moving party's state of mind is in issue. The only way to counter a moving party's affidavit as to the person's state of mind or intent is to call that person at trial and subject the person to formal examination and cross-examination.

- **Statutory prohibition:** "Summary judgment may be denied in the discretion of the court . . . where a material fact is an individual's state of mind, or lack thereof, and such fact is sought to be established solely by the individual's affirmation thereof."

c. Complex Litigation

In general, courts have been reluctant to grant summary judgment in certain types of complex litigation, especially antitrust litigation. This resistance, however, has been substantially eroded by the Supreme Court's 1986 decision in **Matsushita Elec. Indus. Co. v. Zenith Radio Corp.,** *supra,* a complex antitrust suit.

i. The *Matsushita* Decision

The Court upheld a summary judgment motion granted on the basis of no showing of an antitrust conspiracy. The Court indicated that because the defendant successfully showed a lack of motive to conspire, the court reasonably could infer no conspiracy. The plaintiff had failed to respond with a competing showing of either facts or inference.

ii. Impact of *Matsushita:* Competing Inferences

The *Matsushita* decision is significant because it represents a significant inroad on the judiciary's long-standing resistance to granting summary judgment in complex cases. More narrowly, *Matsushita* indicates that summary judgment should be denied only when the trier of fact is confronted with two equally plausible competing inferences.

6. Partial Summary Judgment: Rules 56(g) and 54(b)

a. Partial Summary Judgment

Courts may grant partial summary judgment if they cannot grant summary judgment on the entire action. By this method, the court can reduce the number of claims or issues that need be tried to the jury. **Rule 56(g).**

b. Final Judgment

In a multi-claim case, the court may enter a final judgment on the claim that has been resolved by summary judgment. This permits a losing litigant to bring a direct appeal from the claim decided by the summary judgment motion. *See* **Rule 54(b)** and **28 U.S.C. § 1291.**

■ CHAPTER REVIEW CHECKLIST

Your civil procedure examination will not likely contain a problem relating to voluntary dismissal, involuntary dismissal, or default. However, you might wish to review the circumstances in which courts permit these dismissals, and the consequences of such resolution of the litigation. You are very likely to be tested on summary judgment procedure—along with jurisdictional problems, summary judgment is a fairly predictable examination question. Summary judgment problems need not be difficult to answer if you methodically analyze the relationship of the party seeking the motion and the burdens each litigant must satisfy either to have the court approve or reject the motion.

To answer a problem relating to a summary judgment motion, ask:

1. **Who is asking the court for a dismissal on summary judgment (the "movant")?**

2. **Who is opposing the summary judgment motion (the "adverse party" or "non-movant")?**

3. **What is the material fact that is the subject of the summary judgment motion?**

   Note: Your law professor will have to supply some statement of the applicable substantive law in order for you to identify what constitutes the "material fact" for purposes of the summary judgment motion.

   Note: The movant basically has to take the position that there is *no genuine issue as to this material fact,* and therefore the movant is entitled to a judgment *without having to go to trial.* The point of summary judgment is that in absence of a factual dispute, A TRIAL IS UNNECESSARY.

4. **Who carries what burdens of persuasion at trial? (Refer to Table 8–1.)**

- Does the movant on the summary judgment motion also carry the burden of persuasion at trial?

- Does the non-movant carry burden of persuasion at trial?

5. **Has the summary *judgment movant satisfied its initial burden of production?* (*See* Table 8–1.)**

   - What materials, if any, has the movant for summary judgment supplied to the court in support of its motion (just allegations in pleadings? affidavits?)

   - What is the nature of the support or evidence? What does it show the court? Does the evidence suggest that the non-moving party has failed to produce any evidence to support its case and burdens at trial?

6. **Has the burden of production shifted to the non-movant? (*See* Table 8–1.)**

   - Has the non-movant failed to respond? Relied only on its pleadings?

   - What materials, if any, has the non-movant for summary judgment supplied to the court in support of its motion (just allegations in pleadings? affidavits? discovery materials?)

   - What is the nature of the support or evidence? What does it show the court?

   - Does the non-movant need to request a continuance to obtain more discovery information to respond to the summary judgment motion?

7. **Is the moving party entitled to a summary judgment? Has the moving party carried its ultimate burden of persuasion on the motion? (*See* Table 8–1.)**

   - What is the applicable evidentiary standard at trial (and thus for summary judgment)?

   - Does the resolution of the factual question involve a witness's credibility? State of mind?

- Is the court required to draw inferences from the summary judgment materials in order to decide the motion? Are there competing inferences that should disallow summary judgment?

- Reviewing the entire setting of the case, entire record and summary judgment materials, is summary judgment appropriate?

  — Is it clear that a trial will be unnecessary?

  — Is there any doubt as to the existence of a genuine issue for trial (if there is, resolve this doubt against granting the summary judgment motion).

IX

Pretrial Judicial Management

■ ANALYSIS

■ CHAPTER OVERVIEW

- This chapter explores various pretrial case management techniques that judges may use to ensure the just, speedy, and inexpensive resolution of litigation.

- Traditionally, litigants were the masters of their own dispute and conducted their litigation with very little supervision or involvement of the court system or judicial personnel.

- The modern—although controversial—trend is for judges to take a more active role in supervising and managing their dockets. This "managerial" role is controversial precisely because it transforms the traditional concept of a judge as a neutral arbiter into an active participant in the litigation.

- In federal practice, active judicial case management is highly encouraged by the Judicial Conference of the United States, and through the Federal Rules.

- Congress, in the **1990 Civil Justice Reform Act,** required every federal district court to conduct a docket assessment and prepare a report and reform plan. The reform plans include various pretrial case management techniques.

- **Rule 16** is the primary means for pretrial judicial case management. The Advisory Committee on Civil Rules amended **Rule 16** as part of the 1993 rule-revision package. The amendments expanded the nature and scope of a judge's pretrial authority and duties.

- The pretrial conference rule requires judges to conduct pretrial conferences to schedule and supervise discovery, motion practice, joinder of parties and claims, and other appropriate matters.

- **Rule 16** also provides wide discretion for the judge to consider a range of subjects for disposition at the pretrial conference.

- The court will hold a final pretrial conference as close as practicable to trial. The court issues a final, binding trial order on matters agreed to at that conference and it supercedes all previous pretrial pleadings.

- Lawyers may be sanctioned for not appearing at pretrial conference, or not preparing for and participating in the conference in good faith.

- Judges also are assisted in managing their case dockets through the use of special masters and magistrate judges. **Rule 53** governs the appointment of masters and the scope of their authority. Federal statute provides for the appointment of magistrate judges, who are not Article III judges and who sit for fixed terms.

A. JUDICIAL CASE MANAGEMENT, GENERALLY

1. Traditional Model of Litigation, Judicial Function, and the Adversary System

The traditional model of litigation, described by Professor Abram Chayes, is characterized by five features: (1) the lawsuit is bipolar—between a single plaintiff and single defendant, (2) the litigation is retrospective, concerning past events, (3) the right and the remedy are interdependent, (4) the lawsuit is a self-contained episode, and (5) the process is party-initiated and party-controlled. *See* Abram Chayes, *The Role of the Judge in Public Law Litigation*, 89 Harv. L. Rev. 1281 (1976).

2. Development of Modern Public Law Litigation

Although many state cases and some federal litigation still resemble the traditional model, most litigation does not. Professor Chayes posited the modern litigation paradigm of "public law" litigation. *Id.* Characteristics of the public litigation model include:

- a sprawling and amorphous litigation, including multiple parties and multiple claims;

- a litigation that changes over the course of the dispute resolution process;

- a litigation suffused and intermixed with negotiating and mediating processes at every point;

- a judge who is the major figure in organizing and dominating the case, as well as continuing involvement in administration and implementation of relief.

Paradigmatic public law litigation of the 1960s and 1970s includes cases involving institutional reform of prison systems, mental health facilities, school desegregation, employment discrimination, and civil rights actions. In the 1990s, commentators have suggested that mass tort litigation is a new form of public law litigation.

3. Modern Case Management Movement—Managerial Judges

The "judicial case management" movement originated in the development of the modern sprawling, amorphous case involving multiple parties and multiple claims. Additionally, liberal discovery rules inspire numerous disputes among attorneys concerning pretrial access to information. These pretrial disputes often require the active intervention or supervision by a judicial officer. Once involved, judges often assume the roles of mediators, negotiators, or trial planners—functions well removed from the traditional concept of the neutral, disengaged judge (the "mere referee").

a. Mandated Case Management

Active case management is a method of implementing the values embodied in **Rule 1,** which requires administration of the Federal Rules to achieve the *speedy, efficient and inexpensive* resolution of civil disputes.

i. Rules 1 and 16 Amendments

The Advisory Committee on Civil Rules amended **Rule 1** in 1993 to add the requirement that federal courts *administer* the Federal Rules to accomplish the three goals. Prior to 1993, federal judges only were required to construe the rules to achieve these ends. The amendment, along with revisions to **Rule 16,** (*see* discussion *infra*) were intended to prod federal judges into active case management.

b. Criticisms of Judicial Case Management

The "judicial case management movement" is not universally approved or lauded, for a number of reasons.

i. Traditional Role of Judge

Active judicial case management transgresses the traditional notion of the role and function of the judge as a neutral arbiter of disputes, who only decides questions framed by adversarial litigants.

ii. Rejection of Adversarial System

Judicial case management undermines or subverts the adversarial system by permitting the litigation to be judicially directed, rather than controlled by the litigants. Under the judicial case management model, the judicial system has an independent interest in the litigation and judge shares power with the parties in processing the lawsuit.

iii. Disservice to Litigants

Some managerial judges may place the court's interests in expeditious dispute resolution above the litigants' interests. Thus, judges concerned about congested dockets may impair litigants' interests through docket-clearing techniques, under the guise of calendar control or other supervisory powers. Judges also may improperly pressure parties to settle.

4. Civil Justice Reform Act of 1990

Congress enacted the **Civil Justice Reform Act** in 1990, which required every federal judicial district to create a CJRA Advisory Committee. These committees were required to conduct an assessment of the district's docket and write a report and plan for reform. By the end of 1993, all ninety-four federal district courts complied with the CJRA and implemented plans incorporating a wide array of judicial case management techniques. Many of the CJRA recommendations also have been implemented by local rules of court (*see* **Rule 83**).

a. Cornerstone Principles

Six cornerstone principles animated the CJRA legislative program for managerial reform of the federal courts:

(1) building reform from the "bottom up,"

(2) promulgating a national, statutory policy in support of judicial case management,

(3) imposing greater controls on the discovery process,

(4) establishing differentiated case management systems,

(5) improving motions practice and reducing undue delays associated with decisions on motions, and

(6) expanding and enacting the use of alternative dispute resolution.

5. The Manual for Complex Litigation

In addition to a judge's powers to manage and control a litigation under **Rule 16** and other inherent powers (discussed *infra*), the Federal Judicial Center publishes a *Manual for Complex Litigation* (4th ed. 2004) which contains numerous recommendations to federal judges for organizing and supervising complex litigation. The *Manual's* recommendations do not have the status of Federal Rules of Civil Procedure and are not binding on the parties, unless the judge formally incorporates a recommended procedure into a court order.

B. PRETRIAL CONFERENCE: RULE 16

The pretrial conference rule is the chief means through which a federal judge manages and controls the course of a litigation. In theory, a federal judge may schedule as many pretrial conferences as the judge deems appropriate to the litigation. Prior to 1993, there was no requirement for any pretrial conference or scheduling order, and many federal judges did not wish to use their time in this fashion. The 1993 amendments to **Rule 16** now affirmatively require that the judge prepare a scheduling order, even in the absence of an early pretrial conference. Local district courts may exempt certain cases from this requirement, and many courts have exempted routine simple cases, such as Social Security appeals, from this rule. In addition, the Advisory Committee Note indicates that the 1993 changes were to alter the focus of pretrial conferences to encompass all aspects of case management, and not merely the conduct of trial.

1. Objectives of the Pretrial Conference: Rule 16(a)

Judges have discretionary power to order attorneys or unrepresented parties to appear at a pretrial conference. The purposes of pretrial conference include:

- expediting the disposition of the action;

- establishing early and continuing control so that the case will not be protracted because of a lack of management;

- discouraging wasteful pretrial activities;

- improving the quality of the trial through more thorough preparation; and

- facilitating settlement of the case.

2. Initial Pretrial Scheduling Conference and Order: Rule 16(b)

After the lawyers have met and conferred at the outset of the litigation to discuss mandatory informal exchange of discovery, as well as subsequent formal discovery, the lawyers must submit a report to the court. **Rule 26(f)** (*see* discussion *supra*). After receiving the lawyer's report, the court either may arrange a conference in person with the lawyers, or by other means such as telephone or mail.

a. Timing of the Scheduling Order

The court must issue a scheduling order within 90 days after the appearance of the defendant in the lawsuit or within 120 days after the plaintiff serves the complaint on the defendant.

b. Content of the Scheduling Order

The scheduling order must limit the time:

(1) to join other parties and amend the pleadings;

(2) to file motions, and

(3) to complete discovery

The scheduling order also may include:

(4) modifications of the times for disclosures of mandatory information required to be exchanged under **Rule 26(a)** and **26(e)(1)** and of the extent of permissible discovery;

(5) disclosure or discovery of electronically stored information;

(6) agreements concerning claims of privilege or work product immunity; and

(7) the date or dates for other pretrial conferences, a final pretrial conference, and trial.

c. Modifications of Scheduling Order

A scheduling order may not be modified except upon a *showing of good cause* and by leave of a district judge or if authorized by local rule, by a magistrate judge.

3. Subjects for Consideration at Pretrial Conferences: Rule 16(c)

Rule 16(c) was substantially amended in 1993 to greatly expand the nature and scope of subjects a court may take action regarding, at pretrial conference. These revisions reflect an endorsement and encouragement of increased judicial case management. Judges may take appropriate actions to:

- the formulation and simplification of the issues, including the elimination of frivolous claims or defenses;

- the necessity or desirability of amendments to the pleadings;

- the possibility of obtaining admissions of fact and of documents which will avoid unnecessary proof, stipulations regarding the authenticity of documents, and advance rulings from the court on the admissibility of evidence;

- the avoidance of unnecessary proof and of cumulative evidence, and limitations or restrictions on the use of testimony under **Rule 702** of the **Federal Rules of Evidence;**

- the appropriateness and timing of summary adjudication under **Rule 56;**

- the control and scheduling of discovery, including orders affecting disclosures and discovery pursuant to **Rule 26** and **Rules 29** through **37;**

- the identification of witness(es) and documents, the need and schedule for filing and exchanging pretrial briefs, and the date or dates for further conferences and for trial;

- the advisability of referring matters to a magistrate judge or master;

- settlement and the use of special procedures to assist in resolving the dispute when authorized by statute or local rule;

- the form and substance of the pretrial order;

- the disposition of pending motions;

- the need for adopting special procedures for managing potentially difficult or protracted actions that may involve complex issues, multiple parties, difficult legal questions, or unusual proof problems;

- an order for a separate trial pursuant to **Rule 42(b)** with respect to a claim, counterclaim, cross-claim, or third-party claim, or with respect to any particular issue in the case;

- an order directing a party or parties to present evidence early in the trial with respect to a manageable issue that could, on the evidence, be the basis for a judgment as a matter of law under **Rule 50(a)** or a judgment on partial findings under **Rule 52(c);**

- an order establishing a reasonable limit on time allowed for presenting evidence;

- such other matters as may facilitate the just, speedy, and inexpensive disposition of the action.

4. Pretrial Orders

The court may issue any pretrial orders as a result of pretrial conferences. The order controls the course of the proceedings, unless the court modifies the order by a subsequent order. **Rule 16(e).**

5. Final Pretrial Conference and Pretrial Order: Rule 16(e)

a. Timing

The final pretrial conference takes place as close to the time of trial as reasonable under the circumstances. A final pretrial conference is not absolutely required, and the judge will determine if a final pretrial conference is appropriate.

b. Attendance

The final pretrial conference must be attended by at least one lawyer who will try the case for each side, and by any unrepresented parties.

c. Duties

Lawyers attending the final pretrial conference must be prepared, in good faith, to discuss the case and any subjects listed in **subsection (c).** Lawyers participating in any pretrial conference must have authority to enter into stipulations and make admissions regarding all matters that the participants may reasonably anticipate being discussed. **Rule 16(c).**

- **Settlement.** The court may require that a party or its representative be present or reasonably available by telephone in order to consider possible settlement of the dispute. **Rule 16(c).** *See also* **G. Heileman Brewing Co. v. Joseph Oat Corp.,** 871 F.2d 648 (7th Cir. 1989).

d. Final Pretrial Order

The court will issue a final pretrial order memorializing the actions concluded at the pretrial conference, which are absolutely binding on the subsequent trial. *See* **Payne v. S.S. Nabob,** 302 F.2d 803 (3d Cir. 1962). The final pretrial order may be modified *only to prevent manifest injustice. See* **Smith Contracting Corp. v. Trojan Constr. Co.,** 192 F.2d 234 (10th Cir. 1951) (justice required granting defendant leave to amend an answer to set up a counterclaim, where no prejudice to plaintiff by late assertion of counterclaim).

6.   Duties and Sanctions: Rule 16(f)

a.   Duties

Parties and their attorneys are required to:

(1)   obey scheduling and pretrial orders;

(2)   appear on behalf of a party at a scheduling or pretrial conference, *see* **G. Heileman Brewing Co. v. Joseph Oat Corp.,** 871 F.2d 648 (7th Cir. 1989);

(3)   be prepared to participate in the conference, and

(4)   participate in good faith.

b.   Sanctions for Failure to Comply with Pretrial Conference Duties

A court may sanction a party or lawyer who fails to comply with duties relating to pretrial conferences. Another party may seek a sanction by motion, or the judge may sanction the offending lawyer on the judge's own initiative.

i.   "Orders that Are Just"

The judge may make any orders that are just, or available under the discovery sanctioning provisions contained in **Rule 37(b)(2)(A)(ii)–(vii)** (*see* discovery sanctions, *supra*).

ii.   Attorney's Fees

The court also may order an attorney to pay any reasonable expenses and attorney's fees incurred in connection with non-compliance, unless the judge finds that the attorney's noncompliance was *substantially justified* or other circumstances make award of expenses *unjust.* **Rule 16(f)(2).**

C.   EXTRAJUDICIAL PERSONNEL: MASTERS AND MAGISTRATES

1.   Special Masters: Rule 53

"Special masters" are court-appointed personnel who assist the court in performing a wide array of functions. Special masters have a long history in

English law, although their use in civil litigation was disfavored. Under the old **Federal Equity Rule 59,** the appointment of a special master was to be used in exceptional circumstances only. **Rule 53** was effectively re-written and extensively amended effective December 1, 2003, to reflect the modern practice of appointment of special masters, and the various tasks that special masters perform.

a. Modern Special Masters under the Federal Rules

A court may appoint a special master in any pending action. Masters can be appointed to perform duties consented to by the parties, hold trial proceedings, and address pre-trial and post-trial matters. Masters can be appointed to serve as referees, auditors, examiners, assessors, trial planners, or any other role for which the court seeks assistance. **Rule 53(a).**

b. Orders Appointing Special Masters; Appointment of Magistrate Judges

The court must give the parties notice and an opportunity to be heard prior to the appointment of a special master. The court must issue an order appointing a special master that delineates the scope and authority of the special master, as well as the method and terms for determining the special master's compensation. **Rule 53(b).** A matter may be referred to a magistrate judge under the special master rule only when the order referring the matter to the magistrate judge expressly provides that the reference is made under **Rule 53. Rule 53(h).**

c. Special Master's Authority

Special masters have authority to regulate all proceedings and take appropriate actions to perform assigned duties. These include authority to:

(1) hold and regulate hearings;

(2) do all acts and take all measures necessary for the efficient performance of the master's duties;

(3) require production of all evidence relating to matters within the scope of the mater's duties;

(4) rule on the admissibility of evidence (unless otherwise directed by the order of reference);

(5) put witnesses or parties under oath and examine them.

- Parties may request that a special master make a record of evidence offered and excluded.

- Special masters may impose any non-contempt sanctions as provided by **Rules 37** or **45. Rule 53(c)(2).**

d. Evidentiary Hearings, Orders, Reports

A special master may conduct evidentiary hearings and compel, take, and record evidence. **Rule 53(c).** The special master may issues orders, **Rule 53(d),** and must issue a report to the court as required by the special master's order of appointment. **Rule 53(e).** A court subsequently may act on the special master's report, affording the parties an opportunity to be heard on the report, to object, and to modify the report. **Rule 53(f).** The court must decide *de novo* all objections to findings of fact or law made or recommended by a special master. **Rule 53(f)(3), (4).**

e. Special Master Compensation

The appointing court has the power to determine and fix the special master's compensation based on the terms stated in the order of appointment. **Rule 53(g).**

2. Magistrate Judges: 28 U.S.C. §§ 631–639 and Rule 72

The **Federal Magistrates Act of 1968** created a system of federal magistrates. Federal magistrates may serve in a wide array of functions and capacities as defined both by statute and by the Federal Rules. A 1990 amendment to the Act provides that magistrates be designated as "United States magistrate judges."

a. Constitutional Status of Magistrate Judges

Magistrate judges are not Article III judges and do not enjoy life tenure or the salary protections of Article III judges. Magistrate judges, however, perform many of the same functions as Article III judges, including conducting trials by consent of the parties. There is some controversy whether magistrates are unconstitutional, but the consensus of expert witnesses at the time of enactment of the **Magistrates Act** was that the legislation creating magistrates was constitutional.

b. Powers and Functions of Magistrate Judges

The scope of magistrates authority is very broad.

i. **Parties' Consent**

When the parties consent, a magistrate judge may "conduct any and all proceedings in a jury or non-jury civil matter and order entry of judgment in the case."

ii. **Discovery, Pretrial Motions, Other Matters**

Magistrates may conduct and supervise discovery, make rulings relating to pretrial motions (subject to review by the district judge), or conduct any other proceedings delegated by the district court.

X

Trial

■ **ANALYSIS**

■ CHAPTER OVERVIEW

- This chapter concerns three aspects of trial procedure: the right to a trial by jury; the sequence or phases of a trial; and post-trial motions and the grounds for challenging trial results.

- Juries are the finders of fact and judges make rulings of law. Historically, juries tried all cases involving legal questions, while any equitable actions were tried solely to a judge.

  — The Seventh Amendment to the Constitution preserves the right to a jury trial in suits at common law in any controversy exceeding twenty dollars.

  — The Seventh Amendment guarantee to a right to a trial by jury applies only in federal court. The Seventh Amendment has not been *"incorporated"* under constitutional principles and made applicable to the states through the Fourteenth Amendment.

- Therefore, theoretically, a person is not constitutionally guaranteed a right to a jury trial unless a state provides for a jury trial right in the state's constitution.

- The federal right to a jury trial is not absolute and a party may waive that right either directly, or indirectly by failing to make a timely demand for a jury.

  — A plaintiff must make a *jury demand* in the complaint. If the defendant or other third party asserts a counterclaim, cross-claim, or other claim, the party must make a jury demand on that claim or the right to a jury trial on the claim is waived.

- Under modern federal pleading practice, a party may assert both legal and equitable claims in the same action. When a party asserts both legal and equitable claims, the legal claims must be tried to a jury first, and the equitable claims must be tried to the judge subsequently.

- The size and composition of juries varies in federal and state practice. Many state courts use juries of fewer than twelve jurors, although federal courts still adhere to the twelve juror rule. In state courts lawyers typically examine prospective jurors to see if they are qualified, impartial jurors, in a proceeding called the *"voir dire"*; in federal courts, judges conduct the *voir dire*.

- The trial of a civil suit typically consists of six stages: opening statements; presentation of the evidence; closing argument; jury instructions; jury deliberation and verdict; and post-trial motions and judgment.

- Rules of substantive law and evidence determine the party's allocation of the *burdens of production, persuasion,* and *proof.*

  — In deciding the case, jurors are permitted to draw *rational inferences* from evidence. But there must be some evidence for the jurors to draw this inference.

  — If a party does not satisfy its burden of production on an issue, the adverse party is entitled to a *judgment as a matter of law* and the judge is permitted to *direct a verdict* (old name) in favor of the adverse party. **Rule 50(a).** The "directed verdict" effectively takes the case away from the jury. Judgments as a matter of law are constitutional and do not violate the losing party's Seventh Amendment right to a jury trial.

- Similarly, after a jury returns a verdict, the judge may conclude that no reasonable jury could have reached the same conclusion because the evidence to support the jury verdict was lacking. In this instance, the judge may render a *judgment notwithstanding the jury's verdict* (now renamed "judgment as a matter of law," **Rule 50(b)**).

  (1) In order for a losing party to move for a judgment notwithstanding the verdict, that party has to have made a prior directed verdict motion at the close of evidence during trial.

  (2) A judgment notwithstanding the verdict effectively takes away a jury's verdict or decision.

  (3) Judgments notwithstanding the verdict are constitutional and do not deprive the formerly successful litigant of its right to a jury trial.

- A losing party must assert post-trial motions in an expeditious and timely fashion. A losing party may challenge the trial result, and request a new trial, on the grounds that the jury verdict was *incoherent,* or there was some procedural error or mistake that tainted the jury's ability to render a verdict, or that the verdict was *against the weight of the evidence.*

— A court may either grant or deny a losing party's request for a new trial. In granting or denying the request, the court also will indicate whether it would conditionally recommend a new trial if the appellate court reverses the district judge's decision.

• A losing party may ask the court to set aside a judgment on grounds that are discovered after the court renders its judgment. The grounds for setting aside a judgment include *mistake, excusable neglect, newly discovered evidence, or fraud.*

• Certain kinds of jury misconduct may provide a ground for a new trial.

• Federal judges have the authority to reduce the size of a jury award (*"remittitur"*), but not to increase the size of a jury award (*"additur"*). Many states, however, recognize both *remittitur* and *additur.*

A. CHOOSING THE TRIER: JUDGE OR JURY?

1. The Province of the Judge and Jury

Traditionally, the jury is the "finder of fact" and the judge applies the law. This development of the judge-jury relationship evolved over a lengthy period into this modern dichotomy. For example, in colonial America, juries could decide questions of law, especially in criminal cases. Prior to 1850, juries in many jurisdictions could decide questions of both fact and law.

a. Historical Basis for Choice of Trier: The Institution of Trial by Jury

Modern American jury practice derives from the development of the jury in England. William the Conqueror introduced the jury system in England in the eleventh century. By the end of the fifteenth century the jury was the central method of fact-finding (replacing the medieval practice of trial by ordeal). By the seventeenth century, juries served as checks against the absolutist Stuart kings.

b. Historical Function of the Jury

Originally jurors were chosen on the basis for their fitness as a witness with knowledge and background about the local community. Jurors were entitled to decide a case based on personal knowledge even when this contradicted testimony at trial. Jurors could consult and communicate directly with the parties in an inquisitorial fashion. Over time this inquisitorial role shifted to that of impartial finder-of-fact, and jurors became dependent on evidence the parties presented at trial.

i. American Colonial Practice

The English jury system was imported into the American colonies and served as a check on oppressive British rule in the colonies. The populist, lay jury embodies a long-standing tradition of serving as a bulwark against government oppression. The jury ("of peers") also traditionally is viewed as a fair and equitable arbiter of the law, and more democratic.

ii. Philosophical Basis for Jury Ascendancy

For centuries, reliance on the jury was based in various natural law philosophies. With the waning of natural law theory in the nineteenth century, mistrust of juries increased and the respective roles of jurors and judges became more sharply delineated.

c. Criticisms of Jury Structure and Practice

Notwithstanding its long privileged historical lineage, the jury in contemporary practice frequently is under attack.

i. Juries as an Oppressive, Unregulated Force

Populist juries are viewed as an oppressive force—unknowledgeable, unpredictable, and operating in a largely unregulated manner.

ii. Jury Nullification

Jury critics point to the phenomenon of *jury nullification,* when juries essentially disregard the factual evidence presented at trial, disregard the law, and use their power to "send a message" through their verdict. Jury nullification is more of a phenomenon in criminal trials than in civil cases, because of the enhanced control the civil judge typically may exert over the outcome of the case through **Rule 50.**

iii. Waste of Resources

Jury trials also are perceived as a waste of time and resources, consuming a disproportionate part of societal resources. The costs of jury trials do not outweigh the benefits derived from them; bench trials are equally efficacious and less costly.

iv. Lack of Expertise

Juries also have been criticized as lacking the expertise to render intelligent judgments in complex civil cases. Additionally, juries may render verdicts based on improper criteria or sympathies.

d. Modern Jury Functions

Modern jury functions include:

(1) determining facts;

(2) determining the legal consequences of the facts through application of the law as the judge instructs the jury; and

(3) presenting the results of the jury's deliberation in a verdict.

e. Modern Judicial Functions

Modern judicial functions include:

(1) ruling on pretrial motions and preliminary issues; including determining threshold issues such as questions relating to jurisdiction, joinder, pleading, and defenses;

(2) determining the structure of the trial;

(3) determining questions of admissibility of evidence and exclusion of evidence;

(4) determining questions of privilege and immunity;

(5) taking "judicial notice" of undisputed and uncontroverted facts;

(6) determining the sufficiency of evidence relative to the allocation of burdens of production, persuasion, and proof;

(7) determining the rules of substantive law to be applied;

(8) determining how to instruct the jury concerning the substantive law and what type of verdict to be rendered; and

(9) determining whether a jury's determination is unreasonable or needs to be reduced or increased.

2. Sources of the Right to a Jury Trial

There are three sources for the right to a jury trial: (1) the Seventh Amendment or state constitutional provisions; (2) statutorily-created rights providing for a jury trial; and (3) discretionary jury panels in equity proceedings.

a. Federal Constitutional Right to Jury Trial

i. Federal Court: The Seventh Amendment Right to Trial by Jury

The Seventh Amendment to the Constitution, effective in 1791, provides: *"In suits at common law, where the value in controversy shall exceed twenty dollars, the right to trial by jury shall be preserved, and no fact tried by a jury, shall be otherwise re-examined in any court of the United States, than according to the rules of the common law."*

(a) **"Preservation of right."** The Seventh Amendment *does not create* a right to trial by jury. Rather, it *"preserves"* the right as it existed at the time the amendment was ratified in 1791. This does not mean that jury trials are frozen only as to those actions that existed at common law in 1791. Rather, this language provides the interpretative basis for modern federal courts to determine what contemporary statutory causes of action are entitled to a jury trial. (*see* discussion and examples *infra*).

- **Rule 38** also preserves "the right of trial by jury as declared by the Seventh Amendment . . . to the parties inviolate."

- Although the Seventh Amendment *preserves* the right to a jury trial in federal cases, this right is far from absolute or sacrosanct in federal practice.

- **Jury demand and waiver.** The federal right to a jury is waivable. **Rule 38(d).** A party desiring a jury trial must make a jury demand in a timely fashion. **Rule 38(b);** *see also* discussion *infra*.

(b) **Implementation of the right to a jury trial: Problem created by the merger of law and equity.** With promulgation of the Federal Rules in 1938, the rules merged actions at law and equity into one "civil action." A party could now assert any legal or equitable claims in a unified federal complaint.

(c) **Consequences of the merger of law and equity for jury trial right.** The merger of law and equity permitted the presentation of a single form of action in a unitary federal lawsuit. However, the merger did not abrogate the differences between the substantive and remedial rules of the two systems. Actions at law are entitled to be tried to a jury; equitable claims to a judge.

(d) The equitable "clean-up" doctrine. Before the merger of law and equity, equity practice developed the "clean-up" doctrine which allowed a court with equity jurisdiction to decide ("clean-up") any incidental legal issues involved in the litigation.

ii. **Applying The Seventh Amendment Guarantee in Modern Non-Statutory Cases**

In determining whether litigants are entitled to a jury, federal courts focus on the *nature of the issue* involved in the litigation.

(a) Legal issues raised by plaintiff. If the underlying issue involved in the case is legal (i.e., money damages are sought), then the litigant is entitled to a jury trial on the legal issue. **Ross v. Bernhard,** 396 U.S. 531 (1970). This applies even if the type of action historically is based in equity procedure, such as a class action or interpleader proceedings.

(b) Legal issues raised by defendant in answer. A jury trial is required even if a legal issue is raised by the defendant's answer, as through assertion of a legal counterclaim. **Beacon Theatres, Inc. v. Westover,** 359 U.S. 500 (1959).

(c) Legal and equitable claims: The *Beacon Theatres* rule. In actions that contain both legal and equitable claims, if there is a common factual issue then the legal issue must be tried first to a jury. The judge may then rule on the equitable claim. *Beacon Theatres, Inc., id.* The rationale for this rule is based on the theory that if the equitable claim were tried to the judge first and it had a preclusive effect on the common legal issue, then the litigant would be denied its jury trial right on the legal issue. In order to prevent this, the legal issue must be tried to the jury first. *Id.*

- **Departure from the equitable clean-up rule.** The *Beacon Theatres* holding represents a repudiation of and departure from the old equitable clean-up doctrine. The *Beacon Theatres* rule embodies a modern preference for jury trials.

- **Determining whether an issue is legal or equitable.** To apply the *Beacon Theatres* rule, courts must characterize the nature of an issue as legal or equitable. In many instances this presents no problem, because the issue has retained its legal or equitable nature since the eighteenth century (for example, fraud has always been an equitable claim). But modern litigation sometimes involves legal claims that did not exist as a "suit at common law" in 1791. Thus, federal courts determine whether the modern issue is sufficiently analogous to a common law action in 1791, to be able to characterize the modern issue as legal.

- **Flexible approach.** Federal courts have taken a very flexible approach to characterizing modern legal issues as either legal or equitable.

- **Nature of the remedy.** Courts also look to the form of remedy to assist in characterizing an issue. For example, actions seeking injunctive relief historically are equitable and do not require a jury. However, the nature of a remedy is not absolutely dispositive, and if modern law has created a new remedy, a jury trial may be required.

- **Example.** A claim seeking an accounting of business profits was entitled to a jury trial, even though an accounting is a traditional equitable form of relief. Under modern practice, special masters may assist the court in making an accounting. The availability of the offices of a special master removes the historical reason for referring actions seeking an accounting solely to a judge. **Dairy Queen, Inc. v. Wood,** 369 U.S. 469 (1962).

(d) Complexity exception. The Supreme Court also has suggested that there may be a "complexity exception" to the Seventh Amendment right to a trial by jury. **Ross v. Bernhard,** *supra.* In addition to evaluating whether an issue is legal or equitable, courts also may assess the "practical abilities and limitations of juries." *Id.* Some cases are so complex that a jury cannot reasonably decide the issues. The Supreme Court has not elaborated further on this standard and lower federal courts are split concerning applicability of this "complexity" standard.

iii. Right to Trial by Jury in Statutory Actions

When Congress creates a new right of action it may expressly or impliedly create a right to a jury trial. *See* **Beacon Theatres, Inc. v.**

Westover, *supra.* Congress has the power to confer a jury trial right broader than the Seventh Amendment guarantee. Congress also expressly or impliedly may deny a jury trial. Further, a statute may be silent concerning a jury trial right.

(a) **Statute provides jury trial right.** If the federal statute provides a right to a trial by jury, then there is no Seventh Amendment problem.

(b) **Statute does not provide jury trial right: New causes of action.** The right to a jury trial is not restricted to those actions at common law that existed in 1791.

(c) **Legal or equitable nature of claim.** If a statute does not provide for a jury trial right, then the jury trial right depends on whether the issues are legal or equitable in nature. Since most liability statutes codify common law rights, the right to a jury trial is not a problem. A problem exists when Congress declares an action as equitable, although historically the issue would have been tried to a jury in a common law suit. A jury trial problem also exists when the statute creates a cause of action, but is silent concerning whether a jury trial is available. In these instances, courts may review legislative history to ascertain congressional intent concerning the preference for a jury or non-jury proceeding.

(d) **No jury trial right: Actions before administrative agencies involving "public rights."** Statutes providing for proceedings before administrative boards or specialized courts that do not include a jury right have been upheld against constitutional attack. This applies only to situations involving the government under a statute creating enforceable public rights. *See* **Atlas Roofing Co. v. Occupational Safety & Health Review Commn.,** 430 U.S. 442 (1977) (upholding power of OSHA to levy civil penalties for violators of environmental laws); **Katchen v. Landy,** 382 U.S. 323 (1966) (upholding summary jurisdiction of the bankruptcy courts); **NLRB v. Jones and Laughlin Steel Corp.,** 301 U.S. 1 (1937) (upholding ability of National Labor Relations Board to make conclusive findings of fact).

(e) **No jury trial right: Foreign Sovereign Immunities Act and explicit congressional preference.** Claims brought under the

1976 Foreign Sovereign Immunities Act, Pub. L. No. 94–583, 90 Stat. 2891 (1976), are not entitled to a jury trial. The statute provides district court jurisdiction for actions against foreign governments and their instrumentalities, explicitly limiting jurisdiction to non-jury proceedings. The legislative history clearly indicates congressional intent for non-jury proceedings in order to promote uniformity and international comity, which might be impaired by aberrant jury decisions. Four federal circuit courts have upheld the non-jury provision against Seventh Amendment challenges. *See, e.g.,* **Goar v. Compania Peruana de Vapores,** 688 F.2d 417 (5th Cir. 1982); **Rex v. Cia. Peruana de Vapores, S.A.,** 660 F.2d 61 (3d Cir. 1981), *cert. denied,* 456 U.S. 926, **Williams v. Shipping Corp. of India,** 653 F.2d 875 (4th Cir. 1981), *cert. denied,* 455 U.S. 982; **Ruggiero v. Compania Peruana de Vapores,** "Inca Capac Yupanqui," 639 F.2d 872 (2d Cir. 1981).

(f) Jury trial right: Actions before administrative agencies involving private rights. If Congress does not create a new right of action involving public rights, and simply re-classifies a pre-existing common law cause of action implicating private rights, then a litigant is entitled to a jury trial. *See* **Granfinanciera, S.A. v. Nordberg,** 492 U.S. 33 (1989) (bankruptcy trustee's right to recover a fraudulent conveyance from a party was a private rather than a public right).

(g) Jury trial right: Remedial actions in federal district court with common law analogs. Litigants have a right to a trial by jury if Congress designates the federal district court to provide remedial relief, but is silent concerning a jury trial right. Courts are especially likely to find a jury trial right if there is a common law analog to the newly created cause of action. In such instances, courts may even override legislative intent arguments that Congress did not intend to provide a jury trial right.

■ EXAMPLES AND ANALYSIS

Example 1. Civil rights actions. An African–American woman brought a housing discrimination claim under Title VII of the 1968 Civil Rights Act. The statute was silent as to a jury trial right. She sought an injunction, compensatory and punitive damages, and attorney's fees. Her request for injunctive relief was dropped and the trial involved only money damages. The Supreme Court held that the defendant had a right to a jury trial because Title VII had created a statutory right "in the nature of a suit at common law." **Curtis v. Loether,** 415 U.S. 189 (1974). The Court rejected the argument that Congress did not intend to provide jury trials under the Act in order to avoid prejudice and delay, finding the legislative history to be sparse and ambiguous.

Note: Jury trial right: Other civil rights actions. Although **Curtis v. Loether** resolved the issue of a jury trial right under Title VII claims, this decision did not decide the availability of a jury trial right under other civil rights statutes. A litigant suing under a civil rights statute must show that Congress expressed a preference for a non-jury trial, supported by legitimate concerns about the ability of a jury to decide the case.

Example 2. Truckdrivers seeking backpay for a union's alleged breach of the duty of fair representation have a right to trial by jury. **Chauffeurs, Teamsters and Helpers Local 391 v. Terry,** 494 U.S. 558 (1990). The truckdrivers' action against the union encompassed both equitable and legal issues. The remedy of backpay is legal in nature and the money damages are a type of relief traditionally awarded by courts of law.

Example 3. A landlord sought recovery of real property under the District of Columbia Code. The Court Reform and Procedure Act of 1970 repealed a jury trial right in such actions. The Supreme Court held that the Seventh Amendment required a jury trial, regardless of Congress's intent to reduce delay and expense, because an action for the recovery of real property is analogous to a suit at common law. **Pernell v. Southall Realty,** 416 U.S. 363 (1974).

Contrast: Civil penalty statutes. The Supreme Court has held that in actions under federal statutes providing for civil penalties, an alleged violator is entitled to a jury trial to determine whether a violation has occurred and civil penalty is appropriate. On the other hand, the judge may assess the amount of the penalty, consistent with congressional intent that a judge perform this function. **Tull v. United States,** 481 U.S. 412 (1987).

iv. Right to Jury Panel in Equitable Actions: Rule 39(c)

The right to a jury panel in equitable actions historically is based in the equity advisory jury. The Chancellor had discretion to empanel a jury to render an advisory verdict. These verdicts were not binding and the Chancellor could enforce or disregard the advisory jury's conclusions. Equity juries determined questions for which they were thought especially suited, such as assessing witness credibility. Modern federal and state practice has retained the equity advisory jury to assist the judge in any issue the judge requests. Advisory juries may decide equitable issues for which there is no jury right, or try cases where the parties have waived their jury right. *See* **Rule 39(c).**

- **Binding nature of advisory verdicts.** In federal court judges have discretion to accept or disregard an advisory jury's verdict. This is true in most state courts. In a few state courts, advisory jury verdicts are binding unless the verdict is set aside on a post-trial motion. In some state courts, a judge may disregard an advisory jury's verdict only on a showing of good cause.

b. Right to Jury Trial in State Court

The federal constitutional right to a jury trial is not binding on the states because the Seventh Amendment has not been "incorporated" through the Fourteenth Amendment, as have many other provisions of the Bill of Rights. *See* **Chicago, Rock Island & Pacific Ry. Co. v. Cole,** 251 U.S. 54 (1919); **Walker v. Sauvinet,** 92 U.S. (2 Otto) 90, 23 L. Ed. 678 (1875).

i. State Constitutional Provisions

Most state constitutions contain a right to trial by jury. In state practice, the right to a jury trial typically is determined with reference to the date of the ratification of the state constitutional provisions. Since most states have merged law and equity and have constitutional or statutory provisions identical or similar to the Seventh Amendment, the same law-and-equity problems that exist in federal court are replicated in state court.

- **Avoidance of jury trial issue.** Some states avoid the right-to-jury issue by providing for a jury trial in all actions, including equity claims. Georgia, North Carolina, Tennessee, and Texas provide for a right to trial by jury in equity cases.

ii. **Approaches to Implementing State Jury Trial Right**

The states have adopted three approaches to implementing a jury trial right through state constitutional and statutory provisions.

(a) **Preservation of right.** Some states preserve the right to trial by jury (as declared by the Constitution or statute), without attempting to define the cases in which the right exists. This is the basic approach embodied in **Rule 38(a)** (*see supra*).

(b) **Equity exclusion.** Some states provide for a right to trial by jury in all cases except equity actions.

(c) **Enumeration of cases.** Some states enumerate the specific types of cases that are entitled to a jury trial. Often this enumeration reflects the historical distinctions of actions at law and equity.

c. **Conflicts between Federal and State Jury Trial Right**

i. **Actions Asserting Federally-Created Rights in State Court**

If a federal statute confers a jury trial right as an integral part of the relief, then federal rather than state law applies regarding the jury function. This is especially true when Congress has indicated a strong federal policy in favor of a jury trial in a particular case. **Dice v. Akron, Canton & Youngstown R.R. Co.,** 342 U.S. 359 (1952) (Ohio state courts obliged to conduct a jury trial on the issue of fraudulent release in a **Federal Employers' Liability Act** litigation).

ii. **Actions Involving State-Created Rights in Federal Court**

In federal diversity cases, federal jury standards apply. Although state law characterizes the state claim as legal or equitable, federal law determines whether the case is entitled to a jury trial. *See* **Byrd v. Blue Ridge Rural Elec. Coop. Inc.,** 356 U.S. 525 (1958) (discussed *supra* in Chapter III on Applicable Law); **Herron v. Southern Pacific Company,** 283 U.S. 91 (1931) (state law cannot alter the character or function of federal courts).

3. **Tactical Considerations in Deciding the Trier**

Unless a party makes a demand for a jury, or waives the right, the case will be tried to a judge in a bench trial. The judge also has the power to empanel an advisory jury under state and federal provisions (*see* discussion *supra*). In assessing whether to make a jury demand, a party will evaluate both institutional and psychological factors.

a.   Institutional Factors

i.   Docket Congestion and Delay

In many jurisdictions, litigants often are able to conduct a bench trial faster than a jury trial (because summoning, qualifying, and empanelling a jury takes time, as does the presentation of the case to a jury). The trial calendar may be longer than the judge trial calendar. A judge often can deliver a verdict more quickly than a deliberating jury. Thus, a litigant seeking an expeditious resolution of a dispute may waive a jury trial in favor of a bench trial. Conversely, a defendant seeking to coax a plaintiff into settlement negotiations might demand a jury trial.

ii.   Expense

Jury trials are expensive. Jury trials take longer because of jury selection (*voir dire*), presentation of evidence to the jury, lengthier opening and closing arguments, jury instructions, and jury deliberation. Jury trials typically generate larger attorney and witness fees. For all these reasons, litigants may elect to waive a jury trial in favor of a bench trial.

b.   Psychological Factors

Empirical studies suggest that judges and juries would agree in upwards of eighty percent of cases. However, attorneys weigh various psychological factors in choosing to present a case to a judge or jury. Among the factors considered include:

(1)   the nature of the case;

(2)   characteristics of the parties and the witnesses;

(3)   emotional content of the litigation;

(4)   types of jurors in the jury pool;

(5)   background and disposition of the judge; and

(6)   assessment of whether the lawyer is likely to be more effective before a judge or jury.

4. Demand or Waiver of Jury Trial: Rule 38(b), (d)

In a few states, a jury trial is used unless the parties request a bench trial. In most states, however, and federal court, the right to trial by jury is waived unless a litigant demands a jury within the time period provided by rule. Both plaintiffs and defendants have the right to make a jury demand. The loss of the right to a jury trial because of a failure to make a jury demand does not violate the Seventh Amendment (and therefore is not unconstitutional). **Moore v. United States,** 196 F.2d 906 (5th Cir. 1952).

a. Justification for Waiver of Jury Trial Right

The loss of a jury trial right for failure to make a timely jury demand permits judicial docket management and case control. Court require certainty concerning which cases require juries in order to manage jury and judge trial calendars.

b. Jury Demand in Federal Court

A party requesting a jury trial must make an affirmative demand and failure to do so results in a waiver. **Rule 38(b), (d).**

i. How Made; Timing

A jury demand must be made in writing and served on the opposing party. The jury demand may be made at any time after the commencement of an action, *but no later than 14 days after the service of the last pleading directed to such issue.* **Rule 38(b).**

(a) Counterclaims. In federal court, as a practical matter, jury demands are governed by the complaint and answer so a jury demand must be made within 14 days of service of the answer. If the defendant asserts a counterclaim requiring a reply, there may be additional time to make a jury demand, depending on the relationship of the counterclaim and the case-in-chief. If the counterclaim raises new issues not contained in the complaint and answer, then the plaintiff effectively has 14 days to make a jury demand after service of the answer, and the defendant an additional 14 days to make a jury demand after service of the reply.

(b) Late jury demands. Courts consider the following factors to determine whether to order a jury trial, in its discretion (*see infra*) for parties who have submitted a late jury demand:

- whether the jury demand has been made in a reasonable time after expiration of the specified time period;

- whether the failure resulted from inadvertence, mistake, or excusable neglect;

- whether permitting a late motion will prejudice the adverse party.

ii. Specified Issues

A litigant may effectively extend the time for making a jury demand by requesting a jury for only specified issues. This provides the responding party with time within which to make a jury demand on the issue. **Rule 38(c).**

iii. Withdrawal of Jury Demand

A jury demand may only be withdrawn on the consent of all the parties. This is to protect those parties who have relied on the jury demand and prepared their case for presentation to a jury (rather than a judge). **Rule 38(d).**

iv. Removed Cases: Rule 81(c)(3)

A timely express demand for a jury trial in state court secures the right to a trial by jury in federal court. A demand need not be made, however, if the state court does not require an express jury trial demand. *But see* **Segal v. American Cas. Co.,** 250 F.Supp. 936 (D. Md. 1966) (plaintiffs not entitled to jury on removal where no demand was necessary under state law, and federal demand was untimely).

v. Discretionary Jury Trial: Rule 39(b)

If parties fail to make a timely jury demand and have waived their right to a jury trial, they may request that the court exercise its discretion and order a jury trial anyway. **Rule 39(b).** Some federal courts have indicated that there should be good grounds for exercise of this discretion. *See* **Segal v. American Cas. Co.,** *supra;* **Arnold v. Chicago, Burlington & Quincy R.R. Co.,** 7 F.R.D. 678 (D. Neb. 1947).

B. IMPLEMENTATION OF THE JURY TRIAL RIGHT

1. Selection and Composition of the Jury

The selection and composition of juries varies in state and federal practice. In federal practice, district courts implement the jury right through local rules, pursuant to authority in **Rule 83.**

a. Jury Pools; Size

State and federal courts determine the methods for summoning jurors and geographic area from which jurors are drawn to constitute the jury pool or array. Generally, federal courts draw a jury pool from a wider geographic area than do local state courts.

i. Jury Size in State Court

States constitutionally may use a jury with six or perhaps fewer members in criminal cases. *See* **Williams v. Florida,** 399 U.S. 78 (1970); **Duncan v. Louisiana,** 391 U.S. 145 (1968). In some states, juries of fewer than six members are allowed in civil trials. In Virginia, three-member juries are permissible by party consent. *See* **Painter v. Fred Whitaker,** 235 Va. 631, 369 S.E.2d 191 (1988).

ii. Jury Size in Federal Court: Rule 48

Rule 48 provides that a federal court shall seat a jury of not fewer than six and not more than twelve members, and that all jurors shall participate in the verdict unless excused from service. Many federal courts, through local rulemaking authority conferred by **Rule 83,** use six-person juries in civil actions. *See* **Colgrove v. Battin,** 413 U.S. 149 (1973) (upholding local rule permitting six-person jury in civil cases as not contravening the **Rules Enabling Act, 28 U.S.C. § 2072**).

b. Empanelling the Jury; *Voir Dire;* Challenges

i. Empanelling the Jury

State courts draw jury pools from property and tax lists, local residency, and such. Federal jury pools are summoned from voter registration lists, with supplemental sources (such as driver's licenses, public utilities lists, state tax rolls, telephone lists) when necessary to ensure adequate representation. *See* **28 U.S.C. §§ 1861–66.**

(a) **Composition of the jury pool.** The jury pool is supposed to be drawn from a cross-section of the community, without systematic or intentional exclusion of any groups. This does not mean that every jury pool or jury must contain representatives of every social, economic, religious, racial, political, and geographical segments of the community. **Thiel v. Southern Pac. Co.,** 328

U.S. 217 (1946) (improper jury panel selection where court clerk intentionally excluded all daily wage earners from jury service, regardless of whether actual hardship existed).

(b) Blue ribbon juries. So-called blue ribbon juries consist of jurors selected for their above-average intelligence, presumably to decide complex litigation. The Supreme Court has upheld a New York state statute empowering a judge to empanel such blue ribbon juries. **Fay v. New York,** 332 U.S. 261 (1947).

(c) Jury formation. Juries are selected from the jury pool (or array). Prospective jurors are randomly selected from a jury wheel (similar to a lottery drawing) equal to the number of the final jury, and are questioned by the judge or attorneys. If a juror is disqualified, a new prospective juror is selected from the jury pool. This process continues until a full jury is assembled.

ii. Voir Dire: Rule 47(a)

Voir dire is the process of questioning jurors for suitability to sit on a jury. In state courts, judges or the attorneys conduct the voir dire, or the judge may conduct the voir dire with suggestions from the attorney. In federal court, judges have discretion to determine the method of voir dire, although most federal judges conduct the voir dire. *See* **Rule 47(a).**

iii. Challenges to Jurors

Jurors may be disqualified from a jury for two reasons: either "for cause" or through a "pre-emptory challenge."

(a) Challenges for cause. A challenge for cause removes a prospective juror who evidences bias or other prejudice that might impair the juror's ability to fairly and impartially weigh the evidence and render a verdict. In order to disqualify, the state of mind of the juror must lead to the inference that the juror will not or could not act with impartiality. For example, jurors may be stricken if they know the lawyers, parties, or witnesses involved in the litigation; if a juror owns stock in a defendant corporation; or if the juror holds religious beliefs that would not allow the juror to render a decision in the case.

- Each party has an unlimited number of challenges for cause.

- The trial judge determines challenges for cause.

(b) Pre-emptory challenges. Pre-emptory challenges allow an attorney to disqualify or strike a juror without having to give a reason. Attorneys typically use pre-emptory challenges to remove jurors the attorney believes will not be sympathetic to the client.

- Most state courts limit the number of pre-emptory challenges. In federal courts each side has three pre-emptory challenges. *See* **28 U.S.C. § 1870.**

- Pre-emptory challenges may not be used to exclude jurors on the basis of race or gender, either in civil or criminal litigation. **J.E.B. v. Alabama,** 511 U.S. 127 (1994); **Edmonson v. Leesville Concrete Co., Inc.,** 500 U.S. 614 (1991); **Batson v. Kentucky,** 476 U.S. 79 (1986).

- *Batson* **analysis.** The Supreme Court has construed *Batson* to require the following three-step analysis for pre-emptory challenges (*see* **Purkett v. Elem,** 514 U.S. 765 (1995)):

  - The opponent of a pre-emptory challenge must make out a prima facie case of racial discrimination;

  - the proponent of the pre-emptory challenge must come forward with a race-neutral explanation for the strike; and then

  - the trial court must decide whether the opponent of the strike has proved purposeful discrimination.

C. THE SCOPE AND ORDER OF TRIAL

1. Order of Trial in Jury Cases

After a jury is selected and the judge informs the jurors of their duties, a jury trial typically is presented as follows:

(a) Plaintiff's opening statement (no arguments permitted; attorney may only present a road map of what the evidence will show);

(b) Defendant's opening statement (no arguments permitted; attorney may only present a road map of what the evidence will show);

(c) Plaintiff's presentation of direct evidence; defendant's cross-examination; and plaintiff's re-direct examination;

(d) Defendant's motion for a judgment as a matter of law under **Rule 50(a)** (formerly a directed verdict);

(e) Defendant's presentation of direct evidence; plaintiff's cross-examination; defendant's re-direct examination;

(f) Plaintiff's presentation of rebuttal evidence;

(g) Defendant's presentation of rebuttal evidence;

(h) Plaintiff or defendant's motions for judgment as a matter of law under **Rule 50(a)** (formerly a directed verdict);

(i) Plaintiff's opening final argument;

(j) Defendant's closing or final argument;

(k) Plaintiff's closing final argument;

(l) Judge's instructions to the jury;

(m) Jury deliberations and verdicts;

(n) Post-trial motions for judgment as a matter of law (renewed motion under **Rule 50(b)**), and/or new trial motion (for verdicts against the weight of the evidence).

- **Mistrials: New trial motions.** New trial motions may be made at any point during the trial if based on an error so great that the jury verdict is tainted (mistrial).

- **Non-jury trials.** In bench trials the court dispenses with many of the formal proceedings in jury trials, such as opening and closing arguments. In addition, bench trials do not require jury instructions or deliberation.

2. Allocating Burdens of Production, Persuasion, and Proof

The term "burden of proof" actually encompasses three different types of burdens, which "shift" during the course of trial. These are the burdens of production, persuasion, and proof.

a. Burden of Production

The burden of production refers to the requirement that a party come forward or produce some threshold level of evidence in support of a claim needed to satisfy the standard of proof. Typically the initial burden of production is on the plaintiff. If a plaintiff fails to satisfy its burden of production on a claim, the plaintiff loses. However, a plaintiff may satisfy its burden of production, but nonetheless lose the case for failing to ultimately persuade the fact-finder. The burden of production must be met for the case to go to the fact-finder (usually the jury). If the plaintiff fails, the plaintiff will suffer a "directed verdict," (*see* discussion *infra*), or may even lose prior to trial as a result of a summary judgment motion (*see* Chapter XIII, *supra*).

b. Burden of Persuasion

If the plaintiff satisfies the burden of production, it also must satisfy the burden of persuasion and convince the fact-finder that the plaintiff should prevail based on the weight of the evidence. The defendant will produce its own evidence, or attempt to cast doubt on the plaintiff's evidence by attacking witness credibility or reliability. If the fact-finder is convinced that the plaintiff's evidence is not sufficiently reliable or credible, the defendant will win.

i. Persuasion Standards

Plaintiffs and the prosecution must satisfy one of three standards in civil and criminal cases. These standards assess the quantity and quality of the evidence proffered:

(a) **Preponderance of the evidence.** A preponderance is usually considered to be more than fifty percent. This is the typical standard of persuasion in almost all civil litigation.

(b) **Clear and convincing evidence.** Something more than a preponderance, but less than a reasonable doubt. This higher evidentiary standard of persuasion applies in libel and slander actions, as well as child custody cases.

(c) **Beyond a reasonable doubt.** This is the prosecution standard in criminal cases.

c. Shifting Burdens

Typically the burden of production and persuasion rests on the party asserting a claim, so the plaintiff carries both burdens. In some actions, however, once the burden of production has been satisfied, the burden of persuasion shifts to the opposing party. A defendant carries the burden of production and persuasion on counterclaims.

- **Example.** In employment discrimination cases under **Title VII** of the **Civil Rights Act,** once an employee has made out a prima facie case of discrimination, the burden of persuasion shifts to the employer to prove by clear and convincing evidence that its actions were not race related.

3. Opening Statements

The plaintiff's lawyer typically makes the opening statement because the plaintiff carries the burden of proof (*see* discussion *infra*). If the defendant carries the burden of proof as to all issues (a trial solely on affirmative defenses), then the defendant has the right to make the opening statement. In most jurisdictions the defendant has an option to make an opening statement after the plaintiff, a choice guided by tactical considerations. Attorneys may not make arguments during opening statements, but only may provide the jury with a road map of what the evidence will show.

4. Presentation of Evidence: Direct and Cross–Examination

Each side presents its case in direct examination and rebuttal (if necessary) through witness testimony or by offering other evidence into the record, such as documents or exhibits. A party questions its own witnesses through direct examination. The opposing party has the opportunity to cross-examine the same witness. The major purpose of cross-examination is to impeach or impair the credibility or reliability of a witness's testimony. The party then may "rehabilitate" its witnesses by re-direct examination and the defendant may conduct a re-cross-examination. The scope of cross-examination is limited by the scope of the direct examination.

a. Rules of Evidence

The presentation of evidence is governed by rules of admissibility. Testimony or other evidence (such as exhibits or documentary evidence) will be admitted into the record unless the opposing party objects. A major function of the trial judge is to rule on objections to the admissibility of evidence. Trial lawyers must interpose evidentiary objections at trial, in order to establish a basis for appeal. On the other hand, constant objections disrupt the flow of trial and may have an adverse impact on the jury. Judges often will hold "side-bar" discussions with the attorneys to hear arguments on objections to evidence outside of the jury's hearing.

b. Role of the Judge

The traditional function of the trial judge is to rule on evidentiary questions as a neutral umpire. However, in some jurisdictions judges take an active role in questioning the witnesses, in addition to the attorney's examination.

5. Closing Argument

In final arguments, the attorneys summarize the evidence and draw out the logical implications of the evidence for the jury. Final argument is in three parts. The plaintiff, who typically carries the burden of production and persuasion, speaks first and last. If the defendant carries the burden of proof, the order of closing is reversed. In many jurisdictions, the court limits the length of closing argument.

a. Proper Closing Argument

Attorneys permissibly may summarize the facts of the case, from evidence offered at trial, and any reasonable inferences that may be drawn from that evidence.

b. Improper Closing Argument

In closing arguments, attorneys may not make:

(1) arguments from matters not in evidence;

(2) appeals to passion or racial or religious prejudice;

(3) references to the financial ability of parties;

(4) remarks about the defendant's insurance coverage;

(5) remarks about treating the plaintiff as they would like to be treated;

(6) distortions of the evidence to arrive at unjustified inferences.

D. JUDICIAL CONTROL OF JURY ACTION

1. Enforcing Burdens: Taking Cases from the Jury

a. Judgment as a Matter of Law (Formerly Directed Verdicts and Judgments Notwithstanding the Verdict): Rules 50(a) and (b)

Either party, at the conclusion of the party's presentation of its case, may ask the court to "direct a verdict"; that is, to decide the case in the moving party's favor. If the judge directs the verdict; the case effectively is taken away from the jury, because the case ends and never goes to the jury for decision. Typically the defendant moves for a directed verdict at the conclusion of the plaintiff's presentation of evidence, but it is possible for the court to direct a verdict in the plaintiff's favor if the defendant fails to prove a defense. *See* **Daniel J. Hartwig Assoc., Inc. v. Kanner,** 913 F.2d 1213 (7th Cir. 1990) (directed verdict for plaintiff where defendant failed to prove a defense to a contract).

i. Terminology

State court systems provide for directed verdicts. In 1991, **Rule 50** was amended to change the terms "directed verdict" and "judgment notwithstanding the verdict" to be called "judgment as a matter of law." This change supports the concept that directed verdicts, judgments notwithstanding the verdict, and summary judgment all are governed by identical standards. The singular difference is the time at which these motions typically are raised.

ii. Standard: Directed Verdicts

A judge is to grant a directed verdict if *"there is no legally sufficient evidentiary basis for a reasonable jury to find for the party on that issue."* Directed verdicts are granted where the party carrying the burden of production initially fails to come forward with sufficient evidence in support of its claim, or an issue that is part of the claim.

(a) Evaluation of the evidence. In evaluating the evidence on a directed verdict motion, the court views the evidence in the light most favorable to the non-moving party. Typically the court will view all the evidence, but decide credibility problems in favor of the non-movant.

(b) Quantum and weight of the evidence. Historically courts have used two different tests to assess whether the evidence supports a directed verdict. *The court is not supposed to weigh the evidence,* but rather determine whether the party carrying the burden of proof has produced sufficient evidence to support a favorable verdict.

- **Scintilla test.** A court will not grant a directed verdict if there is a scintilla of evidence—any evidence—on which a jury might possibly render a verdict for the non-movant. In recent times, courts have moved away from the scintilla test.

- **Substantial evidence test.** A court will grant the directed verdict unless there is substantial evidence upon which the jury might decide for the non-movant. The modern trend is for judges to use the substantial evidence test.

(c) Reasonable inferences. On motions for directed verdict and judgment notwithstanding the verdict, courts are permitted to draw reasonable inferences from the evidence. Impermissible inferences require the court (or jury) to span large gaps in the testimony in order to reach a conclusion. *See* **Galloway v. United States,** 319 U.S. 372 (1943).

iii. Constitutionality of Judgments as a Matter of Law

The directed verdict does not violate the Seventh Amendment right to a jury trial because the procedure has analogs at common law, such as the demurrer. *See* **Galloway v. United States,** *supra.* Judgments as a matter of law also withstand constitutional challenge, provided the moving litigant makes a prior directed verdict motion, because JNOVs are viewed as derivative of the directed verdict motion.

iv. Applicable Law Problems: *Erie* Doctrine

The Supreme Court has declined to decide whether state standards for directing a verdict control in federal diversity cases. *See* **Dick v. New York Life Ins. Co.,** 359 U.S. 437 (1959); **Mercer v. Theriot,** 377 U.S. 152 (1964). The lower federal courts are split on this issue. *Compare* **Boeing v. Shipman,** 411 F.2d 365 (5th Cir. 1969) (federal standards apply) *with* **Boynton v. TRW Inc.,** 858 F.2d 1178 (6th Cir. 1988) (state law applies). *See also* **Daniel J. Hartwig Assocs., Inc. v. Kanner,** 913 F.2d 1213 (7th Cir. 1990) (applying Wisconsin directed verdict standards).

v. Judgments Notwithstanding the Verdict: Rule 50(b)

Judgments notwithstanding the verdict (so-called "JNOVs" from the Latin judgment *non obstante veredicto*) are virtually the same as directed verdicts, except the JNOV motion is made after the jury has rendered its verdict. The losing attorney basically asks the court to render a judgment its in favor, despite what the jury has decided. Similar to the directed verdict, the effect of the JNOV is to take the case away from the jury. Also similar to directed verdicts, JNOVs are not a violation of the Seventh Amendment, but they do require the moving party to have made a prior directed verdict motion (*see* discussion *infra*).

(a) Timing. In federal practice a motion for a judgment notwithstanding the verdict is made to the trial judge after the jury renders a verdict. The motion must be made no later than 28 days after the entry of judgment or no later than 28 days after the jury is discharged. **Rule 50(b)**.

- **Requirement of prior directed verdict motion.** The JNOV has no analog at common law (similar to the way in which the directed verdict derives from the common law demurrer). Therefore, in order to withstand constitutional challenge, a party in federal court can make a JNOV motion only if the party previously moved for a directed verdict at the close of evidence. **Rule 50(b).** Even though a defendant can make a **Rule 50(a)** directed verdict motion at the close of a plaintiff's case (and before the defendant's case), a defendant must move for a **Rule 50(a)** directed verdict at the close of evidence (after the defendant's case) in order to file a **Rule 50(b)** JNOV.

- **Contrary state practice.** Because states are not bound by the Seventh Amendment, several states permit litigants to move for a JNOV without having made a prior directed verdict motion.

(b) Standard. The standard for granting a JNOV is that the party carrying the burden of proof at trial failed to support its claim with sufficient evidence, and therefore no reasonable jury could have found the verdict it did.

- **Quantum and weight of the evidence.** Similar to the directed verdict motion, the court is not supposed to weigh the evidence. The court is to evaluate whether, under the requirements of the substantive law and applicable evidentiary burdens, there is any evidence supporting the jury's verdict. In assessing the jury's conclusion, the jury may make reasonable inferences from the evidence, but may not base a decision on mere possibilities. *See e.g.* **Denman v. Spain,** 242 Miss. 431, 135 So.2d 195 (1961) (JNOV for defendant upheld in auto negligence claim on ground that jury verdict impermissibly relied on speculation, conjecture, and mere possibilities). *Compare* **Kircher v. Atchison, Topeka & Santa Fe Ry. Co.,** 32 Cal.2d 176, 195 P.2d 427 (1948) (jury made reasonable inferences concerning how injured plaintiff's hand came to be placed on railroad tracks resulting in injury).

(c) **Conditional rulings on motions for a judgment as a matter of law and new trial motions. Rules 50(c)** and **(d)** provide for the judge to simultaneously rule on a losing party's motion for a judgment as a matter of law, and the losing party's new trial motion. The purpose of the "conditional" rulings is to allow the trial judge to preserve the ability to grant a new trial in the eventuality that an appellate court overturns the judge's ruling on the JNOV. The appellate court independently may order a new trial from a reversal of the trial judge's JNOV. If the judge makes a conditional new trial ruling, the judge must specify the grounds for granting or denying the motion. **Rule 50(c).** *See also* **Neely v. Martin K. Eby Constr. Co.,** 386 U.S. 317 (1967).

(d) **Consequences and benefits of the JNOV.** Because the JNOV is available to reverse a jury's verdict after all the evidence at trial, this reduces pressure on the judge to make an earlier directed verdict ruling. With the JNOV, the judge has the ability to reverse the jury's verdict after all the evidence is in. Also, if a judge orders a directed verdict and an appellate court reverses this ruling, then a new trial must be ordered. If an appellate court reverses a JNOV, however, the appellate court can reinstitute the jury's verdict and there will be no need for a new trial.

2. Instructions and Verdicts

Before the jury retires to deliberate, the jury judge will "instruct" the jury in the law and the jury's fact-finding function.

a. Instructions to the Jury

Practice varies in state and federal court concerning whether the judge instructs the jury before or after the attorneys' closing arguments. **Rule**

51 gives the judge discretion to instruct the jury before or after closing arguments.

i. Form of the Instructions; Objections

In many jurisdictions, the judge permits the attorneys to submit proposed jury instructions. The judge then determines what jury instructions to provide the jury. In most jurisdictions, a party cannot appeal a judge's failure to give a jury instruction the attorney did not request. *See* **Turner Constr. Co. v. Houlihan,** 240 F.2d 435 (1st Cir. 1957).

(a) **Objections.** A party may not appeal if an attorney does not object at the time the judge gave an instruction to the jury. **Rule 51.** *But see* **Wirtz v. International Harvester Co.,** 331 F.2d 462 (5th Cir.), *cert. denied,* 379 U.S. 845 (1964) (judgment reversed for clearly erroneous jury instruction where attorney did not object; *both* parties have duty to ensure that jury instructions are phrased properly). Reversals on the basis of improper instructions, without objections, are rare, although increasing in federal courts. *See, e.g.* **Hunt v. Liberty Lobby,** 720 F.2d 631 (11th Cir. 1983); **MacEdward v. Northern Elec. Co., Ltd.,** 595 F.2d 105 (2d Cir. 1979).

(b) **Form of objections.** Federal courts no longer require formal objections, *see* **Rule 46,** and it is sufficient to make the court aware of the nature of the error in the jury instruction. However, an attorney may not just make a general objection to a jury instruction without specifying a particular defect. *See* **Ratay v. Lincoln Natl. Life Ins. Co.,** 378 F.2d 209 (3d Cir. 1967).

b. Commenting on the Evidence

The ability of judges to comment on the evidence is derived from the common law. A minority of states have retained this power, which includes the ability to express opinions on evidence and witness credibility.

i. Federal Practice

In federal court judges are permitted to comment on the evidence when submitting the case to the jury. **Quercia v. United States,** 289 U.S. 466 (1933). *But see* **Nunley v. Pettway Oil Co.,** 346 F.2d 95 (6th

Cir. 1965) (judge improperly gave opinion on ultimate fact question—amounting to a directed verdict—that was peculiarly for the jury to decide). One federal circuit permits judges to comment on evidentiary matters but not on ultimate facts. *See* **Travelers Ins. Co. v. Ryan,** 416 F.2d 362 (5th Cir. 1969).

ii. State Practice

The majority of states restrict the ability of judges to comment on the evidence:

- in some states, the judge may only make a statement of the applicable law, and may not mention the evidence.

- in some states, the judge may impartially summarize the evidence.

c. Submission to the Jury

After the judge instructs the jury, the jury retires to deliberate and render a judgment.

i. Unanimity Requirement

Federal courts require a unanimous verdict by the jury. The unanimity requirement, however, may lead to stalemated or "hung" juries, requiring a retrial. To avoid this, many states permit less than unanimity in civil trials.

ii. Jury Confusion or Lack of Recall

The jury may request that witness testimony or jury instructions be re-read to them, if the jury is uncertain about its recollection of testimony or is confused about the jury instructions. *See* **Diniero v. United States Lines Co.,** 288 F.2d 595 (2d Cir. 1961), *cert. denied,* 368 U.S. 831 (jury confusion relating to general verdict form accompanied with interrogatories; interrogatories withdrawn to cure jury confusion).

iii. Exhibits and Note-Taking

In the judge's discretion, jurors may take exhibits into the deliberation room and request portions of the trial transcript. In some jurisdictions, judges permit jurors to take notes during trial, which they may then use in deliberations.

d. Forms of Verdicts: Rule 49

There are different methods of submitting the case to the jury. The jury either may render a "general verdict," a "special verdict," or a "general verdict with interrogatories." The choice of the verdict form is in the judge's discretion, **Bartak v. Bell–Galyardt & Wells, Inc.,** 629 F.2d 523 (8th Cir. 1980), and parties are not entitled to any particular verdict form, or particular interrogatories when this verdict form is used. **Miley v. Oppenheimer & Co.,** 637 F.2d 318 (5th Cir. 1981).

i. The General Verdict

The general verdict is the most common form of verdict in which the jury finds for the plaintiff or defendant, but does not disclose the grounds for its decision. The general verdict is criticized for its "all or nothing" quality. It also is impossible to know the basis for the jury's decision, and whether it was based on passion, emotion, prejudice, popular opinion, etc.

ii. Special Verdicts

The Federal Rules provide for two types of special verdicts. Special verdicts are intended to cure the problems of general verdicts, and to enhance judicial efficiency. **Jamison Co. v. Westvaco Corp.,** 526 F.2d 922 (5th Cir. 1976). Special verdicts allow the judge to control for improper jury sympathy or passion.

(a) **Special verdicts: Rule 49(a).** The court submits a list of factual issues to the jury and requests the jury to make findings. The judge then applies the law to the findings to render the appropriate judgment. The jury's findings must be definite, unambiguous, and consistent. If not, the judge can refuse to enter the verdict. **Iacurci v. Lummus Co.,** 387 U.S. 86 (1967).

  • **State practice.** In Texas and Wisconsin the special verdict is the rule, rather than the exception.

(b) **General verdict with interrogatories: Rule 49(b).** The court requests the jury to render a general verdict, but also requests the jury to answer a series of questions. The answers to these questions assists the court in knowing the jury's basis for its general verdict. Depending on the circumstances, the court also may enter the verdict, order a new trial, request further deliberation, or withdraw the interrogatories:

- **Harmonious answers.** If the jury's answers to interrogatories are harmonious, the court will enter a judgment.

- **Consistent answers—inconsistent with general verdict.** If the jury's answers to the interrogatories on a material issue are internally consistent, but inconsistent with the general verdict, the court may either return the questions to the jury for further deliberation, or order a new trial. *See* **Nollenberger v. United Air Lines, Inc.,** 216 F.Supp. 734, *vacated,* 335 F.2d 379 (9th Cir.), *cert. dismissed,* 379 U.S. 951 (1964).

- **Inconsistent answers: Inconsistent verdict.** If the jury's answers to the interrogatories are internally inconsistent and also inconsistent with the general verdict, the court cannot enter a judgment and either must request further deliberation or order a new trial.

- **Jury confusion.** If the jury is persistently confused about answering the interrogatories and rendering a general verdict, the court may withdraw the interrogatories and simply request a general verdict. **Diniero v. United States Lines Company,** *supra.*

e. **Findings of Fact and Conclusions of Law in Non-Jury Cases**

When a case is tried to a judge, the judge is obligated to enter findings of fact and conclusions of law. **Rule 52(a).** In federal court these requirements are mandatory and cannot be waived. States have similar rules for bench trials. This applies even when the judge uses an advisory jury (*see* discussion *supra*).

i. **Purpose**

The major purpose for these requirements is to clarify the basis for the judge's decision and to clearly indicate findings to provide a basis for subsequent res judicata effect of the judgment (*see* Chapter XII on *res judicata* and the binding effects of judgments). *See* **Leighton v. One William Street Fund, Inc.,** 343 F.2d 565 (2d Cir. 1965).

ii. **Federal Practice: Oral Findings—Rule 52(a)**

In federal courts, judges are permitted to make oral findings from the bench. This reduces judicial burdens and the number of written, published opinions.

iii. Attorney Participation

Some judges invite attorneys from both sides to submit proposed findings of fact and conclusions of law, prior to the decision of the case. Some courts decide the case and then ask the winning attorney to submit proposed findings and conclusions. **Heterochemical Corp. v. United States Rubber Co.,** 368 F.2d 169 (7th Cir. 1966). The Third Circuit has rejected this procedure. *See* **Roberts v. Ross,** 344 F.2d 747 (3d Cir. 1965).

iv. Standard of Review

Findings of fact will not be reversed on appeal unless the findings are clearly erroneous. **Rule 52(a)(6).** *See* **Anderson v. City of Bessemer City,** 470 U.S. 564 (1985). The appellate judges must not simply disagree with the judge's findings of fact, but must conclude that the judge's findings are so far off track as to be "clearly erroneous"—a more stringent standard.

E. CHALLENGING ERRORS: GROUNDS FOR NEW TRIALS— RULES 59 AND 61

A litigant who loses at trial either may request a new trial or contest errors on direct appeal from the judgment. The new trial motion allows the judge to correct any errors that might have occurred at trial, rather than having an appellate court reverse the judge. Also, the judge has first-hand knowledge of what occurred at trial, which an appellate court will not. A judge will not order a new trial for "harmless errors" in the court's admission or exclusion of evidence, or any other ruling. **Rule 61.**

1. Discretion

The judge's discretion to order a new trial is very broad. However, most judges exercise this power cautiously, in deference to the jury's function and the time and expense of conducting a new trial.

2. Timing: Rule 59(b)

New trial motions must be made within 28 days after the judgment is entered. **Rule 59(b).** The time for making a new trial motion cannot be enlarged. *See* **Rule 6(b).**

3. New Trial Motion Distinguished from Directed Verdicts and JNOVs: Verdicts Against the Weight of the Evidence

"Where there is substantial evidence in support of the plaintiff's case, the judge may not direct a verdict against him, even though he may not believe his evidence or may think that the weight of the evidence is on the other side; for, under the constitutional guaranty of trial by jury, it is for the judge to weigh the evidence and pass on its credibility. He may, however, set aside a verdict supported by substantial evidence where in his opinion it is contrary to the clear weight of the evidence, or is based on evidence which is false; for even though the evidence be sufficient to preclude the direction of a verdict, it is still his duty to exercise his power over the proceedings before him to prevent a miscarriage of justice." **Garrison v. United States,** 62 F.2d 41 (4th Cir. 1932), quoted in **Aetna Casualty & Surety Co. v. Yeatts,** 122 F.2d 350 (4th Cir. 1941).

4. Grounds for New Trial

Some state rules set out specific grounds for new trials. Where specific grounds are set forth, a judge may not order a new trial "in the interests of justice." *See* **Ginsberg v. Williams.** 270 Minn. 474, 135 N.W.2d 213 (1965).

a. New Trial in Federal Court

The Federal Rules permit a judge to order a new trial for any reason "heretofore granted" in actions at law. **Rule 59(a).** Under this broad mandate, judges have ordered new trials because of prejudicial errors in evidentiary rulings, jury instructions, attorney or juror misconduct, newly discovered evidence, the verdict is against the weight of the evidence, or the verdict is legally excessive or inadequate.

b. Non-Jury Trials

A court may order a new trial after a nonjury trial for any reason for which a rehearing has been granted in a suit in equity.

c. Incoherent Jury Verdicts

A court may order a new trial when the verdict the jury returns, particularly in multiple claim cases, is incoherent or inconsistent. For example, in a case where the court tendered a single verdict form for multiple liability counts based on separate causes of action, the court could not determine whether the jury's single verdict applied to one or both counts. The court also could not reassemble the jury to clarify its decision. Thus, a new trial was appropriate to clarify the first jury's action. **Magnani v. Trogi,** 70 Ill.App.2d 216, 218 N.E.2d 21 (Ill. App. 1966). *See also* **Robb v. John C. Hickey, Inc.,** 19 N.J.Misc. 455, 20 A.2d 707 (1941).

5. Partial and Conditional New Trials

Federal and state judges may order a partial new trial on certain issues. A judge may order a conditional new trial if the judge believes the jury verdict is too small (*see* discussion of *remittitur* and *additur, infra*). This technique avoids the time and expense of completely retrying the entire case. **Rule 59(a)**.

a. Circumstances Not Justifying Partial New Trials

Partial new trials are inappropriate solely on a liability issue if the jury was improperly instructed on the liability standard. **Doutre v. Niec,** 2 Mich.App. 88, 138 N.W.2d 501 (1965).

b. Circumstances Justifying Partial and Conditional New Trials: *Additur* and *Remittitur*

The most common instance for ordering a partial new trial is on the issue of damages. State judges may order a partial new and conditional new trial, limited to the issue of damages, if the judge believes that the jury verdict is legally inadequate or excessive. Where a verdict is believed inadequate, the new trial is for the purpose of determining whether to enhance the verdict through "additur." If the court believes the verdict excessive, the new trial determines whether to diminish the award, through "remittitur." *See* **Fisch v. Manger,** 24 N.J. 66, 130 A.2d 815 (1957).

- **Constitutionality of** *additur* **and** *remittitur.* State courts generally recognize both additur and remittitur. **Fisch v. Manger,** *id.* Remittitur is permitted in federal courts, but not additur. **Dimick v. Schiedt,** 293 U.S. 474 (1935). This is because remittitur only decreases a sum already awarded by a jury, but additur determines an amount that the first jury did not.

6. Constitutionality of New Trial Orders

The judge's ability to order a new trial does not violate the Constitution. This is because the judge effectively is sending the case to a new jury. *See* **Aetna Casualty & Surety Co. v. Yeatts,** 122 F.2d 350 (4th Cir. 1941).

F. POWER TO SET ASIDE JUDGMENT ON GROUNDS DISCOVERED AFTER IT WAS RENDERED: RULE 60

A litigant may move for relief from the judgment based on a series of grounds set forth in **Rule 60.** A motion for relief from the judgment must be made within a reasonable time, and for reasons stated in **Rule 60(b)(1)–(3)**, no more than a year after entry of judgment.

1. Clerical Mistake: Rule 60(a)

A court may correct errors in the judgment that are the result of clerical error, omission, or oversight. This is a ministerial procedure and does not require the case to be reopened or relitigated. This motion may not be used to seek an increase or reduction of a jury award.

2. Other Grounds: Rule 60(b)

a. Timing: Within One Year

Certain grounds for relief from a judgment must be made within one year from the entry of judgment. These include mistake, excusable neglect, newly discovered evidence, or fraud.

i. Mistake, Inadvertence, Excusable Neglect: Rule 60(b)(1)

These grounds existed at the time the Federal Rules were enacted in 1938. Such relief may be granted only when it is reasonable under the circumstances and the mistake, inadvertence, or neglect is not the result of the attorney's gross negligence.

ii. Newly Discovered Evidence: Rule 60(b)(2)

The party seeking relief on this ground must show that the evidence was in existence at the time of trial but that the attorney was unable to discover it despite due diligence in preparing the case. **Patrick v. Sedwick,** 413 P.2d 169 (Alaska 1966). The attorney may not use this ground to develop a new theory or present some new facts.

iii. Fraud, Misrepresentation or Misconduct of the Other Party: Rule 60(b)(3)

The Federal Rule abolishes the distinction between extrinsic and intrinsic fraud. Extrinsic fraud relates to party conduct that prevents the other side from developing its case. Intrinsic fraud refers to conduct during trial, such as the presentation of perjured testimony. **Peacock Records, Inc. v. Checker Records, Inc.,** 365 F.2d 145 (7th Cir. 1966). Some states maintain this distinction and allow a judgment to be reopened only for extrinsic fraud. **Smith v. Great Lakes Airlines, Inc.,** 242 Cal.App.2d 23, 51 Cal.Rptr. 1 (1966). The movant must establish the fraud by clear and convincing evidence.

b. Timing: "Reasonable Time"

Rule 60(b) sets forth a series of grounds for reopening a judgment within a "reasonable time." These include the ground that the judgment is void (*e.g.,* for lack of jurisdiction), has been satisfied, reversal of the law, or changed circumstances that no longer make it equitable to enforce an injunction. These grounds are very limited in scope.

- **"Any other reason."** A litigant also may seek relief from a judgment, within a reasonable time, for "any other reason justifying relief from the operation of judgment." This is the broadest possible ground for relief, preserving the court's equitable power to do justice in individual circumstances. Relief has been limited to "extraordinary circumstances." *See* **Klapprott v. United States,** 335 U.S. 601 (1949). **Rule 60(b)(6).**

G. JURY MISCONDUCT; JUROR IMPEACHMENT OF THE VERDICT

Various errors by the jury or jury misconduct may form the basis for appeal.

1. Jury Misconduct

a. Deception During *Voir Dire*

A juror's lying in answer to questions during voir dire may be a ground for overturning a verdict. The court will determine the extent of prejudice caused by the untruthfulness. A juror's honest but mistaken response to a question on voir dire is not a sufficient ground to invalidate a judgment. **McDonough Power Equip., Inc. v. Greenwood,** 464 U.S. 548 (1984).

b. Misconduct During Deliberation

Juror misconduct includes discussing the case with others (including other jurors) or visiting the site of a claim, when the judge has prohibited such actions. The judge will evaluate the degree of prejudice resulting from improper conversations or viewing. Jurors also may not decide the case from personal knowledge, or decide the case through improper means, such as flipping a coin.

i. Ascertaining Jury Misconduct

(a) Apparent misconduct. If jury misconduct appears on the face of the verdict, the judge may either attempt to cure the defect, or order a new trial. The judge may examine the jurors to adjust the verdict.

(b) **Non-apparent misconduct: The *Mansfield* Rule.** Most often jury misconduct is not apparent from the verdict. The historic eighteenth-century rule, the so-called **Mansfield Rule,** barred jurors from testifying as to what occurred during jury deliberation. Juror affidavits may not be used to attack their verdict. To ameliorate the harshness of this rule, many jurisdictions allow juror affidavits to give testimony to overt acts or prejudicial independent acts of jurors.

- **Overt acts.** Overt acts include "those open to sight, hearing, and other senses and are thus subject to corroboration." **People v. Hutchinson,** 71 Cal.2d 342, 78 Cal.Rptr. 196, 455 P.2d 132 (1969).

- **Federal Rule of Evidence 606(b).** No juror testimony may be used that relates to a juror's mind, emotions, or mental processes during deliberation. A juror may testify "on the question whether extraneous prejudicial information was improperly brought to the jury's attention or whether outside influence was improperly brought to bear on any juror."

■ CHAPTER REVIEW CHECKLIST

Your civil procedure examination will not likely contain a problem relating to jury composition and selection, the actual conduct of trial, and certainly will not contain any question relating to evidentiary matters at trial. The most frequently tested topics include a litigant's Seventh Amendment right to a trial by jury, directed verdicts and judgments notwithstanding the verdict, and motions for new trial. It also is possible to be tested on relief from a judgment.

To answer a problem relating to the right to a trial by jury, ask:

1. **Is the case in state or federal court?**

- If the case is in state court, is there a right to trial by jury? How is it authorized? What is the nature of the right to trial by jury? Is it broader or narrower than the right preserved by the Seventh Amendment?

2. **If the case is in federal court, what is the nature and basis for the claims in the case?**

- Does the litigation include several claims, some that are legal and some that are equitable?

- Is the claim or cause of action one that existed at common law in 1791?

- Is the claim based on a statute?

    — Does the statute codify a legal or equitable claim that existed in 1791?

    — Does the statute create a new cause of action?

    — Where is the claim enforceable? Before an administrative agency? Before an Article III federal district court?

    — Does the statute address private or public rights?

    — Is there congressional intent to provide a jury trial or non-jury proceeding? Does the statute's legislative history explicitly or implicitly indicate a congressional preference?

    — Does the newly-created claim have an analog to an action that existed in 1791?

    — Does the statute pertain to a foreign government or one of its instrumentalities?

    — Does the statute create civil penalties?

    — Does the litigation involve complex facts or issues, suggesting a "complexity exception" to the right to trial by jury?

To answer a problem relating to judgments as a matter of law, ask:

1. **When is the movant requesting a motion for a judgment as a matter of law? Is the motion for a directed verdict? A motion for a judgment notwithstanding the verdict?**

- At what point in the proceedings is the party requesting a judgment notwithstanding the verdict?

    — Has the motion been raised after the plaintiff has presented all the plaintiff's evidence? After both sides have presented their entire cases?

— Has the jury rendered a verdict? Is the losing party asking the judge to decide that the verdict is unreasonable and therefore the judge should render a verdict contrary to what the jury decided?

2. **Who carries the burden of proof on the issue?**

3. **What evidence has the party carrying the burden of proof produced on the issue?**

    • What is the amount and quality of the evidence? Has the party carrying the burden of proof produced more than a mere scintilla of evidence?

    • Will the judge be required to assess the credibility of witnesses or to perform some other jury function, such as assessing demeanor or state of mind?

    • Are there any significant gaps in the evidence, so that the judge would have to make an impermissible inference in order to arrive at a conclusion?

4. **Is that evidence sufficient to defeat a directed verdict and send the case to the jury? Could a reasonable jury, weighing the evidence along with permissible inferences, find for the party carrying the burden of proof? Could a jury reasonably have decided the way the jury did?**

To answer a problem relating to new trial motions, ask:

1. **When is the losing party asking for a new trial motion? Is the new trial motion coupled with a motion for a judgment notwithstanding the verdict?**

2. **Is it appropriate for the judge to issue a conditional new trial ruling, either to preserve the verdict or to permit a new trial if the appellate court reverses the judge's decision on the judgment notwithstanding the verdict?**

3. **Do any grounds for a new trial exist, such as prejudicial errors in evidentiary rulings, jury instructions, attorney or juror misconduct, newly discovered evidence, or the verdict is against the weight of the evidence, or is legally excessive or insufficient?**

4. **Are there appropriate circumstances for a partial or conditional new trial? What issue or issues might be tried again? Does the issue relate**

to liability or damages? If the issue relates to damages, is it appropriate to retry the damages issue to have a new jury determination increasing or decreasing the award?

To answer a problem relating to relief from judgments, ask:

1. **Are there any grounds for the losing party to seek relief from the judgment?** (*i.e.*, **clerical error, mistake, inadvertence, excusable neglect, newly discovered evidence, fraud, misrepresentation, misconduct of the other party, or any other reason?**)

    • If the ground is clerical error, is the error purely ministerial?

    • If the ground is mistake, inadvertence or excusable neglect, how did the attorney conduct him or herself? Do the attorney's actions amount to gross professional negligence, so that the court should not grant relief from the judgment?

    • If the ground is newly discovered evidence, was the evidence in existence at the time of trial? Could the attorney have obtained it?

    • If the ground is fraud, what events constitute the fraud? Is the fraud intrinsic or extrinsic to the proceeding?

2. **Has the party seeking relief from the judgment done this in a timely fashion?**

    • Does the particular ground for seeking relief have to be made within one year of the entry of judgment? Has the motion been made within that time?

    • Does the particular ground for seeking relief need to be made within a "reasonable time"? Has the motion been made within that time?

    • Do extraordinary circumstances exist that should permit relief from the judgment at any reasonable time?

XI

Appellate Review

■ ANALYSIS

■ CHAPTER OVERVIEW

- A litigant may only bring an appeal from a final judgment.

- Most judicial orders that the judge makes during trial are not immediately reviewable by an appellate court, but must await the conclusion of trial and the entry of a final judgment in order for a party to bring an appeal.

- Certain judicial orders, however, may be immediately reviewable and will not have to wait for a final judgment. These orders are called "interlocutory" orders and they are reviewable on "interlocutory appeal."

  — Statutes may define certain orders as immediately appealable. For example, orders relating to injunction are immediately appealable, as are certain orders relating to receiverships and admiralty.

  — An order may be immediately appealable if the trial judge who issues the order certifies his or her own order for immediate review. The judge must state that certain grounds exist requiring that immediate review.

  — An order may be immediately appealable if it falls into a narrow category of orders that are "collateral" to the merits of the dispute, involve an important issue, and if it is not resolved immediately, will cause irreparable harm.

  — Another method of seeking immediate review of a judge's order before final judgment is through a **writ of mandamus,** also called an *"extraordinary writ."*

  — A *writ of mandamus* is an order from a higher court to a lower court judge, ordering the judge to perform his or her duty. An appellate court may issue the writ only in exceptional circumstances, for example, for a trial judge's egregious abuse of discretion.

  — The writ of mandamus is not intended to be used as a "back-door" method of obtaining appellate review for interlocutory orders.

- A losing party may only raise issues on appeal which the party objected to at trial.

- A winning party may not appeal from erroneous findings if those findings were not necessary to the decree.

- The standard of review on appeal depends on whether the alleged error pertains to facts or law, and whether the trial was before a judge or jury.

  — "Harmless errors" are not reversible.

  — Appellate courts review errors of law *de novo*—that is, they determine the question freshly without regard to the findings in the trial court.

  — Rulings committed to a trial judge's discretion are reviewed for abuse of that discretion. An appellate court can reverse the trial judge only if the trial judge was clearly wrong.

  — An appellate court must accord a jury's findings of fact great deference. These findings are typically exempt from review, because of the constitutional guaranty of a right to trial by jury.

  — An appellate court may overturn a judge's findings of fact only if those findings are clearly erroneous, based on a misunderstanding of law, or without evidentiary support.

  — An appellate court may treat mixed questions of law and fact as if they were pure questions of law, and are subject to full review.

- If a trial judge decides one or more claims in a multi-claim litigation, those claims are final for review purposes and an appellate court may review the lower court's determination of those claims.

- The United States Supreme Court has broad discretionary power to choose cases for review. Only a very narrow group of cases are entitled to review of right in the Supreme Court.

A. PERSONS WHO MAY SEEK REVIEW

Typically a losing party may seek appellate review. In certain circumstances (*see infra*), a winning party also may seek appellate review. Finally, in limited circumstances a person or group who was not a party to a litigation may seek to intervene on appeal, although this is highly unusual.

B. THE PROBLEM OF APPEALABILITY: WHEN A DECISION MAY BE REVIEWED

1. The Principle of Finality

In most jurisdictions, litigants (usually the losing party), may only bring an appeal from the entry of a final judgment.

a. Purposes of the Final Judgment Rule

The final judgment rule serves several purposes:

i. Judicial Economy

The final judgment rules enhances judicial economy by saving all objections and claims of error to one appellate proceeding after the trial's conclusion. The final judgment rule thus avoids piecemeal litigation of each and every order a judge issues during a litigation's ongoing proceedings. Also, a litigant who loses an issue may prevail in the case, obviating the need for an appeal.

ii. Delay, Expense, and Harassment

The final judgment rule prevents the delay and avoids the expense that might occur if trial proceedings were stayed pending an immediate appeal of a judge's order. The final judgment rule also prevents adversaries from using interlocutory review as a means to harass the opposing party through repetitive intermediate appeals.

iii. Difference in State Court Practice

Some state courts, such as New York, are unpersuaded by these rationales supporting the final judgment rule. Instead, these jurisdictions believe that immediate resolution of the validity of interlocutory orders may prevent an unnecessary trial. Also, in absence of appellate guidance, judges may issue inconsistent orders. These jurisdictions, then, permit much more liberal interlocutory appeal than the federal courts provide (*see* discussion *infra*).

b. Finality Defined

What constitutes finality for appeal purposes differs from jurisdiction to jurisdiction and usually is defined by statute. Generally, a final judgment is the order that leaves nothing to be done except to execute on the judgment. The final judgment concludes all rights that were the subject of the litigation. Most discovery orders, for example, are not final orders because they are not the subject of the underlying substantive merits of the lawsuit.

c. The Final Judgment Rule in Federal Practice: Rule 54, 28 U.S.C. § 1291, and 28 U.S.C. § 2072(c)

i. Rule 54(a)

A final judgment in federal practice simply includes any decree or order from which an appeal lies.

ii. Jurisdictional Statute: 28 U.S.C. § 1291

This statute confers jurisdiction on appellate courts of all final decisions of the district courts, except those for which the Supreme Court has direct review (*see* discussion *infra*). All aspects of whether a federal court may hear an appeal, such as timeliness and finality, are viewed as involving "jurisdiction over the subject matter." *See* **Firestone Tire & Rubber Co. v. Risjord,** 449 U.S. 368 (1981); **Liberty Mutual Ins. Co. v. Wetzel,** 424 U.S. 737 (1976).

(a) No waiver. Parties may not waive the requirements for an appeal.

(b) Defects in grounds. Neither trial courts nor appellate courts may supply any defects in the grounds for appellate review.

(c) Attorney fee issues undecided. A trial court decision is final for appeal purposes even though issues remain relating to the determination of attorney's fees. **Budinich v. Becton Dickinson & Co.,** 486 U.S. 196 (1988).

iii. Judicial Improvements Act of 1990, Added Subsection 28 U.S.C. § 2072(c)

The Supreme Court may define, by rule, "when a ruling of a district court is final for purposes of appeal under **section 1291**."

d. Exceptions to the Final Judgment Rule

Although the final judgment rule is relatively strict, statutes and doctrine recognize exceptions to the rule whereby an appellate court may have jurisdiction of an interlocutory appeal. Federal statutes recognize four exceptions to the final judgment rule, and state statutes delineate those orders requiring immediate appellate review.

i. Injunctions, Receiverships, Admiralty: 28 U.S.C. §§ 1292(a)(1)–(3)

This statute provides for immediate jurisdiction of appeals of interlocutory orders relating to:

(a) **Injunctions: § 1292(a)(1).** Injunctions (granting, continuing, modifying, dissolving, refusing to dissolve or modify), **Smith v. Vulcan Iron Works,** 165 U.S. 518 (1897), except if the Supreme Court provides for direct review;

- **Denial of motion for summary judgment:** A court's denial of a motion for summary judgment in which a permanent injunction is sought is not immediately appealable under § **1292(a)(1). Switzerland Cheese Assn., Inc. v. E. Horne's Market, Inc.,** 385 U.S. 23 (1966).

- **Practical effect of denying an injunction: Irreparable injury.** Court orders that have the practical effect of refusing to issue an injunction—such as a court's denial of a motion to enter a consent decree enjoining further employment discrimination practices—are immediately appealable if the order might have serious, irreparable consequences. *See* **Carson v. American Brands, Inc.,** 450 U.S. 79 (1981).

- **Compare.** Orders granting or denying stays of legal proceedings on equitable grounds are not automatically appealable under **28 U.S.C. § 1292(a)(1), Gulfstream Aerospace Corp. v. Mayacamas Corp.,** 485 U.S. 271 (1988) (repudiating the *Enelow–Ettelson* doctrine, distinguishing legal and equitable grounds for stays for appellate review purposes).

(b) **Receiverships: § 1292(a)(2).** Appointments of receivers, or refusing to wind up a receivership;

(c) **Admiralty cases: § 1292(a)(3).** Interlocutory decrees determining the rights and liabilities of parties to admiralty cases.

ii. Interlocutory Appeals under 28 U.S.C. § 1292(b)

Appellate courts also have jurisdiction of those orders a district court judge "certifies" for immediate review. The judge has to certify his or her own order in writing—within 10 days of entry of the order—stating that the order appealed from:

- involves a controlling question of law as to which there is substantial ground for difference of opinion; and

- that an immediate appeal may materially advance the ultimate termination of the litigation.

(a) **No stay of proceedings.** If a judge certifies an order for interlocutory review, this does not stay the court's proceedings unless the district judge or court of appeals orders a stay pending determination of appellate review.

iii. The "Collateral Order" Doctrine

The collateral order doctrine is the chief judicially-created exception to the final judgment rule. Refined through a series of Supreme Court cases, *see, e.g.,* **Coopers & Lybrand v. Livesay,** 437 U.S. 463 (1978), and **Cohen v. Beneficial Indus. Loan Corp.,** 337 U.S. 541 (1949), the collateral order doctrine permits immediate review of a trial judge's order that is:

(a) **Final and unrelated to the merits (collateral).**

- The order must be clearly unrelated to the merits, but some orders that are intertwined with the merits may also be reviewed.

(b) **Involves a right "too important" to be denied review.**

- What constitutes an "important" right has been subject to much debate in appellate decisions, but typically involves some non-trivial right that will be lost if resolution of the question must await final appeal.

(c) **Would result in irreparable harm to the person appealing the order, if immediate review were not available.**

- What constitutes irreparable harm is within the trial judge's discretion. The appellate court may borrow the standards for irreparable harm relating to the issuance of injunctions, measuring the severity of the potential injury in absence of an immediate review, the probability of that harm occurring, and the likelihood that effective review will be ineffective if delayed until after a final judgment.

(d) Examples. The "collateral order" doctrine is a frequently litigated issue on appeal to the Supreme Court:

- **Orders immediately appealable as within the collateral order doctrine:**

  - Denial of a motion to impose security costs on plaintiffs in a shareholder's derivative lawsuit (**Cohen v. Beneficial Industrial Loan Corp.,** *supra*).

  - Denial of a motion to quash a subpoena to produce evidence, on the ground that the district court lacked subject matter jurisdiction over the dispute (**United States Catholic Conference v. Abortion Rights Mobilization, Inc.,** 487 U.S. 72 (1988)).

  - Grant or denial of a motion to disqualify an attorney based on alleged conflicts of interest or other grounds (**Richardson–Merrell, Inc. v. Koller,** 472 U.S. 424 (1985); **Firestone Tire & Rubber Corp. v. Risjord,** 449 U.S. 368 (1981)).

  - Denial of a motion to quash subpoena request to President of the United States to produce tape recordings for examination by trial judge (**United States v. Nixon,** 418 U.S. 683 (1974) (traditional contempt avenue to immediate appeal inappropriate in unique circumstances involving the President)).

  - Order directing divestiture of a subsidiary, reserving ruling on specific plan (**Brown Shoe Co. v. United States,** 370 U.S. 294 (1962)).

  - Denial of a motion to proceed *in forma pauperis.*

  - Grant of a motion to require the plaintiff in a class action to send individual notice to all unnamed class members.

- Order of interim attorney's fees to plaintiff in civil rights action, where no final judgment had been entered (**Palmer v. City of Chicago,** 806 F.2d 1316 (7th Cir. 1986)).

- Grant of a motion to recuse the trial judge **In re Cement Antitrust Litigation,** 673 F.2d 1020 (9th Cir. 1981), *affd. sub nom.* **Arizona v. Ash Grove Cement Co.,** 459 U.S. 1190 (1983).

- **Orders not immediately appealable as not within the collateral order doctrine:**

  - Order denying a motion to dismiss based on a forum selection clause in a cruise-line passenger ticket (**Lauro Lines S.R.L. v. Chasser,** 490 U.S. 495 (1989)).

  - Order denying motion to dismiss based on immunity from civil process of extradited person, or on *forum non conveniens* (**Van Cauwenberghe v. Biard,** 486 U.S. 517 (1988)).

  - Order denying request to quash subpoenas directing parties to appear and produce documents (**United States v. Ryan,** 402 U.S. 530 (1971) and **Cobbledick v. United States,** 309 U.S. 323 (1940)).

  - Order denying class certification (**Coopers & Lybrand v. Livesay,** 437 U.S. 463 (1978)).

  - The inapplicability of the collateral order doctrine in regard to class certification orders has been superceded by enactment of **Fed. R. Civ. P. 23(f),** in 1998, which provides for interlocutory appeal of class certification orders.

(e) **Irremediable consequences.** A party may obtain immediate review of a judge's order that has irremediable consequences. **Forgay v. Conrad,** 47 U.S. (6 How.) 201 (1848). This exception to the final judgment rule is rarely used in contemporary practice.

  - **Example.** A district judge ordered a losing party to deliver property immediately to the opposing party, even though the underlying claim was only partially adjudicated. The appellate court had jurisdiction for an immediate appeal, because of the irremediable consequences the losing party might suffer in absence of immediate review. **Forgay v. Conrad,** *id.*

(f) **The "death knell" doctrine.** Historically, several federal circuits developed the "death knell" doctrine as a basis for interlocutory review of orders denying class action certifications, on the ground that such a denial effectively signaled the "death knell" for many small claims holders to pursue relief outside the class action format. *See* **Eisen v. Carlisle & Jacquelin,** 370 F.2d 119 (2d Cir. 1966). This doctrine was extended to orders granting class certification, on a "inverse death knell theory." *See* **Herbst v. International Tel. & Tel. Corp.,** 495 F.2d 1308 (2d Cir. 1974). The Supreme Court has repudiated the death knell doctrine, *see infra.*

(g) **Repudiation of the death knell doctrine.** The Supreme Court repudiated the death knell doctrine in **Coopers & Lybrand v. Livesay,** 437 U.S. 463 (1978). The Court reasoned that the principle vice of the death knell doctrine was that it permitted *indiscriminate* interlocutory review of the trial judge's decisions. The doctrine violates the final judgment rule with an exception encompassing enough to swallow the general rule (*i.e.,* almost every order arguably signals the "death knell" of the litigation).

2. Mandamus: The Extraordinary Writ—28 U.S.C. § 1651(a)

a. Writ of Mandamus Defined

A writ of mandamus is an order from a higher court to a lower court judge to perform the judge's duties (usually, to reverse an order or ruling). In federal practice, all courts may "issue writs necessary or appropriate in aid of their respective jurisdictions and agreeable to the usages and principles of law." **28 U.S.C. § 1651(a).**

b. Party Sued

The party who is the object of the mandamus is the trial judge who issues an order. In mandamus actions, either the judge is named in the case caption, or the case is styled *"In the Matter of. . . . "*

c. Extraordinary Nature

The writ of mandamus is an extraordinary remedy, to be used only in instances of *extreme* or *egregious abuse of discretion.* The writ is viewed as an intrusive invasion of the trial judge's authority during the course of a trial.

- **Example. Leading case authority—La Buy v. Howes Leather Co., 352 U.S. 249 (1957).** A writ of mandamus appropriately issued against a trial judge who essentially abdicated his judicial function in turning over the trial of a complex antitrust lawsuit to a special master.

- **Example. Presidential tapes.** A writ of mandamus is an appropriate means to review a district judge's order to produce tape recordings for judicial inspection prior to determining whether the recordings were subject to a grand jury subpoena. **Nixon v. Sirica,** 487 F.2d 700 (D.C. Cir. 1973).

- **Example. Court-ordered physical exam.** A writ of mandamus is an appropriate means to review an order requiring a defendant to submit to a physical and mental exam. **Schlagenhauf v. Holder,** 379 U.S. 104 (1964).

d. Ninth Circuit Mandamus Standards

The Ninth Circuit has articulated five guidelines to determine whether a mandamus is an appropriate remedy in a particular case (*see* **In re Cement Antitrust Litig.,** 688 F.2d 1297 (9th Cir. 1982)):

(1) whether the party seeking the writ has no other adequate means, such as direct appeal, to attain the relief desired;

(2) whether the petitioner will be damaged or prejudiced in a way that is not correctable on appeal;

(3) whether the district court's order is clearly erroneous as a matter of law;

(4) whether the district court's order is an oft repeated error or manifests persistent disregard for the Federal Rules; and

(5) whether the district court's order raises new and important problems or issues of law of first impression.

Also considered:

- whether the alleged injury justifies mandamus authority;

- whether the mandamus petition presents an issue that may repeatedly evade judicial review; and

- whether there are other compelling factors relating to the efficient and orderly administration of the district courts.

e. Criticism of Mandamus as Alternative Means of Interlocutory Appeal

The writ of mandamus is not intended to provide a "backdoor" means of interlocutory review when no other exception applies to permit immediate review of a judge's orders or rulings. It is intended to apply only to exceptional circumstances of judicial abuse. **La Buy v. Howes Leather Co.** (Justice Brennan, dissenting).

- **Example.** In a criminal case the district court judge ordered discovery for the defendant. The government sought a mandamus to overturn this order. These facts did not constitute the kind of extraordinary circumstances justifying immediate review. **Will v. United States,** 389 U.S. 90 (1967). *See also* **Kerr v. U.S. Dist. Ct.,** 426 U.S. 394 (1976) (**Will** ruling extended to discovery order in civil litigation).

f. State Practice

Some states allow more liberal use than federal courts to provide immediate review of certain issues (such as rulings denying motion to quash service of process for lack of jurisdiction).

3. Contempt

A contempt order is a final judgment and may be appealed immediately. Contempt, then, may supply a route for interlocutory review of other orders that are not typically final or reviewable until final judgment. Discovery orders, for example, fall into this category. A court may order a party to cooperate in some discovery. The initial discovery request and order is not itself immediately appealable, but the party may obtain review by disobeying the court's order to cooperate, and being found in contempt. The contempt route is risky, however, because if the appellate court affirms the trial judge's discovery order, then the contempt stands.

4. Partial Final Judgments: Rule 54(b)

In multi-party, multi-claim litigation, an order finally determining a claim can be immediately appealable. The losing litigant does not have to wait until disposition of the entire case to bring an appeal on the claim that the court has fully determined.

a. Certification Procedure

In a multi-claim case, the court makes an express direction for entry of the judgment on a decided claim and certifies that there is no just reason for delaying an appeal on that claim. **Rule 54(b).**

b. Standards of Review

The appellate court reviews this certification under an *abuse of discretion* standard. The court reviews *de novo* whether the trial court determined a truly separate claim, or merely an alternative theory on a single claim.

i. Two-Party Disputes: Multiple, Separate Claims

Multiple claims are present if the theories of recovery could be separately and concurrently enforced. The claims may be related or rest on overlapping facts.

- **Example.** A complaint setting forth claims under the **Sherman Antitrust Act**, common law inducement to breach of contract, unfair competition, and patent infringement are inherently separable and can be decided independently of each other. **Sears, Roebuck & Co. v. Mackey,** 351 U.S. 427 (1956).

- **Example.** A petitioner's complaint setting forth separate claims of discrimination in hiring, promotion, insurance, and pregnancy policies constituted a single legal theory that applied to one set of facts. **Liberty Mutual Ins. Co. v. Wetzel,** 424 U.S. 737 (1976).

ii. No Just Reason for Delay

Courts assess whether an immediate appeal of a separate claim will simplify the trial or result in repetitive review of the same issues after conclusion of the entire case. Courts also consider the possible prejudicial impact of the separate appeal on the winning party in light of the possibility of an offset if the party losing on the separate claim should win on the remaining claims. *See e.g.,* **Panichella v. Pennsylvania R.R. Co.,** 252 F.2d 452 (3d Cir. 1958) (balancing possibility that defendant might prevail on remaining claims).

iii. Undecided Counterclaims

A defendant's appeal may be appropriate even though the court has not decided a counterclaim arising out of the same transaction. **Cold**

Metal Process Co. v. United Engg. & Foundry Co., 351 U.S. 445 (1956); **Curtiss–Wright Corp. v. General Elec. Co.,** 446 U.S. 1(1980).

C. SCOPE OF REVIEW

1. Issues Subject to Review

The scope of appellate review is limited by a series of general rules and principles.

a. Appeals by Losing Parties: Errors on the Trial Record

To be appealable, an error must appear on the trial record. Alleged errors are presented in the litigant's appellate brief, which will include the relevant portions of the trial transcript relating to the alleged error.

b. Appeals by Losing Parties: Prior Objections at Trial

To be appealable, an attorney must have made a prompt objection to the alleged error at trial including the grounds on which the attorney believes the court erred. This is to give the trial judge an immediate chance to correct or ameliorate any errors at the time they are made during trial. If an attorney does not object at trial, any error is waived. *See* **J.F. White Contracting Co. v. New England Tank Indus. of New Hampshire, Inc.,** 393 F.2d 449 (1st Cir. 1968).

c. Harmless Errors

To be appealable, an error must have affected substantial rights. Appellate courts will not review so-called "harmless errors." **Rule 61. J.F. White Contracting Co.,** *id.*

d. Appeals by Losing Parties: Grounds to Sustain

If a losing party files an appeal based on a trial error, the opposing party (the appellee) may raise any issue that would sustain its favorable judgment below, whether or not it was decided during the trial. *See* **Standard Accident Ins. Co. v. Roberts,** 132 F.2d 794 (8th Cir. 1942). The rules permit a party to file a notice of appeal within 14 days after another party files a notice of appeal. **Federal Rule of Appellate Procedure 4(a)(3).**

e. Appeals by Winning Parties

A winning party may not appeal from a favorable judgment or decree in order to obtain a review of findings the party believes to be erroneous, if those findings are not necessary to the decree. **Electrical Fittings Corp. v. Thomas & Betts Co.,** 307 U.S. 241 (1939); **New York Tel. Co. v. Maltbie,** 291 U.S. 645 (1934).

- **Rationale.** Unnecessary findings will not be given collateral estoppel effect and thus there is no need for appeal because there will be no possible prejudice to the winning party of the alleged erroneous findings.

2. Standards of Review; Harmless Error; Abuse of Discretion

Appellate standards of review are linked to whether the appellate court is asked to review an error of law or fact, and whether the case was tried to a judge or jury.

a. Issues of Law

i. *De Novo* Review

If a case is tried to a jury, then rulings of law receive the fullest scope of appellate review. The appellate court may consider legal rulings *de novo,* or completely fresh. *See* **Bose Corp. v. Consumers Union of the United States, Inc.,** 466 U.S. 485 (1984) (appellate *de novo* review of district court's application of governing constitutional standard in defamation case).

ii. Abuse of Discretion

Rulings that are within a trial judge's discretion are subject to an "abuse of discretion" standard. An appellate court may reverse a trial judge's rulings on law only for clearly erroneous rulings (*see* discussion *infra*).

b. Findings of Fact

Appellate courts accord greater deference to findings of fact, especially where a jury is the fact-finder.

i. Jury's Decision Against the Weight of the Evidence

Appellate courts have extremely limited ability to set aside a jury decision as being against the weight of the evidence. *See* **Corcoran v. City of Chicago,** 373 Ill. 567, 27 N.E.2d 451 (1940).

(a) **Appellate reversal of trial court's order denying new trial.** Appellate courts rarely exercise a power to reverse a trial court's order denying a new trial. *See* **Georgia–Pacific Corp. v. United States,** 264 F.2d 161 (5th Cir. 1959).

- **Reversal of grants or denials of new trials on the ground that the verdict is excessive, or conditioning affirmance upon a remittitur.** Appellate courts may reverse a district court's denial of a new trial on the ground that a verdict is excessive or to condition affirmance upon a remittitur. *See* **Dagnello v. Long Island R.R. Co.,** 289 F.2d 797 (2d Cir. 1961). Appellate courts may review, under an "abuse of discretion" standard, a district court's decision to grant a new trial where a verdict is excessive. *See* **Gasperini v. Center for Humanities,** 518 U.S. 415 (1996).

ii. Clearly Erroneous Standard: General Principles

If a case is conducted as a bench trial, an appellate court will only overturn a judge's findings if those findings are clearly erroneous. **Rule 52(a)(6); Orvis v. Higgins,** 180 F.2d 537 (2d Cir.), *cert. denied,* 340 U.S. 810 (1950) (judge's findings of fact clearly erroneous where contrary to permissible inference that might be drawn from the witness's testimony).

(a) Rationales. The clearly erroneous standard applies because trial judges have the advantage of seeing and hearing the witnesses. Appellate duplication of the trial judge's efforts would only contribute negligibly to the accuracy of fact determination, and at a huge cost in judicial resources. **Anderson v. City of Bessemer City,** 470 U.S. 564 (1985).

- "An appellate court cannot substitute its interpretation of the evidence for that of the trial court simply because the reviewing court 'might give the facts another construction, resolve the ambiguities differently, or find a more sinister cast to actions which the District Court deemed innocent.' " **Inwood Labs., Inc. v. Ives Labs., Inc.,** 456 U.S. 844 (1982).

- "A finding is clearly erroneous when although there is evidence to support it, the reviewing court on the entire evidence is left with the definite and firm conviction that a mistake has been committed . . . If the district court's account of the evidence is plausible in light of the record viewed in its entirety, the court of appeals may not reverse it even though convinced that had it been sitting as the trier of fact, it would have weighed the evidence differently." **United States v. United States Gypsum Co.,** 333 U.S. 364 (1948); **Anderson v. City of Bessemer City,** 470 U.S. 564 (1985).

(b) **No distinctions among types of facts.** The clearly erroneous rule does not distinguish among types of fact, such as "ultimate" or "subsidiary" facts. **Pullman–Standard v. Swint,** 456 U.S. 273 (1982).

(c) **Erroneous view of controlling legal principles.** If a trial judge's findings of fact are made under an erroneous view of controlling legal principles, then the clearly erroneous rule does not apply and the findings may not stand.

(d) **Remand remedies for erroneous findings.** *See* **Kelley v. Southern Pacific Co.,** 419 U.S. 318 (1974):

- If the appellate court determines that a district court judge has made a finding based on an erroneous view of the law, the appellate court remands the case to permit the judge to make missing or additional findings.

- If the appellate court determines that a district court's findings are infirm because of an erroneous view of the law, the appellate court remands the case to the trial judge, unless the record permits only one resolution of the factual issue.

c. Mixed Questions of Law and Fact

Appellate courts treat mixed questions of law and fact as though they were pure questions of law, and therefore are subject to full *de novo* review. If a jury trial was involved, the appellate court will accord greater deference to protect the jury's factual determinations.

i. Distinguishing Law from Fact

Rule 52 does not supply any guidance for distinguishing law from fact, and often this is difficult to do. *See e.g.,* **Pullman–Standard v.**

Swint, *id.* (discriminatory intent in **Title VII Civil Rights** litigation is a finding of fact to be made by trial court, and not a mixed question of law and fact, or pure question of law. An appellate court may reverse only if it concludes the finding is clearly erroneous under **Rule 52(a)(6)**).

d. Preliminary Injunctions: Abuse of Discretion—Review of Facts

Appellate review of a judge's decision granting a preliminary injunction is governed by an abuse of discretion standard. *See* **Roland Machinery Co. v. Dresser Indus., Inc.,** 749 F.2d 380 (7th Cir. 1984). The appellate court assesses whether the judge exceeded the bounds of permissible choice in the circumstances, not whether the appellate court would have decided differently. This standard is not limited, however, only to cases where the judge may be said to have acted irrationally or fancifully. *Id.*

e. Declaratory Judgments

Appellate review of declaratory judgment actions is subject to a two-stage inquiry:

i. Abuse of Discretion

The appellate court will first determine whether the trial court abused its discretion by making the choice to hear a claim for declaratory judgment. **Wilmington Chem. Corp. v. Celebrezze,** 229 F.Supp. 168 (N.D. Ill. 1964).

ii. *De Novo* Review

The appellate court may then determine, even if a declaratory judgment action was proper, that the trial court's opinion was nonetheless erroneous. **National Health Federation v. Weinberger,** 518 F.2d 711 (7th Cir. 1975).

D. APPELLATE PROCEDURE: MECHANICS OF BRINGING AN APPEAL

1. Jurisdictional Nature

A litigant must file an appeal within 30 days of entry of judgment. The time limit for filing appeals is jurisdictional in nature and parties cannot consensually change the time rules. **Torres v. Oakland Scavenger Co.,** 487 U.S. 312 (1988) (**Federal Appellate Rules 3** and **4** are jurisdictional in nature and their requirements are a mandatory prerequisite to appellate jurisdiction). *See also*

Smith v. Barry, 502 U.S. 244 (1992) (informal brief could not serve as functional equivalent of notice of appeal under **Federal Rule of Appellate Procedure 3**). These time limits are rigidly applied.

2. Timing Considerations: Rules 58, 77, 79; Federal Rules of Appellate Procedure 3–5

a. Entry of Judgment

The time limitations are triggered by the *entry of judgment* in conformity with the requirements of **Rule 58**. *See also* **Rule 79(a).**

i. Notice of Entry of Judgment

The clerk of court is required to mail notice of entry of judgment to the parties. **Rule 77(d).** A party also may elect to serve notice formally on an opponent. *Id.*

ii. Events Constituting Final Judgments for Appeal

What events or pro-nouncements constitute an entry of judgment has caused some problems in federal practice.

(a) **General rule.** The general rule is that "[n]o form of words . . . is necessary to evince the rendition [of a judgment]." **United States v. Hark,** 320 U.S. 531 (1944), cited in **United States v. F.M. Schaefer Brewing Co.,** 356 U.S. 227 (1958).

- **Judicial opinions.** A judicial opinion may constitute a final judgment, depending on whether the judge clearly declares his or her intention in the opinion that the opinion is a final judgment. **United States v. F.M. Schaefer Brewing Co.,** *supra.*

- **Unclear intentions.** If a judge's intentions are unclear or leave doubt whether the judge intended the opinion to be his or her final act, then the filing of the opinion will not trigger the time for appeal. **F.M. Schaefer Brewing Co.,** *id.*

- **Example.** A judge's opinion in a tax collection case was not final for appeal purposes where the judge did not state in his opinion the amount or means of determining the amount of the judgment; where the court clerk did not state the judgment amount in the notation on the civil docket, and where counsel of both sides and the judge did not understand the judge's order to be a final act or constitute a final judgment in the case. **F.M. Schaefer Brewing Co.,** *supra.*

(b) **Oral bench rulings: "Premature" appeals.** A judge's oral ruling from the bench may serve as a basis for appeal under **Federal Rule of Appellate Procedure 4(a)(2),** even though the court has yet to enter a final judgment. **Firstier Mortgage Co. v. Investors Mortgage Ins. Co.,** 498 U.S. 269 (1991). Such "premature" notice of appeal from a nonfinal decision can operate as a notice of appeal from the final judgment only when the district court announces a decision that would be appealable if immediately followed by entry of judgment. **Firstier Mortgage Co.,** *id.*

iii. Relationship to Rule 59 Motions to Amend or Modify

If a party files a timely motion to amend or modify a judgment under **Rule 59** (within 28 days of entry of judgment, *see* discussion *supra*), then the time for appeal runs from the entry of the order granting or denying the **Rule 59** motion. *See* **Federal Rule of Appellate Procedure 4(a)(4).**

(a) **Examples.** A litigant's post-trial motion for discretionary pre-judgment interest is a motion to "alter or amend the judgment" that voids a previously filed notice of appeal under **Appellate Rule of Procedure 4(a)(4). Osterneck v. Ernst & Whinney,** 489 U.S. 169 (1989). *But cf.* **Buchanan v. Stanships, Inc.,** 485 U.S. 265 (1988) (post-judgment motion for assessment of costs does not constitute a motion to alter or amend the judgment and does not extend the time to file an appeal).

b. Extensions

Only the district court—and not the appellate court—may grant an extension of time for filing an appeal.

c. Tolling

The timely filing of certain motions tolls the time clock for filing a motion to appeal. These motions include a motion for a judgment notwithstanding the verdict (**Rule 50(b)**); a motion to amend or make additional findings (**Rule 52(b)**); a motion to alter or amend a judgment (**Rule 59**);

or a motion for a new trial (**Rule 59**). Notice of appeal filed before the court has decided any of these motions will not be given effect. Once the court decides the motion a new notice of appeal must be filed. **Federal Rule of Appellate Procedure 4(a)(4).** *See* **Griggs v. Provident Consumer Discount Co.,** 459 U.S. 56 (1982).

E. APPELLATE JURISDICTION OF THE HIGHEST STATE COURTS AND THE UNITED STATES SUPREME COURT

The highest state and federal courts have appellate jurisdiction by constitutional or statutory right, or by discretionary power.

1. Review as of Right

In every state and the federal system, some matters may be directly appealed to the highest court, bypassing intermediate courts of appeal. State and federal courts statutorily define the ability of litigants to bring a direct appeal in the judicial system's highest court, but typically the right of direct review is severely limited—especially in the United States Supreme Court. *See* **28 U.S.C. § 1253.**

a. Repeal of Direct Right of Appeal from District Court Holdings of Unconstitutionality

28 U.S.C. § 1252 provided a direct appeal of any district court decision holding a congressional act unconstitutional in which the United States (or its agencies or employees) was a party. Congress repealed this provision in 1988, acceding to sharp criticism of this appellate jurisdiction. *See* **Brown Shoe Co. v. United States,** 370 U.S. 294 (1962).

b. Direct Appeal from District Court Decisions Where the Supreme Court Would Grant Certiorari

In certain limited situations, the Supreme Court may directly hear an appeal from a district court decision where it also would grant certiorari from an intermediate appellate decision (*see* discussion below). This review bypasses the review by a court of appeals. *See, e.g.,* **United States v. Nixon,** 418 U.S. 683 (1974).

c. State Court Decisions of Federal Claims

The Supreme Court will directly review a state court decision of a federal claim, but that judgment must necessarily turn on the federal question and cannot rest on an independent state ground. If a decision is based on alternative grounds (i.e., one federal and one state-based), then direct review is unavailable. **Zacchini v. Scripps–Howard Broadcasting Co.,** 433 U.S. 562 (1977).

2. Discretionary Review

Almost the entire Supreme Court docket is now determined by discretionary review, granted through the *writ of certiorari. See* **28 U.S.C. §§ 1254(1); 1257(a); Supreme Court Rule 17(a).**

a. Decisions Involving the Validity of State Laws

Appeals from decisions of state and federal courts involving the validity of state laws under the Constitution, treaties, or laws of the United States receive no special treatment and are reviewed, if at all, through grant of a writ of certiorari. *See* **28 U.S.C. §§ 1254** and **1257** (amended in 1988 to eliminate required Supreme Court review).

b. Rule of Four

At least four Justices of the Supreme Court must agree to grant a *writ of certiorari* in order for the full Court to review an appeal. *See* **Harris v. Pennsylvania R.R. Co.,** 361 U.S. 15 (1959).

c. Finality for Purposes of Supreme Court Review

The Supreme Court may review only "final judgments of the highest state court in which the decision could be had." **28 U.S.C. § 1257.** There is some suggestion that "final" for the purposes of Supreme Court review is more flexible than the requirement of finality under **28 U.S.C. § 1291** (*see* discussion *supra*). *See* **Cox Broadcasting Corp. v. Cohn,** 420 U.S. 469 (1975). In general, the Court has suggested that a "technical" definition of finality may give way to a series of pragmatic considerations, including:

(1) when the decision is final from a practical point of view—for example, when the interlocutory decision clearly dictates the final result;

(2) when the federal issue necessarily would survive no matter how the state courts would rule in subsequent proceedings;

(3) when, under state law, subsequent review could be prohibited—for example, in criminal or certain administrative law cases in which

acquittal or decision against the government would not be appeal-able; and

(4) when important federal rights are involved and when delay would erode federal policy.

■ CHAPTER REVIEW CHECKLIST

Appellate review, especially interlocutory appeal, is a good test topic for civil procedure exams. Your law professor is likely to be interested in your general understanding of the final judgment rule and statutes, as well as the exceptions to those rules and statutes. The "collateral order" doctrine is a frequently tested topic. You should concentrate your efforts on the available methods of pursuing appellate relief, including the writ of mandamus. Your law professor also may be interested in your understanding of the different standards of appellate review, and the fact-law distinction. It is highly unlikely that you will be tested on the mechanics of seeking an appeal, or on Supreme Court appellate jurisdiction. However, pay attention to whether an appeal is sought in a *timely* fashion, as federal courts apply the timing rules very rigidly.

To answer a problem relating to the final judgment rule, ask:

1. **Has the claim been fully decided and concluded so that nothing in the litigation remains except to execute on the judgment?**

   - Is there an applicable statute that defines finality for the purposes of filing an appeal?

   - Does the statute liberally permit, or narrowly restrict, the ability to bring an appeal? Does the statute permit interlocutory (or immediate) appeal of a trial judge's rulings?

2. **Is the claim part of a multi-claim lawsuit? Has the particular or individual claim been decided such that an appellate court may review it apart from the remaining claims?**

   - Has the court entered an express certification that the separate claim is ripe for appeal?

   - Is there any just reason for delaying an appeal of the separately decided claim?

   - In what manner or fashion is the decided claim related to the undecided claims in the litigation? What are the theories of recovery for each claim? Are the claims legally or transactionally related?

- Is there a counterclaim based on the plaintiff's claim?

To answer a question relating to interlocutory appeal, ask:

1. **Does the judge's order relate to any of the specific categories that permit interlocutory appeal under federal law (28 U.S.C. § 1292(a))?**

   - Does the order relate to granting, denying, modifying, or amending an injunction?

   - Does the order relate to a matter in an admiralty proceeding?

   - Does the order relate to a matter pertaining to a receivership?

2. If the case is in state court, does a state statute permit immediate appeal of the type of order involved in the problem?

3. **Has the trial judge certified his or her own order for discretionary interlocutory appeal under 28 U.S.C. § 1292(b)?**

   - Does the issue involve a *"controlling question of law for which there is substantial ground for difference of opinion"?*

   - Will an immediate appeal *"materially advance the ultimate termination of the litigation"?*

4. **Does the judge's ruling fall under the "collateral order" exception to the final judgment rule?**

   - Is the judge's order final and unrelated to the merits of the lawsuit?

   - Does the ruling concern an *important right* that may be irretrievably lost if not subject to an immediate appeal?

   - Will irreparable harm occur to the party seeking immediate appeal, if that party must wait until the conclusion of trial to seek appellate review of the judge's decision?

To answer a question relating to a writ of mandamus, ask:

1. **Has the trial judge abused his or her discretion to such a degree that immediate appellate review is appropriate? (28 U.S.C. § 1651)**

- Do the facts present an extraordinary instance of judicial abuse of authority? Is there a pattern of judicial abuse?

2. **Is there any other available method of appeal of the judge's ruling? Is the party seeking mandamus merely as a "back-door" method of appellate review, in absence of any other means of immediate review?**

To answer a question relating to contempt, ask:

1. **Has the court ordered a party to perform some action? Has the party failed to comply? Has the court cited the non-compliant party for contempt?**

To answer a question relating to the appropriate standard of appellate review, ask:

1. **What is the nature of the decision or ruling that is appealed?**

    - Is the party appealing a finding of fact? Who was the fact-finder, a jury or the judge?

        — Was the finding necessary or unnecessary to the court's decree?

    - Is the party appealing a conclusion of law?

    - Does the decision involve a mixed question of law and fact?

2. Who made the fact or legal determination?

    - Was the issue or claim tried by a jury?

    - Was the issue or claim tried by the judge?

XII

The Binding, Preclusive Effect of Judgments

■ ANALYSIS

■ CHAPTER OVERVIEW

- The binding effect of a judgment is generally described by the term *res judicata*, which captures several concepts of preclusion doctrine.

- The major purpose of preclusion doctrine is to bar, prohibit, or preclude the relitigation of claims and issues that have been fully and fairly litigated in a previous lawsuit.

  — The doctrines of *res judicata* serve the interests of litigant fairness and sound judicial economy.

- The term *res judicata* refers to claim preclusion. Both plaintiffs and defendants may assert claim preclusion as *res judicata.*

- The term **collateral estoppel** refers to issue preclusion.

  — A defendant may invoke **defensive collateral estoppel.**

  — A plaintiff may invoke **offensive collateral estoppel.**

  — Applications of offensive collateral estoppel are more circumscribed, however, due to Seventh Amendment concerns in protecting defendants.

  — The collateral estoppel doctrines no longer require **mutuality of estoppel** among the parties to the litigation.

- *Stare decisis* refers to the binding nature of precedent of a prior legal ruling in a case involving the same facts and claims.

  — *The law of the case* refers to the binding nature of an appellate ruling when the appellate court remands a case for further proceedings.

- Preclusion doctrine applies to both judicial and non-judicial judgments.

- Preclusion doctrine extends to intersystem recognition of judgments.

- The Full Faith and Credit Clause of the United States Constitution requires that states give recognition to the valid acts, statutes, and judgments of sister states.

- Federal courts are required to give *res judicata* effect to valid state court judgments, including state settlement agreements.

A. TERMINOLOGY: ISSUE AND CLAIM PRECLUSION DISTINGUISHED

1. *Res Judicata*

The term *res judicata* is broadly used by courts to describe two separate doctrines concerning the preclusive effect of prior judgments. Both doctrines are discussed in greater detail, *infra*.

a. Claim Preclusion

Claim preclusion (true *res judicata*) refers to full relief accorded to the same parties on the same claim or cause of action. Claim preclusion extends to all issues relevant to the claim that were raised, or could have been raised at trial.

i. Merger

When a plaintiff wins, the claim merges in the judgment and the plaintiff cannot seek relief on that claim in a subsequent separate lawsuit. *See, e.g.,* **Rush v. City of Maple Heights,** 167 Ohio St. 221, 147 N.E.2d 599 (1958) (issue of personal injury damages resulting from motorcycle accident could not be litigated in second lawsuit where plaintiff won previous lawsuit arising out of same accident for property damage. Personal injury claim *was merged* in the prior property damage judgment).

ii. Bar

If a plaintiff loses the first lawsuit, the plaintiff's claim is extinguished and the defendant's judgment acts as a bar to the plaintiff seeking subsequent relief on that same claim. *See e.g.,* **Mathews v. New York Racing Assn., Inc.,** 193 F.Supp. 293 (S.D.N.Y. 1961) (defendants' prior successful judgment in earlier assault complaint *barred* subsequent lawsuit by same plaintiff on grounds of assault, kidnapping, false arrest, and false imprisonment, arising from same series of acts and events).

b. Collateral Estoppel or Issue Preclusion

Issue preclusion recognizes that litigation of claims in one lawsuit may resolve issues that are relevant to a subsequent litigation. Issue preclusion bars the relitigation of issues actually adjudicated and essential to the judgment in a prior litigation (*see* discussion *infra*).

c. *Stare Decisis*

Stare decisis refers to the policy of courts adhering to precedent, which is given to actual determinations, but not to dicta.

d. Law of the Case

Law of the case refers to the policy whereby an appellate court's rulings on law are binding on the trial court when cases are remanded for further proceedings.

B. PURPOSES SERVED BY PRECLUSION DOCTRINE

1. Avoidance of Redundant Litigation

Preclusion doctrine avoids or eliminates multiple suits on identical rights or obligations between the same parties. Preclusion doctrine also avoids subsequent redetermination of identical issues of duty and breach.

2. Avoidance of "Claim Splitting" and Judicial Economy

Preclusion doctrine prevents so-called claim-splitting by requiring that litigants prosecute in one action all claims that could or should be litigated, rather than reserving a portion of the lawsuit for some later litigation. *See* **Rush v. City of Maple Heights,** *supra,* and **Mathews v. New York Racing Assn.,** Inc., *supra.*

3. Finality and Avoidance of Harassment

Preclusion doctrine enhances the values of finality to litigation, and avoidance of harassment through the threat of multiple, repeated litigation. Through preclusion doctrine defendants especially may be assured that once a lawsuit is fully and fairly litigated, they will not be subject to relitigation of the same claims in subsequent litigation.

C. CLAIM AND DEFENSE PRECLUSION (RES JUDICATA)

1. Definition

In order to assert claim preclusion, a prior litigation must have occurred. Claim preclusion will then be asserted in a second lawsuit in order to prevent relitigation of claims previously tried to judgment. When a second lawsuit is brought, the judgment in the prior suit is considered conclusive. **Cromwell v. County of Sac,** 94 U.S. (4 Otto) 351, 24 L.Ed. 195 (1876).

a. General Prerequisites (Discussed in Greater Detail, *infra*)

For claim preclusion to operate, the following must exist:

(1) a final judgment;

(2) the judgment must be valid;

(3) the judgment must be "on the merits";

(4) the parties in the subsequent action must be identical to the parties in the first action; and

(5) the claim in the subsequent action must include matters properly considered in the first action.

2. Requirement of Final Judgment

a. Definition of Finality

For the purposes of assertion of res judicata, finality "represents the completion of all steps in the adjudication of a claim, short of execution." American Law Institute, **Restatement Second of Judgments § 13 (1982).**

b. Appeals

Finality for *res judicata* purposes is not affected if a litigant brings an appeal from a judgment, unless the appellate court vacates the judgment and orders a new appeal.

i. Stay of Proceedings

The Court in which *res judicata* is being asserted in a subsequent action may stay its proceedings pending the outcome of the appeal, if the appeal might affect the application of preclusion doctrine.

ii. Discretion to Apply *Res Judicata*

The court in the subsequent action also has the discretion to dismiss the second lawsuit based on the judgment in the first litigation.

3. Requirement of a Valid Judgment

In order to be accorded *res judicata* effect, the judgment in the prior case must be valid. This means that the court rendering the judgment must have had valid subject matter and personal jurisdiction.

a. Collateral Attack

Prior judgments may be collaterally attacked on jurisdictional grounds in a subsequent proceeding if the defendant never raised the jurisdictional defect and defaulted.

4. Requirement of a Judgment on the Merits

For *res judicata* to apply, in a subsequent litigation, the common law rule (followed in many federal courts) is judgment in the first litigation must have been "on the merits."

a. Pretrial Dismissals Unrelated to the Merits

Dismissals in prior lawsuits for reasons that do not relate to the merits of the lawsuit will not bar assertion of the claim(s) in a subsequent lawsuit.

- **Example.** Dismissal for lack of subject matter jurisdiction does not bar a litigant from instituting an identical litigation, involving the same claims and parties, in a court having proper jurisdiction.

b. Pretrial Dismissals Implicating the Merits

A dismissal that implicates the merits of a litigation usually will bar subsequent relitigation of the same lawsuit.

- **Examples.** Dismissals for failure to state a claim upon which relief can be granted, under **Rule 12(b)(6)** (*see* discussion *supra* in Chapter V, Pleading), or on demurrer in state court, may be considered judgments on the merits for which *res judicata* will apply to prevent relitigation of the same claim.

- **Relief from *res judicata* effect of merits dismissals**

  (a) **Changed pleadings.** A litigant can avoid the *res judicata* bar in the subsequent litigation if the litigant pleads new or additional facts or legal theories not pleaded in the first action.

  (b) **Amended pleadings.** A litigant also can avoid the *res judicata* bar if the court grants the litigant the right to amend the complaint at the time of dismissal. If the plaintiff fails to amend or appeal, then *res judicata* will apply to bar relitigation of the same claim(s).

c. Involuntary Pretrial Dismissals

Involuntary dismissals for failure to prosecute or failure to comply with a court rule usually are "with prejudice," meaning that the litigant may not institute a subsequent lawsuit on the same claim and involving the same parties. Typically when a court orders an involuntary dismissal, the court has never considered the merits prior to the dismissal, (*see* **Rule 41(b),** discussed *supra* at Chapter VIII.)

i. Majority Rule: *Res Judicata* Applies

When a litigant suffers an involuntary dismissal, most courts apply *res judicata* to prevent relitigation of the same claim(s) asserted in the dismissed action.

ii. Minority Rule: *Res Judicata* Does Not Apply

A minority of federal courts refuse to apply *res judicata* to involuntarily dismissed lawsuits, on the ground that such dismissals are not adjudications of the claims on the merits.

iii. Ameliorative Possibilities

If a litigant suffers an involuntary dismissal, the litigant either may seek relief from that judgment or appeal the dismissal, which may ameliorate the harshness of the *res judicata* bar.

d. Restatement Approach to Pretrial Dismissals

The American Law Institute's *Restatement Second of Judgments* § **19, Comment (a) (1982)** omits use of the term "on the merits" from its definition of preclusive bar, vesting discretion in the trial judge in the second action to determine whether to give preclusive effect to a litigation that was dismissed before trial.

5. Requirement of Identity of Parties

Res judicata applies in a subsequent lawsuit only to persons who were parties, or *"in privity"* with parties in the first lawsuit. *See* **Mathews v. New York City Racing Assn., Inc.,** *supra.*

a. New Parties in Second Action

If new parties are named in the second action, then *res judicata* will not apply and a separate or new cause of action is presented in the subsequent litigation.

- **Non-identity of parties and collateral estoppel.** If new parties are named in the second action, issue preclusion or collateral estoppel can operate to prevent relitigation of issues resolved in the prior litigation (*see* discussion of collateral estoppel, *infra*).

b. Exception: Class Action Judgments

Class action judgments represent an exception to the "identity-of-parties" requirement for application of *res judicata.* A valid class action judgment is binding on all class members encompassed by the class description, including both the actual class representatives and the absent class members. *See* **Hansberry v. Lee,** 311 U.S. 32 (1940), discussed in Chapter VI, *supra.*

c. Persons in Privity

A person is in privity with a party if the person acquires an interest in the subject matter of the lawsuit after the lawsuit is brought.

i. Traditional Examples of Persons in Privity

Successors in interest are treated as parties for *res judicata* purposes, and are bound by the same judgment as their predecessors in interest. A person may become a successor in interest through such means as contractual assignment of a right, or by legal succession to rights, as through inheritance laws.

ii. Modern Expanded Notions of Privity

Modern courts have expanded the notion of parties in privity to include a wide range of relationships. Expanded concepts of privity are tied to the substantive law defining or regulating the legal relationship.

(a) **Rationale for expanded privity concepts.** The basic principle animating expanded notions of privity is to conserve judicial resources by avoiding a second lawsuit simply because a person was not named in the first lawsuit, even though the person is juridically related to parties in that first lawsuit.

(b) **Examples of modern privity relationships**

- a person (or persons) who control the first litigation are in privity with the named parties to the suit;

- legal representatives, such as guardians or administrators, are in privity with the person they represent;

- employers are in privity with their employees;

- indemnitors are in privity with their indemnitees.

6. Requirement of Scope of Matters Litigated

Res judicata applies both to claims *actually litigated or that could have or should have been litigated* in the first action. Pure **res judicata**, then, (if applicable) works a very harsh effect on litigants to include in the first lawsuit all claims available.

a. Rationale

The major purpose of the "matters litigated" requirement is to prevent claim-splitting and the consequent waste of resources and harassment that attend severing claims into multiple lawsuits. The possibility of a **res judicata** merger or bars forces litigants to plead and adjudicate all possible claims in one lawsuit, or forego subsequent litigation of those claims.

b. Pleading Strategies

Res judicata principles affect pleading strategies. Thus, the failure to plead an available claim may result in the litigant being precluded from asserting that claim independently in a subsequent lawsuit. In many jurisdictions, this principle extends to the mandatory assertion of compulsory counterclaims (*see* discussion of compulsory counterclaims in Chapter VI, *supra*).

c. Definition of a Claim for *Res Judicata* Purposes

Various jurisdictions define what constitutes a "claim" or "cause of action" differently, and use different tests to determine whether *res judicata* should apply. Some jurisdictions define a claim broadly, to encourage the widest possible joinder of parties and claims and avoid multiple lawsuits. Other courts define a claim narrowly, in order to avoid the harsh consequences of *res judicata.*

i. Scope of Relief Test

Some courts look to the scope of relief in the first lawsuit, to determine all the explicit and implicit findings supporting that relief. If relief in a subsequent action would be inconsistent with (or contradict) the relief awarded in the prior action, then a court may give preclusive effect to the first judgment. This focus of this test is very narrow.

ii. Primary Rights Test

This test looks to the legal rights or duties involved in the first lawsuit. A second court will apply preclusion doctrine to prevent multiple successive lawsuits on the same grounds for the same wrong or injury. Several rights can be violated by a single act, and such circumstances can give rise to separate causes of action.

- **Example.** A vehicular accident may present different causes of action arising from a single event—for example, a claim for personal injuries and a claim for property damage to the vehicle. At common law, these would have constituted separate actions of trespass to the person and trespass to a chattel.

- **Example. Contract actions.** In contract disputes, the applicability of *res judicata* may depend on whether a contract is deemed divisible or indivisible, providing for separate rights.

iii. Same Evidence Test

This test simply looks to see whether a litigant will produce and rely on the same evidence in the second lawsuit as in a prior litigation. Courts do not widely use this test to ascertain whether preclusion doctrine should apply, because it is difficult to know how much duplicative evidence is needed before claims overlap to such an extent that preclusion doctrine applies.

iv. Transaction Test

The transaction test requires application of preclusion doctrine to any injury or injuries arising out of the same acts, or series of acts constituting a transaction or occurrence. American Law Institute, *Restatement Second of Judgments* § 24(1) (1982). A litigant must present all such claims in a single lawsuit. **Rules 13(a), (b), and (g).** The transaction test in effect creates a compulsory joinder requirement driven by *res judicata;* **Rush v. City of Maple Heights,** *supra;* and **Mathews v. New York City Racing Assn.,** *supra.*

7. Quality of the Judgment

Preclusion doctrine usually applies to judgments rendered by judicial tribunals at the conclusion of a litigated trial. Some litigation, however, may be resolved without a litigated proceeding, or by non-judicial tribunals such as administrative agencies.

a. Settlements or Consent Judgments

"Consent judgments" often present problems for the application of preclusion doctrine. Consent judgments are an agreement between parties settling an underlying dispute and providing for entry of judgment in a pending or contemplated action. Courts often look to the parties' intent to ascertain the preclusive effect to be given a consent judgment.

i. Consent Judgments as Court Judgments

Some courts treat consent judgments the same as litigated judgments by tribunals—and give these judgments the same preclusive effect as a judgment entered after a trial on the merits.

ii. Consent-Judgment-as-Contract Theory

The preclusive effect of a consent judgment is measured by the intent of the parties. It must be clear that both parties have agreed to reserve an issue or claim, and to precisely state what issue or claim is reserved. The reservation of the issue must be incorporated into the consent judgment itself and be an inherent part of the original complaint.

■ ILLUSTRATION

A sues B. A and B enter into a consent judgment. B believes the litigation is ended. A will not be able to bring subsequent litigation based on the balance of its claims unless A could show that a reservation of those claims was made in A's complaint and in the consent judgment (which B knew and understood). In this way, a court in a subsequent action can be assured that B also intended to continue the litigation.

iii. No Collateral Estoppel Effect

While many courts will give *res judicata* effect to claims resolved by consent agreements, other courts will not permit collateral estoppel to apply to facts subsumed in the consent agreement. This is based on the theory that collateral estoppel effect cannot be given to facts that are not "actually litigated" in a dispute (*see* discussion of collateral estoppel requirements, below). *See* **American Mutual Liability Ins. Co. v. Michigan Mutual Liability Co.,** 64 Mich.App. 315, 235 N.W.2d 769 (1975) (collateral estoppel could apply only if the parties' intention to bind themselves on certain issues of fact was reflected in the consent judgment).

b. Default Judgments

Default judgments are entitled to the same *res judicata* effects as any other judgment. Default judgments are always *res judicata* on the ultimate claim or demand presented in the complaint. **Housing Authority for La Salle County v. Young Men's Christian Assn. of Ottawa,** 101 Ill.2d 246, 78 Ill.Dec. 125, 461 N.E.2d 959 (1984).

i. Collateral Estoppel Effect

Many courts, however, will not give collateral estoppel effect to issues in a complaint that results in a default judgment, especially if the litigant did not have an incentive to litigate. **Housing Authority for La Salle County,** *id.; see also* **American Law Institute, Restatement Second of Judgments § 28(5)(c) (1982).**

c. Judgments of Nonjudicial Tribunals

Whether a court in a subsequent litigation will give preclusive effect to the prior determinations of non-tribunals, such as administrative bodies, depends on the quality, nature, and fairness of the prior hearing.

i. Agencies Acting in a "Judicial Capacity"

The American Law Institute, **Restatement Second of Judgments § 83(2) (1982)** suggests: An adjudicative determination by an administrative tribunal is conclusive under the rules of *res judicata* only insofar as the proceeding resulting in the determination entailed the essential elements of adjudication, including:

(a) Adequate notice to persons who are to be bound by the adjudication;

(b) The right on behalf of a party to present evidence and legal argument in support of the party's contentions and fair opportunity to rebut evidence and argument by opposing parties;

(c) A formulation of issues and fact in terms of the application of rules with respect to specified parties concerning a specific transaction, situation, or status, or a specific series thereof;

(d) A rule of finality, specifying a point in the proceeding when presentations are terminated and a final decision is rendered; and

(e) Such other procedural elements as may be necessary to constitute a sufficient means of conclusively determining the matter in question, having regard for the magnitude and complexity of the matter in question, the urgency with which the matter must be resolved, and the opportunity of the parties to obtain evidence and formulate legal contentions.

ii. Preclusive Effect: Adequate Opportunity to Litigate

"When an administrative agency is acting in a judicial capacity and resolves disputed facts properly before it which the parties have had an adequate opportunity to litigate, the courts have not hesitated to apply res judicata." **United States v. Utah Constr. & Mining Co.,** 384 U.S. 394 (1966).

iii. No Preclusive Effect: Inadequate Prior Proceeding

Federal courts will not give preclusive effect to prior findings made during inadequate proceedings. *See* **Griffen v. Big Spring Independent School Dist.,** 706 F.2d 645 (5th Cir.), *cert denied,* 464 U.S. 1008 (1983) (no federal court application of collateral estoppel to prior findings of state board of education that school teacher's non-renewal was not discriminatorily motivated; state board procedures were not adequate, extensive, or fair).

iv. Arbitration Decisions

Many courts examine the procedural opportunities afforded litigants during the arbitration to determine the preclusive effects to be given an arbitral decision in a subsequent litigation. Arbitration hearings, though, generally lack the essential elements of an adjudicated proceeding. *See e.g.,* **American Ins. Co. v. Messinger,** 43 N.Y.2d 184, 401 N.Y.S.2d 36, 371 N.E.2d 798 (1977).

D. ISSUE PRECLUSION (COLLATERAL ESTOPPEL)

Collateral estoppel refers to the preclusion (or relitigation) of *an issue* (as opposed to a claim) in a subsequent litigation. Collateral estoppel requires that the issue in the first and subsequent litigation is identical, and that the issue was "actually litigated," "necessarily determined," and "essential to the judgment" in the first action. These elements ensure that preclusion will apply only if a litigant had the opportunity to *fully and fairly* litigate an issue. Most collateral estoppel problems focus on what the court decided in the first action.

1. Identical Issue

Identical issues among successive lawsuits are relatively easy to identify when multiple claims arise from a defendant's single wrongful act, but more complex when claims arise out of different acts at different times (where there usually is no identity of issue). *See e.g.,* **Jones v. Morris Plan Bank of Portsmouth,** 168 Va. 284, 191 S.E. 608 (1937).

a. Examples

i. Single Wrongful Act of Defendant (Identity of Issue)

A plaintiff brings a personal injury suit arising out of an automobile accident. In a subsequent lawsuit for loss of consortium brought by the driver's spouse, the issue of the defendant's negligence is identical to both cases.

ii. Acts Occurring at Different Times (No Identity of Issue)

Claiming a tax exemption as a religious organization in one year will not have the benefit of issue preclusion on the exemption in a subsequent year. This is because the group's activities might change from year to year and therefore the exemption issue will not be identical.

iii. Successive Actions on Negotiable Instruments (No Identity of Issue)

In successive actions on bonds or negotiable instruments, issue preclusion will not foreclose relitigation of whether the plaintiff purchased the bonds for value. The issue of bona fide purchase is not identical in the successive litigations, because proof that the plaintiff was a bona fide purchaser of one instrument does not prove how the plaintiff obtained any of the other bonds or instruments. *See* American Law Institute, **Restatement Second of Judgments § 24, Comment (d) (1982).**

b. Different Burdens of Proof

If the burdens of proof differ in successive cases (for example if one litigation is a criminal case and the next a civil litigation), then identity of issues usually will be lacking. However, if there is a higher standard of proof on an issue in the first case ("beyond a reasonable doubt" in criminal cases) then a court may give preclusive effect to that issue in a later civil proceeding. The converse is not true: issue preclusion cannot run from a civil case to a criminal proceeding.

2. Actually Litigated

Preclusive effect will not be given to issues in which a court has not reached a determination of the issue on the merits, as in default or some consent judgments (*see* discussion *infra*). The "actually litigated" requirement ensures that the parties will have engaged in a full adversary presentation of the issue. **Cromwell v. County of Sac,** 94 U.S. (4 Otto) 351, 24 L. Ed. 195 (1876); *see also* American Law Institute, **Restatement Second of Judgments § 28 (1982)** (adopting the "actually litigated" requirement).

a. General Verdicts

Jury determinations rendered on general verdicts sometimes make it difficult to ascertain what the jury decided on one or more issues in the case.

i. Majority View: No Collateral Estoppel

Most courts refuse to give preclusive effect where a jury's findings in a general verdict might have been based on more than one issue in the pleadings.

(a) **Extrinsic evidence rule.** Where the jury's actions are unclear or ambiguous, a court may give preclusive effect to an issue only on extrinsic proof that the jury actually decided the issue. Moreover, the evidence cannot contradict the verdict.

- **Example.** A plaintiff sues a defendant in an action for negligence. The defendant alleges that the plaintiff was contributorily negligent. The jury returns a general verdict for the defendant. It is impossible to know whether the jury found that the defendant was free from negligence, or that the plaintiff was contributorily negligent. If the plaintiff attempts to sue the defendant in a subsequent action, the defendant can only assert issue preclusion if the defendant can show what was the jury's basis for its general verdict. The plaintiff, on the other hand, *cannot* introduce evidence that the plaintiff's alleged contributory negligence was not litigated, because this would contradict the former verdict.

ii. Minority View: Broad Collateral Estoppel Effect

A minority of federal courts give preclusive effect in a second action to all issues actually litigated in the first action that comprise the general verdict.

3. Necessarily Determined and Essential to the Judgment

Similar to the "actually litigated" requirement, the "necessarily determined" standard is to ensure that the parties vigorously litigated the issue in the prior litigation and that it is fair to prevent relitigation in a subsequent lawsuit. *See, e.g.,* **Russell v. Place,** 94 U.S. (4 Otto) 606, 24 L. Ed. 214 (1876).

a. Facts: No Collateral Estoppel Effect

Facts found against the prevailing party in the first litigation are deemed unnecessary, largely because the victorious party has no reason, incentive, or ability to appeal. Thus, the issue is not given collateral estoppel effect because there is no assurance of vigorous prosecution.

i. Historical Test of Ultimate and Mediate Facts

Many courts determined collateral estoppel effect based on whether facts were "ultimate" or "mediate" facts. *See e.g.,* **The Evergreens v. Nunan,** 141 F.2d 927 (2d Cir.), *cert. denied,* 323 U.S. 720 (1944). Criticism of the difficulty in distinguishing between mediate and ultimate facts led to its eventual demise as an operative test. This distinction also was eroded by the availability of special verdicts and general verdicts with interrogatories.

ii. Facts: Modern *Second Restatement* Approach

Courts in a second suit should determine whether the fact on which collateral estoppel is asserted was necessary and important in the first litigation, rather than merely evidentiary. If the fact was necessary and important and the issue was actually litigated, the court in the second action may fairly preclude relitigation in the second lawsuit. American Law Institute, **Restatement Second of Judgments § 27 (1982).** *See, e.g.,* **Synanon Church v. United States,** 820 F.2d 421 (D.C. Cir. 1987) (relying on the *Restatement* approach).

b. Alternative Holdings: Collateral Estoppel Applied

A second court will give full collateral estoppel effect to alternative holdings and there is no need to determine which finding was necessary to the judgment. Courts assume that one issue is no less necessary than any other. Cf. **Malloy v. Trombley,** 50 N.Y.2d 46, 427 N.Y.S.2d 969, 405 N.E.2d 213 (1980) (issue preclusion permitted where judge in bench trial provided complete discussion of each alternative ground for judgment).

• **Example.** If a jury renders a special verdict holding the plaintiff contributorily negligent and the defendant free from negligence, then the defendant is able to collaterally estop the plaintiff on both these issues in a subsequent lawsuit brought by the plaintiff. *See* **Kelley v. Curtiss,** 16 N.J. 265, 108 A.2d 431 (1954).

• **Second Restatement approach.** The American Law Institute suggests that courts not give collateral estoppel effect in such situations because this will encourage appeals. *See* American Law Institute, **Restatement Second of Judgments § 27 (1982).** If an appellate court affirms alternative findings, the **Restatement** would apply collateral estoppel to those issues.

4. Persons Benefited and Bound

a. The Traditional Model

The traditional rule for assertion of collateral estoppel was the same as for *res judicata* or claim preclusion: only parties and their privities could benefit from or could be estopped from relitigating an issue adjudicated in a prior litigation. Non-parties, therefore, could not take advantage of the doctrine of collateral estoppel either to defensively or offensively prevent relitigation of an issue in a subsequent litigation. *See e.g.,* **Ralph Wolff & Sons v. New Zealand Ins. Co.,** 248 Ky. 304, 58 S.W.2d 623 (1933).

i. Rationales for the Traditional Party-Privity Limitation Against Defensive and Offensive Collateral Estoppel

(a) **Defensive use of collateral estoppel: Due process concerns.** Use of collateral estoppel *defensively* (by a prior successful defendant), to prevent relitigation of an issue by a plaintiff who was a non-party to the first action, was perceived as unfair because the non-party never had an opportunity to be heard in the first action. Thus, *due process* prevented application of defensive collateral estoppel because the non-party must be given an opportunity to be heard to have its day in court.

(b) **Mutuality requirement: Offensive collateral estoppel.** The "mutuality" requirement prevented a non-party to the first lawsuit from offensively asserting collateral estoppel, in a subsequent litigation, on an issue against a party to the first lawsuit.

- **Fairness concerns.** The mutuality requirement was based on fairness considerations, mirroring the rationale that since parties could not assert collateral estoppel against a non-party, neither should non-parties be permitted to assert collateral estoppel against a party.

- **The problem of sideline-sitters.** The mutuality requirement also was intended to cope with the problem of potential plaintiffs who could have joined in the first litigation but instead chose to "sit on the sidelines," awaiting the first litigation's outcome. Without a mutuality requirement, a sideline-sitter could take advantage of the winning plaintiff's judgment if the first plaintiff was successful, but would suffer no detriment if the first plaintiff lost (because the sideline-sitter could still sue to have its own day in court).

b. Mutuality Eroded

All federal courts have considerably eroded the doctrine of mutuality, and now recognize both the possibility for defensive and offensive collateral estoppel. Many state courts have not followed the federal lead, and individual state law determines the extent to which the doctrine of mutuality applies, either to assertions of defensive or offensive collateral estoppel.

i. Erosion of Bar Against Defensive Collateral Estoppel

The doctrine of defensive collateral estoppel was first eroded by the California Supreme Court in **Bernhard v. Bank of America Natl. Trust & Sav. Assn.,** 19 Cal.2d 807, 122 P.2d 892 (1942). The United States Supreme Court endorsed this inroad—thereby permitting assertions of defensive collateral estoppel in federal actions—in **Blonder–Tongue Labs., Inc. v. University of Ill. Found.,** 402 U.S. 313 (1971).

(a) Rationale for erosion of the bar against defensive collateral estoppel. Defensive collateral estoppel is now recognized as a means of preventing a defendant from being harassed by serial

litigation. If a defendant has been sued on an issue and won, then the defendant ought to be able to assert its favorable judgment on that issue to prevent subsequent plaintiffs from suing on the identical issue.

ii. Erosion of Bar Against Offensive Collateral Estoppel

The Supreme Court ultimately abandoned the doctrine of mutuality in situations where non-party plaintiffs seek to invoke offensive collateral estoppel. *See* **Parklane Hosiery Co., Inc. v. Shore,** 439 U.S. 322 (1979).

(a) **Fairness concerns relative to the defendant.** In abandoning the mutuality requirement for assertions of offensive collateral estoppel, the Supreme Court requires that the court in the second action determine whether the defendant will be unfairly prejudiced by the non-party plaintiff's offensive use of a prior plaintiff's favorable judgment against the defendant. Considerations include:

- **Foreseeability of subsequent lawsuit.** Could the defendant, at the time of the first lawsuit, have foreseen the subsequent litigation so that the defendant would have fully and aggressively litigated the issue for which the non-party plaintiff asserts offensive collateral estoppel in the second suit?

- **Sideline-sitters.** Could the plaintiff in the second lawsuit (who was not a party to the first lawsuit) have easily joined in that first litigation? If the plaintiff could have easily joined but chose not to—to sit on the sidelines and await a favorable plaintiff's outcome—then the second court may not apply offensive collateral estoppel to give the sideline-sitter the benefit of the favorable judgment.

- **Aberrational first judgment.** Was the judgment in the first action typical or consistent with similar judgments on similar issues, or was the judgment in the first action so aberrational that it would be unfair to offensively apply it to preclude relitigation by a defendant in a subsequent litigation?

- **Different procedural opportunities.** Are there procedural opportunities available in the second action that were not available in the first, such that a different result might be reached in the second suit if the defendant were not offensively precluded by the first judgment?

- **Note.** The possibility of a jury trial subsequent to an equitable non-jury determination is not such a "procedural opportunity" that will prevent offensive assertion of collateral estoppel. **Parklane Hosiery, Inc.,** *supra.*

c. Collateral Estoppel and Non-Parties

i. Multidistrict Litigation

In cases transferred and consolidated pursuant to the multidistrict litigation statute, **28 U.S.C. § 1407** (*see* Chapter II, *supra,* on subject matter jurisdiction), transferee courts may not, consistent with due process, apply defensive collateral estoppel to bar relitigation of identical liability issues litigated in a prior lawsuit arising from an accident. *See* **Humphreys v. Tann,** 487 F.2d 666 (6th Cir. 1973), *rev'g.* **In re Multidistrict Civil Actions Involving the Air Crash Disaster Near Dayton, Ohio, on March 9, 1967,** 350 F.Supp. 757 (S.D. Ohio 1972).

ii. Non-Parties Assuming Control over Litigation

If non-parties assume control over a litigation in which they have a direct financial or pecuniary interest, they may be precluded from relitigating issues resolved in the first lawsuit. *See* **Montana v. United States,** 440 U.S. 147 (1979). The relationship among the parties and non-parties need not be a formal legal relationship, such as guardian and child.

iii. Non-Intervenors

Persons who have notice of an action (especially an employment consent decree), a reasonable opportunity to intervene, and who were adequately represented may not subsequently collaterally attack a prior negotiated consent decree to which they were not parties. *See* **Civil Rights Act of 1991 § 108, Pub. L. No. 102–166, Tit. I, § 108, 105 Stat. 1071, 1076.** This congressional Act was intended to overturn the Supreme Court's holding in **Martin v. Wilks,** 490 U.S. 755 (1989), permitting such collateral attack by non-intervening persons with an interest in the consent decree.

d. Limitations on Collateral Estoppel

i. Seventh Amendment Concerns

Application of offensive collateral estoppel does not violate a litigant's Seventh Amendment right to a jury trial when a second, legal action, follows a first, equitable action. **Parklane Hosiery, Inc. v. Shore,** *supra.*

ii. Courts of Limited or Exclusive Jurisdiction

Federal courts formerly were split concerning whether they were required to give preclusive effect to state decisions where the substantive law vests exclusive jurisdiction of those claims in the federal courts.

(a) **Older position: Preclusion denied.** At least one early federal circuit decision refused to give preclusive collateral effect to a state determination of antitrust claims and remedies. **Lyons v. Westinghouse Elec. Corp.,** 222 F.2d 184 (2d Cir. 1955).

(b) **Preclusion of underlying facts.** Federal courts will give preclusion to underlying facts, reserving to the federal court determination of the ultimate legal issue. **Becher v. Contoure Labs., Inc.,** 279 U.S. 388 (1929).

(c) **Modern position—preclusion permitted.** Federal courts currently will apply preclusion doctrine even where issues exclusively within the federal court's jurisdiction are implicated. *See* **Matsushita Elec. Indus. Co. v. Epstein,** 516 U.S. 367 (1996).

iii. Change of Law

Collateral estoppel will not apply if there is a change of law between the first and second lawsuits, such that it would change the operative facts. *See* **Commissioner of Internal Revenue v. Sunnen,** 333 U.S. 591 (1948).

- **Example.** In a first lawsuit, a husband seeks a tax refund for royalties he believes not taxable to him by virtue of a patent licensing agreement made to his wife. The court finds the agreement valid and that the plaintiff husband is entitled to a refund. The tax law then changes concerning what must be shown in order to prove a valid agreement for assignment of royalties. In a subsequent litigation to recover a tax refund, the husband may not assert his prior judgment as collateral estoppel on the issue of the validity of the assignment, but must produce new evidence under the changed law. *See* **Commissioner of Internal Revenue v. Sunnen**, *id.*

E. INTERSTATE AND INTERSYSTEM PRECLUSION

1. Interstate Preclusion; Full Faith and Credit Clause

The United States Constitution requires that states give "full faith and credit" to the judgments of sister states. **U.S. Const. Art IV § 1.** Remember that some states require mutuality for application of preclusion doctrine, while others have abandoned mutuality requirements. State courts disagree whether they must give the same preclusive effect to a judgment as would the state that rendered the judgment or whether they are free to apply their own preclusion rules. Some states give non-mutual preclusive effect to another state's judgment that the rendering state would not have treated as preclusive. *See, e.g.,* **Hart v. American Airlines, Inc.,** 61 Misc.2d 41, 304 N.Y.S.2d 810 (1969) (New York court gives non-mutual preclusive effect in circumstances in which the Texas court would not have done so).

2. State–Federal Preclusion

The full faith and credit statute, **28 U.S.C. § 1738** imposes the same general principles on federal courts, requiring them to accord full faith and credit to state court decisions. *See* **Matsushita v. Epstein,** *supra.*

a. Exclusive Federal Court Jurisdiction: The *Marrese* Test

In construing statutory full faith and credit, federal courts must apply a two-part test to determine whether to give preclusive effect to a state court determination in a subsequent lawsuit over which federal courts have exclusive jurisdiction (*see* **Marrese v. American Academy of Orthopaedic Surgeons,** 470 U.S. 373 (1985)).

i. Apply State Preclusion Law

The federal court first must determine whether state claim preclusion law would preclude the federal lawsuit. If the state would not bar the federal lawsuit, there is no preclusion.

ii. Exception to 28 U.S.C. § 1738

If the state would bar the federal lawsuit, then the court must ascertain whether the relevant federal law contains an explicit or implicit exception to **28 U.S.C. § 1738** denying preclusive effect to the state judgment.

> **(a) Example. State class actions releasing exclusive federal claims.** Federal courts must give full faith and credit even to state-approved class action settlements that release claims exclusively within the federal court's jurisdiction. *See* **Matsushita v. Epstein,** *supra* (releasing federal securities claims within the exclusive jurisdiction of federal courts; no explicit or implicit exception to **28 U.S.C. § 1738** in federal securities laws).

b. State Adjudication of Fourth Amendment or Habeas Corpus Claims

Federal courts will give preclusive effect to state court determinations of alleged constitutional violations or habeas corpus claims in subsequent federal civil rights actions (under **42 U.S.C. § 1983**), provided that the litigant had a full and fair opportunity to litigate the issue in the prior proceeding. *See* **Allen v. McCurry,** 449 U.S. 90 (1980).

i. Failure to Raise Constitutional Issues in Prior Litigation

A federal court may preclude a plaintiff from subsequently raising federal constitutional issues that could have been litigated in the prior state proceeding, but were not. **Migra v. Warren City School Dist. Bd. of Ed.,** 465 U.S. 75 (1984) (**Section 1983** civil rights actions do not imply an exception to **28 U.S.C. § 1738**).

c. Decisions of Administrative Agencies

Statutory full faith and credit does not require that federal courts give preclusive effect to prior decisions of state agency findings of fact in **Title VII** actions. *See* **University of Tennessee v. Elliott,** 478 U.S. 788 (1986).

i. Congressional Intent Required to Defeat Presumption in Favor of Preclusion for State Administrative Decisions (*Astoria Federal Savings & Loan Assn. v. Solimino*, 501 U.S. 104 (1991))

A presumption favoring preclusion for state administrative decisions applies unless "administrative preclusion would be inconsistent with Congress's intent in enacting the particular statute." *Id.*

3. Federal–State Preclusion

Neither constitutional nor statutory full faith and credit rules apply to situations where state courts are asked to give preclusive effect to prior federal judgments. However, no one has seriously challenged the general requirement that state courts give preclusive effect to prior federal judgments. The requirement that state courts are bound by such judgments is variously supported by the **Supremacy Clause** or the **Article III** "case and controversy" doctrine.

a. Applicable Preclusion Rules

In general, most commentators and the **Restatement Second of Judgments** agree that federal law controls the choice of preclusion rules. *See* American Law Institute, **Restatement Second of Judgments § 87 (1982)**. However, the **Restatement** also suggests that federal law ought to mandate application of state preclusion rules if such rules are important to effectuate substantive state policies. *Id.*

■ CHAPTER REVIEW CHECKLIST

Your civil procedure exam may contain an examination problem relating either to pure *res judicata*—claim preclusion—or to collateral estoppel—issue preclusion. Your professor is unlikely to test on related doctrines such as *stare decisis,* or law of the case. You should focus your efforts on recognizing and understanding the basic differences between claim and issue preclusion. Your professor also may create a preclusion problem involving interstate or intersystem preclusion, which will first require you to ascertain the applicable preclusion law to solve the problem.

The best way of approaching a preclusion problem is to sort out the multiple lawsuits involved in the fact pattern. You cannot have a preclusion problem unless you have at least two litigations: a first litigation, and then a second lawsuit in which someone is seeking to invoke either *res judicata* or collateral estoppel. To break down or analyze a preclusion problem, the following approach is suggested.

To answer a problem relating to preclusion doctrine, first examine the facts and ask about the first litigation:

1. **What kind of proceeding did the first litigation involve?**

   - Was the first proceeding a litigated adjudication before a judge or jury?

   - Did the first litigation involve a proceeding other than an adjudicated trial, such as a proceeding before an administrative agency, or an arbitration board?

2. **What claims did the litigants present in the first lawsuit?**

   - What claims did the plaintiff assert in the complaint?

   - What defenses did the defendant assert in the first lawsuit?

3. **Who were the actual parties to the first lawsuit?**

   - Are there any people who might be considered "in privity" with those parties?

   - Are there other non-parties interested in the litigation?

4. **Was the first lawsuit litigated to a judgment?**

   - Was it settled by a consent agreement?

   - Did the defendant default?

   - Was the case settled?

   - Was the dispute resolved by arbitration?

5. **How was a judgment rendered?**

   - Who won the first lawsuit? Who lost?

   - What claims or defenses did the first lawsuit resolve?

   - Was the judgment rendered by a judge or a jury?

   - If the judgment was rendered by a jury, is it possible to determine what the jury decided? Did the jury return a general verdict, a special verdict, or a general verdict on interrogatories?

   - Are the jury findings ambiguous or uncertain? Could the jury decision rest on alternative grounds?

To resolve whether preclusion (either claim preclusion or issue preclusion) should apply in a second litigation, examine the facts and ask about the second or subsequent litigation:

1. **In what forum is the second litigation being pursued? Is the second litigation in the same forum, or a different state court, or a federal court?**

- Do rules of interstate or intersystem preclusion apply?

2. **Are the parties in the second lawsuit the same as the parties in the first lawsuit?**

3. **Who is seeking to assert preclusion doctrine?**

   - Is the plaintiff seeking to offensively assert claim or issue preclusion?

   - Is the defendant seeking to defensively assert defensive claim or issue preclusion?

4. **What is the nature of the second lawsuit?**

   - What claims or defenses are being asserted in the second lawsuit?

   - Are the claims identical to the claims raised in the first lawsuit?

   - Does the judgment in the first lawsuit bar relitigation of a plaintiff's claim in the second lawsuit?

   - Did the first lawsuit result in a final judgment, "on the merits"?

   - Were the claims in the first lawsuit fully and fairly litigated?

   - Did the judgment in the first lawsuit merge all the plaintiffs' claims (and prevent assertion of a separate claim in the second suit)?

   - Has the plaintiff attempted to split his or her claims across more than one lawsuit? Is a defendant's claim a compulsory counterclaim that should have been raised in the prior litigation?

5. **Is one litigant seeking to collaterally estop another from relitigation of an issue that was allegedly tried to conclusion in the first lawsuit?**

   - Does the second lawsuit present an identical issue that was litigated in the first lawsuit?

   - Was that issue actually decided? How can you tell?

   - Was that issue necessary to the judgment? Are there possible alternative grounds for the prior judgment?

6. **If a plaintiff in the second litigation was not a party to the first litigation, but is seeking to invoke offensive collateral estoppel against the defendant, ask:**

    •   Could the plaintiff in the second litigation have joined in the first, but instead chose to sit out on the sidelines and wait for a favorable result?

    •   Could the defendant have foreseen subsequent litigation when it defended the first lawsuit? Did the defendant vigorously defend itself in the first litigation?

    •   Was the judgment in the first lawsuit so aberrational that it would be unfair to collaterally estop the defendant in the second lawsuit?

    •   Are there different procedural means available in the second lawsuit that were not available in the first, that might result in a different outcome? (other than a jury trial).

APPENDIX A

Sample Exam Questions

■ PROBLEM I

Hawker Siddeley, a Canadian corporation with its principal place of business in Canada, manufactures railroad cars. It has no offices or agents in Minnesota, though it did have a business arrangement with Unity Railway Supply Company ("Unity"), an Illinois corporation. Hawker Siddeley employed Unity to promote Hawker Siddeley's products in the United States and to refer potential customers to Hawker Siddeley's Canadian offices. Unity did not have authority to enter or bid on contracts or quote prices on behalf of Hawker Siddeley; in fact, Hawker Siddeley has made only one sale (worth less than $1,000) to a Minnesota purchaser in the last fifteen years. Although there is no precise evidence on this point, Hawker Siddeley concedes it is quite likely that many of its railcars (and wheels) have traveled on tracks in Minnesota.

Hawker Siddeley's cars and wheels are manufactured in compliance with standards established by the Association of American Railroads (AAR). All cars used in the interchange service market must comply with AAR standards. "Interchange service" refers to the capacity for railcars to be transferred from one railroad to another. The AAR's standards promote interchange by establishing requirements relating to both standardization and quality of equipment. The market covered by the AAR interchange service agreement is rather large; almost all railroads in Mexico, Canada, and the forty-eight contiguous United States are either members of, or signatories to, the AAR agreement. In order to receive AAR approval, Hawker Siddeley had to submit its plans, products, and premises to testing and inspection.

In 1979, Hawker Siddeley sold a railcar to a Canadian division of North American Car Corporation ("North American") in Canada. In 1983, North American entered a management and services agreement with General Electric Railcar Services Corporation ("Gerasco"), a Canadian corporation whose principal place of business is Alberta, Canada, that allowed GERASCO to lease the car on North American's behalf. In June 1984, GERASCO leased the car to Potash Company of America ("PCA"), a Canadian corporation whose principal place of business is in Connecticut. Soo Lines, which would haul the railcars, is a Delaware corporation with its principal place of business also in Connecticut.

PCA used the railcar to transport potash. On February 1, 1986, while Soo Line was transporting the railcar on its tracks for PCA, the train derailed near Winona, Minnesota and damaged railcars, track, and freight. From post-accident investigations, Soo Line determined that the accident was caused by a defective wheel on PCA's railcar. In June 1989, Soo filed suit against Hawker Siddeley in Minnesota state court under theories of strict product liability and negligence. The Minnesota long-arm statute extends jurisdiction to the fullest extent permitted by the Due Process Clause, **Rostad v. On–Deck, Inc.,** 372 N.W.2d 717 (Minn.) (en banc), *cert. denied,* 474 U.S. 1006 (1985). Hawker Siddeley responded by removing the case to federal district court, filing a motion to dismiss for lack of personal jurisdiction, and an affirmative defense based on sovereign immunity. Hawker Siddeley also moves to implead North American, GERASCO, and PCA.

■ QUESTIONS

(1) What arguments will counsel for Hawker Siddeley make in support of its motion to dismiss for lack of personal jurisdiction? What arguments will counsel for Soo Line make in opposition to the motion to dismiss for lack of personal jurisdiction?

(2) Can Hawker Siddeley remove the case to federal court? On what possible grounds? How should Soo Lines respond to Hawker Siddeley's removal?

(3) If the federal removal is good, can the federal court hear the impleaded claims based on common law contract and tort theories of liability? Are there any jurisdictional problems with Hawker Siddeley's attempted impleader actions?

■ PROBLEM II

Western Trails, Inc., the owner of a private campground resort, sued Camp Coast to Coast, a corporation that arranges reciprocal visitation privileges for individual members of licensed campground resorts such as Western Trails. For an annual fee plus use fees, licensed resort members who have purchased a Coast to Coast membership may visit other private affiliated resorts and pay Coast to Coast for each night stayed at the other resort. Western Trails sued after Coast to Coast promulgated a rule, known as the Primary Product Rule, governing the sale of Coast to Coast memberships by affiliated resorts. The suit was brought in federal district court in Illinois.

The Primary Product Rule provides that no licensed resort shall offer Coast to Coast memberships to any person living greater than 250 miles from any resort for so long as (1) greater than 60% of the members of the resort live outside a radius of 250 miles from the resort and (2) during the preceding 12 months, the members of the resort visited other licensed resorts more than the resort hosted visiting members of other licensed resorts.

Western Trails alleges that Coast to Coast designed the rule in conspiracy with other licensed resorts in order to restrict price competition in the sale of resort memberships. Western contends that Coast to Coast deliberately formulated the rule to discriminate against low-priced resorts. Coast to Coast answers that the rule was designed to prevent "free rider" situations in which a resort sells memberships to purchasers who live a great distance from the resort and who have no intention of regularly using the resort, but who purchase the membership in the resort as a means of gaining inexpensive access to other licensed resorts in the Coast to Coast network.

Western Trails sought production of documents relating to the development, formulation, and application of the Primary Product Rule. Western Trails sought these documents in order to prove that the rule was designed to discriminate against resorts that offer resort memberships for a relatively low price. The requested documents fall into four categories:

   (a)   A map and a number of charts created by or for Coast to Coast's outside general counsel, Berliner. The data relates to the number of members of each resort affiliated with Coast to Coast, the percentage of members who live greater than or less than 250 miles from the resort, the number of nights the resort hosted visiting members of other licensed resorts, and the number of nights the members of each resort visited other resorts.

(b) Various documents and memoranda between Berliner and Coast to Coast concerning the Primary Product Rule or the resorts' requests for exemptions from the rule. The documents do not contain any legal advice to Coast to Coast concerning the subject matter contained in the documents.

(c) Preliminary drafts of letters to affiliates of Coast to Coast, and drafts of other communications, prepared or reviewed by Berliner, that were to be published to third parties, for the purpose of providing business advice.

(d) Preliminary drafts of letters and memoranda exchanged between Coast to Coast and its counsel, and communications between Berliner and lawyers in the law firm of Pillsbury, Madison & Sutro, relating to legal advice provided to Coast to Coast.

In response to the production requests, Coast to Coast produced some materials, and inadvertently released a report that consisted of a tabulation of the percentage of members of each licensed resort who live inside and outside of a radius of 250 miles of the resort. Coast to Coast now refuses to produce the four categories of requested documents on the grounds that the documents are protected under the attorney-client privilege and the work product doctrine. Western Trails moves to compel production of the documents, arguing that none of the materials are protected, and further contending that Illinois state law limits attorney work product protection to opinion work product, only.

■ QUESTIONS

(1) Discuss generally the scope and protections afforded by the attorney-client privilege and the work product doctrine. What effect, if any, does the inadvertent disclosure of the report have on the invocation of the privilege and immunity?

(2) How should the court rule on Western's contention that the Illinois state law on attorney work product immunity applies to limit that protection to opinion work product, only?

(3) Assuming that the federal court does not apply the Illinois work product doctrine, discuss whether the privilege or immunity applies as to each category of requested documents, or whether the court should compel disclosure.

■ PROBLEM III

Boatman's Bank of Belton hired Donald H. Frieze in October 1979 when Frieze was forty years old. During his employment with Boatman's, Frieze primarily made and collected loans. Frieze advanced from making simple consumer loans to making more sophisticated commercial and real estate loans. Boatman's always rated Frieze as either competent or superior on his performance evaluations. In May 1986 Boatman's made Frieze assistant vice-president, but his duties did not change. In November 1986, the head of the loan department told Frieze to prepare a stock appraisal for a loan file. Frieze had reviewed the customer's appraisal of the stock, but had not prepared his own appraisal. Angered by the department head's request, Frieze prepared the stock appraisal and signed it, "[P]ersonally by God looked up by me—D.H. Frieze." Later that month, Frieze was terminated. He was told that he was being discharged because of the defiant notation he made on the stock appraisal. Frieze admits that making the notation was unprofessional.

Boatman's did not hire another loan officer when it discharged Frieze. The department head and two other loan officers absorbed Frieze's work. One was thirty-four, one was thirty-seven/and one was thirty-one. Almost five months after Frieze was discharged, the department head resigned to take another position at another bank, and the two other employees were promoted to vice-president positions. In May 1987 Boatman's hired John Dix Wellington as a management trainee. He was twenty-four years old and had no banking experience. Wellington began working in the loan department in September 1987, but did not make his first loan until February 1988. Wellington did not begin making commercial and real estate loans until 1989, more than two years after Boatman's discharged Frieze.

Frieze brought an action in federal district court under the **Age Discrimination in Employment Act, 29 U.S.C. §§ 621–634** (1982 & Supp. III 1985). He asserted that Boatman's stated reason for discharging him was a pretext and Boatman's really fired him because of his age.

Boatman's moved for summary judgment, submitting an affidavit from the former vice-president indicating that Frieze was discharged because of the defiant notation that he had made on the stock appraisal. Frieze responded with an affidavit contending that the absorption of his work by other members of the loan department, the promotions of his younger co-workers, and the hiring of Wellington demonstrate the bank's age discrimination. Frieze's affidavit also stated that four years earlier the vice-president had said to him that Frieze "had waited too long . . . to start [his]effort towards becoming president of a bank and

[Frieze] would never make it." The district court denied Boatman's summary judgment motion and the case went to trial.

At the conclusion of the trial, a jury returned a verdict in favor of Frieze, and Boatman's filed a motion for judgment notwithstanding the verdict and in the alternative a motion for new trial. After considering the motions, the district court entered judgment on the jury verdict for Frieze and denied Boatman's motions for JNOV and a new trial.

■ QUESTIONS

(1) Was the district court correct in denying Boatman's summary judgment motion?

(2) Could Boatman's have immediately appealed the denial of its summary judgment motion?

(3) Should the Court of Appeals reverse the denial of the JNOV and the new trial motion? If so, what recourse does Frieze have?

■ PROBLEM IV

On June 19, 1989 Samuel Winston was arrested in connection with a drug violation. On this same day his wife Maryann, who suffered recurrent psychiatric and substance abuse problems, was intoxicated and taken to the crisis unit of Crozer–Chester Medical Center in Pennsylvania. The family had been living in a shelter for homeless persons, and the couple's three-year-old son Samuel Jr. was taken into custody by the Children and Youth Services (CYS) of Delaware County, Pennsylvania.

Two days later there was a "right-to-detain" hearing relating to Samuel Jr.'s custody, before a Master of the Court of Common Pleas. Because Mr. Winston remained incarcerated and Mrs. Winston was hospitalized, the Master continued Samuel Jr. in custody of the CYS. Mr. Winston was released on bail on June 30, 1989 and on July 11, 1989 after an adjudicatory hearing, the boy was adjudicated dependent and given to the care of CYS which placed him in foster care. That order provided for visitation by his parents, as arranged by CYS. CYS thereafter advised Mr. and Mrs. Winston that they would have scheduled visitation with their son for one hour every two weeks at the CYS office "during the time that the Agency determined that supervised visitation was necessary." At Mr. Winston's request, visits were extended by CYS to one-and-a-half hours in August, and in September, to two hours a week.

On August 23, 1989, the parents, dissatisfied with the limitations on visits imposed by the CYS, filed a class action lawsuit in the Eastern District of Pennsylvania federal court under **42 U.S.C. § 1983,** alleging that the visitation restrictions violated federal statutory and constitutional rights. They sought declaratory and injunctive relief and named as defendants CYS, Pennsylvania's Department of Public Welfare, and Mr. John F. White, Jr., the Secretary of the Department, in his official and individual capacity.

The federal **Adoption Assistance and Child Welfare Act of 1980, 42 U.S.C. §§ 620–28, 670–79(a)** (1988) provides that in order for states to be eligible to receive federal funds to make needed improvements in child welfare services, the state shall have a plan approved by the Secretary which provides that in each case reasonable efforts will be made (A) prior to the placement of a child in foster care, to prevent or eliminate the need for removing the child from his home, and (B) to make it possible for the child to return to his home.

The family continued to have severe domestic difficulties. They were evicted from the shelter because of Mr. Winston's confrontation with the director and Mrs. Winston was hospitalized again for psychiatric problems. Mr. Winston had weekly visits with his son during October, November, and December, and the boy was taken for periodic visits with his hospitalized mother. Samuel Jr. was returned to his father's custody on December 19, 1989 under agency supervision and pending periodic state court review. Mrs. Winston was released from the hospital in January 1990. In March 1990, she and her husband were given legal custody of their son.

In the meantime, the federal action proceeded. Plaintiffs moved for an extension of time in which to file for class certification so that they could determine the size and characteristics of the class. On November 27, 1989, the court entered an order granting the motion and extending plaintiffs' time for 90 days to file for class certification. Nonetheless, the next month, before the allotted time had expired, the court denied plaintiffs' request for class certification, and dismissed the lawsuit. The Winstons then filed an individual lawsuit in Pennsylvania state court, alleging violation of state, federal, and constitutional rights, and seeking injunctive compensatory relief against the CYS, the Department of Public Welfare, and Mr. White and other Department of Welfare officials.

■ QUESTIONS

(1) Was the district court correct in denying class certification? What problems, if any, might the Winstons have faced in pursuing this action as a class litigation?

(2) Are the Winstons precluded from bringing their subsequent state court lawsuit? What arguments might the defendants assert to dismiss on preclusion grounds?

(3) Would the Winstons have been entitled to a jury trial? What additional information might you need to answer this question?

■ PROBLEM V

On November 15, 1991, the United States filed a verified *in rem* complaint seeking the forfeiture of various real and personal properties which, the government alleged, had been used to operate an extensive stolen car enterprise. This civil forfeiture action was commenced under **18 U.S.C. § 981(a)(1)(A),** which provides, in pertinent part: [T]he following property is subject to forfeiture to the United States: (A) Any property, real or personal, involved in a transaction or attempted transaction in violation of section 5313(a) or 5324 of title 31, or of section 1956 or 1957 of this title, or any property traceable to such property. The government alleged that the *in rem* defendants—"all assets" of four named corporations, including Statewide Auto Parts, Inc., plus seven identified parcels of real property—had been used to commit, and facilitate the commission of, violations of various subsections of **18 U.S.C. § 1956,** the federal money-laundering statute, violations which emanated from trafficking in stolen automobiles bearing illegally-altered vehicle identification numbers, and from related mail fraud and bribery offenses.

Simultaneously with filing the complaint, the government applied for a warrant to seize the *in rem* defendants. This application, which was submitted to Judge Nickerson *ex parte,* was accompanied by a 93–page, 337–paragraph declaration from Nassau County police detective Thomas Keteltas, who purported to detail the claimants' scheme of "laundering" stolen automobiles by passing off late-model automobiles as "rebuilt salvage." Detective Keteltas swore to the truth of his declaration before Judge Nickerson, and Judge Nickerson signed the seizure warrant. Within the next four days, United States marshals seized the Statewide premises, hung "Out of Business" signs outside the building, interrupted telephone service, and sealed the premises. A UPS "Next Day Air Letter" sent to

Statewide on November 27 was marked "RETURN TO SHIPPER" with the notations "THIS PACKAGE HAS BEEN RETURNED BECAUSE: Closed up by F.B.I." and "Out of business."

On November 25, 1991, Statewide sought an order to show cause "[w]hy an Order should not be entered by this Court, . . . releasing Defendant STATEWIDE'S property, both real and personal, which has been attached by the United States Marshal . . . and dismissing Plaintiff's Complaint against STATEWIDE AUTO PARTS, INC. for insufficiency and unconstitutionality." Judge Nickerson ordered the government to respond and set argument for December 4, 1991. Along with the order to show cause, Statewide submitted an affidavit of Edward P. Muro, Statewide's secretary-treasurer, which stated that the Keteltas declaration, "while perhaps appearing to be of substance at first blush, upon closer scrutiny is revealed to be just a collection of unsubstantiated speculations and innuendoes as relate to STATEWIDE that hardly justify the imposition of the extreme penalty of extinction." While the Edward Muro affidavit called into question some of the legal conclusions drawn by the government, it did not dispute any of the factual allegations contained in the Keteltas declaration.

Detective Keteltas then submitted a supplemental declaration which indicated that more than a dozen individuals—including Muro—had been arrested on November 19 by the Nassau County Police Department for crimes related to the automobile-laundering scheme. This supplemental declaration further detailed the ongoing criminal activity which had been taking place on the premises of the various named corporations, including Statewide.

Judge Nickerson heard oral argument on the order to show cause on December 4, 1991. Noting that "[t]he object of our motion really is to have the Court allow our clients to continue doing business until the trial of this action," Statewide's attorney argued to the district court that since there was no emergency or exigent circumstance justifying a pre-notice seizure, the property should be summarily returned to Muro and Statewide. However, no evidence other than the already-submitted affidavits was presented. Judge Nickerson declined to vacate the seizure; he did, however, accord Muro and Statewide further opportunity to make evidentiary submissions. Statewide's attorney represented that he would make a further submission on his clients' behalf on December 6. On December 6, however, Statewide submitted only the affidavit of its attorney, which did little more than repeat the arguments set forth in the Edward Muro affidavit. Even then, no evidentiary hearing was requested. On December 16 Judge Nickerson denied Statewide and Muro's motions, concluding that [N]one of the papers submitted on behalf of the movants has refuted the substance of the statements made by Detective Keteltas in his declaration in support of the warrant or in his supplemental declaration submitted upon the motions.

■ QUESTION

You are an associate in the law firm representing Statewide and Mr. Muro. They wish to bring an appeal challenging Judge Nickerson's ruling on your previous motions. A senior partner has asked you to draft a memorandum concerning possible theories of appeal. In particular, the partner wishes you to set out (a) your understanding of the issues on appeal, (b) pertinent current law and any legal standards or tests, (c) how the law applies to the facts in this case, (d) what additional information you might need to structure your appeal, and (e) your assessment of both the strengths and weaknesses of your appeal.

■ PROBLEM VI

During the course of a bitter strike against the New York Daily News by nine of the ten trade unions representing New York newspaper employees, the New York News Inc., then—publisher of the Daily News, and the Tribune, the News' parent company, commenced an action against defendants asking for damages and injunctive relief under the Racketeer Influenced and Corrupt Organizations Act, and on various state law grounds. They named as defendants the Newspaper and Mail Deliverers' Union of New York and Vicinity, which was one of the News' striking unions, the Allied Printing Trades Council of New York State, which is the umbrella organization for the News' ten newspaper workers' unions, and a number of individual officials and members of the Drivers' Union. Theodore W. Kheel was not named as a defendant. The complaint alleged that defendants participated in a criminal conspiracy that had as its object either (1) to coerce the News into settling the ongoing strike on unfavorable terms that would require it to continue to employ undesirable workers and to compensate workers for unearned overtime, or (2) to coerce Tribune into selling the News to a group of private investors with members of the unions representing the News' striking workers receiving a financial interest in the sale.

The complaint described defendants' participation in a "campaign of violence" directed against news dealers and advertisers in an effort to prevent the news dealers from selling the Daily News and advertisers from buying advertising space in the newspaper. Allegedly, the intended result of this campaign was to bring the News to the "verge of collapse." The complaint detailed various racketeering acts engaged in by defendants, such as conspiracy to commit extortion, attempted murder, arson, violence and extortionate threats of violence. The complaint also described the buyout plan in which Kheel, a non-party, allegedly participated. Although Kheel was not named as a defendant, his name appeared throughout the complaint, particularly in the section alleging the buyout plan. According to the complaint, the Allied Council had acted as a spokesperson for the ten newspaper unions through its President, George McDonald, and its "purportedly unpaid advisor, Theodore W. Kheel," and had coordinated the negotiating strategies and strike-related activities of the unions.

The complaint alleged that as a part of and in furtherance of the unlawful plan defendants had sought to exploit the situation they had created through the campaign "for their personal benefit and the personal benefit of certain persons affiliated with them including Kheel." It alleged that within a week of the strike and the commencement of the violence Kheel—operating behind a facade of respectability—embarked upon a plan and scheme to personally benefit from such campaign of violence and threats that he was condoning and facilitating. This plan and scheme envisioned utilizing the violence and threats to coerce the Tribune into selling the News to a group of unidentified private investors represented by him (and possibly including Kheel himself) and the unions. The complaint proceeded to allege in detail Kheel's active participation in the unlawful buyout scheme through which defendants and others conspired to acquire an interest in the News through illegal means.

Kheel filed a motion to intervene for the purpose of moving under **Rule 12(f)** of the Federal Rules of Civil Procedure to strike from the complaint the allegations that referred to him. Kheel contended that these allegations had no basis in fact and that plaintiffs knew that the allegations had no basis in fact. Before any action was taken on Kheel's motion, Tribune sold the Daily News to a subsidiary of Mirror Group. The new owner reached new collective bargaining agreements with the nine striking Daily News unions. As part of these arrangements, the parties agreed to terminate the litigation by signing reciprocal releases and stipulating to dismissal of the case with prejudice. The parties agreed "to refrain from all conduct inconsistent with the parties' intent of resolving all disputes arising out of the bargaining relationships that existed at the News."

■ QUESTIONS

(1) How should the district court rule on Kheel's motions to intervene as of right and permissively?

(2) Assuming that the court had construed Kheel's motion to intervene to assert a **Rule 12(f)** motion, would this have been a proper motion?

■ PROBLEM VII

Mr. James T. Conti, a Toledo, Ohio resident, brought suit in state court asserting allegations of false representation in connection with his recruitment for a high-level administrative position at Pneumatic Products' (Pnuematic) office in Florida. Pneumatic is a Delaware corporation, a manufacturer and seller of air drying systems, with its principal place of business in Ocala, Florida. H. Michael McCurry, Pneumatic's president and chief executive officer during 1990, is a Florida resident.

In late 1989 or early 1990, Conti, while in Ohio, responded to a *Wall Street Journal* advertisement for a directory of executive recruiting firms. The directory included a listing for Management Recruiters, an executive recruiting firm headquartered in Cleveland, Ohio. In early March 1990, Conti mailed a letter and resume to Management Recruiters, which were placed in a file maintained for unsolicited resumes. Late in March 1990, McCurry asked Management Recruiters to perform an executive search for the position of vice-president of engineering at Pneumatic's facility in Ocala, Florida. Roger Holloway, the owner of Management Recruiters, had in the past solicited prospective employees for Pneumatic from various parts of the United States. McCurry made numerous representations about the financial health of Pneumatic to Holloway, which Holloway assumed were truthful. Management Recruiters contacted Conti and later forwarded his resume to Pneumatic. Acting on behalf of Pneumatic, Holloway made several phone calls to Conti and sent Pneumatic literature to him. During this same time that he was talking with Holloway, Conti also had several telephone conversations with employees at Pneumatic headquarters.

Management Recruiters arranged for Conti to travel to Florida to meet with McCurry and other Pneumatic officials on two occasions. Pneumatic made Conti's travel arrangements and sent plane tickets to Conti in Ohio. After Conti returned to Ohio from these interviews, Pneumatic conducted extensive negotiations with him. During these negotiations, Pneumatic either directly or through Management Recruiters mailed employment offers and related material to Conti in Ohio. Shortly following Conti's second trip to Florida, Pneumatic offered him the position, and he accepted in May 1990. Although Pneumatic apparently did not want Conti to start work before mid-June, Conti asked to be placed on the payroll in May because he was unemployed. Thus his employment with Pneumatic began May 21, 1990, and for the first month he was in Ohio doing work preparatory to his move to Florida. Pneumatic paid Conti a salary for that month. Conti began work in Pneumatic's facility in Ocala, Florida, on June 18, 1990. On October 5, 1990, the position of vice-president of engineering was eliminated and Conti was terminated.

Conti filed a complaint in Ohio against Pneumatic and McCurry for fraudulent misrepresentation, promissory estoppel, breach of fiduciary duty, and breach of contract. He alleged that the defendants made fraudulent misrepresentations to him regarding Pneumatic's financial condition, both directly during his visits to Florida and indirectly during telephone calls to him in Ohio by Pneumatic's agent, Management Recruiters. He asserted that he detrimentally relied on these misrepresentations in deciding to accept Pneumatic's offer, leave his employment in Ohio, and reject another job offer.

Pneumatic sells industrial drying systems all over the United States. Sales are made either to authorized distributors for resale or directly by Pneumatic to the end user. Pneumatic is not licensed to do business in Ohio, it does not maintain an office or employees in Ohio, and it does not own any property in Ohio. Pneumatic does, however, sell its products in Ohio through two distributors. These two Pneumatic representatives are responsible for soliciting business for Pneumatic in Ohio. The annual sales of one of these distributors to Ohio customers totals approximately $900,000. From time to time, Pneumatic sends its employees into Ohio for consultation with these distributors.

Ohio Revised Code § 2307.382 (A) provides, in pertinent part that: A court may exercise personal jurisdiction over a person who acts directly or by an agent, as to a cause of action arising from the person's: . . . (3) Causing tortious injury by an act or omission in this state; (4) Causing tortious injury by an act or omission outside of this state if he regularly does or solicits business, or engages in any other persistent course of conduct, or derives substantial revenue from goods used or consumed or services rendered in this state; . . . (6) Causing tortious injury in this state to any person by an act outside this state committed with the purpose of injuring persons, when he might reasonably have expected that some person would be injured thereby in this state; (7) Causing tortious injury to any person by a criminal act, any element of which takes place in this state, which he commits or in the commission of which he is guilty of complicity.

■ QUESTIONS

(1) The defendants have moved to dismiss the case for lack of personal jurisdiction. What arguments will the defendants make in support of their motion to dismiss? What arguments will the Plaintiff make in opposition to the motion to dismiss?

(2) Assuming the lawsuit had been brought in federal court naming Pneumatic Products and McCurry as defendants, how should a federal district court rule on a **12(b)(7)** motion by the defendants?

(3) Assuming again that the lawsuit was brought in federal court, could Pneumatic Products and McCurry assert a claim against Management Recruiters? Could Management Recruiters assert a claim against Pneumatic Products and McCurry? If Pneumatic Products and McCurry do assert a claim against Management Recruiters, could Conti also assert his claims against them, as well?

APPENDIX B

Sample Exam Answers

■ PROBLEM I

(1) Hawker Siddeley's Arguments on Its Motion to Dismiss for Lack of Personal Jurisdiction: Hawker Siddeley will argue that personal jurisdiction is improper because it lacks minimum contacts with the forum state and that assertion of jurisdiction would be unfair and not comport with due process. State courts employ a two-part test to determine whether a court has valid jurisdiction over a non-resident party: (1) whether the facts satisfy the state's long-arm statute, and (2) whether the non-resident has minimum contacts with the forum state, so that the court's exercise of jurisdiction would be fair and in accordance with due process. **World–Wide Volkswagen Corp. v. Woodson** (1980). Since the Minnesota long-arm statute extends jurisdiction to the fullest extent permitted by the Due Process Clause, the federal court need only assess the second part of this test.

Sufficient contacts exist when the defendant's conduct and connection with the forum state are such that he should reasonably anticipate being haled into court there, and when maintenance of the suit does not offend "traditional notions of fair play and substantial justice." **International Shoe Co. v. Washington.** In assessing the defendant's reasonable anticipation, "there must be some acts by which the defendant purposefully avails itself of the privilege of conducting activities within the forum state, thus invoking the benefits and protections of its laws." **Burger King v. Rudzewicz; Hanson v. Denckla.**

The court also must evaluate (1) the nature and quality of the contacts with the forum state; (2) the quantity of the contacts with the forum state; (3) the relation of the cause of action to the contacts; (4) the interest of the forum state in providing a forum for its residents; and (5) the convenience of the parties.

Hawker Siddeley's contacts with Minnesota are insufficient to support an assertion of personal jurisdiction. The defective railcar was sold in Canada; Hawker Siddeley has had negligible sales in Minnesota, and maintains no business practice in the state. It has not availed itself of the laws of the state. Even if many Hawker Siddeley cars passed through Minnesota, this results from the actions of third parties, and cannot be considered a contact by Hawker Siddeley with the state. Hawker Siddeley receives no financial benefits because its railcars can travel through Minnesota. Once the car was sold to North American, Hawker Siddeley lost control over it; the fact that the accident occurred in Minnesota is the type of fortuitous occurrence that alone will not support jurisdiction. Hawker Siddeley's employment of an agent to increase sales in the United States is not a contact with Minnesota; Hawker Siddeley's contract with Unity had no direct or indirect relationship with either the accident or anyone in Minnesota.

The fact that its railcar derailed in Minnesota is not enough to subject it to a lawsuit there; this in effect would subject Hawker Siddeley to a lawsuit anywhere a customer used one of its railcars. The Supreme Court in *World–Wide Volkswagen* rejected the concept that every seller of a chattel would in effect "appoint the chattel as its agent for service of process." In addition, the mere "unilateral activity of those who claim some relationship with the non-resident defendant cannot satisfy the requirement of contact with the forum state." **Hanson v. Denckla.**

Although Hawker Siddeley has availed itself of the Minnesota market, this contact is too attenuated to support an assertion of jurisdiction consistent with fair play. Hawker Siddeley's one sale in the market worth less than $1,000, and minimum contacts analysis does not permit contact with a market to substitute for contact with a forum.

Soo Line's Arguments in Opposition to the Motion to Dismiss for Lack of Personal Jurisdiction. Hawker Siddeley had significant contact with Minnesota by virtue of its compliance with AAR standards and requirements. In order to receive AAR approval, Hawker Siddeley had to submit its plans, products, and premises to testing and inspection. There is virtually no market in the United States for railcars that do not comply with AAR standards. Hawker Siddeley also introduced the railcar into the stream of commerce, **Grey v. American Radiator; Asahi Metals Industry Co. v. Superior Court of California,** and thus reasonably may be held accountable in the forum in which its product causes damage or injury.

Hawker Siddeley identified and purposefully targeted a discrete market, and thus it could reasonably expect to be haled into court anywhere within the interchange service market. **World–Wide Volkswagen.** In **Asahi Metals,** a plurality of the Supreme Court held that "conduct of the defendant may indicate an intent or purpose to serve the market in the Forum state, for example, designing the product for the market in the forum state. . . . " Under Asahi standards, it is not unfair to subject this Canadian corporation to Minnesota federal court jurisdiction for tortious injury within the state.

(2) Hawker Siddeley Removal to Federal Court. A defendant who is sued in state court may remove the case to the federal district court (and the division of that district court) where the state action is pending. **28 U.S.C. § 1441(a).** The case must be one in which the plaintiff originally could have sued in federal court, but chose not to do so. There is no federal question involved in this lawsuit, which is based on state strict products liability and negligence theories. Soo Lines, a Delaware corporation with its principal place of business in Connecticut, could have originally sued Hawker Siddeley, a Canadian corporation, in federal court on diversity grounds. **28 U.S.C. § 1332.**

If diversity grounds were not available on these facts, Hawker Siddeley possibly could attempt to assert federal question jurisdiction by invoking a sovereign immunity defense as a Canadian corporation. However, Soo Lines could argue that grounds for federal jurisdiction must be found in the plaintiff's complaint. Therefore, Hawker Siddeley's assertion of jurisdiction based on an anticipated defense would violate the "well-pleaded complaint" rule, which requires that the grounds for jurisdiction be located in the plaintiff's claims and not in the defendant's answer or any anticipated defense. **Louisville & Nashville v. Mottley.** If removal were attempted on this ground, then Soo Lines could petition for remand under **28 U.S.C. § 1447(c) and (d).**

(3) Impleader of North American, GERASCO, and PCA; Impleaded Claims. The supplemental jurisdiction statute, **28 U.S.C. § 1367(a)** permits addition of claims forming part of "one constitutional case or controversy," as well as so-called "pendent parties." Congress promulgated the supplemental jurisdiction statute in 1991 in order to codify the Supreme Court's holdings in **United Mine Workers v. Gibbs** (pendent claims), and **Owen Electric Co. v. Kroger** (ancillary jurisdiction), and to repudiate the Supreme Court's rejection of the concept of pendent parties in **Finley v. United States.** The only limitation on supplemental party and claim joinder is that such joinder may not violate the requirements of diversity jurisdiction. **28 U.S.C. § 1367(b).** Hence, following the *Owen* rule, parties (and claims) may not be impleaded pursuant to **Federal Rule 14** if the addition of such parties (or claims) could not have been joined originally (that is, would violate the *Strawbridge* complete diversity rule).

There seems to be no problem with joining state-based tort or contract theories in a federal action based on the court's valid diversity jurisdiction. **28 U.S.C. § 1367(a).** Arguably, the tort and contract claims may be said to form a part of "one constitutional case or controversy" arising from the railcar derailment in Minnesota and the related servicing, management, and leasing of the railcars. With regard to joinder and possible supplemental jurisdiction problems, North American and GERASCO are Canadian corporations. In order to implead these two companies as third-party defendants, Hawker Siddeley must have some theory of derivative liability supporting the impleader of these parties, based on its management, services, and leasing contracts. **Federal Rule 14.** Assuming a theory of derivative liability, then impleader of these two entities should present no jurisdictional issues for impleader.

PCA, however, is a Canadian corporation with its principal place of business in Connecticut, making it nondiverse from the original plaintiff Soo Lines, which also has its principal place of business in Connecticut. As such, these facts bring PCA within the *Owen* rule and **28 U.S.C. § 1367(b).** Although the defendant Hawker Siddeley may join PCA as a third-party defendant, Soo Lines cannot amend its complaint to assert a claim against PCA, since Soo Lines could not originally have sued PCA.

Note: These problems are based on **Soo Line R. v. Hawker Siddeley Canada,** 950 F.2d 526 (8th Cir. 1991).

■ PROBLEM II

(1) Scope of Attorney–Client Privilege and Work Product Immunity: The purpose of attorney-client privilege is to promote complete and candid communication between clients and attorneys in order that attorneys may render informed, sound legal advice. **Upjohn Co. v. United States.** The privilege is an exception to the fundamental principle that discovery should be liberal and broad in the furtherance of the search for truth. Thus, the privilege applies only when necessary to promote frank and open attorney-client communications. Courts narrowly construe the privilege, therefore, limiting the protection to "confidential communications between an attorney and his client relating to a legal matter for which the client has sought professional advice."

The attorney-client privilege applies only if (1) the asserted holder of the privilege is or sought to become a client; (2) the person to whom a communication was made (a) is a member of the bar of a court, or his subordinate and (b) in connection with the communication is acting as a lawyer; (3) the communication relates to a fact of which the attorney was informed (a) by his client (b) without the presence of strangers (c) for the purpose of securing either (i) an opinion of law or (ii) legal services or (iii) legal assistance in some legal proceeding, and not (d) for the purpose of committing a crime or tort; and (4) the privilege has been (a) claimed and (b) not waived by the client.

The party asserting the privilege bears the burden of proving each element of the privilege. Attorney-client communications concerning business matters are not within the attorney-client privilege, but the privilege is not lost if business advice is simply incorporated into legal advice of counsel.

The attorney work product doctrine, on the other hand, protects a "zone of privacy within which to think, plan, weigh facts and evidence, and candidly evaluate a client's case, and prepare legal theories." The purpose of the doctrine is to protect the integrity of the adversary trial process by shielding adversaries' thoughts and plans concerning the case. The scope of the doctrine is confined to materials prepared in anticipation of litigation or for trial. *See* **Hickman v. Taylor, Federal Rule of Civil Procedure 26(b)(3).** There is no protection unless the document was initially prepared in contemplation of litigation or in the course of preparing for trial. The privilege does not shield from discovery documents that are prepared in the regular course of the compiler's business, rather than specifically for litigation, even if it is apparent that a party may soon resort to litigation.

With regard to both attorney-client privilege and work product immunity, both inadvertent and deliberate disclosure of privileged communications waives the privilege and immunity.

(2) *Erie* **Problem:** Illinois state law limits attorney work product protection to opinion work product only, a scope of the immunity more limited than under federal work product doctrine. Federal law extends work product protection to both ordinary and opinion work product, although ordinary work product immunity may be overcome upon a showing of substantial need and an inability to obtain the requested materials by independent means.

The Illinois state work product doctrine is inconsistent with federal doctrine, and as such presents an Erie problem. The scope of federal work product protection is defined by **Federal Rule of Civil Procedure 26(b)(3)** and case law construing that rule. As such, the conflicting Illinois state rule presents an Erie problem best resolved by **Hanna v. Plumer,** where a **Federal Rule of Civil Procedure (Rule 4)** was in direct conflict with a Massachusetts state rule on service of process. In **Hanna** the Supreme Court indicated that if Congress enacts a Federal Rule of Civil Procedure pursuant to the rulemaking power vested by the **Rules Enabling Act, 28 U.S.C. § 2072,** then the Federal Rule must prevail and be applied over any conflicting state rule.

In this instance, Congress has enacted **Federal Rule of Civil Procedure 26(b)(3)** as a federal codification of the **Hickman v. Taylor** work product immunity. Federal work product immunity is a validly enacted doctrine under the Rules Enabling Act, and implements the *Hanna* rationale supporting uniform federal procedure among the federal district courts. The conflicting Illinois work product doctrine, limiting the immunity solely to opinion work product, must yield to the federal doctrine.

(3) Application of Attorney–Client Privilege and Work Product Immunity to Categories of Information Requested (a) Maps and Charts Created by Outside Counsel: It is unlikely that the data contained in the charts, which was collected from third parties, is confidential information concerning Coast to Coast. Attorney-client privilege attaches to communications from an attorney to a client only if the attorney's communication would reveal confidential client information. The charts are not privileged because they contain no confidential information concerning Coast to Coast and the information contained in the charts is collected from the resorts and members of the resorts. Moreover, Coast to Coast has not made a sufficient showing that the charts were created by or under the supervision of the outside counsel Berliner in the course of rendering legal advice rather than business advice.

The charts and maps also are not protected under the work product immunity. These documents were prepared in the ordinary course of Coast to Coast's business; they were not prepared in anticipation of litigation. The function served by the documents was not preparation for trial, even though Coast to Coast may have been aware that promulgation of the rule could give rise to some unidentified litigation with affected resorts.

(b) Documents and Memoranda Between Outside Counsel and Coast to Coast Concerning Primary Product Rule: The memoranda do not enjoy protection under the attorney-client privilege or work product immunity because they communicate advice provided in the ordinary course of Coast to Coast's business. These memoranda do not convey thoughts, mental impressions, opinions, legal theories or strategies that were prepared in anticipation of litigation. As a general rule, corporate dealings are not made confidential merely by funneling them routinely through an attorney. To the extent that Berliner, as outside counsel, was acting in a business capacity, there is no protection for these communications.

(c) Preliminary Drafts of Letters to Affiliates, etc., Published to Third Parties for the Purpose of Providing Business Advice: If Coast to Coast intended that the information communicated to outside counsel Berliner would be revealed to third parties by publication of the final drafts of the documents, the preliminary drafts may not be privileged. Communications from a client to an attorney are not presumed to be confidential simply because of an attorney-client relationship. Further, none of the documents appear to have been drafted or reviewed in connection with providing a legal opinion or for the legal assistance in a legal proceeding, but rather for the purpose of providing business advice. In addition, none of the documents enjoy protection under the work product immunity, since none were prepared in anticipation of litigation or in the course of trial preparation. Rather, the documents were prepared in the ordinary course of Coast to Coast's business.

(d) Preliminary Drafts of Letters and Memoranda Exchanged Between Coast to Coast, Its Counsel, Berliner, Pillsbury Lawyers Relating to Legal Advice: These documents are protected under the attorney-client privilege. Coast to Coast intended that communications to counsel relating to preliminary drafts of letters to third parties be kept confidential. Coast to Coast retained discretion to refrain from publishing in whole or part the letters drafted and reviewed by counsel. All these documents directly or indirectly reveal confidential communications relating to legal advice provided to Coast to Coast.

Note: These problems are based on **Western Trails v. Camp Coast to Coast, Inc.,** 139 F.R.D. 4 (D.D.C. 1991).

■ PROBLEM III

(1) Denial of Boatman's Summary Judgment Motion. A litigant may move for summary judgment under **Federal Rule of Civil Procedure 56** and a court is required to grant a summary judgment if the pleadings and other supporting materials *"show that there is no genuine issue as to any material fact and that the moving party is entitled to a judgment as a matter of law."* However, where witness credibility or demeanor is involved, or competing inferences, courts are reluctant to grant summary judgment. *See, e.g.,* **Cross v. United States** (2d Cir. 1964); **Lundeen v. Cordner** (8th Cir. 1966).

Until 1986, there was a great deal of confusion in the lower federal courts concerning the appropriate allocation of burdens of production, persuasion, and proof on a summary judgment motion. In a 1986 trilogy of cases the Supreme Court attempted to clarify the burdens on the movant and adverse party in a summary judgment proceeding. *See* **Celotex Corp. v. Catrett; Anderson v. Liberty Lobby, Inc.,** and **Matsushita Electric Industrial Corp. v. Zenith Radio Corp.** (1986). The major insight of the *Celotex* and *Anderson* decisions was to relate burdens of production and proof on the summary judgment motion to the party that carries those burdens at trial.

After **Celotex,** if the non-movant carries the burden of persuasion at trial, then the party moving for summary judgment may satisfy its initial burden by showing affirmative evidence negating an essential element of the non-moving party's claim, or that the non-moving party's evidence is either absent or insufficient to establish an essential element of the non-moving party's claim. Once satisfied, the burden then shifts to the party opposing the summary judgment to produce information showing the existence of a genuine issue of material fact that should be tried to a jury. **Celotex.**

In this case, the material fact in issue centered on the reason for Frieze's dismissal from his job. Frieze carried the burden of proof at trial to prove his claim that his dismissal resulted from age discrimination as prohibited by the federal age discrimination act. Boatman's, as the summary judgment movant, thus met its initial burden of production with the affidavit from the former vice-president indicating that Frieze was discharged because of the defiant notation that he had made on the stock appraisal (that is, affirmative evidence negating an essential element of the non-moving party's claim).

At this point, Frieze then carried the shifted burden of producing information indicating the existence of a genuine issue of fact relating to age discrimination as the basis for his dismissal. Frieze's affidavit, contending that the absorption of his work by other members of the loan department, the promotions of his younger co-workers, and the hiring of Wellington, arguably satisfied this burden of supporting alternative grounds demonstrating the bank's age discrimination.

The court was correct in denying Boatman's motion for summary judgment and permitting the case to be tried to a jury. The reasons for Frieze's discharge are genuinely in issue and subject to inferences to be drawn from the employer's and employee's conduct. When a party is unable to establish the existence of a central act or event directly through affidavits, documents, or other evidence, courts generally may not allow inferences to be taken into account on summary judgment. *See e.g.,* **Cross v. United States** (2d Cir. 1964). In addition, Justice Brennan, dissenting in **Celotex,** indicated the undesirability of resolving a claim through a summary "trial by affidavits" in the place of a jury trial.

(2) Boatman's Possible Interlocutory Appeal of Denial of Summary Judgment Motion. The Federal Rules of Civil Procedure and related statutory provisions allow appeals only from final judgments of the federal district courts. *See* **Federal Rule 54** and **28 U.S.C. § 1291.** A denial of a summary judgment motion is not a final judgment for appeal purposes, because the denial permits the litigation to move forward to trial.

The denial of a summary judgment motion also is not immediately appealable under any statutory provisions ameliorating the final judgment rule. Such a denial is not injunctive in nature, nor does it relate to a receivership, or an action in admiralty. *See* **28 U.S.C. § 1292(a).** Moreover, the district court judge did not certify the order denying summary judgment for immediate review by an appellate court, pursuant to **28 U.S.C. § 1292(b).**

Denial of the summary judgment motion also probably is not reviewable under the collateral order doctrine articulated by the Supreme Court in **Cohen v. Beneficial Industrial Loan Corp.** (1949) and **Coopers & Lybrand v. Livesay** (1978). The collateral order doctrine permits immediate review of a trial judge's order that is (a) final and unrelated to the merits (collateral), (b) involves a right "too important" to be denied review, and (c) would result in irreparable harm to the person appealing the order, if immediate review were not available.

Denials of summary judgment motions are routine court orders that are not intrinsically collateral, but are intertwined with an assessment of the merits of the litigation. Boatman's cannot contend that in absence of immediate review it loses the important "right" not to have to be subjected to a jury trial, because the "right" not to have to go to trial is not a "right" courts conventionally have construed as requiring immediate appeal. Moreover, Boatman's will not suffer irreparable harm from the court's denial of its summary judgment motion, because it retains the right to renew its motion for insufficiency by moving for a directed verdict or for a judgment as a matter of law even after a jury verdict.

Finally, the only remaining route for immediate review of the district court's denial of the summary judgment motion would be through a writ of mandamus seeking reversal of the judge's order. **28 U.S.C. § 1651.** The writ of mandamus, however, is reserved only for instances of extraordinary abuse of a judge's discretion, **La Buy v. Howes Leather Co.,** which these facts do not suggest.

(3) Denial of Boatman's Motion for a JNOV and New Trial. The court of appeals should reverse the trial court's denial of Boatman's request for a JNOV. The court should reverse and remand the case to the district court, with an order to enter a judgment for Boatman's.

A judgment as a matter of law (formerly a judgment notwithstanding the verdict) under **Federal Rule of Civil Procedure 50(b)** should be granted only when all the evidence points one way and is susceptible of no reasonable inferences sustaining the plaintiff's position. In deciding whether Boatman's is entitled to a JNOV, the appellate court has to consider the evidence in a light most favorable to Frieze, assume all conflicts in the evidence were resolved by the jury in Frieze's favor, assume Frieze proved all facts his evidence tends to prove, and give Frieze the benefit of all favorable inferences to be drawn from the proven facts.

A jury could not reasonably infer Frieze was discriminated on the basis of age. It is not the appellate court's role to assess the soundness of Boatman's decision to terminate Frieze; the court's role is to ascertain whether the record contains evidence from which a reasonable jury could have concluded that age discrimination was a determining factor in Frieze's dismissal.

The absorption of work by other members of the loan department does not create a reasonable inference of age discrimination because some of the members were under forty. Employers often distribute a discharged employee's duties to other employees performing related work for legitimate reasons. Boatman's distributing Frieze's work to other members of the loan department does not increase or decrease the likelihood that Boatman's discharged Frieze because of his age. Although Frieze is entitled to the benefit of all reasonable inferences, an inference is reasonable only if it can be drawn from the evidence without resort to speculation.

Boatman's hiring of Wellington also does not create a reasonable inference of age discrimination. Boatman's only hired Wellington nearly five months after Frieze's discharge and another employee resigned from the bank; given Wellington's total lack of experience and the time lag, the jury could not reasonably infer Boatman's hired Wellington to replace an experienced loan officer like Frieze. Finally, the comments made to Frieze do not create a reasonable inference of age discrimination because the persons making the comments did not take part in the decision to discharge Frieze, and because the remarks were made more than four years before the decision to discharge Frieze.

Note: These problems are based on **Frieze v. Boatmen's Bank of Belton,** 950 F.2d 538 (8th Cir. 1991).

■ PROBLEM IV

(1) Class Certification Issues. Arguably, the district court erred in denying the Winstons' request for class certification before permitting them to complete discovery of factual information relating to class certification issues. This is especially so when the court granted the plaintiffs an additional ninety days to complete such pre-certification discovery

Problems the Winstons might have faced in certifying a class action depend, in part, on whether their complaint alleged that CYS's visitation limitations were facially constitutionally improper, or as applied to them. If the complaint alleged that CYS's actions were constitutionally deficient as applied, then it might be difficult for the Winstons to adduce facts in support of a class.

However, the Winstons might have pursued a class constitutional challenge attacking the facial validity of CYS's visitation policy. A class probably could have been certified because the CYS policies are generally applicable to all parents and their children who are CYS clients. Since the Winstons' complaint requested injunctive and declaratory relief, the class would be certifiable under **Federal Rule 23(b)(2),** the classic injunctive relief provision of the class action rule.

To secure such certification, the proposed class initially would have to certify the **Rule 23(a)** threshold requirements of numerosity, commonality, typicality, and adequacy of representation. The Winstons would need to show that numerous other parents (probably more than forty) had been or would be subject to the restrictive CYS visitation limitations; that other parents had experienced similar visitation restrictions; and that the Winstons' experience was typical of other parents and children supervised through the CYS. In addition, the Winstons would need to demonstrate they would vigorously pursue relief on behalf of the proposed class; that the class was relatively free from conflicts-of-interest; and had retained experienced, capable class counsel.

At least one problem with the proposed class action concerns the viability of the Winstons as class plaintiffs, since Samuel Jr. was returned to his parent's custody. This action, in essence, rendered the Winstons' claims moot. However, when a class has been certified, the mootness of the class representative's claim does not affect the court's Article III jurisdiction. **Sosna v. Iowa.** Although the need for an injunction on behalf of the Winstons is no longer live, their request for class declaratory relief remains viable and the court (or class counsel) could appoint another class representative to challenge CYS's visitation policy.

(2) Preclusion of the Subsequent State Court Lawsuit. Whether a state court may entertain a subsequent lawsuit by the Winstons depends on the nature of the federal court's order in dismissing the Winstons' federal lawsuit, which the facts do not indicate. This question involves the possible application of intersystem preclusion doctrine, that is, whether a prior successful federal litigant may preclude relitigation in a subsequent state court. In this instance, the federal court dismissed the plaintiff's case prior to class certification, raising difficult questions relating to the fairness of applying preclusion doctrine to a non-litigated action. In addition to fairness concerns, the application of preclusion principles depends on the nature and quality of the prior judgment, identity of the parties or their privities, and identity of the claims and issues in the two lawsuits.

The defendants will argue that *res judicata* applies to bar relitigation in state court of the same claims the federal court dismissed in the prior lawsuit. If the federal district court dismissed the Winstons' complaint *with prejudice,* then the defendant CYS might attempt to preclude subsequent state relitigation if the state lawsuit met the requirements for claim preclusion or *res judicata.* This, in turn, depends on whether the state litigation involves the same parties suing on the same claims as in the federal case. *Res judicata* would then apply to those claims that were or could have been litigated in the first action, because a judgment *merges* all claims and *bars* subsequent relitigation.

On the other hand, if the federal district court dismissed the case without prejudice, then the Winstons most likely would be free to institute a state action based on the same claims, including any federal constitutional challenges to the CYS visitation policies. Finally, if the district court did not indicate the nature of its dismissal (either with or without prejudice), then **Federal Rule 41(b)** provides that a dismissal operates as an adjudication on the merits, except for dismissals based on a lack of jurisdiction, improper venue, or failure to join a party under **Rule 19.** Since the court apparently dismissed this case for reasons other than these listed defects, the order would serve as an adjudication on the merits, even though the court never reached the class certification issue.

The Winstons could attempt to controvert application of preclusion doctrine by alleging that their state complaint included new parties, claims, and issues not alleged in the federal complaint. In addition, they could argue that the more appropriate disposition of the federal court should have been to retain but abstain jurisdiction in favor of permitting the state court to resolve essentially state-based family and administrative law issues.

(3) Right to a Jury Trial. If the Winstons' lawsuit had gone forward in federal court, their right to a jury trial would be governed by federal constitutional and statutory provisions. The Seventh Amendment to the United States Constitution preserves the right to a trial by jury in suits at common law where the value exceeds twenty dollars. The Supreme Court, in a series of cases beginning with **Beacon Theaters v. Westover,** has construed the Seventh Amendment to provide a jury trial right for civil claims that existed at common law as of the date of ratification of the Seventh Amendment in 1791, or actions analogous to those at common law then. Moreover, the Seventh Amendment does not bind states, because the Supreme Court has not "incorporated" the Seventh Amendment through the Fourteenth Amendment to apply to states. Thus, the Winstons' right to a jury in state court would depend on whether the state constitution provided a jury for the Winstons' claims.

The Winstons' complaint alleges constitutional challenges to CYS's visitation policies and statutory claims under **42 U.S.C. § 1983,** the general federal civil rights statute. To determine whether the Winstons would be entitled to a jury, we would need to know the specific provisions of the civil rights statutes that applied to their claims, and whether those provisions explicitly permitted a jury trial.

For actions that did not exist at common law a federal statute may explicitly provide for a jury trial right. If Congress is silent concerning a jury trial right, as in some **§ 1983** litigation, the Supreme Court has variously ruled whether a litigant is entitled to a jury. For example, the Court has held that defendants have a right to a jury trial in **Title VII** discrimination cases because Congress had created a statutory right "in the nature of a suit at common law." **Curtis v. Loether.**

Although **Curtis v. Loether** resolved the issue of a jury trial right under Title VII claims, this decision did not decide the availability of a jury trial right under other civil rights statutes. A litigant suing under a civil rights statute must show that Congress expressed a preference for a non-jury trial, supported by legitimate concerns about the ability of a jury to decide the case. Moreover/the Supreme Court has held that in actions under federal statutes providing for civil penalties, an alleged violator is entitled to a jury trial to determine whether a violation has occurred and civil penalty is appropriate. **Tull v. United States.**

Finally, the Winstons filed a complaint seeking declaratory and injunctive relief. **Rule 23(b)(2)** injunctive class actions traditionally are equitable in nature, typically tried to a judge rather than a jury. Although the declaratory judgment is not an equitable remedy, these actions traditionally are tried to a judge rather than a jury We also would need to know whether the Winstons' complaint sought any additional relief, such as compensatory damages, and whether such damages were central or incidental to the equitable claims. If the Winstons' complaint requested compensatory damages, the court would need to try the legal issues first. If compensatory damages were not incidental, then the class action might not be able to be certified as a **(b)(2)** action.

Note: These problems are based on **Winston v. Children and Youth Services,** 948 F.2d 1380 (3d Cir. 1991).

■ PROBLEM V

Memorandum

TO: **Senior Partner**
FROM: **Law Student**
RE: **Prejudgment Property Seizures and Due Process; Statewide's Arguments for Appeal**

This memorandum examines the issues and legal principles relating to the government's ability to seize property prior to trial, consistent with the due process requirements of the Fifth and Fourteenth Amendments. The property seizure in this problem was authorized by the federal civil forfeiture statute, **18 U.S.C. § 981(a)(1)(A).** The Fifth and Fourteenth Amendments to the United States Constitution provide that the federal and state governments may not deprive any person of life, liberty, or property without due process of law. Because federal agents seized Statewide's assets, the Fifth Amendment and federal law apply directly to this problem.

(a) Issue on Appeal. The issue on appeal is whether the government's seizure of Statewide's assets, without a prior hearing or prompt post-seizure hearing, violated Statewide's due process rights.

(b) Current Legal Standards Relating to Prejudgment Property Seizures. The Supreme Court has articulated current standards governing the validity of statutory pre-judgment seizures in **Fuentes v. Shevin** (1972), **Mathews v. Eldridge** (1976), and **Connecticut v. Doehr** (1991). **Fuentes** and **Mathews** govern prejudgment property seizures by governmental entities; *Doehr* applies to private property seizures (*e.g.,* through a property lien). The seizure of Statewide's assets involves a governmental seizure and therefore comes within the **Fuentes** and **Mathews** (as opposed to **Doehr**) precedents.

The Due Process Clause of the Fifth Amendment generally has been read to require the government to afford procedural safeguards *before* it deprives a person of one of the fundamental rights enumerated in the clause. In certain limited circumstances, however, process may be postponed until *after* deprivation where an important governmental interest is accompanied by assurances that the deprivation is warranted. In general, seizure statutes that provide opposing parties a hearing before a neutral official, based on sworn factual testimony, and require a pre-seizure bond, will withstand constitutional scrutiny.

Mathews v. Eldridge sets forth a balancing test to determine whether a pre-hearing seizure of property violates due process. The **Mathews** calculus instructs federal courts to determine the constitutional adequacy of an *ex parte* procedure by balancing (a) the private interest involved, (b) the risk of erroneous deprivation of that interest through the procedures utilized, as well as the probable value of additional procedural safeguards, and (c) the government's interest, including the function involved and the fiscal and administrative burdens that additional or substitute procedural safeguards would entail.

In assessing the strength of the government's interest in obtaining a pre-notice seizure, federal courts look to whether "exigent" or "extraordinary" circumstances are present. **Fuentes v. Shevin.** Exigent circumstances are present when (1) the seizure is necessary to secure an important governmental or public interest, (2) very prompt action is necessary, and (3) a government official initiated the seizure by applying the standards of a narrowly drawn statute. *Id.*

(c) Application of Legal Standards to Facts of Seizure of Statewide's Assets
Statewide's Private Interest. Statewide's property interest affected by the government's actions is the ownership, possession, and operation of an ongoing business. Commercial property interests typically have not enjoyed the same privileged protection as private residences, but the government shut down Statewide completely instead of pursing some less-intrusive means, such as entering into an occupancy agreement, or appointing a receiver to run the business during the pendency of the forfeiture proceedings. While the commercial property interest involved may be less substantial than a private residential property interest, the invasion of that interest is far greater here because the government's *ex parte* seizure was unaccompanied by any attempt to preserve the claimants' property rights.

Risk of Error and Value of Additional Procedures. The court held an *ex parte* probable cause determination before a judicial officer, Judge Nickerson, based on a lengthy (and supplemental) declaration by a Nassau County police detective alleging in detail Statewide's supposed illegal activities. Federal courts have held that such *ex parte* hearings before a judicial officer reduce the possibility of erroneous property deprivations, although a pre-seizure notice and opportunity to be heard would have further minimized the risk. In addition, within almost two weeks of the seizure, Judge Nickerson held a post-seizure hearing in which Statewide's secretary-treasurer had the opportunity to contest the seizure under the statutory provisions. Statewide should argue on appeal that the statute's failure to provide pre-seizure notice and opportunity to be heard renders the statute constitutionally defective.

The Government's Interest. The government's interests are in stopping trafficking in stolen motor vehicles and motor vehicle parts, halting financial transactions designed to facilitate and conceal the proceeds of an auto theft scheme, and ensuring that the district court maintains *in rem* jurisdiction over defendants. Under conventional standards, no compelling exigent circumstances justified the government's seizure of Statewide's assets. Statewide should argue that the mere allegations of ongoing criminal activity, standing alone, do not justify pre-notice seizure and the shutdown of a thriving business. Moreover, the government cannot justify such a prejudgment seizure based on a fear that the defendants might waste or remove any valuable assets. The government might have taken a less drastic means for limiting the dissipation of Statewide's assets, as for example by appointing a receiver to run Statewide during the pendency of proceedings.

(d) Additional Information Needed to Structure an Appeal. Due process requires notice and *the opportunity* to be heard at a meaningful time. After the seizure of Statewide's assets, Statewide was given an opportunity to be heard promptly. Muro presented counter-arguments by paper affidavit only, but never requested an evidentiary hearing in the district court. Furthermore, Muro presented little of evidentiary value for the district court to vacate or modify the seizure, or that any greater process would have altered the result at this stage of the forfeiture action. Further information countering the detective's conclusory allegations would better support a post-seizure appeal for modification of the seizure order.

(e) Assessment of Strengths and Weaknesses of Appeal. Statewide's greatest strengths are the lack of a compelling, exigent governmental interest in the pre-notice seizure, coupled with the possibility of less intrusive means to preserve the company's assets during the civil proceedings. Statewide's greatest weakness is the company's failure to offer any factual information to counter the government's supporting affidavits, or any suggestions concerning how additional process would have altered the district court's conclusion.

Note: This problem is based on **United States v. All Assets of Statewide Auto Parts, Inc.,** 971 F.2d 896 (2d Cir. 1992).

■ PROBLEM VI

(1) Kheel's Motion to Intervene as of Right and Permissively. Intervention as of Right: The district court should deny Kheel's motion to intervene as of right. In order to intervene as of right under **Federal Rule of Civil Procedure 24(a)(2)**, an applicant must (1) timely file an application, (2) show an interest in the action, (3) demonstrate that the interest may be impaired by the disposition of the action, and (4) show that the interest is not protected adequately by the parties to the action. The failure to satisfy any of these requirements is sufficient grounds to deny the application.

Moreover, in order to intervene as of right, the movant must possess "an interest relating to the property or transaction which is the subject of the action," **Federal Rule 24(a)(2)**, which interest must be direct, substantial, and legally protectable.

Kheel's motion to intervene does not satisfy these requirements because Kheel's interest in protecting his reputation is not related to the conspiracy alleged in the proceedings and because disposition of the case would not impair Kheel's ability to protect his interest by other means, such as a defamation suit under state law. Moreover, Kheel's purported interest—to pursue **Rule 11** sanctions against the plaintiffs—is not a cognizable interest for intervention purposes. Persons have no legally protectable interest in moving for **Rule 11** sanctions and Kheel's interest in an abuse-free judicial system is not a "significantly protectable interest" within the meaning of **Rule 24(a)(2).**

Permissive Intervention. The district court also should deny Kheel's motion to intervene permissively. Under **Rule 24(b)(2),** an applicant may be permitted to intervene in an action "when an applicant's claim or defense and the main action have a question of law or fact in common." A federal district court has broad discretion to grant or deny permissive intervention. Kheel's claim and the underlying cause of action do have a common question of fact to the extent that Kheel's claim will rely on proof that he did not engage in the conduct the plaintiffs alleged in their complaint. But, a district court also may consider whether permitting intervention permissively would "unduly delay or prejudice the adjudication of the rights of the original parties."

In this instance, allowing Kheel to permissively intervene would have these effects. Even assuming that a motion for **Rule 11** sanctions contains an issue of fact common to the underlying action, the parties here agreed to settle the suit and to "refrain from all conduct inconsistent with the parties' intent of resolving all disputes arising out of the bargaining relationships that existed at the News." In order to determine whether **Rule 11** sanctions are appropriate, the district court would have to delve into facts supporting allegations in the complaint. This would revive the disputed issues the parties agreed to put aside, and would continue an inquiry into an action that the parties voluntarily dismissed. Moreover, in responding to the **Rule 11** motion for sanctions, the plaintiffs likely would have to argue the validity of the allegations in the complaint. Because the settlement might be jeopardized by permitting intervention of right, this potential prejudice supports the conclusion to deny Kheel's intervention.

(2) Kheel's Original Attempt to Intervene with a Motion to Strike. Kheel's original motion to intervene was for the purpose of striking allegations from the plaintiff's complaint pertaining to him. **Federal Rule 12(f)** provides that upon a party's request (within certain time limits after the service of a pleading) a court may strike from pleadings any "insufficient defense or any redundant, immaterial, impertinent, or scandalous matter." Procedurally, Kheel would not be able to seek **Rule 12(f)** relief from the court unless he satisfied the **Rule 24** requirements for intervention and the court granted him party status with a right to fully participate as an intervening party (including the right to submit pleadings, papers, and motions).

On the merits, Kheel might have had a difficult time prevailing on his motion to strike the allegations about him in the complaint. Generally, federal courts disfavor and rarely grant motions to strike allegations from the opposing party's pleadings. Motions to strike are often viewed as a dilatory tactic, although since Kheel originally was not named as a party-defendant, this rationale is largely absent. As an outsider to the litigation, Kheel has little incentive to delay the course of the litigation.

Federal courts will not strike allegations from a pleading unless their presence will prejudice the adverse party. Generally, the question whether allegations are prejudicial turns on whether the pleadings will be made available to the jury (in some instances the pleadings themselves become part of the evidence and may be shown to the jury). This usage is limited by evidence rules, and irrelevant or prejudicial matters independently may be excluded under the evidence rules. Regarding scandalous allegations, the party would carry the burden of convincing the court that the allegations are obviously false and unrelated to the subject matter of the action.

Note: These problems are based on **New York News, Inc. v. Kheel,** 972 F.2d 482 (2d Cir. 1992).

■ PROBLEM VII

(1) Motion to Dismiss for Lack of Personal Jurisdiction: Defendant's Arguments in Support of Their Motion. The defendants, Pneumatic and McCurry,

Florida residents, will argue that the Ohio state court lacks personal jurisdiction over each for two reasons. First, the provisions of the Ohio long-arm statute do not reach their actions or contacts with the forum state. Second, the Ohio state court's exercise of personal jurisdiction over either would offend traditional concepts of fair play and substantial justice embodied in the Due Process Clause of the Fourteenth Amendment.

To validly assert jurisdiction over a non-resident defendant, a state's statutory long-arm provisions must apply to the defendant's conduct or affiliating contacts with the state. In addition, a state's assertion of long-arm jurisdiction must comport with federal constitutional due process principles. **World–Wide Volkswagen v. Woodson; International Shoe Co. v. Washington.**

In this case, the Florida defendants will argue that none of their actions come within any of the statutory grounds for asserting jurisdiction because they did not commit any criminal acts within the state, nor did they injure Conti in Ohio by any act or omission within the state. Furthermore, the corporation does not regularly solicit business or engage in a persistent course of conduct, or derive substantial revenue from goods used or consumed in the state. Lastly, the defendants could not reasonably have expected that Conti would be injured in Ohio by their actions in using a nationwide executive recruiting firm to search for a new vice-president for their engineering facility in Florida.

On constitutional grounds, the defendants will argue that Ohio cannot assert general jurisdiction over them. A proper exercise of general jurisdiction requires that a defendant's contacts with the forum state be of such a "continuous and systematic" nature that the state may exercise personal jurisdiction over the defendant even if the action is unrelated to the defendant's contacts with the state. **Helicopteros Nacionales v. Hall.**

Pneumatic, the corporate defendant, will argue that it is not licensed to do business in Ohio, does not maintain an office or employees in Ohio, and does not own property in Ohio. Pneumatic sells its products all over the United States, either through distributors for resale or directly to the end user. Although the distributors sell Pneumatic products worth about $900,000 annually in Ohio, the distributors are only occasionally visited by Pneumatic employees for consultation. The nature of these Ohio contacts do not amount to "continuous and systematic" business conduct to support an assertion of general jurisdiction over the corporation. Moreover, none of the facts alleged support an assertion of general jurisdiction over the individual defendant, McCurry.

The defendants also will argue that Ohio cannot assert specific jurisdiction over them. Some federal courts have recognized that a state may exercise specific jurisdiction over a non-resident defendant in a lawsuit arising out of or related to the defendant's contacts with the forum. Other federal courts have endorsed a "but for" test that examines whether a plaintiff's injuries would have occurred "but for" the defendant's actions. Standards for specific jurisdiction also frequently require that a defendant must purposefully avail himself of the privilege of acting in the forum state, **Burger King v. Rudzewicz,** or cause a consequence in the forum.

Pneumatic and McCurry will argue that their contacts with Ohio were random, fortuitous, and attenuated, and these contacts therefore cannot satisfy the tests for specific jurisdiction. They did not purposefully recruit an Ohio resident to fill the position of vice-president of engineering at their facility in Florida. Instead, they contacted a local executive recruiting firm headquartered in Florida to conduct and recruit a candidate.

Conti, the plaintiff, unilaterally initiated the events that resulted in his being considered for a position with Pneumatic. Conti ordered a directory of executive recruiting firms and then sent Management Recruiters his resume. Pneumatic and McCurry only learned of Conti's interest in the position through Conti's unilateral action. The defendants will argue that a forum resident's contact with an out-of-state defendant alone is insufficient to automatically establish jurisdiction over the defendant. **Hanson v. Denckla; Burger King.**

Plaintiff's Arguments in Opposition to the Motion to Dismiss on Personal Jurisdiction Grounds

Conti will respond that the defendants' tortious recruitment actions in Ohio and Florida caused him injury in Ohio; thus subsections (3), (4), and (6) of the Ohio long-arm statute reach these actions to permit assertion of personal jurisdiction. Beyond the reach of these statutory bases for assertion of jurisdiction, Conti additionally will argue that the Ohio court's assertion of personal jurisdiction comports with constitutional due process standards.

Regarding general jurisdiction, Conti will counter that even apart from the Ohio-related acts of the defendants in recruiting him for the vice-president's position, Pneumatic had constant, well-established and long-standing commercial ties with Ohio. Conti will argue that Pneumatic's nationwide sale of its products, including a distribution chain in Ohio, plus $900,000 in annual revenues derived from the state, are sufficient to support an assertion of general jurisdiction unrelated to the underlying cause of action.

Regarding specific jurisdiction, Conti will argue that the defendants' activities constituted a purposeful availment of the privilege of acting in Ohio to recruit him for an employment position, ultimately causing him injury there. Pneumatic knowingly authorized its agent, Management Recruiters, to look outside Florida for a candidate to fill the position. Thus, the defendants paid for and mailed airline tickets to Conti in Ohio, mailed other materials directly to him in Ohio, conducted extensive contract negotiations with him in Ohio through Management Recruiters, mailed the employment contract offer letter to Ohio—and that this collection of contacts is sufficient to establish personal jurisdiction over the defendants in Ohio. Conti also will argue that Management Recruiters had authority to act on behalf of Pneumatic and therefore Pneumatic is liable for the fraudulent representations made by Management Recruiters in Ohio to Conti.

(2) Defendant's Rule 12(b)(7) Motion to Dismiss for Failure to Join a Party Under Rule 19. The district could should deny the defendants McCurry and Pneumatic's motion, unless under applicable state law the court cannot grant full and fair relief to all the litigants in absence of Management Recruiters as a defendant in the lawsuit.

The theory behind the defendant's **Rule 12(b)(7)** motion is that Conti, as plaintiff, has failed to join a person necessary for a just adjudication as a defendant; namely, Management Recruiters. Management Recruiters has not been joined because, as a corporate citizen of Ohio, the company is nondiverse from the plaintiff Conti (also a citizen of Ohio for diversity purposes). Therefore, if Management Recruiters must be joined in the litigation, its presence would destroy diversity and the lawsuit would have to be dismissed. **Federal Rule 19(a).**

The question, then, is whether Management Recruiters is merely a necessary party to the dispute, or indispensable (such that the case would have to be dismissed if Management Recruiters were required to be joined). Whether a person is a necessary or indispensable party is determined with reference to applicable state law governing the relationship of the defendants, McCurry and Pneumatic, to Management Recruiters. It seems highly unlikely that the defendants hold any joint interest, right, or liability stemming from their relationship. However, the contractual relationship between Pneumatic and Management Recruiters might create an agency relationship including such liability. On balance, it seems that even if Management Recruiters might be construed as a "necessary party" to the litigation because of an agency relationship, the court probably can achieve complete justice among the parties in Management Recruiters' absence.

If, under applicable state law, Management Recruiters were deemed a party indispensable to a just resolution to the litigation, then the federal court would have to make a determination under **Rule 19(b)** whether, "in equity and good conscience" the litigation could proceed in Management Recruiters' absence, or whether justice required that the lawsuit be dismissed altogether. The court would make this determination based on its assessment of the four factors delineated in **Federal Rule 19(b).** However, since it seems highly unlikely that Management Recruiters is an indispensable party, **Rule 19(b)** would not apply.

(3) Supplemental Jurisdiction over Additional Parties and Claims Under 28 U.S.C. § 1367. All three variations of joinder of Management Recruiters involve a determination of the federal court's possibility of supplemental jurisdiction over Management Recruiters. These inquiries are governed by the federal supplemental jurisdiction statute, **28 U.S.C. § 1367,** which has codified the common law doctrines of ancillary, pendent claim, and pendent party jurisdiction.

(a) Joinder of Management Recruiters by McCurry and Pneumatic. The defendants already named as parties, McCurry and Pneumatic, could possibly join Management Recruiters by way of "impleader" under **Federal Rule 14(a).** This joinder would have to be predicated on a theory that Management Recruiters, as Pneumatic's agent, is or could be liable to the defendants if Conti prevails in the case-in-chief. The supplemental jurisdiction statute would permit such assertion of jurisdiction against Management Recruiters under **28 U.S.C. § 1367(a)** and **(b)** because the statute permits pendent claim and pendent party jurisdiction over parties and claims added under **Rule 14,** provided that those parties and claims form part of one "constitutional case or controversy." The facts here seem to support the conclusion that the defendant's potential claims against Management Recruiters form one case or controversy with the facts relating to Conti's claims against the defendant.

(b) Management Recruiter's Claims Against McCurry and Pneumatic. Assuming the existence of substantive grounds under their contractual relationship, once Management Recruiters is joined or impleaded into the litigation, Management Recruiters could assert any claims it had against the two original defendants. Basically, Management Recruiters stands in the position of a third-party plaintiff, filing its claims against the original co-defendants. **Rule 14(a)** permits such claims by impleaded third parties, and the supplemental jurisdiction statute would support this assertion of ancillary jurisdiction, **28 U.S.C. § 1367,** because Management Recruiters' claims would form part of one "constitutional case or controversy" under the statutory standard.

(c) Conti's Claims Against an Impleaded Management Recruiter. If the original defendants did successfully implead Management Recruiters under **Federal Rule 14,** Conti probably would be barred from amending its complaint to assert claims against Management Recruiters. This is because Conti could not have sued the nondiverse Management Recruiters initially. Therefore, this assertion of jurisdiction is barred both by the supplemental jurisdiction statute (**28 U.S.C. § 1367(b)** and pre-existing doctrinal law (**Owen Kroger**)).

Note: These problems are based on **Conti v. Pneumatic Products Corp.,** 977 F.2d 978 (6th Cir. 1992).

APPENDIX C

Glossary

A

Abuse of Discretion A standard of appellate review that permits a higher court to reverse a lower court judge's ruling for only the most egregious violation or misuse of authority.

Ad Damnum Clause The paragraph of a complaint, usually at the end of the complaint, that sets forth the pleader's request for damages. The *ad damnum* clause will set forth the nature of the relief requested (such as *compensatory, exemplary,* or *special damages,* see infra) and the amount of damages sought.

Advisory Opinions An advisory opinion is a request from litigants to a court requesting that the court issue a ruling on a legal question because the courts have not previously ruled on that issue. Hence, litigants seek advisory opinions to elicit a judicial interpretation of the law when no precedent already exists. Almost all courts refuse to issue advisory opinions because the request does not present a real case or controversy. The prohibition against issuing advisory opinions is one of the doctrines of non-justiciability. (*see* "justiciability" *infra*).

Additur The ability of a judge or an appellate court to increase the amount of damages that a jury awards a winning party in a lawsuit. Federal courts prohibit additur on the grounds that it violates the right to a trial by jury, by increasing (and therefore changing) the amount already awarded by a jury. Many states, however, permit *additur*.

Admissions A statement of agreement by a party to a litigation as to the truth of a factual allegation. The effect of an admission is to conclusively establish the matter for trial, unless the court permits an amendment or withdrawal of the admission. Facts or allegations admitted by a party do not need to be proved by production of factual information at trial. Admissions reduce the scope of trial and therefore are a means of judicial economy. Admissions are chiefly sought during discovery (*see infra*), and are governed by **Federal Rule 36** (Request for Admissions) (*see infra*).

Affirmative Defenses Affirmative defenses are legal arguments that a defendant may raise in opposition to a plaintiff's claims, either to avoid or dismiss those claims. **Federal Rule 8(c)** lists affirmative defenses including accord and satisfaction; arbitration and ward; assumption of risk; contributory negligence; duress; estoppel; failure of consideration; fraud; illegality; injury by fellow servant; laches; license; payment; release; *res judicata;* statute of frauds; statute of limitations; and waiver. This list is not exhaustive of affirmative defenses in either federal or state practice. State statutory and common law may create additional affirmative defenses.

Ancillary Jurisdiction Jurisdiction over a claim added to a lawsuit that lacks an independent subject matter base. In federal law, ancillary jurisdiction traditionally extended to additional claims that had some "logical nexus" to the claims asserted in the original case between the plaintiff and the defendant. Federal law now provides for ancillary jurisdiction over cross-claims, counterclaims, and third-party claims through the federal supplemental jurisdiction statute, **28 U.S.C. § 1367,** although the statute does not use the term "ancillary" jurisdiction. The claims sought to be added must form "one constitutional case or controversy"

Amendments A method of changing or revising claims or allegations stated in a pleading. Allegations in complaints,

answers, and replies may be amended under **Federal Rule 15,** subject to limitations set forth in that rule and interpretative law. Amendments usually seek to change misnomers or mistakes, but the amendment rule may not be used to substitute new parties. In general, amendments to change parties are severely limited.

Amicus Curiae Literally, a "friend of the court." Someone who is not a party to the lawsuit, but whom the court permits to file a brief and make an argument to further enlighten the court concerning how or why the court should rule. *Amici* present their arguments in an *amicus curiae* brief, and must obtain the leave of court to do so. Often courts will permit amicus status to persons when it denies permissive intervention (*see infra*).

Answer One of the three forms of pleadings permitted under **Federal Rule 7,** in addition to the complaint and reply. The answer sets forth the defendant's response to the plaintiff's claims, and may also set forth affirmative defenses and counterclaims.

Appellate Jurisdiction The jurisdiction of a higher court to review orders, decisions, and judgments of a lower court. Most appellate courts have appellate jurisdiction limited to review orders that constitute final judgments (*see* "final judgments," *infra*). Appellate courts may have jurisdiction to review certain intermediate judicial orders (also known as "interlocutory orders," *see infra*). Appellate courts operate under different standards of review; typically, abuse of discretion (*see supra*); harmless error (*see infra*); and clearly erroneous (*see infra*).

Arbitration A consensual form of alternative dispute resolution by a nonjudicial body of arbitrators (usually three), chosen by the parties, to hear evidence and render an arbitral decision. Arbitration may be either binding or non-binding on the parties. An arbitration is a nonjudicial proceeding and is not subject to the strict rules of evidence. Arbitration decisions have no binding precedential value, but may be used as persuasive authority in a subsequent arbitration.

Attorney–Client Privilege One of the common law privilege doctrines (similar to that of physician-patient; clergy-penitent; etc.), that protects communications from a client given to an attorney during a professional representation. Attorney-client privilege attaches when the attorney agrees to represent the client and extends beyond the end of the representation. An attorney is duty-bound not to disclose any information the client provides the lawyer, except for information relating to ongoing or future crimes, fraud, or torts. The attorney may not disclose, however, any information about past crimes, fraud, or torts (or any other retrospective information). All states recognize the attorney-client privilege, and **Federal Rule 26** also protects attorney-client privileged information from disclosure during discovery or trial.

Attorney Work Product Immunity Attorney work product immunity is a judicially-created protection for the work produced by an attorney and the attorney's associates in anticipation of litiga-tion. The immunity protects from disclosure ordinary work product, such as witness statements, or the attorney's opinion work product, such as the attorney's opinions, mental impressions/legal strategies, etc. Most states recognize some form of attorney work product protection and the Federal Rules protect attorney work product in **Federal Rule 26(b)(3)** (trial preparation materials). *See also* **Hickman v. Taylor.**

Averment At common law, a positive statement contained in a declaration (complaint) with an offer of proof. In modern practice, averments typically refer to allegations in a complaint.

Avoidance At common law, an avoidance is an allegation of statement of new matter, in opposition to a former pleading/which, admitting the facts alleged in such former pleading, shows cause why they should not have their ordinary effect.

B

Bar In preclusion doctrine, the rule by which a losing litigant in a first action is prohibited from relitigating the claim again in a second action. The judgment in the first action *bars* relitigation of the same claim in the second action. Bar is a rule of claim preclusion, or *res judicata.*

Bench Trial A trial conducted by the judge and without a jury. Actions at equity typically are tried by a judge and not a jury. Certain federal statutory actions are tried solely to a judge. Also, if a litigant fails to make a "jury demand," (*see infra*), the case will be conducted as a bench trial.

Beyond a Reasonable Doubt The burden of proof in a criminal prosecution; in contrast to the civil standards of "clear and convincing evidence" or "preponderance of the evidence" (*see infra*).

Burden of Persuasion Generally, the plaintiff or proponent carries the ultimate burden of convincing the factfinder (either a jury or judge) that the plaintiff is entitled to a favorable verdict on its claims, based on the evidence. The burden of persuasion also may refer to the obligation of a movant, on a particular motion, to convince the judge that the movant is entitled to a grant of that motion. Thus, for example, a movant for summary judgment also carries the ultimate burden of persuasion on the motion, which may be tied to which party carries the burden of persuasion on the issue at trial (*see* "summary judgment," *infra*).

Burden of Production The obligation of a party to produce or come forward with some factual support for allegations, claims, or arguments at trial or made in a motion. The burden of production may "shift" from one litigant to another. Thus, once a plaintiff satisfies its burden of production on its claims, the burden of production shifts to the opposing party to produce evidence avoiding or dismissing the plaintiff's evidence. The burden of production applies at trial and in motion practice.

Burden of Proof The burden of proof rests with the proponent of a claim or defense. In some instances, statutory law may determine which parties carry what burdens of proof on a claim. In most civil trials the burden of proof typically rests with the plaintiff, who must satisfy this burden in order to avoid the judge dismissing the case for failure to supply sufficient evidence in support of the claims. Defendants carry the burden of proof on any counterclaims asserted in the answer, as well as for affirmative defenses.

C

Capacity Refers to the legal competence of a party to sue on the party's own behalf, or on behalf of someone else (in a representative capacity). State law usually determines capacity and federal capacity is determined by the law of the individual's domicile (**Federal Rule 17(b)**). Infants, minors, and incompetents usually lack capacity to sue on their own behalf, and may be represented by a "guardian ad litem" (*see infra*). **Federal Rule 17(b)** also states capacity rules for artificial entities, such as corporations, partnerships, and unincorporated associations.

Certiorari Jurisdiction Discretionary appellate jurisdiction of the United States Supreme Court. Technically, the *writ of certiorari* is a request from a higher court to a lower court for the records in a case. In Supreme Court practice, four Justices must vote to grant the writ of certiorari in order to hear an appeal. (*see* "Rule of Four," *infra*).

Chancery In England, the Lord Chancellor's Court, a division of the High Court of Justice. The Chancery was responsible for the development of equity practice and procedure in England. In the United States, chancery courts are courts of equity.

Choice-of-Forum Clauses Contractual provisions designating, in advance of litigation, a particular court or venue for adjudication of a dispute if a dispute arises under the contract. Forum selection clauses are valid and upheld in almost all states, and are presumptively valid as a matter of federal law. A few states, however, do not recognize contractual forum selection clauses.

Choice-of-Law Clauses Contractual provisions designating, in advance of litigation, the applicable body of law, if a dispute arises under the contract. Choice-of-law clauses are valid and upheld in almost all states, although a few states do not recognize the validity of choice-of-law clauses.

Claim Preclusion A form of preclusion doctrine, also known as *res judicata,* (*see infra*), that prevents relitigation of claims decided on the merits and fully and fairly litigated in a first trial. The doctrine applies to all claims actually litigated and that could have or should have been litigated. All such claims are said to be *merged* (*see infra*) into the judgment, and therefore *barred* from relitigation (*see supra*).

Class Action A form of aggregate joinder of parties and claims, constituting representational litigation. The chief characteristic of the class action is that most class claimants are *absent* or *unnamed*, and their interests in the litigation are represented by their *class representatives* and *class counsel.* Most (but not all) states provide for class action litigation, and **Federal Rule 23** is the federal class action rule. Class actions may be constituted as *mandatory classes,*

opt-out classes, or *settlement classes.* Because class actions are representational litigation and absent class members will be bound by the class judgment, class action procedure requires numerous due process protections for these absent class members.

Class Certification The procedure by which a judge makes the determination whether a litigation meets the requirements to go forward as a class action. The judge will certify the class as soon as practicable after commencement of the proceedings. **Federal Rule 23(c).** Under federal procedure (and in many states), threshold requirements for class certification include numerosity, commonality, typicality, and adequacy of the class representatives and class counsel. **Federal Rule 23(a).** In addition, the judge will determine whether the class may be maintained either as a *mandatory class* or as an *opt-out class* (*see infra*).

Clear and Convincing Evidence A standard of proof at civil trial, requiring something more than a mere "preponderance" of the evidence (*see infra*), but less than evidence "beyond a reasonable doubt" (*see supra*).

Compensatory Damages Also called *actual damages;* the legal conversion of harm into monetary or pecuniary relief. Compensatory or "actual" damages are to be distinguished from other types of damages that are not compensatory in nature, such as *exemplary* or *punitive* damages (*see infra*).

Compulsory Counterclaim A claim that an adverse party has against the original claimant, arising out of the same transaction or occurrence that is the subject matter of the original party's claim, which must be asserted in answer to the claim or it will be forfeited through operation of waiver, estoppel, or *res judicata*. **Federal Rule 13(a)** governs federal compulsory counterclaims and many states have compulsory counterclaim rules. The compulsory counterclaim rule is in the interests of judicial efficiency and economy.

Compulsory Joinder Parties who must be joined in order for the court to achieve a just adjudication. Parties who are deemed "indispensable" to the litigation because they hold a joint right or interest, must be joined or the court must dismiss the case. **Federal Rule 19** governs parties who must be joined for a just adjudication, and many states have compulsory joinder rules.

Confession and Avoidance At common law, a pre-emptory plea (*see infra*) whereby the defendant admits to the plaintiff's allegations (the "confession"), but asserts some other grounds for "avoiding" culpability, such as the defendant's minority. The confession and avoidance has been abolished under the Federal Rules of Civil Procedure, but modern analogs to this plea are found in the defendant's ability to assert affirmative defenses under **Federal Rule 8(c)** (*see supra*).

Consolidation A procedural means of aggregating separate lawsuits into one forum or court for a joint trial. **Federal Rule 42(a)** governs consolidation of cases in federal court and requires that all the cases to be consolidated must be pend-

ing in the judicial district prior to consolidation. Although the consolidated cases are tried jointly, they retain separate identities, separate counsel, and separate relief.

Code Pleading The method of pleading claims or causes of action under state rules, typically requiring the pleader to set forth both the legal grounds for relief and the detailed factual allegations in support of those claims. The Federal Rules of Civil Procedure do not require code pleading, but simply rather "notice pleading." (*see infra*).

Collateral Attack A means of seeking another court's review of a prior court's determination of an issue or a claim. This is in contrast to a direct attack (*see infra*), by which a losing party seeks appellate review of a lower court determination. In intersystem state practice, collateral attacks are limited by the constitutional requirements of the Full Faith and Credit Clause, which requires that sister states recognize the judgments of sister courts.

Collateral Estoppel In preclusion doctrine, refers to issue preclusion or the prohibition against relitigating the same issues previously determined in a prior litigation. The rules relating to assertion of collateral estoppel are matters of state and federal common law. Defendants may defensively assert collateral estoppel to prevent a plaintiff from relitigating an issue that defendants previously litigated and won. Plaintiffs, with some constitutional limitations, may offensively assert collateral estoppel to prevent defendants from relitigating an issue on which prior plaintiffs have prevailed. The principles relating to collateral estoppel (and its limitations) are set forth in the Supreme Court case, **Parklane Hosiery Co. v. Shore.**

Collateral Order Doctrine In federal practice, a doctrine of *interlocutory appeal* (*see infra*) that is an exception to the *final judgment rule* (*see infra*). In order for an appellate court to have jurisdiction over a lower court order under this doctrine, the order must be "collateral" to the main issues in the case—that is, separate from the merits of those issues. The order also must involve an important issue that cannot await a final judgment for resolution, because the issue effectively will be forfeited or unresolvable at that time.

Collusive Joinder The attempt to impermissibly add or join parties to a litigation, or to assign a contract right, in order to create federal diversity jurisdiction when it otherwise would not legitimately exist. Federal statute prohibits such attempts to collusively create federal subject matter jurisdiction. **28 U.S.C. § 1359.** The federal statute does not prohibit collusive joinder to defeat diversity jurisdiction, however, although some federal courts extend the doctrine to include such attempts.

Common Law Law that is derived from custom or precedent, rather than from statutes.

Complaint The pleading that a plaintiff uses to set forth claims in a lawsuit. Usually, filing a complaint with the court plus service of process on the defendant, initiates a lawsuit. The complaint is one of the three recognized pleadings under **Federal Rule 7(a)** (in addition to the answer (*see supra*) and the reply (*see infra*)).

Complete Diversity Rule A rule governing federal diversity subject matter jurisdiction (*see infra*), that requires that all the parties to the lawsuit on both sides be from different states or countries than every other party. The rule derives from the Supreme Court case **Strawbridge v. Curtiss.** The presence of a nondiverse party destroys the court's subject matter jurisdiction. A nondiverse party may be dropped from the lawsuit to confer valid jurisdiction, except if the party is necessary for a just adjudication (*see infra*). There are certain statutory exceptions to the complete diversity rule, such as interpleader actions. In addition, the class action rule (*see supra*) is an exception to the complete diversity requirement because only the named class representatives need be diverse from the defendants.

Conciliation A form of consensual informal alternative dispute resolution that employs a "conciliator" or facilitator to meet with the disputing parties and arrange a resolution of their dispute. Conciliation is a private, nonjudicial means of dispute resolution, outside the auspices of the court system.

Concurrent Jurisdiction The simultaneous authority of different courts over the subject matter of a dispute, to render a binding decision in the litigation. Federal and state courts possess such simultaneous, overlapping jurisdiction over almost all subject matters. Parallel federal and state courts also may exercise concurrent jurisdiction. The ability of one court to restrain another court's exercise of jurisdiction is severely limited by the federal Supremacy Clause and the federal **Anti–Injunction Act, 28 U.S.C. § 2283.**

Counterclaim A claim that an adversary may assert against the opposing party. Counterclaims may be mandatory if they arise out of the same transactions or events that gave rise to subject matter of the main action, under **Federal Rule 13(a)** (*see* "compulsory counterclaims," *supra*). Counterclaims also may be permissive if they do not arise out of the same transaction or occurrence that gave rise to the subject matter of the opposing party's claim, under **Federal Rule 13(b)** (*see* "permissive counterclaims," *infra*).

Cross–Claim A claim asserted against a co-party to a lawsuit that arises out of the transaction or occurrence that is the subject matter either of the original action or a counterclaim relating to any property that is the subject matter of the original action. **Federal Rule 13(g)** provides for cross-claims.

D

Damages A form of legal relief, usually monetary recovery, as compensation for a loss or injury sought for liability under various claims or causes of action. Substantive law provides for the types of available damages including, for example, compensatory damages, exemplary damages, special damages, punitive damages, etc.

Declaration At common law, the form of pleading analogous to the modern complaint, setting forth the pleader's claims or causes of action.

Default A type of judgment that a court may award for the failure of the defendant to appear in a lawsuit and present a legal defense. Default judgments are judgments on the merits and are binding, and enforceable. Other courts must give default judgments preclusive effect, unless the default was based on a lack of the rendering court's valid jurisdiction. **Federal Rule 55** governs default judgments in federal court.

Defensive Collateral Estoppel. A form of issue preclusion, asserted by a defendant in a second lawsuit to prevent the plaintiff in the second suit from relitigating an issue previously determined in the defendant's favor in a prior adjudication between the parties. Courts regularly uphold assertions of defensive collateral estoppel, which no longer requires "mutuality" of estoppel in order to be given effect.

Demurrer A form of common law pleading seeking to dismiss the plaintiff's claims for lack of legal sufficiency. The Federal Rules of Civil Procedure have abolished the technical common law demurrer, but the modern analog is contained in **Federal Rule 12(b)(6),** the motion to dismiss for failure to state a claim upon which relief can be granted. Some states that have retained either common law or code pleading still use the demurrer.

Denials One form of response by a defendant to the claims and allegations in the plaintiff's complaint, in which the defendant disputes the plaintiff's claims. Denials are governed by **Federal Rule 8(b)** and **(d).** There are various forms of denials, including the evasive denial (*see infra*); the general denial (*see infra*), and the specific denial (*see infra*).

Deponent The person who is subject to an oral examination, on the record, prior to trial for the purpose of making a record of that person's testimony. Deponents may be parties to the lawsuit, non-party witnesses, or expert witnesses. Non-party deponents typically are summoned to a deposition by use of a *subpoena* (*see* **Federal Rule 45**). Rules governing the examination of deponents are found in **Federal Rules 30–32.**

Deposition One of the five formal discovery methods which consists of conducting an oral examination of a party, non-party, or expert witness involved in a lawsuit. Depositions are conducted on the record, under oath, and may be used subsequently at trial for impeachment and other purposes. Depositions are subject to time, place, and manner restrictions. Rules governing the conduct of depositions are found in **Federal Rules 30–32.**

Dilatory Plea At common law, a responsive pleading that challenged the court's right to hear the case. These pleas included challenges to the court's jurisdiction, variances between the declaration (*see supra*) and the writ (*see infra*); and pleas that the case be suspended for some other technical fault, such as the minority of one of the parties. Dilatory pleas did not challenge the merits of the plaintiff's claims. The modern Federal Rules of Civil Procedure have abolished the various forms of common law pleas, including the dilatory plea. **Federal Rule 7(c).** Some of the grounds for these challenges are now found in **Federal Rule 12,** and some states that use common law pleading have retained the dilatory plea.

Direct Attack A method of challenging a judge's order or jury verdict through appeal to a higher court, within the same court system, following a final judgment in a lawsuit. Direct attack is distinguished from a "collateral attack" (*see supra*), whereby a litigant seeks to challenge a judicial order or jury verdict in some other jurisdiction, rather than a higher court within the same court system.

Directed Verdict A procedural means by which a judge takes the case away from the jury prior to jury deliberation. A judge may "direct a verdict" if the party who carries the burden of proof on an issue fails to adduce sufficient credible evidence in support of the claim. Many states have directed verdict rules and the directed verdict has been renamed, in federal practice, as a "judgment as a matter of law." **Federal Rule 50.** Litigants typically move for directed verdict during the course of trial, either at the close of the plaintiff's presentation of its case-in-chief, or again after the presentation of all the evidence. Directed verdicts do not violate a litigant's Seventh Amendment right to a trial by jury.

Discovery The means of obtaining factual information prior to trial. Prior to the Federal Rules, discovery was limited chiefly to private investigation. The modern Federal Rules provide for five formal discovery devices: depositions; interrogatories; production of documents and inspection of premises; request for admissions; and requests for physical and mental examinations. **Federal Rules 30–36.** 1993 amendments to the Federal Rules also require certain mandatory disclosures at the outset of the litigation. **Federal Rule 26(a).** The scope of discovery is very broad and generally limited only by privileges, immunities, or protective orders. **Federal Rule 26(c)** (*see* attorney-client privilege and attorney work product, *supra*; protective orders, *infra*).

Dismissal With Prejudice The dismissal of an action that effectively operates as a decision on the merits, resulting in a loss of rights that may be given *preclusive* or *res judicata* (*see infra*) effect if the litigant seeks to reinstitute legal proceedings.

Dismissal Without Prejudice A voluntary withdrawal or temporary abandonment of a lawsuit, reserving the right to subsequently refile and pursue the action. *See **voluntary dismissal**, (infra).*

Diversity Jurisdiction One of the two bases for federal court subject matter jurisdiction, provided for in **Article III** of the Constitution and **28 U.S.C. § 1332.** Diversity jurisdiction requires that the plaintiffs and defendants be from different states or countries, and that the claims be worth or exceed $75,000. In lawsuits involving multiple parties, all the litigants on both sides of the suit must satisfy the "complete diversity rule" (*see supra*). **Strawbridge v. Curtiss.**

Domicile A person's fixed place of abode, and where the person has the intention to remain. A person's domicile is used to determine their citizenship for diversity jurisdictional purposes. **Mas v. Perry.** The concept of domicile is to be distinguished from that of "residence," which denotes a more temporary place of living. For legal purposes, a person may have many residences, but only one domicile.

E

Early Neutral Evaluation A method of alternative dispute resolution whereby parties to a dispute meet with a judge or court surrogate (such as a magistrate) to evaluate the strengths and weaknesses of a case, and to make recommendations concerning settlement or the future conduct of the litigation. Early neutral evaluation is intended to assist the expeditious and inexpensive resolution of disputes.

Erie **Doctrine** The method of determining applicable law in federal diversity lawsuits, named for the Supreme Court case (**Erie Railroad v. Tompkins**) in which the doctrine was articulated. According to the doctrine, federal courts must apply state substantive and federal procedural rules.

Equity The application of general principles of justice and fairness to relieve, correct, or supplement remedies at law. The Chancery Court in England (*see supra*) developed a separate system of equitable principles and procedure, alongside the common law system. The Federal Rules of Civil Procedure merged the separate systems of law and equity into one form of action, the civil action. **Federal Rule 2.** A few states still retain the separate legal and equity systems, as well as separate equity courts.

Evasive Denial A defendant's response to allegations in a complaint whereby the defendant "neither admits not denies" the plaintiff's allegations. **Federal Rule 8(b)** does not prohibit evasive denials, but some states by statute specifically prohibit the use of evasive denials.

Ex Parte; Ex Parte **Hearing** At the insistence of one party only, without the presence of the other party, and without advance notice to the other party An *ex parte hearing* is one conducted by a judge with only one party to the dispute, and is to be contrasted with an adversarial (between parties) proceeding.

Exclusive Jurisdiction Power vested by the Constitution or statute over certain subject matter, that may be adjudicated solely by a particular court. For example, the federal district courts have exclusive jurisdiction—exclusive of state courts—of admiralty and maritime cases. **28 U.S.C. § 1333.** Exclusive jurisdiction is in contrast to concurrent jurisdiction (*see supra*).

Exemplary Damages Also called *punitive damages* (*see infra*). Damages to punish a wrongdoer as an example to others not to do likewise. The availability of punitive damages differs from state to state; some states prohibit exemplary damages, and other states limit or cap the amount of exemplary damages that a litigant may recover from the defendant. An award of exemplary damages must comport with the requirements of the Due Process Clause. **BMW v. Gore.**

Federal Common Law Law that federal courts may determine applies to certain limited cases involving federal interests, such as water-right disputes between states, or commercial paper. Federal courts also may create federal common law if Congress, through a federal statute, authorizes the courts to create and apply such federal common law. An example is the creation of federal labor law under the federal labor relations statutes. The *Erie* decision (*see supra*) declared, however, that there is no "general federal common law," and that federal courts must apply state substantive law in most diversity cases.

Federal Question Jurisdiction One of the two bases for federal subject matter jurisdiction. (*see* also "diversity jurisdiction," supra). **Article III** of the Constitution and **28 U.S.C. § 1331** (the general federal question statute) provide that federal courts have subject matter jurisdiction over cases or controversies that arise under the Constitution, laws, or treaties of the United States. Many federal statutes also confer original federal question jurisdiction on United States federal district courts. With regard to federal statutes, this is sometimes referred to as the federal courts' "arising under" jurisdiction.

F

Field Code The original reform of common law pleading in the United States in 1846, after David Dudley Field, an appointed commissioner on a New York state panel to reform the system of pleading. The Field Code radically modified and simplified pleading, and the Field Code became a reform model for other states. The Field Code was a nineteenth-century precursor of the modern Federal Rules of Civil Procedure.

Final Judgment Rule A rule requiring that a judicial decree or order must be final in order for an appellate court to review that order, decree, or judgment. Federal district courts have appellate jurisdiction only from final orders or judgments, not from interlocutory orders (*see infra*). **Federal Rule 54(a); 28 U.S.C. § 1291.** There are very limited exceptions to the final judgment rule, set forth in **28 U.S.C. § 1292** (immediate appeal of orders involving injunctions, receiverships, and admiralty cases, as well as judicially certified orders). The so-called collateral order doctrine is a judicially-created exception to the final judgment rule (*see supra*).

Fluid Recovery A type of possible court-ordered relief, usually in a class action settlement, by which parties agree to a non-compensatory form of relief such as the creation of a research fund to avoid future injurious conduct, or medical monitoring of potentially-injured claimants.

Forms of Action At English common law, the basis for each legally cognizable claim. Each form of action had a corresponding "writ." (*see infra*). The plaintiff's lawyer had to swear out the appropriate writ for each form of action, which governed commencing the case, the substantive requirements of

the case, the manner of trial, and the remedy or sanction for a judgment. The modern Federal Rules of Civil Procedure abolished all common law forms of action. **Federal Rule 2.**

Forum Non Conveniens The common law doctrine permitting a case to be dismissed because the plaintiff's choice of forum is an inconvenient or inappropriate venue in which to try the lawsuit. In some jurisdictions, an alternative forum must exist before the court will dismiss the litigation on *forum non conveniens* grounds. Some states do not recognize or permit the doctrine of *forum non conveniens*. A federal court may either dismiss a case under federal common law principles of *forum non conveniens* (articulated in **Gulf Oil Company v. Gilbert**), or the court may transfer the case to another federal district court where the litigation could have been brought. **28 U.S.C. § 1404(a).**

Full Faith and Credit The constitutional and statutory requirement that federal and state courts give the same recognition and effect to the acts, records, and judicial proceedings of sister states as would the state itself. *See* **Article IV § 1** of the **Constitution; 28 U.S.C. § 1738.**

G

General Denial A defendant's response to the plaintiff's complaint which broadly denies every single allegation in the complaint, including such introductory matters as the facts and grounds for the court's jurisdiction. A general denial is permitted under the Federal Rules, but some court systems prohibit use of the general denial.

Guardian Ad Litem A person appointed by the court to represent the interests of another; most typically a person lacking legal capacity, such as an infant, minor, or incompetent (*see* "capacity," *supra*).

H

Harmless Error A standard of appellate review that directs appellate courts not to grant a new trial or modify a jury verdict for errors or defects occurring at trial, including the exclusion of evidence, which do not affect the substantial rights of the parties or were not inconsistent with substantial justice. **Federal Rule 61.**

Heightened Pleading A judicially-created doctrine in some federal courts which requires the plaintiff to set forth its claims, in certain types of cases, with a greater degree of particularity than is generally required under the notice-pleading system (*see infra*). The Supreme Court has rejected any "heightened pleading" requirement for civil rights complaints against munici-palities. **Leatherman v. Tarrant County.** Some federal district courts require pleading with greater specificity in securities actions, and other types of civil rights litigation.

I

Immunity In general, an exemption from a legal obligation. States and their political subdivisions may claim *sovereign immunity* from suit based on the **Eleventh Amendment** to the Constitution and various common law doctrines of sovereign immunity. In federal practice, such immunity may be raised as an affirmative defense, by way of avoidance. Also, *attorney work product immunity* is a method of avoiding disclosure of information during discovery, as covered by that doctrine (*see* "attorney work product immunity," *supra*).

Impleader A method of joining a person to a lawsuit who is not already named as a party, and who is or may be liable to one or more of the original parties to the action. This joining of an outsider to the litigation is called "impleader," and the person who is joined is "impleaded" into the action. This practice also is called third-party practice (*see infra*). The person who seeks to join or implead a non-party is called the third-party plaintiff, and the person who is impleaded into the action is called the third-party defendant. Federal impleader is governed by **Federal Rule 14.**

In Camera **Proceeding** Literally, in chambers. A hearing held by a judge in chambers, rather than in open court before a jury. In discovery proceedings, frequently used to permit the judge to inspect or review documents privately without fear of disclosure of information to the opposing side.

In Personam **Jurisdiction** To make someone personally liable; the power or authority of the government to issue a valid and binding judgment over parties to a litigation, based on their contacts or affiliating circumstances with the jurisdiction. Personal jurisdiction over an *in personam* action may be conferred by consent, presence, or contacts with the jurisdiction. State assertions of personal jurisdiction over non-resident defendants must comport with the due process requirements of the **Fourteenth Amendment (International Shoe Company v. Washington).** Federal courts also must have valid *in personam* jurisdiction over federal defendants.

In Rem **Jurisdiction** Literally, jurisdiction over a thing, usually referring to property Refers to the power or authority of a state to issue a valid, binding judgment over a defendant based on the presence of property in the jurisdiction, or property at issue in the litigation. Pure *in rem* jurisdiction, as a basis for a court's jurisdiction, is rare, although it still exists. Federal admiralty and maritime jurisdiction is a remaining example of pure *in rem* jurisdiction, in which the government seizes the vessel as the basis for federal jurisdiction.

Indispensable Party At common law, a party possessing some joint legal right or interest whose presence is absolutely required in the lawsuit in order for the court to render complete and substantial justice to all the parties. Substantive law determines whether a person was "indispensable" to a litigation. If a party is deemed indispensable to the lawsuit and cannot not be joined for any reason (such as a lack of jurisdiction), then the court is required to dismiss the case. Under federal practice, the concept of the indispensable party is now embodied in **Federal Rule 19(a),** although a federal court may allow a litigation to go forward without the party if it so determines that the court may reach a fair judgment in "equity and good con-

science" without the party's presence. **Federal Rule 19(b).**

Inferences The act of forming a conclusion from premises or information presented to the fact-finder, either on a motion to a judge, or to the jury at trial. Fact-finders are permitted to draw *reasonable inferences* from the evidence, but such inferences may not tax credibility or span cavernous gaps in the evidence. **Galloway v. United States.**

Injunction An equitable remedy restraining a person from an act, compelling redress to an injured party, or restraining or compelling certain future conduct. As an equitable remedy, a party seeking an injunction must not have adequate remedy at law and must show that in absence of the injunction the person will suffer irreparable harm. There are various forms of injunctions such as temporary restraining orders, preliminary injunctions, and permanent injunctions. **Federal Rule 65.**

Interlocutory Appeal An intermediate appeal of a court order, prior to final judgment. In general, interlocutory appeals are prohibited by the final judgment rule (*see supra*). The law discourages interlocutory appeals as inspiring piecemeal litigation, and fostering additional expense, delay, and harassment. However, appellate courts will hear interlocutory appeals under certain limited exceptions to the final judgment rule, such as orders involving injunctions, receiverships, and actions in admiralty. Federal courts also will hear appeals from interlocutory orders that come within the *collateral order* exception to the final judgment rule (*see supra*).

Interlocutory Order A judicial order that a judge issues during the course of proceedings and prior to a final judgment in a case. Judges routinely issue numerous interlocutory orders during pretrial proceedings, including rulings on **Rule 12** motions, discovery motions, motions for summary judgment, requests for protective orders, and so on.

Interpleader An equitable joinder device wherein a person faced with the possibility of conflicting claims of liability or ownership asserted by two or more potential plaintiffs can secure a binding judgment against all those plaintiffs. Interpleader is usually sought by insurance companies to resolve all competing claims against a policy. The fund for which there are competing claims is called the "stake," and the party seeking interpleader is said to be the "stakeholder." In federal practice, interpleader is governed both by **Federal Rule 22** ("rule interpleader"), and statute, **28 U.S.C. § 1335** et seq. ("statutory interpleader"). The two possible forms of interpleader differ in their jurisdiction and service requirements.

Interrogatories One of the five methods of formal discovery to obtain information prior to trial. Interrogatories consist of a set of questions directed to parties to the lawsuit, which are supposed to be answered by the party but typically are answered by the party's lawyer and then signed by the party. In federal practice, the form and mode of interrogatories is governed by **Federal Rule 33;** federal and local rules limit the number of interrogatories that may be served on the opposing party.

Intersystem Preclusion The doctrine concerning the binding effect that federal courts are required to give to state court judgments (and vice versa), governed by the **Full Faith and Credit Clause** to the Constitution (**Article IV § 1**) (*see supra*), as well as by statute, **28 U.S.C. § 1738.** These provisions also govern the binding effect of judgments in sister state courts (intersystem preclusion doctrine).

Intervention The ability of a non-party to a lawsuit to join the litigation when that non-party has an interest in the litigation that is not adequately represented by the existing parties, which may be impaired or impeded if not represented. In federal practice, there are two types of intervention: intervention as of right under **Federal Rule 24(a)** (*see infra*), and permissive intervention under **Federal Rule 24(b)** (*see infra*). A person who is permitted to join the lawsuit under these circumstances is called an "intervenor," and acquires party status, although the court may limit the intervenor's participation in the litigation.

Intervention as of Right One of the two forms of intervention (*see supra*) permitted under the Federal Rules. A non-party to a lawsuit can permissively intervene when a federal statute confers a conditional right to intervene, or when the applicant's claim or defense and the main action have a question of law or fact in common. Permissive intervention is discretionary with the court. **Federal Rule 24(b).**

Involuntary Dismissal A courts dismissal of a plaintiff's action for failure to prosecute or go forward with an action. In federal practice, involuntary dismissal for failure to prosecute the action is governed by **Federal Rule 41(b).** Litigants also may suffer an involuntary dismissal for utter failure to cooperate with discovery orders or for failure of a lawyer to attend a pretrial conference. Involuntary dismissals may be with or without prejudice to subsequently reinstitute the action. *See also default* under **Federal Rule 55** (*supra*).

Issue Preclusion Also known as collateral estoppel. A form of *res judicata* that prohibits a litigant from relitigating an issue that previously has been fully and fairly litigated in a prior proceeding. There are two types of issue preclusion or collateral estoppel: *defensive collateral estoppel,* (*see supra*), and *offensive collateral estoppel,* (*see infra*). Subject to due process constraints, federal courts permit both offensive and defensive assertions of collateral estoppel (issue preclusion). Some state courts do not recognize one or both of these doctrines, but rather adhere to the "mutuality" rule (*see infra*).

J

Judgment as a Matter of Law A judgment the court may order, without allowing the case to go to jury deliberation, when there is no genuine issue of material fact in dispute between the parties, or when the party who carries the burden of proof at trial has failed (at trial) to adduce sufficient evidence in support of its claims. A moving party, therefore, may be entitled to a judgment as a matter of law on a summary judgment motion under **Federal Rule**

56 (*see infra*), or after presentation of evidence at trial, under **Federal Rule 50.** Trial judgments as a matter of law used to be denominated as "directed verdicts" (*see supra*), and judgments notwithstanding the verdict (*see infra*).

Judgment Notwithstanding the Verdict A judgment by the court, upon a motion by the losing party at trial after a jury verdict, vacating the jury verdict in favor of the losing party based on the ground that no reasonable jury could have decided as the jury did. Commonly called the **JNOV,** from the Latin phrase judgment *non obstante veredicto*. In effect, a judgment notwithstanding the verdict "takes away" the jury's verdict in favor of the judge's contrary assessment of the evidence In federal practice, JNOVs are now called "judgments as a matter of law." **Federal Rule 50(b)** (*see supra*).

Judicial Case Management Active supervision by a judge over the conduct of pretrial and trial proceedings, including case settlement. **Federal Rule 16** (Pretrial Conferences; Scheduling; Management) provides the chief rule basis for active judicial case management. Proponents favor it as enhancing the inexpensive, speedy, and just resolution of disputes. Judicial case management is criticized as impairing the status of the judge as neutral arbiter of disputes.

Jury Demand A request by a party to a dispute for a trial by jury (rather than by the judge—a so-called bench trial, *see supra*). Either the plaintiff may make a jury demand for its claims, or the defendant may make a jury demand for its counterclaims. The right to a trial by jury is not absolute and may be waived for failure to make a jury demand in a timely manner. **Federal Rule 38(b)** governs the timing of a litigant's right to a jury demand.

Justiciability A controversy or dispute that is capable of being resolved by the judiciary, rather than the legislative or executive branches. In order to be capable of judicial resolution, the case or controversy must present an actual, concrete dispute between adverse individuals with *standing* to sue. The controversy also must be *ripe* for resolution, not *moot,* and not *collusively* pursued by the litigants. In addition, the dispute must not present a *political question* or seek an *advisory opinion* (*see supra*).

K

Klaxon **Rule** The rule requiring federal district courts, in diversity cases, to apply the choice-of-law rules of the state in which the federal courts sits, to determine the applicable law. For *Erie* purposes (*see supra*), choice-of-law rules are substantive. So-called after the Supreme Court case, **Klaxon v. Stentor.**

L

Laches An equitable defense that bars a person from seeking judicial relief if that person has excessively delayed in seeking redress for the claim. Laches is one of the affirmative defenses listed in **Federal Rule 8(c).**

Limited Fund Class One of the mandatory class actions under **Federal Rule 23(b)(1)(B),** based on the potential prejudice to the class of plaintiffs if individual actions were permitted to exhaust the defendant's resources prior to resolution of all the plaintiffs' claims against those resources. The parties seeking certification of a limited fund class carry the burden of proving the existence of the defendant's limited fund.

Limited Issues Class A type of class action authorized under **Federal Rule 23(c)(4),** which permits a judge to certify a classwide determination of separate issues in a litigation, such as negligence; or defenses, such as state of the art defense.

Local Action A lawsuit that must be filed in a particular jurisdiction with which it has a specific connection; for example, a suit over title to real property (where the property is located). Local actions should be contrasted with *transitory actions,* (*see infra*).

Local Rules The power and authority of federal district courts to promulgate procedural rules, in addition to the Federal Rules of Civil Procedure, provided that those local rules are not inconsistent or in conflict with the general federal rules. **Federal Rule 83.**

Lodestar Formula A judicially-created method for determining and approving attorney's fees in certain statutory and other actions (such as class actions). The lodestar formula combines both an adjusted hourly rate with court-determined multipliers for risk, novelty of claims, and importance of results.

Long–Arm Statutes Statutes enacted by state legislatures setting forth the grounds for state assertion of personal jurisdiction over non-resident defendants. Called "long-arm" statutes because they figuratively represent the ability of the "long-arm" of the state to reach outside its territorial boundaries and subject a non-resident to the authority of its courts. Very detailed long-arm statutes are called *Illinois-style* long-arm statutes. Long-arm statutes that permit state assertions of jurisdiction to the full extent of the Constitution are called *California-style* long-arm statutes.

M

Magistrate A civil official with certain assigned judicial powers and functions. In federal practice, United States Magistrate Judges perform tasks assigned by statute (**28 U.S.C. § 631** et seq.) and **Federal Rules 72–75**. Magistrate judges are not Article III judges but are appointed for a fixed term. Magistrate judges may try all misdemeanors and may conduct any other pretrial proceedings requested by the federal district judge. Magistrates also may conduct consent trials.

Mandamus An order from a higher court to a lower court judge to perform certain duties, typically sought by a *writ of mandamus.* A higher court will issue the writ of mandamus only for egregious abuse of power or misconduct on the part of the lower court judge. Mandamus is not intended to provide a "backdoor" method of seeking interlocutory appeal of a judge's orders, short of final judgment (*see supra*).

Mandatory Classes In class action procedure, classes of claimants who are bound by class and who may not exclude themselves from the class. **Federal Rule 23** recognizes two possible mandatory classes: the **Rule 23(b)(1)** classes (also called *prejudice classes*), and the **(b)(2)** classes (seeking *injunctive* or *declaratory* relief). Mandatory class members are viewed as sharing homogenous interests in the action, as opposed to heterogeneous members of a **(b)(3)**, non-mandatory, opt-out class.

Mass Tort Litigation Any form of tort litigation that seeks to aggregate claims of individual tort claimants into a larger litigation unit. The most common procedural means of aggregating claims include class actions (*see supra*), consolidations (*see supra*), or multidistrict litigation (*see infra*). Examples of mass tort litigation include litigation involving asbestos, Agent Orange, the Dalkon Shield, DES and Bendectin, silicone breast implants, heart valves, blood products, lead paint, and so forth.

Mediation A form of private alternative dispute resolution that consensually employs the offices of a designated "mediator." The mediator meets with the parties to attempt a resolution of the dispute without recourse to litigation. Mediated disputes are non-binding, have no precedential value, and are not subject to judicial rules and procedure.

Merger (1) In *claim preclusion* doctrine (*see supra*), the rule whereby all claims that a plaintiff *could have* or *should have* raised in a former litigation are merged into the judgment. The doctrine of merger operates to bar subsequent litigation of a claim already litigated, or one that could have been litigated. (2) Referring to the abolition of the distinction of separate actions at law and equity achieved by the **Federal Rules of Civil Procedure** (*see* **Federal Rule 2**). The Federal Rules commonly are considered as having "merged" law and equity.

Mootness One of the doctrines of justiciability (*see supra*) whereby a claim or issue already has been resolved and therefore there is no ripe, actual case or controversy for the court to decide. A "moot" case presents a "non-justiciable" controversy and is a ground for dismissing a lawsuit.

Multidistrict Litigation ("MDL") A procedural method for transferring and consolidating separate cases filed in different federal judicial districts, for coordinated pretrial proceedings. **28 U.S.C. § 1407.** The **Judicial Panel on Multidistrict Litigation** determines which controversies are suitable for multidistrict treatment. After the multidistrict litigation court has completed pretrial proceedings, the statute requires that the cases be returned to their originating districts for trial. A very high percentage of cases transferred for MDL treatment settle and do not return to the originating courts.

Mutuality of Estoppel A common law doctrine developed in the context of collateral estoppel, to prevent unfair usage of collateral estoppel in a subsequent litigation. The mutuality doctrine is based on the idea that no person should benefit from a prior judgment if that person stood to lose nothing by it—commonly referred to as the problem of the "sideline sitter." Similarly, no person should be disadvantaged by a

prior judgment if the person lacked the opportunity to present evidence or argument at the first trial. The doctrine of mutuality for both defensive and offensive collateral estoppel has been eliminated in federal court (**Parklane Hosiery Co. v. Shore**). Many states, however, retain the doctrine of mutuality.

N

Necessary Party A person needed for a just adjudication in order to give complete relief or to prevent unfairness to parties to the litigation. However, absence of a necessary party from a lawsuit does not require dismissal of the suit (in contrast to *indispensable parties*, see supra). In federal practice, the concept of the necessary party is embedded in **Federal Rule 19(a).**

Negative Pregnant A form of evasive denial in which the defendant's denial effectively includes an affirmative implication that is favorable to the adversary.

New Trial Appropriate when the court's or jury's examination of the contested issues of fact and law cannot be determined between the litigating parties. In federal practice, a motion for a new trial may be presented as part of a motion for a "judgment as a matter of law" (*see supra*) after presentation of the evidence or jury verdict (*see* **Federal Rule 50(b)**). The court also may *conditionally* grant a new trial motion, based on the appellate court's review of the court's ruling on the judgment as a matter of law. (**Federal Rule 50(b)**). Federal courts also may grant new trials based on newly discovered evidence or proof of juror bias. **Federal Rule 59(a).**

Nonpositive Denial A form of response by the defendant (usually in the defendant's answer) by which the defendant indicates that the defendant lacks knowledge or information upon which to form a belief as to the truth of the allegation.

Notice A component of due process necessary in order for a court to assert a valid, binding judgment over defendants; intended to apprise the defendant of the pendency of an action. There are two basic forms of notice: (1) *actual notice* which is direct communication to the party to be notified, and (2) *constructive notice,* which the law treats as actual notice, such as recordation of a property deed. Notice under federal law and in most states is accomplished by service of process on the defendant. **Federal Rule 4.**

Notice Pleading The form of pleading permitted under the Federal Rules of Civil Procedure, intended merely to give notice to the defendant of the filing and pendency of an action. Notice pleading does not require the specificity of common law pleading, and is intended to cure the numerous "traps for the unwary" involved with common law pleading under the "forms of action" (*see supra*) and writs (*see infra*). For example, the Federal Rules merely require "a short and plain statement showing that the pleader is entitled to relief." **Rule 8(a)(2).**

O

Offensive Collateral Estoppel A form of claim preclusion, asserted by a plain-

tiff to prevent relitigation of an issue determined in the plaintiff's favor in a prior proceeding. Federal courts now permit assertions of offensive collateral estoppel, without a showing of mutuality (*see infra*), subject to certain due process protections for the defendant. *See* **Parklane Hosiery Co. v. Shore.** Some states still do not permit offensive assertions of collateral estoppel in absence of mutuality of estoppel.

Opt–Out Classes In federal class action procedure, a heterogeneous class of claimants who retain the right to exclude themselves ("opt-out") from the class and thus avoid the binding nature of the class judgment. **Federal Rule 23(b)(3).** Opt-out classes must satisfy additional requirements for certification, including a finding of the predominance of common issues over individual issues, and that the class is a superior method of resolving the dispute.

Original Jurisdiction The authority and power of trial courts to adjudicate a dispute, as distinguished from appellate jurisdiction (*see supra*). The Supreme Court has original jurisdiction over all cases "affecting ambassadors, other public ministers, and those in which a state shall be a party." **U.S. Const., Art. III § 2, cl. 2.** Many federal statutes set forth the original jurisdiction of the federal district courts. State statutes set forth the original jurisdiction of state trial courts.

P

Partial Summary Judgment The ability of a judge to grant a dismissal of separate claims in a multi-claim lawsuit, provided those claims present no genuine issue of material fact and the movant is entitled to a judgment as a matter of law (*see* **"summary judgment,"** *infra*). **Federal Rule 56(g).** A judge's order granting partial summary judgment is a final order (*see infra*) for appellate jurisdiction. **Federal Rule 54(b).**

Pendent Party A person who is not originally named in a lawsuit but who is added because that person has a logical nexus to the original parties and claims. The Supreme Court rejected pendent party jurisdiction for many years (*see* **Aldinger v. Howard** and **Finley v. United States**), but Congress legislatively overturned these decisions and federal practice now permits joinder of pendent parties under the *supplemental jurisdiction* statute (*see infra*), as long as the parties and claims form part of one constitutional case or controversy. **28 U.S.C. § 1367.**

Pendent Claim A state claim joined to federal claims in a diversity-based federal lawsuit. Judicially-created doctrine permits pendent claims provided those claims arose from a "common nucleus of operative facts" with the federally-based claim. **United Mine Workers v. Gibb.** Congress codified the doctrine of pendent claim jurisdiction in the *supplemental jurisdiction* statute (*see infra*). provided that the state and federal claims form part of one constitutional case or controversy.

Permissive Intervention The ability of a non-party to join a lawsuit if a federal statute confers a conditional right to intervene or the applicant's claim or defense and the main action have a question of law or fact in common. Permissive intervention is in the court's discretion and the court may limit the permissive intervenor's participation in the litigation. In lieu of permissive intervention, some courts grant applicants status as an *amicus curiae* (*see supra*).

Personal Jurisdiction Power or authority of a court over the parties to the dispute and to render a valid, binding judgment against a defendant. Because of territorial sovereignty and fairness concerns, states must obtain valid personal jurisdiction over a non-resident defendant in order to issue a judgment against them. **International Shoe Co. v. Washington.** Such assertions of personal jurisdiction must comport with the requirements of **Fourteenth Amendment** due process. Assertions of personal jurisdiction may be based on presence, property, consent, or an array of affiliating circumstances with the forum (*see in personam jurisdiction,* supra).

Plea in Abatement At common law, a plea that took the form of a motion to dismiss that did not go to the merits of the case, such as misjoinder. Such pleas often were characterized as *dilatory pleas* (*see supra*). The Federal Rules of Civil Procedure abolished the common law pleas, **Federal Rule 7(c),** but analogs to pleas in abatement may be found in **Federal Rule 12(b).** Some states have retained common law pleas.

Plea in Bar At common law, a plea that took the form of a motion to dismiss an action because of a substantial and fatal defect such as lack of jurisdiction, res judicata, or double jeopardy. The Federal Rules of Civil Procedure abolished all common law pleas, **Federal Rule 7(c),** but analogs to the *plea in bar* may be found in **Federal Rule 12(b).**

Plea in Replication At common law, a successive round of pleading by which the plaintiff responded to the defendant's pleas (e.g., a traverse (*see infra*) or confession and avoidance (*see supra*)), with the plaintiff's own pleas mirroring those of the defendant. Modern practice under the Federal Rules of Civil Procedure has abolished all common law forms of pleas, **Federal Rule 7(c).** The Federal Rules do not permit multiple, successive rounds of pleading. **Federal Rule 7(a).**

Political Questions A type of dispute that presents a *non-justiciable controversy* (*see supra*) because it is better committed to another branch of government. Federal courts will not hear (and will dismiss) cases that involve political questions. Historically, federal courts would not decide cases relating to legislative redisricting, because these disputes were denominated as political questions best resolved by federal and state legislative bodies.

Preclusion Doctrine Referring to the doctrines of *res judicata* (*claim preclusion, see supra*), and *collateral estoppel* (*issue preclusion, see supra*). Also generically used to refer to the obligation of federal and state courts to give recognition to the judgment of sister courts under the Full Faith and Credit Clause and statute (**Art. IV § 1; 28 U.S.C. § 1738**). The preclusion doctrines prevent relitigation of claims and issues already fully and fairly litigated in a prior proceeding, subject to various doctrinal limitations.

Pre-emptory Challenges Challenges that a lawyer may make during jury selection—*voir dire* (*see infra*)—to disqualify and remove a juror without having to state any reason. Pre-emptory challenges differ from challenges *for cause,* in which the attorney must state the grounds for disqualification, such as juror bias.

Pre-emptory Pleas At common law, the pre-emptory plea, or plea in bar, was a defendant's denial of the plaintiff's claims on the merits. One form of pre-emptory plea, if the defendant denied the plaintiff's allegations, was the *traverse* (*see infra*), which squarely placed the issue in contest. Another form of pre-emptory plea was the *confession and avoidance* (*see supra*) whereby the defendant would admit to the plaintiff's allegations (the "confession"), but assert some other grounds for "avoiding" culpability, such as the defendant's minority. Pre-emptory pleas have been abolished under the modern Federal Rules of Civil Procedure, but these pleas have modern analogs in federal practice in both the defendant's denials (*see supra*), or affirmative defenses (*see supra*).

Preponderance of the Evidence The usual measure for the burden of proof in most civil trials, requiring that the evidence in support of the claim outweighs the other evidence. "Preponderance" is usually conceived as requiring at least 51% percent, but is variously described as evidence that is more or the most satisfying, has a greater probability of truth, or that "preponderates."

Pretrial Conference A meeting of the judge and attorneys, and sometimes the parties, prior to trial to discuss the nature of the litigation, set motion and discovery schedules, engage settlement, and dispose of any other pretrial matters. Attorneys are required to attend pretrial conference and appear with authority to settle. In federal practice, pretrial conferences are now required for all civil cases, except those exempted by local rule. **Federal Rule 16.** If the case is to go to trial, the judge frequently will conduct a final pretrial conference and produce a "pretrial order." (*see infra*).

Pretrial Order A judicial order setting forth the agreement of the parties and the court concerning the conduct of the trial. The final pretrial order is binding on the parties and amendments to, or relief from, the final pretrial will be granted only in exceptional circumstances. The final pretrial order indicates such matters as party admissions, stipulations, order of witnesses, pretrial evidentiary rulings, and designation and admissibility of exhibits. **Federal Rule 16.**

Privity; Parties in Privity The relationship of persons in connection with a particular transaction, property, right or thing, that carries with it the benefits or burdens of the relationship. The concept of *parties in privity* is important for the preclusion doctrines of *res judicata* (*see infra*) and *collateral estoppel* (*see supra*).

Protective Order An order from a court to protect persons during discovery proceedings from annoyance, embarrassment, oppression, undue burden or expense; or to protect proprietary trade secret information from disclosure. In federal practice, protective orders are governed by **Federal Rule 26(c),** and the person seeking the protective order must show good cause for its issuance.

Provisional Remedies A temporary remedy in aid of a civil action to preserve the value of an ultimate judgment from waste during pendency of the proceedings. Examples of provisional remedies include attachment, garnishment, injunctions (*see supra*), appointment of a receiver, etc.

Punitive Damages *See* **"exemplary damages,"** *supra.*

Q

Quasi In Rem **Jurisdiction** (1) In modern practice, a lawsuit as if against property, but actually against a person. The most common form of *quasi in rem* jurisdiction is attachment of a debt (an intangible property). The Supreme Court has declared that all assertions of *quasi in rem* jurisdiction are subject to the same due process requirements as *in personam* jurisdiction (*see supra*), because *quasi in rem* jurisdiction is merely an elliptical way of referring to *in personam* jurisdiction. **Shaffer v. Heitner.** (2) Technically, a suit to adjudicate the rights of specific persons in specific property, i.e., to partition or divide up property between owners—as opposed to a true *in rem* proceeding to adjudicate a claim as against everyone else (e.g., to quiet title).

R

Real Party in Interest The person who possesses a substantive right to enforce a claim, even though that enforcement may be for another person's benefit (*see, e.g., **guardian ad litem**, supra*). In federal practice, every action must be brought by the real party in interest. **Federal Rule 17(a).** Some states have abolished the concept of the real party in interest.

Rebutter At common law, a form of successive defensive pleading to a plaintiff's *plea in replication* (*see supra*). The common law plea of rebutter has been abolished in modern federal practice. **Federal Rule 7(c).**

Redaction Term used to describe the editing of documents, during discovery, to protect from disclosure sensitive or proprietary information. Judges may order parties to a dispute to redact documents prior to disclosure.

Rejoinder At common law, a form of successive defensive pleading consisting of a defendant's reply in response to a plaintiff's plea. The common law rejoinder has been abolished in modern federal practice. **Federal Rule 7(c).**

Remand The procedure for sending an improperly removed case back to state court after an attempted removal of the case (*see **removal**, infra*). Remand is governed by **28 U.S.C. § 1447(b).**

Relation–Back Doctrine The doctrine by which a plaintiff (or defendant) may amend a pleading to change claims or parties after expiration of a statute of limitations, so that those claims are not time-barred. The amendment effectively *relates back* to the date of the filing of the original claims. In federal practice, relation-back of time-barred amendments is permitted under limited circumstances set forth in **Federal Rule 15(c)** and cases construing that rule.

Remittur The common law doctrine permitting a judge to reduce a jury's excessive award. A judge denies the losing party's motion for a new trial conditioned on the winning party's acceptance of a reduced award. If the winning party does not agree, then the judge orders a new trial. In federal practice, remittur is permitted as not violative of the **Seventh Amendment** right to a jury, because the reduced amount is already included in the larger amount the jury determined. Federal courts do not recognize the opposite practice of *additur*, however (*see supra*).

Removal Jurisdiction The ability of a state court defendant to move a state civil litigation to the federal district court in that jurisdiction if either federal question or diversity grounds exist for federal court jurisdiction. Federal removal is governed by **28 U.S.C. § 1441** et seq. and is solely a state defendant's right. An improperly removed case may be **remanded** back to state court. There is no analogous procedure for moving cases from federal to state court, or so-called *reverse-removal*.

Reply One of the three forms of pleading permitted under **Federal Rule of Civil Procedure 7(a).** A plaintiff may file a reply only if the defendant sets forth a counterclaim in its answer. The reply constructively serves as the plaintiff's answer to the counterclaim.

Request for Admissions One of the five methods of formal discovery (*see* *supra*), governed by **Federal Rule 36.** These requests essentially ask the responding party to admit or deny the truthfulness of statements made in the requests. Any party admissions are deemed **admitted,** that is, conclusively determined for trial purposes and need not be proved by factual evidence at trial. Request for admissions may seek the respondent to admit to statements or opinions of fact, the application of law to fact, or the genuineness of documents.

Res Judicata The term generically used to describe the collection of preclusion doctrines, including both *claim preclusion* (*see supra*) and *issue preclusion* (*see supra*). More narrowly and accurately, pure *res judicata* refers to claim preclusion (*see supra*).

Ripeness One of the doctrines of *justiciability* (*see supra*) requiring that a dispute, on the facts and procedurally, present a real controversy that is ready for determination by the court.

Rule of Four The Supreme Court informal rule whereby four Justices must affirmatively vote to grant a *writ of certiorari* to hear an appeal of a lower court decision, (*see Certiorari* Jurisdiction, *supra*).

Rules of Decision Act The congressional Act (**Section 34** of the **Judiciary Act of 1789**) requiring that federal courts apply, as the decisional law in federal diversity cases, the substantive state law where the federal court sits. **28 U.S.C. § 1652.**

Rules Enabling Act The congressional statute which authorizes the federal judiciary to promulgate federal rules of civil procedure provided that those rules do not "abridge, enlarge, or modify" any substantive rights. **28 U.S.C. §§ 2071–72.**

S

Severance In federal practice, the ability of the court to order a separate trial of any claim, cross-claim (*see supra*), counterclaim (*see supra*), or third-party claim (*see infra*) in the interests of convenience and to avoid prejudice. The severance of claims for separate trials must not violate the Seventh Amendment right to a trial by jury. **Federal Rules 20(b); 42(b).**

Service of Process Part of the mechanics of commencing an action and satisfying the due process requirements for providing the opposing party with notice (*see supra*) of the action. Service of process is the technical means of subjecting persons or property to a court's jurisdiction. State law prescribes the permissible modes of service and the persons with capacity to effect service. **Federal Rule 4** governs the various permissible manners of federal service of process.

Settlement Classes In class action procedure, a class that is certified as part of the settlement deal, sometimes only after the parties negotiated the settlement. The Supreme Court has held that settlement classes must satisfy the same certification requirements as class actions that a court certifies for litigation, except for the manageability requirement. **Amchem Prods. v. Windsor; Ortiz v. Fibreboard.**

Speaking Demurrer At common law, a demurrer that raises matters not mentioned in the pleading to which the demurrer is addressed. In modern federal practice, the analog of the speaking demurrer is the ability to turn a **Federal Rule 12(b)(6)** motion to dismiss for failure to state a claim into a *summary judgment* motion (*see infra*) by including matters outside the motion itself (such as a copy of the contract in a contract dispute).

Special Damages Damages that are the proximate result of the defendant's conduct but that occur only because of the plaintiff's specific situation. Distinguished from *general damages,* which are damages that are the natural, expected result of the defendant's conduct. In federal practice, any special damages must be specially pleaded. **Federal Rule 9(g).**

Special Master A judicial officer or "surrogate" appointed by a judge to assist the judge on a particular case by performing some particular task, such as an accounting in a complex commercial litigation. The powers of a special master are defined by statute and the master typically files a special master's report with the court. **Federal Rule 53.**

Specific Denial Numbered paragraphs in a defendant's response to the plaintiff's complaint that refer to each allegation or averment, and specifically admit or deny those allegations. Specific denials are contrasted to the "general denial" (*see supra*).

Standing One of the doctrines of *justiciability* (*see supra*), requiring that the person bringing the lawsuit have a personal stake in the outcome, and have suffered an actual injury for which the law can supply redress.

Stare Decisis The doctrine of following precedent for the sake of serving continuity and consistency in the law.

Statute of Limitations A statute that sets a time limit within which a claimant must file an action based on some substantive right, or the action will be barred. State law fixes the time period for particular types of claims, such as actions in contract, property, and tort. In federal practice, either federal statute sets limitations periods or, if not, federal law may "borrow" analogous state limitations periods. Also, in federal practice, the statute of limitations is an affirmative defense under **Federal Rule 8(c).** A pleader may amend its pleadings to avoid the bar of a statute of limitations through use of the *relation-back* doctrine (*see supra*) under **Federal Rule 15(c).**

Stipulation An agreed upon statement. In pleading and motion practice, lawyers may agree to "stipulate" to certain facts (**stipulated facts**), which then do not need to be proved by evidence.

Subject Matter Jurisdiction The power or authority of a state or federal court over the particular subjects in dispute, to issue a valid, binding judgment in the litigation. Both state and federal subject matter jurisdiction is defined by constitutional and statutory provisions. State and federal courts may exercise *concurrent* subject matter jurisdiction (*see supra*), or some matters are within the federal court's exclusive jurisdiction (*see supra*).

Summary Judgment A dispositive motion prior to trial in which the movant may have the case dismissed because there is no genuine issue as to a material fact and the movant therefore is entitled to a judgment as a matter of law. **Federal Rule 56(c).** Either the defendant or plaintiff, or both, may move for a summary judgment. If granted, the case does not go to trial. The court also may grant partial summary judgment in a multi-claim case (*see supra*), or summary judgment as to issues in the case. **Federal Rule 56(g).**

Supplemental Jurisdiction The general term capturing the concepts of *ancillary, pendent claim,* and *pendent party* jurisdiction. In federal practice, supplemental jurisdiction over additional parties or claims lacking an independent jurisdictional basis is now governed by federal statute. **28 U.S.C. § 1367.**

Supplemental Pleadings In federal practice, the ability to add additional pleadings or allegations to original pleadings, setting forth transactions or occurrences or events that have happened since the date of the original pleading. Such supplemental pleadings only may be filed "upon reasonable notice and upon such terms as are just." Supplemental pleadings typically may not set forth new matter. **Federal Rule 15(d).**

Surrebutter At common law, one of the many types of pleas in replication (*see supra*) in successive rounds of responsive pleading. The Federal Rules of Civil Procedure have abolished the common law pleas, **Federal Rule 7(c),** as well as successive rounds of pleading, **Federal Rule 7(a).**

Surrejoinder At common law, one of the many types of pleas in replication (*see supra*) in successive rounds of responsive pleading. The Federal Rules of Civil Procedure have abolished the common law pleas, **Federal Rule 7(c),** as well as successive rounds of pleading, **Federal Rule 7(a).**

T

Tag Jurisdiction Another term for so-called *transient jurisdiction* (*see infra*), or the ability of a state to assert jurisdiction over a person who, while temporarily in the state, is served with process (or "tagged") in an action (provided that the person has not been fraudulently induced into the forum). Transient or "tag" jurisdiction has a long historical lineage and the Supreme Court has approved such jurisdiction. **Burnham v. Superior Court.**

Territorial Jurisdiction The ability of a federal or state court to assert authority over a defendant to issue a valid, binding judgment against that person in an action. Territorial jurisdiction is closely tied to concepts of state sovereignty, and is one of the oldest traditional bases for asserting personal jurisdiction (*see supra*). Territorial jurisdiction may be asserted against a person based on property or other presence in the state, as well as consent. **Pennoyer v. Neff.**

Third–Party Claim The claim of a person who has been added or "impleaded" (*see supra*) into a lawsuit, against original parties to the lawsuit, based on some interest in or substantive right to recovery in the action. In federal practice, third-party claims are governed by

Federal Rule 14. A person seeking to assert a third-party claim becomes the *third-party plaintiff,* and must file a *third-party complaint.*

Third–Party Practice Referring to the ability of original litigants in a lawsuit to bring additional parties into the litigation who are or might be liable to the original parties. In federal practice, third-party practice is governed by **Federal Rule 14.** Both plaintiffs and defendants may "implead" (*see supra*) or bring additional third parties into the lawsuit. The third parties may then assert claims against the original parties, by filing *third party complaints.*

Transient or Transitory Jurisdiction A doctrine of territorial power or jurisdiction that permits the assertion of valid jurisdiction over persons temporarily within a state, who are served with process in a pending action (*see* **tag jurisdiction,** *supra*). Transient or transitory jurisdiction has a long historical heritage, and the Supreme Court has approved it. **Burnham v. Superior Court.**

Traverse At common law, a pre-emptory plea (*see supra*) by which the defendant denied the plaintiff's allegations, which squarely placed the facts in issue for trial. Modern practice under the Federal Rules of Civil Procedure has abolished the traverse, but its modern analog is found in the ability of the defendant to deny the plaintiff's allegations through a denial under **Federal Rule 8(b).**

V

Venue The proper place of trial; generally, the place where the events of a civil action arose. State law statutorily defines appropriate venue, and federal venue is governed by a complicated series of particular rules relating to the status of the parties to the dispute. **28 U.S.C. § 1391** et seq. If venue is improperly chosen, the federal court may cure defective venue by transferring the case to the appropriate venue. **28 U.S.C. § 1406.** Additionally, litigants in the federal system may, in the interest of convenience to the parties and justice, transfer a case to a more convenient venue. **28 U.S.C. § 1404** (*transfer or change of venue*).

Voir Dire From the Latin, "to speak the truth." The process of selecting a jury by oral and written examination by lawyers or the court to test the qualifications of prospective jurors to render an impartial judgment in a litigation. During voir dire, lawyers have the ability to "challenge" or attempt to disqualify prospective jurors on two grounds: *challenges for cause,* and *pre-emptory challenges* (*see supra*).

Voluntary Dismissal The ability of a plaintiff to freely withdraw a complaint filed in an action, before service of process on the defendant, usually without the court's permission and without prejudice to refiling the lawsuit again. If the defendant has been served, the court must grant permission to voluntary dismiss the lawsuit, unless all the parties agree to the dismissal by stipulation (*see supra*). **Federal Rule 41(a).** To be contrasted with *involuntary dismissals* (*see supra*).

W

Work Product Immunity *See attorney work product immunity, supra.*

Writ At common law, the method of instituting or commencing a legal action, based on the various common law *forms of action* (*see supra*). Every particular form of action had a corresponding writ, and the failure of the plaintiff's lawyer to "swear out" the appropriate writ could result in the plaintiff's case being dismissed on a demurrer (defective writ).

Writ of *Mandamus See mandamus, supra.* The writ is the court order from a higher court to a lower court judge, ordering the judge to perform his duties. In federal practice, the writ of mandamus is considered an extraordinary remedy that is not to be used as a "back-door" means for accomplishing interlocutory appellate review of a judge's decision. **28 U.S.C. § 1651; LaBuy v. Howe.**

Table of Cases

References are to pages.

Table of Statutes

References are to pages.

Table of Federal Rules

References are to pages.

FEDERAL RULES OF APPELLATE PROCEDURE

FEDERAL RULES OF EVIDENCE

FEDERAL EQUITY RULES

Table of Restatements of the Law

References are to pages.

Index

References are to Pages